FIFTH CANADIAN EDITION

ESSENTIALS OF MANAGING HUMAN RESOURCES

Eileen B. Stewart
British Columbia Institute of Technology

Monica Belcourt
Professor of Human Resource Management
York University

Catherine Fitzgerald
Okanagan College

George W. Bohlander
Professor Emeritus of Management
Arizona State University

Scott A. Snell
Professor of Business Administration
Darden Graduate School of Business
University of Virginia

NELSON / EDUCATION

NELSON / EDUCATION

Essentials of Managing Human Resources, Fifth Canadian Edition

by Eileen Stewart, Monica Belcourt, Catherine Fitzgerald, George W. Bohlander, and Scott A. Snell

Vice President, Editorial Higher Education:
Anne Williams

Acquisitions Editor:
Alwynn Pinard

Marketing Manager:
Dave Stratton

Developmental Editor:
Luciano Nicassio

Photo Researcher:
Jessie Coffey

Permissions Coordinator:
Jessie Coffey

Content Production Manager:
Christine Gilbert

Production Service:
Integra Software Services Pvt. Ltd.

Proofreader:
Integra Software Services Pvt. Ltd.

Indexer:
Jeanne Busemeyer, Hyde Park Publishing Services

Manufacturing Manager—Higher Education
Joanne McNeil

Design Director:
Ken Phipps

Managing Designer:
Franca Amore

Interior Design:
Peter Papayanakis

Cover Design:
Trinh Truong

Cover Image:
Hand with box with grass image: italianestro/iStockphoto; Asian business woman: tunart/ iStockphoto; female doctor: LattaPictures/iStockphoto; man in restaurant: Blend Images/ Masterfile

Compositor:
Integra Software Services Pvt. Ltd.

Printer:
RR Donnelley

Library and Archives Canada Cataloguing in Publication

Essentials of managing human resources/Eileen Stewart ... [et al.]. —5th Canadian ed.

Includes bibliographical references and index.
ISBN-13: 978-0-17-650692-6

1. Personnel management— Textbooks. I. Stewart, Eileen B., 1943-

HF5549.E85 2013   658.3
C2012-907795-X

ISBN-13: 978-0-17-650692-6
ISBN-10: 0-17-650692-6

BRIEF CONTENTS

DETAILED CONTENTS

PREFACE

The fourth edition of *Essentials of Managing Human Resources* was published just as the Great Recession was clearly upon us, and the issues that led to the upheaval are still with us: continuing global economic instability, skill shortages, mounting government debt, and intense global competition. Nonetheless, organizations are very aware of the need to focus on their people: the people who make or break company success. Attracting and engaging scarce talent is not easy, but it must happen if the economic scene is to improve.

With this ongoing focus on the people in a company—the company's "human resources"—it is important to understand what types of people practices are needed to create the engaged workforce. This book is written to help you understand the HR "language"—the practices, processes, and systems integral to the success of the people in the organization, and therefore, the success of the organization. For example, one of the more important systems in an organization is recruiting capable and skilled people.

This textbook builds on concepts you have learned or been introduced to in either a general management or a general organizational behaviour course. It is written for students who will become (or are) supervisors and line managers and HR professionals. Since the text covers the major human resources management processes and systems, it will provide a good overview if you are thinking about moving into the HR profession.

The book has been authored by experienced instructors recognized by students for many years for their excellence in teaching and facilitating learning. The authors are also active HR practitioners who share business stories throughout the text to make the materials interesting for students.

Essentials of Managing Human Resources is a shorter and a more relevant book for general business students with simpler language. It is important, however, to remember that the field of HR has its own jargon, or specialized language. Therefore, one goal of this book is to help you learn the terminology so that you can deal with HR issues in a more informed way.

Finally, this book is designed to cover all the materials you will need for a good general understanding of all the HR activities in a company, as well as your role in managing people. It shows how theory applies to managers and HR practices in the 21st century. Further, the book has stories about all types of organizations: profit, nonprofit/voluntary, public sector; those that are unionized and non-unionized; and those that are small and large.

WHAT'S NEW IN THE FIFTH EDITION

Building on the successes of the fourth edition, and incorporating suggestions from users of the text, the following changes have been made:

- Each chapter has content and questions that illustrate the integrated and strategic nature of human resources management.
- Approximately 99% of the references have been updated, with 95% since 2010.
- A "Small Business (SME) and HRM" feature in each chapter applies learning outcomes to small- and medium-sized enterprises—those that employ up to 300 employees.
- Updated HRM Close-ups appear in each chapter.
- At Work with HRM, HRM and the Law, and HRM and Ethics chapter features, which are full of practical examples, have been revised for students.
- There is updated content in all chapters to help students acquire the tools and skills to be successful employees.
- The text reflects current Canadian research from professional journals/periodicals and academic journals.

- New cases are presented in each chapter, with focus on Canadian companies.
- New critical thinking questions and end-of-chapter materials appear in each chapter.
- Additional Web sites are identified within each chapter.
- Data and information from the 2011 Census are used.

FEATURES OF THE BOOK

Each chapter contains the following materials:

- **Learning outcomes** are listed at the beginning of each chapter, with reference icons indicating the objective within the chapter.
- An **HRM Close-up** that relates a story about a supervisor's experience in human resources management opens each chapter.
- **Manager's Toolkit** boxes contain tools and resources for handling HR matters, including tips for supervisors.
- **At Work with HRM** boxes feature real-world applications relating to a specific topic with critical thinking questions at the end.
- **HRM and the Law** boxes help explain the legal implications of HR.
- **HRM and SME** boxes provide stories about organizations that have fewer than 300 people. (There are more than one million such enterprises.)
- **Ethics in HRM** boxes highlight sensitive issues supervisors might face.
- An **Emerging Trends** box provides information about trends in relation to each chapter theme.
- **Key terms** appear in boldface and are defined in margin notes. The key terms are also listed at the end of the chapter and in the Glossary.
- **Figures with graphs** and **research information** appear throughout the chapters.
- **Illustrations** reinforce points and maintain reader interest.
- A **Summary** at the end of each chapter reinforces the learning objectives.
- A **Need to Know/Need to Understand** box at the end of each chapter helps to identify key topics.
- **Review Questions** and **Critical Thinking Questions** promote basic recall as well as stimulate critical thinking questions for discussion.
- **Developing Your Skills** contain both text-based and Web-based experiential exercises.
- Two **case studies** in each chapter present current HRM issues in real-life settings that allow for critical analysis.
- **Notes and References** are included for further research and information.
- **Web site addresses**, indicated with a computer symbol in the margin, are provided throughout the text.

SUPPLEMENTARY MATERIALS

For Instructors

The Nelson Education Teaching Advantage (NETA)

The **Nelson Education Teaching Advantage (NETA)** program delivers research-based instructor resources that promote student engagement and higher-order thinking to enable the success of Canadian students and educators.

Instructors today face many challenges. Resources are limited, time is scarce, and a new kind of student has emerged: one who is juggling school with work, has gaps in his or her basic knowledge, and is immersed in technology in a way that has led to a completely new style of learning. In response, Nelson Education has gathered a group of dedicated instructors to advise us on the creation of richer and more flexible ancillaries and online learning platforms that respond to the needs of today's teaching environments. Whether your course is offered in-class, online, or both, Nelson is pleased to provide pedagogically driven, research-based resources to support you.

In consultation with the editorial advisory board, Nelson Education has completely rethought the structure, approaches, and formats of our key textbook ancillaries and online learning platforms. We've also increased our investment in editorial support for our ancillary and digital authors. The result is the Nelson Education Teaching Advantage and its key components: *NETA Engagement, NETA Assessment, NETA Presentation,* and *NETA Digital.* Each component includes one or more ancillaries prepared according to our best practices and may also be accompanied by documentation explaining the theory behind the practices.

NETA Engagement presents materials that help instructors deliver engaging content and activities to their classes. Instead of Instructor's Manuals that regurgitate chapter outlines and key terms from the text, NETA Enriched Instructor's Manuals (EIMs) provide genuine assistance to teachers. The EIMs answer questions like *What should students learn?, Why should students care?,* and *What are some common student misconceptions and stumbling blocks?* EIMs not only identify the topics that cause students the most difficulty, but also describe techniques and resources to help students master these concepts. Dr. Roger Fisher's *Instructor's Guide to Classroom Engagement (IGCE)* accompanies every Enriched Instructor's Manual. (Information about the NETA Enriched Instructor's Manual prepared for *Essentials of Managing Human Resources,* Fifth Canadian Edition is included in the description of the IRCD below.)

NETA Assessment relates to testing materials. Under *NETA Assessment,* Nelson's authors create multiple-choice questions that reflect research-based best practices for constructing effective questions and testing not just recall but also higher-order thinking. Our guidelines were developed by David DiBattista, a 3M National Teaching Fellow whose recent research as a professor of psychology at Brock University has focused on multiple-choice testing. All Test Bank authors receive training at workshops conducted by Prof. DiBattista, as do the copyeditors assigned to each Test Bank. A copy of *Multiple Choice Tests: Getting Beyond Remembering,* Prof. DiBattista's guide to writing effective tests, is included with every Nelson Test Bank/Computerized Test Bank package. (Information about the NETA Test Bank prepared for *Essentials of Managing Human Resources,* Fifth Canadian Edition is included in the description of the IRCD below.)

NETA Presentation has been developed to help instructors make the best use of PowerPoint® in their classrooms. With a clean and uncluttered design developed by Maureen Stone of StoneSoup Consulting, NETA Presentation features slides with improved readability, more multi-media and graphic materials, activities to use in class, and tips for instructors on the Notes page. A copy of *NETA Guidelines for Classroom Presentations* by Maureen Stone is included with each set of PowerPoint slides. (Information about the NETA PowerPoint® prepared for *Essentials of Managing Human Resources,* Fifth Canadian Edition is included in the description of the IRCD below.)

Instructor's Resource CD

Key instructor ancillaries are provided on the *Instructor's Resource CD* (ISBN 0-17-666078-X) giving instructors the ultimate tool for customizing lectures and presentations. (Downloadable web versions are also available at **www.stewart5ce.nelson.com**) The IRCD includes:

- **NETA Engagement:** The Enriched Instructor's Manual was written by Eileen Stewart, British Columbia Institute of Technology. It is organized according to the textbook chapters and addresses eight key educational concerns, such as typical stumbling blocks students face and how to address them. Other features include lecture outlines, answers to end-of-chapter material, critical thinking questions, and notes for the end-of-chapter case studies.

- **NETA Assessment:** The Test Bank was written by Catherine Fitzgerald, Okanagan College and Roger Wheeler, Okanagan College. It includes multiple-choice questions written according to NETA guidelines for effective construction and development of higher-order questions. Also included are context specific questions, true/false, and essay questions. Test Bank files are provided in Word format for easy editing and in PDF format for convenient printing whatever your system.

  The Computerized Test Bank by ExamView® includes all the questions from the Test Bank. The easy-to-use ExamView software is compatible with Microsoft Windows and Mac OS. Create tests by selecting questions from the question bank, modifying these questions as desired, and adding new questions you write yourself. You can administer quizzes online and export tests to WebCT, Blackboard, and other formats.

- **NETA Presentation:** Microsoft® PowerPoint® lecture slides for every chapter have been created by Eileen Stewart, British Columbia Institute of Technology. There is an average of 25 slides per chapter, many featuring key figures, tables, and photographs from *Essentials of Managing Human Resources,* Fifth Canadian Edition. NETA principles of clear design and engaging content have been incorporated throughout.

- **Image Library:** This resource consists of digital copies of figures, short tables, and photographs used in the book. Instructors may use these jpegs to create their own PowerPoint presentations.

- **DayOne:** Day One—Prof InClass is a PowerPoint presentation that you can customize to orient your students to the class and their text at the beginning of the course.

Instructor's Website

Our text website (**www.stewart5ce.nelson.com**) is filled with a whole set of useful tools. Instructors will find all the key instructor resources in electronic format: PowerPoint collections, Enhanced Instructor's Manual, and Test Bank files. Students will also find a host of valuable resources including self-assessment quizzes, weblinks, and CBC Videos.

DVD with CBC Videos

For the Fifth Canadian Edition we have included a DVD (0-17-666079-8) featuring new clips from the CBC's *The National.* Each clip has been carefully selected for every chapter. These clips are a great way to conclude teaching a chapter because they require students to draw connections and articulate the relationships between the clip and the chapter concepts. These videos are also available to your students through the companion website at **www.stewart5ce.nelson.com**.

For Students

Companion Website

A companion website, **www.stewart5ce.nelson.com**, is one of the most comprehensive websites available in human resources management. It includes test-yourself exercises and weblinks divided by subject: Organizations and Associations; Statutes, Regulations, and Government Agencies; and Career Development, concerning job analysis, recruitment, compensation, and health and safety. It also features new CBC videos from *The National.* These videos are a great way to apply the material you have learned in class with real world scenarios provided by Canada's leading news program. Our videos are intended for students who are enrolled in courses using *Essentials of Managing Human Resources*, Fifth Canadian Edition. Access is therefore granted only to those submitting valid passwords. To access these videos, a userid and password is required. The userid is "hrmessentials5ce" and the password can be obtained by turning to page 334 of the text. Note the first word on the page: it will be the password for the CBC Videos.

ACKNOWLEDGMENTS

This fifth edition could not have happened without the hard work of many people, particularly the users of earlier editions. We are grateful to the supervisors and HR practitioners who have shared their stories and helped influence the thinking.

Thanks to people such as Lewisa Anciano, Coast Capital, and John Beckett, B.C. Maritime Employers Association, for your contributions. And thanks also to those that provided guidance and support throughout—Mory Mosadegh and Deb Broznitsky.

Many thanks to Deborah Sanborn and to the featured individuals for their work on "HRM Close-ups."

The efforts of the Nelson Education team were excellent. Thanks to Evelyn Veitch, Anne Williams, Jackie Wood, Alwynn Pinard, and Luciano Nicassio for their guidance, wisdom, and patience.

The authors and publisher also wish to thank those people who reviewed this project during its development and provided important insights and suggestions:

Philip Hanan, *TriOS College*

Shari Ann Herrmann, *Kwantlen Polytechnic University*

Dave Inkster, *Red Deer College*

Joseph LeBlanc, *Eastern College*

Louis Masson, *Southern Alberta Institute of Techonology (SAIT)*

Cheryl Meheden, *University of Lethbridge*

Susan Milton, *Conestoga College*

Eddy Ng, *Dalhousie University*

James O'Brien, *Western University*

Chris Roubecas, *Southern Alberta Institute of Techonology (SAIT)*

Veronica Utton, *Seneca College of Applied Arts & Technology*

Chantal Westgate, *McGill University*

Leslie Wilder, *Red River College*

Our greatest thanks go to our families, particularly this author's son, Jason Robertson, and daughter-in-law, Andrea McLean. They have provided help, support, research, and encouragement that were most welcome for the project to succeed. And the previous authors' spouses—Michael Belcourt, Ronnie Bohlander, and Marybeth Snell—have also provided invaluable guidance and assistance. We are grateful to all of them for their enthusiasm and guidance.

Eileen B. Stewart
British Columbia Institute of Technology

Monica Belcourt
York University

George W. Bohlander
Arizona State University

Scott A. Snell
The Pennsylvania State University of Virginia

ABOUT THE AUTHORS

EILEEN B. STEWART

Eileen Stewart continues to teach part time at the British Columbia Institute of Technology (BCIT), where she was program head, Human Resource Management Programs, for a number of years. She is a senior human resources professional with extensive experience in all areas of human resources management (HRM), including labour relations in both the public and private sectors. As the HR executive, she has managed human resources units in several of British Columbia's large public-sector organizations. With a diverse background that includes mining, banking, education, and municipal government, Ms. Stewart has a strong overall business orientation.

After receiving a B.A. in economics and commerce from Simon Fraser University, British Columbia, she joined Teck Mining as its first personnel manager. She then moved to BCIT, where she specialized in labour relations. She obtained her senior management experience at BCIT, as director of personnel and labour relations; the University of British Columbia, as director of human resources; and the City of Vancouver, as general manager of human resources.

While working full time, Ms. Stewart completed her M.B.A. at Simon Fraser University. She currently teaches HRM courses at BCIT and continues to provide consulting services to private, public, and not-for-profit organizations.

Ms. Stewart is active in the HR community through her continued involvement with the B.C. Human Resources Management Association (BC HRMA), where she chairs the Leadership Forum. She was recognized by BC HRMA in 2012 with the Award of Excellence for the HR Professional of the Year. She has also served as president of the BC HRMA, as well as in other executive roles, for several years. In addition to her professional involvement, she chairs the Research Advisory Council of the Women's Health Research Institute and sits on the Board of Directors, B.C. Women's Hospital and Health Centre Foundation, where she is vice-chair. Previously, she was chair of the Board of Directors, YWCA of Vancouver, for two years.

CATHERINE FITZGERALD

Catherine Fitzgerald is a professor in the management and human resource management (HRM) options with the Okanagan School of Business, at Okanagan College, with more than 25 years of combined teaching experience with Western Canadian universities and colleges. Ms. Fitzgerald has played a leadership role in the development, delivery, and evaluation of 13 human resources management classroom and online courses with the resource support and knowledge-sharing of Okanagan College colleagues and industry partners.

Since 1987, Ms. Fitzgerald has managed a successful HR practice. She has assisted both private- and public-sector organizations in dealing with resource allocation and service delivery changes resulting in workforce adjustments.

Ms. Fitzgerald has completed certificates in leadership, human resources management, information technology, organizational learning and development, career development, conflict management, and negotiation. She has a master of arts degree from the School of Management, J.F.K. University. She also holds the designation of Certified Human Resource Professional and Certified Canadian Counsellor and is currently pursuing her Ph.D. in Management at the Sobey School of Business, Saint Mary's University.

Ms. Fitzgerald has authored instructors' and students' learning support materials for the Nelson Education textbook series in HRM. She has reviewed both textbooks and journal articles for Canadian and international publishers as well as presented HRM papers at national and international conferences.

Ms. Fitzgerald has been recognized by WorkSafe BC for her contribution to the safety of young workers and by BC HRMA for her leadership and excellence in HRM.

MONICA BELCOURT

Monica Belcourt is a full professor of Human Resources Management at York University. Her research is grounded in the experience she gained as director of personnel for CP Rail, director of employee development, National Film Board, and as a functional HR specialist for the federal government. Dr. Belcourt alternated working in Human Resources Management with graduate school, obtaining an M.A. in Psychology, an M.Ed. in Adult Education, and a Ph.D. in management. She also holds the designation of Certified Human Resource Professional. Dr. Belcourt has taught HRM at Concordia, UQUAM, McGill, and York, where she founded and manages the largest undergraduate program in HRM in Canada. She created Canada's first degrees in human resources management: B.HRM, B.HRM (honours), and a Masters in HRM (www.atkinson.yorku.ca/mhrm).

As director of the International Alliance for HR Research, Dr. Belcourt manages these programs: The Research Forum in the *Human Resources Professional*, the Applied Research Stream at the annual conference; the *HRM Research Quarterly*, the best theses (M.A. and Ph.D.) awards program, and a funding program for HR research (www.yorku .ca/hrresall).

Dr. Belcourt is series editor for the Nelson Education Series in HRM, which includes eight texts to date: *Performance Management through Training and Development, Occupational Health and Safety, Human Resources Management Systems, Recruitment and Selection in Canada, Compensation in Canada, Strategic Human Resources Planning, Research, Measurement and Evaluation in HRM*, and *The Canadian Labour Market*. Additionally, she is lead author of the best-selling book, *Managing Human Resources*, published by Nelson Education, from which this text is adapted.

Active in many professional associations and not-for-profit organizations, Dr. Belcourt was the president (2003–2004) of the Human Resources Professionals Association of Ontario and serves on the national committee for HR certification. She is a past board member of CIBC Insurance and the Toronto French School. She is also a frequent commentator on HRM issues for CTV, *Canada AM*, CBC, *The Globe and Mail, The Canadian HR Reporter*, and other media.

GEORGE W. BOHLANDER

George W. Bohlander is professor emeritus of Management at Arizona State University (ASU). He teaches undergraduate, graduate, and executive development programs in the field of human resources and labour relations. His areas of expertise include employment law, training and development, work teams, public policy, and labour relations. He received his Ph.D. from the University of California at Los Angeles and his M.B.A. from the University of Southern California.

Dr. Bolander is the recipient of six outstanding teaching awards at ASU and has received the Outstanding Undergraduate Teaching Excellence Award given by the College of Business at ASU. In 1996, Dr. Bohlander received the prestigious ASU Parents Association Professorship for his contributions to students and teaching.

Dr. Bolander is an active researcher and author. He has published more than 40 articles and monographs covering various topics in the human resources area: these range from labour–management co-operation to team training. His articles appear in such academic and practitioner journals as *Labor Studies Journal, Personnel Administrator, Labor Law Journal, Journal of Collective Negotiations in the Public Sector, Public Personnel Management, National Productivity Review, Personnel*, and *Employee Relations Law Journal*.

Before beginning his teaching career, Dr. Bohlander served as personnel administrator for General Telephone Company of California. His duties included recruitment and selection, training and development, equal employment opportunity, and labour relations.

He was very active in resolving employee grievances and in arbitration preparation. Dr. Bohlander has also worked with such organizations as the U.S. Postal Service, Kaiser Cement, McDonnell Douglas, Arizona Public Service, American Productivity Center, Rural Metro Corporation, and Del Webb. He is also an active labour arbitrator. He continues to be a consultant to both public- and private-sector organizations.

SCOTT A. SNELL

Scott A. Snell is professor of Business Administration at the Darden Graduate School of Business at the University of Virginia. During his career, Dr. Snell has taught courses in human resources management, principles of management, and strategic management to undergraduates, graduates, and executives. He is actively involved in executive education and serves as faculty director for Penn State's Strategic Leadership Program as well as faculty leader for programs in human resources, developing managerial effectiveness, and managing the global enterprise. In addition to his teaching duties, Dr. Snell serves as director of research for Penn State's Institute for the Study of Organizational Effectiveness.

As an industry consultant, Professor Snell has worked with companies such as Arthur Andersen, AT&T, GE, IBM, and Shell Chemical to redesign human resources systems to cope with changes in the competitive environment. His specialization is the realignment of staffing, training, and reward systems to complement technology, quality, and other strategic initiatives. Recently, his work has centred on the development of human capital as a source of competitive advantage.

Dr. Snell's research has been published in the *Academy of Management Journal, Human Resource Management Review, Industrial Relations, Journal of Business Research, Journal of Management, Journal of Managerial Issues, Organizational Dynamics, Organizational Studies, Personnel Administrator, Strategic Management Journal,* and *Working Woman.* He is also co-author of *Management: The Competitive Edge,* with Thomas S. Bateman. In addition, Dr. Snell is on the editorial boards of *Journal of Managerial Issues, Digest of Management Research, Human Resource Management Review,* and *Academy of Management Journal.*

Dr. Snell holds a B.A. in psychology from Miami University, as well as M.B.A. and Ph.D. degrees in business administration from Michigan State University. His professional associations include the Strategic Management Society, Academy of Management, and the Society for Human Resource Management.

1

PART

HRM Challenges and the Legal Context

1

CHAPTER

THE CHALLENGES OF HRM

OUTCOMES

After studying this chapter, you should be able to

1 Define human resources management (HRM).

2 Identify the processes and practices of HRM.

3 Explain the importance of HRM to the line manager.

4 Discuss the relationship between the line manager and the HR practitioner.

5 Describe current business issues facing organizations and the impact on people in organizations.

6 Outline the key demographic and employee concerns.

7 Illustrate the link between business strategy and HRM strategy.

OUTLINE

HRM CLOSE-UP

"I need to help people understand the important business issues before new ideas can be implemented, all the time being positive and supportive of their need and ability to contribute with fresh thinking."

Tania Goodine always felt she'd like to manage people and develop a team. At university, she chose an undergrad degree in psychology, studied marketing, and then completed her M.B.A. Although her first job was as a marketing officer, Goodine soon headed up a team of her own and found herself doing two things she loves: marketing and people management.

At Libro Financial Group, a credit union with 300 employees throughout southwestern Ontario, Goodine's title is vice-president, Brand. She has responsibility for the identity of the credit union—its reputation in the community, its advertising and marketing programs, and its communications to employees and members.

In contrast to her early days at Libro, Goodine must now get work done through other people. Doing so means spending much of her day developing and coaching people, and helping to solve problems.

"It's always worth it," she says. "Investing time with people, no matter how challenging the conversation, is always worth the time and effort. In a service business, all you have are your people," she says. "They are earning business and keeping business. Therefore all the human resources processes and programs we have in place are critical to our success as a company."

Training at Libro is flexible, and employees complete programs at their own pace. Embracing individual differences and developing people to their full potential is Goodine's goal. "I believe people want to do a good job, and when they're not, there's almost always a legitimate reason. Sometimes, it's simply a training issue. It's almost never that they're unwilling," she explains.

The newest employees sometimes provide the greatest challenges for Goodine. They come to the organization with fresh ideas and eagerness, and it can be a fine balance to harness an employee's energy without shutting the person down.

Courtesy of Tania Goodine

Tania Goodine, vice-president, Brand, Libro Financial Group.

"I need to help people understand the important business issues before new ideas can be implemented, all the time being positive and supportive of their need and ability to contribute with fresh thinking. Exploring social media is one example of that, where we work to establish business objectives and guidelines to manage risk, and then I get out of the way of creative ideas!"

Libro has a prescribed performance management process involving regular feedback with staff. As a result, there are no surprises when it comes to evaluating how a person is doing in their job. "I also look for opportunities to have people hold a mirror up to themselves," Goodine explains. "When employees can see a behaviour themselves, it makes learning and development so much easier."

The most valuable advice Goodine received as a new manager was during a supervisory training session. A leader explained that everybody carries around a personal knapsack of things. It is therefore important to recognize individual differences and vary your style accordingly. Sometimes, a manager needs to be more direct, and sometimes, a softer approach is needed. "Set the tone from day one," says Goodine. "To get trust, you have to give it. Take the time to know people and try to connect in a genuine way."

INTRODUCTION

While the economy has not fully recovered from the Great Recession, it is generally agreed that it was the most severe recession since the days of the Great Depression in the late 1920s.[1] There is no clear evidence as to what created the recession, but it does appear to be triggered by both the housing market and financial system in the United States.[2] What might have been a bad recession turned really bad when the stock market nosedived and created distrust in the banking and stock-market sectors.[3] As money throughout the world became tighter, companies that needed large amounts of cash flow began to experience difficulty in paying bills. Further, problems in sectors that were already in difficulty, such as the auto industry, became even more pronounced. The global economy contracted by 2.1% with 17 million people in the world losing their jobs.[4]

Along with the global economic contraction, major countries spent trillions of dollars (trillion has 12 zeros!) to stimulate their economies. This infusion of dollars continues in 2012 with the European Union (EU) providing cash bailouts for Greece and Spain. There are worries about whether the EU will survive.[5]

However, by the end of the first quarter of 2012, there was confidence that the Canadian economy was on the upswing, with companies looking toward hiring and making some capital investments.[6] This is critical because at the same time, both the federal and provincial governments are beginning to deal with the deficits that have accumulated since the economic slowdown.

The information being presented to you, particularly relating to the legal framework of employment and the various HR processes and practices, will be relevant no matter what is occurring in the economy. By the time you are reading this, given that there is still global instability, the trends facing organizations may have shifted. It will be important for you, your classmates, and your instructor to consider what is happening on the world stage as you read what is being presented here.

The managing of people in an organization remains key to the business agenda—perhaps even more so now. New phrases, such as "human capital," "intellectual assets," and "talent management," have crept into business jargon to emphasize the value that the people in the organization have. As Tania Goodine says in the opening vignette, it is important to recognize the individual differences of each employee and to adapt her style accordingly. But what is human resources management (HRM) and why is it important?

Just for a moment, imagine an organization without people. No employees, no supervisors, no managers, executives, or owners. It's a pretty tough assignment. Without people, organizations would not exist. And while this idea may not be much of a revelation, it brings home the point that organizations are made up of people. Successful organizations are particularly good at bringing together different kinds of people to achieve a common purpose. This goal is the essence of human resources management. As students, you are the future of any organization—whether you become employees, supervisors, managers, or owners.

Human resources management (HRM)
An integrated set of processes, practices, programs, and systems in an organization that focuses on the effective deployment and development of its employees

WHAT IS HUMAN RESOURCES MANAGEMENT?

Outcome 1

What is human resources management (HRM)?

Human resources management is more than hiring, paying, and training people. **Human resources management (HRM)** is an integrated set of processes, practices, programs, and systems in an organization that focuses on the effective deployment and development of its employees.

The word "employee" is also intended to cover a contract worker, a person from another organization who is working on a project, or anyone in another similar working relationship. This expansion of the term is indicative of the new workplace that is far more fluid and flexible than the workforce 10 to 20 years ago.

Managers use a lot of words to describe the importance of people to their organizations. The term "human resources" implies that people are as important to the success of any business as other resources, such as money, materials, machinery, and information.

WHAT ARE THE HRM PROCESSES AND PRACTICES?

Outcome 2

What are the HRM processes and practices?

Before there can be a discussion about why to study HRM, let's look at the various individual systems and processes that fit together. There are some very traditional activities as well as some new and emerging activities. You will also notice that this book is structured on the typical HR activities in an organization.

1. *Organizational, work, and job design*—determining what tasks need to be done, in what order, with what skills, and how individual tasks fit together in work units. For example, in the HRM Close-up, Goodine has to ensure that the tasks are coordinated in a way to get the work done by her team.
2. *HR Planning*—ensuring that people in the organization are the right people with the right skills at the right time in the right place. In the HRM Close-up, Goodine has to plan when it is necessary to add more staff.
3. *Recruitment and selection*—sourcing, attracting, and hiring the people with the necessary skills and background. Goodine had to find and hire the people who can best represent the company and do the work as expected.
4. *Training and development*—providing the resources to assist employees in developing the necessary knowledge and skills to do their job today and in the future. Goodine indicated that training is in a flexible format and that she spends a good portion of each day coaching and helping staff develop to their full potential.
5. *Performance management*—ensuring that there are appropriate mechanisms in place to provide feedback to employees regularly. To ensure that the business objectives are being met, Goodine and Libro provide regular feedback so that there are no surprises during review time.
6. *Rewards and recognition*—developing and administering a variety of rewards and recognition components, including pay and benefits, that will attract, retain, and engage employees. Being in the financial services business, Libro will need to ensure that its compensation program can attract and retain the calibre of staff it desires.
7. *Occupational health and safety*—ensuring that the safety and health of employees are maintained. Goodine and others in the company need to ensure that the physical premises have a safe and healthy work environment.
8. *Employee and labour relations*—ensuring that there are positive and constructive relations between the employees and their supervisors or managers and/or union representatives. Goodine notes that part of her job is to recognize individual differences in staff and adjust her management style accordingly.

While the above lists the more traditional areas, a number of areas are emerging as the field of HR grows and responds to the concerns of both employees and employers. Some of these are (1) organizational development and learning (an extension of training and development); (2) high-performance work groups or teams (an extension of job design and performance management); (3) flexible work arrangements (ways to engage employees and address demographic issues); and (4) HRMS—human resources management systems. HRMS will be discussed more fully in this chapter's section under "Technology and Quality." These processes and activities and their relationship to the organization and the employees are shown in Figure 1.1. Throughout this text, you will also be provided with information that links organizational performance with the various people practices, thereby reinforcing the requirement to have HR processes that fit the organization.

WHY STUDY HUMAN RESOURCES MANAGEMENT?

Outcome 3

Why is HRM important to the line manager?

To work with people in any organization, it is important to understand human behaviour and to be knowledgeable about the various systems and practices available to effectively use as well as build a skilled, knowledgeable, and motivated workforce. At the same time, managers must be aware of economic, technological, social, and legal issues that either help or hinder their ability to achieve organizational success.

The line manager or supervisor is the key link between the employee and the organization. Therefore, the manager must have a thorough knowledge and understanding of contemporary HRM and how these practices influence the output of any organization. You are the managers and employees of tomorrow: studying HRM will help you understand your roles and responsibilities in helping to manage your company's people—its human resources.

In the process of managing human resources, increasing attention is being given to the individual needs of the employees. Organizations understand that the individual and collective knowledge that employees possess and use are significant assets of any organization.[7] Thus, this book will not only emphasize the importance of the contributions that HRM makes to the organization but will also show how, through good people management in an organization, the individual and our overall society are improved. Consider how you feel and behave if your work isn't enjoyable and you don't feel that you understand your role in the organization or that your work doesn't appear to be valued. You might respond in a variety of ways, including being unconcerned about a customer complaint. By acting in this way, you are not contributing to the success of the organization, which includes your own success. If enough people do this, our overall productive capacity as a society will decrease.

In addition, employees and the public at large are demanding that employers demonstrate greater social responsibility in managing their people. Complaints that some jobs are deadening the spirit and injuring the health of employees are not uncommon. Complaints of discrimination against women, visible minorities, the physically and mentally challenged, and the elderly with respect to hiring, training, advancement, and

FIGURE 1.1 Overall Framework for HR

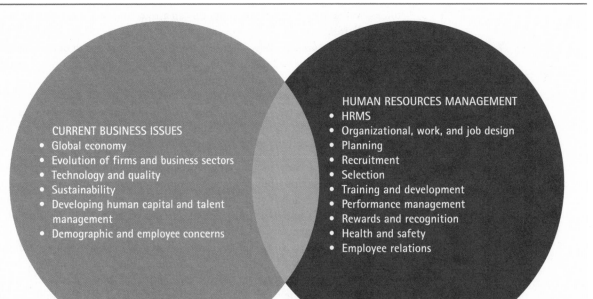

CURRENT BUSINESS ISSUES
- Global economy
- Evolution of firms and business sectors
- Technology and quality
- Sustainability
- Developing human capital and talent management
- Demographic and employee concerns

HUMAN RESOURCES MANAGEMENT
- HRMS
- Organizational, work, and job design
- Planning
- Recruitment
- Selection
- Training and development
- Performance management
- Rewards and recognition
- Health and safety
- Employee relations

compensation are being levelled against some employers. Issues such as comparable pay for dissimilar work, the high cost of health benefits, daycare for children of employees, and alternative work schedules are ones that many employers must address as our workforce grows more diverse.

THE PARTNERSHIP OF LINE MANAGERS AND HR PROFESSIONALS

Role of the Line Manager

Outcome 4

What is the relationship between the line manager and HR practitioner?

Managing people depends on effective supervisors and line managers. Although HR professionals may have responsibility for coordinating programs and policies pertaining to people-related issues, managers and employees themselves are ultimately responsible for making the organization successful. All line managers, in effect, are people managers— not the HR professional or HR unit. It is through the effective leadership of the line manager or supervisor that the talent or "intellectual capital" of the organization is enhanced. Remember that it is the line manager who directly interacts with the employees and is responsible for the effective contribution of those employees to the organization. In a recent survey of the world's most admired companies, it was noted that the most successful organizations recognize that the key driver of their success were employees.[8] In order to keep employees motivated and engaged, these organizations understood that the leadership had to be effective and that managers had to take a key role in coaching and were very influential on how the employees viewed their role in the organization.[9] Therefore, when an organization wishes to place an increased emphasis on the growth and development of its people, it is the line manager who is front-and-centre in identifying the gaps in any skill sets. It is only then that the HR practitioner can offer some ways and means of bridging the gap.

It is also important to understand that the supervisor or manager has "line authority"—being directly responsible for the product or service. Unlike line managers who are directly responsible for a product or service, HR professionals are typically "staff"—people who help and support the line manager. HR professionals may have "functional authority"; that is, they have the legitimate authority in HR areas, such as recruitment strategies or developing organizational programs, to recognize employees. In today's organizations, most HR professionals no longer have total functional authority and are expected to provide advice and guidance to the line. However, there might be a situation that could have very serious consequences for the organization. In this case, the HR professional will be expected to provide advice in a strong and influential way, ensuring that the line manager understands the impact on the organization prior to taking action.

Readers of this book will become line managers, supervisors, and employees as well as HR professionals. This text is oriented toward helping people manage people more effectively and understanding the various HR processes, whether they become first-line supervisors or HR professionals. Students now preparing for careers in organizations will find that the study of HRM provides a background that will be valuable in managerial and supervisory positions. Discussions concerning the role of the HR department can provide a better understanding of the functions performed by this department. A familiarity with HRM will help facilitate closer co-operation between HR professionals, whether they are part of the organization or are a contracted service, and will provide an opportunity to more fully use the expertise of HR professionals. For example, an HR professional can assist the supervisor in developing steps to improve the performance of a particular employee. The consequences for the supervisor of developing a poor approach could result in the employee either not improving the performance or the employee feeling unsupported or criticized by the supervisor's approach. In either situation, the primary objective of improving performance would not be achieved.

Role of the HR Professional

It is important for line managers to understand the role or function HR professionals play, whether these individuals are part of the organization or are external resources retained by the organization. HR practitioners are increasingly becoming more professional and are being trained with common bodies of knowledge and information. Besides knowing how to recruit and pay people appropriately, HR professionals need sound business knowledge, good problem-solving and influence skills, and personal credibility (trust and the ability to build personal relationships). The HR practitioner's primary role in today's organizations is to help equip the line manager with the best people practices so that the organization can be successful. HR professionals can provide service activities, such as recruiting and training. Further, they can be active in policy formulation and implementation in such areas as workplace harassment, healthy work environments, and change management. Lastly, an HR professional can be an employee advocate by listening to employee concerns and ensuring that the organization is aware of and responding to those concerns.

HR professionals are expected to fulfill their role by actively involving others in the organization, particularly the supervisors and managers, in the development and design of HR programs. For example, a company may want the HR professional to develop an overall recruitment approach to attract individuals with key skill sets. This approach would then generate a pool of applicants with the required skills. However, it would be the line manager who would actually select the best person from this pool.

Dave Ulrich,[10] a leading expert and author on human resources practices, states that an HR professional must focus on delivering value to the various stakeholders in any organization—the line managers, the investors, and the employees. Above all else, HR professionals must be able to integrate business skills, HR skills, and skills in helping employees handle change so that their organization can build and maintain a competitive advantage through its people.

In the highly competitive hospitality industry, it is important that hotel managers work closely with HR professionals to hire and retain capable employees.

Taxi/Getty Images

The Ongoing Partnership

As we next look at the competitive and social challenges facing human resources management, it is important to reinforce the idea that managing people is not something that occurs in a back room or is done by HR professionals alone. Managing people is every manager's responsibility and obligation, and successful organizations are those that equip their line managers with a thorough understanding of good HRM practices—either through having an HR unit or retaining expertise when needed. The key is to find ways to develop and utilize the talents of employees so that the employees reach their greatest potential. If an organization has an HR unit, the HR professionals can provide guidance and assistance as internal consultants to the line manager or to help design and deliver programs and services to better equip employees, supervisors, and managers to contribute to organizational success. Even without an HR professional, the manager is still responsible for effective human resources management.

In organizations that have an HR unit, HR managers assume a greater role in top-management planning and decision making, a trend that reflects the growing awareness among executives that HRM can make important contributions to an organization's success. And HR professionals have a critical role to play in facilitating the success of managers by helping them align HR practices to business outcomes.[11] A recent study conducted by Aon Hewitt indicated that successful organizations were paying close attention to talent management, including a fully dedicated executive in charge of talent management.[12] For additional information on the studies conducted by Aon Hewitt in this area, visit its Web site: **www.aon.com**.

Let's reconsider the comments made by Goodine in the HRM Close-up. The organization has more than 300 employees and an HR unit with an HR manager. But many smaller organizations often wonder when they should hire an HR professional. Frequently, when an organization has 75 to 100 employees, the owners or senior management may decide that it would be best to have professional assistance. Figure 1.2 shows what the relationship between HR and other business units might be in a small organization. Even smaller organizations, those with fewer than 75 employees, will frequently retain an independent HR practitioner. When doing so, this is typically done through the owner or president, and the line manager may not have much interaction with the HR expertise.

If Jack needed to hire a customer service agent, he would work with Sarita in confirming the job requirements, identifying possible recruitment sources, doing the final interviewing, and making the decision on which candidate to hire. Sarita, on the other hand, would assist Jack as required, including the development of appropriate interview questions and conducting reference checks.

Aon Hewitt
www.aon.com

FIGURE 1.2 Relationship of HR to Other Business Units

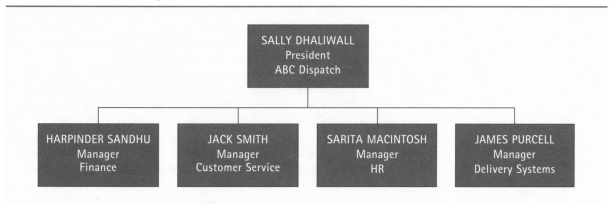

In a larger organization, the HR department may have several professionals to work with employees, supervisors, and managers. Frequently, a particular HR person might be assigned to Jack Smith and be the key contact for all HR services.

CURRENT BUSINESS ISSUES AND THE CHANGING NATURE OF WORK

Outcome 5

What are the current business issues?

Conference Board of Canada
www.conferenceboard.ca

Society for Human Resource Management (SHRM)
www.shrm.org

HR People & Strategy
www.hrps.org

Organizations such as the Conference Board of Canada (**www.conferenceboard.ca**), the Society for Human Resource Management (**www.shrm.org**), and the HR People & Strategy (**www.hrps.org**) conduct ongoing studies of the most important competitive trends and issues facing firms. As we go forward into a new global environment, some of the business challenges are considerably different than they were just a few years ago.

1. Global economy
2. Evolution of firms and business sectors
3. Technology and quality
4. Sustainability
5. Developing human capital and talent management
6. Demographic and employee concerns

Issue 1: Global Economy

The Canadian economy is primarily built on exports, including those in natural resources such as oil, gas, mining, and forestry. Because of this, for years many Canadian companies have been involved in the global markets. As Canada has moved into other goods and services to export, many companies have created global operations or worked collaboratively with foreign companies to sell Canadian products. Canadian exports were valued at close to $460 billion in late 2011.[13] This figure represents approximately 35% of Canada's gross domestic product (GDP).[14] At Work with HRM 1.1 provides insights about a number of Canadian companies that are successful in the global marketplace.

Perhaps one of the more dramatic changes for a Canadian company in the global marketplace has been Research in Motion (RIM). It had been Canada's darling of the tech world ever since the introduction of the BlackBerry. However, through competitors such as Apple and Samsung, the share price for RIM went from $55 in April 2011 to $7 in July 2012—a decrease of more than 600%![15] This dive followed the bankruptcy of Nortel Networks—another tech legend in Canada. The Board at RIM has changed executive leadership, and what will happen is yet to be seen.

Impact of Globalization

Globalization
Moving local or regional business into global marketplace

By partnering with firms in other regions of the world and using information technologies to coordinate distant parts of their businesses, companies such as Bombardier, General Electric, and SNC Lavalin have shown that their vision for the future is to offer customers "anything, anytime, anywhere" around the world. But **globalization** is not just something of interest to large firms. While estimates vary widely, 70 to 80% of the Canadian economy today is affected by international competition. This means, for a small distributor in Kamloops, British Columbia, or a small manufacturer in Alliston, Ontario, that the competition today is no longer the distributor or manufacturer in the next town or province. Trade agreements that allow a freer flow of goods and services mean that competitors may be located anywhere around the world. For example, Finning International, one of the world's largest dealers in Caterpillar heavy equipment, based in Vancouver, British Columbia, generates close to $6 billion in annual revenue from its worldwide markets of which about 50% is from equipment sales in South America and the United Kingdom.[16] In order to remain competitive, managers of today's organizations,

AT WORK with HRM 1.1

OUR GLOBAL SUCCESS: GREAT EMPLOYEES!

Many Canadian companies acknowledge that their success in the global marketplace is attributable to the people they have hired. Firms such as Avison Young, E.C.S. Electrical Cable Supply, Robotec, and Delcan were honoured in early 2012 for being in the top 50 Best Managed Companies in Canada.

Avison Young, a Canadian-owned commercial real-estate venture, is proud of its investment in people. It provides specialized training and workshops that allow its staff to provide exceptional service to the clients. Further, it highlights the importance of collaboration to achieve the best expertise and intellectual capital. It also believes that its culture of team-orientation helps it keep the most talented in the commercial real-estate business.

With operations as far away as Dubai, E.C.S. Electrical Cable Supply provides wire and cable products to specialty markets, such as shipping, mining, and critical life support with portable cables. It is successful because its professionals have deep knowledge of the various industries and superb customer service capabilities. To help with the deepening of its knowledge base, the company provides personal development and encourages everyone to take an active part in the company's success.

Likewise, Robotec, a Quebec-based company that designs and manufactures innovative hydraulic systems that handle bulk solids or unusual items, provides equipment and service to projects in more than 20 countries. Because it employs people with specialized trades such as machinists, it actively recruits the best and then continues with their development to ensure that they will stay.

Delcan, with headquarters in Toronto and operations in South Africa, the United Kingdom, Israel, Hong Kong and the United States, provides superior technology infrastructure and engineering services to such projects as wetland restoration, traffic control systems, and water systems. It attributes its success and growth to the dedication, innovation, and skills of its employees. Delcan's people are engaged because of a competitive compensation program and career advancement.

CRITICAL THINKING QUESTIONS:

1. What other businesses in your geographic area have a global marketplace?
2. What types of skills might their employees need for them to continue being global players?

Sources: Adapted from "Congratulations to Canada's 50 Best Managed Companies of 2011," *The Financial Post*, February 21, 2012, http://business.financialpost.com/2012/02/21/congratulations-to-canadas-50-best-managed-companies-of-2011 (accessed April 15, 2012); "Culture," www.avisonyoung.com/about/culture (accessed April 15, 2012); "A Company that Works for You," www.ecswire.com/careers/a_company_that_works_for_you (accessed April 15, 2012); "About Us," http://rotobec.com/en (accessed April 15, 2012); and "I can impact projects around the world," http://www.delcancareers.com/Homepage.aspx (accessed April 15, 2012).

both large and small, must ensure that they manage their human resources in the most productive, efficient, and effective way possible.

Canada began to show signs of economic recovery in early 2012, and a modest growth in GDP of 2.6% was predicted.[17] With an improved economy, the labour gap (to be discussed later) will become ever more pronounced as people begin to move to new organizations.

Effect of Globalization on HRM

When managers start to "go global," they have to balance a complicated set of issues related to different geographies, cultures, laws, and business practices. Human resources issues underlie each of these concerns and include such things as identifying capable expatriate managers who live and work overseas; designing training programs and development opportunities to enhance the managers' understanding of foreign cultures and work practices; and adjusting compensation plans to ensure that pay schemes are fair and equitable across individuals in different regions with different costs of living.

So, while managing across borders provides new and broader opportunities for organizations, it also represents a quantum leap in the complexity of human resources management. Whether you are working for a large multinational company or a small parts distributor, HRM in other countries has an impact on you. Chapter 11 focuses on international human resources management.

Issue 2: Evolution of Firms and Business Sectors

While the U.S. economy has been in a longer recession than Canada, the two economies are closely linked since approximately 72% of Canada's GDP is exported to the United States.[18] As a result, many firms and certain sectors in North America have been impacted more than others. For example, those companies in Canada that mine and produce gold have done well over the last several years as the price of gold has gone from approximately $1,000 per ounce in early 2010 to more than $1,700 per ounce in early 2012—a 70% increase in the commodity price in two years.[19] Even with the rise in gold prices, other mining sectors have not grown. Teck Resources, for example, saw its share price go from $40 in early 2010 to $32 a few months later to $62 in early 2011 and then back to $35 in early 2012.[20] These wide variances create difficulties when planning for expansion and further investment.

And it isn't just the price of the natural resource on the world market that continues to be volatile; it is also the price per share and, therefore, the value of the company that continues to be affected. It is important to reflect on the stock market over the last several years. Before the recession, the Toronto Stock Exchange had a value of over 15,000 points, then plunged to 7,500 points, and in the first quarter of 2012 improved to 12,000 points.[21] In addition to the slow recovery in the stock market, the banking systems in North America are still very restrictive on their lending requirements and thus not encouraging companies to reinvest any cash on hand.

While the prices of oil and gas have been strong even through the recession, Canada's ability to produce isn't easy given the environmental concerns about extracting and shipping. In order to improve this situation and create a stronger oil industry, the major companies in the oil sands in Alberta have pledged a more collaborative approach with the creation of the Canada Oil Sands Innovation Alliance which will advance science on tailings ponds, land disturbance, and water use.[22]

In addition to oil, gas, and mining, the manufacturing sector, particularly in Ontario and Quebec, declined significantly during the recession and has yet to recover. While the impact on those provinces was highlighted due to the economy, problems in the manufacturing sector have been around for several years.[23] Much of the decrease is attributable to the auto and auto parts industries as well as clothing. There is no doubt that the auto industry has suffered greatly in both Canada and the United States. Even with the large economic stimulus dollars from both the Canadian and U.S. governments, some of these manufacturers did not survive—GM products Pontiac and Oldsmobile among them. And the manufacturing sector wasn't helped when Caterpillar shut its locomotive plant in London, Ontario, in early 2012. The company had had a dispute with its union, the Canadian Auto Workers, and locked out the workers in January 2012. Only a month later Caterpillar closed the plant, stating that it was no longer cost-competitive on a world scale.[24]

On the other hand, new manufacturing is also taking place in places such as Alberta. With the development of the oil sands, new plants are being built to manufacture intricate and complex pipe modules. It isn't the traditional type of mass manufacturing, but a new type where one module is made at a time to specifications, a basic "building block" of refineries and petrochemical plants.[25]

Managing Costs

Companies continue to be pressured to lower costs and improve productivity to maximize efficiency in order to be globally competitive. Labour costs are one of the largest expenditures of any organization, particularly in service and knowledge-intensive companies. Organizations have tried a number of approaches to lower costs, particularly labour costs. These include downsizing and outsourcing, each of which has a direct impact on HR policies and practices.

Downsizing
The planned elimination of jobs

Downsizing is the planned elimination of jobs. The pain of downsizing and layoffs can be felt throughout Canada, even as the economy improves. Some downsizing is a result of governments taking decisions to reduce the cost of government. In late 2011, for example, the federal government announced that it was going to lay off staff throughout the government service.[26] One of the first agencies to be affected was the Canadian Broadcasting Corporation (CBC) which announced a reduction of 650 jobs in an attempt to handle a budget reduction of $200 million.[27]

Virtually every major corporation within the country has undergone some cycle of downsizing. What is intriguing about the current economic climate is that there is a continual concern about a labour shortage as the Canadian economy recovers and therefore some companies are being particularly careful about how they reduce or eliminate work.

A number of lessons were learned in earlier downsizing situations, so organizations are being much more careful about where the operations are reduced. For a number of years, the general approach was to do an across-the-board reduction or to eliminate individuals based on performance. However, studies have demonstrated that it can take between 6 and 18 months for a company to realize savings from job cuts.[28] Without a well-designed downsizing approach, the company may find that its best and brightest have left.[29]

Organizations always attempt to be more creative in order to minimize the amount or type of downsizing. For example, Anderson Water Systems took advantage of a federal program involving work-sharing and encouraged people to use any banked overtime. Likewise, staff at Innotech-Execaire Aviation participated in the work-share program where people worked 50% less.[30] Again, attempting to minimize the impact on individuals while dealing with any financial realities is in the longer-term best interests of the organization and the people.

If jobs and employees have to be eliminated, the manner in which the action is taken also has to be carefully planned. As much attention needs to be paid to those people who will still be employed as to departing employees. It is the people who are still employed will help the company recover from recessionary times, it is important that they feel that the company has treated everyone well. Companies will provide outplacement services (discussed in more detail in Chapter 9) to help employees deal with the transition, particularly during times of economic turmoil.[31]

Outsourcing and Employee Leasing

Outsourcing
Contracting outside the organization for work that was formerly done by internal employees. The small-business owner saves money, time, and resources by outsourcing tasks such as accounting and payroll.

Outsourcing means hiring someone outside the company or bringing in a company to perform tasks that could be done internally. Companies often hire the services of accounting firms, for example, to take care of financial services. Interest in outsourcing has been spurred by executives who want to focus their organization's activities on what they do best. Increasingly, activities such as maintenance, security, catering, and payroll are being outsourced in order to increase the organization's flexibility and to lower overhead costs. Sometimes, there is a perception that people working for outsourcing firms are not paid well. This is not necessarily accurate—it depends on the service and/ or products expected. For example, there may be a situation where an organization needs a senior manager and will contact firms that provide such individuals who might work full-time but not for the same organization.[32]

While the use of outsourcing continues, there are examples of where outsourced work is returning to the home company. Sears Canada has established new call centres in Saskatchewan and Ontario, and brought the work back from the Philippines.[33] It has done so to provide an improved level of customer satisfaction, particularly for repair calls. Likewise, American Express Canada returned some activities to Canada from other countries. Furthermore, in some cases, using outsourced services can help with a business transformation, such as is occurring in Russia, where outsourcing has not traditionally been done.[34] However, since there is always a risk when outsourcing, here are some important things to examine:

1. What does the company want to outsource and why?
2. Who are the service providers and what will be the evaluation criteria?
3. What are the risks of outsourcing and how will the risks be mitigated?[35]

In some situations, a large portion of a company is outsourced in order to create a new business. This occurred with both Hydro One Inc. (formerly Ontario Hydro) and B.C. Hydro, where a number of their customer service areas were outsourced. As an alternative to layoffs and outsourcing, some companies are exploring the idea of employee leasing, where employees are let go and then hired by a leasing company that contracts back with the original company. The Bank of Montreal outsourced its human resources processing services (payroll and benefits administration, HR call centres, and employee records) to Exult, a company specializing in outsourcing, in a contract that saw the transfer of 100 BMO employees to Exult.

In addition to downsizing, outsourcing, and employee leasing, organizations are making more use of contract workers and part-time workers as a way to contain costs. All of these are HRM concerns as managers work to ensure that these individuals understand the mission of the organization and are actively engaged and committed to the organization.

Issue 3: Technology and Quality

Advancements in technology have enabled organizations to improve processes (both production and administrative), reduce costs, and improve quality. With computer networks, unlimited amounts of data can be stored, accessed, and used in a variety of ways, from simple record keeping to controlling complex equipment. The effect is so dramatic that, at a broader level, organizations are changing the way they do business. Use of the Internet to transact business for both large and small companies is now a way of doing business and is transforming the way traditional brick-and-mortar companies do business. For example, Amazon's vision was to be a company that sent books directly without you having to go to a bookstore. Not only did Amazon create a new business model, but its success led to the bankruptcy of a huge bookseller, Borders.[36] Likewise, the law firm of Cassels Brock & Blackwell is making as much use of technology as possible to become more efficient. One thing that creates headaches for lawyers is retrieving information. To streamline this step, a more robust and content-rich system was developed for both storage and retrieval. The firm is also making use of document-drafting software and is field-testing digital dictation on the lawyers' smartphones.[37] Organizations are connected via computer-mediated relationships, and they are giving rise to a new generation of "virtual" workers who work from home, hotels, cars, or wherever their work takes them. The implications for HRM are, at times, mind-boggling.

It is hard to imagine that the Web is only 20 years old and yet the impact has been huge. For example, there are blogs, instant messaging, and now "cloud" computing; music is now downloaded and shared; there are online communities where people who share common interests can come together; news feeds are 24/7; e-mail and e-books are well established; and there is Google.[38] Can you remember when "to google" wasn't a verb or you couldn't access it to answer a question! Google now dominates the search engine competition, enabling more and more information to be retrieved faster and faster.[39] Cloud computing is a growing trend and is expected to create 14 million jobs worldwide, with more than 70,000 in Canada.[40]

Further, it is important to remember the impact that technology and the Internet have had on the way people work. Specifically, people can live in one location and "work" in another. A good example is the owner-operator of Legal Services

Telework
Conducting work activities in different locations through the use of technology

Working in Canada
www.workingincanada.gc.ca

Monster.ca
www.monster.ca

Workopolis
www.workopolis.com

Manpower
www.manpower.ca

International—a firm in British Columbia that provides legal services in the United States. The owner is a lawyer in the United States and does all the service provisions using technology.[41] This kind of work is sometimes called **telework**, where people may have their job structured to allow them to work from home and to work at any time. While telework may be on the decline in the United States, there is evidence that it is very profitable. Recent research suggests that 75% of employees who work from home earn more than $65,000 per year.[42] Canadian businesses have been reluctant to embrace the idea of telework on a large scale; however, more firms are planning to do so to ease work scheduling and increase productivity.[43] Part of the reason for this occurring is that companies, such as MTS Allstream, can reduce the physical space required for their employee base.[44]

In addition, social networks such as Facebook and Twitter enable organizations to better communicate and share information with staff in multiple locations.[45] According to recent statistics, 45% of hiring managers use all types of social media to check job seekers.[46]

As a consequence, the skills necessary to be successful are different. For example, this text provides you with Web sites for additional information. You can access **www. workingincanada.gc.ca** for information on trends in jobs and occupations, earnings, and work prospects in Canada. Likewise, some of you will get work after you finish school by posting your résumé online through **www.monster.ca**, **www.workopolis.com**, or **www. manpower.ca**, or by featuring your résumé on your own home page.

Figure 1.3 provides information about the skills that are important for contributing to innovation in the workplace.

FIGURE 1.3   Innovation Skills

The Conference Board of Canada, as a nonprofit applied research organization, helps identify skills necessary to help organizations be more innovative and productive. Here are some of those skills:

Creativity and continuous improvement skills—necessary to generate ideas
- Seeking different points of view and exploring options
- Being adaptable
- Asking questions
- Putting forward own ideas
- Demonstrating trust in other's ideas

Risk-taking skills—necessary for being entrepreneurial
- Being open to opportunities for change
- Assessing risk
- Encouraging others to bring new ideas forward
- Accepting failures
- Learning from failures

Implementation skills—necessary to turn ideas into processes, products, and services
- Accessing and applying knowledge
- Adapting to changing requirements
- Using the right tools and technologies
- Using measurements to show progress and outcomes
- Adopting a "can-do" attitude
- Tolerating mistakes when trying out new ideas
- Making change visible

Source: Adapted from the *Conference Board of Canada Innovation Skills Profile (ISP)* found at http://www.conferenceboard.ca/hcp/hot-topics/innovation.aspx. Reproduced with permission from the Conference Board of Canada.

Influence of Technology in HRM

Human resources management system (HRMS)
Technology system that provides data and information for purposes of control and decision making

Information technology has, of course, changed the face of all business processes in Canada and abroad. Perhaps the most central use of technology in HRM is an organization's **human resources management system (HRMS)**. An HRMS not only provides data for HR professionals, but it also provides information for the entire organization and includes self-service options for employees.[47] In this sense, such systems have moved beyond simply storing and retrieving information to include broader applications, such as producing reports, forecasting HR needs, assisting in strategic planning and career and promotion planning, and evaluating HR policies and practices. These systems are designed as a resource to be used by the line manager and the HR practitioner to make the best decisions for the organization.

The impact of technology within HR has been both pervasive and profound. Technology allows firms to store and retrieve large amounts of information quickly and inexpensively. It also enables them to rapidly and accurately combine and reconfigure data to create new information and institutionalize organizational knowledge. For example, companies will use data to determine employee attrition or, in the case of Capital One Financial, to analyze the characteristics of its most successful employees, including what schools they went to and what courses they took.[48] Through networks and the Internet, managers can communicate more easily and selectively with others in remote parts of the world, thereby allowing for even better use of the information at their disposal. With the advances of cloud computing, such connectivity is even more powerful as organizations no longer need to rely upon equipment with large capacities. Access can be easy and seamless with just appropriate software, billing-for-use, and use driven by the user.[49] As you probably already know, technology can be a potent weapon for lowering administrative costs, increasing productivity, speeding response times, improving decision making, and enhancing service. It may also be vital for coordinating activities with parties external to the firm. Ultimately, technology can provide a data and communications platform that helps HR staff link and leverage the firm's human capital to achieve a competitive advantage.

Technology influences HRM in three basic ways.

The first is its operational impact; that is, automating routine activities, alleviating administrative burden, reducing costs, and improving productivity internal to the HR function itself. The most frequent uses of technology in HRM include automating payroll processing, maintaining employee records, and administering benefits programs. Another

A person working in a pharmaceutical laboratory needs not only technical skills but also skills in working with others.

new advance in this area is making use of both cloud computing and social media systems to provide information for conducting performance reviews.[50] Organizations are also making use of social media to share goals and help employees understand their contribution in achieving those goals.[51]

The second way technology influences HR is by enhancing services to line managers and employees. Initially, security was a big concern, particularly in relation to employees having access to their own information. However, since online security has improved so much, companies have created more and more applications of employee self-service. In this way employees can bypass HR and handle information about themselves directly. Examples of this are accessing pay statements and updating personal information, such as change of address.[52]

The third influence of technology on HR is the Internet as it has revolutionized our ability to access and use information. Almost every well-known organization, including Canada Post, RONA, Hewlett-Packard (Canada), and IBM Canada, is using the Internet to do everything from reading current job postings, to applying online, to creating "virtual" worlds for training and development purposes. The ever-evolving technology allows users internal to an organization to not just use external social networks such as Facebook, but also internal collaboration tools, such Chatter and Jive.[53] Pitney Bowes has created its own internal collaboration platform, called IdeaNet, where employees throughout the world can connect, make suggestions, and build upon each other's ideas. Finally, technology has a transformational impact by redefining the activities that HR undertakes. James Raybould, director at LinkedIn, describes the influence of using data to analyze various HR processes and to make decisions based on solid information, not conjecture. In doing so, companies have been able to identify bottlenecks and improve abilities to attract and retain talent.[54]

Manager's Toolkit 1.1 provides helpful current Web site addresses for the supervisor or manager.

Quality

Meeting customer expectations and providing excellent customer service are essential for any organization. In addition to focusing on internal management issues, managers must also meet customer requirements of quality, innovation, variety, and responsiveness. These standards often separate the winners from the losers in today's competitive world. How well does a company understand its customers' needs? How fast can it develop and get a new product to market? How effectively has it responded to special concerns? "Better, faster, cheaper"—these standards require organizations to constantly align their processes with customer needs. Management approaches, such as quality management, Six Sigma, and Lean, which are outlined below, provide comprehensive approaches to responding to customers. These have direct implications for HR: the requirement to hire staff that can work in teams, the necessity of having compensation systems that support quality objectives, and the need to have performance management systems that recognize the importance of customer satisfaction and service excellence.

The attention to quality began about 20 years ago with total quality management (TQM) and was based on a management philosophy that focused on understanding customer needs, doing things right the first time, and striving for continuous improvement. Pioneered by Deming, a number of studies have demonstrated the strong positive link between a focus on quality and higher customer satisfaction.[55] TQM is still practised in many countries. For example, companies in India, such as Tata Steel, have used TQM approaches to make its coal washers more efficient and thus produce more timely product for its customers.[56] Since continuous improvement was primarily incremental in its approach, organizations began to use the concept of re-engineering or business process improvement to redesign significant processes. It was felt that everyone in the organization had to be involved to make products or services that fit the purpose.[57]

MANAGER'S TOOLKIT **1.1**

A GUIDE TO INTERNET SITES

The Internet offers managers and HR professionals a vast amount of resources for research, news, recruitment, and networking with people and organizations. Listed below are some Internet sites related to the HR field. Their addresses (URLs) are printed here for reference, but once you get started, it's easier to access the rest by following the links to related sites.

GENERAL HR SITES

www.workforce.com

This site posts articles regarding the latest trends and topics in human resources. It also provides links to HR specialist consultants.

www.hrreporter.com

An excellent Canadian resource for current news, information on the latest trends and practices, expert advice, experiences and insights from HR practitioners, research, and resources.

www.kickstarthr.com

This Canadian site provides all the necessary tools and strategies to attract and retain staff.

www.hrVillage.com

This is an excellent source of up-to-date human resources information, featuring online articles, discussion forums, and links to related sites.

SPECIALIZED SITES

www.canoshweb.org

This site offers a variety of information regarding safety and health in the workplace, reports and statistics, and industry trends. It also provides online access to the workers' compensation legislation in Canadian jurisdictions.

www.hrsdc.gc.ca/eng/labour/labour_law/index.shtml

This site provides online access to federal statutes and regulations, with links to provincial employment legislation.

www.statcan.gc.ca

The Statistics Canada site offers daily news updates, census information, and free tabular data on various aspects of the Canadian economy.

www.cchra.ca

This site provides information about membership in Canadian HR associations, information resources, links to relevant HR sites, and information about the HR professional designation: Certified Human Resources Professional (CHRP).

In addition to the above sites, this book's Web site, **www.stewart5Ce.nelson.com**, provides useful and up-to-date links to accompany this text.

Six Sigma
A process used to translate customer needs into a set of optimal tasks performed in concert with one another

Companies such as Motorola, GE, and Home Depot then adopted a more systematic approach to quality, called Six Sigma, which includes major changes in management philosophy and HR programs. **Six Sigma** is a statistical method of translating a customer's needs into separate tasks and defining the best way to perform each task in concert with the others. In addition, using Six Sigma makes the improvements through diagnosing and solving problems.[58] The approach can also be used for internal organizational processes that deal with internal "customers." For example, Six Sigma has been used in a number of North American organizations to create work environments that are healthier and safer.[59] What makes Six Sigma different from other quality efforts is that it catches mistakes before they happen.

Lean is similar to Six Sigma but is a more inclusive organizational system of workplace improvements that reduce costs, improve overall quality and production, and improve working conditions.[60] It was pioneered by Toyota as a way to continually find waste that creeps into every aspect of a knowledge worker's job.[61] While those organizations that have made use of its principles are strong advocates of the approach, many companies do not realize the cost-saving results they anticipated. A recent study suggested that the lack of success is based on the need for the entire business culture to change in order to achieve the desired outcomes.[62] For example, Caterpillar is identified as an example of an organization that has created a different business culture through the use of Lean. As one expert says, it is a persistent and relentless effort to create a long-term environment that allows front-line staff to generate and implement solutions.[63]

Benchmarking
Finding the best practices in other organizations that can be brought into a company to enhance performance

Benchmarking looks at the "best practices" in other companies, whether they are competitors or not. By looking at other companies, managers and employees can assess whether something could be used in their organization to improve overall performance. For example, Royal Bank is involved in benchmarking customer service practices with other financial institutions in North America.

Key to all of these techniques are good HR practices. One reason that HR programs are so essential to programs such as Six Sigma is that they help balance two opposing forces. Six Sigma's focus on continuous improvement drives the system toward disequilibrium, while Six Sigma's focus on customers, management systems, and the like provides the restraining forces that keep the system together. HR practices help managers balance these two forces. Hence, the manager plays a key role in motivating employees to care about quality and helping the company foster a work environment that will allow employees to succeed in quality initiatives. Read At Work with HRM 1.2 to learn more about the effect of the work environment on quality and productivity.

Another approach to overall quality in an organization is The Baldrige Award for Performance Excellence, sponsored by the National Institute of Standards and Technology in the United States. This award looks at excellence from a systems perspective with detailed criteria in the areas of leadership; strategic planning; customer focus; measurement and knowledge management; workforce focus; process management; and results. In Canada, the awards are managed through Excellence: Canada and companies as small as Print Audit, which provides print management solutions to increase document security and reduce costs, and as large as American Express Canada have been recipients.[64]

The Baldrige Performance Excellence Program
www.nist.gov/baldrige

AT WORK **with HRM 1.2**

CULTURE CREATES EFFICIENCY!

As mentioned in the text, making use of initiatives that promote quality and efficiency is very dependent on the environment and culture of the company. So what happens when there isn't trust?

Union Gas, headquartered in Ontario, realized that it wasn't going to see the improvements its parent company in the U.S. wanted without improving the trust at all levels in the organization, including with the executives. Specialized assistance was brought in to help managers identify how they could best support their staff and the organization overall.

While the change didn't happen overnight, Union Gas is now exceeding all its goals, including improved productivity. It achieved this in part by having all senior management meetings focus on strategy, financial performance, employee engagement, and organizational culture. This enabled senior managers to focus on the right work. The improved culture and high level of employee engagement was largely achieved through the efforts of front-line managers.

To help these individuals, Union Gas invested in their training and leadership development.

Likewise, Zappos, an exceptional online retail store, made headlines with its high level of productivity with a very unusual culture. Zappos focuses on superior customer service while allowing its employees to do what is necessary to ensure that the tasks get done and the customers are totally satisfied. In this way it has created a "flat" culture where there is little gap between front-line employees and management. Results are emphasized, but so is fun. This relaxed atmosphere allows Zappos to show superb organizational performance. The CEO of Zappos, Tony Hsieh, has now taken the culture one step further, saying that the mission of the organization is to deliver happiness!

CRITICAL THINKING QUESTION:

Is use of any quality improvement initiatives just another management fad to get more work out of people? Explain the reasons for your answer.

Sources: Adapted from Virginia Galt, "When management needs a tune-up—or an overhaul," *Report on Business*, March 1, 2012, B10; Neil McEachern, "The Impact of Culture on Productivity," *PeopleTalk*, Fall 2011, 36; and Tony Hsieh, "Delivering Happiness," presentation to BCHRMA Annual Conference, April 27, 2012.

**Standards Council
of Canada**

www.scc.ca

Quality Digest

www.qualitydigest.com

Excellence: Canada

www.nqi.ca

Before we leave the discussion on quality, there is some new research that suggests certain business processes might be better if they weren't standardized. As so often happens with great and new ideas, managers might go overboard and use a certain technique on everything. However, some output in variability may be better for organizational performance than not. For example, the Ritz-Carlton, a global hotel chain noted for its exceptional service, found that certain routines in creating a great guest experience weren't working. For example, staff always saying "good morning" felt stuffy in some situations. To make the interaction with guests seem more natural and spontaneous, the company changed one of its value statements to "I build strong relationships and create Ritz-Carlton guests for life." This change led to encouraging the employees to sense customers' needs and respond accordingly.[65]

Visit the following sites for the most current information about quality initiatives: **www.scc.ca**, **www.qualitydigest.com**, and **www.nqi.ca**.

Issue 4: Sustainability

As the world progresses further into the 21st century, more and more attention is being paid to the health of our planet and to the sustainability of economic growth. The world population is increasing, natural resources are declining, and the climate is changing. People are realizing that there might be finite limits to how much humankind can be sustained. With this, businesses are examining the threats and opportunities that are presented by these concerns.

Some of the threats are in the oil and gas industry where, on the one hand, there is increased demand for its products, but on the other hand, a desire to reduce the world's reliance on fossil fuels for energy. Canada's economy has benefitted greatly from our ability to export oil and gas on the global markets. Change to that would cause dislocation to both the employees and government revenues. A recent study undertaken by Deloitte indicated that Canada needed to pay attention to finite resources and sustainability as well as the skill sets of the labour force to be a healthy and viable economy in the future.[66]

On the other hand, with more focus on sustainability, there are new industries and companies on a global level looking at "clean" technology. Canada appears to be well positioned to move forward on the innovation front. For example, Westport, a Canadian company that specializes in natural gas engines, has partnerships throughout the world to provide engine technology that is better for the environment. It worked with Beijing during the 2008 Olympics to supply 3,000 natural gas engines to produce the additional power required.[67] Currently, it is estimated that 44,000 people in Canada work in clean technology areas and that the numbers are expected to grow five times by 2020.[68]

Besides the environment, climate change is also on businesses' agenda. N-Solv Corp., a Calgary-based company, has developed technology that can extract bitumen from oil sands without using water—thereby reducing greenhouse gases by 85%.[69] Likewise, the Forest Products Association of Canada has helped to introduce imaginative thinking into forest products such that more value can be gained from wood waste—for example, transforming pulp-mill waste into methanol, which can then be used in manufacturing a number of products.[70] By doing this, the waste product does not spew into the atmosphere.

As new business opportunities are created, new jobs and careers will also be created. For example, some of the newer careers are environmental engineers and technologists, conservation biologists, and environmental communications officers. In addition, TD Bank Group has created a "chief environment officer," to ensure that there is a focus on the environment and that it is embedded in the bank's strategy. The bank is not just reducing the amount of paper used but helping to protect critical forest habitat.[71]

To recognize the achievements of organizations that promote and take action for the "greening" of their businesses, Corporate Knights has been tracking, measuring, and ranking Canadian companies for several years. In this fashion, it has honoured a number of companies for being good corporate citizens in relation to the environment and the ability to be sustainable. The top 10 for 2011 include Mountain Equipment Co-op, Enbridge, Vancouver City Savings, and Nexen Inc.[72]

Read HRM and SME 1.1 to learn more about sustaining small businesses.

HRM and SME 1.1

CHALLENGING TIMES FOR SMALL BUSINESSES

Canada's future economic health continues to depend on small businesses—some of which grow into success stories such as Research in Motion (RIM). While RIM is currently struggling, it did start out as small and was for a number of years very successful.

So, how do small businesses succeed in challenging times? One way organizations have been helped is through the Challenge Contest sponsored by Telus Corporation and *The Globe and Mail*. The contest is to award a small business grant by the small business identifying its biggest challenge and how $100,000 would help it succeed. Recently, Sandberg Labs in Alberta received the award that allowed the owners to feel enthusiastic again about the company they purchased in 2010. Sandberg Labs is a soil- and feed-testing company with a focus on determining the amount of organic matter in soils. The award allowed the owners to purchase an automated machine for testing and also to make use of Lean to improve the flow of work. The purchase of the new machine increased the testing output by 14 times and by applying the Lean principles, the owners were able to reduce the amount of movement between operations by 87%. These changes enabled Sandberg Labs to stop being a dinosaur working with "museum pieces" and to become a contemporary business providing a valuable service.

Not only did Sandberg get money to buy equipment, it also received great advice from the judges. Among the advice received was the direction about creating a new image focused on promoting the ethics and honesty of the people running the business. In addition, the award provides coaching for individuals running small- and medium-size businesses.

CRITICAL THINKING QUESTIONS:

1. Would more awards sponsored by private enterprise help small businesses succeed? Why or why not?
2. There are number of government-sponsored resources to help small businesses. Should there be more? Why or why not?

Sources: Adapted from Judy Gerstel, "From museum pieces to modern science," *The Globe and Mail*, February 29, 2012, B8; "The Challenge," *The Globe and Mail*, www.theglobeandmail.com/report-on-business/small-business/sb-growth/the-challenge/contest (accessed April 23, 2012).

Issue 5: Human Capital and Talent Management

Human capital
The individual's knowledge, skills, and abilities that have economic value to an organization

The idea that organizations "compete through people" highlights the fact that success increasingly depends on an organization's ability to manage "human capital." **Human capital** is an overall term used to describe the value of knowledge, skills, and capabilities that may not show up on a company's balance sheet but nevertheless have tremendous impact on an organization's performance. There is no doubt that the knowledge, skills, and abilities of people are becoming increasingly important—particularly in a world of service-oriented work on a global and 24/7 basis.[73]

Human capital is intangible and elusive, and cannot be managed the way organizations manage jobs, products, and technologies. One reason for this is that employees, not the organization, own their own human capital. If valued employees leave a company, they take their human capital with them, and any investment the company has made in training and developing those people is lost. Once again, it is important to emphasize that the supervisor/manager is the link between the organization and the employees. Therefore, managers are key in helping the organization maintain and develop its human capital.

To build human capital in organizations, managers must begin to develop ways of ensuring superior knowledge, skills, and experience within their workforce and to find ways to distribute this "capital" throughout the organization. Managers need to recognize that each person is different and to draw out and build upon those capabilities.[74] In addition, employees need opportunities for development on the job. Therefore, managers have to do a good job of providing developmental assignments to employees and making certain that job duties and requirements are flexible enough to allow for growth and learning. To successfully develop people, supervisors and managers have to "let go."

Further, more and more organizations are recognizing that sets of knowledge capabilities—**core competencies**—are part of their human capital. These competencies are necessary in order to be different from their competition and provide ongoing value to their customers. For example, a core competency might be as follows: *Focus on customer—* ability to make an effort to identify internal and external customers and understand what adds value for them; to create an environment that appreciates delivery of good customer service.

While many core competencies, such as focus on customer or active listening skills, are similar from one organization to another, each organization will develop its own set and define the competency to fit that organization. Thus, the combination of competencies of all employees in that organization makes it stand out from its competition.

Once competencies are identified, organizations, through senior leadership, have to find ways of using and improving the competencies that exist and ensure that they are used in all HR processes and activities.[75] This effort has to go beyond the investment in employee development. Too often, employees have skills that go unused and thus skills become outdated. Some of this can be eliminated by leveraging what people have by sharing and helping others learn.[76] Efforts to empower employees and encourage their participation and involvement utilize the human capital available more fully. Jason Parks, owner of Profab Welding in Alberta, says, "I put my people first and when business was slow, we found a way for people to learn skills from each other which enabled us to expand into new specialty areas."[77]

Studies have consistently demonstrated that an organization's strategic assets include its human capital and that firms with a focus on building and enhancing that capital demonstrate higher profitability and stronger overall organizational performance.[78] Developmental assignments, particularly those involving teamwork, can also be a valuable way of facilitating knowledge exchange and mutual learning. Effective communications (whether face to face or through information technology) are instrumental in sharing knowledge and making it widely available throughout the organization. As Dave Ulrich, considered one of the foremost management gurus of our time, noted,

> When employees find meaning at work, they care enough about it to develop their competence; they work harder and are more productive; they stay longer and are more positive about their work experience. But there is more: when employees are more positive, customers generally respond in kind. Employee attitude is a key lead indicator of customer attitude, and satisfied customers help the businesses they patronize to survive and thrive.[79]

As companies continue to focus on their human capital, the concept of **talent management** has evolved. This is concerned about leveraging the competencies in the organization by ensuring that the competencies are in the right places in the organization and then measuring the impact of those competencies against goals. Given the breadth of the concept, companies will look at various HR practices that have to be more clearly integrated than what might be found in many organizations. The HR practices that need to be considered in order to attract, keep, and engage employees include such things as:

having a profile of top talent
providing opportunities for professional and personal development
creating a sense of purpose in work
ensuring that there is work–life balance
making the workplace supportive for women
recognizing, acknowledging, and celebrating the unique contributions of each person
ensuring that the rewards are appropriate for retaining talent.[80]

For additional online resources that help small organizations develop their human capital, see **www.humancapitalonline.com** or **www.inc.com**.

Core competencies
A combination of knowledge, skills, and characteristics needed to effectively perform a role in an organization

Talent management
Leveraging competencies to achieve high organizational performance

Human Capital Online
www.humancapitalonline
.com

***Inc.* (Small Business Ideas and Resources for Entrepreneurs)**
www.inc.com

Issue 6: Demographic and Employee Concerns

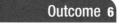

Statistics Canada

www.statcan.gc.ca

In addition to the competitive challenges facing organizations, managers in general, and HR professionals in particular, need to be concerned about changes in the makeup and expectations of their employees. Some of these issues will be discussed here and others will be discussed in other chapters.

Among the most significant challenges to managers are the demographic changes occurring in Canada. You can find current information about the labour force through Statistics Canada (**www.statcan.gc.ca**). Because they affect the workforce of an employer, these changes—in employee background, age, gender, and education are important topics for discussion.

Diversity of Backgrounds

Canadian workers will continue to be a diverse group. According to a recent report by Statistics Canada, it is predicted that 33% of the labour force will be foreign born and that 15% of the labour force will belong to a minority group.[81] Most of the immigration is from Asia—a sharp contrast to immigration that occurred 40 years ago, which was primarily from European countries. Immigrants tend to settle in large urban areas such as Toronto, Montreal, and Vancouver. It has also been predicted that by 2031, over 50% of the population in Toronto, Montreal, and Vancouver will be visible minorities with more than 70% of all immigrants settling in those three cities.[82] The majority of immigrants coming to Canada are from China, South Asia, Korea, and the Arab countries.

To ensure that skilled immigrants have access to employment opportunities, a number of partnerships have developed such as the Toronto Region Immigrant Employment Council (TRIEC) and the Assisting Local Leaders with Immigrant Employment Strategies (ALLIES), which is modelled after TRIEC. The purpose of these agencies is to help immigrants make use of their skills and talents in the workforce so that Canada can become more prosperous as a nation.[83]

Aboriginal people make up 3.8% of the population and are predicted to be 5% of the population by 2031.[84] Of particular note is the number of Aboriginal youths and the efforts of organizations to find ways to better involve Aboriginal people in the workforce. To assist with this, the Aboriginal Human Resource Council has a mandate to advance the full labour-market participation of Aboriginal people. Employers such as RBC, Syncrude, and IBM Canada are actively involved in the Council's programs and as advocates to other employers. To learn more, access the Council's Web site at **http://aboriginalhr.ca**.

More about the recruitment and selection of immigrants and Aboriginal people will be discussed in Chapter 4.

Aboriginal Human Resources Council

http://aboriginalhr.ca

Generations at Work

The working-age population in Canada is becoming older—there are more individuals than ever before in the older age brackets (ages 45 to 64) and fewer individuals than ever in the younger brackets. According to the 2011 census, the employment rate for the 45 to 64 age bracket is 71%, with 11% of the people over 65 having jobs.[85] The 45 to 64 age bracket accounted for over 28% of Canada's total population of 34.5 million in 2011, compared with only 20% in 1991.[86] And the 55 to 64 year age group now accounts for 18% of the workforce.[87] Further, by 2021, it is expected that approximately 25% of the workforce will be over 55.[88]

The age distribution throughout the Canadian workforce means that there can be several generations working together—all with different values and expectations. It is predicted that there can be as many as six generations in the workplace, which means that organizations will need to find ways for everyone to work together in a positive and healthy manner.[89]

A recent study by PricewaterhouseCoopers identified that with older people working longer and with younger, eager-for-advancement people moving into roles with more responsibility, Gen X employees (born between 1960 and 1981) are not getting the promotions they expected.[90] Further, Gen Y employees (born between 1982 and 2000) want to know the company's vision and want the culture articulated, especially in being more than just profit oriented. Gen Y staff want the company to be socially responsible.[91] As a result, employers will need to be very vigilant about understanding the needs, wants, and values of the different age cohorts in their organization. Figure 1.4 provides a summary of the generational differences, including those individuals who are 65 but perhaps not yet retired.

Companies are responding in a number of ways to this demographic shift. More attention is being paid to the corporate culture and ensuring that staff fit well with the culture and values of the organization. Culture is important as it drives the company's performance and results. For example, HP Advanced Solutions, a Victoria-based subsidiary of HP, has a culture which encourages a number of different approaches to career advancement, including temporary assignments and job shadowing.[92] Read Manager's Toolkit 1.2 to find out about some of the other HR practices affected by an aging population.

Skills and Labour Shortage

With the aging of the workforce and fewer new entrants, there is a concern about shortages—and primarily for skilled workers. The current economic climate is improving, and the shortages are becoming more problematic. And the situation is not just about the

FIGURE 1.4   Generations at Work

	Veterans (Born 1930–1941)	Boomers (Born 1943–1960)	Gen X (Born 1960–1981)	Gen Y/Millennials (Born 1982–2000)
Work ethic values	Respect authority	Question authority Question work ethic of younger people Efficient	Intolerant of bureaucracy Hardworking and bottom-line oriented	Loyal Tech savvy Optimistic Need challenging work Involved in green causes and social activism Like extrinsic rewards Achievement oriented
Interactive style	Very independent	Team player	Independent	High socialization Need positive reinforcement Technologically dependent E-mail, social networking, less face time
Idea of work	Expected	Adventure	Challenge	Means to end Want interesting work and not motivated to do boring work Energetic
View of work rewards	Get what deserve	Expect money and promotion	Prefer freedom and flexibility	Instant feedback Recognition when due
Work and family life	Dependable	Thrive on adrenaline	Socially responsible	Need work–life balance Told by parents that they were special

Sources: Adapted from "How five generations can work together," Troy Media, September 8, 2010, www.troymedia.com/blog/2010/09/08/how-five-generations-can-work-together (accessed April 20, 2012); Misty Harris, "Clash of cultures on the way?" *Vancouver Sun*, March 22, 2012, B3; Harvey Schachter, "Five myths about Gen Y workers," *The Globe and Mail*, April 2, 2012, B7; Sarah Boesveld, "Public resignations popular with Gen Y," *Vancouver Sun*, August 13, 2011, C5; and "Value through your people," PricewaterhouseCoopers, 2012.

WORKING TOGETHER!

With more older workers staying in the workforce and with a slow economy, tensions can arise from younger workers who are eager to move ahead. And depending on how an organization handles this matter, the tensions can be reduced, resulting in a highly productive and healthy organization.

There are two key steps. The first step is to recognize that there are differences between the generations (see Figure 1.4). The second step is to accept those differences and the idea of younger employees working or interacting with more senior and seasoned employees.

For example, I Love Rewards Inc., a Toronto-based company that designs and implements incentive solutions for small- and medium-sized companies, understands the nature of its workforce and that it has three generations of employees. To assist in creating a harmonious work environment, it has a democratic environment that allows Gen Ys to work on important projects. Further, the CEO states that if you want an organization that is flat with no hierarchy and no command-and-control style of management, you have to be very careful in hiring people who can work and be comfortable in that type of environment.

It also means providing a bit more flexibility for younger workers who have much more complexity in their lives. Gen Ys are likely to have young children who need quality childcare at an affordable price—hard to come by. This means that Gen Ys may not seem as dedicated to their work when, in fact, they have multiple demands on their time.

Another way to provide older workers with meaningful work and yet find ways to move younger workers into more responsible roles is to assist with a "transitional career"—something different than what they are currently doing and that will provide a bridge into full-time retirement. This approach can also include creating more flexible work schedules and assisting younger workers in a mentorship arrangement. While an older worker may not be able to keep up with the physical demands of a job, or have health issues that could be problematic for an organization, it doesn't mean that there isn't a role for that person. Companies may need to be more creative in finding suitable work that is both engaging and rewarding for both the company and the person.

Finally, as has been noted elsewhere, Canada is experiencing skills shortages in a variety of industries so making the best use of all our workforce participants is an imperative.

Sources: Adapted from Marjo Johne, "An office with liberty and justice for all?" *Report on Business*, June 16, 2011, B10; Harvey Schachter, "Five myths about Gen Y workers," *The Globe and Mail*, April 2, 2012, B7; Paul Kershaw, "Generation Squeeze's seismic shift," *Vancouver Sun*, October 31, 2011, A9; and Misty Harris, "Retirement takes on a new meaning," *Vancouver Sun*, March 12, 2012, B2.

number of workers—shortages are occurring where people do not have the skills that are required for a changing economic base. A recent survey by the Bank of Canada found that 27% of employers reported a labour shortage in 2012.[93]

Some industries are more greatly affected by shortages than others. The mining industry is expanding and will need more than 100,000 skilled workers over the next 10 years as many of the existing employees will be leaving. To help handle this situation, firms such Tetra Tech, a mining engineering services company, is hiring people just graduating from university and training them.[94] The company also pays for specialized software training. Likewise, Cabo Drilling Corp., in B.C., pays slightly higher bonuses to encourage retention.[95] Unfortunately, some organizations feel that the problem can be addressed either by doing more advertising or by dedicating more people to recruitment activities. However, as was stated a few paragraphs ago, there are fewer new entrants due to fewer people being born.

To deal with these shortages, an employer can do a number of things including providing more mentoring for Millennials, ensuring that the management style in the organization is suitable for both tech-savvy workers and workers who are less tech-savvy, and encouraging older workers to stay and share their knowledge and expertise.[96] Recent projections indicate a continuing shortage of people with technical, engineering, and information technology skills as well as for jobs such as professional truck drivers.[97]

Part of the concern about a shortage of labour is that the economy could also slow in its growth. This is because the labour-force participation rate—the percentage of the population working—is forecast to decline as the population ages.[98]

One way the labour shortage is being addressed is through changes in federal government policy. Specifically, in late 2011, Canada expanded the number of foreign students who could acquire permanent residency and earn their Ph.D. here. It is anticipated that through this measure, students will remain in Canada to work once their education is completed.[99] In addition, Canada added a "fast track" program for temporary foreign workers with the necessary skills to gain permanent resident status. Again, the initiative is anticipating that people who are familiar with living and working in Canada will want to stay.[100]

Gender Distribution of the Workforce

According to Statistics Canada, 62% of women over 25 are working.[101] Employers are under constant pressure to ensure equality for women with respect to employment, advancement opportunities, and compensation. And since the rate is so high during women's child-bearing years, employers also need to accommodate working mothers and fathers through parental leaves, part-time employment, flexible work schedules, job sharing, telecommuting, and childcare assistance. Employers are also finding that many working people are now faced with being caregivers to aging parents. Thus, the whole area of "dependent care" is creating issues in organizations that will require creative solutions. In addition, because more women are working, employers are more sensitive to the growing need for policies and procedures to eliminate sexual harassment in the workplace. Some organizations have special orientation programs to acquaint all personnel with the problem and to warn potential offenders of the consequences. Many employers are demanding that managers and supervisors enforce their sexual harassment policy vigorously.

Rising Levels of Education

The educational attainment of the Canadian labour force has steadily risen over the years. Not coincidentally, the most secure and fastest-growing sectors of employment over the past decade have been in those areas requiring higher levels of education. As organizations become more sophisticated and use more technology, there is less and less employment available for unskilled workers. The more education a person has, the greater the chances are of having work. The participation rate for those individuals with high school was 75% compared to 83% for university graduates. People with Grade 3 or less have about a 45% participation rate.[102] What is also notable is that more and more people are combining school and work—over 60% of full-time students are also working, and most are employed in retail, grocery stores, or food outlets.[103] Also, the earnings of university graduates continue to be 72% higher than those of high-school graduates, and work prospects and opportunities increase with the amount of education.[104]

It is important to observe that while the educational level of the workforce has continued to rise, there is a widening gap between the educated and noneducated, leading to different types of work experiences. At the lower end of the educational spectrum, many employers are coping with individuals who are functionally illiterate—unable to read, write, calculate, or solve problems at a level that enables them to perform even the simplest technical tasks, such as reading an operating manual or reading safety procedures. The topic of literacy will be discussed in more detail in Chapter 5, but it is important to know that it is estimated poor literacy skills may have cost the Canadian economy as much as $80 billion in lost opportunities.[105] On the other hand, there is also some

As more and more employees strive to balance the demands of their jobs with the needs of their families, employers are responding by offering greater flexibility, such as part-time work and parental leave.

evidence that a university degree is now the new high-school diploma and students may not have the appropriate human capital skills required.[106]

The Changing Nature of the Job and Cultural Changes

The era of the full-time ongoing job seems to have disappeared. Nearly half of all jobs created during the last two decades were nontraditional—that is, part-time, temporary, or contract work. As job security erodes, so do pension plans and health-care benefits, particularly for part-timers. About 20% of the working population work part time and almost all do so voluntarily. Further, more than 15% of Canadians are self employed.[107] With the change in the traditional notion of "job," companies, however, place high value on team-structured work and on projects, something that also leads to new issues in creating effective HR processes.

The attitudes, beliefs, values, and customs of people in a society are an integral part of their culture. Naturally, their culture affects their behaviour on the job and the environment within the organization, influencing their reactions to work assignments, leadership styles, and reward systems. Like the external and internal environments of which it is a part, culture is undergoing continual change. HR processes and systems, therefore, must be adjusted to accommodate and integrate these changes.

Employee Rights, Ethics, and Privacy

Over the past few decades, legislation has radically changed the rules for managing employees by granting them many specific rights. Among these are laws granting the right to equal employment opportunity, union representation if desired, a safe and healthy work environment, minimum working conditions (hours of work, wages, vacations, etc.), and privacy in the workplace. More information on employee rights will be presented in both Chapter 2 and Chapter 9.

With the various business scandals that continue to plague North America, increased attention is being paid to business ethics. This topic will be explored more fully in Chapter 9; however, Ethics in HRM 1.1 describes employees' views of ethics.

HR managers and their staffs, as well as line managers, generally recognize the importance of discretion in handling all types of information about employees. The *Personal Information Protection and Electronic Documents Act* (PIPEDA) is a federal law that deals with the collection, use, and disclosure of personal information (note that Quebec is the only province with similar laws, although Ontario and others have draft legislation in place). This law requires federally regulated organizations holding personal information on customers or employees to obtain their consent before they use, collect, or disclose this information. Chapter 2 will describe more on privacy.

Changing Attitudes toward Work

With the different expectations of people, as discussed in "Generations at Work" (Figure 1.4), it means that there are also changing attitudes toward work and what will motivate people. Organizations that create supportive and inclusive cultures are seen as great workplaces where people want to do their best. Also, more and more evidence is being accumulated to demonstrate that these organizations outperform on the stock market and have done so consistently even through the Great Recession.[108] For example, Digital Extremes, recently named one *Financial Post*'s Ten Best Companies to Work For, receives high praise from employees for its parent leave top-up and skills development support with tuition subsidies.[109] TD Bank Financial Group was also recognized for its top-up payments to both parents and even for adoptive parents.

Another well-established trend is for employees to define success in terms of personal self-expression and fulfillment of potential on the job. They are frequently less obsessed with the acquisition of wealth and now view life satisfaction as more likely to result from balancing the challenges and rewards of work with those of their personal lives. Though most people still enjoy work and want to excel at it, they tend to be focused on finding interesting work and may pursue multiple careers rather than being satisfied with just "having a job." People also appear to be seeking ways of living that are less complicated but more meaningful.

These new lifestyles cannot help but have an impact on the way employees are motivated and managed. Research has demonstrated that employees who are actively mentored report higher job and personal satisfaction, and organizational commitment.[110] On the other hand, the recession also made people re-examine the importance they put on work: 47% said that family was now more important while 37% said that work wasn't as important as it once was.[111]

ETHICS **in HRM 1.1**

ETHICS START AT THE TOP!

More and more focus is being put on leadership and ethics. No matter how much a company does to attract, retain, and engage employees, if the leaders do not conduct themselves ethically, people will not stay.

And ethics can take many different forms. For example, according to a recent survey by Aon Hewitt, ethics includes people being honest and fair, and the organization producing reasonable services or products at a reasonable price.

Another aspect of ethics is ensuring that the organization has a whistle-blower policy and that people are encouraged to bring concerns to senior managers. But this isn't always the case. For example, even with enhanced regulatory requirements around whistle-blowing, employees can experience negative reactions. This happened at Citigroup when the vice-president of consumer lending expressed concern about the quality of the mortgages being bought from other companies. When no response came from superiors, the person tried once more by alerting the board of directors. Unfortunately, the person was terminated, and it is now a matter of history as to what happened to mortgage lending in the U.S.

Ethics Resource Center, a nonprofit organization dedicated to improving ethical practices, has recently identified how leaders can enhance ethical practices. Among these are the following:

- Create a strong ethical culture where senior leaders demonstrate that integrity is a priority.

- Ensure that the ethics training is strong and that the ethics program is visible.

- Top executives need to behave ethically as others will observe and follow.

- Talk about the value of ethics at all times, and encourage employees to bring any wrongdoing to the attention of their leaders.

QUESTION:

Are there other ideas you have for how leaders can enhance ethical practices? Explain your reasons.

Sources: Adapted from David Crisp, "Respect, good leadership (ethics) and quality people," *Canadian HR Reporter*, September 12, 2011, www.hrreporter.com/blog/Strategic-HR/archive/2011/09/12/respect-good-leadership-(ethics)-and-quality-people (accessed April 21, 2012); Susan Ladika, "Whistle While You Work," *Workforce Management*, April 1, 2012, www.workforce.com/article/20120401/NEWS02/120409999/0/7xd7o3s (accessed April 21, 2012); Steve Watkins, "Take These Steps to Improve Weakening Leader Ethics," *Investors Business Daily,* March 29, 2012, news.investors.com/articleprint/606024/201203291305/improve-ethical-culture-to-keep-wrongdoing-low.aspx (accessed April 21, 2012).

Balancing Work and Family

Work and the family are connected in many subtle and not-so-subtle social, economic, and psychological ways. Because of the new forms that the family has taken—for example, the two-wage-earner and the single-parent family—work organizations find it necessary to provide employees with more family-friendly options. "Family friendly" is a broad term that may include flexible work schedules, daycare, part-time work, job sharing, parental leave, executive transfers, spousal involvement in career planning, assistance with family problems, and teleworking. Another emerging issue is that of eldercare. Many employees not only balance work and childcare but are also responsible for aging parents.

Pfizer Canada and Manitoba Hydro were recently awarded "Top Family-Friendly Employers" for their initiatives supporting parents with young families. Some of the initiatives include flexible work schedules, maternity and parental leave top-ups, and compassionate care leave.[112] Further, other studies have demonstrated that flexible work schedules create higher levels of job satisfaction and less likelihood that employees will look for other work.[113]

There is also the issue of today's workforce being responsible for caregiving—and not just of young children. Many employees are looking after family members with disabilities or aging parents. Saskatchewan Government Insurance is recognized as a leader in not only providing work scheduling flexibility for caregiving but in continuing full salary while employees have to be off.[114] Although provincial employment standards legislation and Employment Insurance (EI) provide for time and pay, both are at reduced rates. Provisions of this kind help people stay productive while at work as they do not have to worry when time off is needed.

For additional insights on trends and issues, read Emerging Trends 1.1.

EMERGING TRENDS **1.1**

1. ***Continued development of clean technologies***. More and more innovations are occurring with waste, and as a result, more "greening" is happening. Aspera Recycling in Toronto, for example, is finding ways of taking 230 million tons of carpeting a year and making the waste useful. Some of the carpeting is used in projects such as Habitat for Humanity. Most, however, becomes other products such as plastic patio furniture. Likewise, Blue Fuel Energy, for example, is making use of CO_2 to create methanol.

continued

2. **Creating more environmentally friendly office environments**. Along with the ongoing development of clean technologies, more offices are looking at acquiring LEED certification that the physical space has been designed and built to be as environmentally healthy and energy efficient as possible. For example, Earth Rangers in Ontario created an open concept workspace that incorporated some of the mechanics of the structure while creating workspaces that allowed people to function in a more informal atmosphere.

3. **Enhancing work flexibility**. Partly in response to the values and expectations of younger workers, but also as a way to minimize traffic congestion and increasing public transit, organizations are rethinking the daily commute. For example, Cisco, a global producer of networking equipment, allows 85% of its employees to telework with no set work schedule.

4. **Increased attention to the culture of an organization**. Partly due to the changing demographics and partly due to the talent shortage, organizations are placing more emphasis on ensuring that they have cultures that are welcoming, supportive, and will engage employees. For example, SaskCentral, a financial services co-operative in Regina, was recently named the Best Employer in Medium-Sized Companies for its culture of empowerment and caring.

5. **Retention of older workers**. As the skill shortage becomes more acute, and as older employees want to work longer, organizations will place more emphasis on identifying what talents they have in older workers and how any untapped skills can be used. By not looking at underutilized skills, the organization may experience reduced performance over time.

6. **Acceleration of technology**. The changes in technology are happening more quickly than ever. Broadcast TV is under attack by viral TV; e-commerce and B2B business are threatening the bricks-and-mortar businesses; and libraries and references are being replaced by Wikipedia.

Sources: Adapted from "Report on Green Solutions," *The Globe and Mail*, April 20, 2012; Nick Rockel, "The office gets a blast of fresh air," *Report on Business*, January 25, 2012, B16; Cindy Krischer Goodman, "Welcome to the new workplace," *Vancouver Sun*, November 26, 2011, C6; "Canada's Best Workplaces, 2012," *The Globe and Mail*, GPTW1; Ed Frauenheim, "Stressed & Pressed," *Workforce Management*, January 2012, 18–22; Ian Henry, "Baby boomers aren't all alike," *Canadian HR Reporter*, April 25, 2012, 11; and Jeremy Gutsche, Trendhunter, Opening Plenary Speaker, BCHRMA Conference, April 26, 2012.

BUSINESS STRATEGY AND HRM STRATEGY

Outcome 7

What is the link between business strategy and HRM strategy?

As you can see, there are many issues facing supervisors and managers, as well as HR professionals, in today's business environment. In order to effectively manage these issues, an organization develops a business strategy to enable it to achieve a high level of performance. The strategy helps the organization determine what business or businesses it will be in, why it exists, what its key goals are, and what actions it needs to take to realize those goals.

It is important to recognize the distinction between *corporate strategies* and *business strategies*. Corporate strategy deals with questions such as these: Should we be in business? What business should we be in? Corporate strategies are company-wide and focus on overall objectives, such as long-term survival and growth. There are two main types of corporate strategies. The first is a restructuring strategy, to ensure long-term survival. Under this option, we can find turnaround situations (Harmac Mill), divestitures (the Gillette empire getting rid of the Montreal Canadiens), liquidation (Circuit City), and bankruptcy (Magna Entertainment).

The second corporate strategy is growth. Organizations can grow incrementally (by adding new products or new distribution networks). For example, Procter & Gamble added skin care lotion and hair conditioners for babies, and began to distribute to drugstores as well as grocery stores. Organizations can gain new customers by expanding internationally as Finning International Ltd. did when it started selling and renting Caterpillar equipment to the United Kingdom and Chile. Growth can also be achieved through mergers and acquisitions, such as when Rogers Communications acquired Fido and Best Buy Canada acquired Future Shop.

Unlike corporate strategy, business strategy focuses on one line of business and is concerned with the question "How should we compete?" Michael Porter has developed a classification system that helps us understand five ways in which a business unit can compete.[115] Let us illustrate his model by analyzing how hamburgers are sold. Restaurants can compete by being a low-cost provider (McDonald's); by trying to differentiate their products in a way that will attract a large number of buyers (e.g., Burger King introducing the Whopper); by being a best-cost provider through giving more value for the money (e.g., East Side Mario's sells hamburgers, but on a plate in an attractive environment); by focusing on a niche market based on lower cost to a select group of customers (e.g., offering fish burgers or vegetarian burgers); or by offering a niche product or service customized to the tastes of a narrow market segment (MBRGR in Montreal sells a hamburger sprinkled with truffle shavings and fries for $100).

Part of any business strategy is to be competitive. However, to be competitive, an organization needs to think about its people as part of its competitive advantage. Thus, the people in the organization need to be managed in a manner that enables achievement of the business strategy.

While people have always been central to organizations, today's employees are critical in helping to build a firm's competitive advantage. Competitive advantage is the capacity or quality that gives an organization an edge over its competition. The advantage could be productivity, price, quality, delivery, or service. Therefore, the focus of current HRM thinking and research is identifying and implementing people processes and systems that can make a particular firm stand out above the rest. Thus, the HR practices are expected to develop the employees' abilities and to motivate employees such that the organization is successful. There is also a body of knowledge that suggests these practices do not necessarily lead to the organizational results desired if these HR practices do not fit the needs of the organization and are not helpful to managers.[116] Therefore, for HR processes to lead to organizational success, the HR systems must be supported, used, and highly regarded. This strategy identifies the role the line manager plays in, for example, management development.

An HR strategy aligned with the business strategy is particularly critical in organizations whose products or services rely upon the knowledge, skills, abilities, and competencies embedded in the employees—the knowledge workers. Research has confirmed that the better an organization makes use of the knowledge held by all the people in the organization, the better the organization's overall performance.[117] As a result, the HR areas of recruitment, learning and development, and retention—or "talent management"—become crucial to the attainment of the business goals.

For example, companies such as CIBC are intentionally designed to increase the value that employees add to the bottom line and to customer satisfaction. CIBC actively involves employees in day-to-day decisions, such as determining what specific steps can be taken to reduce customer complaints. Further, companies such as the Four Seasons Hotels invest a great deal to hire and train the best and brightest employees in order to gain advantage over their competitors.

Human resources management strategy
Identifying key HR processes and linking those to the overall business strategy

What then is the link between business strategy and a human resources strategy? As stated earlier, a **human resources management strategy** involves the development and implementation of HR practices that ensures the human capital (employees) contribute to the achievement of business objectives.[118] When one company buys another company, often the success of the new business revolves around how well the people side of the merger was handled. This was a critical issue when Aon, a worldwide risk management company, bought Hewitt, a very successful HR consulting firm. Aon knew that the success of the merger was dependent on how well the two businesses integrated their people. To help with team building, it created "Pass It On." This initiative sought to combine the components of employee engagement, community service, and client relationships to facilitate an understanding that the 60,000 employees throughout the world are empowered to get results for their clients and communities.[119]

Organizations of all sizes, public or private, will undertake a set of HR practices that enhance the employees' contribution for organizational success—the success as defined by the business strategy. Thus, all managers play a tremendous role in developing and maintaining effective HR practices and assisting the organization in acquiring a competitive advantage. If a manager believes that employees must be carefully monitored, when the business strategy suggests that employees need to be empowered, then it is highly unlikely the business will succeed. When a company (or a line manager) doesn't link the people processes and practices with the business objectives, the company will be unable to leverage its knowledge capabilities and will not be innovative enough to achieve the necessary competitive advantage.[120] For example, if a company wished to focus on providing superb customer service, then the company would have an employee selection process that hired people with those skills. Further, it might also have a training and development program that reinforced the expectations regarding customer service. And it would also have a performance management system that rated how well the employees did in customer service. For example, Lowe's identified the HR processes necessary for business success, developed appropriate HR linkages to business results, and instituted a measurement system that could determine if the desired results were being achieved.[121] Likewise, Teck Resources identified that one of its key business results is responsible resource development, and to achieve that, it must protect the safety of its employees. Part of its HR strategy is to use safe behaviour as a competency and to ensure its training reflects the "safety first" mindset. Also, Coast Capital has values that include being innovative and working collaboratively. Again, its HR strategy provides managers with tools to encourage innovation and develop teams.[122]

While "competing through people" may be a key theme for human resources management, the idea remains only a framework for action. On a day-to-day basis, managers frequently focus on specific business challenges and issues, and may not always focus as critically on the people issues. You can see from Figure 1.1 that HRM helps blend many aspects of management–business pressures, such as technology and the global market, with the changing nature of the workforce. By balancing what are sometimes competing demands, HRM plays an important role in getting the most from employees for organizational success and providing a work environment that meets the employees' short- and long-term needs.

SUMMARY

1. Define human resources management (HRM).
   - Integrated set of processes, programs, and systems that focus on effective deployment and development of employees.

2. Identify the processes and practices of HRM.
   - Organizational, work, and job design
   - HR planning
   - Recruitment and selection
   - Orientation, training, and development
   - Performance management
   - Recognition and rewards—developing and administering a variety of components, including pay and benefits that will attract and retain employees
   - Occupational health and safety
   - Employee and labour relations

3. Explain the importance of HRM to the line manager.
   - Line manager is key link between employee and organization.
   - Helps you understand roles and responsibilities in managing employees.
   - People have always been central to organizations, but their strategic importance is growing in today's knowledge-based industries.

4. Discuss the relationship between the line manager and the HR practitioner.
   - Every manager's job is managing people.
   - Successful organizations equip their line managers with a thorough understanding of HRM.
   - HR professionals help the line manager be a good people manager by providing advice as well as direct services.
   - Combining expertise of HR professionals with the experience of line managers can develop and utilize the talents of employees to their greatest potential.

5. Describe current business issues facing organizations and the impact on people in organizations.
   - Globalization is creating pressure for managers to effectively manage people.
   - Evolution of firms and business sectors will focus on maximizing utilization of employees.
   - Technology has enabled organizations to focus on quality and customer.
   - Environment and climate change is creating both threats and opportunities.
   - Businesses are concerned about their human capital and talent management.
   - Demographics are creating challenges in managing people with different expectations and values.

6. Outline the key demographic and employee concerns.
   - There is a diverse and aging workforce with increased female participation.
   - Different generations are working side by side with differing values and expectations.
   - There will be a shortage of labour in the not too distant future.
   - The work landscape is changing with more part-time and self-employed people.
   - Employees have more rights.

7. Illustrate the link between business strategy and HRM strategy.
   - Business strategy involves formulation of company's mission, goals, and action plans.
   - Part of any business strategy is to be competitive; to be competitive, an organization needs to think about its people as part of its "competitive advantage."
   - HRM strategy focuses on linking and aligning the HRM practices to the business strategy.
   - The HR practices and programs will reflect the particular strategy, such as growth.

NEED TO KNOW

- Definition of HRM
- Names of HR processes and practices
- Definition of strategic human resources management
- Nature of employee expectations and concerns

NEED TO UNDERSTAND

- Impact of current business issues on HRM
- Link of business strategy and HRM strategy
- Role of line managers in responding effectively to the expectations and concerns of employees

KEY TERMS

benchmarking 19
core competencies 22
downsizing 13
globalization 10
human capital 21

human resources management (HRM) 4
human resources management strategy 31
human resources management system (HRMS) 16

outsourcing 13
Six Sigma 18
talent management 22
telework 15

REVIEW QUESTIONS

1. Define human resources management.
2. Name and describe the eight HRM processes.
3. What is the relationship between the line manager and an HR professional?
4. Identify the current business issues facing Canadian organizations.
5. What is the important link between a business strategy and the HR strategy?

CRITICAL THINKING QUESTIONS

1. Are people always an organization's most valuable asset? Why or why not? What might other strategic or valuable assets that a company might have?
2. The manufacturing sector in Canada continues to undergo rapid changes. What are some of the changes, and how are companies responding to the impact that these are having on their employees?
3. Identify a situation in which, if a particular person left an organization, the organization's expertise or competitive advantage might drop rapidly.
4. You are managing a small business and are faced with reducing costs; which would you do and why: outsource or downsize?
5. You and some of your classmates have been discussing the future of Research in Motion (RIM). Access at least three news Web sites and determine what is the company's status. Prepare a one-page summary of the information.
6. The Federal Government announced in 2012 that the age to collect Old Age Security (OAS) was changing from age 65 to 67 starting in 2023. What is the implication of this change for you? For your parents?

DEVELOPING YOUR SKILLS

1. In groups, debate this statement: "Employees are an expense and their numbers should be reduced."
2. As discussed in this chapter, Canada is changing some of its approaches to immigration. What would be the human resources implications if Canada decided to significantly reduce the number of immigrants?
3. Working in groups of three to four, create a list of ways in which you have encountered technology in your job search, hiring, training, etc. Assess your experiences: were they primarily positive or negative? Why?
4. Listed below are a number of Web sites that provide information about jobs. Look at each site. After doing so, identify which one(s) would be more useful to you when looking for work. Why?

   www.hrdc-drhc.gc.ca
   www.monster.ca
   www.careeronestop.org
   www.careers.ca
   www.bcjobs.ca
   mb.workinfonet.ca
   www.workopolis.com

5. Earlier in the chapter, you were introduced to the idea that certain skills are required to be successful in today's organizations. To determine your skills, attitudes, and behaviours for contemporary organizations, access the Skills Credentialing Tool for Individuals through the Conference Board of Canada. Access the online tool at **www.conferenceboard.ca/topics/education/default.aspx** and follow the instructions.

Case Study 1

Growth and Sustainability?

These two words almost seem contradictory, but that is what Canada is facing. On the one hand, it is important that the economy does not stagnate and that businesses prosper. On the other hand, can growth be sustained over the long term?

These are issues that every organization—small or large in the country—considers every day. One of the ways in which progress can be made is through research and development. While there have been stories over the years about some of the questionable research areas, there is no doubt that without experimentation, innovation and breakthroughs would not occur. For example, the person who invented the Ski-Doo was the same individual whose innovations eventually led his company to becoming a global force in the rail and aircraft manufacturing industry—Bombardier.

Partners in the research and development arena include government, private enterprise, and educational institutions. Places such as the University of Guelph recently opened a new laboratory to research infectious microbes that can move between animals and humans. Another example is the nanoscale laboratory at the Université de Sherbrooke, where tiny microelectric devices are made to explore the possibility of doctors using biochips to treat patients based on an individual biological profile.

In late 2011 an expert panel on research and development that was commissioned by the federal government identified that the government needed to enhance its support of small and medium enterprises (SMEs) to grow into larger and more globally competitive organizations. The report acknowledged that, on the basis of the size of Canada's economy, the government had been very generous. It also said, though, that research and development investment by businesses was not as good as it could be. One recommendation was to create the Industrial Research and Innovation Council to oversee and deliver the government's innovation programs instead of the multitude of government agencies that had been involved. The 2012 Federal budget began to streamline the manner in which R&D funds are allocated which it anticipates will provide more dollars for research.

Sources: Adapted from "Innovation Canada," *The Globe and Mail*, April 25, 2012, CF1-6; "Federal R&D Panel reports with six major recommendations" October, 17, 2011, http://rd-review.ca/eic/site/033.nsf/eng/home (accessed April 25, 2012); and "Federal budget to outline R&D funding changes," *CBC News*, March 27, 2012, www.cbc.ca/news/business/story/2012/03/27/nrc-changes-budget.html (accessed April 25, 2012).

Questions

1. What are the pros and cons of having the federal government involved in supporting research and development?
2. There has been much media attention on pharmaceuticals that slow-down manufacturing of drugs once the patents run out. What could be done to encourage on-going manufacturing even when the revenues begin to diminish?
3. Do you think businesses ought to be *required* to conduct research and development? Why or why not?

Case Study 2

No Sleet or Snow!

Canada Post is an organization in transition and evolving into something different. And it isn't easy. For years, Canada Post has had a monopoly on mail delivery. However, with the advent of technology, individuals and organizations have a variety of ways of sending and receiving "mail."

As a Crown corporation with a new CEO, the primary challenge appears to be in employees (and their unions) understanding that the organization has an opportunity to create its own future. Deepak Chopra, CEO, states, "We have an opportunity to create the right conditions from a cost structure, work flexibility and pension perspective to free-up some cash to invest …" Among Canada Post's financial issues is a home mail delivery decrease of 17% and an almost $5 billion annual pension deficit. Further, in 2011, Canada Post had a $253 million loss in revenue—the first loss in 16 years.

Even though there are 200,000 new homes built in Canada each year, Canada Post still has to plan for mail delivery whether mail is available for delivery or not. And in terms of any HR planning, it is important to remember that many employees retire at 55 with more than 25 years of service and that without the revenues it used to enjoy, Canada Post can no longer provide high wages with high retirement benefits.

One business model being considered is for Canada Post to allow itself to become a place where people can get their mail digitally. By becoming a secure Web site, Canada Post could allow people to get their bills in one place instead of having to access 20 or 30 different Web sites to download their bills. Since Canadians are heavy users of technology, it makes sense that people could access one site instead of having to go to multiple sites.

Another area of growth for Canada Post is its parcel delivery. In order to achieve efficiencies, it is moving to hand-held devices for delivery purposes and working with Canada Customs to streamline clearances at border crossings. This is an area where there is heavy competition, but currently Canada Post has 90% of the delivery market for eBay purchases in Canada—strong performance with the ability to build upon its successes.

All of the above is being supported by the "Postal Transformation" project that is modernizing Canada Post's physical and electronic network. Even though it is highly automated already, new state-of-the-art equipment will allow it to sort and deliver mail more quickly. In addition to its physical plant, dollars are being invested in the technology so that all electronic networks can be fully enhanced. These changes will provide the platform for Canada Post to realize its business objectives.

Sources: Adapted from Steve Ladurantaye, "A seismic shift from paper to pixels," *The Globe and Mail*, April 14, 2012, B3; "Postal Transformation at Canada Post," Canada Post, www.canadapost. ca/cpo/mc/aboutus/corporate/postaltransformation/default.jsf (accessed April 23, 2012); and Barrie McKenna, "Canada Post in the red for first time in 16 years," *Report on Business*, May 2, 2012, B1.

Questions

1. What are the opportunities and threats for Canada Post as it transforms itself?
2. What HRM issues arise at Canada Post with these changes?
3. What are the HR implications if Canada Post does not make changes?

NOTES AND REFERENCES

1. "The Legacy of the Great Recession," Center on Budget and Policy Priorities, April 10, 2012, www.cbpp.org/cms/index.cfm?fa=view&id=3252.

2. David B. Grusky, Bruce Western, and Christopher Wimer, editors, *The Great Recession* (New York: Russell Sage Foundation, October 2011).

3. John B. Judis, "Stop Blaming Wall Street," *National Post*, July 21, 2011, FP1.

4. Brian Keeley and Patrick Love, "From Crisis to Recovery," *OECD Insights*, Organisation for Economic Co-operation and Development, 2010.

5. "Spanish Stock Market Plunges to Three-Year Low," *The Guardian*, April 13, 2012, www.guardian.co.uk/business/2012/apr/13/spanish-stock-market-plunges; and Larry Elliott, "The Single Currency Has Arrived at a Three-Pronged Fork in the Road," *The Guardian*, April 15, 2012, www.guardian.co.uk/business/2012/apr/15/single-currency-three-pronged-fork-road.

6. Jeremy Torobin, "Business Optimism Takes Off," *The Globe and Mail*, April 10, 2012, A1.

7. Mike Cook, "Keeping the People You Need in the Outsourced Economy," *About.com Human Resources*, accessed April 15, 2012, http://humanresources.about.com/od/retention/a/lead_retention.htm.

8. "Lighting the Path to Success" (presentation by Hay Group, Vancouver, April 18, 2012).

9. Ibid.

10. Dave Ulrich, "Why HR Should Be at the C-Suite Table," Forbes, May 30, 2011, www.forbes.com/sites/karlmoore/2011/05/30/dava-ulrich-on-why-hr-should-be-at-the-c-suite-table/.

11. Mary Kay Vona, *The Seven Tall Tales of Talent Management*, Aon Hewitt, 2010.

12. Ibid.

13. Statistics Canada, "Canadian International Merchandise Trade: Annual Review 2011," *The Daily*, April 4, 2012.

14. "Gross Domestic Product at Basic Prices by Industry, January 2012," Statistics Canada, accessed April 15, 2012, http://www.statcan.gc.ca/tables-tableaux/sum-som/l01/cst01/gdps04a-eng.htm.

15. Iain Marlow and Omar El Akkad, "RIM's Hard Choices," *Report on Business*, April 14, 2012, B8; and RIM stock information, http://quotes.wsj.com/RIMM.

16. *Powered for Success, 2011 Annual Report*, Finning International, February 2, 2012.

17. "Canada's Economy to See Moderate Growth in 2012, Recovery 'Fragile': Flaherty," *Financial Post*, April 10, 2012, http://business.financialpost.com/2012/04/10/canadas-economy-to-see-moderate-growth-in-2012-recovery-fragile-flaherty/; and "RBC Economic and Financial Outlook," Royal Bank of Canada, March 2012.

18. "Imports, Exports and Trade Balance of Goods on a Balance-of-Payments Basis, by Country or Country Grouping," Statistics Canada, April 12, 2012, www.statcan.gc.ca/tables-tableaux/sum-som/l01/cst01/gblec02a-eng.htm.

19. "London Fix Historical Gold," Kitco, accessed April 16, 2012, www.kitco.com/scripts/hist_charts/monthly_graphs.plx.

20. "Teck Resources Historical Prices," Yahoo Finance, accessed April 16, 2012, http://ca.finance.yahoo.com/q/hp?s=TCK-B.TO&a=0&b=12&c=1995&d=3&e=16&f=2012&g=d&z=66&y=0.

21. TSX, The Canadian Stock Exchange, accessed April 16, 2012, www.tmx.com.

22. Christine Dobby, "Oil Sands Industry's Co-operative Spirit Helps Polish Public Image," *Financial Post*, March 9, 2012, E6.

23. "The Evolution of the Canadian Manufacturing Sector," Statistics Canada, accessed April 12, 2012, www.statcan.gc.ca/pub/11-010-x/2009008/part-partie3-eng.htm.

24. Tavia Grant, "The Caterpillar Shutdown's Stark Warning for the Industrial Heartland," *The Globe and Mail*, February 22, 2012, A8.

25. Gordon Pitts, "Oil Sands Fuel a New Manufacturing Boom—in Alberta," *The Globe and Mail*, March 8, 2012, www.theglobeandmail.com/report-on-business/economy/manufacturing/oil-sands-fuel-a-new-manufacturing-boom-in-alberta/article2359563.

26. Richard Blackwell, "CEOs in Tune with Ottawa's Deficit Plan," *Report on Business*, December 19, 2011, B1.

27. Guy Dixon, "CBC to Cut 650 Jobs in Fighting $200-Million Shortfall," *The Globe and Mail*, April 5, 2012, www.theglobeandmail.com/news/arts/television/cbc-to-cut-650-jobs-in-fighting-200-million-shortfall/article2392282.

28. Robert I. Sutton, "What's the Best Strategy for Astrigo?" *Harvard Business Review*, March 2009, 40.

29. Madhav Murti, "Outsourcing Opportunities in Bad Economy," *Canadian HR Reporter*, January 26, 2009, accessed July 24, 2012, www.hrreporter.com/ArticleView.aspx?l=1&articleid=6628.

30. Sarah Dobson, "Layoffs Change with the Times," *Canadian HR Reporter*, January 25, 2010, accessed April 17, 2012, www.hrreporter.com/articleview/7498-layoffs-change-with-the-times.

31. Martin Kingston, "Setting Up a Safety Net for Terminated Workers," *Canadian HR Reporter*, April 9, 2012, 11.

32. Sarah Dobson, "Use of Interim Managers an Escalating Trend," *Canadian HR Reporter*, September 20, 2010, accessed April 17, 2012, www.hrreporter.com/articleview/8238-use-of-interim-managers-an-escalating-trend.

33. Sean Silcoff, "Busy Signals: Why Call Centres Came Back," *The Globe and Mail*, March 14, 2012, B3.

34. Eugeny Sokolove, "Transformation through Outsourcing," *The Moscow Times*, April 17, 2012, www.themoscowtimes.com/business/business_for_business/article/transformation-through-outsourcing/456840.html.

35. Smita Vasudevan, "Growing Outsourcing Risks," *Global Services*, May 27, 2011, www.globalservicesmedia.com/Strategies-and-Best-Practices/Risk-Management/Growing-Outsourcing-Risks/24/13/10964/GS110527859658.

36. Marilyn Adama and Nicolas Rapp, "Bytes Beat Bricks," *Fortune*, July 4, 2011, 13.

37. Virginia Galt, "Tech Tools Lift Workers' Heads above the Data Flood," *The Globe and Mail*, March 8, 2012, B20.

38. Dan Worth, "The World Wide Web Turns 20—How It's Changed the World Forever," V3·co·uk, August 5, 2011, www.v3.co.uk/v3-uk/analysis/2099398/world-wide-web-changed-world-forever.

39. Wugang Zhao, "Competition in Search Engine Market," *Journal of Business Strategies* 28, no. 2 (Fall 2011): 123–50.

40. Scott Simpson, "Cloud Computing Could Touch Off Global Job Boom," *The Vancouver Sun,* March 7, 2012, C1.

41. Darah Hansen, "Technology Helps Make Commuting Virtual," *The Vancouver Sun*, December 6, 2011, C2.

42. Derek Sankey, "Teleworking Becomes Part of the Environment," *The Vancouver Sun,* August 27, 2011, D10.

43. Amanda Silliker, "More Firms Plan to Offer Teleworking over Next Few Years: Survey," *Canadian HR Reporter*, August 15, 2011, 15; and Nick Rockel, "Why Everyone's Not on Board with Telework," *The Globe and Mail*, January 11, 2012, B11.

44. Sarah Dobson, "Telework Declines in U.S.: Work at Work," *Canadian HR Reporter*, September 12, 2011, 14; Meg McSherry, "Numbers Down, but Still Strong Selling Point," *Workforce Management*, April 2012, 15.

45. Jason Magder, "Keeping Everybody in the Loop," *The Vancouver Sun*, July 2, 2011, D6.

46. Darah Hansen, "Social Media Explosion Sparks Debate among Employers," *The Vancouver Sun*, June 7, 2011, C3.

47. Ian Turnbull, "The Evolution of HR Technology: 'Sexy' Is Out, Functionality Is In," *Canadian HR Reporter*, November 1, 2010, accessed April 18, 2012, www.hrreporter.com/articleview/8374-the-evolution-of-hr-technology-sexy-is-out-functionality-is-in.

48. Joseph Walker, "Analyzing People Data Gives New Edge to HR Departments," *Report on Business*, April 18, 2012, B22.

49. David Vanheukelom, "HR Tech's Future (and Present) in the Cloud," October 20, 2011, www.hrreporter.com/articleview/11414-hr-techs-future-and-present-in-the-cloud.

50. Nick Rockel, "Giving the Boot to Traditional Performance Reviews," *The Globe and Mail*, March 7, 2012, B6.

51. Carly Weeks, "Time to Adapt to Social Media—or Face the Consequences," *The Globe and Mail*, October 13, 2011, B18.

52. Turnbull, "The Evolution of HR Technology."

53. Harpaul Sambhi, "Internal Social Networks Can Drive New Ways of Thinking," *Canadian HR Reporter*, April 17, 2012, www.hrreporter.com/blog/Social-HR/archive/2012/04/17/internal-social-networks-can-drive-new-ways-of-thinking.

54. Walker, "Analyzing People Data Gives New Edge to HR Departments."

55. S. Thomas Foster Jr., Cynthia Wallin, and Jeffrey Ogden, "Towards a Better Understanding of Supply Chain Quality Management Practices," *Journal of Production Research* 49, no. 8 (April 15, 2011): 2285–300.

56. Fasil Taddese and Hiroshi Osada, "Process Techno-Innovation Using TQM in Developing Countries Empirical Study of Deming Prize Winners," *Journal of Technology Management & Innovation* 5, no. 2 (2010): 46–65.

57. Vidhu Shekhar Jha and Himanshu Joshi, "Relevant of TQM or Business Excellence Strategy Implementation for Enterprise Resource Planning—A Conceptual Study," ERP

Implementation, accessed April 18, 2012, www.slideshare.net/anupipal/application-oftqmandbusinessexcellencemodelstowards42121, 2011.

58. Mike Boucher, "Preventing Lean Six Sigma Failures," *Canadian HR Reporter*, March 26, 2012, 15.

59. The term "Six Sigma" is a registered trademark of Motorola. It is based on the Greek letter *sigma*, used as a symbol of variation in a process (the standard deviation).

60. Boucher, "Preventing Lean Six Sigma Failures."

61. Bradley R. Staats and David M. Upton, "Lean Knowledge Work," *Harvard Business Review*, October 2011, 101–10.

62. John D. Stoll, "Study Downplays Effects of Lean Manufacturing," *Canadian HR Reporter*, September 28, 2011, www.hrreporter.com/articleview/11322-study-downplays-effects-of-lean-manufacturing.

63. Staats and Upton, "Lean Knowledge Work."

64. "All Canada Awards for Excellence," Excellence Canada, accessed April 18, 2012, www.nqi.ca/en/awards/All_CAE_Recipients_Alpha.

65. Joseph M. Hall and M. Eric Johnson, "When Should a Process Be Art, Not Science?" *Harvard Business Review*, March 2009, 58–65.

66. "Major Changes Needed for Prosperous Future: Report," *Canadian HR Reporter*, April 3, 2012, www.hrreporter.com/articleview/12722-major-changes-needed-for-prosperous-future-report.

67. "Clean Technologies," *The Globe and Mail*, February 27, 2012, SDTC1.

68. Ibid.

69. "SDTC-Supported Innovators," *The Globe and Mail*, February 27, 2012, SDTC5.

70. "Innovative Practices Transform Wood Waste into Valuable Products," *The Globe and Mail*, February 27, 2012, SDTC5.

71. "Banking on Green Initiatives," *Financial Post*, April 17, 2012, FP6.

72. "2011 Best 50 Corporate Citizens of Canada," *Corporate Knights Magazine,* Spring 2011, 30.

73. Alan Erskine, "Human Capital Management," *Management Services* (Spring 2012): 12–13.

74. PwC, "Workforce Inclusion: Maximizing Business Performance," *Advisory: People and Change*, June 2011.

75. Joan Hill, "Competency Model Helps HR Add Value," *Canadian HR Reporter*, January 30, 2012, 20.

76. Robert E. Ployhart, Chad H. Van Iddekinge, and William I. Mackenzie Jr., "Acquiring and Developing Human Capital in Service Contexts: The Interconnectedness of Human Capital Resources," *Academy of Management Journal* 54, no. 2 (2011): 353–68.

77. "Client Satisfaction and Better Business Results Start with Motivated Employees," *Canadian Small Business Week*, October 2011, 14.

78. Ali Akbar Ahmadi, Freyedon Ahmadi, and Shaghayegh Shakeri, "The Survey of Relationship between Intellectual Capital (IC) and Organizational Performance (OP) within the National Iranian South Oil Company," *Interdisciplinary Journal of Contemporary Research in Business* 3, no. 5 (September 2011): 369–80.

79. Dave Ulrich and Wendy Ulrich, *The Why of Work* (New York: McGraw Hill, 2010), 5.

80. M.S. Srinivasan, "An Integral Approach to Talent Management," *The XIMB Journal of Management* (September 2011): 81–90.

81. Statistics Canada, "Study: Projected Trends to 2031 for the Canadian Labour Force," *The Daily*, August 7, 2011, www.statcan.gc.ca/daily-quotidien/110817/dq110817b-eng.htm.

82. *Projections of the Diversity of the Canadian Population*, Statistics Canada, June 2010.

83. "ALLIES," The McConnell Foundation, accessed April 21, 2012, www.mcconnellfoundation.ca/en/programs/allies.

84. Statistics Canada, "Population Projections by Aboriginal Identity in Canada," *The Daily*, December 7, 2011, www.statcan.gc.ca/daily-quotidien/111207/dq111207a-eng.htm.

85. "Work–Employment Rate," Human Resources and Skills Development Canada, April 2012, www4.hrsdc.gc.ca/.3ndic.1t.4r@-eng.jsp?iid=13#M_3.

86. Statistics Canada, "Population Estimates by Sex and Age Group as of July 1, 2011," September 28, 2011, www.statcan.gc.ca/daily-quotidien/110928/t110928a4-eng.htm.

87. Anne Milan, "Age and Sex Structure: Canada, Provinces and Territories, 2010," Statistics Canada, July 2011.

88. John Morrissy, "1 in 4 Workers Will be over 55 in 2021," *Financial Post*, August 18, 2011, FP2.

89. Misty Harris, "Clash of Cultures on the Way?" *The Vancouver Sun*, March 22, 2012, B3.

90. "Value through Your People," PricewaterhouseCoopers, 2012; and Walter Immen, "Gen X Workers Feeling the Promotion Pinch," *Report on Business*, March 16, 2012, B12.

91. "The Fine Art of Leading Gen Y," *Canadian Business*, February 20, 2012, 10–13.

92. Amanda Silliker, "4 Generations Pose Challenges for Workplaces," *Canadian HR Reporter*, December 5, 2011, 6.

93. Tavia Grant and Richard Blackwell, "Canada's Growing Labour Gap," *Report on Business*, April 10, 2012, B1.

94. Alison Martell, "Miners Fight Labour Shortages with Bonuses, Training," *The Globe and Mail*, March 7, 2012, B19.

95. Ibid.

96. Jock Finlayson, "Readying for the Reality of an Aging Workplace," *PeopleTalk*, Fall 2011, 44–45.

97. Richard Blackwell, "From Coast to Coast, a Skills Crisis in the Making," *Report on Business*, March 5, 2012, B1.

98. John Morrissy, "Growth of Labour Force Slowing," *The Vancouver Sun*, August 8, 2011, F2.

99. Kim Pemberton, "Canada Eases Immigration Rules to Allow More Foreign Students," *The Vancouver Sun*, November 3, 2011, A7.

100. Steven Chase, "Wanted: Immigrants with Experience," *The Globe and Mail*, November 3, 2011, A1.

101. Statistics Canada, "Labour Characteristics by Age and Sex," March 2012, www.statcan.gc.ca/daily-quotidien/120405/t120405a001-eng.htm.

102. Statistics Canada, "The Canadian Labour Market at a Glance," January 30, 2009, 54.

103. Ibid., 56.

104. Statistics Canada, "Fast Facts—Education: Is It Worth Completing University?" December 19, 2011, www.statcan.gc.ca/edu/edu02_0019-eng.htm.

105. "Literacy Skills a Foundation of National Productivity and Prosperity," *The Globe and Mail*, March 26, 2012, B6.

106. Joanne Laucius, "The Devaluation of Higher Learning, *The Vancouver Sun*, June 11, 2011, C2.

107. Ted Wannell and Jeannine Usalcas, "Labour Force Survey: 2011 Year-End Review," *Perspectives on Labour and Income*, Statistics Canada, March 23, 2012.

108. Mary Teresa Bitti, "The Culturally Rich Get Richer," *National Post*, November 4, 2011, JV1; and Michael Burchell and Jennifer Robin, "Canada's Best Workplaces 2012," *The Globe and Mail*, April 19, 2012, GPTW8.

109. Financial Post, *Ten Best Companies to Work for 2011*.

110. Lisa Baranik, Elizabeth A. Roling, and Lillian T. Eby, "Why Does Mentoring Work? The Role of Organizational Support," *Journal of Vocational Behaviour* 76, no. 3 (June 1, 2010): 366–73.

111. "Recession May Be Changing Americans' Attitudes toward Work," *Bloomberg Businessweek*, October 22, 2010, accessed April 21, 2012, www.businessweek.com/lifestyle/content/healthday/644692.html.

112. "Pfizer, Manitoba Hydro among 20 Firms Recognized for Family-Friendly Culture," *Canadian HR Reporter*, December 8, 2011, www.hrreporter.com/articleview/11909-pfizer-manitoba-hydro-among-20-firms-recognized-for-family-friendly-culture.

113. Claudine Kapel, "Tackling the Challenge of 'Time Famine,'" *Canadian HR Reporter*, December 5, 2011, www.hrreporter.com/blog/Compensation-Rewards/archive/2011/12/05/tackling-the-challenge-of-time-famine.

114. Sarah Dobson, "Compassionate Care Top-ups Very Rare," *Canadian HR Reporter*, December 5, 2011, www.hrreporter.com/articleview/11884-compassionate-care-top-ups-very-rare.

115. Michael E. Porter, *On Competition* (Boston, MA: Harvard Business Press, 2008).

116. J. Barton Cunningham and Jim Kempling, "Promoting Organizational Fit in Strategic HRM: Applying the HR Scorecard in Public Service Organizations," *Public Personnel Management* 40, no. 3 (Fall 2011): 193–213.

117. Rosdi Intan-Soraya and Kok-Wai Chew, "Framework for Human Resource Management in the Knowledge Economy: Building Intellectual Capital and Innovative Capability," *International Journal of Business & Management Science* 3, no. 2 (December 2010): 251–73.

118. Nadeem Malik and Muhammad Aminu, "The Role of Human Resource in New Globalized World," *Interdisciplinary Journal of Contemporary Research in Business* 2, no 11 (March 2011): 318–30.

119. Richard Rothschild, "Aon's Premier Partnership Kicks Up Camaraderie," *Workforce Management*, November 3, 2011, www.workforce.com/article/20111103/NEWS02/111109993/aons-premier-partnership-kicks-up-camaraderie.

120. Intan-Soraya and Chew, "Framework for Human Resource Management in the Knowledge Economy."

121. Cedric T. Coco, Fiona Jamison, and Heather Black, "Connecting People Investments and Business Outcomes at Lowe's," *People & Strategy* 34, no. 2 (2011): 28–33.

122. Presentations to HRMA Leadership Forum, February 2011 and March 2012.

CHAPTER 2

THE LEGAL FRAMEWORK OF HRM

OUTCOMES

After studying this chapter, you should be able to

1 Explain the impact of laws on the behaviour and actions of supervisors and managers.

2 Discuss the legal framework of HRM in Canada.

3 Describe discrimination and harassment in the workplace.

4 Outline the line manager's role in creating a work environment that is free from harassment and discrimination.

5 Identify the general types of employment laws in Canada.

6 Illustrate the difference between employment equity and pay equity.

7 Describe the differences between diversity and employment equity.

OUTLINE

HRM CLOSE-UP

"The lack of exposure to human resource realities can blindside you."

Launched in 1996, Outpost has carved a niche for itself in the travel magazine business. Adventure travel is its focus and the journalists write about off-the-beaten-track excursions to interesting and unusual places.

For the magazine's editorial director and publisher, most of today is spent reviewing a story about a 75-km trail hike on Vancouver Island, calling potential advertisers, and finalizing a deal with a tour company for coveted back cover advertising space. But Matt Robinson must also set aside time for human resources management because his responsibilities cover all aspects of the magazine's operation.

Though admittedly a "hands-off" manager, Matt does acknowledge that a good 15% of his time is spent interacting with the people who work for him. "We are small and therefore have to be nimble with staffing," explains Robinson. "The people who work for us are often part-time contract, freelance, or casual, and we also manage up to 12 student interns from colleges and universities annually."

Managing interns may seem straightforward, but there are things a manager has to be aware of when accepting interns. Robinson describes the legal considerations to do with workers' compensation, saying that if a magazine compensates an intern during their unpaid internship, that payment, although intended to show appreciation for the work, may interfere with that student's school insurance coverage, transferring liability back to the company. "Small companies with nominal staff wouldn't necessarily know about this," commented Robinson. "It's hard to stay on top of all the legalities of human resources. It's best to read up a little here and there so that you have the knowledge you need to avoid legal issues in the future."

Robinson has sought legal advice from time to time for help with tasks such as drawing up contracts. He says that other responsibilities related to managing people, for example, maintaining a safe office environment, providing staff the proper tools to do their jobs, and ensuring everyone has time for a proper lunch. He also cautions that "the lack of exposure to human resource realities can blindside you."

Years ago, Robinson had an issue with an employee using a company computer inappropriately during work time. Although the laws are not entirely defined regarding use of the Internet during work hours, it is important to inform staff of company policies related to personal blogging, signing on to Facebook,

Courtesy of Matt Robinson

Matt Robinson

texting, and twittering during business hours. It is also important to let staff know that the company's Web administrator has access to company electronic mail and that copies of that mail are saved as standard business practice.

Hiring the right person for the right job can be the best way to avoid legal problems down the road. "We're all salespeople," says Robinson, "especially in a job interview. It can take 60 days to start seeing things in terms of an employee's work performance." Doing research, asking for references, and spending quality time checking those references will pay off in the long run. "Be careful also about giving recommendations for past employees," he adds, "because that can come back to haunt you as well!"

For new people managers, Robinson has some solid advice: "Take the time to know something about human resources. It may be true that the strongest irons are forged in the hottest fires, but an HR issue can be a fire that's a little too hot!" He acknowledges that entrepreneurs are at the highest risk because they want to get things done quickly and are not in the practice of prevention. "You want to offer a fair day's pay for a fair day's work and have fun doing it, but the proper parameters have to be there."

INTRODUCTION

Outcome 1

What is the impact of laws on the behaviour and actions of supervisors and managers?

As the HRM Close-up shows, there is no doubt that employment laws affect line managers and what they are expected to do to successfully manage the people they are responsible for. Laws have been written to protect the employer and the employees; these laws reflect the values of society, and in some situations, laws have been enacted because of poor management practices. Therefore, it is important for supervisors to understand the legal context in which they have to operate. Managers, supervisors, and employees can no longer behave and act in certain ways without severe consequences. When managers ignore the legal aspects of HRM, they risk incurring costly and time-consuming litigation, negative public attitudes, and damage to organization morale.

And some of the laws address not just legal issues—the issues can also be emotional. For example, human rights legislation is paramount over other laws and concerns all individuals regardless of their gender, race, religion, age, marital status, disability, family status, sexual orientation, national origin, colour, or position in an organization. All employees, including supervisors and managers, should be aware of their personal biases and how these attitudes can influence their dealings with one another. It should be emphasized that whether the supervisor unintentionally or intentionally acts a certain way, the supervisor is responsible for any illegal actions. Being ignorant of the law is not a valid excuse. As Matt Robinson indicates, entrepreneurs are at the highest risk as they want to get things done quickly. This chapter will focus on the various employment laws at both the federal and provincial levels that affect how a manager practises human resources management.

Beyond legislation, there is also an expectation in today's society that treating employees in certain ways is just "good business." Thus, the concept of diversity management in a multicultural society has become part of business simply because it makes good business sense. It is important to remember that we have gone beyond what is required by law in our human resources management practices.

THE LEGAL FRAMEWORK OF HRM

Outcome 2

How does the legal framework in Canada work?

Canada has two distinct sets of laws that govern: federal and provincial. Federal laws apply to everyone who resides in Canada. For example, everyone must pay income taxes. Other laws are handled at the provincial level. For example, the provinces are responsible for determining who can get a driver's licence. While this chapter will discuss specific employment laws, other kinds of laws, such as common law (our body of law that has developed from judicial decisions), contract law (the laws that relate to legal and binding agreements, such as the purchase of a car), and government regulations (called statutory law), can also have an impact on HR. For example, common law establishes the basic employee–employer relationship of trust. Contract law governs a person engaged in a fee-for-service activity for a company. Statutory law creates employment conditions, such as providing minimum wages or holidays with pay (e.g., Canada Day on July 1).

There are a total of 14 different jurisdictions (government authorities), which means 14 different sets of laws.

Federal legislation applies to only about 10% of Canadian workers, those who are employed by federal government departments and agencies, Crown corporations, and other businesses and industries under federal control, such as banks, airlines, railway companies, and insurance and communications companies. Examples of these companies are CIBC, Scotiabank, Air Canada, WestJet, Bell, and CBC.

In addition, each province and territory has its own legislation that covers employment standards, human rights, labour relations, and worker health and safety. Companies covered under provincial legislation include the corner 7 Eleven, the local McDonald's, and others such as Canadian Tire, RONA, and Walmart. Although there is a great deal of similarity across provinces and territories, there are some notable variations in minimum wage and vacation entitlement, for example. Also, some aspects of human rights legislation differ from one jurisdiction to another. Some provinces and territories have employment equity legislation, and others do not. For example, Ontario and Quebec have stringent pay equity legislation. In Alberta and British Columbia, however, there is no such legislation. Therefore, any pay equity adjustments are the decision of the organization.

Although federal law regulates both Employment Insurance (EI) and the Canada Pension Plan (CPP), all employers and employees are covered, not just federal employees. EI provides for wage payment should you lose your job, and CPP provides for a small pension when you retire. Quebec has its own pension plan, which is similar to the Canada Pension Plan. Changes to EI over the last several years have had an impact on human resources practices in organizations. For example, compassionate care benefits are available to employees who need time off to care for or support a family member who is gravely ill or at risk of dying within six months.[1] Further, a total of 35 weeks is available for parental leave, which can be used by either parent or shared between them.[2]

Federal Employment Laws

Canada Labour Code

aws-lois.justice.gc.ca/eng/
acts/L-2

**Canadian Human
Rights Act**

Laws-lois.justice.gc.ca/eng/
acts/h-6

**Personal Information
Protection and Electronic
Documents Act (PIPEDA)**

Laws-lois.justice.gc.ca/eng/
acts/P-8.6

For companies that are federally regulated, there are two basic employment laws: the **Canada Labour Code** and the **Canadian Human Rights Act**. The Canada Labour Code covers basic employment conditions, labour relations, and health and safety in the federal sector. The Canada Industrial Relations Board administers this law.

Like the Canada Labour Code, the *Canadian Human Rights Act* applies to all federal government departments and agencies, Crown corporations, and businesses and industries under federal jurisdiction, such as banks, airlines, railway companies, and insurance and communications companies. It is administered by the Canadian Human Rights Commission, which makes decisions on complaints involving discrimination and harassment. The concept of a certain level of basic human rights is part of the very fabric of Canadian society. It is also an area that is constantly expanding. For example, in June 2011, the *Canadian Human Rights Act* was applied to all First Nations communities.[3]

Of increasing concern for managers and HR professionals is privacy legislation. There are two primary laws—one that applies to only federally regulated companies (e.g., bank, airlines, etc.) and one that extends the federal legislation to provinces and businesses within the provinces. These laws are the **Personal Information Protection and Electronic Documents Act (PIPEDA)** and provincial legislation commonly called the "Personal Information Privacy Act." These acts have a direct influence on how companies and managers handle employee information and the rights of employees regarding this information. Both acts enhance the protection granted to employees on their personal information that a company retains. Organizations can use the information (such as social insurance number) only for its intended purpose (to remit premiums to the Canada Pension Plan). Organizations can no longer collect personal information without disclosing the full use to employees. Further, organizations must seek written permission from the employee to disclose personal information. For example, if you want to get a car loan, your employer is obliged to seek your written authorization to disclose your pay to the lending agency.

These acts have been most noted in the monitoring of e-mails, use of social media, and Web site visits of employees while at the worksite. More information on this will be covered in Chapter 9, Management Rights, Employee Rights, and Discipline.

As businesses look outside of Canada for new employees, they have become more familiar with the *Immigration and Refugee Protection Act* when they wish to recruit and hire people who are not citizens or permanent residents of Canada. This topic will be discussed in Chapter 4, "Human Resource Planning, Recruitment, and Selection."

Provincial Employment Legislation

Each province and territory has relatively similar legislation that provides certain rights and guarantees regarding employment. For example, each province has maximum limits regarding hours per day or hours per week that a person can work before the organization is obliged to pay overtime wages. Similarly, the health and safety of workers are also covered by provincial legislation. In addition, provinces and territories have legislation dealing with

FIGURE 2.1   Major Employment Laws in Canada

Jurisdiction	Basic Employment Conditions	Labour Legislation	Occupational Health and Safety and Workers' Compensation	Human Rights
Federal	Canada Labour Code	Canada Labour Code	Canada Labour Code	Canadian Human Rights Act
Alberta	Employment Standards Code	Labour Relations Code	Occupational Health and Safety Code	Human Rights Act
British Columbia	British Columbia Employment Standards Act	Labour Relations Code	Workers' Compensation Act	Human Rights Code
Manitoba	Employment Standards Code	Labour Relations Act	Workplace Safety and Health Act	Human Rights Code
New Brunswick	Employment Standards Act	Industrial Relations Act	Occupational Health and Safety Act	Human Rights Act
Newfoundland and Labrador	Labour Standards Act	Labour Relations Act	Occupational Health and Safety Act	Human Rights Act
Nova Scotia	Labour Standards Act	Trade Union Act	Occupational Health and Safety Act	Human Rights Act
Nunavut	Labour Standards Act	Labour Standards Act	Safety Act/Workers' Compensation Act	Human Rights Act
Ontario	Employment Standards Act	Labour Relations Act, 1995	Occupational Health and Safety Act/Workplace Safety and Insurance Act	Human Rights Code
Prince Edward Island	Employment Standards Act	Labour Act	Occupational Health and Safety Act	Human Rights Act
Quebec	Act Respecting Labour Standards	Labour Act	Act Respecting Occupational Health and Safety	Charter of Human Rights and Freedoms
Saskatchewan	Labour Standards Act	Trade Union Act	Occupational Health and Safety Act	Saskatchewan Human Rights Code

Note: Web sites for legislation can be found in the Appendix at the end of this chapter.

human rights and legislation that covers unions and their relationships with employers. In the following sections, you will get information about these major types of employment laws whether they are provincial or federal. Figure 2.1 provides a summary of the various federal and provincial employment laws referred to in the previous two sections.

HUMAN RIGHTS LEGISLATION

The legislation that has had the most far-reaching impact on employment conditions has been in the area of human rights. Although the original human rights legislation was at the federal level, all provinces have enacted similar laws. The basic foundation of human rights legislation is that "all individuals should have an opportunity equal with other individuals to make for themselves the lives that they are able and wish to have and to have their needs accommodated, consistent with their duties and obligations as members of society, without being hindered in or prevented from doing so by discriminatory practices based on race, national, or ethnic origin, colour, religion, age, sex, sexual orientation, marital status, family status, disability, or conviction for an offence for which a pardon has been granted."[4] While the legislation is designed to protect individuals, it does not cover every situation. For example, until 2008, "age" was defined to be the ages between 19 and 65 in most jurisdictions. However, most jurisdictions eliminated the "65," which means that, in most cases, the notion of "mandatory retirement" would now be illegal. In order to still have a mandatory retirement policy, the organization would have to demonstrate that it was a BFOR (bona fide occupational requirement), such as the physical demands of the work of a firefighter.[5] The concept of BFOR will be discussed later in this chapter.

Human rights legislation is enforced through human rights commissions (or tribunals) and is achieved via a complaint process (explained in more detail later). Since human rights legislation is paramount over other employment laws, the decisions of these commissions and tribunals have a huge influence over all types of employment issues. It is important to note that commission decisions have changed expectations regarding the proper treatment of employees. As a result, organizations now have higher standards to meet. For example, a recent human rights decision found that employers can be considered discriminatory if they fail to make accommodation for childcare responsibilities.[6]

Since this legislation has had a profound effect on the employment landscape, the latter part of this chapter will discuss its impact in more detail. Web sites for accessing the legislation can be found in the Appendix at the end of this chapter.

Discrimination

Outcome 3

What are discrimination and harassment?

The essence of human rights legislation is to prohibit discrimination on the basis of race, religion, gender, age, national or ethnic origin, disability, or family or marital status. The majority of provincial human rights legislation also covers sexual orientation. Figure 2.2 provides a partial listing of prohibited grounds of discrimination in employment for federal, provincial, and territorial jurisdictions. Note that some jurisdictions include pardoned convictions (e.g., federal, British Columbia, Ontario, and Quebec) and records of criminal convictions (British Columbia, Quebec, Prince Edward Island, and Yukon Territory) as prohibited grounds. A person's political beliefs are protected in some jurisdictions, such as British Columbia, Manitoba, Quebec, and Prince Edward Island. The complete list of prohibited grounds can be found at the Canadian Human Rights Commission Web site in its publications link (**www.chrc-ccdp.ca**).

Systemic discrimination
The exclusion of members of certain groups through the application of employment policies or practices based on criteria that are not job related

Many employment barriers are hidden, unintentionally, in the rules and procedures that organizations use in their various human resources management practices. These barriers, referred to as **systemic discrimination**, have prevented the progress of these designated groups. Inequity can result if these barriers discourage individuals based on their membership in certain groups rather than on their ability to do a job that the employer needs done. An example of systemic discrimination would occur when an employer's workforce represents one group in our society and the company recruits new employees by posting job vacancies within the company or by word of mouth among the employees. This recruitment strategy is likely to generate a candidate similar to those in the current workforce, thereby unintentionally discriminating against other groups of workers in the labour market. A better approach might be to vary recruitment methods by contacting outside agencies and organizations.

Bona fide occupational qualification (BFOQ)
A justifiable reason for discrimination based on business reasons of safety or effectiveness

Employers may be permitted to discriminate if employment qualifications are based on a **bona fide occupational qualification (BFOQ)** or bona fide occupational requirement (BFOR). For example, a recent Canadian Human Rights Tribunal decision upheld Air Canada's right to retire pilots at age 60.[7] A BFOQ is justified if the employer can establish its necessity for business operations. Business necessity is a practice that includes the safe and efficient operation of an organization. In other words, differential treatment is not discrimination if there is a justifiable reason. However, it should be pointed out that it is difficult for many employers to establish legitimate BFOQs. A law firm recently lost its ability to retire partners when the B.C. Human Rights Tribunal determined that the individual was more like an employee and that no BFOQ existed.[8] Therefore, a supervisor will probably be asked to carefully examine job requirements and demonstrate that a

FIGURE 2.2   A Partial List of Prohibited Grounds of Discrimination in Employment

This partial list provides comparative information on the prohibited grounds of discrimination covered by federal, provincial, and territorial human rights legislation in Canada. In some instances, prohibited grounds for employment differ from those for the provision of services. The complete list can be found through the Canadian Human Rights Commission.

Prohibited Ground	Jurisdiction	Comments
Race or colour		
Employment	All jurisdictions	
Provision of Service	All jurisdictions	
Religion		
Employment	All jurisdictions	Manitoba's Code and Yukon's Act read "religion or creed, or religious belief, religious association or religious activity." In addition, Saskatchewan prohibits discrimination on the basis of "religious creed." Ontario uses the term "creed." Nunavut's Act says "creed [and] religion."
Provision of Service	All jurisdictions	Manitoba's Code and Yukon's Act read "religion or creed, or religious belief, religious association or religious activity." In addition, Saskatchewan prohibits discrimination on the basis of "religious creed." Ontario uses the term "creed." Nunavut's Act says "creed [and] religion."
Physical or mental disability		
Employment	All jurisdictions	Quebec uses the phrase "handicap or use of any means to palliate a handicap." Ontario has prohibition on the basis of "both current and previous disabilities as well as the perception that one may have or have had a disability." Nunavut uses the word "disability."
Provision of Service	All jurisdictions	Quebec uses the phrase "handicap or use of any means to palliate a handicap." Ontario has prohibition on the basis of "both current and previous disabilities as well as the perception that one may have or have had a disability." Nunavut uses the word "disability."
Dependence on alcohol or drugs		
Employment	All jurisdictions	Policy to accept complaints in British Columbia, Alberta, Saskatchewan, Manitoba, Ontario, New Brunswick, and Prince Edward Island
		Included in "handicap" ground in Quebec
		Provisions dependence only in New Brunswick and Nova Scotia
		Included in "disability" ground in the Yukon, Alberta, and Nunavut
Provision of Service	All jurisdictions	Policy to accept complaints in the Northwest Territories and Manitoba
		Previous dependence only in New Brunswick and Nova Scotia
		Included in "handicap" ground in Quebec
		Included in "disability" ground in the Yukon, Alberta, and Nunavut

Source: CHRC, *Prohibited Grounds of Discrimination in Canada*, http://www.chrc-ccdp.ca/pdf/prohibit_en.pdf. Canadian Human Rights Commission. Reproduced with the permission of the Minister of Public Works and Government Services, 2012.

certain characteristic is absolutely essential. The federal government, for example, has been allowed to hire only women as guards in prisons for women; however, a retail store specializing in women's fashions would not be allowed to hire only women. Frequently, the HR professional and the line manager would work together to review job requirements to determine if the qualifications met the BFOQ requirement. For recruitment and hiring purposes, it is important that job requirements not create a discriminatory situation.

Likewise, even the process of hiring can be considered discriminatory if inappropriate questions are asked. This area will be discussed more fully in Chapter 4.

This partial list provides comparative information on the prohibited grounds of discrimination covered by federal, provincial, and territorial human rights legislation in Canada. In some instances, prohibited grounds for employment differ from those for the provision of services. The complete list can be found through the Canadian Human Rights Commission.

Most of the decisions made by the Supreme Court of Canada, human rights tribunals, and arbitrations have looked at whether the discrimination was "intentional" or "unintentional." Intentional discrimination is very clear and direct, such as a requirement that only males five feet nine inches and taller could apply. On the other hand, some discriminatory employment situations are unintentional. An example of unintentional discrimination is the requirement that a firefighter be able to run a certain distance within a fixed amount of time.

A Supreme Court decision several years ago changed this approach from previous court decisions.[9] The case involved a female forest firefighter in British Columbia who was terminated after performing successfully on the job for three years. As a consequence of a coroner's report, new fitness standards had been instituted requiring that all firefighters be able to run 2.5 km in 11 minutes. The person failed the standard on four attempts and was terminated, even though she had been doing the work successfully. The Court decided that the test was discriminatory since females have a lower aerobic capacity than males and would therefore be unable to meet the standard. The decision went on to establish a new approach to BFOQ. From now on, an employer is required to demonstrate that it is impossible to accommodate individuals discriminated against without undue hardship. This means that whatever the standard is, the employer must provide for individual accommodation, if possible.[10]

Another concept that has arisen from human rights decisions is that of reasonable accommodation. **Reasonable accommodation** involves adjusting employment policies and practices so that no individual is denied benefits, is disadvantaged with respect to employment opportunities, or is blocked from carrying out the essential components of a job because of race, colour, disability, or any of the other prohibited grounds of discrimination. This is a legal obligation so as new prohibited grounds are added to any human rights legislation, they, too, become eligible for reasonable accommodation. In an interesting case dealing with someone getting ill from their physical environment, the tribunal determined that the person was hypersensitive and as such needed accommodation to work remotely from home.[11] Specifically, an employer needs to thoroughly investigate and consider methods by which the employee's characteristic (e.g., family status, gender, disability) can be accommodated in the workplace, including whether the specific tasks can be organized in a way to deal with the characteristic. The employer cannot just make assumptions.[12] For example, if someone does not have the necessary degree of hand-eye coordination to do detailed electronics work, the employer may be obliged to reconfigure the tasks so that the person can do the work. Whether an employer can accommodate the work to fit the individual needs is ultimately a decision made by human rights tribunals. Ethics in HRM 2.1 describes what happens when the concept of disability is used to justify inappropriate behaviour.

It is no longer acceptable for employers to assume that all employees will "fit in" no matter what their special needs. Employers must find the means to alter systems to meet the needs of their employees as long as this does not cause them "undue hardship." However, undue hardship may be something different for a small organization compared with a large organization. For example, it may be a hardship for a small firm to modify a washroom to accommodate a person in a wheelchair, but it may be reasonable to expect a large organization, with its own building, to renovate or install a washroom that can accommodate a wheelchair.

Reasonable accommodation may include redesigning job duties; adjusting work schedules; providing technical, financial, and human support services; and upgrading facilities. The City of Toronto developed award-winning facilities in its Barrier Free Access

Reasonable accommodation
Attempt by employers to adjust the working conditions and employment practices of employees to prevent discrimination

Ability Society

www.abilitysociety.org

Abilities Magazine

www.abilities.ca

Canadian Council on Rehabilitation and Work

www.ccrw.org

Mental Health Works

www.mentalhealthworks.ca

program, which was designed to allow people with disabilities accessible passage throughout city facilities. There are many not-for-profit organizations in Canada that support and encourage employment opportunities for people with disabilities. Among those are Ability Society (**www.abilitysociety.org**), Abilities (**www.abilities.ca**), and Canadian Council on Rehabilitation and Work (**www.ccrw.org**). While many employers tend to think of accommodation in terms of physical disabilities, it is important to remember that the duty to accommodate includes all the prohibited grounds of discrimination, including mental illness. Therefore, it is important that employers carefully listen to any employee who says, "I am stressed." It may be that the individual has a mental illness or disorder.[13] Organizations such as Mental Health Works (**www.mentalhealthworks.ca**) can provide advice and guidance regarding workplace issues.

Reasonable accommodation benefits all employees. The provision of allowances for childcare expenses when employees take company-sponsored courses not only removes a barrier that blocks many women but also may assist any employee with sole parenting responsibilities. The flexible work schedules adopted by some companies in northern Canada benefit First Nations employees who are prepared to work unusual hours in exchange for significant breaks away from the worksite in order to take part in traditional hunting and fishing activities. Many other employees also benefit from these flexible work schedules. Further, with the cultural and religious diversity of the Canadian population, more and more employers are being asked for accommodation for religious purposes. A Toronto law office, for example, created a reflection room for religious accommodation at work.[14] At Work with HRM 2.1 provides two accommodation cases that were decided by the courts.

Reverse Discrimination

Reverse discrimination
Giving preference to members of certain groups such that others feel they are the subjects of discrimination

In pursuing initiatives to avoid discrimination, employers may be accused of **reverse discrimination**, or giving preference to members of certain groups such that others feel they are being discriminated against. For example, if a company feels that it has too few women employees, it may take active steps to hire more women. By hiring more women, however, the company may hire fewer men, opening itself to criticisms that it is discriminating against men. When these charges occur, organizations are caught between attempting to correct past discriminatory practices and handling present complaints that they are being unfair. If an organization is required to comply with any type of employment equity legislation (discussed later), it can be quite legal to discriminate and hire certain individuals.

ETHICS **in HRM 2.1**

WAS THE STEALING JUSTIFIED?

In mid-2011, an employer was allowed to fire a person for stealing even though it was argued that the person had a drug dependency and therefore needed to be accommodated. The employee had stolen thousands of dollars worth of copper wire to support a cocaine habit. The ruling determined that while one of his addictions might be some form of disability, the employer had not discriminated on the basis of that disability. The judge also noted that the employee had chosen not to go through

expensive drug rehabilitation that reinforced that the stealing was done deliberately and not on the spur of the moment. While the employee eventually sought help, it was only done so after the police investigation began.

QUESTION:

Do you think that the employee ought to have been accommodated and allowed to continue the employment? Why?

Source: Tom Blackwell, "Decision to fire addict for stealing upheld," *National Post*, August 18, 2011, A4.

Businesses today are actively seeking skilled and capable people with physical challenges.

Janet Kimber/The Image Bank/Getty Images

In some cases, organizations may identify the need to hire a certain proportion of people from specific groups, such as visible minorities. While these organizations may state that they wish to find a larger pool of qualified applicants from a particular group, the organizations may, in fact, create a type of quota system for hiring. If it is perceived that there are hard numbers attached to hiring, then it is easy for individuals not in a targeted group to feel that they are being discriminated against. Charges of reverse discrimination have occurred in the fire and police services as those organizations try to achieve a workforce more reflective of the residents in their communities.

Harassment

Outcome 4

What is the role of the line manager?

Harassment
Any unwanted physical or verbal conduct that offends or humiliates the individual

Besides prohibiting discrimination, human rights legislation prohibits harassment. Some provinces protect only against sexual **harassment**, while other provinces prohibit any type of workplace harassment. Harassment is any unwanted physical or verbal conduct that offends or humiliates a person.[15] Harassment can take many forms and can be one incident or several incidents. It is not acceptable, for instance, for one co-worker to strike another, and it is not acceptable to make personal comments that are offensive to the other person. When dealing with harassment in the workplace, a manager needs to ask whether a "reasonable person" would consider a certain behaviour or action as harassment. If the answer is yes, then the supervisor is expected to act accordingly. It is interesting to note that what is considered harassment

AT WORK **with HRM 2.1**

SHOULD ACCOMMODATION BE DONE?

- A recent case, which was settled without a hearing, dealt with what someone can say at work regarding one's own religion. During lunch breaks, a particular employee, a Jehovah's Witness, would preach to other employees about their beliefs. Employees complained to the employer. It was concluded that while an employer needed to accommodate someone's religious beliefs, the accommodation did not extend to imposing one's beliefs on others in the workplace.

- The Alberta Human Rights Commission found that Livingstone Range School Division #68 had not been obliged to accommodate a teacher who indicated chronic fatigue. The case involved how much teaching and what type of teaching the person could do. The teacher worked with children who had special needs and found that if a student had severe physical challenges, it was very fatiguing to work full time. However, if the teacher worked less than full time or with a student with fewer challenges, then the fatigue was manageable through longer breaks. Whenever the teacher informed the supervisor of needing less strenuous work, the supervisor accommodated the situation. When there was a change in supervisor, the teacher expected longer breaks without needing to inform the new supervisor of the condition. The evidence presented during the hearing verified that the teacher at no time indicated that there was a medical condition that required accommodation and did not submit any medical information to support the need for accommodation. The commission determined that without clear medical information to indicate a physical disability that required accommodation, the employer was not obligated to accommodate.

CRITICAL THINKING QUESTION:

Do you think these were appropriate decisions? Why or why not?

Sources: Shannon Klie, "Pitting human rights against each other," *Canadian HR Reporter*, March 14, 2011, http://www.hrreporter.com/articleview?&articleid=9738&headline=pitting-human-rights-against-each-other (accessed October 21, 2011); and Human Rights Tribunals of Alberta, *Shimp vs. Livingstone Range School Division #68*, October 19, 2010, http://www.hrreporter.com/articleview?&articleid=9738&headline=pitting-human-rights-against-each-other (retrieved October 21, 2011).

in today's workplace was sometimes considered acceptable behaviour not long ago. For example, it used to be acceptable to call someone a name that reflected the person's ethnic background.

While for some time, discussions of harassment have focused on sexual harassment, in the last several years the focus has been on general harassment in the workplace. Specifically, organizations have developed policy statements and guidelines for dealing with harassment in the workplace.

The Canadian Human Rights Commission defines harassment as follows:

Harassment is any unwanted physical or verbal conduct that offends or humiliates you. Such conduct can interfere with your ability to do a job or obtain a service. Harassment is a type of discrimination. It can take many forms, such as

- threats, intimidation, or verbal abuse;
- unwelcome remarks or jokes about subjects like your race, religion, disability, or age;
- displaying sexist, racist, or other offensive pictures or posters;
- sexually suggestive remarks or gestures;
- inappropriate physical contact, such as touching, patting, pinching, or punching;
- physical assault, including sexual assault.

HRM and the Law 2.1

WAS "SEXTING" HARASSMENT?

In 2011, a case between an employee and business owner was decided by the British Columbia Human Rights Tribunal that cost the company $30,000. The specifics of the case involved an individual who had had a relationship with the owner of the company. During the relationship, each person would frequently text the other with messages that were of a sexual nature. Eventually the relationship ended, but the texting by the owner continued. The employee both verbally and by text said that the texting created uncomfortable feelings and requested that the owner stop texting. The texts did not stop, and the employee became stressed and took a leave of absence. After several months when the texting continued, even after threats of contacting the police, the employee left the company. The employee then filed a human rights complaint alleging that the employee was forced to leave the company due to sexual harassment. The company maintained that the relationship was consensual and that the employee had participated in the texting and that quitting work had nothing to do with the texting. The tribunal determined that the employee had clearly stated that the relationship had ended, that there were feelings of harassment with the ongoing texting, and that the texting had to stop. The tribunal ordered back pay of almost $15,000 plus damages of $12,500 and costs of $2,900.

What do you think of the decision? Were the costs appropriate? Why?

Sources: Extract from British Columbia Human Rights Tribunal, *McIntosh v. Metro Aluminum Products and another*, 2011 BCHRT 34, February 15, 2011; and Jeffrey R. Smith, "Worker awarded $30,000 in 'sexting' case," *Canadian HR Reporter*, April 11, 2011, http://www.hrreporter.com/articleview?articleid=9968&headline=worker-awarded-%2430000-in-sexting-case-%28legal-view%29 (accessed October 21, 2011).

Harassment will be considered to have taken place if a reasonable person ought to have known that the behaviour was unwelcome.[16]

What this means for supervisors is that they are expected to work with employees to ensure that they are behaving and acting in an acceptable fashion. For example, HRM and the Law 2.1 describes the impact of a harassment complaint that involved text messaging between an employee and the owner of a company.

It is important for organizations to have policies dealing with harassment. For example, CBC/Radio-Canada has an extensive policy dealing with anti-harassment and discrimination.[17] It includes not only definitions and examples, but information about how complaints are filed and handled.

In another example, Seneca College's discrimination and harassment policy states:

It is the Policy of Seneca College that all employees and students have a right to work and study in an environment that asserts the personal worth and dignity of each individual.

In order to achieve this objective, Seneca College will not tolerate any form of discrimination and/or harassment in its employment, educational, accommodation or business dealings. Every member of the College community has the right to file a complaint of discrimination/harassment.[18]

Its policy defines harassment as:

Engaging in a course of vexatious comments or conduct related to one or more of the prohibited grounds that is known or might reasonably be known to be unwelcome/unwanted, offensive, intimidating, hostile, or inappropriate, which adversely affects the employment or academic status of the individual.[19]

Seneca's policy is very far-reaching as it applies to students, faculty, and staff, and visitors to the campus as well as corporations and vendors who do business with the college.

For harassment policies to succeed, confidentiality is necessary, and so is a method for filing complaints. Without organizational commitment to zero tolerance of harassment, such policies are meaningless. It is also important to remember that harassment is against the law. As the Province of Saskatchewan reminds employers:

> If you violate the *Code* you could be liable for the harm caused by discrimination.[20]

Manager's Toolkit 2.1 presents some suggestions for developing an effective harassment policy.

The concepts of harassment in the workplace are being broadened to include **psychological harassment**, such as bullying, yelling at subordinates, excluding employees from certain activities, and making derogatory comments. Psychological harassment, which can create a poisoned work environment, is based on grounds other than those prohibited in human rights legislation. Several jurisdictions, Quebec, Ontario, and Saskatchewan among them, have legislation prohibiting psychological harassment. In November 2010, Manitoba changed its health and safety regulations to include psychological harassment, and Ontario has changed its health and safety legislation to include workplace violence.[21]

Psychological harassment
Repeated and aggravating behaviour that affects an employee's dignity, psychological, or physical integrity that results in a harmful work environment

Enforcement of Human Rights Legislation

The federal government and each province and territory have a commission or similar agency to deal with complaints concerning discriminatory practices covered by legislation. For example, the Canadian Human Rights Commission (CHRC) (**www.chrc-ccdp.ca**) deals with complaints from those employees and businesses covered by the *Canadian Human Rights Act*. These commissions can act on their own if they feel that there are sufficient grounds for a finding of discrimination. The agencies also have the ability to interpret the act. Figure 2.3 presents a flowchart of the process used at CHRC to resolve complaints. You will note that the process includes a very early step of resolution and preventive mediation. Other human rights commissions operate in a similar fashion.

The steps are as follows:

1. Inquiry—Individual contacts the CHRC about launching a complaint, and the CHRC determines if the allegations fall within its jurisdiction.
2. Early Resolution and Preventive Mediation—A CHRC representative determines if it is the correct agency and if so, encourages the parties to seek resolution by using its trained specialists in mediation.

Canadian Human Rights Commission (CHRC)

www.chrc-ccdp.ca

MANAGER'S TOOLKIT **2.1**

GUIDELINES FOR HAVING AN EFFECTIVE ANTI-HARASSMENT POLICY

1. Encourage employees to come forward with complaints.
2. Provide a clear definition of harassment.
3. Provide guidelines for individuals about making a complaint.
4. Provide a step-by-step procedure for making a complaint.
5. Maintain confidentiality.
6. Guarantee fair and prompt action.

Additional resources from the various human rights commissions are available at the following Web sites:

- www.albertahumanrights.ab.ca (Province of Alberta)
- www.bchrt.bc.ca (Province of British Columbia)
- www.manitobahumanrights.ca (Province of Manitoba)
- www.ohrc.on.ca (Province of Ontario)
- www.shrc.gov.sk.ca (Province of Saskatchewan)

Source: Adapted from "Guidelines for Developing an Anti-Harassment Policy," September 2011, Yukon Human Rights Commission. Adapted and published with permission.

FIGURE 2.3 Canadian Human Rights Commission Disputes Resolution Process

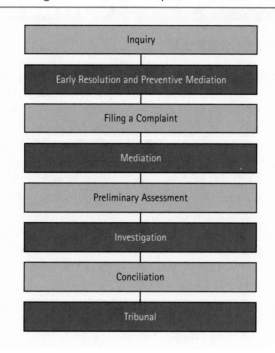

Source: *CHRC: Overview-Resolving Disputes: Dispute Resolution Process*, Canadian Human Rights Commission. Reproduced with the permission of the Minister of Public Works and Government Services, 2012.

3. Filing a Complaint—If the matter hasn't been resolved in Step 2, and if the individual wishes to pursue the matter, a complaint is filed. The CHRC can decide to deal with the complaint or it can be dismissed. If the CHRC will hear the complaint, a review is done to determine if mediation would work.
4. Mediation—Specialists are assigned by the CHRC to assist the parties in finding a mediated solution. This is a voluntary and confidential step.
5. Preliminary Assessment—If the parties are not willing to be involved in mediation (or if mediation is not appropriate), the complaint is referred to the Investigation Division to determine next steps. This stage of the process can once again include mediation or a decision to have a full investigation.
6. Investigation—An investigation, which includes the gathering of any documents and other evidence, is made; a report analyzing the information, along with a recommendation as to the further handling of the case, is then prepared. The report is submitted to the commissioner. The commission can dismiss the case, refer it to conciliation, or refer to the tribunal for a final and binding decision. When a case is referred to a tribunal, there is no guarantee that the complaint will be upheld. For example, the Bank of Montreal was alleged to have terminated a long-service employee due to a physical disability and that occurred after it had already provided accommodation. The tribunal determined through the evidence submitted that the person had been terminated due to poor performance and not for any disability.[22]

Any person who obstructs an investigation or a tribunal, or fails to comply with the terms of a settlement, can be found guilty of an offence that may be punishable by a fine and/or jail sentence. A person found to have discriminated can pay a fine up to $40,000 with an additional $10,000 if any hate message was involved.[23]

HRM and SME 2.1

INTENTIONAL OR LOOSE TALK?

The consequences of discrimination complaints can be particularly damaging for small- to medium-size businesses. For example, a metal manufacturing company in Ontario was fined almost $35,000 for racial discrimination. The case revolved around two individuals who were told to stop speaking Punjabi in the lunchroom during their breaks. During the hearing the tribunal confirmed that while language isn't a prohibited ground, it is a substitute for race or ethnic origin—both of which are prohibited grounds. The tribunal also determined that the general manager's behaviour and actions tended to differentiate based on ethnic background. Part of the award included $10,000 for "loss of dignity and stress."

In Quebec, an employer was fined $7,500 for the questions asked of an applicant. While the employer wanted to know if the individual had any religious objections to certain types of work and asked specifically if the person was a Muslim. During the hearing, the employer explained there was an attempt to determine whether there were any constraints on the person working during certain times. However, the tribunal determined that the employer had repeatedly asked specific questions about being a Muslim and that these questions had no relevance in determining whether the person could do the job.

Sources: Connie Reeve and Lisa Carty, "Recent Decisions from the Human Rights Tribunal of Ontario," *Blakes Bulletin on Labour and Employment*, November 2011; and Jeffrey R. Smith, "A Little Bit of Conversation Can Be Expensive," *The Canadian HR Reporter*, May 12, 2011, www.hrreporter.com/blog/Employment-Law/archive/2011/05/12/a-little-bit-of-conversation-can-be-expensive.

Provincial human rights laws are enforced in a similar manner to that used in the federal system. The majority of cases are resolved at the investigation stage. If no agreement can be reached, the case is presented to the province's human rights commission. The members of the commission study the evidence and then submit a report to the minister in charge of administering human rights legislation. The minister may appoint an independent board of inquiry, which has similar powers to a tribunal at the federal level. Failure to comply with the remedies prescribed by the board of inquiry may result in prosecution in provincial court. Individuals may be fined between $500 and $1,000, and organizations or groups between $1,000 and $10,000. These levies may vary across provinces. The impact of fines can be particularly difficult on small and medium businesses as is seen in HRM and SME 2.1.

EMPLOYMENT STANDARDS LEGISLATION

Outcome 5

What are the general types of employment laws in Canada?

All federal, provincial, and territorial jurisdictions have passed employment standards laws specifying the minimum obligations of employers. The names of the laws usually include the words "employment standards" or something similar. However, the minimum obligations for federal companies are covered under the *Canada Labour Code*.

Usually included in this type of legislation are items such as hours of work, minimum wages, overtime pay, vacation pay, public holidays, and who is covered by the legislation. Standards vary between provinces. In Manitoba, for instance, "domestic workers" are covered. However, a person is defined as a domestic worker only if the person works more than 24 hours per week for a family doing cooking, cleaning, and childcare for the entire family. The legislation also typically reflects the views of the respective government with regard to its social policy. For example, British Columbia's legislation provides the right for a person to take a limited number of days off to tend to childcare needs. Other jurisdictions, such as Ontario, have no such provision. Both British Columbia and Ontario have legislation that provides nine statutory or public holidays. There is usually a separate

Ontario Employment Standards

www.labour.gov.on.ca

Manitoba Employment Standards

www.gov.mb.ca/labour/standards

New Brunswick Employment Standards

www2.gnb.ca/content/gnb/en/departments/post-secondary_education_training_and_labour/labour.html

branch or agency that administers and interprets the legislation for both employers and employees. All the Web sites are listed in the Appendix at the end of this chapter, but you may want to look at several of the following: **www.labour.gov.on.ca**, **www.gov.mb.ca/labour/standards**, and **www2.gnb.ca/content/gnb/en/departments/post-secondary_education_training_and_labour/labour.html**.

This legislation is important as it applies to all employers, whether they are unionized or not. And because it specifies minimum obligations of employers, every employer—large or small—needs to be aware of the legislation. It is particularly important during difficult economic times that employers take note of their legal obligations. For example, in Ontario, pregnant employees and employees on parental leave are protected by both employment standards and human rights legislation, in relation to termination or layoff.[24]

An agency or commission that both interprets and enforces the law administers the legislation. For example, if employees feel that they are not receiving the right amount of vacation pay, they can contact the agency and find out what the right amount should be. If they are getting the wrong amount, then the agency can contact the employer and start an investigation. Further, if the complaint is significant and might have an impact on employees throughout Canada, sometimes the courts will hear the case, as has happened. This is the situation where a class-action lawsuit against the Bank of Nova Scotia claims that more than 5,000 employees were unfairly treated when overtime compensation was denied.[25] Other similar lawsuits against financial institutions have occurred in the last several years.

LABOUR RELATIONS LEGISLATION

Labour relations legislation governs both the process by which a trade union acquires bargaining rights and the procedures by which trade unions and employers engage in collective bargaining. In some jurisdictions, such as Ontario, the legislation (*Labour Relations Act*, 1995) applies primarily to workplaces in the private sector but also to certain parts of the public sector (e.g., municipal workers, hospital employees, school boards). Ontario also has separate legislation for certain types of employers in the public sector, such as hospitals and Crown corporations.[26] However, in other jurisdictions, such as British Columbia, the legislation can apply to any workplace—whether it is in the public or private sector. Labour relations legislation applies only to unionized employees and to employers with unionized employees. Currently, approximately 4.2 million employees (or 29% of the Canadian workforce) belong to a union primarily in public administration and education (68%) with less than 15% being in trades. Unionization continues to decline in Canada.[27]

Labour relations legislation is usually administered through an agency called the Labour Relations Board, which is responsible for administering and enforcing the legislation. This board makes decisions on a variety of complaints from either a union or an employer. An employer might complain about the location of a trade union's picket, or union members might complain that the union has not fairly represented them. The people making these decisions are hired by the board and are usually lawyers or have some type of legal training.

More information on labour relations legislation will be covered in Chapter 10.

HEALTH AND SAFETY LEGISLATION AND WORKERS' COMPENSATION

As you will see later in this book, the health and safety of employees is a responsibility of employers. This responsibility is governed by legislation that describes the expected standards for health and safety in the workplace, as well as outlining the role and involvement of employees in health and safety. Recent changes to this type of legislation have

Construction workers must adhere to strict guidelines in order to meet workplace safety regulations.

Photodisc Collection/Getty Images

not only increased responsibility for employers, but have also placed more onus for a healthy and safe work environment on employees.[28] Violations of health and safety statutes are administered through a government agency, frequently called the Workers' Compensation Board. As part of the legislation, workers can receive a monetary payment if they are injured at work. Thus, the employer is responsible not only for the health and safety of the workplace but also for financial compensation if the worker is injured on the job.

Additional information on health and safety legislation will be covered in Chapter 8.

EMPLOYMENT AND PAY EQUITY

Outcome 6

What is the difference between employment and pay equity?

Central to Canada's economic growth and prosperity in a highly competitive global marketplace will be a barrier-free environment in which all Canadians can fully explore and develop their career potential. Labour force statistics, described in Chapter 1, indicate changing patterns of immigration, the rising labour force participation rates of women, and an aging population with a proportionately higher incidence of disabilities. Women, visible minorities, First Nations people, and people with disabilities make up more than 60% of Canada's labour force, and their numbers continue to rise. These designated-group members entering Canada's labour pool constitute a vital resource, and their full participation in the workplace will be fundamental to an organization's ability to understand and respond to the needs of a rapidly changing marketplace.

Employment Equity

Employment equity
A distinct Canadian process for achieving equality in all aspects of employment

Equity by definition means fairness or impartiality. In a legal sense, it means justice based on the concepts of ethics and fairness and a system of jurisprudence administered by courts and designed primarily to decrease the rigidity of common law. The implementation of **employment equity** has involved the establishment of policies and practices designed to ensure equitable representation in the workforce and to redress past discriminations as they relate to employment and employment practices.

The Law on Employment Equity

The *Employment Equity Act* requires that the federal government, federal agencies, and Crown corporations with 100 employees or more and that are regulated under the Canada Labour Code must implement employment equity and report on their results. Some of the companies that are covered by the Employment Equity Act are the Royal Bank, Rogers Foods Ltd., General Electric Canada, Brinks Canada Limited, and Metro Vancouver Port Authority. Under the act the employer is required to develop plans to better represent certain **designated groups** (women, visible minorities, Aboriginal peoples, and people with disabilities). In creating the plan, the employer must identify and remove any employment barriers, such as a keyboarding test for jobs in which no keyboarding is required. Further, the plan must have a timetable for achieving these changes. Although this law does not extend to the provinces, the federal government, through its Federal Contractors Program, expects organizations that do business with the federal government, such as Sheraton Winnipeg Hotel, SAP Canada, Mustang Survival Company, and Atlantic Industries, to implement employment equity principles.[29]

While there are no specific provincial acts pertaining to employment equity, the concept of employment equity is rooted in federal and provincial employment standards legislation, human rights codes, and the *Canadian Charter of Rights and Freedoms*. Employment equity involves the identification and removal of systemic barriers to employment opportunities that adversely affect designated groups. It also involves the implementation of special measures and reasonable accommodation (discussed earlier under "Discrimination"). The employment equity legislation identified four designated groups in Canada that had not received equitable treatment in employment—women, visible minorities, First Nations peoples, and people with disabilities—recognizing that they faced significant, but different disadvantages in employment. Some of the disadvantages included high unemployment, occupational segregation, pay inequities, and limited opportunities for career progress. While there has been progress since the introduction of the legislation in the mid-1980s, some of the original concerns have not been advanced very far.

While women have an employment rate of 62%,[30] employment for women tends to be concentrated in retail trade, banking, education, and health care (68%).[31] On the other hand, women tend to be under-represented in construction (1.6%), but they are close to being equally represented (4.4%) with men (4.5%) in recreation and cultural jobs.[32]

While the number of Aboriginal people is only about 3.8%[33] of the population, the numbers of young Aboriginal workers will increase, and in western Canada, they will account for a substantial portion of labour market growth. However, many Aboriginal people face major employment barriers, which may be compounded by low educational achievement and lack of job experience, as well as language and cultural barriers. In urban centres, many Aboriginal workers are concentrated in low-paying, unstable employment. Economic self-sufficiency and participation in the economy are seen as essential to Aboriginal development. At Work with HRM 2.2 describes the success of several organizations in assisting Aboriginal people to become an integral part of their workforces.

Visible-minority groups vary in their labour force profiles and in their regional distributions. Toronto and Vancouver have large visible-minority populations. Studies have shown that Latin Americans and Southeast Asians experience lower-than-average incomes, higher rates of unemployment, and reduced access to job interviews, even for those persons with the same qualifications as other candidates. Systemic barriers that have a negative employment impact on visible minorities can include culturally biased aptitude tests, lack of recognition of foreign credentials, and excessive levels of language requirements. Recent statistics indicate that although visible minorities, 84% of whom are immigrants, possess higher educational achievements, they also have the highest unemployment rates and tend to work in jobs with low skill requirements and receive less training while employed.[34]

Designated groups
Women, visible minorities, Aboriginal peoples, and persons with disabilities who have been disadvantaged in employment

AT WORK **with HRM 2.2**

SUCCESS!

Human Resources and Skills Development Canada has recognized several organizations in its annual report for the work done to enhance employment for First Nations people. The Canadian Museum of Nature in Ottawa provided workshops that focused on Aboriginal Awareness issues with the objective of increasing the number of Aboriginals working at the museum. Nasittuq Corporation, which operates and maintains the North Warning System of radar, continued to identify opportunities where Aboriginals could be trained in trades, technical, and professional categories. The Bank of Montreal created a scholarship and internship program to provide Aboriginal youth with the opportunity to do a summer internship while still in school. The intention of the program is to offer Aboriginal youth work in financial services when they graduate.

Canada Mortgage and Housing Corporation received special recognition for the following efforts:

- providing lunch and learn sessions during a National Aboriginal Awareness Week

- posting job openings in outreach organizations representing Aboriginal communities

- advertising in Aboriginal newspapers and on Aboriginal Web sites

The organization has created a culture of belonging for all its employees.

CRITICAL THINKING QUESTIONS:

1. What has the company you are working for (or have recently worked for) done to assist visible minorities, people with disabilities, and Aboriginal people in getting hired?

2. Is there more that they could do? If so, please explain.

Source: Adapted from Human Resources and Social Development Canada, *Employment Equity Act: Annual Report 2009*.

Of the employable people with disabilities, only about 51% are actively participating in the workforce.[35] People with disabilities face attitudinal barriers, physical demands that are unrelated to actual job requirements, and inadequate access to the technical and human support systems that would make productive employment possible. A number of modifications such as job redesign, number of hours of work, and appropriate parking can assist people in more actively participating in the workforce.[36] The employment experiences of people with disabilities are also dependent on the extent of the limitations, as perceived by the person. In most cases, people with minor limitations do not experience as many barriers as those with more extreme limitations.[37]

As mentioned earlier in the chapter, these employment practices can unintentionally preclude certain segments of our population from employment opportunities. Manager's Toolkit 2.2 gives examples of suggested solutions to systemic barriers.

Benefits of Employment Equity

Employment equity makes good business sense since it contributes to the bottom line by broadening the base of qualified individuals for employment, training, and promotions, and by helping employers to avoid costly human rights complaints. Most provinces now take an active approach to ensuring that there is appropriate representation in their workforces. For example, the Manitoba Civil Service Commission believes that a diverse employee base can better serve the citizens of Manitoba.[38] Likewise, organizations such as Atlantic Tractors and Equipment in Nova Scotia and New Brunswick find that through employment equity initiatives, they are able to attract young women to work for them.

Human Resources and Social Development Canada administers the federal *Employment Equity Act* and as part of that administration recognizes organizations that have made special efforts to achieve a workforce that is representative of our population. In the annual reports produced each year, organizations are recognized for their efforts,

EXAMPLES OF EMPLOYMENT PRACTICES

1. *Word-of-mouth recruiting.* While this is a common form of making job opportunities known to family and friends, this can be an effective tool for sourcing designated group members if the information is shared widely and to a variety of different communities.

2. *Job requirements.* Employers that require Canadian experience may be eliminating visible minorities, particularly recent immigrants. It is important to review the experience required and determine if having previous work in a Canadian environment is necessary for job success.

3. *Training and development.* It is important to review the organization's approach to training of its employees. Training opportunities that are linked to seniority, wage levels, and type of work could limit the participation of designated group members.

Source: *Guidelines for the Employment Equity Act and Regulations: Guideline 6*: Employment Systems Review, Human Resources and Social Development Canada, Labour Program.

Human Resources and Skills Development Canada (HRSDC)

www.hrsdc.gc.ca

such as those described in At Work with HRM 2.2. As stated by Paul Kilala, director, Canada Mortgage and Housing Corporation, "I am proud to be part of CMHC's Ethno Marketing Strategy that aims to provide our literature and programs in languages other than English and French. I know that the information needs of immigrants (having been one myself) are greatest immediately when they arrive. I am particularly honored to be of assistance to them."[39]

For additional information on the Employment Equity Act, visit HRDC's Web site at **www.hrsdc.gc.ca**.

First Nations University is a unique university in Canada that focuses on the educational needs of Aboriginal people.

Pay Equity

As a result of a 1978 amendment to the *Canadian Human Rights Act*, pay equity became law. Federal pay equity law makes it illegal for federally regulated employers to discriminate against individuals on the basis of job content. The focus of pay equity legislation is to narrow the wage gap between men and women, on the basis that women's work historically has been undervalued and therefore underpaid relative to work primarily done by men. For example, the average hourly wage of males who worked full time in 2011 was $24.61, compared with $21.45 for women.[40] Even when organizations work on reducing any wage gaps, there can still be a perception of unfairness and inequity.[41]

Pay equity means equal pay for work of equal value and is based on two principles. The first is equal pay for equal work. Equal pay for equal work means that if a woman and a man are doing substantially the same work for the same organization or company, they must receive the same wage unless the difference in pay is due to seniority, temporary training assignment, or merit.[42] Equal pay for equal work is regulated through basic employment conditions legislation, usually called an Employment Standards Act.

The second principle of pay equity is equal pay for work that may be comparable in value to the organization. Pay equity compares the value of and pay of different jobs. This means that male and female workers must be paid the same wage rate for jobs of comparable value, such as a nurse (historically, female-dominated work) to an electrician (historically, male-dominated).

Implementation of pay equity is based on comparing jobs performed mostly by women with jobs performed mostly by males. Comparisons require the use of a gender-neutral job comparison system to evaluate the jobs in the organization.[43] The value of the work is based on the skills and effort required, the responsibilities of the job, and the conditions under which the work is performed. It is important to remember that the comparisons are made on job content, not on the performance of the employee. The comparison must be done in such a way that the characteristics of "male" jobs, such as manual skills of a machinery repairperson, are valued fairly in comparison with the characteristics of "female" jobs, such as the dexterity skills of a typist.[44] For example, under pay equity, Canadian National Railways would need to compare the work of an accounts payable clerk with that of a person who repairs the train cars.

The federal pay equity legislation applies to the workforce under its jurisdiction and covers all organizations regardless of number of employees. The system is complaint-based, meaning that complaints can be raised by an employee, a group of employees, or a union.[45] However, it can take years for complaints to be resolved. For example, it took 28 years to resolve a pay equity case involving Canada Post! The case was originally filed with the Canadian Human Rights Tribunal in 1983 and involved pay comparisons with clerical workers (primarily female) to operations jobs, such as letter carriers (primarily male). The tribunal initially upheld the complaint, and then the issue went through years of various appeals. Finally in 2005, a decision that upheld the complaint was made, and it was appealed to the Supreme Court of Canada. In November 2011, the Court reinstated the original award, worth about $150 million, and the award will be implemented.[46]

In Ontario the legislation covers public- and private-sector employers with 10 or more employees. Like the federal legislation, Ontario's legislation is complaint-based. There is no pay equity legislation in either Alberta or British Columbia.

For more information on pay equity, check the following Web sites:

- www.payequity.gov.on.ca/en/index.php
- www.chrc-ccdp.ca
- www.gov.ns.ca/lae/payequity

Even though there have been recent changes in some of the employment legislation described in these, changes will continue as Canadian social values change. See Emerging Trends 2.1 for things to watch.

Pay equity
The practice of equal pay for work of equal value

Ontario Pay Equity Commission
www.payequity.gov.on.ca/en/index.php

Canadian Human Rights Commission
www.chrc-ccdp.ca

Nova Scotia Pay Equity Commission
http://www.gov.ns.ca/lae/payequity

EMERGING TRENDS **2.1**

There have been several recent significant court decisions that may have an impact on the rights of both employees and employers. Here are a few items to consider:

1. ***Pre-employment screening***. Given the impact of a poor hiring decision, more employers are making use of pre-employment credit checks, criminal record checks, driving history, and verification of academic credentials.

2. ***Medical notes from doctors***. For years, employers have had to accept one-line notes from doctors about the medical condition of an employee. In most situations, employees were disadvantaged as the employers did not have good information about their health (or disability) and made decisions based on what they had. In 2008, the Supreme Court of Canada determined that an employee could be evaluated by a doctor of the firm's choosing.

3. ***Legislation***. The need to accommodate people with disabilities is expanding. For example, Ontario has recently enacted legislation under its *Accessibility for Ontarians with Disabilities* Act that will apply to all employers within the province. The legislation outlines certain standards aimed at making Ontario fully accessible by

2025. Further, there have been recent challenges as to whether obesity and smoking are treated as disabilities.

4. ***Psychological harassment***. The issue of bullying and harassment is not just a workplace health and safety issue. Through courts and tribunals, increasingly decisions are made that demonstrate an expectation of a respectful and civil work environment.

5. ***Inclusion of mental stress in workers' compensation legislation***. As more and more court cases, as well as tribunal decisions, deal with the impact of bullying and harassment, provincial health and safety legislation is broadening coverage for workplace mental stress. The objective of the expanded coverage is to create a healthy work environment.

6. ***Use and misuse of technology.*** There have been more court cases involving employee blogs as blogs can divulge confidential and sensitive information. Also there are situations where the language is offensive and the information inaccurate. In addition, employers may also need to consider how accessible they want employees to be with PDAs as constant use could attract overtime claims.

Sources: Adapted from Howard Levitt, "Workplace Law: Recent Judgments a Sign of the Times," *The Vancouver Sun*, January 10, 2009, 15; Sarah Dobson, "Perfect legal storm brewing with psychological safety in workplace," *The Canadian HR Reporter*, November 1, 2010, http://www.hrreporter.com/articleview?&articleid=8381&headline=perfect-legal-storm-brewing-with-psychological-safety-in-workplace (accessed November 2, 2011); Sarah Dobson, "Battling the bulge bias: Summit," *The Canadian HR Reporter*, February 14, 2011, http://www.hrreporter.com/articleview?&articleid=9512&headline=battling-the-bulge-bias-summit (accessed November 2, 2011); Ken Cahoon, "Pre-employment screening: What is necessary?" *The Canadian HR Reporter*, July 18, 2011, http://www.hrreporter.com/articleview?&articleid=10784&headline=pre-employment-screening-what-is-necessary (accessed November 2, 2011), Rob Shaw, "Provincial bill expands coverage for workplace mental stress," *The Vancouver Sun*, November 4, 2011, A4; and Amanda Silliker, "Ontario's AODA deadline just around the corner," *Canadian HR Reporter*, October 24, 2011, 1.

DIVERSITY

Outcome 7

What are the differences between diversity and employment equity?

Diversity management
The combination of organizational policies and practices that supports and encourages employee differences in order to reach business objectives

Managing diversity goes beyond Canadian employment equity legislation's four designated groups in addressing the need to create a fair work environment. The terms "diversity management" and "employment equity" are often used interchangeably, but there are differences. **Diversity management** is voluntary; employment equity is not. Managing diversity is a broader, more inclusive concept encompassing such factors as religion, personality, lifestyle, and education. Many organizations are not only focusing on diversity, but are ensuring that the workplace is also inclusive—ensuring not only that people are hired, but also retained and developed. An inclusive environment leads to growth, new markets, higher profits, and a more loyal customer and employee base.[47] A November 2011 report released by Deloitte Canada, a professional services firm, noted that a diverse workforce not only is better for our society but also encourages innovation and creativity for enhanced economic growth.[48]

According to Statistics Canada, about 25% of our total population by 2031 will be immigrants.[49] In this context, diversity management is not merely a legal obligation but rather a business requirement for company success. Diversity is also not just about racial and cultural background—it is about accepting and understanding differences. One of the more progressive firms is Accenture, a global management consulting, technology services, and outsourcing firm with about 1,000 employees in Canada and 236,000 employees worldwide. Since the company does business in about 120 different countries, it wants to ensure that it attracts and retains the best and brightest.[50] Other organizations take inclusion a step further by supporting transgendered employees. See At Work with HRM 2.3 for a fuller description of TD Bank's leading-edge approach to inclusion.

Statistics show that the ethnocultural profile of Canada has been changing since the 1960s and will continue to change dramatically given the federal government's immigration policy. According to the most recent census data (2006), 20% of the Canadian population is visible minorities or Aboriginal.[51] The top five nonofficial languages (i.e., neither French nor English) spoken by Canadians are, in ranked order, Chinese (all dialects), Italian, German, Punjabi, and Spanish.[52]

CEOs in Canada recognize the importance of diversity in their overall business strategy. As Canadian companies compete in the global marketplace, it is important that organizations need to do more than just have a diverse workforce—they need to ensure that those employees are engaged and developed.[53] The importance of having diversity and inclusion is not just about established organizations. The Pan Am Games, which will be held in Canada (Toronto) in 2015, have developed diversity policies that will cover everything from governance to employees to volunteers. These policies recognize the

---

AT WORK **with HRM 2.3**

TRANSGENDER AND TD BANK

It has only been a few years, but already TD Bank is standing out among employers that truly endeavour to have an inclusive workplace. In 2009, TD developed what was seen as groundbreaking guidelines and benefits to support workers going through a gender change. The guidelines covered a variety of topics, including appropriate language, use of words, and bathroom rules. A great deal of emphasis was placed on the roles of supervisors and co-workers in supporting the employee.

This type of support has also provided a great recruitment tool for the bank. A recent hire noted being drawn to work at the bank and commented on feeling totally accepted during the interview process. While sexual orientation is not specifically mentioned in human rights legislation, cases determined by the Supreme Court of Canada have included sexual orientation as part of the prohibited grounds on harassment and discrimination.

As employers in Canada continue to seek qualified and experienced staff, more companies are looking at how inclusive their organizations really are. These companies are undertaking significant re-examinations of their policies and how the words play out in actions in relation to gay, lesbian, bisexual, and transgender. Only through education and open conversation will employers realize an inclusive environment where differences are recognized and celebrated

CRITICAL THINKING QUESTION:

Can you think of other initiatives that organizations can adopt to help create a positive work environment that supports diversity?

Source: Adapted from Darah Hansen, "Companies are changing to support transgender employees," *The Vancouver Sun*, August 13, 2011, C3.

economic impact of the Games to people who might have been under-represented in large projects in the past. As Ian Troop, CEO of TO2015, says, "Toronto 2015 will be the first Pan/Parapan American Games to mandate a comprehensive and inclusive diversity policy providing business opportunities to our many multicultural communities. We have adopted diversity as a standard practice in our day-to-day business."[54]

While CEOs may recognize the importance of diversity, there are still ample examples of immigrants struggling to gain employment opportunities in their chosen field of study or experience. A variety of studies indicate that well-educated immigrants have difficulty finding employment in their chosen field and that it can be exacerbated by how "English sounding" their names might be.[55] There is, therefore, a continuing need to create programs and other ways to tap into a vital and talented component of our population and maximize the country's human capital.

It is important to remember that in Canada, diversity also includes Aboriginal peoples. PTI Group, a company headquartered in Edmonton, Alberta, specializes in the provision of modular accommodations and catering services at worksites. It won the 2011 Premier's Award of Distinction for its work to develop recruitment partnerships and hands-on training for Aboriginal youth. These initiatives resulted in employment opportunities for 150 Aboriginal people with a retention rate of 94%.[56] To highlight the importance of diversity in organizations, MediaCorp created the Canada's Best Diversity Employers list. Among the 2012 employers are Hewlett-Packard Canada, Home Depot Canada, Stantec Consulting, and the YMCA of Greater Toronto.[57] Another example of diversity success is described in At Work with HRM 2.4, which showcases the business successes of an Aboriginal group in the interior of British Columbia.

Creating an Environment for Success

Transforming an organizational culture into one that embraces diversity and is inclusive can be a complex and lengthy process. Diversity and inclusion initiatives should be taken slowly so that everyone can understand that this change is an evolutionary process and that expectations should be realistic.

Leadership is one of the most important variables in an organization's ability to successfully incorporate the value of diversity into its business strategy. Good management is key to creating a workplace that values all employees and the talents and skills that they bring.[58]

AT WORK **with HRM 2.4**

BUSINESS SUCCESS FOR ABORIGINALS

Chief Clarence Louie is very proud of the successes his community has achieved. As Chief and Administrator of the Osoyoos Indian Band and C.E.O. of Osoyoos Indian Band Development Corporation, he has provided leadership and vision for the Band to excel in a number of enterprises. He has been recognized with numerous awards, including Chairman of the National Aboriginal Economic Development Board.

During the last 25 years the Band has created a large and successful business enterprise on the Band's

32,000 acres of land. The Band businesses include Nk'Mip vineyards, Nk'Mip Gas & Convenience Store, Nk'Mip construction, Oliver Readi Mix, Nk'Mip Golf Course, Nk'Mip Campground & RV Park, the first Aboriginal winery in North America—Nk'Mip Cellars and Nk'Mip Desert Cultural Centre—an eco-cultural centre that promotes Okanagan Native heritage and culture. All of the Band's business interests are handled through the Osoyoos Indian Band Development Corporation of which Spirit Ridge Vineyard Resort and

continued

Spa is its premium accommodation. The Band also has a strategic alliance with the owners of Mt. Baldy Ski Resort.

The variety of businesses provides the Band with numerous jobs and countless career opportunities for its members. The Osoyoos Indian Band prides itself in having low unemployment rates, a healthy economic outlook and the potential for more business development. Chief Louie is a strong believer in helping individuals with their education and expanding their areas of interest. He also has a vision of developing his community into one of the greatest First Nations communities of North America.

Recently, the Band won the First Nations Financial Management Board certification. This is a distinguished designation that will allow the Band to borrow money for infrastructure at rates that apply to municipalities. Not only will the Band be able to borrow at lower rates of interest, but it will also have easier access to capital. With such access, the Band will be in a better position to fully develop its 45-hectare Senkulmen Business Park.

Chief Clarence Louie

Osoyoos Indian Band, www.oib.ca (retrieved January 16, 2009).

Sources: Adapted from Osoyoos Indian Band, www.oib.ca and www.oibdc.com (accessed October 26, 2011); and Don Cayo, "B.C. bands reap certification rewards," *The Vancouver Sun*, December 30, 2011, C2.

As part of its commitment to its staff and clients, KPMG, a global consulting firm, understands the importance of skilled immigrants and actively reaches out to its various immigrant communities with an open recruiting process. It is proud to say that 15% of its workforce received its postsecondary education outside Canada.[59] Likewise, Diavik Diamond Mines Inc., headquartered in Yellowknife, Northwest Territories, is actively involved with Northern communities in co-operative ventures providing scholarships, stay-in-school programs, and community-based training.[60]

Diversity is more than just ethnic and cultural background. At Work with HRM 2.5 describes how diversity is in the basic fabric of the business at Coast Capital Savings.

Training is essential to the success of diversity implementation. A number of companies, including Loblaw, have created a variety of different diversity programs. Loblaw created an inclusion council, composed of senior leaders, that focuses on ensuring that the staff in its stores reflects the ethnicities of the communities. Further Loblaw has launched an "inclusion toolkit," which trains and supports managers in recruiting and hiring diverse candidates.[61]

Breaking down barriers is also an important initiative when creating diversity initiatives. For example, Cameco of Saskatchewan (one of the 100 Top Employers in Canada) has partnered with "Women in Mining" and the Mining HR Council to identify employment barriers in the mining industry that women face.[62]

An added advantage of establishing a diversity initiative is its impact on employee retention. Keeping well-qualified and skilled employees is an important goal, considering

AT WORK with HRM 2.5

WE JUST DO IT!

"We don't have any special programs or approaches to diversity," says Lewisa Anciano, vice-president, people, at Coast Capital Savings. "We are a model for others as the people see that we have a workforce that is very reflective of our clients—particularly with the number of women in senior management roles."

Coast Capital Savings, headquartered in Surrey, B.C., is one of Canada's largest credit unions with over $12 billion in assets and 454,000 members. It is distinguishing itself in the marketplace by its focus on financial services for individuals and local communities, as well as being consistently ranked in the top of the Best Managed Companies in Canada.

There are no diversity programs, and yet everyone is comfortable with each other. With a true belief in people, and tied to its business strategy, the company also functions as a local community supporter through its charitable giving program.

Noted for taking action, Coast Capital has a strong belief in having women in leadership roles. Currently, six of the nine senior executive leaders are women. And diversity is more than just about gender

and ethnicity—it is about everyone being unique. The company's focus is on performance and results, not gender or cultural background. People are valued for contributing to the company's success. "Much of this can be attributed to president and CEO, Tracy Redies," says Anciano. "She truly embraces diversity and ensures the right people are hired for our culture."

With a business that provides financial services in a highly competitive market, it is important that Coast Capital has employees who understand the market and what customers want. Says Anciano, "We have an integrated people strategy with our business strategy to ensure we have the workforce that can provide the greatest service to our customers."

CRITICAL THINKING QUESTIONS:

1. What are the similarities between TD Bank (At Work with HRM 2.3) and Coast Capital in relation to their diversity approaches?

2. Would the approach at Coast Capital be successful at TD Bank? Why or why not?

Source: Interview with Lewisa Anciano, November 2011.

---

the amount of resources, both in time and money, spent on recruiting and hiring new employees. The above-mentioned report by Deloitte's also identified that Canada's economic health is hampered when barriers exist for foreign-born workers and companies don't see retaining these individuals as success factors for their business.[63]

When establishing diversity initiatives, an overall review of policies and employment practices must be considered. The use of an employee attitude survey may prove beneficial in finding areas of systemic or perceived discrimination. The success indicators used most often by Canadian organizations are changes in staff attitudes, particularly in relation to lesbian, gay, bisexual, and transgender (LGBT), increases in promotions for minority employees, reduction in turnover of minority employees, reduction in number of harassment suits, improved recruitment statistics for minorities, and improvements in productivity.[64] A final element in achieving success in the implementation of diversity initiatives is having a performance indicator regarding diversity so that it can be measured, monitored, and rewarded.[65]

Measuring management's performance with regard to diversity initiatives will instill those values in the minds of all employees and demonstrate that valuing diversity is part of day-to-day business. Key to achieving success in diversity objectives is setting an example and creating an atmosphere that respects and values differences. Many Canadian organizations have recognized the competitive advantage gained by embracing diversity within their business strategies and doing so will continue to assist Canada in its economic sustainability.

SUMMARY

1. Explain the impact of laws on the behaviour and actions of supervisors and managers.
   - Accepted practices and behaviours of supervisors and managers toward their employees are governed through a variety of employment legislation at both the provincial and federal levels.
   - Various laws establish certain minimum requirements regarding working conditions as well as providing protection of basic human rights.

2. Discuss the legal framework of HRM in Canada.
   - There are two distinct sets of legislation—federal and provincial.
   - The *Canadian Charter of Rights and Freedoms* is the cornerstone of contemporary employment legislation.

3. Describe discrimination and harassment in the workplace.
   - Discrimination is denying someone something because of race, ethnic background, marital status, or other prohibited grounds under human rights legislation.
   - Harassment is any behaviour that demeans, humiliates, or embarrasses a person.
   - Discrimination and harassment are illegal under human rights legislation.

4. Outline the line manager's role in creating a work environment that is free from harassment and discrimination.
   - Supervisor or manager needs to ensure that unacceptable behaviours are dealt with.
   - Supervisor is expected to work with employees to ensure that they are behaving and acting in an acceptable fashion.
   - Line manager is key link in creating an appropriate work environment.

5. Identify the general types of employment laws in Canada.
   - Employment standards legislation describes the basic obligations of employers.
   - Labour legislation governs both the process by which a trade union acquires bargaining rights and the procedures by which trade unions and employers engage in collective bargaining.
   - Health, safety, and workers' compensation legislation describes the expected standards for health and safety in the workplace and the impact if an employee is injured.
   - Human rights legislation prohibits discrimination on the basis of such areas as race, ethnic origin, marital status, and gender.
   - Human rights legislation is paramount over other employment laws.
   - Human rights legislation also protects individuals from all types of harassment.

6. Illustrate the difference between employment equity and pay equity.
   - Employment equity refers to the employment of individuals in a fair and unbiased manner.
   - Four groups in Canada (women, visible minorities, Aboriginal peoples, and people with disabilities) have been designated as those needing help to fix past wrongs.
   - The federal government and some provinces have passed legislation to help achieve a more equitable workforce.
   - Pay equity means equal pay for work of equal value.
   - Pay equity examines job content and compares dissimilar work in an organization.

7. Describe the differences between diversity and employment equity.
   - Managing diversity not only incorporates but also goes beyond employment equity.
   - The goal of diversity management is to make optimal use of an organization's multicultural workforce in order to realize strategic business advantages.

NEED TO KNOW

- Relationship of *Canadian Charter of Rights and Freedoms* to employment laws
- Names of employment laws and what they do
- Definition of harassment and discrimination
- Purpose and definition of employment and pay equity
- Definition of diversity

NEED TO UNDERSTAND

- Impact of legislation on managerial actions
- Relationship of bona fide occupational requirements to discrimination
- Impact of reasonable accommodation on managerial action
- Relationship of managerial behaviours to harassment and discrimination
- Harassment as a form of discrimination
- Impact of employment practices and managerial decisions on fair employment opportunities
- The link between diversity and business strategy

KEY TERMS

bona fide occupational qualification (BFOQ) 45

designated groups 57

diversity management 61

employment equity 56

harassment 49

pay equity 60

psychological harassment 52

reasonable accommodation 47

reverse discrimination 48

systemic discrimination 45

REVIEW QUESTIONS

1. What are three employment laws in your province? Provide examples.
2. Which of the laws described pertain to providing minimum standards in relation to hours of work before overtime pay is required?
3. How would you react to a comment that a company discriminates against women by having a height requirement to do certain types of work?
4. Explain why employment equity is needed in organizations. What are the arguments for and against it?
5. Describe the purpose of the *Employment Equity Act* and discuss some of its provisions.
6. Describe the process involved in implementing an employment equity plan. How would you evaluate its success?
7. Define pay equity and discuss how it is related to discrimination.
8. Describe the ways in which an organization can optimize the use of a multicultural workforce.

CRITICAL THINKING QUESTIONS

1. While the process for filing a complaint of harassment or discrimination in the workplace appears clear, many employees or potential employees would choose not to file. Identify some reasons why someone might not file a complaint.
2. Organizations are concerned with ensuring that the workplace is respectful and that people behave civilly to one another. What does a respectful and civil workplace look like to you?
3. You see a job ad to work at your college bookstore. Part of the job requires that the person be able to occasionally lift books onto a top shelf. You have back problems that preclude you from lifting more than 10 kg. Would lifting more than 10 kg be a justifiable BFOQ? Why or why not?

4. You have recently been hired as a supervisor to work in a food products packaging plant that has 100 employees with many different cultural backgrounds. The owner wants your help in ensuring that the work environment is inclusive. What would you suggest?

5. A friend of yours has heard you are taking a business course that focuses on human resources management and wants some help. Your friend, a practising Muslim, wishes to be able to pray regularly at work. The organization at which your friend works has a large office complex with more than 500 employees. Is this a case for reasonable accommodation? Why or why not?

6. After receiving several complaints of bullying, the manager of a large appliance store decides to establish an anti-harassment policy. What should be included in the policy? How should it be implemented?

DEVELOPING YOUR SKILLS

1. Much attention has been placed on the issue of harassment and bullying in the workplace. The cornerstone to addressing this is achieving organizational awareness. Training can assist in raising this awareness. Working in groups of three or four, develop the outline of a training session that would raise awareness for a company with 200 employees. The outline should include (1) topics to be covered; (2) specific examples of harassment and/or bullying; (3) how complaints are to be made and to whom; and (4) who would attend the training.

2. Companies are concerned about appropriate workplace behaviours and want to ensure that abusive behaviours do not occur. Watch this YouTube video: Abusive Behaviour in the Workplace, at **http://www.youtube.com/watch?v=dzHJBoVxgSE**. Working in groups of two or three, determine whether you have encountered abusive behaviour at work. If so, what did you do and why? Were any of the suggestions in the video used? Would those have worked?

3. The word "ageism" reflects attitudes and assumptions about older people and their abilities and skills—particularly in the workforce. As a result, older people are often stereotyped and not hired or promoted. It is estimated that within a few years, 20% of the Canadian population will be over 55. Working in groups of two or three, reflect on what you've learned in Chapter 1 about the shrinking Canadian workforce and what you've learned in this chapter about discrimination. From these reflections, identify at least five actions a company could take to retain older workers.

4. Working in pairs, list as many jobs as you can in which an employer could hire only male applicants based on a BFOQ.

5. Using any search engine, conduct a search using the phrase "workplace diversity" or "workplace inclusion." Note the number of matches. Review the first 10 matches and determine if they would be helpful resources. Prepare a one- to two-page summary of the results of your search, indicating whether the sites were useful.

6. Access the employment standards legislation in your province (see Appendix for URLs). Identify what is covered and determine how complaints are handled. Determine whether the current minimum wage is listed in the legislation. If not, where are you directed to find the minimum wage? Where did you find it?

Case Study  1

Discrimination?

Joe works in a large mining operation in Saskatchewan. He has been with the company for a number of years. He started as a labourer and over time was promoted to a supervisory position.

As the mining business continued to grow, the senior management decided it was important to have a more diverse workforce—90% of the workforce were men, primarily of European background. In doing so, the senior management met with all the supervisors, explained what they were trying to achieve, and engaged the supervisors in discussions regarding barriers. All the supervisors were supportive of the direction the company wished to take.

Shortly after the supervisory meeting, a female employee filed a complaint of gender discrimination against Joe. Based upon the company's own procedures, an investigation was launched. The investigation concluded that Joe did not discriminate but did identify that Joe was not properly fulfilling his responsibilities as a supervisor, especially in relation to training employees about appropriate behaviour at work. As a result, Joe was reassigned to another job that the company felt he could do. Joe was not pleased with the reassignment and began to show his anger and unhappiness at work. He also tended to say things to people (particularly women) whom he felt were "out to get him."

Several months after Joe's reassignment, several female workers complained to the senior managers about the hostile environment that was developing. Again, another investigation was done and it concluded that Joe had been retaliating against those that had complained earlier. Joe was instructed to stop the behaviour and also to take a new training course that focused on creating a civil workplace.

Joe's new role included training employees on how to operate a certain machine. Among the new trainees was a woman who asked lots of questions. Joe tended to answer the questions sharply and he was less than helpful. Again, another complaint was launched about Joe's discriminatory behaviour. The company is once again starting another investigation.

Questions

1. Are these incidences of discrimination? Why or why not?
2. What should be considered in this current investigation?
3. If you were the senior management, what would you do?

Case Study 2

Discipline or Harassment?

In 2010, the province of Ontario amended its Health and Safety Act to include new provisions regarding workplace violence and harassment. As a result of the changes, ABC company conducted training sessions for all employees that covered the concepts of harassment, physical violence, verbal abuse, and awareness of how a person's words and actions can affect others at work.

Marsha, a long-service employee, attended the training. During her employment, she had received several disciplinary and non-disciplinary warnings for various reasons, including yelling and shouting at her supervisor, and swearing at co-workers. In addition to the training on workplace violence and harassment, she was also required to attend anger management counselling.

Shortly after the training, Marsha verbally threatened a fellow employee with harm. The employee reported the threat, and an investigation was made of the incident. Given Marsha's work issues, the anger management and workplace violence training, and the subsequent threat, ABC decided to terminate her employment. Marsha grieved the decision, alleging harassment, and the case was referred to an arbitrator.

At the hearing, the employer stated that the new legislation put a higher test of "reasonableness" on the employer and that it needed to take concrete action when verbal threats were made. The company further indicated that the employee had a history of inappropriate behaviour at work and did not take responsibility for her actions. The union argued that the company, by pursuing discipline, was harassing Marsha.

Questions

1. What do you think the arbitrator decided? Why?
2. Do you feel that the new legislation puts an added burden of responsibility on employers? Why or why not?
3. If you were the arbitrator, how would you decide? Explain your reasons.

APPENDIX

Web Sites for Employment Legislation

1. Federal Government
   - Canada Labour Code: **http://laws.justice.gc.ca/en/L-2**
   - Canadian Human Rights Act: **http://laws-lois.justice.gc.ca/eng/acts/h-6**
2. Province of Alberta
   - Employment Standards Code: **http://www.qp.alberta.ca/documents/Acts/ E09.pdf**
   - Labour Relations Code: **http://www.alrb.gov.ab.ca/alrb_code.htm**
   - Occupational Health and Safety Act: **http://www.employment.alberta.ca/ SFW/295.html**
   - Alberta Human Rights Act: **http://www.qp.alberta.ca/documents/Acts/ A25P5.pdf**
3. Province of British Columbia
   - Employment Standards Act: **http://www.bclaws.ca/Recon/document/ID/ freeside/00_96113_01**
   - Labour Relations Code: **http://www.bclaws.ca/Recon/document/ID/ freeside/00_96244_01**
   - Workers' Compensation Act: **http://www.bclaws.ca/Recon/document/ID/ freeside/96492_00**
   - Human Rights Code: **http://www.bclaws.ca/Recon/document/ID/ freeside/00_96210_01**

4. Province of Manitoba
   - Employment Standards Code: **http://www.gov.mb.ca/labour/standards/index.html**
   - Labour Relations Act: **http://web2.gov.mb.ca/laws/statutes/ccsm/l010e.php**
   - Workplace Safety and Health Act: **http://web2.gov.mb.ca/laws/statutes/ccsm/w210e.php**
   - Human Rights Code: **http://web2.gov.mb.ca/laws/statutes/ccsm/h175e.php**
5. Province of New Brunswick
   - Employment Standards Act: **http://www.gnb.ca/labour**
   - Industrial Relations Act: **http://www.gnb.ca/labour**
   - Occupational Health and Safety Act: **http://www.gnb.ca/leg1_e.asp**
   - Human Rights Act: **http://www.gnb.ca/0062/ PDF-acts/h-11.pdf** (to download copy of legislation)
6. Province of Newfoundland and Labrador: All statutes are accessible through **http://www.assembly.nl.ca** with links to each law.
7. Province of Nova Scotia: All statutes are accessible through **http://nslegislature.ca/legc/index.htm**
8. Province of Ontario: All statutes are accessible through **http://www.e-laws.gov.on.ca/navigation?file=home&lang=en** with links to each law.
9. Province of Prince Edward Island: Electronic versions of the legislation can be accessed by downloading PDF files from **http://www.gov.pe.ca/law/statutes/**.
10. Province of Quebec: All statutes are accessible through **http://www2.publicationsduquebec.gouv.qc.ca/home.php** with links to each law.
11. Province of Saskatchewan: Electronic versions of the legislation can be accessed by downloading PDF files from
    - Labour Standards Act: **www.qp.gov.sk.ca/documents/English/Statutes/Statutes/L1.pdf**
    - Human Rights Code: **http://www.shrc.gov.sk.ca/human_rights_code.html**
12. Government of Nunavut: All statutes are accessible through **http://www.justice.gov.nu.ca/apps/authoring/dspPage.aspx?page=CURRENT%20CONSOLIDATIONS%20OF%20ACTS%20AND%20REGULATIONS&letter=*** with links to each law.

NOTES AND REFERENCES

1. Service Canada, "Employment Insurance Compassionate Care Benefits," accessed October 14, 2011, www.servicecanada.gc.ca/eng/ei/types/compassionate_care.shtml#Definition.
2. Service Canada, "Employment Insurance Maternity and Parental Benefits," accessed October 14, 2011, www.servicecanada.gc.ca/eng/ei/types/maternity_parental.shtml#eligible.
3. "Canadian Human Rights Act Takes Effect in First Nation Communities—AFN Calls on Canada to Work with First Nations," June 16, 2011, www.afn.ca/index.php/en/news-media/latest-news/canadian-human-rights-act-takes-effect-in-first-nation-communities-afn.
4. *Canadian Human Rights Act*, Section 2, Purpose of Act, September 21, 2011, http://laws-lois.justice.gc.ca/eng/acts/h-6/page-1.html#h-2.
5. "Ontario Allows Mandatory Retirement of Firefighters at 60," *Canadian HR Reporter*, May 31, 2011, www.hrreporter.com/articleview?&articleid=10393&headline=ontario-allows-mandatory-retirement-of-firefighters-at-60.
6. Shannon Klie, "Must Accommodate Child Care: Tribunal," *Canadian HR Reporter*, September 6, 2010, accessed October 17, 2011, www.hrreporter.com/articleview?&articleid=8200&headline=must-accommodate-child-care-tribunal.
7. Susan Pigg "Mandatory Retirement Upheld at Air Canada," *The Toronto Star*, July 11, 2011, www.thestar.com/business/companies/article/1023259--mandatory-retirement-upheld-at-air-canada.
8. Tom Gorsky, "Law Firm's Mandatory Retirement Policy Retired," *Canadian HR Reporter*, September 12, 2011, 5.
9. Canadian Human Rights Commission, "Bona Fide Occupational Requirements and Bona Fide Justifications under the *Canadian Human Rights Act*: The Implications of *Meiorin* and *Grismer*," October 5, 2010, accessed October 17, 2011, www.chrc-ccdp.ca/discrimination/occupational-eng.aspx.
10. For students who wish to understand in more detail the *Meiorin* case, access http://www.chrc-ccdp.ca/publications/1999_lr/page1-eng.aspx.

11. Jeffrey R. Smith, "Employer Insensitive to Hypersensitivity," *Canadian HR Reporter*, June 20, 2011, www.hrreporter.com/articleview?&articleid=10582&headline=employer-insensitive-to-hypersensitivity.

12. Jeffrey R. Smith, "Drug-Addicted Nurse Reinstated after Stealing Drugs from Work," *Canadian HR Reporter*, May 9, 2011, www.hrreporter.com/articleview?&articleid=10212&headline=drug-addicted-nurse-reinstated-after-stealing-drugs-from-work-%28legal-view%29; and Fasken Martineau, "Labour, Employment and Human Rights National Update," February 22, 2012.

13. Naome Howe, "Life, Interrupted," *Canadian HR Reporter*, August 9, 2010, accessed October 18, 2011, www.hrreporter.com/articleview?articleid=8098&headline=life-interrupted.

14. Sarah Dobson "Calm amidst the Storm," *Canadian HR Reporter*, July 12, 2010, accessed October 18, 2011, www.hrreporter.com/articleview?&articleid=8033&headline=calm-amidst-the-storm.

15. Definition of Harassment, Canadian Human Rights Commission, accessed October 21, 2011, www.chrc-ccdp.ca/discrimination/what_is_it-en.asp.

16. "Harassment: What Is It and What to Do about It," accessed October 21, 2011, www.chrc-ccdp.ca/publications/what_is_it-eng.aspx.

17. CBC Radio-Canada, "Policy 2.2.15: Anti-discrimination and Harassment," February 1, 2010, accessed October 21, 2011, www.cbc.radio-canada.ca/docs/policies/hr/harassment.shtml.

18. Seneca College Policy, "Discrimination and Harassment," accessed October 21, 2011, www.senecac.ca/policies/dh.html.

19. Ibid.

20. Saskatchewan Human Rights Commission, "A Guide to Human Rights for Employers," 2011.

21. "Manitoba Targets Psychological Harassment in the Workplace," *Canadian Employment Law Today*, November 2, 2010, accessed October 21, 2011, www.employmentlawtoday.com/ArticleView.aspx?l=1&articleid=2345; and Ontario Ministry of Labour, "Preventing Workplace Violence and Workplace Harassment," accessed February 26, 2012, www.labour.gov.on.ca/english/hs/sawo/pubs/fs_workplaceviolence.php.

22. *Taramatie Roopnarine, Complainant-and-Bank of Montreal* (2010), T1405/03109, accessed October 21, 2011, http://chrt-tcdp.gc.ca/aspinc/search/vhtml-eng.asp?doid=1002&lg=_e&isruling=0.

23. *Canadian Human Rights Act*, paras. 53 and 54, accessed October 21, 2011, http://laws-lois.justice.gc.ca/eng/acts/H-6/FullText.html.

24. Shannon Klie, "Poor Economy No Excuse for Discrimination," *Canadian HR Reporter*, May 18, 2009, 1.

25. Jeff Gray, "Overtime Lawsuit against Scotiabank Gets Green Light," *The Globe and Mail*, June 7, 2011, B6.

26. Ontario Ministry of Labour, "Laws," accessed October 21, 2011, www.labour.gov.on.ca/english/lr/laws/index.

27. "Unionization 2010," Statistics Canada, accessed October 21, 2011, www.statcan.gc.ca/pub/75-001-x/2010110/article/11358-eng.htm.

28. For more detailed information on changes to health and safety legislation, refer to the discussion papers from British Columbia ("Protecting Young Workers: Focus Report"), www.worksafebc.ca/publications/reports/focus_reports/Default.asp; and Work Safe Alberta, www.employment.alberta.ca/SFW/274.html, both accessed October 22, 2011.

29. Human Resources and Skills Development Canada, *Employment Equity Act: Annual Report 2009*, accessed October 22, 2011, www.hrsdc.gc.ca/eng/labour/equality/employment_equity/tools/annual.shtml.

30. Statistics Canada, "Labour Force Characteristics by Age and Sex," October 7, 2011, accessed October 22, 2011, www.statcan.gc.ca/daily-quotidien/111007/t111007a1-eng.htm.

31. Statistics Canada, "Employment by Industry and Sex," accessed October 22, 2011, www40.statcan.gc.ca/l01/cst01/labor10a-eng.htm.

32. Ibid.

33. Statistics Canada, "Aboriginal Identity Population by Age Groups," accessed October 22, 2011, www12.statcan.ca/census-recensement/2006/dp-pd/hlt/97-558/pages/page.cfm?Lang=E&Geo=PR&Code=01&Table=1&Data=Count&Sex=1&Age=1&StartRec=1&Sort=2&Display=Page.

34. Diane Galarneau and René Morisette, *Immigrants' Education and Required Job Skills*, Statistics Canada, accessed October 22, 2011, www.statcan.gc.ca/access_acces/alternative_alternatif.action?l=eng&loc=../pdf/10766-eng.pdf; and Statistics Canada, "Study: Job-Related Training of Immigrants," *The Daily*, August 30, 2011, www.statcan.gc.ca/daily-quotidien/110830/dq110830d-eng.htm.

35. Statistics Canada, *Participation and Activity Limitation Survey of 2006: Labour Force Experience of People with Disabilities in Canada*, accessed October 22, 2011, www.statcan.gc.ca/pub/89-628-x/89-628-x2008007-eng.htm.

36. Ibid.

37. Ibid.

38. "Diversity and Employment Equity," Manitoba Civil Service Commission, accessed October 22, 2011, www.gov.mb.ca/csc/employment/emplequity.html.

39. Human Resources and Skills Development Canada, *Employment Equity Act: Annual Report 2009*, (page 17), accessed October 22, 2011, www.hrsdc.gc.ca/eng/labour/equality/employment_equity/tools/annual.shtml.

40. Statistics Canada, "Average Hourly Wages of Employees by Selected Characteristics and Profession," September 2011, www40.statcan.gc.ca/l01/cst01/labr69a-eng.htm.

41. Claudine Kapel, "Improving Perceptions of Pay Fairness," *Canadian HR Reporter*, October 17, 2011, http://www40.statcan.gc.ca/l01/cst01/labr69a-eng.htm.

42. Ontario Pay Equity Commission, "Guideline #12—Permissible Differences in Com, accessed October 22, 2011, www.payequity.gov.on.ca/en/resources/pe_guidelines/ge_12.php.

43. Ontario Pay Equity Commission, "Guideline #9—Gender Neutral Job Comparison," accessed October 22, 2011, www.payequity.gov.on.ca/en/resources/pe_guidelines/ge_9.php.

44. Ibid.

45. Department of Justice, accessed October 22, 2011, www.justice.gc.ca/eng/index.html.

46. Kathryn May, "Female Canada Post Workers Awarded $150 Million after 28-Year Legal Fight," *The Vancouver Sun*, November 18, 2011, C2.

47. Ratna Omidvar, "Moving beyond Diversity to Inclusion, *Canadian HR Reporter,* July 18, 2011, 17.

48. Bill Currie, Larry Scott, and Alain Cote, "The Future of Productivity: An Eight-Step Game Plan for Canada," Deloitte, November 2011.

49. Statistics Canada, "Study: Projected Trends to 2031 for the Canadian Labour Force," *The Daily*, August 17, 2011, accessed February 26, 2012, www.statcan.gc.ca/daily-quotidien/110817/dq110817b-eng.htm.

50. Mario Johne, "The Hunt for Talent at an Emerging Giant," *The Globe and Mail Canada's Top 100 Employers*, October 7, 2011, E6.

51. Statistics Canada, "Selected Trends," accessed October 25, 2011, www12.statcan.gc.ca/census-recensement/2006/dp-pd/92-596/P1-2.cfm?Lang=eng&T=PR&PRCODE=01&GEOCODE=01&GEOLVL=PR&TID=0.

52. Statistics Canada, "Population by Mother Tongue (2006 Census)," accessed October 25, 2011, www40.statcan.gc.ca/l01/cst01/demo11a-eng.htm.

53. "Many Global Businesses Have Non-representative Management Teams," *Canadian HR Reporter*, February 21, 2011, www.hrreporter.com/articleview?&articleid=9572&headline=many-global-businesses-have-non-representative-management-teams.

54. "Diversity Policy Developed for Pan Am Games 2015," *Canadian HR Reporter*, March 7, 2011, accessed October 25, 2011, www.hrreporter.com/articleview?&articleid=9679&headline=diversity-policy-developed-for-pan-am-games-2015.

55. Danielle Harder, "Newcomer Success: Is It Better to Be 'More Canadian'?", *Canadian HR Reporter*, February 28, 2011, www.hrreporter.com/articleview?&articleid=9620&headline=newcomer-success-is-it-better-to-be-more-canadian; and Douglas Todd, "Employers Favour English-Sounding Names," *The Vancouver Sun,* October 14, 2011, A1.

56. "PTI Group Wins 2011 Premier's Award of Distinction," accessed October 25, 2011, www.ptigroup.com/news_item.php?list=26.

57. "Support for Diversity and Inclusion Grows as Canadian Employers Take Action," *The Globe and Mail*, February 21, 2012, B11.

58. Michael Bach, "A Little Recognition Goes a Long Way," *Canadian HR Reporter*, October 24, 2011, www.hrreporter.com/articleview?&articleid=11521&headline=a-little-recognition-goes-a-long-way.

59. Ibid.

60. Gail Johnson, "Wanted: Workers with a Healthy Sense of Adventure," *The Globe and Mail*, October 7, 2011, E8.

61. "Employers Recognized for Exceptional Workplace Diversity," *Canadian HR Reporter*, February 23, 2011, www.hrreporter.com/articleview?&articleid=9574&headline=employers-recognized-for-exceptional-workplace-diversity.

62. "Cameco Chosen as One of Canada's Best Diversity Employers for 2011," accessed October 26, 2011, www.eluta.ca/diversity-at-cameco.

63. Rita Trichur, "Employment Barriers Faced by Immigrants Hamper Productivity," *The Globe and Mail*, November 1, 2011, B7; and Deloitte, "The Future of Productivity."

64. Amanda Silliker, "LGBT Staff Still Face Bias," *Canadian HR Reporter*, December 19, 2011, 1.

65. Amanda Silliker, "Making Manager Accountable for Diversity," *Canadian HR Reporter*, August 15, 2011, www.hrreporter.com/articleview?&articleid=10997&headline=making-managers-accountable-for-diversity.

PART **2**

Attracting and Selecting People for the Organization

Chapter 3: Defining and Designing the Work

Chapter 4: Human Resource Planning, Recruitment, and Selection

CHAPTER 3

DEFINING AND DESIGNING THE WORK

OUTCOMES

After studying this chapter, you should be able to

1 Explain the supervisor's role in defining and designing work.

2 Discuss the relationship between job requirements and HRM processes.

3 Explain the relationship between job analysis and a job description.

4 Define and describe the sections in a job description.

5 Describe the uses of information gained from job analysis.

6 Define employee contribution and describe the relationship of job design to employee behaviours and contributions.

7 Discuss the different types of work designs to increase employee contribution.

OUTLINE

HRM CLOSE-UP

"If you don't know what your strengths and weaknesses are, how do you formulate a plan?"

"I was wearing a lot of hats and realized I had to start putting those hats on other people's heads!" says Dawn Mucci, founder and president of The Lice Squad. A rather odd comment from someone who spends her day advising kids not to share hats, hair accessories, or other headgear in order to prevent the spread of *Pediculus humanus capitis*—human head lice.

Realizing the need to help frantic families deal with this common pest, Mucci set up shop in 2001 with a desk, phone, and computer. She fielded calls, provided in-home head lice removal service, and screened schoolchildren. It wasn't long before she needed a team of on-call contractors to handle client service. Four years later, the first full-time hire was an office manager.

"What I needed was a carbon copy of me," Mucci comments. "I had a long list of duties but needed to allocate more of my time on training, selling franchises, and developing the company."

When the demand grew for her proprietary non-pesticide head-lice product and high-quality nit comb, Mucci's next hire was a product distribution manager. Following that was a bookkeeper—a position she describes as the most important mainly because accounting was not one of her core strengths.

Mucci knows her company will continue to grow but rather than ramp up staff and wait for the business, she waits for business volume to warrant new positions. She also tends to hire part time at the outset. This strategy has worked well for her and makes good business sense. "I can't spend money on salaries until there's a job that is going to bring in revenue, increase sales, or create goodwill for the company," she explains.

Dawn Mucci, founder and president of The Lice Squad, Ontario, and her team.

Contracted positions also help to fill in the gaps. Jobs such as Web development, information technology, and graphics design have definite ebbs and flows so shorter-term contracts work best for Mucci.

The Lice Squad's office employees have written job descriptions so that they understand what has to be accomplished each workday. Mucci admits to being an easygoing boss and appreciates employees setting their own goals. "I make sure we all share the overall goal of the company," Mucci explains, "but I like my staff to seek out opportunities themselves and show initiative. I also expect learning curves as well as the odd ruffle!"

Running a relatively small operation that is growing and developing requires flexibility and compromise. Jobs at The Lice Squad can change depending on the person in the job. Mucci appreciates feedback and input. "Since I am now less focused on the day-to-day details, my office manager is often the one to suggest things that could be done better."

And for Mucci, hiring the right person is critical. "Everyone has skills—tasks they are good at doing. But if they are not passionate about the work at hand, it doesn't matter what skill level they bring to the job."

And with a business that revolves around head lice, making sure that the hat fits is an ongoing challenge. Mucci is on a mission to rid the world of head lice—and that's a job description you won't find anywhere else.

INTRODUCTION

Just as The Lice Squad has evolved and Mucci had to determine who was going to do what, other organizations are looking at how work is arranged to make them more competitive.

Organizations are transforming themselves in an attempt to become more effective. Companies such as Karo, a Calgary-based branding agency, are paying attention to the structure and culture of their organizations. Karo practises what it preaches by creating teams—smaller and more interconnected groups within its organization—to deliver results to its clients.[1] There is an emphasis on smaller scale, less hierarchy, fewer layers, and more decentralized work units.

As organizations reshape themselves, managers want employees to operate more independently and flexibly to meet customer demands. To do this, managers require that decisions be made by the people who are closest to the information and who are directly involved in the product or service delivered. The objective is to develop jobs and basic work units that are adaptable enough to thrive in a world of high-speed change.

This chapter will discuss how jobs can be designed to best contribute to the objectives of the organization and at the same time satisfy the needs of the employees who perform them. You will learn about the role of the line manager in defining and designing work, and the terminology used to describe how jobs are defined. Several innovative job design and employee contribution techniques that increase job satisfaction while improving organizational performance are discussed. Teamwork and the characteristics of successful teams are highlighted. The chapter concludes by briefly discussing the future design of organizational work.

THE LINE MANAGER'S ROLE IN DEFINING WORK

Outcome 1

What is the supervisor's role in defining and designing work?

The line manager or supervisor is the primary individual who determines what tasks and activities need to be performed, and in what order, to reach the company's goals or objectives. Therefore, it is critical that the line manager understands what steps need to be implemented to maximize organizational performance. The line manager will take an active role in determining what skills and abilities are needed to successfully perform the work. The line manager is the most knowledgeable person about the work to be done and the skills necessary to do the work. Therefore, the line manager will play an integral role in developing and/or writing a job description.

RELATIONSHIP OF JOB REQUIREMENTS AND HRM PROCESSES

Outcome 2

What is the relationship between job requirements and HRM processes?

Job
A group of related activities and duties

Position
Specific duties and responsibilities performed by only one employee

Work
Tasks or activities that need to be completed

A number of HRM processes, such as recruitment and training, make use of information about the work or job. A **job** consists of a group of related activities and duties. Ideally, the duties of a job should consist of natural units of work that are similar and related. They should be clear and distinct from those of other jobs to minimize misunderstanding and conflict among employees and to enable employees to recognize what is expected of them. For some jobs, several employees may be required, each of whom will occupy a separate position. A **position** consists of the specific duties and responsibilities performed by only one employee. In a city library, for example, four employees (four positions) may be involved in reference work, but all of them have only one job (reference librarian).

In many ways, the words "job" and "position" are relics of the industrial age. As organizations need to be more flexible and adaptable, and utilize their people resources well for a competitive advantage, managers also need to think in terms of "work." By thinking of "**work**," employers have more flexibility to define what needs to be done and when, and to change employee assignments on a short-term basis.

You will recall from Chapter 1 that you were introduced to the concept of "competencies"—characteristics or behaviours necessary for successful work performance in an organization. Competencies become very important when focusing on "work" compared to job. Instead of organizations focusing on job descriptions, companies will use "work profiles" or "contract work" to describe the work to be done. Further, the concept of "roles" is also linked to competencies. Your "role" is the part you play in the organization, and it will have certain expected behaviours. For example, your role as a customer service representative includes active listening as an expected behaviour. You will continue to see more references to work and work processes, project management, tasks, and task analysis than to "job."

Whether thinking in terms of "job" or "work," a manager needs to describe what tasks need to be done, in what order, the skills a person needs to successfully perform the work requirements, and the role a person plays in the company. This is the essence of organizational success. For all HR processes, you will need to have this type of information.

Job Analysis

Outcome 3

What is the relationship between job analysis and a job description?

Job analysis
Process of obtaining information about jobs by determining the duties, tasks, or activities, and the skills, knowledge, and abilities associated with the jobs

Job analysis is sometimes called the cornerstone of HRM because the information it collects serves so many HRM processes. **Job analysis** is the process of obtaining information about jobs (or work) by determining what the duties, tasks, or activities of those jobs are and the necessary skills, knowledge, training, and abilities to perform the work successfully. The procedure involves undertaking a systematic approach to gathering specific job information, including the work activities, worker attributes, and work context.[2] The ultimate purpose of job analysis is to improve organizational performance and productivity. Figure 3.1 illustrates how job analysis is done and what the information is used for.

Job analysis is concerned with objective and verifiable information about the requirements of a job (compared to "job design," which reflects subjective opinions about the ideal requirements of the job). The outcome of a job analysis is a written job description. It should be as accurate as possible if it is to be of value to those who make HRM decisions. These decisions may involve any of the HR processes—from recruitment to termination of employees. Job analysis is not done in a vacuum: it is important that the organization's goals and strategies be known and understood. Without the organizational context or an understanding of the organization as a whole, the requirements identified may not reflect foreseeable future requirements. A proactive strategic approach would link the jobs to the organization's performance.[3]

Trained HR people typically undertake job analysis; however, a line manager who has good analytical abilities and writing skills can also do it. The HR professional can provide assistance to the manager in gathering the relevant information by ensuring that appropriate questions are asked and that the job is not inflated. It is also valuable to have the person doing the work (and the supervisor or team leader) review the data gathered to ensure that it is accurate and complete.

Job data can be collected in a range of ways: through interviews (asking questions, such as "What duties do you perform every day?" or "What tools do you use to complete these duties?"), questionnaires (forms that ask you to write down tasks performed, purpose of job, equipment, and materials used, and so on), observation of someone doing the work, an employee log (a diary of work activities during a time), or any combination of these methods. Review Manager's Toolkit 3.1 for some sample questions that could be posed either in an interview or on a questionnaire.

Frequently, in larger organizations a uniform approach is used to collect the data, such as asking people to fill out a questionnaire that requests only a list of work activities. Ethics in HRM 3.1 describes what can happen if a job is inflated.

For links to a variety of resources on job profiles, writing job descriptions, and conducting a job analysis, go to **www.job-analysis.net** and **http://alis.alberta.ca**.

Job-Analysis.Net work
www.job-analysis.net

Alberta Career Profiles
http://alis.alberta.ca

FIGURE 3.1   The Process of Job Analysis

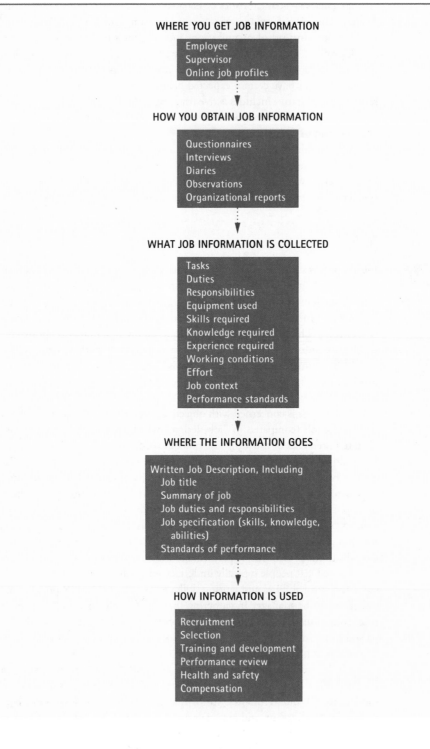

Job Descriptions

Outcome 4

What are the sections in a job description?

Once all the information on a particular job has been collected, it is organized into a **job description**—a written document. This description includes the types of duties or responsibilities, and the skills, knowledge, and abilities, or competencies (job specifications) needed to successfully perform the work. Since no standard format applies to job

MANAGER'S TOOLKIT 3.1

JOB ANALYSIS QUESTIONS

Here are some sample questions when conducting a job analysis.

1. In a brief statement (three to four sentences), describe the basic purpose of your position. Do it in a way that answers "Why does my position exist?"

2. What are the most important responsibilities of your position, and how much time do you spend on each of these? Please list each main responsibility in order of importance. Start each statement with an action verb; some examples are "provides," "determines," "verifies."

3. What are the key tasks for each of the responsibilities? What percentage of your time each month do you spend on each task?

4. What are the physical surroundings and/or hazards of your position? (This can include travel, exposure, danger, and environmental risks.)

5. Describe the mental and physical effort you expend in performing your work. For example, do you have long periods of intense concentration? Is there a lot of routine? Is the position physically demanding? Please include the frequency of the effort.

6. What are the knowledge and basic skills required to successfully fulfill the responsibilities?

7. Describe two or three of the more difficult problems you must solve to your job done. Include situations that are a constant challenge as well as situations that require judgment and time to consider alternative solutions before problems can be resolved.

Job description
A document that lists the tasks, duties, and responsibilities of a job to be performed along with the skills, knowledge, and abilities, or competencies needed to successfully perform the work

descriptions, they tend to vary in appearance and content from one organization to another. However, the typical headings are the following:

1. Job title
   Provides an indication of what the duties might be or the nature of the work. For example, the title might be "night supervisor," "salesperson," "lab assistant," or "team leader."
2. Summary of job
   Two to three sentences describing the overall purpose of the job; it answers the question "Why does this job exist?"
3. Duties and responsibilities
   Individual statements, usually listed in order of importance, of the key duties and responsibilities; you would expect to see between 10 and 15 statements.
4. Job specification
   Two to three sentences describing the knowledge, skills, and abilities.
5. Performance standards
   A prioritized list outlining several expected results of the job.
6. Date
   A time reference, which allows the organization to think about the currency of the information when it is used for a variety of HR processes.

Job specifications
Statement of the needed knowledge, skills, and abilities of the person who is to perform the position; the different duties and responsibilities performed by only one employee

The specific skills, knowledge, and abilities that are required to successfully perform the job become the **job specifications**. Skills relevant to a job can include education and experience, specialized training, and specific abilities, such as manual dexterity. If there were any physical demands to the job, such as walking long distances or reaching high shelves, these would also be part of the job specifications. Many organizations now view job specifications as including "employability" skills and knowledge, such as problem-solving abilities. For a more complete list of employability skills, see Figure 5.2 in Chapter 5.

ETHICS **in HRM 3.1**

INFLATING THE JOB

At some point in your working life, you will be asked to describe your job, perhaps when being interviewed by a job analyst or by answering questions on a form. Most employees have a reasonable expectation that their answers will affect their lives in significant ways. The information obtained may be used to reclassify the job to either a higher or lower pay level. Most employees believe that standards of performance may change, and the employer will expect them to work faster or to do more, although that is not the goal of job analysis. As a result of these beliefs and expectations, employees have a vested interest in "inflating" their job

descriptions, by making the job sound very important and very difficult. Thus, night clerks in hotels become auditors, and receptionists become administrators. Making a job sound more important than it is may reflect an employee's sincere belief in the significance of his or her contribution, or it may be an attempt to lobby for higher pay.

QUESTION:

As a manager, how can you ensure that job information is correct if the employee and you view the job differently?

Manager's Toolkit 3.2 provides an example of a job description for the manager of retail operations at a sports arena. Note that this particular job description includes specific HR responsibilities, as noted in the first section under "People Management." This sample job description includes both job duties and job specifications and should satisfy most of the job information needs of managers who must recruit, interview, and orient a new employee.

Job descriptions are of value to both the employees and the employer. From the employees' standpoint, job descriptions that include standards of performance can be used to help them learn their job duties and to remind them of the results they are expected to achieve.

Problems with Job Descriptions

While many managers consider job descriptions a valuable tool for performing HRM activities, several problems are frequently associated with these documents, including the following:

1. If they are poorly written, using vague rather than specific terms, they provide little guidance to the jobholder (e.g., "other duties as assigned").
2. They are sometimes not updated as job duties or specifications change.
3. They may violate the law by containing specifications not related to job success (e.g., "must be single between the ages of 25 and 35").
4. They can limit the scope of activities of the jobholder.
5. They do not contain standards of performance, which are essential for selecting, training, evaluating, and rewarding jobholders.
6. They can be the basis for conflict, including union grievances, when expected behaviours are not included.

Writing Clear and Specific Job Descriptions

When writing a job description, it is essential to use statements that are concise, direct, and simply worded. Unnecessary words or phrases should be eliminated. Typically, the sentences that describe job duties begin with a present-tense and

SAMPLE JOB DESCRIPTION

Position: Manager, Retail Operations
Reports to: Director, Retail Operations
Date: February 2013

SUMMARY

The manager, retail operations, is responsible for all aspects of retail operations for game nights and events. The manager ensures the store, booths, and kiosks are staffed with well-trained sales and service professionals and are visually attractive with appropriate merchandise for the customer environment. While staff development, sales, and service are primary focus areas, administrative activities such as payroll and scheduling are also part of this role.

ESSENTIAL DUTIES AND RESPONSIBILITIES

People Management

1. Recruit, train, motivate, and develop a professional and knowledgeable part-time and on-call service and sales workforce.

2. Coach and communicate with employees in a fair and consistent manner (e.g., mentoring sessions, performance evaluations).

3. Work closely with senior retail management and human resources regarding disciplinary and other sensitive employee issues.

4. Identify and implement employee recognition and incentive programs.

5. Ensure staff are trained in all key areas of the business.

Business Management

1. Ensure selling areas are open for business on time and are clean and visually attractive.

2. Identify opportunities for increasing revenue.

3. Create sales and promotional programs.

4. Work with marketing staff regarding event details, such as expected attendance levels, merchandise deals, internal and external event contacts.

5. Produce sales reports.

Administration

1. Schedule staff in a fair and consistent manner.

2. Input payroll information into payroll time-management system.

3. Monitor payroll against budget and sales.

4. Develop and maintain an employee manual.

REQUIRED EXPERIENCE AND QUALIFICATIONS (JOB SPECIFICATIONS)

1. Four to six years retail experience, with at least two years' supervisory experience.

2. Degree or diploma in business administration or related field.

3. Excellent leadership skills with the ability to coach, mentor, and motivate a sales service team.

4. Excellent communication, interpersonal, and problem-solving skills.

5. A solid understanding of the business and customer environment.

6. Must be able to identify and implement new business opportunities and promotions.

7. Flexible and adaptable.

8. Computer literate with a working knowledge of MS Word, MS Excel, point-of-sale software, and electronic mail systems.

9. Must be able to work evenings and weekends.

STANDARDS OF PERFORMANCE

1. Meets on a weekly basis with all staff to review sales results.

2. Orients new staff during the first shift on customer-service requirements.

3. Meets or exceeds monthly sales targets.

4. Submits sales within 24 hours of each event.

5. Trains staff on any new procedures within one week.

6. Keeps customer satisfaction levels at 80% or above.

action-oriented verb, with the implied subject of the sentence being the employee performing the job. An example for an accounting clerk for a small company might read: "Deposits cheques on a daily basis" or "Prepares month-end financial statements by the 10th of the following month." (Note that these two statements include performance standards.) The term "occasionally" is used to describe those duties that are performed once in a while. The term "may" is used in connection with those duties that are performed only by some workers on the job. Other examples of action-oriented, present-tense verbs include "coordinates," "handles," "researches," "conducts," "generates," and "evaluates." You can obtain a list of verbs used in job descriptions at **www.job-analysis.net**.

Even when set forth in writing, job descriptions and specifications can still be vague. To the alarm of many employers, however, today's legal environment has created what might be called an "age of specifics." Human rights legislation requires that the specific performance requirements of a job be based on valid job-related criteria. Decisions that involve either job applicants or employees and that are based on criteria either vague or not job related are increasingly being challenged successfully. Managers of small businesses, where employees may perform many different job tasks, must be particularly concerned about writing specific job descriptions. Or in a very small business, such as Aquinox Pharmaceuticals in British Columbia, the focus is not so much on writing a job description but identifying the core activities and then describing the attributes needed to be successful.[4]

When preparing job descriptions, managers must be aware of human rights legislation. Written job descriptions must match the requirements of the job. Position descriptions may need to be altered to meet reasonable accommodation. Reasonable accommodation is used most frequently to match religious or disability needs, although any prohibited ground for discrimination under human rights legislation would have to be considered for reasonable accommodation. The 2010 case *Fiona Johnstone and Canada Border Services* made it clear that reasonable accommodation for family status reasons is valid.[5] Job descriptions written to match the needs for reasonable accommodation reduce the risk of discrimination. The goal is to match and accommodate human capabilities to job requirements. For example, if the job requires the jobholder to read extremely fine print, to climb ladders, or to memorize stock codes, these physical and mental requirements should be stated within the job description.

Human rights legislation requires that specific job requirements be based on valid job-related criteria. For example, pilots must have a certain level of eyesight.

Standards of Performance

Standards of performance
Set out the expected results of the job

This section is the least likely to be included in a job description; however, it often provides the most valuable data for both the manager and employee. **Standards of performance** set out the expected results of the job—what you are expected to accomplish, as well as how much and how fast. Look again at the sample job description above—it has several performance standards. From the employer's standpoint, written job descriptions can serve as a basis for minimizing the misunderstandings that occur between managers and their subordinates concerning job requirements. They also establish management's right to take corrective action when the duties covered by the job description are not fulfilled as required by performance standards.

JOB ANALYSIS IN A CHANGING ENVIRONMENT

The traditional approach to job analysis assumes a static job environment and large organizations in which jobs remain relatively stable even though incumbents who might hold these jobs perform them differently. Here, jobs can be meaningfully defined in terms of tasks, duties, processes, and behaviours necessary for job success. This assumption, unfortunately, discounts technological advances that are often so accelerated that jobs, as they are defined today, may be obsolete tomorrow. Furthermore, downsizing, the adoption of teams, the demands of small organizations, or the need to respond to global change can alter the nature of jobs and the requirements of individuals needed to successfully perform them. For organizations using "virtual" jobs or "virtual" teams, there is a shift away from independently performed jobs with narrow job specifications and descriptions to a focus on the relationships among workers and their work environments.[6] In a dynamic environment where job demands rapidly change, job analysis data can quickly become inaccurate, and outdated job analysis information can hinder an organization's ability to adapt to change. Likewise, large organizations can find that the job information is outdated if it is not regularly reviewed and adjusted as needs change.

For organizations that operate in a fast-moving environment, several novel approaches to job analysis may accommodate needed change.

First, managers might adopt a future-oriented or strategic-oriented[7] approach to job analysis where managers have a clear view of how jobs should be restructured to meet future organizational requirements.

Second, organizations might adopt a competency-based approach to job analysis in which emphasis is placed on characteristics or behaviours of successful performers rather than on standard job duties and tasks and so on. As was described in Chapter 1, these competencies would be customized to the organization's culture and strategy, and include the tailoring of broad competencies such as communication skills, decision-making ability, project management, conflict resolution skills, adaptability, and self-motivation. Competencies are developed using a top-down rather than a bottom-up approach, with the goal of integrating organizational and human resources management objectives, strategies, and systems.[8] Neither of these two approaches are without concerns, including the ability of managers to predict future job needs accurately, and the need for job analysis to comply with human rights legislation.

A third and perhaps more practical method might be to have a "living job description," a description that is updated as the job changes. The line manager and employee would then ensure that substantial changes in duties, responsibilities, skills, and other work characteristics are documented on an ongoing basis. A type of "living job description" is a behavioural job description: one that describes how the work is to be done and what results are expected. Often, these descriptions also describe typical issues and problems that may occur and the results that can be expected in dealing with the issues. By doing this, the manager and employee can also establish standards of performance. These descriptive and evaluative job descriptions can be linked to the organization's online performance management system, allowing for continuous updating by all users.

Determining the work to be done involves an approach that links the organization's future goals with work information gathered from the people who actually do the work.

Jon Riley/Getty Images

In order to have the "right people with the right skills at the right time," contemporary managers must take the time to think about the work and the skills required to do the work. Organizational success depends on capable people. Managers want to be sure that they have the correct number of employees and the correct skills mix. Clearly identifying the work duties and the skills needed to perform the work can help managers achieve that objective. It is important to remember that the purpose of identifying who does what is to bring all the talent together, mobilizing that talent for organizational success.[9]

USES OF INFORMATION FROM JOB ANALYSIS

Outcome 5

What are the uses of information gained from job analysis?

As stated earlier in the chapter, a variety of HRM processes make use of the output of job analysis: recruitment, selection, legal issues, training and development, performance reviews, health and safety, and compensation. These are discussed below.

Recruitment

Recruitment is the process of locating and encouraging potential applicants to apply for job openings. Because job specifications establish the qualifications required of applicants for a job opening, they serve an essential role in the recruiting function as they define "who" will be successful doing the job and provide a basis for attracting qualified applicants.

Selection

After you have located individuals who are interested in working for you, you must now hire someone. Selection is the process of choosing the individual who has the relevant qualifications and who can best perform the job. Therefore, a manager will use the information on the job description as a basis to compare the skills and abilities of each applicant.

Legal Issues

In the past, job specifications used as a basis for selection sometimes bore little relation to the duties identified in the job description. Many examples can be cited of job requirements that do not match the actual duties of a job: the requirement that applicants for a labourer's job have a high-school diploma; the requirement that firefighters be at least six feet tall; the requirement that applicants for the job of truck driver be male. These kinds of job specifications discriminate against members of certain designated groups, many of whom have been excluded from these jobs.

Given changes to our society and the various employment laws, employers must be able to show that the job specifications used in selecting employees for a particular job relate specifically to the duties of that job. Because line managers usually help define the job specifications, they must ensure that the job requirements recruit the best candidate and do not discriminate. Managers must be careful to ensure that they do not hire employees on the basis of "individualized" job requirements that satisfy personal whims but bear little relation to successful job performance. Read HRM and the Law 3.1 to understand more about the legal implications of inappropriate job requirements.

Training and Development

Any discrepancies between the knowledge, skills, and abilities (referred to as KSAs) demonstrated by a jobholder and the requirements contained in the description and specification for that job provide clues to training needs. Also, if the job specification section contains competencies (such as "focuses on customer" or "demonstrates excellent customer service skills"), these competencies could provide the basis for training. As line managers are often responsible for training the new employee, accurate job specifications and descriptions are essential. Also, as career development is often a concern for both the manager and the employee, the formal qualification requirements set forth in higher-level jobs serve to indicate how much more training and development are needed for employees to advance to those jobs.

HRM and the Law 3.1

JOB DESCRIPTION TENSIONS

Tensions may arise in the workplace out of family-related or disability-related limitations on an employee's availability and ability for work.

In 2011, a female banquet manager, a single parent with a young child, was terminated. The job entailed being available for functions and events, which would sometimes require long and irregular hours. The manager understood these requirements when she accepted the job. The employer had concerns about her performance after she left early from an event due to childcare obligations. The employer expressed further concerns about her changing childcare situation. The banquet manager claimed that her employer refused to continue to employ her because of assumptions made about her ability to work; the employer claimed that her employment was terminated due to her poor performance. The question before the human rights tribunal was whether the employer could show that long and irregular hours were a bona fide occupational job requirement. The tribunal found that family status was a factor in the dismissal and concluded that there was no evidence that the employee would be unable to meet the long and irregular hours required. The employee was awarded $12,000.

Another 2011 case involved the termination of a senior poultry plant employee who was returning to work after a shoulder injury from a motor vehicle accident. The employee had provided manual labour at the poultry processing plant for 15 years. He informed his employer that he would be able to work only three days a week with no heavy lifting. After 10 months he was laid off. The employee claimed that he had been discriminated against because of his disability, and the employer claimed that the employee couldn't establish a steady work schedule. The question before the human rights tribunal was whether there had been an explanation for the employee's layoff. The tribunal said that the plant didn't meet its duty to accommodate and awarded the employee $7,500.

CRITICAL THINKING QUESTION:

Do you think these decisions were appropriate? Provide and explain reasons for your answer.

Sources: *Cavanaugh v. Sea to Sky Hotel & Mohajer (No. 2)*, 2010 B.C.H.R.T. 209 (CanLII) Aug. 16, 2010; and *Sarain v. Wingtat Game Bird Packers Inc.*, [2011] B.C.H.R.T.D. No. 84, April 6, 2011.

Job analysis can be used to determine the type and level of training required to perform the job.

Photodisc Collections/Getty Images

Performance Reviews

The job requirements contained in the job analysis provide the criteria for evaluating the performance of the jobholder. These individual performance standards are linked to the business performance goals and strategies incorporated in the performance management systems, as discussed in Chapter 6. Evaluating an employee's performance is a major responsibility of the line manager. As the workplace evolves due to rapid advances in digital communication technology and workers work in more distributed ways, performance reviews become an increasingly important method for managers to monitor and evaluate worker activities and performance. The results of the performance evaluation may reveal whether certain requirements established for a job continue to be valid. For example, a job description may require an employee to word-process at the rate of 30 words per minute (wpm), but the performance review may determine that 60 wpm is necessary. If the criteria used to evaluate employee performance are vague and not job related, employers may find themselves being charged with unfair discrimination.

Health and Safety

The job analysis identifies the health and safety–related physical and mental capabilities required to perform the job, and the work environment conditions in which the job is performed. It describes the existing and potential safety and health hazards associated with workplace injuries or illnesses, which are particularly important in redesigning jobs to improve employee wellness and eliminate or reduce exposure to hazards. Creating a healthy organizational culture is discussed in Chapter 8.

As mentioned in Chapter 2, the 2011 Air Canada pilots case of discrimination due to the mandatory retirement age of 60 was dismissed. The Canadian Human Rights Tribunal determined that extra staffing, scheduling, and health and safety requirements would constitute an undue hardship for the airline and that mandatory retirement of pilots at age 60 is a BFOR.[10]

Compensation

Job descriptions are often used solely for compensation purposes. In determining the rate at which a job is paid, the relative worth of the job is one of the most important factors.

This worth (*pay rate*) is based on what the job demands of an employee in skill, effort, and responsibility, as well as on the conditions and hazards under which the work is performed. Systems that measure the worth of jobs are called *job evaluation systems* (see Chapter 7). Job descriptions and job specifications are used as sources of information in evaluating jobs. Often, the HR department designs these job evaluation systems. Ultimately, however, it is the line manager who makes pay decisions based on performance relative to the standards of performance that have been established.

DESIGNING THE JOB

Outcome 6

What is the relationship of job design to employee behaviours and contributions?

Job design
Process of defining and organizing tasks, roles, and other processes to achieve employee goals and organizational effectiveness

An outgrowth of job analysis, **job design** is the process of defining and arranging tasks, roles, and other processes to achieve employee goals and organizational effectiveness. For example, organizations engaged in self-management teams, continuous improvement, or process re-engineering may revamp their jobs in order to eliminate unnecessary job tasks or find better ways of performing work. Job design should facilitate the achievement of organizational objectives and at the same time recognize the capabilities and needs of those who are to perform the job. Job design is concerned with appropriately altering and modifying the job so that there is a good person–job fit and person–organization fit. Improving the quality of work life facilitates positive worker attitudes and behaviours, leading to organizational effectiveness. Historically, the focus has been on analyzing and defining specific jobs within physical "brick and mortar" structures. Today, with the rapid advances of communication technology, the meaning of the word "job" is in flux with workers working in more distributed, unconstrained work environments.[11] These fundamental changes in the relationships between workers, the type of work they do, how they perform their work, when the work is scheduled, and the organizational environment are increasing the use of non-standard employment forms and non-traditional strategies for job design. Job design strategies can include the following:

- job rotation (in which people move from one job to another to learn new tasks)
- job enlargement (in which a person's job expands in the types of tasks he or she is expected to perform)
- leadership teams (in which a leader takes on multiple responsibilities and activities rather than one well-defined functional leadership role)
- job enrichment (in which a person's job takes on higher-order responsibilities)
- job crafting (in which a person initiates, shapes, and customizes his or her work)[12]

Non-traditional employment forms are discussed later in this chapter. As Figure 3.2 illustrates, job design is a combination of four basic considerations: (1) the organizational objectives the job was created to fulfill; (2) industrial engineering considerations, including ways to make the job technologically efficient; (3) ergonomic concerns, including workers' physical and mental capabilities; and (4) employee attitudes and behaviours that influence their contributions. Employee contributions are reflected in the participation of employees in making job improvements or enhancing operational decisions.

Job Design and Job Characteristics

Job characteristics model
An approach to job design that recognizes the link between motivational factors and components of the job to achieve improved work performance and job satisfaction

Job design studies explored a new field when behavioural scientists focused on various job dimensions that would improve simultaneously the efficiency of organizations and the job satisfaction of employees. The **job characteristics model** proposes that three psychological states of a jobholder result in improved work performance, internal motivation, and lower absenteeism and turnover. The motivated, satisfied, and productive employee is one who (1) experiences meaningfulness of the work performed, (2) experiences responsibility for work outcomes, and (3) has knowledge of the results of the work performed. When these three psychological states are achieved, the employee is more strongly motivated to continue doing the job well.

FIGURE 3.2 Basis for Job Design

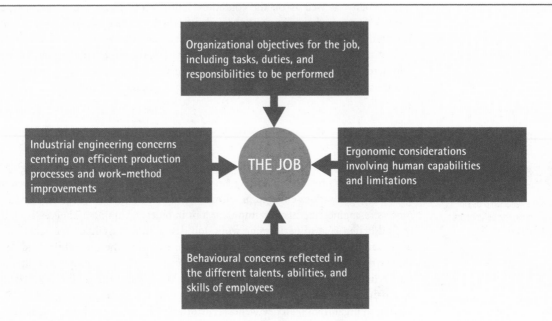

There are five job characteristics in this model:

1. *Skill variety.* The degree to which a job entails a variety of different activities, which demand the use of a number of different skills and talents by the jobholder.
2. *Task identity.* The degree to which the job requires completion of a whole and identifiable piece of work—that is, doing a job from beginning to end with a visible outcome.
3. *Task significance.* The degree to which the job has a substantial impact on the lives or work of other people, whether in the immediate organization or in the external environment.
4. *Autonomy.* The degree to which the job provides substantial freedom, independence, and discretion to the individual in scheduling the work and in determining the procedures to be used in carrying it out.
5. *Feedback.* The degree to which carrying out the work activities required by the job results in the individual being given direct and clear information about the effectiveness of his or her performance.

The job characteristics model seems to work best when certain conditions are met. One of these conditions is that employees must have the psychological desire for the autonomy, variety, responsibility, and challenge of enriched jobs. When this personal characteristic is absent, employees may resist the job redesign effort. Job redesign efforts almost always fail when employees lack the physical or mental skills, abilities, or education needed to perform the job. Forcing enriched jobs on individuals who lack these traits can result in frustrated employees. The advances in information technology resulting in increased flexible work arrangements have expanded the scope of these characteristics to employees doing front-line work.[13]

Designing Work for Group Contributions

Although a variety of group techniques have been developed to involve employees more fully in their organizations, all these techniques have two characteristics in common—enhancing collaboration and increasing synergy. By increasing the degree of collaboration in the work environment, these techniques can improve work processes and organizational decision making. By increasing group synergy, they underline the adage that the contributions of two or more employees are greater than the sum of their individual efforts. Research has shown that working in a group setting strengthens employee commitment to an organization's goals, increases employee acceptance of decisions, and encourages a co-operative approach to workplace tasks. Two collaborative techniques are discussed below: employee empowerment and employee teams.

Role of Management

Leadership issues arise at several levels when employees are involved in decision making. At both the executive and management levels, there needs to be clear support for employee involvement and teams as there may be changes required in processes and actions to support this new way of doing business. For many years, managers and supervisors have played the role of decision maker. Thus, organizations will need to redefine the role of supervisor when employees are participating more in the operations of the company. For example, Mike Moore Construction works closely with its owners, subtrades, and partners to ensure that everyone from management to labourer is involved in workplace decisions and practices.[14] Decisions within the company are based on a process of inclusion.

Therefore, when designing work for either individual or group contributions, it is critical that the organization be clear on what is expected of managers and supervisors and the skills necessary to be successful. Further, the organization needs to carefully consider its overall design and structure. Research has demonstrated that the organizational structure and context (size, centralization, and hierarchical levels) are key determinants of behaviours in the organization.[15] If the organization wants a more committed and engaged workforce, then the way in which it is structured—who reports to whom and who makes decisions—will greatly influence the effectiveness of the leaders.

Organizations have found that the success of employee involvement depends on first changing the roles of managers and team leaders. With fewer layers of management and a focus on team-based organizations, the role of managers and supervisors is substantially different. Managers are expected to be open to suggestions, actively support two-way communication, and encourage risk taking. Rather than autocratically imposing their

Employee empowerment: Leveraging the full capabilities of all employees. This group is working on a way to improve their product delivery system.

Photodisc/Getty Images

demands on employees and closely watching to make sure that the workers comply, managers share responsibility for decision making with employees. Typically, "team leader" has replaced the term "manager."

In a growing number of cases, leadership is shared among team members. Some organizations rotate team leaders at various stages in team development. Alternatively, different individuals can assume functional leadership roles when their particular expertise is needed most.

A clear example of the role senior managers play in creating an involved organization is described in At Work with HRM 3.1.

Employee Empowerment

Outcome 7

What are the different types of work designs to increase employee contribution?

Employee empowerment
Granting employees power to initiate change, thereby encouraging them to take charge of what they do

Employee empowerment is a technique for involving employees in their work through a process of inclusion. Empowerment encourages employees to become innovators and managers of their own work, and involves them in their jobs in ways that give them more control. Empowerment has been defined as pushing down decision-making responsibility to those close to internal and external customers. Job crafting is another strategy where workers do not wait for management initiatives but customize, modify, and craft their own work to meet both their needs and the organization's goals.[16] Empowerment and job crafting strategies are more fluid in nature, a departure from other job design methods that are generally top-down and fixed in nature. Interviews with employees in both a small service organization and a large manufacturing organization found that senior employees felt more constrained than front-line employees to craft their jobs even though they had greater autonomy and power.[17]

AT WORK **with HRM 3.1**

BEST EMPLOYER

Would you like to work for Canada's #1 company? "Yes" is the answer most of us would give. EllisDon, an Ontario-based construction company, earned this distinction as the first-place employer in 50 Best Employers in Canada—2012 and as one of Canada's Top 100 Employers—2012. The company has placed high in studies done by Aon Hewitt for 10 years.

But what led to this honour?

EllisDon has a practice of encouraging employees to tackle projects with autonomy. Brian Waltham, vice-president for Southwestern Ontario, states: "When you come to work here, you are given authority to do things the way you want right off the bat. At some other businesses, you do not control your own destiny. Managers actively work to ensure that staff have the resources to do their jobs as expected and challenge employees to grow in their jobs. In addition,

the company hires people who excel in this type of work environment."

Other workplace elements that put certain employers ahead of others include aligning employees' values with organizational values, fostering an environment of integrity and respect, and displaying ethical conduct. Hard work and thinking out of the box are required to achieve these.

Check out Aon Hewitt's Best Employers Studies Canada for current information on the top employers in Canada: **https://ceplb03.hewitt.com/bestemployers/canada/pages/index.htm.**

CRITICAL THINKING QUESTION:

What would your current or past company need to do to go out of its way to meet the needs of the employees?

Sources: Adapted from "50 Best Employers in Canada Offer Flexibility, Demonstrate Integrity, According to Hewitt Associates," CNW TEBEC, January 3, 2008, http://www.newswire.ca/fr/story/293217/50-best-employers-in-canada-offer-flexibility-demonstrate-integrity-according-to-hewitt-associates; "EllisDon Celebrates Ten Years as One of Canada's Top Employers," accessed March 15, 2012, www.ellisdon.com/news/?i=587; Aon Hewitt, "2012 List of the Best Employers in Canada," accessed March 15, 2012, https://ceplb03.hewitt.com/bestemployers/canada/pages/currentlist2012.htm.

While defining empowerment can become the first step to achieving it, in order for empowerment to grow and thrive, organizations must encourage these conditions:

- *Participation.* Employees must be encouraged to take control of their work tasks. Employees, in turn, must care about improving their work process and interpersonal work relationships.
- *Innovation.* The environment must be receptive to people with innovative ideas and must encourage people to explore new paths and to take reasonable risks at reasonable costs. An empowered environment is created when curiosity is as highly regarded as technical expertise.
- *Access to information.* Employees must have access to a wide range of information. Involved individuals make decisions about what kind of information they need to perform their jobs.
- *Accountability.* Empowerment does not involve being able to do whatever you want. Empowered employees should be held accountable for their behaviour toward others. They must produce agreed-upon results, achieve credibility, and operate with a positive approach.

Additionally, employee empowerment succeeds when the culture of the organization is open and receptive to change. An organization's culture is created largely through the philosophies of senior managers and their leadership traits and behaviours. In an empowered organization, effective leadership is exemplified by managers who are honest, caring, and receptive to new ideas, and who treat employees with dignity and respect, and as partners in organizational success. Further, for empowerment to work, it must be aligned directly with the strategy of the organization and individual accountability throughout the entire enterprise.

However, some organizations will have difficulty instilling the concept of empowerment as managers are sometimes unwilling to give up power or give employees the authority to make decisions. For more information on how to encourage employee empowerment, access the resources and information at the American Society for Quality (**www.asq.org**).

Manager's Toolkit 3.3 gives some additional examples of employee empowerment.

American Society for Quality (ASQ)

www.asq.org

Employee Engagement

A relatively new concept resulting from employee empowerment is that of employee engagement—the employee who is committed and dedicated to the organization—where the organization has truly captured the total person in achieving organizational outcomes. The concept has evolved from the practitioner community requiring further empirical research. Engagement is used to refer to the interplay of attitudes, behaviours, and dispositions that relate to organizational outcomes such as turnover and productivity. Several HRM consulting firms such as Aon Hewitt and Towers Watson conduct engagement surveys and publish studies identifying factors that drive employee engagement. These studies present a wide array of drivers and definitions that makes the term "engagement" complicated. Some of the drivers include the organization's reputation for social responsibility, leadership trust and integrity, nature of the job, and total rewards. Certain studies focus on particular drivers and their impact on specific organizational outcomes, such as employee turnover, absenteeism, tenure and retention, customer satisfaction, loyalty, sales, company productivity, and financial performance. Organizations become involved in Top Employer surveys to have an independent external assessment of their employees' engagement compared to other organizations.

Aon Hewitt

http://www.aon.com

Towers Watson

www.towerswatson.com

Aon Hewitt, a global HR consulting and outsourcing solutions business of Aon Corporation, conducts an annual national Canadian workplace study that measures employee engagement. Cisco Canada has been recognized as one of Canada's top employers from 2009 to 2012 because the employees wanted to take and actually took leadership roles in improving the company's business results as well as contributing to

MANAGER'S TOOLKIT **3.3**

EXAMPLES OF EMPLOYEE EMPOWERMENT

Many types of organizations have successfully empowered their employees. Examples include such diverse companies as DuPont, Walmart, Costco, and Home Depot. Empowered employees have made improvements in product and service quality, reduced costs, increased productivity, and modified or, in some cases, designed products.

- Novotel, a mid-scale international hotel chain, offers a high standard of customer service at seven hotels in Canada and more than 400 around the world. Its human resources philosophy is based on building and developing a culture of collaborative relationships that encourage and empower team members to engage in decision making. Teams can take risks without having to get management permission. The chain's open-door program allows employees to discuss concerns with management at any level. Every employee's input is valued and plays an integral part of Novotel's business success.

- Aecon, a Toronto-based international construction company, creates a learning environment that encourages innovation and continuous improvement. With a focus on talent management, it provides technical and soft skills training, a mentorship program, performance appraisals, career progression, and cross-divisional experiential learning.

- Ikea, a furniture retailer, listens to, encourages, and supports staff as part of its shared value system. It also incorporates environmental stewardship into its products and daily operations. Staff are empowered to remove damaged goods without checking with a supervisor.

- Ing Direct, a direct commercial bank, empowers employees through open and transparent communication. Ing takes steps to create an environment where all employees can thrive and focus on creating a quality experience for their customers.

Sources: Adapted from "Canada's Best Employers," *Macleans*, October 11, 2011, www2.macleans.ca/2011/10/20/the-best-employers-3/; Novotel Hotels, "Novotel Named One of the 50 Best Employers in Canada by Aon Hewitt's 2012 Best Employers Studies," press release, accessed December 1, 2011, www.accor.com/fileadmin/user_upload/Contenus_Accor_Presse/Country/North_America/PR_2011/1110_PR_Novotel_50_Best_Employers_in_CA_2012.pdf; "Talent Management, Aecon," accessed December 1, 2011, www.aecon.com/Careers/Employer_of_Choice/Talent_Management; Aecon Group, "Aecon Named One of Canada's Best Employers for Fifth Consecutive Year," news release, October 24, 2011, www.aecon.com/Media_Room?articleView=individual&articleID=873; and Richard Yerma and Kristina Leung, "Employer Review: IKEA Canada Limited Partnership, Chosen as One of Hamilton-Niagara's Top Employers for 2012," Mediacorp Canada Inc., 2012, accessed July 24, 2012, www.eluta.ca/top-employer-ikea-canada.

social responsibility initiatives.[18] Cisco's work environment promotes employee engagement by encouraging collaboration, teamwork, and giving back to the community.[19] Employees are encouraged to speak out and find solutions to problems. Cisco provides mentoring, training, and career programs: after two to four years, employees are encouraged to consider job moves that will provide them with opportunities for career growth.[20]

Another way for management to view engagement is by ensuring that workers are treated fairly and equitably. According to organizational justice theory,[21] workers' evaluative assessments of fairness can influence their attitudes and behaviours. Three dimensions define organizational justice: distributive justice, procedural justice, and interactional justice.[22] Procedural justice proposes that organizational decision-making processes should be consistent, ethical, and fair. Related engagement drivers would include employee voice, autonomy and fairness in decision making, and the offering of worker learning and skill development opportunities. Distributive justice proposes that the consequences of decisions be perceived by workers as fair, equitable, and equally applied. This idea supports engagement drivers such as fair total compensation and clear career paths within the organization. Interactional justice, concerned about interpersonal treatment, proposes that workers should be treated with respect and provided adequate explanations concerning their work. This idea supports the importance of such engagement drivers as leadership that cares about worker well-being, good relationships among managers and co-workers, and organizational pride. With increased organizational fairness, workers are likely to view their managers and organization more positively.

To achieve a high level of employee engagement, it is critical that the leadership practices focus on key engagement and organizational justice drivers. But why do employees want to be engaged? A further study by Psychometrics Canada, a Canadian firm specializing in employee assessments, provided information about what makes employees engaged and what leaders can do to improve engagement. Figure 3.3 identifies a number of areas for consideration.

Further, engagement leads to less frustration at work, thereby creating greater impact at the work level, something that becomes increasingly important during a tough economic situation. A job design approach that integrates engagement drivers and organizational justice will reduce problems that lead to a lack of employee engagement.

Employee Teams

Employee teams
An employee-contributions technique in which work functions are structured for groups rather than for individuals, and team members are given discretion in matters traditionally considered management prerogatives, such as process improvements, product or service development, and individual work assignments.

During the past decade perhaps one of the more radical changes to how work is done has been the introduction of **employee teams**. Employee teams are a logical outgrowth of employee involvement, the philosophy of empowerment, and employee engagement. While many definitions of teams exist, we define an employee team as a group of employees working together toward a common purpose whose members have complementary skills, the work of the members is mutually dependent, and the group has discretion over tasks performed. Furthermore, a team seeks to make members of the work group share responsibility for the group's performance. Inherent in the concept of employee teams is that employees, not managers, are in the best position to contribute to workplace improvements.

FIGURE 3.3 Work Design and Engagement

Work Design and Engagement
Psychometrics Canada Inc. conducted a study on the perspectives of human resources professionals on employee engagement in the Canadian workplace. The recent study showed that when employees are engaged, they demonstrate higher levels of performance, commitment, and improved work relationships. Some themes for increasing engagement are identified below.

What Makes Employees Engaged?
Positive work relationships with co-workers and management.
Good fit between skills, job requirements, and organization's culture.
Regular feedback on employee performance.
Opportunities to learn new skills.
Employees having control over their work.
Celebrations of progress.
Communication of direction and strategy of the organization.
Presence of a role model and/or mentor.

What Can Leaders Do to Improve Employee Engagement?
Design jobs to include employees' skills and strengths.
Listen to and incorporate employee opinions.
Communicate clear expectations.
Give recognition and praise.
Provide learning and career development opportunities.
Provide resources and support in finding solutions to problems.
Clarify roles and decision-making authority.
Provide flexible work schedules and workloads.

Source: Adapted from "Engagement Study: Control Opportunity & Leadership, 2011," as seen online at http://www.psychometrics.com/docs/engagement_study.pdf. Used with permission of Psychometrics Canada Ltd.

Virtual team
A team with widely dispersed members linked together through computer and telecommunications technology

Two issues that are important in the design of work for teams are as follows: (1) the appropriate use of teams; and (2) the types of teams.[23] Job tasks that require specialized individual expertise may be inappropriate for teams. Teams should be used when the work is amenable to teamwork and is adequately structured and supported.[24] Transitioning to distributed workplaces requires more effort on the part of managers to ensure that practices and processes capitalize on team communication, collaboration, and collective knowledge. Teams can operate in a variety of structures, each with different strategic purposes or functional activities. Figure 3.4 describes six different team forms.

One form, the **virtual team**, also called a distributed team, consists of dispersed team members who need to meet regularly but do not require high levels of interdependencies among members. Communication technology is integrated so that workers are able to constantly consult each other. Managers must establish common communication processes and practices that work effectively as well as create a sense of collaborative communication. Organizations such as Dow Chemical, SAS, and the Ontario Public Service have utilized virtual teams for training, product development, and product market analysis.[25] Virtual teams provide these organizations access to previously unavailable diverse and collective expertise and knowledge. More organizations are forming leadership teams to address the challenges faced by those in leadership roles. A cross-national study of senior leadership teams suggests that particular attention needs to be given to the design, dynamics, and performance of these senior-level teams.[26]

Regardless of the structure or purpose of the team, here are a few of the characteristics of successful teams:

- commitment to shared goals and objectives
- consensus decision-making
- open and honest communication
- shared leadership
- climate of co-operation, collaboration, trust, and support
- valuing of individuals for their diversity
- recognition of conflict and its positive resolution

FIGURE 3.4   Work Design and Types of Teams

Surgical teams require coordinated interaction among all members in real time with the responsibility and accountability for outcomes lying primarily with one person. Appropriate for work that requires a high level of individual insight, expertise, and/or creativity but is too large or complex to be handled by any one member working alone.

Coacting groups are individual members who do not depend upon what the others do; the output of a group is simply the aggregation of members' individual contributions. Appropriate only when there is little need for interdependent work by group members.

Face-to-face teams have members with complementary expertise, experience, and perspectives who work together interdependently in real time to generate a product for which they are collectively accountable. Appropriate for a wide variety of tasks for which creating a high-quality product requires coordinated contributions in real time.

Virtual, or distributed, teams use communication technologies to exchange observations, ideas, and reactions at times of their own choosing. Teams are collectively responsible and accountable for work products and are useful when it is difficult for team members to meet regularly and the work does not require high levels of interdependence.

Leadership teams include all significant leaders who share responsibility for leading an entire organization or a large organizational unit. This kind of team addresses the expanding pace and scope of leadership.

Sand dune teams are dynamic and fluid social systems that change in number and kind of members as business requirements and opportunities change. Well suited for fast-changing environments.

Source: Adapted from Greg R. Oldham, J. Richard Hackman. "Not what it was and not what it will be: The future of job design research," *Journal of Organizational Behavior* 31 (2010): 463–479. Copyright © 2010 John Wiley & Sons, Ltd.

Unfortunately, not all teams succeed or operate to their full potential. Therefore, in adopting the work team concept, organizations must address several issues that could present obstacles to effective team function: these include authoritarian leadership and aggressive communication styles, inadequate resources and support, and poor work design.[27] For example, new team members must be retrained to work outside their primary functional areas, and compensation systems must be constructed to reward individuals for team accomplishments. Another consideration is that work teams alter the traditional manager–employee relationship. Managers often find it hard to adapt to the role of leader rather than supervisor and sometimes feel threatened by the growing power of the team and the need to hand over authority. Furthermore, some employees may have difficulty adapting to a role that includes traditional supervisory responsibilities. As team members become capable of carrying out processes, such as strategic planning, that were previously restricted to higher levels of management, managers must be prepared to design work that utilizes their newfound expertise. In designing work teams, special attention needs to be given to the more fluid relationships and communication among workers and their work activities.[28]

Future Design of Organizational Work

There have been changes in jobs and work contexts over the past few decades. Globalization, technology, and demographics have given rise to new questions about how, where, when, and what work is done. Organizations have been responding by replacing traditional (permanent full-time, full-year) jobs with a range of non-traditional employment forms and flexible arrangements such as these:

contract or freelance work	mobile work
e-work	home-based work
temporary work	flextime or flexyear
job or work sharing	time-limited projects
telework	partnership arrangements or talent
compressed workweek	pooling

The increasing use and convergence of social, mobile, and cloud computing technologies are creating unique ways to work. These types of work forms are so new that their definitions have yet to be agreed upon. These contingent employment options are associated with improved work–life balance as well as increased job insecurity. Vosko, Zukewich, and Cranford have developed a model that captures the growing diversity of employment options: they classify mutually exclusive employment forms, wage and salary workers (full-time permanent, full-time temporary, part-time permanent, part-time temporary), and the self-employed (full-time own account, part-time own account, full-time small business owners/employers, part-time small business owners/employers, unpaid family workers).[29] Future job design will shift its focus away from traditional jobs, where individuals worked independently within bounded organizational structures, toward the more dynamic fluid relationships among workers and their work activities that utilize networked communication technology. Future job design practices will require more attention to job crafting, the broader organizational context and culture (e.g., technology, work flow, decentralization, and control systems), distributed teams, the social and relational aspects and attributes of work, diversity, and the linking of competencies, work, and organizational strategy.[30] For information about what might be in the future for job/work design, read Emerging Trends 3.1.

It is important for line managers to understand employee empowerment, employee involvement, and employee teams as they will be asked to help create and support these types of work relationships. And since such arrangements can change the role of line managers, they need to be comfortable with and accepting of the changes. Increasingly,

EMERGING TRENDS **3.1**

1. ***Diversity and generational differences.***
   Managers and supervisors will continually be challenged by the changing nature and mix of their workers. The Millennials are entering the workplace in significant numbers, and research suggests that they hold different work values and motivations from the Gen X and Baby Boom generations. High self-esteem and assertiveness, two of the Millennium generation's characteristics, have implications with respect to designing jobs: members of this cohort expect praise and noncritical feedback, and prefer initiating, negotiating, and creating their work. They are less motivated than earlier generations to meet organizational goals. Most of the Canadian Baby Boom generation is continuing to work part time or members are returning to work during their retirement years. They are working in a wide range of employment forms and for diverse reasons. This situation raises questions that range from how to design work to meet the motivations and needs of this large aging population to how to design work so that the different generations can best work together. In designing work, caution needs to be taken to ensure that generations are not viewed too narrowly as homogenous groups and that recognition is given to the broader aspects of human diversity.

2. ***Increasing use of competencies.*** As work becomes more fluid, organizations will incorporate the core competencies needed for success in each job. These competencies will be the skills, knowledge, abilities, and other behaviours (KSAOs) that lead to the organization's desired results. Competencies are developed top-down by senior managers to ensure that they are strategic, future oriented, and linked to the organization's strategy. An attempt is made to distinguish the KSAOs of top performers.

3. ***The emergence of "job architecture."***
   Managers will want to link strategic jobs with organizational performance outcomes, to put a focus on competitive advantage. As organizations change and evolve, there will be certain critical points that require a business-led view of the structure of the organization. By using a job architecture model, the roles, skills, and careers of the individuals can be effectively managed, and the various HR processes can be more clearly integrated.

4. ***Job crafting and organizational context.*** With the increased uncertainty and change in work environments and in the workforce (in the form of more diversity), when designing future work, special attention will need to be given to the social and collaborative aspects of work, the changing workplace contexts, and the process by which workers craft their jobs.

Sources: Adapted from Jean Twenge, "Generational Changes and Their Impact in the Classroom: Teaching Generation Me," *Medical Education* 43 (2009): 398–405; Mo Wang and Kenneth Shultz, "Employee Retirement: A Review and Recommendations for Future Investigation," *Journal of Management* 36 (2010): 172–206; Jean Pignal, Stephen Arrowsmith, and Andrea Ness, "First Results from the Survey of Older Workers, 2008," *Statistics Canada Perspectives on Labour and Income*, accessed November 30, 2011, http://www.statcan.gc.ca/pub/89-646-x/89-646-x2010001-eng.pdf; Jungwee Park, "Retirement, Health, and Employment among Those 55 Plus," *Statistics Canada Perspectives on Labour and Income*, accessed November 30, 2011, http://www.statcan.gc.ca/pub/75-001-x/2011001/pdf/11402-eng.pdf; David Harrison and Stephen Humphrey, "Designing for Diversity or Diversity for Design? Tasks, Interdependence, and within-Unit Differences at Work," *Journal of Organizational Behavior* 31 (2010): 328–37; Michael Campion et al., "Doing Competencies Well: Best Practices in Competency Modeling," *Personnel Psychology* 64, no. 1 (Spring 2011): 225–62; "Job Architecture—The Key to Good Organizational Health," Watson Wyatt World Wide, March 2009, accessed July 23, 2012, http://www.watsonwyatt.com/research/pdfs/EU-2009-11541.pdf; Brian Becker and Mark Huselid, "SHRM and Job Design: Narrowing the Divide," *Journal of Organizational Behavior* 31 (2010): 379–88; Adam Grant et al., "Putting Job Design in Context: Introduction to the Special Issue," *Journal of Organizational Behavior* 31 (2010): 145–57; and Adam Grant and Sharon Parker, "Redesigning Work Design Theories: The Rise of Relational and Proactive Perspectives," *Academy of Management Annals*, accessed November 30, 2011, http://iwp.dept.shef.ac.uk/files/docs/GrantParker_WorkDesign-Annals.pdf.

the role of the line manager is to find ways to help, support, and expand employee involvement within the company. Without the manager's support and encouragement in creating employee involvement opportunities, there is little chance that such initiatives will succeed. HRM and SME 3.1 explores the challenges and opportunities faced by small business owners and their mobile workforce.

HRM and SME 3.1

CLOUD COMPUTING

Recent interview surveys have been conducted with Canadian small business owners and their mobile workers. Mobile workers are individuals who perform their work in multiple locations that range from customer sites to home offices, using a range of networked communication technologies to remain in contact with their work. Their ability to expand their use of laptops, e-book readers, smartphones, tablets, and other hand-held mobile devices with cloud computing is creating an increasingly contingent and flexible workforce. According to a forecast from IDC's Mobile Enterprise Group, the global mobile worker population will increase from 919.4 million in 2008 to more than 1.19 billion in 2013, representing nearly 35% of the worldwide workforce.

Is mobile communications technology enhancing small business productivity and innovation and workers' work–life balance, or is it draining business resources and employee health? What are the challenges and opportunities faced by small business owners and their mobile workers? The following narratives, taken from the interviews, reveal some important insights into the changing ways workforces are deployed and managed, and the very means as to how, when, and where employees conduct their work. What are these stories telling us?

Mobile Worker: The new experiences and using leading-edge learning applications are exciting but can lead to working longer hours. I enjoy the freedom, control, independence, and autonomy I have over my work. I would never go back to working a regular office job. I frequently work alone and do not always receive support resources and feedback from my manager or co-workers. Communication is often strained, and relationships can be difficult to build. The travelling lifestyle and constantly changing work environments can be stressful. The owner says that family time is important, yet often asks me to work longer hours. I feel trapped by the demands of my job. I guess everyone does it; it's expected. I find that the boundaries are increasingly blurred between my work and family time. I had hoped that technology would allow me more time with my family. At times I feel insecure about career and finances as I do not receive health-care or pension benefits. I don't feel I have a relationship with my employer. It would be nice to have more friendships at work, but I find I am constantly working with different people and in different environments.

Small Business Owner: Our small business growth is in non-traditional markets. We have decentralized work as well as expanded into six countries while still staying connected through networked technology. Networked technology has allowed us to work faster and more effectively. I find that adapting to new technology, processes, and management practices is a constant challenge for everyone in this company. I feel oddly insecure, anxious, and cut off when my Internet connection goes down. I am frustrated at not knowing what the workers are doing or how well they are doing it. We use a wide range of flexible staffing and compensation options that allow us to acquire people with specialized skills, but workers have told me that they feel it is confusing and inequitable. Contract workers seem to be working independently without collaborating with other workers. Coping with being mobile myself as well as managing an increasingly mobile workforce has me constantly rethinking about how to best redesign work. I feel I am always "connected" to technology. I just can't seem to preserve any quality nonwork time with my family or for my own personal development.

Sources: Stephen Drake, Justin Jaffe, and Raymond Boggs, "World Wide Mobile Worker Population 2009-2013 Forecast," IDC Mobile Enterprise Group, June 2010, www.workshifting.com/downloads/2010/07/29/Worldwide%20Mobile%20Worker%20Population%202009-2013%20Forecast.pdf (accessed March 15, 2012).

SUMMARY

1. Explain the supervisor's role in defining and designing work.
   - Line manager or supervisor is the primary individual who determines what work needs to be done.
   - Line manager takes an active role in determining what skills and abilities are needed to successfully perform the work.

2. Discuss the relationship between job requirements and HRM processes.
   - HRM processes, such as recruitment or training, make use of information about the work or job.
   - A job consists of a group of related activities and duties.
   - A position consists of the specific duties and responsibilities performed by only one employee.

3. Explain the relationship between job analysis and a job description.
   - Job analysis is the process of obtaining information about jobs (or work) by determining what the duties, tasks, or activities are.
   - The outcome is a job description—a written document that contains a number of elements.
   - A job description is a written description listing the types of duties and the skills (job specifications) needed to successfully perform the work.

4. Define and describe the sections in a job description.
   - Job title—indication of what the duties might be or the nature of the work.
   - Summary of job—two to three sentences describing the overall purpose of the job.
   - List of duties and responsibilities—statements of the key duties and responsibilities.
   - Job specifications—statement of the needed knowledge, skills, and abilities or competencies of the person who is to perform the work.

5. Describe the uses of information gained from job analysis.
   - Job specifications establish the qualifications required of applicants for a job opening and play an essential role in the recruiting function.
   - Information on the job description is used as a basis for comparing the skills and abilities of each applicant in the selection process.
   - Managers must be careful to ensure that they do not hire employees on the basis of "individualized" job requirements that satisfy personal whims but bear little relation to successful job performance.
   - Requirements contained in the job description and specifications provide clues to training needs.
   - The pay of a job is based on what the job demands in skill, effort, and responsibility, as well as the conditions and hazards under which the work is performed.

6. Define employee contribution and describe the relationship of job design to employee behaviours and contributions.
   - Job design is the process of defining and arranging tasks, roles, and other processes to achieve the employee's goals and organizational effectiveness.
   - Job design strives to incorporate the behavioural needs of employees, which leads to improved performance.
   - Employee contribution is the degree to which employees are involved in making critical work-process or organizational decisions.
   - Job design can enhance or take away from the employee's ability to participate in decision making.

7. Discuss the different types of work designs to increase employee contribution.
   - Employee empowerment is a method of involving employees in their work and encouraging them to take charge of what they do.

- Employee involvement groups are groups of 5 to 10 employees doing similar or related work who meet together regularly to identify, analyze, and suggest solutions to shared problems.
- Employee teams are groups of employees who assume a greater role in the production or service process.
- Non-traditional employment forms and arrangements are addressing employee and employer needs for work flexibility.

NEED TO KNOW

- Definition of job analysis, job description, job specification, standards of performance, and job design
- Definition of employee and group contributions
- Definition of employee involvement, employee empowerment, and employee engagement

NEED TO UNDERSTAND

- Relationship of job requirements to recruitment, selection, training, performance evaluation, health and safety, and compensation
- Relationship between job analysis, job descriptions, job specifications, and standards of performance
- Role of line manager in designing jobs for maximum employee contributions
- Ways to encourage employee involvement

KEY TERMS

employee empowerment 92

employee teams 95

job 78

job analysis 79

job characteristics model 89

job description 81

job design 89

job specifications 81

position 78

standards of performance 85

virtual team 96

work 78

REVIEW QUESTIONS

1. What is the difference between a job analysis and job description?
2. What are the problems associated with a written job description?
3. What are the uses of information from job analysis?
4. What are the types of employee and group contributions?
5. What are the different forms of teams?
6. What job information would you collect when conducting a job analysis?
7. What are two non-traditional employment forms?

CRITICAL THINKING QUESTIONS

1. You have just been hired as a customer service representative at a branch of a large bank. The branch manager is considering creating a non-traditional work schedule for everyone. The manager has asked for your advice about what to consider to ensure its success—and the continued strong performance of the branch. What would you say?
2. Assume that you are a new supervisor in a hotel and you have been asked to prepare a job description for room attendant. What would you include as five key duties and what would you list as three key skills? Would you involve the current room attendant in the preparation of the job description? Why?

3. You are working for a company that has recently created a number of work teams. Your boss has been assigned to head up one of the teams. What advice would you give so that the team and your boss create a high-performing team?

4. You are working as a manager for a new recreational resort that has no written job descriptions. From your observation, it appears that many of the employees are not always sure what to do, and sometimes, there is overlap in tasks and activities between employees. What arguments would you use to convince your boss to develop written job descriptions?

5. You are a small business owner in the catering business. What might be some work design issues you would need to consider to recruit and keep top performers?

6. How is the increasingly mobile workforce changing how, when, where, and what work is done? What are the opportunities and challenges faced by managers and mobile workers?

DEVELOPING YOUR SKILLS

**Human Resources and
Skills Development
Canada**

www.hrsdc.gc.ca

1. In groups of four or five, identify the job specifications (knowledge, skills, and abilities) for the position of college instructor. (You will have approximately 20 minutes to complete the exercise.) Each group will then present its findings to the rest of the class. Discuss and compare the requirements and develop a single list of job specifications.

2. Access the Web page of the National Occupation Classification (NOC) system that is managed by Human Resources and Skills Development Canada (**http://www5. hrsdc.gc.ca/NOC/English/NOC/2011/AboutNOC.aspx**). Familiarize yourself with the various job classification information. Search through the various job titles and find a job description that interests you. Prepare a one-page summary describing the key duties and skills, and explain what training and experience you would need in order to be hired.

3. Each student will bring one job description to class. In a small group, critique each other's descriptions based on the information and examples in the chapter. What changes can you make to ensure that each description is both measurable and future oriented?

4. Use the job analysis questions in Managers Toolkit 3.1 to interview someone, perhaps another student who is working, about his or her job position. What did you discover about the job analysis interview process and the information required?

5. Access and use current research about a nonstandard work option (e.g., telework, mobile work, flexible schedules) that you would like your current or future employer to consider. Write a one-page proposal to your employer that illustrates the benefits of your chosen employment form (e.g., teleworkers are more satisfied than office workers).

6. Bring a past or current job description to class. In a small group, refer to Figure 3.2 to discuss how you would change your jobs so that they are a better job–environment fit.

Case Study ❶

But My Job Has Changed

Job descriptions are a critical tool used for job orientation and training and, importantly, in annual employee performance evaluations. When the duties and responsibilities listed in the job description do not reflect current job content, employee/management disagreements can arise, as this case illustrates.

Both employees and managers agree that Brenda Batten has been an exceptional employee. As a senior technical representative (STR) for Blackhawk Aironics, she is valued for her knowledge in airplane instrumentation. One manager described her as "simply an expert in the complex technology of satellite weather systems."

Recently, Blackhawk Aironics implemented a new work reorganization plan. STRs such as Brenda now work largely by telecommuting with managers and engineers at company headquarters and with customers scattered throughout North America. Additionally, under the new work plan, STRs were given more freedom to deal directly with customers and engineers without supervisory intervention. This freedom greatly facilitated customer service needs and demands in an aviation market everyone considers highly dynamic.

Brenda's current job description reflects the technical dimensions of her position but not the telecommuting requirements now performed. Personal competencies such as decision making, self-motivation, problem solving, and communication skills are not covered.

Brenda met with her manager, Martin Eaton, for her annual performance review. Unfortunately, unlike past meetings, which were highly satisfactory, this meeting quickly developed into a disagreement. At the centre of the controversy were the factors to be used to measure Brenda's new job demands. Martin wanted to place major emphasis on the tasks and duties listed in her current job description. As he explained to Brenda, "I hardly see you anymore, and I have no objective criteria or performance data by which to measure those behaviours you now use." Brenda, in response, acknowledged that some things in the current job description were still important aspects of her job, but overall the current job description did not capture the full scope of her new duties and responsibilities. Brenda concluded that she was satisfied with Martin's evaluation of the technical aspects of her job, but she was clearly not pleased with the overall evaluation of her performance. As she told Martin, "It's simply not fair; you just don't know what I do now."

Source: From BELCOURT/BOHLANDER/SNELL. *Managing Human Resources*, 6E. © 2011 Nelson Education Ltd. Reproduced by permission. www.cengage.com/permissions

Questions

1. Given the facts of this case, is it possible for Brenda and Martin to reach a satisfactory result? Explain.
2. How could an organization go about identifying and measuring the personal competencies of employees?
3. How could the company prevent this problem from occurring in the future? Explain.

Case Study 2

Revitalizing Your Workspace

Air Miles, the consumer rewards company, recently relocated its headquarters in North York to downtown Toronto. In the preparation, designing, and planning, it decided that it wanted workspace that would incorporate several of its key themes for its staff. These themes were health and well-being, and employee engagement. In making the move, the company contemplated that as many as 10% of the staff might not make the move. However, what they experienced was less than 1% not moving. As Bryan Pearson, president and CEO of Air Miles, stated, "It is a testament to the design of the building and the facilities provided."

The new facility features ergonomic furniture, more windows, and an on-site fitness facility. The company acknowledges that it didn't want to cut certain costs as it understood that it was making an investment in its employees. It knew that if employees were healthier, they would be more productive and would be happier and more motivated. To engage employees in the process, Air Miles began communicating its intentions 15 months before the move. In addition, staff were encouraged to provide input on size of space, design of space, and more. The employees would be moving into a slightly smaller space and a more open environment.

Air Miles is thrilled as the staff are highly energized and engaged, interacting and socializing well with one another. And even with the open concept, the noise level is lower than in the old environment. It seems that people are more respectful and considerate of one another. As Pearson concludes, "You need to know what kind of environment you want to create for your staff and how you want to treat them."

Source: Adapted from Sarah Dobson, "Getting Workspace into Shape," *Canadian HR Reporter*, January 12, 2009, www.hrreporter.com/ArticleView.aspx?l=1&articleid=6598 (accessed March 22, 2012).

Questions

1. What arguments could be advanced both for and against involving employees in the redesign of office space?
2. Empowerment and engagement is mainly a motivational tool. Do you think the new offices will continue to keep employees engaged? What more might Air Miles have to do?
3. How might a manager in the former location react to managing in a more open environment?

NOTES AND REFERENCES

1. "Work," Karo Persuasive Experiences, accessed March 25, 2012, www.karo.com/portfolio.
2. Juan I. Sanchez and Edward L. Levine, "The Rise and Fall of Job Analysis and the Future of Work Analysis," *Annual Review of Psychology* 63 (November 30, 2011).
3. Greg R. Oldham and Richard R. Hackman, "Not What It Was and Not What It Will Be: The Future of Job Design Research," *Journal of Organizational Behavior* 31 (2010): 463–79.
4. Jason Robertson (Director, Business Development, Aquinox), interview by the author, February 2012.
5. Fiona Johnstone and Canadian Human Rights Commission and Canada Border Services [Indexed as *Fiona Johnstone v. Canada Border Services*], file no. T1233/4507, Ottawa, Ontario, August 6, 2010, accessed March 15, 2012, www.chrt-tcdp.gc.ca/aspinc/search/vhtml-eng.asp?doid=1021&lg=_e&isruling=0.
6. Oldham and Hackman, "Not What It Was and Not What It Will Be."
7. Ibid.
8. Michael A. Campion et al. "Doing Competencies Well: Best Practices in Competency Modeling," *Personnel Psychology* 64, no. 1 (Spring 2011): 225–62.
9. Brian Becker and Mark Huselid, "SHRM and Job Design: Narrowing the Divide," *Journal of Organizational Behavior* 31 (2010): 379–88.
10. *Vilven and Kelly v. Air Canada and Air Canada Pilots Association* (2011), Canadian Human Rights Tribunal FILES: T1176/5806, T1177/5906 & T1079/6005 accessed October 12, 2011, http://chrt-tcdp.gc.ca/search/files/t1079_6005ed081110.pdf.
11. Oldham and Hackman, "Not What It Was and Not What It Will Be."

12. Justin M. Berg, Amy Wrzesniewski, and Jane Dutton, "Perceiving and Responding to Challenges in Job Crafting at Different Ranks: When Proactivity Requires Adaptivity," *Journal of Organizational Behavior* 31 (2010): 158–86.

13. Oldham and Hackman, "Not What It Was and Not What It Will Be."

14. "Moore Wins 2011 OGCA Doug Chalmers Award," *Daily Commercial News*, September 26, 2011.

15. Frederick P. Morgeson, Erich C. Dierdorff, and Jillian L. Hmurovic, "Work Design In Situ: Understanding the Role of Occupational and Organizational Context," *Journal of Organizational Behavior* 31, nos. 2–3 (February 2010): 351–60.

16. Severin Hornung et al., "Beyond Top-Down and Bottom-Up Work Redesign: Customizing Job Content through Idiosyncratic Deals," *Journal of Organizational Behavior* 31, nos. 2–3 (February 2010): 187–215.

17. Berg, Wrzesniewski, and Dutton, "Perceiving and Responding to Challenges in Job Crafting at Different Ranks."

18. "Cisco Ranked among Top Three Best Employers in Canada," *Cisco's Technology News Site*, January 8, 2010, accessed November 27, 2011, http://newsroom.cisco.com/dlls/2010/prod_010810b.html.

19. Cisco Systems, *CSR Report 2010: Our People*, accessed November 28, 2011, www.cisco.com/web/about/ac227/csr2010/our-people/index.html.

20. "EllisDon, Cisco Canada, and WestJet were among top employers for the Greater Toronto Area," *Canadian HR Reporter*, November 24, 2011, www.hrreporter.com/ArticleView?articleid=11793&headline=ellisdon-cisco-canada-and-westjet-among-top-employers-for-gta.

21. Jerald Greenberg, "Organizational Justice: Yesterday, Today, and Tomorrow," *Journal of Management* 16 (1990): 399–432.

22. Yochi Cohen-Charash and Paul Spector, "The Role of Justice in Organizations: A Meta-analysis," *Organizational Behavior and Human Decision Processes* 86 (2011): 278–321.

23. Oldham and Hackman, "Not What It Was and Not What It Will Be."

24. Richard R. Hackman and Nancy Katz, "Group Behavior and Performance," in *Handbook of Social Psychology*, 5th ed., ed. S. T. Fiske, D. T. Gilbert, and G. Lindzey (New York: Wiley, 2010).

25. J. Wagner Consulting, "Building Effective Virtual and Remote Teams: An OD Perspective," (presentation, November 1, 2011), www.odnetwork.org/resource/resmgr/2011_conf_ppts/building_effective_virtual_a.pdf.

26. Oldham and Hackman, "Not What It Was and Not What It Will Be."

27. Mark Gorkin, "Key Components of a Dangerously Dysfunctional Work Environment," *Workforce Management*, accessed October 21, 2011, www.workforce.com/archive/feature/22/22/18/223747.php.

28. Oldham and Hackman, "Not What It Was and Not What It Will Be."

29. Leah F. Vosko, Nancy Zukewich, and Cynthia J. Cranford, "Precarious Jobs: A New Typology of Employment," *Perspectives on Labour and Income* 4, no. 10 (October 2003), Statistics Canada Catalogue no. 75-001-XIE, accessed October 15, 2011, www.statcan.ca/english/freepub/75-001-XIE/01003/ar-ar_200310_02_a.htm.

30. Oldham and Hackman, "Not What It Was and Not What It Will Be."

CHAPTER 4

HUMAN RESOURCE PLANNING, RECRUITMENT, AND SELECTION

OUTCOMES

After studying this chapter, you should be able to

1 Discuss the steps in human resource planning.

2 Describe the relationship between planning, recruiting, and selecting people to work with the organization.

3 Compare the advantages and disadvantages of recruiting from within the organization.

4 Outline the advantages and disadvantages of external recruitment.

5 Explain the objectives of the selection process.

6 Describe the typical steps in the selection process.

7 Identify the various sources of information used for selection decisions.

8 Discuss the different methods and types of questions for conducting an employment interview.

9 Illustrate the value of different types of employment tests.

OUTLINE

HRM CLOSE-UP

Jennifer Mills, co-CEO, Precision BioLogic Inc.

At Precision BioLogic Inc. (PBI), in Dartmouth, Nova Scotia, 60 employees fulfill traditional responsibilities of jobs in areas such as sales, manufacturing, product development, quality control, administration, and management. But the company's organization chart is far from traditional. On paper, it looks like a living organism with functional cells and pods and many offshoots showing relationships between job functions.

The organic structure is reflective of the company's business that is developing and manufacturing products used by medical lab technicians to diagnose people with blood clotting or bleeding disorders. Employees work in teams in a non-hierarchical structure that recognizes that each person plays a key role in the customer relationship.

"You won't find terms like 'boss,' 'subordinate,' or 'direct report' at PBI," explained co-CEO Jennifer Mills. "I have broad responsibility for the operations of our company, but it doesn't mean I'm any more important than anyone else."

Bosses at PBI are referred to as "Primary Supports" since the term implies a two-way support relationship rather than a one-way "telling-and-directing" relationship. And when it comes to recruiting, the company takes much care and time in the process.

"When I myself was hired," said Mills, "the process took many months. It began with lunch with the CEO, and then I had meetings or lunches with members of the management team. I had so many meetings, lunches, and dinners that when I finally received the job offer, my husband quipped, 'Did he give you a job offer or a marriage proposal?'"

This kind of focus and care in recruiting and selection ensures that Precision BioLogic finds an ideal match. Many people are involved in the process, including team members, colleagues, and the primary support person, who all meet with the candidate before a decision is made.

"Hire for FIT!" exclaims Mills. "Culture fit is the most important aspect. We have a unique culture and when people haven't worked out, it's rarely been that they do not have the right skills or knowledge—it's normally because they don't fit with the culture."

The culture at PBI is described as collaborative with lots of communication and good humour. At the centre of its values chart are the words "'trust, curiosity, and fun.'"

"We are curious about what our customers are looking for, and we are curious about our employees and what they need to be successful," said Mills. "Knowing this is the best way for our company to be successful."

When a job needs filling, the company prepares a role dimension, a compensation range, and a job profile that is essentially a "personality profile" for the role. Recruits then complete their own personality profile and the two are compared. Differences are explored in order to determine a fit. This profiling is designed to indicate qualities such as a person's level of sociability, whether the person is a multi-tasker or prefers a single focus, and whether the person is more likely to enjoy working with data or with people.

Of course, job skills, education, and experience count, but according to Mills, if "a role personality goes against the candidate's natural personality, it's not likely going to be a good fit. In fact, when we first adopted this system, we had all our staff complete the profiles. Nearly all of them said that the survey described them very accurately. And there's no judgment in the profiling. People's personalities are not right or wrong, just distinct and different."

If someone indicates unhappiness in a job, Mills refers again to the personality profiling. She once had an accountant who wasn't feeling fulfilled. "We discovered that she was highly sociable and put her on the office social committee," she said. "It gave her the ability to access this part of her personality without having to change her chosen career. Awareness is really helpful. We can make subtle shifts to help staff."

For most of its hiring, Precision BioLogic works with a recruiting agency. The agency knows the company and its culture very well and does much of the groundwork to prepare a short list of candidates. The agency uses Internet, professional networking tools like LinkedIn, and other online posting sources to identify potential recruits.

Anticipating staffing requirements is a key part of the executive team's strategic planning process. This way, they can stay ahead of the curve and allow for the careful approach needed in hiring. And if they do encounter an unforeseen crunch, the company can reassign staff internally where possible. "Everyone is willing to chip in and help out," states Mills, "which also provides development opportunities."

INTRODUCTION

In earlier chapters we stressed that the structure of an organization and the design of the work within it affect the organization's ability to reach its objectives. These objectives, however, can be achieved only through the efforts of people. It is essential that work within the organization is done by people who are qualified to do the work and most likely to best perform the work. To achieve this, defining the core competencies for any work is critical to the recruitment and selection processes, and this starts with the line manager, who is also encouraged to think about current and future people requirements. Jennifer Mills clearly understands the importance of finding the right person for the company. Precision BioLogic uses a variety of ways to find (recruit) and then pick (select) the people who have the attitudes desired to make the firm successful. And it is important that this process supports both operational and strategic planning.

Employment recruiting and selection continue to be one of the top concerns of all levels of management within an organization. Despite the economic challenges of the last several years, almost all organizations are finding it increasingly difficult to secure qualified and appropriate applicants to fill job openings. According to recent studies, most employers have entered a period in which jobs ranging from the unskilled to the professional and highly technical are harder to staff; this condition is not likely to improve in the near future, especially for small businesses.[1] No longer can managers rely solely upon unsolicited applications to fill openings nor can they be sloppy in making hiring decisions. This chapter will discuss the process of planning for staffing requirements and then finding, attracting, and selecting applicants.

HUMAN RESOURCE PLANNING

You will recall from Chapter 1 that a company becomes competitive by means of its people. Therefore, it is essential that an organization look strategically at its people and the skills they require to accomplish the strategic and operational goals of the organization.

But what is meant by "strategic"? While strategy has many definitions, we will use the one you might have learned in a management course. Strategic plans tend to be broader in scope, longer in time frames (two to three years), provide overall direction, and apply to the entire organization. Basically, a company's strategy lies in determining its key goals and the actions it needs to take to achieve those goals. Strategic HRM, as noted in Chapter 1, includes all the HR policies, processes, and practices that help the company achieve those goals through its employees. Therefore, it is important that the line manager links the goals of the company to the skills of the people employed.

In linking goals to skills, the line manager will need to anticipate the current and future needs of the company and develop the road map to get there. What the manager is really doing is ensuring that the company has people with the right skills for the present and for future organizational growth.[2] This is called **human resource planning**. Human resource planning is a process to ensure that the people required to run the company are being used as effectively as possible, where and when they are needed, in order to accomplish the organization's goals. Depending on the organization, the process might also be called manpower planning or employment planning. No matter which phrase is used, the purpose is still the same: to have the right people with the right skills in the right jobs at the right time. Given the economic uncertainty, organizations sometimes may want to ignore this. However, it is even more important in difficult financial circumstances to ensure that they have the appropriate staff to achieve success in both the short term and into the future.[3]

Human resource planning
Process that the people required to run the company are being used as effectively as possible, where and when they are needed, in order to accomplish the organization's goals

Linking HR Planning to Strategic Planning

Organizations will undertake strategic planning where major objectives are identified and comprehensive plans are developed to achieve the objectives. Because strategic planning involves the allocation of resources, including the people resources of the organization, HR planning is aligned to ensure that the objectives are met. And from the overall organizational objectives, divisions and/or departments will also set objectives that support the attainment of organizational objectives. Thus, the line manager will need to make plans not only for business objectives but plans for the necessary staffing resources. For example, if the organization has strategically decided to enter a new market, it needs to ensure that it has the people with the right skill sets to gain a foothold in that market. Consequently, the HR plan must have an activity that assesses the skill of current employees and possibly a recruitment activity that attracts new employees with the necessary skills.

Likewise, through HR planning, all HR processes, systems, and practices can be aligned to the overall business strategy. In doing this, the organization ensures that it has the people capabilities to adjust to changes in the environment. One area of strategic HR planning that is receiving much attention is succession planning. Organizations are concerned about developing leaders for the future and are focusing efforts on leadership development so that the leaders have the competencies necessary that can keep pace with the direction and overall strategy of the organization.[4] In the best companies, such as Fairmont Hotels, BMO, and IBM, virtually no distinction exists between strategic planning and HR planning; the planning cycles are the same, and HR issues are seen as inherent in the management of the business. Another example is the entry of Target into Canada by acquiring Zellers. Target has decided that its business needs to have additional staff to be successful and is planning to have 50% more people employed at each store than did Zellers.[5]

Importance of HR Planning for Staffing Needs

Why is it important for the line manager to be involved in human resource planning? Consider these facts about the Canadian labour force:

- In 2011, close to 19 million Canadians were in the labour force out of a population of about 35 million.
- The workforce is aging—in 2011 close to 17% of the workforce were 55 or older, and by 2031 it is projected that 25% of the workforce will be 55 or older.
- In 2011, the percentage of foreign-born workers was 21% and is expected to rise to 33% in 2031.
- Workers are delaying retirement resulting in an employment rate increase from 22 to 34%.
- Labour shortages are predicted for the information and communications technology sector.
- Today, 35% of workers are part time or self-employed, with the self-employed around 15% of total employment.[6]

These dramatic shifts in the composition of the labour force require that managers become more involved in planning their staffing needs, since such changes affect not only employee recruitment but also methods of employee selection, training, compensation, and motivation. As illustration of the impact of changes in the workforce, companies such as the PTI Group in Alberta have determined that the hiring of Aboriginal people(s) is a strategic imperative. PTI supplies remote-site services such as food services and worker accommodations, particularly within the resource industry. Since much of its work in Canada occurs on or near Aboriginal land, the company decided that it was in its long-term best interests to create employment opportunities for the local communities. In doing so, PTI has also partnered with Northern Alberta Institute of Technology to create training programs where it can employ the graduates.[7] Without doing its own workforce planning, PTI would not have known there was a problem.

An organization may incur several intangible costs as a result of inadequate or no people planning. For example, inadequate planning can cause vacancies to remain unfilled.

The resulting loss in efficiency can be costly, particularly when lead time is required to train replacements. Situations also may occur in which employees are laid off in one department while applicants are hired for similar jobs in another department.

Realistically, planning occurs more systematically in medium and larger organizations. Small, entrepreneurial organizations tend to approach HR staffing needs on a more short-term basis. These businesses tend to spend most time creating the business and give little time to creating staffing plans.[8]

An example of a small organization that does pay attention to its staffing needs is Digitcom Canada, recently awarded the Avaya SME Canadian Business Partner award. The company's president considers its success is because of the 35 people dedicated to providing telecommunications service and support. Digitcom focuses on hiring the best, and it ensures that these highly qualified people remain through ongoing training and a culture of respect.[9]

Statistics Canada provides a variety of different reports that can be helpful in HR planning. The "Population Pyramid" Web site at **www.statcan.gc.ca/kits-trousses/animat/edu06a_0000-eng.htm** is animated to demonstrate the changes in population, including projections to the mid-21st century, from which organizations can determine their own trends in relation to their staffing needs.

**Statistics Canada
Population Pyramids**

www.statcan.gc.ca/
kits-trousses/animat/
edu06a_0000-eng.htm

Outcome 1

What are the steps in human resource planning?

Trend analysis
Quantitative approach to forecasting labour demand on an organizational index

Management forecasts
Opinions and judgments of supervisors or managers and others that are knowledgeable about the organization's future employment needs

HR Planning Approaches

Since the overall outcome of HR planning is to have the right people with the right skills at the right time in the right jobs, there is a need to forecast the demand for employees. Forecasting can be done through quantitative approaches, such as a **trend analysis**, or through qualitative approaches, such as **management forecasts**.

A trend analysis will forecast employment requirements on some type of organizational index, such as sales or units of production. Previous years' experiences will be analyzed and projections will be made for the future. In management forecasts, the opinions and judgments of people who are knowledgeable about the organization's future needs will develop scenarios that can be used for planning purposes.

Besides forecasting the demand for employees, an organization will also need to look at the supply of employees. This activity includes looking both internally, in the organization, and externally, to the larger labour market. Two techniques to assess the internal

A research scientist has knowledge and company-specific skills that are directly linked to the company's strategy.

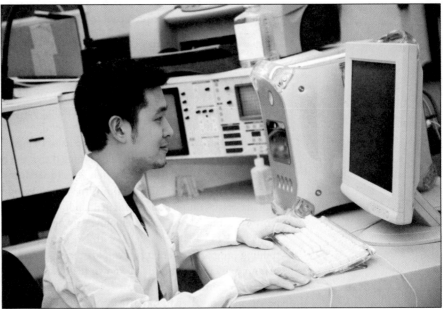

© 2009 Jupiterimages Corporation

Staffing table
Graphic representations of organizational jobs along with the numbers of employees currently occupying those jobs and future employment needs

Markov analysis
Method for tracking the pattern of employee movements through various jobs

Skills inventory
Information about the education, experiences, skills, etc. of staff

supply are **staffing tables** and **Markov analysis**. Staffing tables are graphic representations of all organizational jobs, along with the numbers of employees currently occupying those jobs (and perhaps also future employment requirements derived from demand forecasts). Markov analysis shows the percentage (and actual number) of employees who remain in each job from one year to the next, as well as the proportions of those who are promoted, demoted, or transferred, or who leave the organization.

While staffing tables and Markov analysis focus on numbers of employees, another technique focuses on the skill mix or **skills inventory**. When assessing the organization's supply, organizations will identify the key skills or core competencies necessary for organizational success. Without knowing the core competencies required for business success, the other HR processes may not be successful. All other HR needs are based on the identified competencies of employees to ensure good organizational performance. Organizations such as Hewlett-Packard and DuPont Canada use HR information and enterprise systems to assist in this task. Figure 4.1 describes the steps in the planning process.

Results of HR Planning

The outcome of HR planning is to achieve a usable balance between the demand for and supply of employees. It is here that organizations can see the results of good HR planning. The demand for and supply of labour is very much a function of the economic environment. For example, with what is being called the "Great Recession," which started in 2008, many organizations found that they had to modify their plans and did not need as many people. While the overall economic climate in North America, particularly in Canada, is improving, many organizations are being very cautious about adding staff. However, some organizations in Canada do see employment growth in the areas of information technology, engineering, business development, and sales/marketing.[10]

But HR planning is not a guarantee that there might not come a time when the organization has too many employees for its immediate or long-term needs. This situation can be the result of severe economic conditions, as mentioned in Chapter 1, or major company collapses, such as Blockbuster's bankruptcy in 2011. In either case, a company may be faced with terminating or laying-off employees. However, there are other ways that an organization can balance its employee complement without having to terminate people or hire more staff.

FIGURE 4.1   The HR Planning Steps

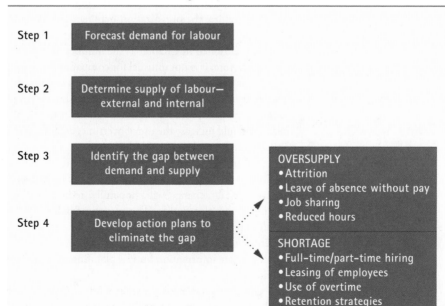

Ways to Deal with an Oversupply of Labour

Some organizations have decided that since employees are key to their success, any need to reduce employee numbers would be done by attrition. Attrition is the natural departure of employees through people quitting, retiring, or dying. Usually, organizations can estimate how many people leave and for what reasons. Therefore, an organization may be able to avoid downsizing because it knows that people will leave. This was easier to do when people left the organization at the age of retirement—usually 65. However, with many people postponing retirement, it is more difficult to predict what the natural attrition rate will be.

Not all attrition is good. If too many people leave—high turnover—it can cost the company more money than intended. Replacing an employee is a costly and time-consuming activity. It is estimated that the costs of turnover can be as high as two times the annual compensation, particularly in high-demand skill areas or professionals.[11] And the costs are not just financial: they can include the loss of key knowledge. One of the more serious business issues of the 21st century has been the concern with retaining key employees.

If the organization can predict that the excess supply of employees is more short-term, it may suggest that some employees take a leave of absence (without pay), job-share, reduce working hours (and pay); or, it can redeploy people to units that have a need. Generally speaking, most organizations do not stop hiring because of economic pressures. Frequently, there may be too many people in one area of the business and not enough in another area. By utilizing a number of strategies, an organization can minimize the need to terminate employees.

While much has been written about the impending overall labour shortage, what is also being said is that there is an oversupply of unskilled labour and/or a mismatch with the skills available and the skills desired.

Ways to Deal with Shortages of Labour

Even though human resource planning frequently focuses on the surplus of employees, currently much of the attention has been on projected labour shortages—particularly in certain occupations and industries. For example, British Columbia is projecting that there will be almost 62,000 more jobs than people to fill them by 2020, with a shortage of skilled trades much sooner.[12] Further, the need for additional employees may be short-term or temporary, and, therefore, the organization will not want to hire for the longer term. Therefore, the organization may request that employees work extra hours, such as during peak periods.

As mentioned in Chapter 1, the number of part-time employees has increased a great deal. Therefore, it is not unusual for companies to hire part-time staff to cover for absences of regular, full-time employees. Likewise, organizations will utilize the services of a temporary employment agency to acquire short-term staff, particularly in areas where a certain type of expertise is required, such as software programmers. In addition, an organization could increase the use of overtime, enhance retention strategies, and as mentioned in Chapter 1, employees could be leased.

In early 2012, the federal government announced that there would be a more flexible immigration system to enable people with skilled trades qualifications to enter Canada.[13] This change will, hopefully, reduce critical shortages in the trades, such as plumbers and electricians. The government has further stated that this revised system would allow employers to determine who has the skills necessary instead of the government.[14]

For more information on HR planning, see *The HRM Guide* at **www.hrmguide.net/canada**.

Once a manager knows what work is to be done and the skills required to do the work successfully, the task of finding and selecting the right people begins.

The HRM Guide
www.hrmguide.net/canada

RECRUITMENT

Outcome 2

What is the relationship between HR planning, recruitment, and selection?

Recruitment
The process of locating and encouraging potential applicants to apply for jobs

Once an organization has determined its needs, it must then recruit potential employees. The line manager, together with available HR professionals, will identify where a company might look for these candidates. **Recruitment** is the process of locating and encouraging potential applicants to apply for existing or anticipated job openings. The purpose of recruitment is to have a large pool of potentially qualified applicants. Figure 4.2 provides an overview of the recruitment process.

Some organizations will have an ongoing recruitment effort. For example, IMV Projects, a Calgary-based engineering services firm, actively looks for staff all the time. It feels that if it has great talent, other great talent will be attracted when an opportunity arises.[15]

This process informs the applicants about the qualifications required to perform the job and the career opportunities the organization can offer its employees. Whether or not a particular job vacancy will be filled by someone within the organization or from outside will, of course, depend on the availability of people, the organization's HR practices, and the requirements of the job to be staffed.

One of the biggest challenges for organizations is to continue the recruitment process even during difficult economic times. As mentioned in the section on HR planning, and in Chapter 1 regarding the business environment and demographics, there is still a shortage of people with certain skill sets for certain types of industries. Therefore, it is important to focus on employee retention as well as on accessing new talent. Given the demographics of the workforce, from people who are choosing not to retire to those just coming out of school, it is important to understand what employees expect and want from the organization in order to retain them. While organizations want people to stay, companies also want them to be engaged and want to stay.[16]

In some cases, there is a need for the organization to consider its "branding" from a future employer perspective. For those of you who have not had a course in marketing, "branding" refers to the need to have a total and holistic approach to how the marketplace sees the company or products. There is a desire to have a uniform image come into the consumer's mind when the company or product is visible. Many companies are now

FIGURE 4.2 The Recruitment Process

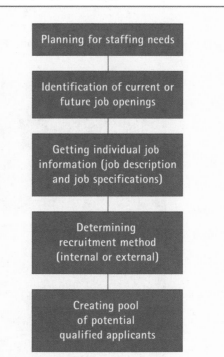

transferring the concept of "branding" to their employment framework—to have a uniform image come into prospective employees' minds (and of existing employees) when the company name is mentioned. By using a branding approach to all aspects of employment, contemporary organizations can create an opportunity to retain their key talent.

Recruiting Within the Organization

Outcome 3

What are the advantages and disadvantages of internal recruiting?

Most public-sector organizations, and many private-sector organizations, try to follow a policy of filling job vacancies above the entry-level position through promotions and transfers from within the organization. By filling vacancies in this way, an organization can capitalize on the investment it has made in recruiting, selecting, training, and developing its current employees. Promotion-from-within policies at CIBC and Canada Mortgage and Housing Corporation have contributed to the companies' overall growth and success.

Advantages of Recruiting from Within

Promotion serves to reward employees for past performance and is intended to encourage them to continue their efforts. Promoting from within makes use of the people who already know the organization and the contribution they have made. It also gives other employees reason to anticipate that similar efforts by them will lead to promotion, thus improving morale within the organization. This is particularly true for members of designated groups who have encountered difficulties in finding employment and have often faced even greater difficulty in advancing within an organization. Most organizations have integrated promotion policies as an essential part of their employment equity programs.

Transfers can also serve to protect employees from layoff or to broaden their job experiences. This strategy becomes more noticeable as organizations become flatter with fewer layers between front-line employees and executives. Furthermore, the transferred employee's familiarity with the organization and its operations can eliminate the orientation and training costs that recruitment from the outside would entail. Most important, the transferee's performance record is likely to be a more accurate predictor of the candidate's success than the data gained about outside applicants.

Methods of Locating Qualified Internal Job Candidates

The effective use of internal sources requires a system for locating qualified job candidates and for enabling those who consider themselves qualified to apply for the opening.

By filling job vacancies from within, organizations can capitalize on investments made in developing current employees.

Keith Brofsky/Photodisc: Green/Getty Images

Qualified job candidates within the organization can be located by using computerized record systems and internal job postings.

HUMAN RESOURCE MANAGEMENT SYSTEMS   Information technology has made it possible for organizations to create databases that contain the complete records and qualifications of each employee within an organization. Combined with increasingly user-friendly search engines, managers can access this information and identify potential candidates for available jobs. Organizations have developed résumé-tracking systems that allow managers to query an online database of résumés. Companies such as Oracle and SAP Canada are leaders in developing technology for staffing and skills management. Similar to the skills inventories mentioned earlier, these information systems allow an organization to rapidly screen its entire workforce to locate suitable candidates to fill an internal opening. These data can also be used to predict the career paths of employees and to anticipate when and where promotion opportunities may arise. Since the value of the data depends on its being kept up-to-date, the systems typically include provisions for recording changes in employee qualifications and job placements as they occur.[17]

SUCCESSION PLANNING   As mentioned earlier, many organizations have done some succession planning—the process of identifying, developing, and tracking key employees for future promotions or transfers. Therefore, when a job opening occurs in a particular part of the organization, it might make use of the succession plan and put the employee into the vacancy. Succession plans rely upon the organization identifying its long-term goals, outlining the competencies required to achieve those goals, and making sure that the employee is developed in order to assume other roles and take on other responsibilities.

INTERNAL JOB POSTING   Organizations may advertise about job openings through a process referred to as **internal job posting**. In the past, this process has consisted largely of posting vacancy notices on company employment boards in an HR department or common area, such as lunchroom. In addition, internal advertising can also be done through a company's intranet, e-mails, or other types of internal memos, and company newsletters. Increasingly, companies such as Xerox are developing computerized job posting systems and maintaining voluntary lists of employees looking for upgraded positions. As part of the overall approach to assessing internal staff and their skill sets, organizations will use technology, including Web-based solutions, to determine whether any staff have the necessary skills for a certain role.[18]

Internal job posting can provide many benefits to an organization. However, these benefits may not be realized unless employees believe the process is being administered fairly. Furthermore, it is more effective when internal job posting is part of a career development program in which employees are made aware of opportunities available to them within the organization. For example, the organization may provide new employees with literature on job progression that describes the lines of job advancement, training requirements for each job, and skills and abilities needed as they move up the job-progression ladder.

Internal job posting
Method of communicating information about job openings

Limitations of Recruiting from Within

Sometimes, certain jobs that require specialized training and experience cannot be filled from within the organization and must be filled from the outside. This situation is especially common in small organizations. Also, for certain openings it may be necessary to hire individuals from the outside who have gained the knowledge and expertise required for these jobs from another employer.

Even though the company may encourage that job openings be filled from within the organization, potential candidates from the outside should be considered in order to prevent the inbreeding of ideas and attitudes. Applicants hired from the outside, particularly for certain technical and managerial positions, can be a source of new ideas and may bring with them the latest knowledge acquired from their previous employers. Indeed, excessive reliance on internal sources can create the risk of "employee cloning." Furthermore, it is not uncommon for firms in competitive fields, such as high technology or retailing, to attempt to gain secrets and managerial talent from competitors by hiring away their employees.

Recruiting Outside the Organization

> **Outcome 4**
>
> What are the advantages and disadvantages of external recruiting?

Frequently, organizations will decide to fill positions by bringing people in from outside the organization. Thus, when a mid-level manager of the organization leaves, a chain reaction of promotions may subsequently occur, creating other openings throughout the organization. The question, therefore, is not whether to bring people into the organization, but rather at which level they are to be brought in.

Usually, external recruitment is organized and coordinated by an HR department with the line manager frequently giving suggestions about where to recruit, such as an ad in a newspaper or professional journal. However, if there is no HR department. These line managers need to be aware of such things as labour-market conditions and where to recruit.

Organizations such as RONA, Scouts Canada, and the Bank of Montreal will often focus on external recruitment for senior management positions. In many of these cases, hiring someone from the outside is seen as bringing in new ideas, different styles, new energy, and earlier successes.[19]

Advantages and Disadvantages of External Recruitment

Like recruiting from within, external recruitment has advantages and disadvantages.

One advantage of bringing someone in from outside the organization is that the individual brings certain unique skills that the company needs now. Likewise, it is possible to bring in people with a variety of different experiences and perspectives.

A disadvantage to external recruitment is the lack of solid information about the person's performance on the job. That information is available only through second-hand sources, such as what the applicant volunteers and what references might say. Also, the person may also not know the industry or organization, necessitating more extensive orientation and training. Further, there may be constraints in the organization, such as salary levels, that prevent the organization from accessing a large pool of applicants. Significant costs are usually associated with external recruitment. These costs include the amount of time, the cost of advertising (sometimes as much as $9,000 per newspaper), and the cost of familiarizing the person with the organization. Lastly, there may also be legislative requirements, such as employment equity, which lead to certain applicant pools.

The Labour Market

> **Labour market**
> Area from which applicants are recruited

The **labour market**, or the area from which applicants are recruited, will vary with the type of position to be filled, the amount of compensation to be paid, and as mentioned earlier, the economic environment. Recruitment for executives and technical personnel who require a high degree of knowledge and skill may be national or even international in scope. Most colleges and universities, for example, conduct national employment searches to fill top administrative positions. Recruitment for jobs that require relatively little skill, however, may encompass only a small geographic area—such as within Winnipeg. The reluctance of people to relocate may cause them to turn down offers of employment, thereby eliminating them from employment consideration beyond the local labour market.

The condition of the labour market may also help to determine which recruiting sources an organization will use. During periods of high unemployment, organizations may be able to maintain an adequate supply of qualified applicants from unsolicited résumés alone. A tight labour market, one with low unemployment, may force the

Human Resources and Skills Development Canada Labour Market Information

www.hrsdc.gc.ca/eng/ workplaceskills/labour_ market_information/ index.shtml

employer to advertise heavily and/or seek assistance from local employment agencies. How successful an organization has been in reaching its employment equity goals may be still another factor in determining the sources from which to recruit. Typically, an employer at any given time will find it necessary to utilize several recruitment sources, including apps for smartphones and social media sites.[20]

For a number of years, Canada has relied on immigration to assist in meeting the demand for labour. While other countries may be reducing the number of immigrants, Canada has set a target for 2012 about the same as 2011.[21] In addition, the department responsible for immigration, Citizenship and Immigration Canada, has worked with businesses to create processes that are more responsive to labour market shortfalls. Information about provincial labour market conditions and what occupations may be of interest to immigrants can be found on the Web site of Human Resources and Skills Development Canada (**www.hrsdc.gc.ca/eng/workplaceskills/labour_market_information/index.shtml**). These changes are intended to allow applicants into Canada that have the skills that are in short supply. As mentioned in Chapter 1, Canada has an aging population with insufficient younger workers to fill the work requirements in the future. Further, as more and more individuals become part of a global talent pool, companies will seek a number of ways to recruit beyond one's home country.

The dynamics of the labour market mirror the general economy: when there is a poor economic climate with many people unemployed, there is potentially a larger pool of applicants. Likewise, if the economy is strong with few unemployed, the pool of applicants may be much smaller. There are also training and education programs that aim to provide an appropriate number of skilled applicants so that most of those graduates can be hired—such as nurses and other medical specialists. This does not mean that everyone is always hired, though, as the person may not have the skills needed by a particular employer. However, employers who make good use of their HR planning activities will continue to look for qualified applicants whether the economy is good or poor.

Outside Sources of Recruitment

The outside sources from which employers recruit will vary with the type of position to be filled. A software developer, for example, is not likely to be recruited from the same source as a retail service person. Trade schools can provide applicants for entry-level positions, though these recruitment sources are not as useful when highly skilled employees are needed. Networking, referrals from previous and existing staff, information from customers/clients, and involvement in the community are a few ways that organizations seek people outside the organization. A variety of new and creative recruitment approaches continues to evolve with the expanded use of social networks such as LinkedIn, Facebook, and Twitter.

Some of the major outside sources of recruitment are described below.

LinkedIn
www.linkedin.com

Facebook
www.facebook.com

Twitter
http://twitter.com

ADVERTISEMENTS   One of the frequent methods of attracting applicants is through advertisements. Whether through Web sites, newspapers, or trade journals, other media used include radio, television, billboards, posters, and e-mail blasts. And it is no longer unusual to see an ad on the side of a bus. Advertising has the advantage of reaching a large audience of possible applicants. Some degree of selectivity can be achieved by using newspapers and journals directed toward a particular group of readers. Professional journals, trade journals, and publications of unions and nonprofit organizations fall into this category.

Well-written advertisements highlight the major assets of the position while showing the responsiveness of the organization to the job and career needs of the applicants. Among the information typically included in advertisements is a statement that the recruiting organization is an equal-opportunity employer. It is important that the advertisement is eye-catching whether in print media or in an Internet environment. As Manager's Toolkit 4.1 illustrates, the preparation of online recruiting advertisements requires creativity in developing design and message content.

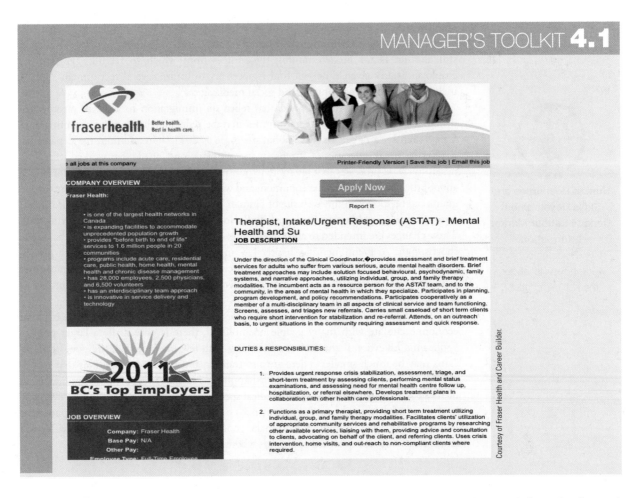

MANAGER'S TOOLKIT **4.1**

Courtesy of Fraser Health and Career Builder.

**Human Resources and
Skills Development
Canada**

www.hrsdc.gc.ca

Service Canada Job Bank

www.jobbank.gc.ca

JobServe

www.jobserve.ca

Canada's Human Resources and Skills Development (HRSDC) (**www.hrsdc.gc.ca**) is responsible for administering the Employment Insurance program through its Service Canada agency, found in most communities. Individuals who become unemployed must register at one of these offices and be available for "suitable employment" in order to receive their weekly employment insurance cheques. Service Canada has created a national job bank that lists information about jobs across the country province by province. The database can be searched by type of job and geographic area within the province (**www.jobbank.gc.ca**).

In addition, HRSDC provides assistance to employers in approving special work permits to enable people from other countries to move to Canada for employment. While approvals of special permits have become more difficult during the recession, Canada still has a shortage of skilled workers in industries such as oil, gas, and information technology.[22]

INTERNET   The Internet is the most commonly used search tactic by job seekers; 60% of Canadians with Internet access have gone online in search of a job. Both companies and applicants find the approach cheaper, faster, and potentially more effective. At Work with HRM 4.1 describes how JobServe links companies with people who have the necessary skills.

There is no doubt that the Internet has had an impact on print advertising in the newspapers. Not that many years ago a person would see 5 to 10 pages of career ads in all the major newspapers. Now, you might not find more than 1 or 2 pages once a week. Further, many companies use their Web sites to announce job openings. For example, Mountain Equipment Co-op posts detailed information about job openings at its Web site along with a savable application form. Likewise, WestJet and CIBC actively use their company Web sites to encourage people to consider working for them. Canadian recruiting

AT WORK **with HRM 4.1**

JOBSERVE

JobServe, Canada's first online job site, helps link job seekers with jobs that match their needs and skills. According to the company, the process is fast and effective, and very simple for those with little time to pursue jobs.

The job seeker searches for career opportunities by category (such as advertising) and then by location (such as Alberta—all cities). All available positions are then listed for that location. Once the job seeker finds the appropriate position(s), the person applies with some basic information online and uploads both a cover letter and résumé. Recruiting companies post jobs, listing skills required. Very sophisticated software matches job seekers to the posted opportunities. Within minutes of a company posting a job, the application-matching software sends a notification by e-mail to the job seekers whose profiles match it, giving a detailed job description, salary, etc. The job seeker can reply by e-mail or by an internal messaging system. Recent technology enhancements include RSS feeds, job search through mobile devices, and YouTube.

Jobserve.com prides itself in having technology that can get the match of the right candidate with the right job. It has more than 200,000 postings and processes over one million applications each month. Employers can search the résumé database at any time they wish. The service is free for job seekers, but the companies pay a fee based on the number of jobs advertised.

CRITICAL THINKING QUESTIONS:

1. What do you think is making Internet recruiting so popular?
2. What are the potential problems that can happen with Internet recruiting?

Monster
www.monster.ca

Workopolis
www.workopolis.ca

NiceJob
www.nicejob.ca

working.com
working.com

sites include Monster.ca (**www.monster.ca**), Workopolis (**www.workopolis.ca**), NiceJob (**www.nicejob.ca**), and working.com (**www.working.com**), a site that provides information about job opportunities throughout Canada.

Employers claim that the Internet is faster (with some job applicants responding within 30 minutes of the job posting); that it generates higher-quality candidates; and that it is cheaper (by as much as 80%) than traditional advertising media. An Internet posting can be as low as $50 per month compared to a newspaper ad of $6,000 per day, with Monster and Workopolis being about $750 per job posting. An interesting side benefit of Internet job searching is the amount of time someone might be unemployed. According to a recent study, it was determined that a person is unemployed 25% less time by making use of Internet job postings.[23] Given the difficult employment landscape, this can be a great help to people locating work sooner.

Both companies and job seekers find the approach is cheaper, faster, and potentially more effective. It is estimated that there are more than 4,000 Web sites where applicants can submit their employment backgrounds and potential employers can check for qualified candidates. A capability like this can help companies find the people with the competencies that are required in today's dynamic business environment.

CareerBuilder, an internationally focused online recruitment advertiser, recently stated that employers need to use current technology for effective recruitment. According to one of its studies, 28% of Canadian employers use social media sites to seek potential job applicants. Further, even though few people secure a job through these sites, 22% of job applicants actively use LinkedIn and Facebook to identify job opportunities.[24] It is therefore important that employers develop a strategic approach to the use of social media as a recruitment tool.

As demonstrated on the previous page, there is a need to prepare Internet advertisements in a careful way so that the Web site does attract the qualified people you are seeking. Manager's Toolkit 4.2 provides tips for creating such a Web site.

MANAGER'S TOOLKIT 4.2

DEVELOPING EFFECTIVE WEB SITE ADVERTISEMENTS

1. Understand the target applicant pool. Answer questions such as these: What has been the recruitment needs over the last several years? What jobs have been hardest to fill?

2. Focus on what makes your organization different and a great employer. Talk about the unique features of its culture and work environment or any special career advancement programs.

3. Provide stories and other testimonials, including pictures, of current employees and why they think the company is great.

4. Make sure that the site is easy to use—for both the company and job applicants. The Web site must provide value to the recruitment activities.

5. Link your site to other sites and career search engines so that your site can be optimal. It is also helpful to track the number of hits so that the organization can gauge the site's effectiveness.

6. Tailor the message and information to the target audience.

7. Look at the site from the job seeker's perspective. Make sure that whatever job titles are used will be known to the typical job seeker.

Sources: Adapted from Paul Dodd, "Putting your best foot forward on the web," *Canadian HR Reporter*, April 25, 2011, www.hrreporter.com/articleview/10080-putting-your-best-foot-forward-on-the-web (accessed January 7, 2012); "Recruitment Display Ads Not One-Size-Fits-All," *TalentMinded*, December 20, 2011, http://talentminded.com/recruitment-display-ads-not-one-size-fits-all/ (accessed January 7, 2012); and Susan Grant, "Technology streamlines recruitment," *Canadian HR Reporter*, April 11, 2011, www.hrreporter.com/articleview/9962-technology-streamlines-recruitment (accessed January 7, 2012).

But having a Web-based ad is not sufficient. The organization must also have the means to easily and quickly process the number of applications that can come from their own sites or other job search engines. To help organizations screen large amounts of information from online sources, companies have integrated front-end career Web sites with their own databases. This type of software can pull the right data from all candidates and organize the data that makes the review of the applicants more efficient; it can also provide recruitment statistics.[25] In addition, résumés are stored and the software is sophisticated enough to connect candidates directly to the hiring manager. Some of the technology in use, particularly in larger organizations, enables the job application to be moved electronically from one step to another, thus ensuring that a good candidate isn't lost due to lengthy delays.

Companies, such as RONA, Bombardier, Finning Canada, and Hydro One, and organizations, such as the federal government and the Ontario government, use the Internet to attract people. Employers indicate that the reason is to increase the opportunity to attract the people with the right skill sets for their organizations.

As mentioned at the beginning of the chapter, social media networking sites have been very much in the forefront for job seekers. As of late 2011, Facebook had created apps where employers can post jobs inside the 800-million member social network.[26] Such a situation has created an incredibly large labour pool for little in recruitment costs.

EMPLOYMENT AGENCIES   Employment agencies, including executive search firms and temporary employment agencies, attempt to match applicants with the specific needs of a company. A fee is charged to the employer for services that are tailored to the employer. By law, job seekers cannot be charged for help in finding work. It is common for such agencies to specialize in serving a specific occupational area, such as office staff or technical computer people. Private agencies usually focus on clerical, technical, and junior–middle management whereas executive search firms tend to focus on senior and executive management. These agencies may charge an employer 25 to 30% of the annual salary if they find a candidate who gets hired. Since these agencies differ in the services they offer, job seekers would be wise to take the time to find a recruiter who is knowledgeable, experienced, and professional. When talking with potential recruiters, individuals should discuss openly their philosophies and practices with regard to recruiting strategies, including advertising, in-house recruiting, screening procedures, and costs for these efforts.

Executive search firms (also called "headhunters") are employment agencies that typically focus on senior-level and executive-level managerial positions. The search tends to be very focused to that specific employer. The fees charged by the agencies to the employer may range from 30 to 40% of the annual salary for the position to be filled. The employer pays this fee.

As noted earlier, it is increasingly common to bring in new chief executive officers (CEOs) from outside the organization. A large number of these new CEOs are placed in those positions through the services of an executive search firm. Since high-calibre executives are in short supply, many different types of organizations from not-for-profits to public sector agencies will use executive search firms to fill their top positions. To get a sense of the range of organizations that use executive search firms, access the sites of OdgersBerndtson (**www. odgersberndtson.ca**) and Korn/Ferry (**www.kornferry.com**).

Agencies that provide temporary employees are one of the fastest-growing recruitment sources. Companies such as Imperial Oil Ltd., Home Depot, and SaskTel use temporary employees extensively. "Temps" are typically used for short-term assignments or to help when managers cannot justify hiring a full-time employee, such as for vacation fill-ins, for peak work periods, or during an employee's parental or sick leave.

Increasingly, temps are being employed to fill positions once staffed by permanent employees. At Hydro-Québec, for example, "long-term temporaries" have replaced permanent hires as a staffing practice. Employees are hired for one- to three-year terms. This practice is growing because temporaries can be laid off quickly, and with less cost, when work lessens. The use of temporaries thus becomes a viable way to maintain proper staffing levels. Also, the employment costs of temporaries are often lower than those of permanent employees because temps are usually not provided with benefits and can be dismissed without the need to file employment insurance claims.

The drawbacks of contract employees are that their commitment to the company is lower than that of full-time employees, and they may take confidential information to their next employer, possibly a competitor.

Check out the Web sites of Angus One Professional Recruiters (**www.angusone.com**), Olsten Staffing Services (**www.olsten.com**), Adecco (**www.adecco.ca**), and Manpower, one of Canada's largest temporary agencies (**www.manpower.ca**), to find out more about employment agencies.

EDUCATIONAL INSTITUTIONS   Educational institutions are a source of young applicants with formal training but relatively little full-time work experience. High schools are usually a source of employees for clerical and blue-collar jobs. Community colleges, with their various types of specialized training, can provide candidates for technical jobs. These institutions can also serve as a source of applicants for a variety of white-collar jobs, including those in the sales and retail fields. Some management-trainee jobs are staffed from this source. Humber College in Etobicoke, Ontario, and the B.C. Institute of Technology offer a Human Resource Management training program. For technical and managerial positions, universities are generally the primary source. It is important for employers to be aware of what attracts students to employers. Universum, a global survey company, conducts research on students' perceptions of employers. Part of the survey asks about the ideal company. The top "ideal companies" in Canada for 2011 were the Government of Canada, Apple, Google, Bank of Canada, and Air Canada.[27]

OPEN HOUSES AND JOB FAIRS   Organizations may also use open houses and job fairs to recruit new employees—particularly if the organization is expanding or is looking for particular types of skills. For example, with the shortage of skilled trades, an organization might participate in a job fair at an educational institution that graduates tradespeople.

OdgersBerndtson
www.odgersberndtson.ca

Korn/Ferry
www.kornferry.com

Angus One Professional Recruiters
www.angusone.com

Olsten Staffing Services
www.olsten.com

Adecco
www.adecco.ca

Manpower
www.manpower.ca

Or the organization might have an open house where potential applicants are encouraged to visit the company and see what might be available. Seasonal resort operations such as Whistler/Blackcomb in British Columbia use open houses at the start of each ski season as a way to attract people with a variety of skills. In 2011, combining the concept of an open house with the use of technology, a job fair was created where 20 employers from a wide array of industries (e.g., financial services, insurance, and retail) attracted over 18,000 job applicants throughout Canada.[28] While the event had virtual employer booths describing the opportunities, job seekers could access the information at any time during the event, no matter where they lived or worked. This ability represents an example of the evolving use of technology in recruitment.

EMPLOYEE REFERRALS   The recruitment efforts of an organization can be aided by employee referrals or recommendations made by current employees. Managers have found that the quality of employee-referred applicants is normally quite high, since employees are generally hesitant to recommend individuals who might not perform well. According to a management professor, 88% of employers rate employee referrals as their #1 source of quality candidates.[29] The effectiveness of this recruitment effort can be increased by paying commissions or bonuses to employees when they make a successful "recruitment sale." An organization, however, needs to ensure in utilizing employee referrals that it is not creating a situation of systemic discrimination.

UNSOLICITED APPLICATIONS AND RÉSUMÉS   Many employers receive unsolicited applications and résumés from individuals who may or may not be good prospects for employment. Even though the percentage of acceptable applicants from this source may not be high, the source cannot be ignored. Many job search strategies suggest that individuals use this method to introduce themselves to organizations that are of interest to them.[30]

For such an approach to be successful for the job seeker, it might be useful to create a digital résumé. This tool can be exceptionally helpful if the work one is seeking is within the technology or digital world. For a digital résumé to be effective, it might contain visual information, video, and infographics.[31]

Good public relations dictate that any person who contacts an organization for a job be treated with courtesy and respect. If there is no possibility of employment in the organization at present or in the future, the applicant should be tactfully and frankly informed of this fact.

PROFESSIONAL ORGANIZATIONS   Many professional organizations and societies offer a placement service to members as one of their benefits. Listings of members seeking employment may be advertised in their journals or publicized at their national meetings. A placement centre is usually established at national meetings for the mutual benefit of employers and job seekers.

Employers use job fairs as a way to attract applicants.

© Frances Roberts/age fotostock/FirstLight

UNIONS   If a company is unionized and has employees that belong to labour unions, those unions can be a principal source of applicants for blue-collar jobs (such as welders, electricians, and plumbers) and for some professional jobs. Some unions, such as those in the maritime, printing, and construction industries, maintain hiring halls that can provide a supply of applicants, particularly for short-term needs. Employers wishing to use this recruitment source should contact their local union for employer eligibility requirements and applicant availability.

RECRUITMENT FOR DIVERSITY   As organizations continue to develop a diverse workforces, employers will often focus on attracting potential staff in communities of different ethnic and cultural backgrounds. Those employers that fall under the federal employment equity legislation (see Chapter 2) are expected to have a recruitment program that focuses on the designated groups of women, visible minorities, people with disabilities, and First Nations people. While Canada (unlike the United States) does not have a quota system, under employment equity legislation, there is an expectation that over time, those organizations that fall under the legislation will have a workforce reflective of the general population of Canada.

Having a diverse workforce is not just about hiring Canadians. It is important to capitalize on the skills that foreign-born immigrants bring with them. There are still incredible barriers to immigrants finding work. However, a recent report by Deloitte, *Welcome to Canada, What Now?*, encourages employers to take a calculated risk and become more productive by making use of skills brought by immigrants.[32] As stated in the report, Canada is good at attracting people, but organizations tend to want people with Canadian experience. And for Canada to remain competitive on a global basis, it is important to improve productivity since Canada lags behind other countries.

This situation was reinforced by a study by the Royal Bank of Canada, which stated the Canadian economy is losing close to $31 billion by not fully utilizing the skills of foreign-born and educated workers.[33] Of particular note is that 40% of immigrants have at least a bachelor's degree compared to 17% for the Canadian-born population.[34]

The situation of immigrants finding it difficult to locate work was further highlighted by a study done through the University of Toronto. The study indicated that the name of the person led to more or fewer job interviews. Someone with a "foreign-sounding" name was less likely to receive a call for an interview than someone with an anglophone name.[35] And this occurred in the hiring process in Canada's three largest cities: Montreal, Vancouver, and Toronto. This is not only discriminatory; it is affecting Canada's economic health. More information about immigration and recruitment will be discussed in Chapter 11.

While there might be a desire to recruit a diverse workforce, recruiting for small businesses can be especially difficult, as the firm grows from owner-operated into a larger company. Read HRM and SME 4.1 to better understand the difficulties.

HRM and SME 4.1

HOW DO WE PROVIDE LUXURY SERVICE?

It is generally understood that the Canadian economy is driven by small- and medium-size businesses (SMEs). According to a recent report, SMEs account for almost 43% of Canadian GDP and account for close to 62% of employment in the private sector. There are approximately 1.1 million SMEs in Canada of which 95% have fewer than 50 employees.

With a very diverse Canadian workforce, many SMEs see the value of having individuals with different experiences and ways of doing things. One organization in Nova Scotia has actively recruited for diversity as a way of providing exceptional service in luxury hotel. Prince George Hotel in Halifax makes excellent use of new immigrants by offering them

continued

exceptional training and development opportunities. It believes that only through its staff—not its physical appearances—that guests can receive excellent hospitality and memorable service.

The hotel, with its diverse workforce, also offers immigrants a course that focuses on workplace English for their particular job rather than general English language. This course is integrated into the hotel's room attendant training. Such an approach facilitates not only improved language skills, but also improved integration into the Canadian workforce.

Guests have commented on the exceptional service, which includes calling guests by name and opening doors. This level of service is accomplished only through recruiting staff that understand guest experiences and then creating a training program that focuses on the skills and behaviours that create such an exceptional experience.

Sources: Adapted from Business Development Canada, "SMEs at a Glance," August 2011, and Centre for Workplace Skills, *Investing in Skills: Effective Work-Related Learning in SMEs*, 2011.

TRIEC
www.triec.ca

MOSAIC
www.mosaicbc.com

Costi Immigrant Services
www.costi.org

Diversity World
www.diversityworld.com

Canadian Abilities Foundation
www.abilities.ca

Aboriginal Skills and Employment Partnership
www.hrsdc.gc.ca/eng/ employment/aboriginal_ training/index.shtml

Nation Talk
www.nationtalk.ca

As indicated in a recent study of the S&P 500 over the last five years, companies that aggressively sought and supported a diverse workforce outperformed the other companies in the study. As mentioned in Chapter 2 in the section on diversity, it is important for line managers and supervisors to be knowledgeable about and supportive of their organization's objective to have employees with diverse ethnic and cultural backgrounds. Managers need to be held accountable for the success (or failure) of creating a more diverse workforce.[36] Managers may also be actively involved in recruitment "outreach" programs, where they speak at ethnic community centres to let people know about employment opportunities with their company. Other avenues for recruiting designated groups include ethnic community newspapers and TV stations. Maple Leaf Sports and Entertainment recently extended itself into the South Asian community by ensuring that hockey games were broadcast in Punjabi.[37]

A particularly effective organization in bridging the immigrant gap is the Toronto Region Immigrant Employment Council (TRIEC) (**www.triec.ca**). The Council represents an innovative partnership between employers, unions, postsecondary institutions, other community organizations, and government. The organization came into existence in 2003 when the city identified that to have well-settled and satisfied immigrants, it was necessary for immigrants to have successful employment opportunities. The mission of the organization is to create and facilitate solutions to better the integration of immigrants into the regional workforce.[38] It is unique in that it doesn't work directly with immigrants but provides a collaborative approach to engaging the various parties that can help immigrants get settled, find work, and succeed in Canada.

There are also several organizations that help new immigrants, people with disabilities, and First Nations people find work and employers to find potential employees. Among these are MOSAIC (**www.mosaicbc.com**), Costi Immigrant Services (**www .costi.org**), Diversity World (**www.diversityworld.com**), Canadian Abilities Foundation (**www.abilities.ca**), Aboriginal Skills and Employment Partnership (**www.hrsdc.gc .ca/eng/employment/aboriginal_training/index.shtml**), and Nation Talk (**www .nationtalk.ca**).

SELECTION

Outcome 5

What are the objectives of selection?

Once the recruitment process has yielded applicants whose qualifications appear to fit the organization's requirements, you then must assess those qualifications and make a decision on whom to hire—which individual or individuals will perform best on the job. It is usually, the line manager's responsibility to make the final selection decision. If there is an HR department, it will usually play a supporting role by arranging interviews, doing reference checking, administering employment tests, and so on. However, if no HR professional is there to help, the line manager needs to know these steps and their importance.

Matching People and Jobs

Selection
The process of choosing individuals who have relevant qualifications and who will best perform on the job to fill existing or projected job openings

Making hiring decisions is not a scientific process, and, therefore, it cannot be structured to achieve perfect results. However, by being systematic in the selection process, there is a greater possibility of having staff that can be committed to the vision and business plans.[39] **Selection** is the process of choosing individuals who have relevant qualifications to fill existing or projected job openings. Those responsible for making selection decisions should have adequate information on which to base their decisions. Information about the jobs to be filled, and as much relevant information as possible about the applicants themselves, is essential for making sound decisions. The objective is to have information that will predict job performance of the candidate in the organization.

Prior to the selection process, it is important to reconfirm the necessary knowledge, skills, and abilities for the job. As mentioned in Chapter 3, these job requirements are identified through job analysis. Managers can then use selection methods, such as interviews, references, psychological tests, and the like, to assess the applicant's competencies and match these against the requirements of the job and the needs of the organization.[40]

Ordinarily, managers are well acquainted with the requirements pertaining to skills, physical demands, and other factors for jobs in their respective departments. If the interview step includes professionals from the HR department, the HR professional will need to maintain a close liaison with the various departments to become thoroughly familiar with the jobs and competencies needed to perform them.

The Selection Process

Outcome 6

What are the steps in the selection process?

In most organizations, selection is a continuous process. Turnover inevitably occurs, leaving vacancies to be filled by applicants from inside or outside the organization or by individuals whose qualifications have been assessed previously. In some situations, organizations will have a waiting list of applicants who can be called when permanent or temporary positions become available.

The number of steps in the selection process and their sequence will vary, not only with the organization but also with the type and level of job to be filled. Each step should be evaluated on its contribution. The steps that typically make up the selection process are shown in Figure 4.3. Not all applicants will go through all these steps. Some may be rejected after a review of their application form or résumé, or after a preliminary interview.

FIGURE 4.3   Steps in the Selection Process

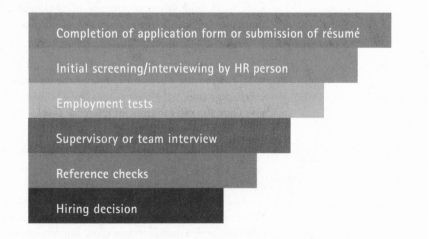

Completion of application form or submission of résumé

Initial screening/interviewing by HR person

Employment tests

Supervisory or team interview

Reference checks

Hiring decision

Note: Steps may vary. An applicant may be rejected after any step in the process.

As shown in Figure 4.3, organizations use several different means to obtain information about applicants. These include application forms and résumés, interviews, tests, and reference checks. Regardless of the method used, it is essential that it conform to accepted ethical standards, including privacy and confidentiality, as well as legal requirements. Above all, it is essential that the information obtained be sufficiently reliable and valid.

Obtaining Reliable and Valid Information

Reliability
The degree to which interviews, tests, and other selection procedures yield comparable data over time and alternative measures

The degree to which interviews, tests, and other selection procedures yield comparable data over time is known as **reliability**. For example, unless interviewers judge the capabilities of a group of applicants to be the same today as they did yesterday, their judgments are unreliable—that is, unstable. Likewise, a test that gives widely different scores when it is administered to the same individual a few days apart is unreliable.

Validity
How well a test or selection procedure measures a person's attributes

In addition to having reliable information pertaining to a person's suitability for a job, the information must be as valid as possible. **Validity** refers to what a test or other selection procedure measures and how well it measures it. In the context of employee selection, validity is essentially an indicator of the extent to which data from a procedure (interview or test, for example) predict job performance. However, whether something is valid depends upon the selection tool's overall reliability. Therefore, whatever selection procedures or tools are used—whether an interview or an employment test—they must be both reliable and valid in order to provide useful information about predicting the applicant's performance in the organization. The procedure or tool used may need to be modified (or not used), or the results carefully evaluated due to cultural differences. For example, companies that screen job applicants for values will not get good information about a person's overall capability to perform the job successfully; the best overall predictor for job performance (and training success) is the person's general mental abilities.[41]

While it is important that all information is both reliable and valid, most organizations are more concerned about the reliability and validity of any employment tests. This topic will be discussed further in the section "Employment Tests."

Sources of Information about Job Candidates

Outcome 7

What are the various sources of information when making a selection decision?

Many sources of information are used to provide as reliable and valid a picture as possible of an applicant's potential for success on the job. This section looks at the usefulness of application forms and résumés, reference checks, employment tests, and interviews.

Application Forms and Résumés

Most organizations require application forms to be completed because they provide a fairly quick and systematic means of obtaining a variety of information about the applicant. Application forms serve several purposes:

- They provide information for deciding whether an applicant meets the minimum requirements for experience, education, and so on.
- They provide a basis for questions the interviewer will ask about the applicant's background.
- They also offer sources for reference checks. For certain jobs, a short application form is appropriate.

As mentioned in the section on Internet sourcing, many organizations no longer are using paper applications and are having you apply for work directly online. In some cases, there is an electronic application and in other cases you merely send your résumé to an e-mail address.

Individuals frequently exaggerate or overstate their qualifications on a résumé. However, the consequences of falsifying information on applications and résumés are frequently severe such as termination. But candidates not only exaggerate; in a tight labour market, candidates sometimes delete advanced qualifications, as described in Ethics in HRM 4.1. Other cases highlight the importance of integrity in job applications. A recent

ETHICS in HRM 4.1

WHEN DOES "STRETCHING" BECOME LYING?

Most candidates for white-collar jobs prepare a résumé and submit it to prospective employers. They also complete the application form, answering questions required by employers for comparison purposes. Some recruitment agencies noticed during the last recession that résumé padding increased. Applicants were "stretching" the dates of their employment, misleading employers about the nature of their duties, and misrepresenting their salaries. When you are writing a résumé, adding three months to your previous employment, saying you were a night auditor instead of clerk, and adding $950 to your last salary might seem relatively harmless.

But what are the facts? Studies of "creative" résumé writing indicate that about 30% of résumés report incorrect dates, 11% misrepresent reasons for leaving, and others exaggerate education attainments or omit criminal records. The probability is that about two-thirds of employers check references. Some former employers give only dates of employment and previous salary ranges.

Most organizations require you to sign a statement saying that the information you supply is true and that if it is not, you will be dismissed. Some cases of résumé padding have been heavily publicized. A Toronto Stock Exchange manager was dismissed for lying about having a master's degree. A member of Parliament listed an ILB on his résumé, which normally stands for International Baccalaureate of Law, but which he claimed stood for Incomplete Baccalaureate of Law. In one heart-wrenching case, a person who was ready to retire was found to have lied about his age decades earlier to get a job. On discovery, he was dismissed and lost his pension. In another case, a Canadian businessman was sentenced to eight months in jail in New Zealand for lying on his résumé: he had listed false qualifications, such as an MBA.

Falsifying a résumé doesn't just happen with "white-collar" jobs. In 2011, a football coach was forced to resign for allegedly overstating his experience as a head coach, and in 2012 a political figure overstated a relationship with the board of trustees at a community college.

In a labour market where too many people are chasing too few jobs, candidates will also lie on their résumés, but do so by dropping experience and educational qualifications. This practice, called "stripping," is used because job seekers are ready to take any job in order to survive or to hold them over until the jobs they really want are available.

Here are some tips for employers when reviewing résumés:

1. Watch for ambiguity—probe on use of general or vague terms.

2. Ask more than once—rephrase similar questions and compare answers.

3. Be factual—ask references to confirm basic information such as employment history.

QUESTION:

Have you overstated your résumé? Explain your reason.

Source: Adapted from "Almost one-half of workers know someone who lied on resume," *Canadian HR Reporter*, September 27, 2011, www.hrreporter.com/articleview/11315-almost-one-half-of-workers-know-someone-who-lied-on-resum (accessed January 9, 2012).

ResumeCompanion

www.resumecompanion.com

Mohawk College

www.mohawkcollege.ca/
student-engagement/student-
graduate-employment/
create-resume.html

survey indicates that 45% of individuals in the 18 to 34 age range "stretch" the truth on their résumés.[42] Ethics in HRM 4.1 also describes these situations.

Résumés are prepared by the applicant and provide job-related information about the job seeker. A résumé will usually contain sections on work experience, education, volunteer activities, and personal interests. In preparing and presenting résumés, applicants can display their creativity in how they present themselves.

Students can practise reading and analyzing résumés online at these sites:

- www.resumecompanion.com
- www.mohawkcollege.ca/student-engagement/student-graduate-employment/
  create-resume.html

Live Career
www.livecareer.com

Career Magazine
www.careermag.com

JobStar
jobstar.org/tools/resume/
index.php

- www.livecareer.com
- www.careermag.com
- jobstar.org/tools/resume/index.php

Many managers remain unclear about the questions they can ask on an application form. While most know they should steer clear of such issues as age, race, marital status, and sexual orientation, other issues are less clear. The following are some suggestions for putting together an application form:

- *Application date*. The applicant should date the application. This piece of information helps managers know when the form was completed and gives them an idea of the time limit (e.g., one year) that the form should be on file.
- *Educational background*. The applicant should also provide grade school, high school, college, and university attendance—but not the dates attended, since that can be connected with age.
- *Experience*. Virtually any questions that focus on work experience related to the job are permissible.
- *Arrests and criminal convictions*. Questions about arrests, convictions, and criminal records are to be avoided. If bonding is a requirement, ask if the individual can be bonded.
- *Country of citizenship*. Such questions are not permitted. It is allowable to ask if the person is legally entitled to work in Canada.
- *References*. It is both permissible and advisable that the names, addresses, and phone numbers of references be provided. (References are covered in more detail below.)
- *Disabilities*. Employers should avoid asking applicants if they have physical disabilities or health problems, if they have ever received psychiatric care or have been hospitalized, or if they have received workers' compensation.

Look at Emerging Trends 4.1 for the latest techniques used in developing résumés.

The Employment Interview

Traditionally, the employment interview has played a very important role in the selection process—so much so that it is rare to find an instance where an employee is hired without some sort of interview. Depending on the type of job, applicants may be interviewed by one person, by members of a work team, or by other individuals in the organization. While researchers have raised some doubts about its validity, the interview remains a mainstay of selection because (1) it is especially practical when there are only a few applicants; (2) it serves other purposes, such as public relations; and (3) interviewers maintain great faith and confidence in their judgments. Nevertheless, the interview can be plagued by problems of subjectivity and personal bias. In such cases, some interviewers' judgments are more valid than those of others in the evaluation of applicants. Remember, the purpose of the interview is to gather relevant information to determine whether the candidate has the skills, abilities, and knowledge to be successful on the job in the organization. However, it is also critical that the interview questions are based on the work requirements (as determined through the job analysis) and specific knowledge required for the job. The interviewer needs to have been appropriately trained to ensure that the interviewer isn't being influenced by the candidate's appearance or how well spoken the candidate is.[43]

Outcome 8

What are the different methods and questions for conducting employment interviews?

Interviewing Methods

Employment or selection interviews differ according to the methods used to obtain information and to find out an applicant's attitudes, feelings, and behaviours. Organizations have a variety of methods to choose from. Further, depending on the number of interviews, more than one method may be used.

1. *Quick response codes (QR).* While the marketing field has used barcodes in linking ads to consumers, organizations can also make use of QR to target applicants with information not easily conveyed in print. Such a tool will move the mobile smartphone to the platform of choice for recruitment.

2. *Smartphone apps.* Both job seekers and employers are making use of apps. Job seekers can apply wherever they happen to be, and employers can manage postings through mobile apps.

3. *Video résumés.* With the evolution of so many different technologies, job seekers, especially those in creative fields, are using video technology to present their résumés. While there can be a number of legal issues associated with this for the potential employer, it has had some appeal for certain organizations. Employers also have tools that allow them to assess the candidates' by using pop-up video comments while reviewing the résumé.

4. *Use of keywords.* Companies that use sophisticated software to match a person's résumé to the opportunities within the organization will frequently screen or use "keywords" in the matching process. The technology behind this is very similar to that used by students when doing an electronic database or Google search.

5. *Increased use of social networks.* More and more job seekers are using their contacts on social networks to get both recommendations and to post their résumés. Likewise, many organizations will search the various social network sites to gather information about applicants.

Sources: Adapted from "The Role of QR Codes," *The Globe and Mail*, December 5, 2011, B10; Sarah Dobson, "Recruitment technology evolving," *Canadian HR Reporter*, April 5, 2010, www.hrreporter.com/articleview/7693-recruitment-technology-evolving (accessed January 9, 2012); Jennifer Ricci, "How is HR using social media?" *Canadian HR Reporter*, November 21, 2011, www.hrreporter.com/articleview/11771-how-is-hr-using-social-media (accessed January 9, 2012); and Michelle V. Rafter, "Six Facebook Recruiting Apps," *Workforce*, December 9, 2011, www.workforce.com/article/20111209/NEWS02/111209953/six-facebook-recruiting-apps (accessed January 9, 2012).

ONE-ON-ONE Most often, the first face-to-face interview occurs between the applicant and an interviewer. The interviewer could be an HR professional or a supervisor. Questions are asked and observations are made of both the interviewer and the applicant. The structure of the questions could be behavioural description interview (BDI), situational, or non-directive. (The different types of questions are explained below.)

Panel interview
An interview in which a board of interviewers questions and observes a single candidate

PANEL OR GROUP INTERVIEW This type of interview involves a panel of interviewers who question and observe a single candidate. In a typical **panel** (or **group**) **interview**, the candidate meets with several interviewers who take turns asking questions. After the interview, the interviewers pool their observations to reach a consensus about the suitability of the candidate. It is reported that when people work together as a team, having some of the team members form the interview panel is particularly useful as questions regarding experience in working in a team can be asked of the candidates.[44] During the interview, the panel may use structured questions, situational questions, BDI questions, or a combination of all three.

TELEPHONE INTERVIEW Generally, organizations are doing more interviews today than they have done in the past. Much of this is caused by the need to make a better hire decision than in the past. Companies have assessed that a poor decision can be very costly and want to minimize the costs. Therefore, many companies use a telephone interview as the first interview in the screening process. This interview can be conducted by someone from the company, or with the advent of technology, companies can use software where applicants are asked to respond to questions by touching a keypad.

INTERNET-BASED INTERVIEW   The increased use of technology has not only helped in creating a way to recruit job applicants, technology has also enabled organizations to pre-screen or assess applicants online. A growing number of organizations have been using online assessment tools to help with the interview process. Some companies will assess online using the GMA (general mental ability) tool or personality profiles. Sometimes, the candidates are asked to answer a series of multiple-choice questions tailored to the job. These answers are compared either with an ideal profile or with the profiles developed on the basis of other candidates' responses. Using computer-based technology can also assist in filtering out unqualified candidates. Monster makes use of online interviewing; given that its business is Web-based services, this practice is consistent with its use of technology.[45] Depending on the company and software in use, a computer interview conducted in conjunction with online tests can measure everything from contradictory responses to time delays related to answering to the applicants' keyboarding skills.

In addition to the benefits of objectivity, some research evidence suggests that applicants may be less likely to engage in "impression management" in computerized interviews than in face-to-face interviews. Using such technology is typically at the initial stages of the interview process.[46]

Types of Interview Questions

Regardless of the type of interview method used, questions must be asked of the applicant. In addition, for an interview to be reliable, the questions must be stated in such a way that the same questions are asked of each applicant. The questions can be very specific to get specific answers (structured), or they can be less structured where broad and open-ended questions are asked. Listed below are the types of interview questions typically used.

STRUCTURED QUESTIONS   Since the objective of an interview is to gather data for making a decision, companies will look at the interview process as an investment and therefore create structured questions to determine if the person has the competencies to do the work.[47] Because structured questions are based on job requirements and an established set of answers against which applicant responses can be rated, they provide a more consistent basis for evaluating job candidates. Structured questions are more likely to provide the type of information needed for making sound decisions. They also help to reduce the possibility of legal charges of discrimination. Employers must be aware that any interview is highly vulnerable to legal attack and that more challenges (human rights and grievances) in this area can be expected in the future. The two main types of structured questions are discussed below.

Behavioural description interview (BDI)
Question about what a person did in a given situation

The leading type of interview question being used is a **behavioural description interview (BDI)**. A BDI question focuses on real-work incidents, not hypothetical situations as a situational interview question does. The BDI format asks job applicants what they did in a given situation. For example, to assess a potential manager's ability to handle a problem employee, an interviewer might ask, "Tell me about the last time you disciplined an employee." Or the format might be this sequence:

1. Describe a situation when you disciplined an employee.
2. What was the action taken?
3. What were the results?

Manager's Toolkit 4.3 provides an example of a BDI question and approach for interviewing someone for a front-desk position in a hotel.

Such an approach to interviewing is based on solid research that past performance is the best predictor of future performance. You will notice that with this type of interview, the questions can produce a variety of responses. The interviewer usually will clarify or ask further questions to get the necessary information. Many more organizations are using BDI questions to better assess the applicant's ability to perform successfully in the organization's environment. If you have recently looked for work, you may have encountered BDI questions.

SAMPLE BDI INTERVIEW QUESTION

You are being considered for work in our hotel. As we encounter difficult situations with our customers, please describe a time you had to tell a customer that there was no reservation for a room. What action did you take? What were the results?

Some additional clarification might be gained from the following questions:

Was there any aspect of your decision that you were uncertain about?

Did the customer have information that you didn't have?

Could anyone overhear the customer?

What decision did you finally make?

This type of interview question is being used more for a number of reasons:

1. Answers can provide a rich source of information. Questions are based on the job requirements directly related to the skills and competencies needed to successfully perform the work.
2. Responses provide a clear view of the candidate's past behaviour and results.
3. Responses provide consistency to selection process due to format of questions.
4. Answers are noted and rated based on previously established guidelines.
5. Provides a high degree of validity when done properly.[48]

Situational question
Question in which an applicant is given a hypothetical incident and asked how he or she would respond to it

Another variation of a structured question is called a **situational question**. With this type of question, an applicant is given a hypothetical incident and asked to respond to it. The applicant's response is then evaluated relative to pre-established benchmark standards. Interestingly, many organizations are using situational questions to select new college graduates. Manager's Toolkit 4.4 shows a sample situational question used to select systems analysts at a chemical plant.

UNSTRUCTURED QUESTIONS These types of questions are broad and open-ended and allow the candidate to talk freely with little interruption from the interviewer. For example, an interviewer might ask: "Tell me more about your experiences on your

SAMPLE SITUATIONAL INTERVIEW QUESTION

QUESTION:

You work in an environment where deadlines are part of everyone's work. The project you are working on has a deadline that you feel is not realistic. What would you do in this situation?

RECORD ANSWER:

_____

_____

_____

SCORING GUIDE:

Good: "I would discuss the situation with my teammates to get feedback on whether my conclusion is accurate."

Good: "I would bring my concern to the project manager and work out a suitable solution."

Fair: "I would let the team know of my concerns but do the best I can."

Poor: "I would ignore my concerns."

last job." Through these questions, the applicant is allowed a great deal of latitude in guiding the discussions. Generally, the non-directive interviewer listens carefully and does not argue, interrupt, or change the subject abruptly. The interviewer also uses follow-up questions to allow the applicant to elaborate, makes only brief responses, and permits pauses in the conversation—the pausing technique is the most difficult for the beginning interviewer to master. A study conducted by the University of Western Ontario indicated that unstructured questions could have inconsistent and subjective responses that can disadvantage minority candidates, particularly for those organizations with employment equity programs.[49]

WHICH TYPE OF QUESTIONS TO USE?   The greater freedom afforded to the applicant in the non-directive interview is particularly valuable in bringing to the interviewer's attention any information, attitudes, or feelings that may often be concealed by more structured questioning. However, because the applicant determines the course of the interview and no set procedure is followed, little information that comes from these interviews enables interviewers to cross-check agreement with other interviewers.

Thus, the reliability and validity of the non-directive interview may be expected to be minimal. Based on experiences in hiring, it is probably a better approach to use both types of questions—structured to get good information about skills and competencies to do the work and unstructured to help in determining the candidate's fit in the organization.[50]

Guidelines for Employment Interviewers

Studies on the employment interview tend to look at questions such as "What traits can be assessed in the interview?" and "How do interviewers reach their decisions?" The purpose of the studies is to assess how an interview can be structured to improve the overall process. Manager's Toolkit 4.5 presents some of the major findings of these studies. It shows that information is available that can be used to increase the validity of interviews.

Training has been shown to dramatically improve the competence of interviewers. If not done on a continuing basis, training should at least be done periodically for managers, supervisors, and HR representatives who conduct interviews. Interviewer training programs should include practice interviews conducted under guidance. Some variation in technique is only natural. However, the following list presents 10 ground rules for employment interviews that are commonly accepted and supported by research findings.

1. *Establish an interview plan.* Determine the areas and specific questions to be covered. Review job requirements, application or résumé data, test scores, and other available information before seeing the applicant.
2. *Establish and maintain rapport.* Greet the applicant pleasantly, explain the purpose of the interview, display sincere interest in the applicant, and listen carefully.
3. *Be an active listener.* Strive to understand, comprehend, and gain insight into what is only suggested or implied. A good listener's mind is alert, and facial expressions and posture usually reflect this fact.
4. *Pay attention to nonverbal cues.* An applicant's facial expressions, gestures, body position, and movements often provide clues to that person's attitudes and feelings. Interviewers should be aware of what they themselves are communicating nonverbally. However, be cautious as to your interpretation of nonverbal cues as some cultures, such as First Nations, are more comfortable with silence.
5. *Provide information as freely and honestly as possible.* Answer the applicant's questions fully and frankly. Present a realistic picture of the job.
6. *Use questions effectively.* To obtain a truthful answer, questions should be phrased as objectively as possible, giving no indication of what response is desired.
7. *Separate facts from inferences.* During the interview, record factual information. Later, record inferences or interpretations of the facts. Compare inferences with those of other interviewers.
8. *Recognize biases and stereotypes.* One typical bias is for interviewers to consider strangers who have interests, experiences, and backgrounds similar to their own to

MANAGER'S TOOLKIT **4.5**

WHAT ARE SOME OF THE FINDINGS FROM RESEARCH STUDIES ON THE INTERVIEW?

1. Understand that there is difficulty in gathering the right information and in making an informed decision.

2. Use appropriate and good questions to get the necessary information. Structured interviews are more reliable than unstructured interviews.

3. Review candidate information (such as résumé) after the interview. To do so prior to interview can lead to certain impressions and therefore certain conclusions, such as where the person went to school.

4. Impressions and judgments need to come from the interview and applications or résumés.

5. Take time to come to a conclusion—don't make early judgments.

6. Observe the behaviour and actions of the candidate during the interview. Sometimes, candidates will behave in a way intended to strengthen their credentials, for example, name-dropping or projecting an image of the ideal candidate.

7. Look for information outside the interview to confirm conclusions and perceptions.

8. Practise asking questions before the interview.

9. Ask questions to determine fit with the organization—particularly about interpersonal skills and motivation.

10. Allow the applicant time to talk that provides a larger behaviour sample.

11. Be aware that nonverbal as well as verbal interactions influence decisions.

Sources: Adapted from Allen Hullcutt, "From science to practice," *Canadian HR Reporter*, June 6, 2011, www.hrreporter.com/articleview/ 10442-from-science-to-practice (accessed January 10, 2012); Scott Erker, "Do's and don'ts of recruitment," *Canadian HR Reporter*, November 15, 2010, www.hrreporter.com/articleview/8457-dos-and-donts-of-recruitment (accessed January 10, 2012); and Brian W. Swider, Murray R. Barrick, T. Brad Harris, and Adam C. Stoverink, "Managing and Creating an Image in the Interview," *Journal of Applied Psychology*, Vol. 96, No. 6 (2011): 1275–1288.

be more acceptable. Stereotyping involves forming generalized opinions of how people of a given gender, race, or ethnic background appear, think, feel, and act. Also, interviewers will sometimes rate one competency, such as leadership, very high and assume that all other competencies are equally as high (halo effect). Likewise, an interviewer may consider all competencies average even though there is evidence of either poor or excellent job performance (central tendency).

9. *Control the course of the interview.* Stick to the interview plan. Provide the applicant with ample opportunity to talk, but maintain control of the situation in order to gather the information required.

10. *Standardize the questions asked.* To increase reliability and avoid discrimination, ask the same questions of all applicants for a particular job. Keep careful notes; record facts, impressions, and any relevant information, including what was told to the applicant. As noted earlier, structured questions and preparation are good ways of ensuring you obtain the information you are seeking.

Employers have found it advisable to provide interviewers with instructions on how to avoid potentially discriminatory questions in their interviews. The examples of appropriate and inappropriate questions shown in Figure 4.4 may serve as guidelines for application forms as well as pre-employment interviews. Complete guidelines may be developed from current information available from the office of the Canadian Human Rights Commission (or check (**www.chrc-ccdp.gc.ca**). Once the individual is hired, the information needed but not asked in the interview may be obtained if there is a valid need for it and if it does not lead to discrimination.

As a final helpful hint for interviews, applicants need to be provided with information on all aspects of the job, both desirable and undesirable (called a realistic job preview), so

Canadian Human Rights Commission

www.chrc-ccdp.gc.ca

FIGURE 4.4　Appropriate and Inappropriate Interview Questions

	Appropriate Questions	Inappropriate Questions
National or ethnic origin	Are you legally entitled to work in Canada?	Where were you born?
Age	Have you reached the minimum or maximum age for work, as defined by the law?	How old are you?
Sex	How would you like to be referred to during the interview?	What are your childcare arrangements?
Marital status	As travel is part of the requirement of our position, would you foresee any problems meeting this obligation?	What does your spouse do for a living? Is there travel involved? Who takes care of the children when you are away?
Disabilities	Do you have any conditions that could affect your ability to do the job?	Do you use drugs or alcohol?
Height and weight	(Ask nothing.)	How tall are you? How much do you weigh?
Address	What is your address?	What were your addresses outside Canada?
Religion	Would you be able to work the following schedules?	What are your religious beliefs?
Criminal record	Our job requires that our employees be bonded.	Are you bondable? Have you ever been arrested?
Affiliations	As an engineer, are you a member of the engineering society?	What religious associations do you belong to?

that they may opt out of the selection process if they feel they would not be satisfied with the job. This reality check helps avoid production losses and costs associated with low job satisfaction which can result in the person leaving the organization.

Employment Assessments

An employment assessment is an objective and standardized way to assess a person's KSAs, competencies, and other characteristics in relation to other individuals.[51] When an organization decides to use a particular employment assessment or test, it is critical that the attribute or skill being tested is used in the work. For example, if someone's keyboarding skills are tested and yet the job doesn't have any tasks that require keyboarding, it would be inappropriate to use that test. Again, the purpose of tests is to gather additional information on the candidate so that job performance in the organization can be predicted.

As mentioned earlier in this chapter, there continues to be concerns about the reliability and validity of employment tests. The concern is focused on whether these tests are biased and appropriate for the job under consideration.[52] In a court decision in 2010, the court held that the written examination of applicants for a firefighter position adversely affected certain minority groups.[53] While an organization is certainly able to design and use any test it so chooses, without ensuring the validity and reliability of the test through on-the-job performance over time, employers are creating legal challenges for themselves.[54]

Organizations use assessments/tests to gather more in-depth information on applicants.[55] However, the information from the assessment will not be useful if there are challenges of bias and discrimination. To better understand the legal implications of pre-employment testing, read HRM and the Law 4.1.

Outcome 9

What is the value of different types of employment tests?

Types of Employment Assessments/Tests

Employment assessments/tests may be classified in different ways. Generally, they are viewed as measuring either **aptitude** (capacity to learn or acquire skills) or **achievement** (what a person knows or can do right now).

HRM and the Law 4.1

WAS THIS DISCRIMINATION?

When making a hiring decision, managers must ensure that the use of pre-employment assessments do not create a complaint of discrimination. In a case involving the Toronto District School Board and an applicant, it was determined by the Ontario Human Rights Tribunal that while the assessment was valid and reliable, pre-employment accommodation needed to be done with that particular applicant.

Specifically, the applicant, with a diagnosed learning disability and attention-deficit disorder, applied for a part-time caretaker role. As part of the screening process, the employer used literacy and numeracy assessments. The applicant informed the school board of the learning disability and asked that there be some accommodation to write the test: specifically, to write in a separate room, to have someone break down the questions so that they could be understood, and to use a calculator. The applicant was informed that the board does not accommodate. The person administering the tests suggested that the applicant just write the tests, see what the results were, and then further consider any accommodation needs. The applicant felt that this was being "set up to fail."

At the time of the application, the job seeker was working with an agency that assists adults with learning disabilities. The executive director of the agency contacted the school board, confirmed the need for accommodation, and indicated that medical documentation could be provided. Even after the documentation was received and reviewed, the school board refused to provide accommodation.

In making its decision, the tribunal first determined that the applicant had been discriminated against in the application process. The tribunal indicated that the applicant had a documented learning disability that makes it difficult to perform on written tests without assistance and that to be forced to do so would mean that the applicant would perform poorly. The tribunal concluded that the applicant had fulfilled the responsibility by informing the school board that accommodation was required. While the tribunal accepted that to do so for a pre-employment screening test would be difficult, such accommodation could have occurred. Finally, the tribunal confirmed that the employer did not seek information about the nature of the disability, as it was required to.

And the consequence of this decision to the Toronto District School Board? The tribunal awarded $7,500 in compensation to the job applicant for injury to dignity.

1. Given what you were informed about in Chapter 2 on accommodation, do you think the decision is reasonable? Why?

2. What are some of the potential issues with other candidates who do not or may not be aware of the ability to seek accommodation when being assessed for a job?

Source: Human Rights Tribunal of Ontario, David Mazzei, Applicant, and Toronto District School Board, Melanie Stoughton and Silvana Filice, Respondents, February 24, 2011, TR-0527-09, 2011 HRTO 400.

Aptitude tests
Measures of a person's capacity to learn or acquire skills

Achievement tests
Measures of what a person knows or can do right now

COGNITIVE ABILITY TESTS   Cognitive ability tests measure mental capabilities, such as general intelligence, verbal fluency, numerical ability, and reasoning ability. A variety of tests— both paper and pencil and computer administered—measure cognitive abilities, including the General Aptitude Test Battery (GATB), the Graduate Management Aptitude Test (GMAT), the Bennett Mechanical Comprehension Test, and the Wonderlic Cognitive Ability. Figure 4.5 shows some items that could be used to measure different cognitive abilities.

Although cognitive ability tests can be developed to measure specialized areas such as reading comprehension and spatial relations, many experts believe that the validity of cognitive ability tests simply reflects their connection to general intelligence. Measures of general mental abilities have been shown to be good predictors of performance, as well as career success and job satisfaction.[56] Generally speaking, while cognitive ability tests are highly predictive of the applicants' performance on the job, frequently these tests are viewed as unfair—by both managers and candidates.[57] Further, there is some evidence suggesting that cognitive ability tests may create lower levels of minority representation.[58]

FIGURE 4.5 Sample Measures of Cognitive Ability

Verbal	1. What is the meaning of the word "surreptitious"?

    a. covert   c. lively
    b. winding   d. sweet

2. How is the noun clause used in the following sentence? "I hope that I can learn this game."

    a. subject   c. direct object
    b. predicate nominative   d. object of the preposition

Quantitative   3. Divide 50 by 0.5 and add 5. What is the result?

    a. 25   c. 95
    b. 30   d. 105

4. What is the value of 144^2?

    a. 12   c. 288
    b. 72   d. 20736

Reasoning   5. _____ is to boat as snow is to _____ .

    a. Sail, ski   c. Water, ski
    b. Water, winter   d. Engine, water

6. Two women played 5 games of chess. Each woman won the same number of games, yet there were no ties. How can this be?

    a. There was a forfeit.   c. They played different people.
    b. One player cheated.   d. One game is still in progress.

Mechanical   7. If gear A and gear C are both turning counterclockwise, what is happening to gear B?

    a. It is turning counterclockwise.   c. It remains stationary.
    b. It is turning clockwise.   d. The whole system will jam.

Answers: 1. a, 2. c, 3. d, 4. d, 5. c, 6. c, 7. b

One of the more interesting uses for measuring general mental ability is with the National Football League. Recently, it began using the Wonderlic to measure the brainpower of its recruits to ensure that they can keep up with both the physical and mental demands of the game.[59]

PERSONALITY AND INTEREST INVENTORIES Whereas cognitive ability tests measure a person's mental capacity, personality tests measure personal characteristics such as extroversion, agreeableness, and openness to experience. While the ability of such tests to predict job performance has been quite low, recent research indicates that people tend to blame themselves and react inappropriately when something goes wrong. This type of awareness can be useful when assessing candidates for managerial roles.[60] Personality tests can be problematic if they inadvertently discriminate against individuals who would otherwise perform effectively. Therefore, although it is generally not recommended that personality tests be used for background information when selecting employees, they can be very useful as part of a career development program.[61]

EMOTIONAL INTELLIGENCE/EMOTIONAL AND SOCIAL COMPETENCE One of the newer, and greatly debated, types of employment tests measures the emotional intelligence of the applicant—particularly for leadership roles. Emotional intelligence (EI) has many definitions, but the one most commonly used describes it as a personal set of qualities that are distinct from cognitive ability and important for success.[62] With the

Some employers use tests, such as keyboarding, to provide additional information for making a selection decision.

debate also comes additional research. The researchers, including those who originally developed the concept, believe that there is more to success at work than mere intellect. As such, the concept of EI is evolving into "emotional and social competence," or ESC. and that ESC consists of personality characteristics and is not just a single measurement.[63] As a result of the emerging research, it is questionable as to whether one type of employment assessment can measure ESC and suggests that what may be better is a set of different tests that measure the broad spectrum of personality and social competence. The research also suggests that emotional and social competence is more appropriately assessed for leadership roles.[64]

PHYSICAL ABILITY TESTS   In addition to learning about a job candidate's mental capabilities, employers may need to assess a person's physical abilities. Particularly for demanding and potentially dangerous jobs like those held by firefighters and truck drivers, physical abilities such as strength and endurance tend to be good predictors of performance on the job, but possibly also of ability to minimize injuries on the job.[65] A physical ability test is not the same as a medical exam. Some organizations may still require a medical exam before actually starting employment to ensure that there is no medical condition that could preclude the employee from successfully performing the work. However, many organizations are no longer doing medical exams due to privacy issues or potential challenges of discrimination.

JOB SAMPLE TESTS   Job sample tests, or work sample tests, require the applicant to perform tasks that are a part of the work required on the job. Like job knowledge tests, job sample tests are constructed from a carefully developed outline that, experts agree, includes the major job functions; the tests are thus considered content valid. They are often used to measure skills for office and clerical jobs. Job sample tests have been devised for many diverse jobs: a map-reading test for traffic control officers, a lathe test for machine operators, a complex coordination test for pilots, an in-basket test for managers, a group discussion test for supervisors, a judgment and decision-making test for administrators, to name a few.

SUBSTANCE ABUSE (DRUG AND ALCOHOL) TESTING   The Canadian Human Rights Commission and some of its provincial counterparts have issued policies on employment-related drug testing. Generally speaking, an employer in Canada, compared to its U.S. counterparts, cannot do random substance abuse testing, even in safety-sensitive work environments, and if it does so the employer is at risk of challenges.[66] Addiction to drugs or alcohol is considered a disability, and the employer is to be guided by legislation and by practices such as workplace accommodation. For example, Rio Tinto Alcan recently lost an arbitration regarding a drug and alcohol abuse policy. The policy provided treatment to employees with substance abuse problems and said that if any impairment was noted on the job, the supervisor had to remove the employee and have the person go through a medical evaluation. The union grieved this latter action, claiming that the medical examination was done without the employee's consent and that the employee could be subject to discipline if refusing to undertake the medical. The arbitration board determined that while the policy had the right intention, the requirement for a medical examination went too far.[67]

If the employer has established that drug testing is job-related—typically, this involves safety issues—the candidate must be informed that job offers are conditional on the successful passing of a drug test and that this test will be required during the course of employment. The employer then has the right to demand a random drug and alcohol test. This right was reaffirmed in a decision in New Brunswick. A pulp and paper company implemented such a policy for safety-sensitive positions. After the policy was implemented, the union grieved the policy, saying that it was unreasonable. The New Brunswick Labour Board upheld the grievance, agreeing with the union. The company appealed the decision to the Queen's Court. After a lengthy hearing, the court agreed with the company that the work environment was dangerous and determined that such a policy was reasonable.[68]

To comply with legal issues in Canada, any policies in relation to substance abuse testing must have a clear and legitimate purpose. As well, the policies must be administered in a reasonable manner, including not being invasive or done in a discriminatory fashion.[69]

Reference Checks

Organizations use a variety of ways to check references, including electronic and telephone. But while references are commonly used to screen and select employees, they have not proved successful for predicting employee performance. Written letters of reference are notoriously inflated, which limits their validity. Generally, telephone checks are preferable because they save time and provide for greater candour. At Intuit, the Edmonton, Alberta, software company that produces Quicken, managerial applicants are asked to provide between five and nine references that are then called and asked specific job-related questions.

An employer has no legal obligation to provide a former employee with a reference. To avoid liability, many employers are providing a perfunctory letter of reference, which supplies only the name, employment dates, last position with the company, and final salary. It is important for employers to be understanding of the handling of reference information so that the employer does not create legal issues for itself. The best way to do this is to have a consent form that the applicant signs that provides the reference names and contact information.[70] By using sources in addition to former employers, organizations can obtain valuable information about an applicant's character and habits. Telephone interviews are most effective, and one key question that is particularly effective in screening is to ask: "Would you rehire this employee?" Some employers prefer to outsource reference checking to professional firms, such as Intelysis Employment Screening Services in Toronto, to obtain as accurate information as possible. A recent survey conducted by Robert Half International, an employment agency, identified that 21% of job seekers were eliminated from consideration after reference checks.[71]

Those individuals supplying references must do so in a responsible manner without making statements that are damaging or cannot be substantiated. To aid employers in ensuring that appropriate reference checks are done, there are a number of companies that

Certain jobs require people who can cope with potentially dangerous situations. The aftermath of this Alberta tornado put workers to the test.

CP PHOTO/Red Deer Advocate/Randy Fiedler

Informed Hiring
www.informedhiring.com

BackCheck
backcheck.net

Hire Performance
www.hireperformance.ca

National Association of Professional Background Screeners
www.napbs.com

provide screening services. Among these are Informed Hiring (**www.informedhiring. com**), BackCheck (**backcheck.net**), and Hire Performance (**www.hireperformance.ca**). With the increasing number of companies that are providing pre-employment screening, the National Association of Professional Background Screeners (**www.napbs.com**) was formed to create and promote standards when screening job applicants.[72]

Inadequate reference checking can contribute to high turnover or difficulties with the employee. Further, organizations could face legal liability issues if inadequate reference checks were done (see Chapter 9). Remember, the reference check is to obtain relevant information to predict whether the person will be a good match with the organization and is capable of performing the work successfully. It is important to remember, though, that reference checking needs to be in relation to the work. For example, Mark's Work Wearhouse in Alberta was banned from having credit checks done on candidates for sales positions.[73] The company indicated that credit checks were important to see whether the salesperson could handle financial responsibilities and identify risk for store theft. The Alberta commission disagreed and determined that this was an invasion of privacy.

A final caution on reference checks: accessing social media sites to see what candidates have posted may not only be inaccurate but it also could be considered an invasion of privacy.[74] There has been sufficient concern on this latter point that the Privacy Commissioner of Alberta issued guidelines for employers using social media for background checks.[75]

Manager's Toolkit 4.6 provides some sample questions to use when doing reference checks.

Reaching a Selection Decision

Although all of the steps in the selection process are important, the most critical step is the decision to accept or reject applicants. Because of the cost of placing new employees on

MANAGER'S TOOLKIT **4.6**

SAMPLE REFERENCE CHECK QUESTIONS

1. How long has the person been employed in your organization?

2. Describe their attendance pattern.

3. Can you give me some examples of how the candidate demonstrated initiative?

4. What are the person's strengths?

5. How did the person get along with others in the work unit?

6. What are some areas the person needs to develop?

7. Was the person successful in their role?

8. Why did the person leave your employment?

9. Would you rehire?

10. Describe the person's ability to work with others or in a team.

Sources: Adapted from Public Service Commission, "The Right Choice!" accessed January 13, 2012, www.psc-cfp.gc.ca/ppc-cpp/acscmptnc-evl-cmptnc/chck-ref-eng.htm; "Sample Reference Check Questions," Best-Job-Interview, accessed January 13, 2012, www.bestjob-interview.com/reference-check-questions.html; and "Conducting Effective Reference Checks," go2hr, accessed January 13, 2012, www.go2hr.ca/ForbrEmployers/Recruitment/ReferenceandBackgroundChecks/tabid/103/Default.aspx.

the payroll, the short probationary period in many organizations, and human rights considerations, the final decision must be as sound as possible. Thus it requires systematic consideration of all the relevant information about applicants. It is common to use summary forms and checklists to ensure that all the pertinent information has been included in the evaluation of applicants.

Summarizing Information about Applicants

Fundamentally, an employer is interested in what an applicant both can do and will do. An evaluation of candidates on the basis of assembled information should focus on these two factors, as shown in Figure 4.6. The "can-do" factors include knowledge and skills, as well as the aptitude (the potential) for acquiring new knowledge and skills. The "will-do" factors include motivation, interests, and other personality characteristics. Both factors are essential to successful performance on the job. The employee who has the ability (can do) but is not motivated to use it (will not do) is little better than the employee who lacks the necessary ability.

Specific criteria must be established under the various factors, especially for the "can-do" factors. For example, if a person is being hired as a call-centre agent, one ability might be to "input data quickly on a computerized system" or the competency of "ability to present a positive voice image." In most call-centre environments, there are performance standards regarding the time it would take to input the average call-centre information and the number of customer complaints. The standards would also identify extremely poor performance. This would then be a specific level below which an applicant would not be deemed suitable for the job.

It is also helpful to remember that summarizing the information about the candidates is not a mechanical process. The decision maker needs to be sure that any employment assessments are appropriate for the work and that any challenges to their use can be defended, that the weighting of any criterion is done consistently for all applicants, and that job performance indicators are appropriate for all stages of the job.[76]

Of primary importance is ensuring that the entire process is well structured. Recent research indicates that by improving the overall structure of the decision process, including structured interview questions, the validity and reliability of the process improves.[77]

A useful approach to ensuring that the criteria are appropriate and conform to legal requirements is the OUCH test: Objective, Uniform in application, Consistent in effect, Has job relatedness.

Making a selection decision is no different than making any other type of management decision: identifying criteria and weighting of the criteria needs to be done. For practice on this, see the exercise at the end of this chapter in "Developing Your Skills."

It is much easier to measure what individuals can do than what they will do. The can-do factors are readily evident from test scores and verified information. What the individual will do can only be inferred. Responses to interview and application-form questions may be used as a basis for obtaining information for making inferences about what an individual will do.

Decision Strategy

The strategy used for making personnel decisions for one category of jobs may differ from that used for another category. The strategy for selecting managerial and executive personnel, for example, will differ from that used in selecting clerical and technical personnel. While many factors are to be considered in hiring decisions, the following are some of the questions that managers must consider:

1. Should the individuals be hired according to their highest potential or according to the existing needs of the organization?
2. At what grade or wage level should the individual be started?
3. Should initial selection be concerned primarily with an ideal match of the employee to the job, or should potential for advancement in the organization be considered?
4. To what extent should those who are not qualified but are qualifiable be considered?
5. Should overqualified individuals be considered?
6. What effect will a decision have on meeting employment equity plans and diversity considerations?

In addition to the above factors, people will typically approach the hiring decision in one of two ways.

One way is a "clinical approach," in which each person involved will use different weights to the applicants' background. This approach can lead to different decisions and frequently demonstrates biases and stereotypes as it is based on personal judgment.

The other type is a "statistical approach," in which criteria for successful job performance are listed and weighting factors are assigned. Information gathered from interviews and assessments are then combined with the person receiving the highest score being offered the job. In this approach, it is important to identify any threshold or cut-off—the point at which a person is no longer considered.

Studies have demonstrated that the statistical approach provides a far better outcome—hiring the best person for the job—than the clinical approach.[78]

The Final Decision

The line manager makes the decision as to who gets hired. Therefore, it is important that the manager understands the importance of the steps necessary to make a good decision. In large organizations, notifying applicants of the decision and making job offers is often

FIGURE 4.6 "Can-Do" and "Will-Do" Factors in Selection

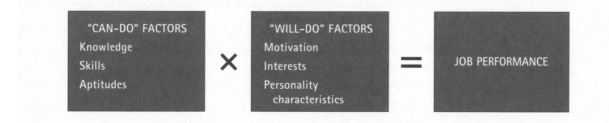

the responsibility of the HR department. This department will confirm the details of the job, working arrangements, wages, and so on, and specify a deadline by which the applicant must reach a decision. In smaller organizations without an HR practitioner, the manager will notify the candidates. Therefore, if there is an HR department, it is valuable to forge a strong partnership with HR in order to gain their valuable technical and legal assistance.

SUMMARY

1. Discuss the steps in human resource planning.
   - Forecast demand for labour in the organization.
   - Determine the supply of labour—both external and internal to the organization.
   - Identify the gap between demand and supply.
   - Develop action plans to close or eliminate the gap.

2. Describe the relationship between planning, recruiting, and selecting people to work with the organization.
   - As organizations plan for their future, supervisors and managers at all levels must play an active role in planning for future people requirements.
   - It is critical that the organization have the right number and types of employees available to implement a chosen business plan.
   - Managers play a key role in planning for the human resources necessary to achieve the business plan.

3. Compare the advantages and disadvantages of recruiting from within the organization.
   - By recruiting from within, an organization can capitalize on previous investments made in recruiting, selecting, training, and developing its current employees.
   - Internal promotions can reward employees for past performance and send a signal to other employees that their future efforts will pay off.
   - A disadvantage can be the inbreeding of ideas and attitudes.

4. Outline the advantages and disadvantages of external recruitment.
   - External recruitment can bring in new ideas and acquire people with specialized skills.
   - Constraints on the organization, such as a legislated employment equity plan, may lead to a different pool of applicants than what the manager may want.

5. Explain the objectives of the selection process.
   - The selection process attempts to get the right person with the right skills at the right time in the right job.

6. Describe the typical steps in the selection process.
   - Typical steps start with the receipt of an application form, then an initial interview, possible employment tests, an interview with the supervisor, reference checks, and then a hiring decision.

7. Identify the various sources of information used for selection decisions.
   - Interviews
   - Application forms or résumés
   - References
   - Employment tests

8. Discuss the different methods and types of questions for conducting an employment interview.
   - One-on-one, where there is only the candidate and one interviewer.
   - Panel or group, where more than one interviewer is present.
   - Telephone, where an initial screening is done.
   - Internet, where a variety of technologies, including video streaming, is used.
   - Unstructured, wherein the interviewer is free to pursue whatever approach and sequence of topics might seem appropriate.
   - Structured, wherein each applicant receives the same set of questions, which have pre-established answers.
   - Situational, in which candidates are asked about hypothetical situations and how they would handle them.
   - Behavioural descriptions of previous work experiences.

9. Illustrate the value of different types of employment tests.
   - More objective than the interview.
   - Can provide a broader sampling of behaviour and skills.

NEED TO KNOW

- Purpose of human resource planning
- Definition of recruitment
- Various recruitment sources
- Definition and purpose of selection
- Typical steps in selection process
- Types of interview methods and questions

NEED TO UNDERSTAND

- Advantages and disadvantages of internal or external recruitment
- Use of tests and interviews in selection decision
- Applications and interview questions in relation to human rights legislation
- Importance of good decision making in hiring

KEY TERMS

achievement tests 135

aptitude tests 135

behavioural description interview (BDI) 130

human resource planning 108

internal job posting 115

labour market 116

management forecasts 110

Markov analysis 111

panel interview 129

recruitment 113

reliability 126

selection 125

situational question 131

skills inventory 111

staffing table 111

trend analysis 110

validity 126

REVIEW QUESTIONS

1. Why is human resource planning important?
2. What are the various approaches to planning?
3. What are the comparative advantages and disadvantages of filling openings from internal sources? from external sources?
4. If you were looking to hire for the following jobs, where might you recruit? (List both internal and external sources.)
   - Call centre operator
   - IT data administrator
   - Sales associate for retail

- Labourer
- Massage therapist
- Electrician

5. Discuss some of the employment problems faced by new immigrants to Canada.
6. What are the interviewing methods described? Which method would you prefer and why?
7. Describe the guidelines for a successful employment interview.
8. What are the criticisms of employment testing?

CRITICAL THINKING QUESTIONS

1. You have recently applied for work at a medium-size home improvement store as an experienced warehouse worker. Part of the screening process will include a group interview with some of the people you would be working with. What questions do you think they will ask you? What questions would you ask of them?
2. You have recently purchased a small company that packages organic greens. The company is getting ready to expand into another province and you need the following positions filled:

   - purchasing agent
   - customer service representative
   - labourer

   Identify two or three key job requirements for each position and then develop the selection criteria for each requirement. What selection tools or techniques would you use to assess each criterion?
3. You have just been asked to assist in hiring a new receptionist for a small graphics company. However, before starting the process, the owner of the company wants to know how much time it will take, what the cost will be, and where candidates might be located. Estimate the number of staff hours and the cost, and determine where applicants might be sourced.
4. You have recently applied for a retail sales position in a clothing store and have been asked to supply the names of references. What would the references say about you for this work?

DEVELOPING YOUR SKILLS

Jung Typology Test

www.humanmetrics.com/
cgi-win/JTypes2.asp

**The Big Five
Personality Test**

www.outofservice.com/bigfive

EasyJob Resume Builder

www.easyjobresumebuilder
.com

resume-now

resume-now.com

1. Here is your opportunity to take personality tests. Access the Jung Typology Test at Human Metrics and access The Big Five Personality Test. Complete each online assessment. Review the results. Is this consistent with your understanding and awareness of yourself? Are there any surprises? If so, what are they?
2. Working in groups of four or five, list three recent times you have been interviewed. Working with this list, identify the type of interview conducted. Determine whether the interview questions were appropriate for the work and whether or not the interview was effective in attracting you to work for the organization.
3. Working in pairs, one person will access **easyjobresumebuilder.com** and click on the link "Resume Samples," and the other person will access **resume-now.com** and click on "Create Resume." For EasyJob Resume Builder, pick one of the related links with sample résumés. Review the sample résumé and then prepare your résumé. For resume-now, follow the instructions and prepare a résumé. Bring your résumé to class. Working in your pair, critique each other's résumé, and identify what is similar and what is different in the formatting of each. Share your findings with the rest of the class.
4. Access the corporate Web site for Bombardier, one of Canada's premier aerospace and transportation companies, at **bombardier.com** and click on the link "Careers." Watch the short video and read the rest of the information about working at Bombardier.

Prepare a one- to two-page summary explaining why you would or would not want to work there. Comment on how effective the video was in helping you make your decision.

Case Study **1**

What an Approach to Recruitment!

Most of us have looked for work by reading newspapers, checking online job postings, attending job fairs, and looking at specific company Web sites. When attending a job fair, have you ever received a promotional item as part of the "pitch"?

Veterans Affairs Canada (VAC) is the agency responsible for providing programs and services to individuals who served in Canada's armed forces. The programs and services are diverse and include the provision of disability pensions, health care, and career transition services. According to the VAC, many of its positions require postsecondary education; therefore, it frequently uses university recruitment as a way to attract the talent it seeks. During the on-campus recruitment sessions, the recruitment team describes types of roles that range from client services agent (point of first contact with VAC) to communications staff to physicians. In addition to information about the various jobs, the agency describes the types of development and mentoring provided.

As part of the recruitment efforts directed toward students, VAC has provided a variety of items as giveaways. Among these are pens, sticky notes, and clocks that VAC determined students would use. It hoped that through these items, students would remember the experience every time they used the item.

However, as VAC is expecting many employees to retire in the next several years, it decided it needed something more to attract the candidates with the skill sets it was looking for. VAC decided that it needed to provide something else that would catch student attention, involve them while speaking to a recruiter, and remember VAC when making decisions about where to seek work. The recruitment team worked with a company that supplies promotional items and determined that a touchable puzzle would do the trick. The puzzle could be swivelled and twisted as well as taken apart and reassembled. Various links in the puzzle have information—the Web address repeated several times, a Canadian flag, and key messages.

But did the approach work?

According to the recruitment team, the puzzle achieved exactly what the team wanted: students paying attention to and following up on career opportunities at Veterans Affairs Canada.

Questions

1. What competitive advantages do you see in using items as giveaways as part of a recruitment process?
2. How effective do you feel such an approach would be over time?
3. If you received a giveaway in a campus recruitment drive by any organization, would that influence you about looking for work there? Why or why not?

Case Study 2

Can We Hire and Still Save Money?

Employers are always challenged by the need to add staff while not having the financial resources to do so. The issue of whether new staff can be productive enough to ensure that the organization prospers is ever present.

But one company did just that. The company, a large retailer in Canada, entered into a long-term relationship with a vendor whose product focused on systematic improvements to quality, reliability, and effectiveness of the stores' service representatives. At the time the relationship started, the company was experiencing more than a 200% turnover in its store staff. The first order of business was to stabilize and reduce turnover.

The company decided that to achieve this, it needed to standardize its hiring practices and processes, and that these needed to be developed and implemented in a centralized manner. Even though the stores were geographically distributed, some without Internet capability, and functioning in a decentralized manner, the management team felt that the hiring practices needed to be consistent throughout the organization.

Part of the solution for the management team was to increase the number of job applicants while finding ways to reduce the time each store manager spent on reviewing applications and eliminating those job seekers that would not be a good prospect.

Because the company focused on using more technology to improve the processes, off-site applications were encouraged through use of kiosks in malls and through its Web site. Within three years, the company had doubled the number of job applicants. Not only were there more applicants, but also the technology allowed the screening process to be streamlined so that local store managers spent less time reviewing individual applications.

In addition to the improvement in application numbers, the overall process of screening using the software interface for online applications reduced the amount of time in screening applications. By screening the applicant to previously identified criteria (determined by the performance of successful employees), only those that met the criteria were referred to the store manager. Along with the referral to the store manager, an interview guide with appropriate questions for the applicant was also provided. The interview guide had the applicant's overall profile, including an assessment of the applicant's ranking on the customer service criterion. While a store manager could hire if the applicant's profile was poor, the manager had to get approval to do so from the regional director. In this fashion a specific rationale had to be made on deviating from the approved guidelines.

Because there was a better fit between the new hire and the company, the company retention rate increased. Prior to the new guidelines, 25% of people quit within the first 30 days. After the guidelines, this loss was reduced to 16%. The retention rates also improved steadily, and the turnover rate was cut in half. Further, the retailer determined that it saved more than $3 million each year due to the transactional costs associated with hiring and termination—these are impressive statistics!

Questions

1. Do you think the primary success was due to the technology or the change in hiring processes? Why?
2. What other suggestions might you have to improve the retention rate?
3. Is technology always the right solution to too many applications? Why or why not?

NOTES AND REFERENCES

1. "Top Talent Getting Harder to Find: Survey, *Canadian HR Reporter*, December 12, 2011, www.hrreporter.com/articleview/11936-top-talent-getting-harder-to-find-survey; and "Data Bank Focus: Hiring Future Leaders," *Workforce*, November 16, 2011, www.workforce.com/article/20111116/NEWS02/111119978/data-bank-focus-hiring-future-leaders.

2. "Is Strategic Human Resource Planning the Same as Human Resource Planning?" *Planning Resource Center*, accessed January 3, 2012, http://work911.com/planning-master/faq/hr-strathrplan.htm.

3. Ian J. Cook, "Increasing Engagement in Tough Times," *HRMA People Talk* 16, no. 3 (Fall 2011): 28–29.

4. Karen Pastakia, "Leadership No Game of Chance," *Canadian HR Reporter*, June 6, 2011, accessed January 3, 2012, www.hrreporter.com/articleview/10440-leadership-no-game-of-chance.

5. Amanda Silliker, "Target Sets Sights on Hiring," *Canadian HR Reporter*, September 26, 2011, accessed January 3, 3012, www.hrreporter.com/articleview/11314-target-sets-sights-on-hiring.

6. Statistics Canada, "Study: Projected Trends to 2031 for the Canadian Labour Force," *The Daily*, August 17, 2011, accessed January 3, 3012, www.statcan.gc.ca/daily-quotidien/110817/dq110817b-eng.htm; Statistics Canada, "Study: Delayed Retirement," *The Daily*, October 26, 2011, accessed January 3, 2012, www.statcan.gc.ca/daily-quotidien/111026/dq111026b-eng.htm; Jameson Berkow, "Canadian IT Sector Facing an 'Alarming' Labour Shortage: Report," *Financial Post*, March 29, 2011, accessed January 3, 2012, http://business.financialpost.com/2011/03/29/canadian-it-sector-to-face-alarming-labour-shortages-study/; and Statistics Canada, "Employment by Age, Sex, Type of Work, Class of Worker and Province," November 2011, accessed January 3, 2012, http://www40.statcan.gc.ca/l01/cst01/labr66a-eng.htm.

7. Shannon Klie, "Aboriginals a 'Strategic Imperative,'" *Canadian HR Reporter*, April 25, 2011, accessed January 4, 2012, www.hrreporter.com/articleview/10088-aboriginals-a-strategic-imperative.

8. "Three-Quarters of Small Businesses Lack Succession Plans," *Canadian HR Reporter*, October 17, 2011, accessed January 4, 2012, www.hrreporter.com/articleview/11461-three-quarters-of-small-businesses-lack-succession-plan-survey.

9. Jeff Wiener, "Digitcom Canada Awarded Avaya's SME Canadian Business Partner of the Year Award," October 21, 2010, accessed January 4, 2012, www.thetelecomblog.com/2010/10/21/digitcom-canada-awarded-avaya%E2%80%99s-sme-canadian-business-partner-of-the-year-award/; and information from the Web site of Digitcom Canada (www.digitcom.ca/).

10. "Steady Employment Growth Expected in 2012," *Canadian HR Reporter*, January 3, 2012, accessed January 4, 2012, www.hrreporter.com/articleview/12030-steady-employment-growth-expected-in-2012-survey.

11. "Employee Turnover—How Much Is It Costing You?" *BC Jobs*, accessed January 4, 2012, www.bcjobs.ca/re/hr-resources/human-resource-advice/recruitment-and-retention/employee-turnover—how-much-is-it-costing-you.

12. Tara Carman, "B.C. Faces Vast Labour Shortages Unless It Can Attract More Workers," *The Vancouver Sun*, February 3, 2102, All.

13. Robert Hiltz, "New Rules to Open Border to Skilled Trades," *The Vancouver Sun*, January 30, 2012, B3.

14. Joe Friesen, "Immigration Overhaul to Let Employers Choose Prospects," *The Globe and Mail*, March 2, 2012, A5.

15. "Winning War for Talent," *Financial Post*, September 28, 2011, D6.

16. Garry Kranz, "Special Report on Employee Engagement Losing Lifeblood," *Workforce*, July 22, 2011, www.workforce.com/article/20110721/TOOLS/307219997.

17. Interested readers can check out the Web sites of these companies at www.oracle.com/applications/peoplesoft-enterprise.html and www.sap.com/canada/index.epx.

18. David Burlington, "Unified Talent Management: The Platform Is the Service," *Workforce Management*, accessed January 22, 2009, www.workforce.com/.

19. Robert Cyran, "Yahoo's Hire Is Slap for eBay," *The Globe and Mail*, January 5, 2012, B11.

20. Michelle V. Rafter, "Facebook: The New Recruit in the Recruiting Game," *Workforce*, December 9, 2011, accessed January 5, 2012, www.workforce.com/article/20111209/NEWS02/111209955/facebook-the-new-recruit-in-the-recruiting-game#.

21. Citizenship and Immigration Canada, "Notice—Supplementary Information for the 2012 Immigration Levels Plan," accessed January 5, 2012, www.cic.gc.ca/english/department/media/notices/notice-levels2012.asp.

22. *CBC News Report*, March 29, 2011, accessed January 6, 2012, www.cbc.ca/news/business/story/2011/03/29/labour-shortages.html?ref=rss.

23. Leigh Goessl, "Study Finds Internet Job Search Reduces Time Spent Unemployed," *Digital Journal*, October 5, 2011, accessed January 6, 2012, http://digitaljournal.com/article/312400.

24. Ian Sullivan, "Recruiting via Social Media? Be Honest, Direct," *Canadian HR Reporter*, October 10, 2011, accessed January 6, 2012, www.hrreporter.com/articleview/11413-recruiting-via-social-media-be-honest-direct.

25. Susan Grant, "Technology Streamlines Recruitment," *Canadian HR Reporter*, April 11, 2011, accessed January 7, 2012, www.hrreporter.com/articleview/9962-technology-streamlines-recruitment.

26. Michelle V. Rafter, "Six Facebook Recruiting Apps," *Workforce Management*, December 9, 2011, accessed January 6, 2012, www.workforce.com/article/20111209/NEWS02/111209953/six-facebook-recruiting-apps.

27. "Government of Canada Most Attractive Employer for Students: Survey," *Canadian HR Reporter*, July 21, 2011, accessed January 7, 2012, www.hrreporter.com/articleview/10815-government-of-canada-most-attractive-employer-for-students-survey; and "Canada's Ideal Employers 2011," *Universum*, accessed January 7, 2012, www.universumglobal.com/IDEAL-Employer-Rankings/The-National-Editions/Canadian-Student-Survey.

28. Robin Waghorn, "Internet Puts Spin on Traditional Career Fair," *Canadian HR Reporter*, November 21, 2011, accessed January 6, 2012, www.hrreporter.com/articleview/11769-internet-puts-new-spin-on-traditional-career-fair.

29. Jennifer Salopek, "Employee Referrals Remain a Recruiters Best Friend," *Workforce*, December 6, 2010, accessed January 7, 2012, www.workforce.com/article/20101206/NEWS02/312069996.

30. "Job Search Strategies," accessed January 7, 2012, www.kellyservices.ca/web/ca/services/en/pages/tip_mar10_search_strategies.html; accessed January 7, 2012, www.sasknetwork.gov.sk.ca/html/JobSeekers/lookingforwork/searchstrategies.htm; Career and Employment Services, University of Manitoba, "Job Search Strategies," accessed January 7, 2012, www.umanitoba.ca/student/employment/media/job_search_workbook.pdf; and other similar resources on job search techniques.

31. Tina Mansfield , "Looking for a Job? Building a Digital Resume," *Backbone*, October 15, 2011, 15–17; Eileen Chadnick, "Giving Your CV a Fresh Boost," *The Globe and Mail*, November 23, 2011, B20. For additional sources on writing résumés, see BC Jobs.ca; Youth Canada, "Writing a Resume," www.youth.gc.ca/eng/topics/jobs/resume.shtml; Monster.ca; and "Canada's #1 Online Resume Builder," accessed January 9, 2012, http://www.resume-now.com/default.asp?lp=rnarsmsm31&cobrand=RSMN&tag=120208162909921&hitlogid=91663265&ref=9061&utm_source=PPCg&utm_medium=SEMK&utm_term=writing+resumes&utm_campaign=Canada&match_type=e&ad=11378631331.

32. Sarah Dobson, "Employers Should Start Taking 'Calculated Risks' and Hire More Foreign Workers: Deloitte," *Canadian HR Reporter*, December 5, 2011, 3.

33. Tavia Grant and Rita Trichur, "Shortchanging Immigrants Costs Canada," *The Globe and Mail*, December 17, 2011, B8.

34. Ibid.

35. Amanda Silliker, "Matthew, You're Hired. Good luck Next Time, Samir," *Canadian HR Reporter*, November 21, 2011, 1; and Wallace Immen, "How an Ethnic-Sounding Name May Affect the Job Hunt," *The Globe and Mail*, November 18, 2011, B21.

36. Amanda Silliker, "Making Managers Accountable for Diversity," *Canadian HR Reporter*, August 15, 2011, accessed January 7, 2012, www.hrreporter.com/articleview/10997-making-managers-accountable-for-diversity.

37. Marina Jiménez, "Scoring Points with Newer Canadians," *The Globe and Mail*, March 13, 2009, L1.

38. "About Us," TRIEC, accessed January 7, 2012, http://triec.ca/about-us/.

39. John Ewing, "The First Steps to Growing Your Company," *Green Industry PRO* 10 (October 2011): 11–12.

40. Farah Naqvi, "Competency Mapping and Managing Talent," *Journal of Management Research* 8, no. 1 (2009): 85–94.

41. Christopher M. Berry, Malissa A. Clark, and Tara K. McClure, "Racial/Ethnic Differences in the Criterion-Related Validity of Cognitive Ability Tests," *Journal of Applied Psychology* 96, no. 5 (2011): 881–906.

42. Anne Fisher, "Are Young Job Seekers Less Ethical or Just Desperate?" *Fortune*, July 12, 2011, accessed January 9, 2012, http://management.fortune.cnn.com/2011/07/12/are-young-job-seekers-less-ethical-or-just-desperate/.

43. Kevin Ryan, "Gilt Groupe's CEO on Building a Team of A Players," *Harvard Business Review*, January/February 2012, 43–46.

44. Heather O'Neill, "Building a Sales Team Starts with the First Impression," *Workforce Management*, October 24, 2011, accessed January 9, 2012, www.workforce.com/article/20111024/NEWS02/111029987.

45. Tim Halloran, director of Recruiting, Monster.com, video accessed January 10, 2012, through YouTube and greenjobinterview.com.

46. Nita Wilmott, "Interviewing Styles: Tips for Interview Approaches," About.com: Human Resources, accessed January 10, 2012, http://humanresources.about.com/cs/selectionstaffing/a/interviews.htm.

47. Murray R. Barrick, Brian W. Swider, and Greg L. Stewart, "Initial Evaluations in the Interview," *Journal of Applied Psychology* 95, no. 6 (2010): 1163–72.

48. Hanna Dunn, "Behavioural Interviews Deserve Accolades," *Canadian HR Reporter*, July 12, 2010, accessed January 10, 2012, www.hrreporter.com/articleview/8031-behavioural-interviews-deserve-accolades.

49. "Interview Format Influences Perception of Hiring Fairness: Study," *Canadian HR Reporter*, May 21, 2010, accessed January 10, 2012, www.hrreporter.com/articleview/7872-interview-format-influences-perception-of-hiring-fairness-study.

50. Wallace Immen, "Want Better Employees? Ask Better Questions," *The Globe and Mail*, January 6, 2012, B14.

51. For additional resources on employment testing, see Robert M. Guion, *Assessment, Measurement and Prediction for Personnel Decisions*, 2nd. ed. (New York: Routledge, 2011).

52. Jana Szostek and Charles J. Hobson, "Employment Test Evaluation Made Easy," *Employee Relations Law Journal* 37, no. 2 (Autumn 2011): 67–74.

53. Arthur B. Smith Jr. and Michael H. Cramer, "Supreme Court Rules on Pre-employment Tests and Disparate Impact," *Texas Employment Law*, July 2010, 6.

54. Yanseen Hemeda and Joan Sum, "Understanding Pre-employment Testing," *Canadian HR Reporter*, November 21, 2011, accessed January 10, 2012, www.hrreporter.com/articleview/11765-understanding-pre-employment-testing.

55. Ashley Shadday, "Assessments 101: An Introduction to Candidate Testing," *Workforce Management*, January 5, 2010, accessed January 10, 2012, www.workforce.com/article/20100105/NEWS02/301059990.

56. Timothy A. Judge, Ryan L. Klinger, and Lauren S. Simon, "Time Is on My Side: Time, General Mental Ability, Human Capital, and Extrinsic Career Success," *Journal of Applied Psychology* 95, no. 1 (2010): 92–107.

57. John J. Sumanth and Daniel M. Cable, "Status and Organizational Entry: How Organizational and Individual Status Affect Justice Perceptions of Hiring Systems," *Personnel Psychology* 64 (2011): 963–1000.

58. Eddy S. W. Ng and Greg J. Sears, "The Adverse Impact in Selection Practices on Organizational Diversity: A Field Study," *The International Journal of Human Resource Management* 21, no. 9 (July 2010): 1454–71.

59. David W. Freeman, "Wonderlic Test on Tap for NFL Hopefuls: What It Is and Who Has Highest Score?" *CBC News*, February 24, 2011, accessed January 13, 2012, www.cbsnews.com/8301-504763_162-20035953-10391704.html?tag=mncol;lst;7.

60. Ben Dattner and Robert Hogan, "Can You Handle Failure?" *Harvard Business Review*, April 2011, 117–21.

61. Rick Smith, "Building on Your Strengths," *HR Professional* 27, no. 1 (January 2010): 22–25.

62. Cary Cherniss, "Emotional Intelligence: New Insights and Further Clarifications," *Industrial and Organizational Psychology* 3 (2010): 183–91.

63. Ibid.

64. Frank Walter, Michael S. Cole, and Ronald H. Humphrey, "Emotional Intelligence: Sine Qua Non of Leadership or Folderol?" *Academy of Management* (February 2011): 45–59.

65. Norman D. Henderson, "Predicting Long-Term Firefighter Performance from Cognitive and Physical Ability Measures," *Personnel Psychology* 3 (2010): 999–1039.

66. Danielle Harder, "Courts Clarify Unresolved Issues in 2009," *Canadian HR Reporter*, February 19, 2010, accessed January 13, 2012, www.hrreporter.com/articleview/ 7564-courts-clarify-unresolved-issues-in-2009; and Jeffrey R. Smith, "Right Idea, Wrong Application for Drug, Alcohol Policy," *Canadian HR Reporter*, August 15, 2011, www.hrreporter.com/articleview/11001-right-idea-wrong-application-for-drug-alcohol-policy-legal-view.

67. Smith, "Right Idea, Wrong Application for Drug, Alcohol Policy."

68. Jeffrey R. Smith, "No Need for History of Workplace Accidents for Random Drug and Alcohol Testing: Court," *Canadian HR Reporter*, December 10, 2010, accessed January 13, 2012, www.hrreporter.com/articleview/8666-no-need-for-history-of-workplace-accidents-for-random-drug-and-alcohol-testing-court-legal-view.

69. David Whitten, "Deconstructing Random Drug, Alcohol Testing," *Canadian HR Reporter*, November 21, 2011, accessed January 13, 2012, www.hrreporter.com/articleview/11775-deconstructing-random-drug-alcohol-testing-legal-view.

70. Ken Cahoon, "Pre-employment Screening—What Is Necessary?" *Canadian HR Reporter*, July 18, 2011, accessed January 16, 2012, www.hrreporter.com/articleview/10784-pre-employment-screening-what-is-necessary.

71. "Survey 21 Percent of Job Seekers Dropped after Reference Checks," *Workforce Management*, June 23, 2010, accessed January 16, 2012, www.workforce.com/article/20100623/ NEWS01/306239996.

72. The National Association of Professional Background Screeners, accessed January 16, 2012, http://www.napbs.com.

73. Shannon Klie, "Tread Carefully with Credit Checks: Privacy Commissioner," *Canadian HR Reporter*, March 22, 2010, accessed January 16, 2012, www.hrreporter.com/ articleview/7670-tread-carefully-with-credit-checks-privacy-commissioner.

74. Daniel E. Martin and Benjamin Austin, "Validation of Moral Competency Inventory Measurement Instrument," *Management Research Review* 33, no. 5 (2010): 437–51; and Michael A. McDaniel, "Gerrymandering in Personnel Selection: A Review of Practice," *Human Resource Management Review* 19, no. 3 (2009): 263–70.

75. Paul R. Sackett and Filip Lievens, "Personnel Selection," *Annual Review of Psychology* 59 (2008): 16.1–16.32.

76. Robert M. Guion, *Assessment, Measurement and Prediction for Personnel Decisions*, 427.

77. Amanda Silliker, "Tread Carefully with Social Media Checks," *Canadian HR Reporter*, January 30, 2012, 1.

78. Ibid.

PART

3

Developing People in the Organization

CHAPTER 5

ORIENTATION, TRAINING, AND DEVELOPMENT

OUTCOMES

After studying this chapter, you should be able to

1. Discuss the systems approach to training and development.

2. Describe the components of a training-needs assessment.

3. Identify the principles of learning and how they facilitate training.

4. Identify the types of training and development methods used for all levels of employees.

5. List some characteristics of an effective orientation process.

6. Describe the special training programs that are currently popular.

7. Explain how a career development program integrates individual and organizational needs.

8. Discuss specialized career development needs.

OUTLINE

HRM CLOSE-UP

"If you leave learning and development completely to staff, it's sometimes hard for them to see the forest from the trees. That's where I can help identify opportunities for them."

Garnett Volk.

Farm Credit Canada is a federal Crown corporation established in 1959 to support agriculture in Canada. Though it first financed mortgages and loans for farmers, the company has greatly expanded its products and services. With more than 100,000 customers nationwide, Farm Credit Canada is 100% committed to supporting the business of agriculture.

From his sales office in Edmonton, Alberta, District Director Garnett Volk heads a sales team of 10 field staff, a business developer, and a customer service manager with support staff. Volk's sales team serves farmers around the Edmonton area, including the communities of Westlock, Barrhead, and Leduc. Often on the road, this group supports farmers through financing land and equipment. Volk himself spent 10 years in the field and has been managing his own team since 2008.

In terms of new employee orientation, Farm Credit Canada runs a corporate-wide program consisting of a three-day session, held about four times a year and delivered in both English and French. New employees are introduced to senior leaders, who present a global vision of the company. Videos, speeches, and various activities help to familiarize staff with the company's operations and best practices.

Some development programs are required for all employees—programs that educate about such things as the Code of Conduct and Ethics, and Health and Safety. These are delivered in various ways, including online and off-site with external training vendors.

"The first day on the job is really about conveying who we are and what we do," says Volk. "It's really important to build comfort with the office team, meeting staff and knowing that they will be supported. I want them to have a kick in their step knowing that they've made a good choice to work here."

Volk uses a detailed checklist for new employee orientation to make sure that all the bases are covered. Staff complete online training, systems knowledge, and job shadowing with peers so there's a lot of information to take in at the start. Volk checks in often—in person and by phone and e-mail to monitor the employees' progress, especially in the early days.

Since most employees are hired with some agricultural industry background, Volk can focus training on systems and financial analysis. These things are also addressed with all staff at twice-yearly district meetings. Corporate partners are brought in to share expertise in areas such as marketing and credit management as well as to discuss new products and share best practices.

Every employee at Farm Credit Canada has an individual development plan using forms on the company's intranet. Volk reviews this twice a year with each member of his team. They meet to discuss the employee's current role and how the employee might progress in his or her career. Although he encourages staff to identify their own learning needs, Volk finds that "if you leave the identification of learning and development needs completely to staff, it's sometimes hard for them to see the forest from the trees. That's where I can help identify opportunities."

Volk has a budget for outside training and has had staff pursue accreditation. One fellow, in particular, was supported with the completion of his CFA, or Certified Financial Advisor, designation. "There is also accreditation for appraisals and we would identify that kind of need when we complete the development plan." Volk looks first at internally offered training before he seeks training outside the company.

There is also training related to a company-wide investment in information technology on the horizon. Farm Credit Canada is testing tablets as these may prove to be particularly helpful in the field. Currently, Volk's sales force uses BlackBerry devices and laptop computers for their work. "We are out of the office with clients at their farms at least one day a week," explains Volk, "and regardless of technology, our customers want and expect the personal connection. They want access to technology, but they want to deal with a person they know and trust."

Asked about his role as a people manager, Volk says that he sometimes wonders whether he's making a difference. "You don't necessarily get positive or negative feedback from staff," he says, "but if you see that your staff are happy and successful in what they do, this is very rewarding."

INTRODUCTION

Orientation
Formal process of familiarizing new employees with the organization, their jobs, and their work unit and embedding organizational values, beliefs, and accepted behaviours

Training
The acquisition of skills, behaviours, and abilities to perform current work

Development
The acquisition of skills, behaviours, and abilities to perform future work or to solve an organizational problem

The ability for an organization to ensure its people continue to learn, grow, and develop has become critical to business success. As we noted in Chapter 1, organizations often compete on competencies—the core sets of knowledge and expertise that give them an edge over their competitors. Frequently, organizations refer to "intellectual capital," which is the combination of the "human capital" (the competencies) and the organizational support that enables the human capital to flourish.[1] Further, as individuals learn (e.g., the human capital increases), the organization has the potential to learn. Only through individuals does the organization gain knowledge.[2] **Orientation**, **training**, and **development** play a central role in enabling, nurturing, and strengthening the human capital in the organization. As Garnett Volk describes in the HRM Close-up, Farm Credit Canada focuses on its orientation, mentoring, and employee development programs to communicate organizational values and encourage a culture of learning.

Further, as will be discussed in this chapter, it is critical that organizations approach their orientation, training, and development needs in a systematic way. Doing so will ensure that there is a clear linkage to the organization's strategic direction. Rapidly changing technologies require that employees continuously hone their knowledge, skills, and abilities (KSAs), or "competencies," to cope with new processes and systems. A carefully designed program can also be a key lever in attracting and retaining people with the key competencies that will keep the organization's competitive advantage. Jobs that require little skill are rapidly being replaced by jobs that require technical, interpersonal, and problem-solving skills. And, as described, the business world is constantly changing, requiring improved skills and abilities.

The manager or supervisor plays a key role in ensuring that the training and development efforts are appropriate and reinforced for the individuals for whom they are responsible. Without the managers' involvement, organizational growth, success, and sustainability could be at risk. Other trends toward empowerment, total-quality management, teamwork, and international business make it necessary for managers as well as employees to develop the skills that will enable them to handle new and more demanding assignments.

APPROACH TO ORIENTATION, TRAINING, AND DEVELOPMENT

Outcome 1

What are the four phases of the systems approach to training?

Since the primary goal of orientation, training, and development is to contribute to the organization's overall goals, orientation, training, and development programs should be structured with an eye to organizational goals and strategies. Unfortunately, many organizations never make the connection between their strategic objectives and their training programs. Instead, fads, fashions, or "whatever the competition is doing" sometimes drives an organization's training agenda. As a result, much of an organization's investment can be wasted—training programs are often misdirected, poorly designed, inadequately evaluated—and these problems directly affect organizational performance.

To make certain that investments in orientation, training, and development have the maximum impact on individual and organizational performance, a systems approach to training should be used. The systems approach involves four phases: (1) needs assessment, (2) program design, (3) training delivery, and (4) evaluation of training. While the word "training" will be used in the discussion on the systems approach, all elements refer to orientation and development as well. Figure 5.1 is a useful model when designing the training programs. Each component of the systems approach will be discussed further in this chapter.

THE SCOPE OF ORIENTATION, TRAINING, AND DEVELOPMENT

Many new employees come equipped with most of the skills and capabilities needed to start work. Others may require extensive training before they are ready to make much of a contribution to the organization. All employees need some type of training and

FIGURE 5.1   Systems Model of Training

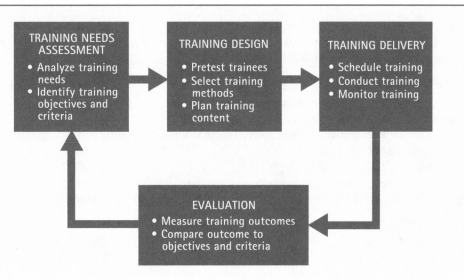

development on an ongoing basis to maintain effective performance or to adjust to new ways of work.

The term "training" is often used casually to describe any effort initiated by an organization to foster learning among its members. However, many experts make a distinction between training and development. Training tends to be more focused and oriented toward acquiring skills, behaviours, and abilities to perform current work, while development tends to be oriented more toward acquiring skills, behaviours, and abilities to perform future work or to solve an organizational problem. These terms tend to be combined into a single phrase—"training and development"—to recognize the combination of activities used by organizations to increase the abilities and capabilities of their employees.

You often hear the word "learning," as well. Learning refers to an ongoing change in behaviour and thinking: ultimately the goal of training and development.

The primary reason that organizations train new employees is to bring their KSAs up to the level required for satisfactory performance. As these employees continue on the job, additional training and development provide opportunities for them to acquire new knowledge and skills. As a result of this training, employees may be even more effective on the job and may be able to perform other jobs in other areas or at higher levels. Increasingly, companies are using training and development and knowledge management strategies that range from leadership development and succession planning to manage anticipated talent shortages.[3] To help you understand the importance of training in today's business environment, refer to Figure 5.2, which lists the skills that many employers seek.

Investments in Training

Conference Board of Canada

www.conferenceboard.ca

According to a Conference Board of Canada survey, Canadian businesses spend about $688 per employee each year on formal training, an amount that has decreased by 40% since the early 1990s.[4] Canadian organizations provided about 25 hours of training annually per employee—a decrease of 11% since 2008.[5] However, organizations that make the Best Employers in Canada lists tend to place a much higher value on the continued learning and development of their employees. For example, in 2012, Cisco Canada was ranked #2 on the Best Employers in Canada list. Cisco provides opportunities for employees to grow into new roles, resulting in low turnover as 70% of the positions are filled internally.[6] With the relative lack of priority Canadian organizations are placing on learning and development, combined with Canada's economic downturn and lagging global competiveness and innovation, the issue of whether training should be legally

FIGURE 5.2   Workplace Skills and Capabilities

Employees want to know what employers are looking for today in skill sets. The Conference Board of Canada researched this topic and prepared the following broad list. While all employers do not look for all of these skills, many employers look for many of these skills.

Fundamental Skills

- Read and understand information presented in different forms (e.g., words, graphs)
- Write and speak so that others understand
- Use relevant knowledge and skills (scientific, technological) to explain and clarify
- Identify the root cause of a problem
- Evaluate solutions to make a decision
- Use numbers to complete tasks, such as making estimates and verifying calculations
- Manage information by locating, gathering, and organizing information using appropriate technology and systems

Personal Management Skills

- Be flexible and adaptable
- Be honest and ethical
- Be responsible for setting goals
- Be able to work safely
- Demonstrate positive attitudes and behaviours, such as dealing with people with honesty and integrity
- Be willing to keep learning

Teamwork Skills

- Understand and contribute to the organization's goals
- Understand and work within the dynamics of the group
- Plan and make decisions with others and support the outcomes
- Respect the thoughts and opinions of others
- Adapt to changing requirements
- Understand the role of conflict in group dynamics and resolve as appropriate

Source: Adapted from Employability Skills 2000+ PDF 2000 E/F (Ottawa: The Conference Board of Canada, 2000, PDF file). Reproduced with permission from the Conference Board of Canada.

enforced arises.[7] Ethics in HRM 5.1 describes the debate surrounding decisions to mandate organizations to provide training and to force employees to take training.

In addition to formal training, more than $180 billion is spent on informal instruction that goes on every day in organizations everywhere. More and more organizations are also providing training on an "as need" basis and are ensuring that it is linked to work experiences. For example, team training would be done as part of a team project on designing a new product. The types of training range from computer application skills to customer service.

The Conference Board of Canada found that the top strategic goals of Canadian organizations were to improve organizational performance, develop leaders, and align learning with business objectives.[8] The question that organizations always ask is this: Will training improve organizational performance? Even though the effectiveness of training initiatives on the KSAs of employees must be measured to ensure their positive impact on the organization's performance, most organizations still struggle to evaluate training effectiveness.[9] A recent study found that 86% of employees reported that job satisfaction, efficiency, quality, and productivity were positively influenced by their participation in a tuition assistance training program, and 94% said that the knowledge they acquired was useful to their jobs.[10] The costs and benefits beyond performance and productivity, such as recruitment and retention, need to be assessed. For training to be effective and transferred to the workplace, it is important that employers provide support—whether it is paying for the training, ensuring the use of the new KSAs on the job, or encouraging workers to increase their skill set.

ETHICS **in HRM 5.1**

LEGISLATING LEARNING?

In recent years, widespread public concern has led to the development and passing of more laws that require workplace training in areas such as health and safety, the environment, and human rights. Although legislation enacted to date deals with strict minimal standards, enforcement, and penalties to employers that do not comply with the training requirements, the larger purpose of the legislation is to widely educate owners, managers, and workers about acceptable safe and non-discriminatory workplace behaviours. Examples of Canadian workplace training that has been legislated federally and provincially include the areas of payroll training taxes, WHMIS, accessibility, and violence.

Only one payroll training tax in North America, the Quebec *Act to Promote Workforce Skills Development and Recognition*, requires employers to spend 1% of payroll on training. The purpose of this act is to improve workforce qualifications and skills through investment in training and concerted action between management, unions, community partners, and the education sector.

Every province requires that employees be trained in the safe handling of potentially hazardous materials or conditions in the workplace (WHMIS). This requirement extends to offices that use printers and copying machines. Further, under workplace health and safety legislation, an employer can be fined or have its insurance rates increased if employees are not trained.

In 2012, the Customer Service Standard of the *Accessibility for Ontarians with Disabilities Act* (Ontario Regulation 429/07) became a legislated requirement, whereby all companies and employers must provide training to all employees, contractors, volunteers, and suppliers of support services who may interact with the public. Regulations that set out three standards and requirements of this legislation will be phased in over time between 2011 and 2021: (1) developing accessibility policies and plans, (2) training employees and volunteers, and (3) considering accessibility when purchasing goods or services.

In June 2010, Bill 168, which amended the Ontario *Occupational Health and Safety Act* to deal with the prevalence of, impact of, and risks associated with workplace violence and harassment, came into effect. It requires organizations to provide training in employer and employee obligations and related workplace policies and programs. Most recently other provinces are requiring training that addresses violence in the workplace, including assessment of the risks of a domestic violence situation spilling over into the workplace.

CRITICAL THINKING QUESTIONS:

1. Do you think mandatory training is right? Why or why not?

2. How would you react if your employer wanted you to participate in a training program that you thought was a waste of time? Why?

Sources: Adapted from "The Benefits of Investing in Québec" Investissement Quebec, October 2011, accessed August 7, 2012, www.investquebec.com/documents/en/secteur/InvestInQuebec.pdf; *An Act to Promote Workforce Skills Development and Recognition*, Éditeur officiel du Québec, April 2012, www2.publicationsduquebec.gouv.qc.ca/dynamicsearch/telecharge.php?type=2&file=/d_8_3/d8_3_a.html; "Accessibility Standards for Customer Service, Ontario Regulation 429/07, 2005," accessed May 1, 2012, www.e-laws.gov.on.ca/html/regs/english/elaws_regs_070429_e.htm; "About the *Accessibility for Ontarians with Disabilities Act*, 2005," Ontario Ministry of Community and Social Services, accessed May 1, 2012, www.mcss.gov.on.ca/en/mcss/programs/accessibility/understanding_accessibility/aoda.aspx; "*Bill 168, Occupational Health and Safety Amendment Act (Violence and Harassment in the Workplace), 2009*," Legislative Assembly of Ontario, accessed May 1, 2012, www.ontla.on.ca/web/bills/bills_detail.do?locale=en&BillID=2181; and "Domestic Violence in the Workplace," WorkSafe BC, accessed May 1, 2012, www2.worksafebc.com/Topics/Violence/Resources-DomesticViolence.asp#Readmore.

SYSTEMATIC ORIENTATION, TRAINING, AND DEVELOPMENT

As mentioned earlier in the chapter, the model shown in Figure 5.1 allows organizations to identify what is needed for employee and organizational performance. Each of these components will be discussed in detail.

Phase 1: Conducting the Needs Assessment

Outcome 2

What are the components of a training-needs assessment?

Managers and HR professionals should stay alert to the kinds of training that are needed, where the training is needed, who needs the training, and which methods will best deliver increased abilities to employees. If workers consistently fail to achieve productivity objectives, this might be a signal that training is needed. Likewise, if organizations receive an excessive number of customer complaints, this might suggest inadequate training.

To make certain that training is timely and focused on priority issues, and that training is the right solution for the concern, managers should approach a needs assessment systematically. You can also think of this as trying to identify the training problem. The needs assessment can occur at the organizational level (examining the environment and strategy of the company to see where training emphasis ought to occur); the task level (reviewing the activities of the work to determine the competencies needed); and the person level (reviewing which employees need training.)

A needs assessment can be done by asking (and answering) four questions:

1. How important is this issue to the success of the organization? If it is important, then proceed to answer Questions 2, 3, and 4.
2. What competencies or knowledge, skills, and abilities do employees *need*?
3. What competencies or knowledge, skills, and abilities do the employees currently *have*?
4. What is the gap between the desired (need) and the actual (have)?

Once answers have been determined, then specific action plans can be developed to address the gap. For example, since the September 11, 2001, attacks, training of airport security personnel has increased substantially. It has also increased for flight crews of airlines, employees in the transportation industry, workers in nuclear power plants, and even security staff at theme parks.

Manager's Toolkit 5.1 provides some suggestions for a simple approach to identifying training needs.

Other training issues tend to revolve around the strategic initiatives of an organization. Mergers and acquisitions, for example, frequently require that employees take on new roles and responsibilities and adjust to new cultures and ways of conducting business. Nowhere is this more prevalent than in grooming new leaders within organizations. Other issues, such as technological change, globalization, re-engineering, and total quality management, all influence the way work is done and the types of skills needed to do it. Still other concerns may be more tactical but no less important in their impact on training. Organizational restructuring, downsizing, empowerment, and teamwork, for example, have immediate training requirements.

Finally, trends in the workforce itself have an impact on training needs. As we mentioned in Chapter 1, employees increasingly value self-development and personal growth, and with this has come an enormous desire for learning. At the same time, as older workers may decide to postpone retirement, training will need to be done for a variety of different generations. Because no company in the private sector can count on stable

Determining the specific training needs of individuals helps determine their abilities before entering a training program.

Goodluz/Shutterstock.com

MANAGER'S TOOLKIT 5.1

CONDUCTING A TRAINING NEEDS ASSESSMENT

This approach is relatively simple and will take about one to two hours.

I. Gather together a group of people with similar jobs into a room with white boards and/or flip charts; have another individual (not part of the group) to act as facilitator.

2. Individually, ask each person to write down their 10 specific training needs. Be sure that the need is specific—such as "how to give feedback to colleagues" and not general like "team building."

3. Individually, each person will tell the whole group what the 10 training needs are. The facilitator will list each need on the white board. Do not list any duplicates. (Note: The facilitator may need to ask clarifying questions to ensure that it is a duplicate.)

4. The group will use some type of voting process to determine the top five training needs. This can be done by giving each participant 10 sticky dots and asking that they vote for no more than three training needs but putting one or more dots by the need. The needs with the most dots would then be the highest-rated ones.

5. Depending on the organization, the group could determine how the training needs will be implemented or the facilitator could use a brainstorming process to identify goals or outcomes for the top five training needs.

6. The facilitator will ensure that notes are taken of the session and that the top one or two needs of each person are recorded. This can be useful for the supervisor to work one-on-one with the employee to build appropriate training opportunities into the employee's performance plan.

employment levels, organizations as diverse as Inco and Boeing are facing situations in which they need to prepare the next generations of employees as the current groups approach retirement.

It is important that the supervisor or manager be knowledgeable about the organization's needs, the requirements of the work, and the capabilities of the person in order to assess that training is the right solution. Training efforts (and dollars) can be wasted if the supervisor has not adequately determined whether training is appropriate. The question to ask here is something like this: "If Joe receives more training on how to handle customer complaints, will his performance improve?" If performance issues are due to ability problems, training may likely be a good intervention. However, if performance issues are due to poor motivation or factors outside an employee's control, training may not be the answer. Ultimately, managers have to sit down with employees to talk about areas for improvement so that they can jointly determine the training and developmental approaches that will have maximum benefit.[11]

Phase 2: Designing the Training Program

Once the training needs have been determined, the next step is to design (or buy) appropriate training programs. The success of training programs depends on more than the organization's ability to identify training needs. Success hinges on taking the information gained from the needs analysis and utilizing it to design first-rate training programs. Experts believe that training design should focus on at least four related issues: (1) instructional objectives, (2) trainee readiness and motivation, (3) principles of learning, and (4) characteristics of instructors.

Instructional Objectives

Instructional objectives
Desired outcomes of a training program

As a result of conducting organization, task, and person analyses, managers will have a more complete picture of the company's training needs. On the basis of this information, they can more formally state the desired outcomes of training through written **instructional objectives**. Generally, instructional objectives describe the desired outcomes of the training: the skills and knowledge the company wants people to have and the behaviours employees should acquire or change. For example, a stated objective for one training program might be "Employees trained in team methods will be able to demonstrate the following skills within six months: Problem-solving, conflict resolution, and effective team meetings."

Frequently, managers will seek external resources to design the training program and write the learning objectives. However, they will contribute help and guidance. It is, therefore, important for managers to be able to describe what they want the person to do or how they want the person to act after completing a training program.

Trainee Readiness and Motivation

Trainee readiness
The consideration of a trainee's maturity and experience when assessing him or her

Two preconditions for learning affect the success of those who are to receive training: readiness and motivation. **Trainee readiness** refers to both maturity and experience factors in the trainee's background. Prospective trainees should be screened to determine that they have the background knowledge and the skills necessary to absorb what will be presented to them. The other precondition for learning is trainee motivation. For optimum learning to take place, trainees must recognize the need for new knowledge or skills, and they must maintain a desire to learn as training progresses. By focusing on the trainees rather than on the trainer or training topic, managers can create a training environment that is conducive to learning. Six strategies can be essential:

1. Use positive reinforcement.
2. Eliminate threats and punishment.
3. Be flexible.
4. Have participants set personal goals.
5. Design interesting instruction.
6. Break down physical and psychological obstacles to learning.

While most employees are motivated by certain common needs, they differ from one another in the relative importance of these needs at any given time. Training objectives that are clearly related to trainees' individual needs will increase the motivation of employees to succeed in training programs. Again, the manager plays a vital role in ensuring that the training is suitable for the person and that the person is ready to take on the training initiative.

Principles of Learning

Outcome 3

What are the principles of learning and how do they facilitate training?

As we move from needs assessment and instructional objectives to employee readiness and motivation, we are shifting from a focus on the organization to a focus on employees. Ultimately, training has to build a bridge between employees and the organization. One important step in this transition is giving full consideration to the psychological principles of learning, that is, the characteristics of training programs that help employees grasp new material, make sense of it in their own lives, and transfer it back to the job.

Because the success or failure of a training program is frequently related to certain principles of learning, managers as well as employees should understand that different training methods or techniques vary in the extent to which they utilize these principles. When investing in effective and efficient training programs, it is important that they incorporate the following principles of learning (see Figure 5.3):

GOAL SETTING   It is important that the goals and objectives for the training are clear.

INDIVIDUAL DIFFERENCES   People learn at different rates and in different ways.

FIGURE 5.3 Principles of Learning

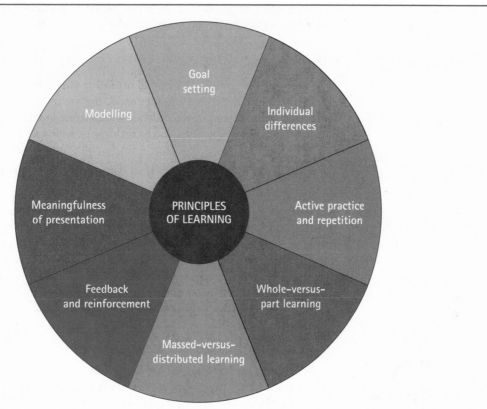

ACTIVE PRACTICE AND REPETITION   Trainees should be given frequent opportunity to practise their job tasks in the way that they will ultimately be expected to perform them.

WHOLE-VERSUS-PART LEARNING   Most jobs and tasks can be broken down into parts that lend themselves to further analysis. Determining the most effective manner for completing each part then provides a basis for giving specific instruction.

MASSED-VERSUS-DISTRIBUTED LEARNING   Another factor that determines the effectiveness of training is the amount of time devoted to practise in one session. Should trainees be given training in 5 two-hour periods or in 10 one-hour periods? In most cases, it has been found, spacing out the training will result in faster learning and longer retention.

FEEDBACK AND REINFORCEMENT   Can any learning occur without feedback? Some feedback comes from self-monitoring while other feedback comes from trainers, fellow trainees, and the like. As an employee's training progresses, feedback serves two related purposes: (1) knowledge of results, and (2) motivation.

MEANINGFULNESS OF PRESENTATION   The material to be learned must be presented in as meaningful a manner as possible so that the trainees can connect the training with things that are already familiar to them.

MODELLING   The old saying "A picture is worth a thousand words" applies to training. Quite simply, we learn by watching.

Behaviour modification
Technique that if behaviour is rewarded, it will be exhibited more frequently in the future

In recent years some work organizations have used **behaviour modification**. This technique operates on the principle that behaviour that is rewarded—positively reinforced—will be exhibited more frequently in the future, whereas behaviour that is penalized or unrewarded will decrease in frequency. For example, in safety training it is possible to identify "safe" behavioural profiles—actions that ensure fewer accidents—as well as unsafe profiles. As a follow-up to training, or as part of the training, managers can use relatively simple rewards to encourage and maintain desired behaviour.

Characteristics of Trainers

The success of any training activity will depend in large part on the skills and personal characteristics of those responsible for conducting the training. Good trainers, whether staff persons or line managers, need to be knowledgeable about the subject, be well-prepared, have good communication skills, and be enthusiastic with a sense of humour.

Phase 3: Implementing the Training Program

Despite the importance of needs assessment, instructional objectives, principles of learning, and the like, choices regarding instructional methods are where "the rubber meets the road" in implementing a training program. A major consideration in choosing among various training methods is determining which ones are appropriate for the KSAs to be learned. For example, if the material is mostly factual, methods such as lecture, classroom, or programmed instruction may be fine. However, if the training involves a large behavioural component, other participative methods, such as on-the-job training, simulation, or interactive virtual training, might work better.

Training and Development Methods

Outcome 4
What are the types of training and development methods used for all levels of employees?

A wide variety of methods are available for training and developing employees at all levels. Some of the methods have a long history of usage. Newer methods have emerged as the result of a greater understanding of human behaviour, particularly in the areas of learning, motivation, and interpersonal relationships. More recently, technological advances, especially in Web 2.0 technologies and social media from blogs to virtual collaboration environments, have resulted in emerging learning approaches that, in many instances, are more effective and economical than the traditional training methods.

The Conference Board of Canada found that, in 2010, 58% of all workplace learning was done in the classroom, a decrease from 2000 where 80% of all learning was instructor-led, face-to-face classroom training. It is now becoming increasingly common for organizations to use several different delivery methods. The two most common delivery methods after instructor-led training are e-learning and collaborative face-to-face learning.[12] Surprisingly, with the growth of Web 2.0 technologies, only 2% of organizations are using online collaborative learning methods, although these are expected to increase as learning becomes increasingly learner driven and collaborative.[13] The awareness and prevalence of informal learning (e.g., seeking information from co-workers or the Internet) continues to grow, prompted by the increased need of organizations to transfer and retain knowledge as leaders from the Baby Boom cohort approach retirement.[14] Informal e-learning through communities of practice, sharing of experiences, and self-learning is growing rapidly.[15]

The following are various types of training approaches that can more or less blend formal, informal, and social learning.

On-the-job training (OJT)
Method by which employees are given hands-on experience with instructions from their supervisor or other trainer

ON-THE-JOB TRAINING   One of the most common methods used for training employees is **on-the-job training (OJT)**. OJT has the advantage of providing hands-on experience under normal working conditions and an opportunity for the trainer—a manager or senior employee—to build good relationships with new employees. Although all types of organizations use it, OJT is often one of the most poorly implemented training methods. Three common drawbacks include (1) the lack of a well-structured training environment, (2) poor training skills of managers, and (3) the absence of well-defined job performance criteria.

Manager's Toolkit 5.2 describes some basic steps that can be taken to address the drawbacks of OJT programs.

MANAGER'S TOOLKIT **5.2**

THE PROPER WAY TO DO ON-THE-JOB TRAINING

P *Prepare*. Decide what employees need to be taught. Identify the best sequence or steps for training. Decide how best to demonstrate these steps. Have materials, resources, and equipment ready.

R *Reassure*. Put each employee at ease. Learn about his or her prior experience, and adjust accordingly. Try to get the employee interested, relaxed, and motivated to learn.

O *Orient*. Show the employee the correct way to do the job. Explain why it's done this way. Discuss how it relates to other jobs. Let the employee ask lots of questions.

P *Perform*. When employees are ready, let them try the job themselves. Give them an opportunity to practise the job and guide them through rough spots. Provide help and assistance at first, then less as they continue.

E *Evaluate*. Check the employees' performance, and question them on how, why, when, and where they should do something. Correct errors, repeat instructions.

R *Reinforce and Review*. Provide praise and encouragement, and give feedback about how the employee is doing. Continue the conversation, and express confidence in the employee's work.

Apprenticeship training
System of training in which a worker entering the skilled trades is given thorough instruction and experience, both on and off the job, in the practical and theoretical aspects of the work

APPRENTICESHIP TRAINING **Apprenticeship training** is used extensively where individuals entering an industry, particularly in the skilled trades, such as machinist, laboratory technician, or electrician, are given thorough instruction and experience, both on and off the job, in the practical and theoretical aspects of the work. Many former fishers left the declining East Coast fishery to join in a seafarers' training program funded by several companies, the federal government, and the Nova Scotia government to learn new skills working in the engine rooms of larger vessels. Magna International, the auto parts giant, pays students to train as millwrights and tool and die makers. Learning is offered variously in shops, laboratories, and classrooms. Employers in the oil industry in Alberta have established an apprenticeship approach to ensure that oil-patch workers have the appropriate training. The Banff World Media Festival and Shaw Media have developed a Global Writers Apprentice Program that provides emerging Canadian writers with the opportunity to gain experience by apprenticing in the story department of a prime-time series.[16]

Co-operative training
Training program that combines practical on-the-job experience with formal education

Internship programs
Programs jointly sponsored by colleges, universities, and other organizations that offer students the opportunity to gain real-life experience while allowing them to find out how they will perform in work organizations

CO-OPERATIVE TRAINING AND INTERNSHIP PROGRAMS Similar to apprenticeships, **co-operative training** and **internship programs** combine practical on-the-job experience with formal education. Typically, co-op programs are offered at colleges and universities where students work for an entire semester as part of their education. While they don't get course credit, they do graduate with an indication that they have been involved in a co-op program. They can thereby demonstrate to prospective employers that they have work experience. The pioneer in co-op education is the University of Waterloo, but there are now co-op programs throughout Canada. Syncrude Canada, Harley-Davidson, and Canadian Microelectronics Corporation are among the many companies that have formed partnerships with education. Further, organizations benefit by getting student-employees with new ideas, energy, and eagerness to accomplish their assignments. Humber College in Toronto, British Columbia Institute of Technology (BCIT) in Burnaby, and many other colleges allow students to earn college credits on the basis of successful job performance and fulfillment of established program requirements.

CLASSROOM INSTRUCTION Classroom instruction enables the maximum number of trainees to be handled by the minimum number of instructors. This method lends itself particularly to training in areas where information can be presented in lectures, demonstrations, films, and videotapes or through computer instruction. A special type of classroom facility is used in "vestibule training." Trainees are given instruction in the operation of equipment like that found in operating departments. The emphasis is on instruction. For example, a checkout clerk in a supermarket first learns how to use the cash register.

SELF-DIRECTED LEARNING   Self-directed learning occurs when individuals work at their own pace at programmed instruction. Such learning typically involves the use of books, manuals, or computers to break down subject matter content into highly organized, logical sequences that demand continuous response on the part of the trainee.

AUDIO-VISUAL   Audio-visual methods are used to teach the skills and procedures required for a number of jobs. An example would be golf and tennis coaches using video or camcorders so that their students can see their mistakes. Video conferencing has also been successful in connecting First Nations communities in remote areas so that they can learn from one another.[17] Telehealth, a shared B.C. Ministry of Health video-conferencing system, connects patients through live video conferencing to clinical, administrative, and educational consultations in more than 100 communities across the province. Video conferencing can deliver faster service, allow for desktop conversations and meetings across distances, and can enhance the management, sharing, and archiving of digital content.[18]

SIMULATION   Simulation is used when it is either impractical or unwise to train employees on the actual equipment used on the job. An obvious example is training employees to operate aircraft, spacecraft, and other highly technical and expensive equipment. The simulation method provides realism in equipment and its operation. For example, before the launch of its first edition, the *National Post* used simulations to train a new workforce by requiring them to produce a mock newspaper with real content and headlines.

E-LEARNING   The simpler, audio-visual, programmed, and computer-oriented training methods just discussed are evolving into what trainers today describe as e-learning. **E-learning** covers a wide variety of applications such as Web-based and computer-based training (CBT) and virtual classrooms. It includes delivery of content via the Internet, intranets and extranets, audiotape, videotape, satellite and broadcast interactive TV, DVD, and CD-ROM. E-learning makes it possible to provide drill and practice, problem solving, simulation, gaming forms of instruction, and certain sophisticated forms of individualized instruction in a way that's more engaging for learners than traditional classroom instruction. It is also cheaper for employers to administer because, in many instances, it can be delivered directly via the employees' computer.

E-learning has become firmly established as a delivery method within organizations: 78% are self paced, 48% are instructor led, 34% are blended, and 27% are collaborative, becoming an alternative, not a replacement to classroom delivery methods.[19] Further, according to Industry Canada, 98% of employees stated that e-learning helped them reach their own personal development goals and 83% of employees stated that e-learning increased their productivity.[20] There are also systems that can track the progress of learners. For example, go to **http://moodle.org** to see how e-learning systems are used in educational institutions to track student progress.

E-learning also allows employees to search through a virtual sea of information in order to customize their own learning in their own time and space. More companies are demanding access to individual training components for employees to use when and where they need them. This approach helps alleviate the boredom trainees can experience during full-blown training courses, and employees are more likely to retain the information when they can immediately put it to use. It is also important to ensure that the strategies and culture of the organization support and encourage e-learning. At Work with HRM 5.1 describes how Telus is promoting learning and development through formal, informal, and social learning delivery methods.

Although e-learning systems can be very sophisticated, they need not be overly expensive. Many e-learning training programs use existing applications that employees are familiar with—for example, PowerPoint, Word, and Adobe Acrobat—and convert them

E-learning
Learning that takes place through electronic media

Moodle
http://moodle.org

AT WORK **with HRM 5.1**

TELUS: FORMAL, INFORMAL, AND SOCIAL LEARNING

Telus is a global telecommunications provider. Its new approach to learning and development has been in response to the shifting demographics, flattened organizational structures, teamwork, knowledge-based economy, and increased use of social media.

Its learning initiatives are formal, informal, and social: classroom communities of practice, e-learning, books, coaching, videos, blogs, webinars, micro-blogs, and wikis. A few of its learning opportunities include career and business conversations with subject matter experts, interactive team collaboration across distances, and a virtual orientation. Throughout 2010, it experienced an increase in participation through the use of social learning as well as a resulting increase in job-related performance. In 2011, its return on investment (ROI) was 68%.

In an interview with the Conference Board of Canada, Dan Pontefract, senior director of Learning and Collaboration, described Telus's success in its learning approach as a result of leadership support, alignment with the organizational strategy, champions, and a gradual and inclusive adoption.

CRITICAL THINKING QUESTION:

Access one of Telus's YouTube videos on Learning 2.0 either on their website or at YouTube .... Two possible locations are http://www.youtube.com/watch?v=kdaDD82geNo/ and http://csrdev.power shiftermedia.com/en/en/areas_of_innovation/team_members/wellness_and_growth_programs/lifelong_learning. Watch and discuss the Telus YouTube video on how learning and development are promoted through social media. Discuss your experiences with these diverse workplace learning methods.

Sources: Adapted from "Telus 2010 Corporate Social Responsibility Report—Life Long Learning," accessed August 1, 2012, http://csr.telus.com/en/areas_of_innovation/team_members/wellness_and_growth_programs/lifelong_learning; "Telus 2010 Corporate Social Responsibility Report—Social Media and Team Members," accessed May 1, 2012, http://csr.telus.com/en/areas_of_innovation/team_members/wellness_and_growth_programs/social_media; and Carrie Lavis, *Learning and Development Outlook 2011; Are Organizations Ready for Learning 2.0?*, Ottawa: The Conference Board of Canada, October 2011.

---

into Flash programs so that they can be easily viewed online with any Web browser. Web-based training can also be revised rapidly, thereby providing continuously updated training material. This capability not only makes it easier and cheaper to revise training curricula, but also saves travel and classroom costs. When combined with other communications technology such as e-mail, teleconferencing, video conferencing, and groupware, Web-based training can be even more effective.

A review of training media can be found at Training Media Review (**www.tmreview.com**). This is a good resource for managers who want to find out about current effective training approaches.

ON-THE-JOB EXPERIENCES   On-the-job experiences present managers with the opportunities to perform under pressure and to learn from their mistakes. Such experiences are some of the most powerful and commonly used techniques. However, just as on-the-job training for first-level employees can be problematic if not well planned, on-the-job management development should be well organized, supervised, and challenging to the participants. Methods of providing on-the-job experience include the following:

a. *Coaching* involves a continuing flow of instructions, comments, and suggestions from the manager to the subordinate.
b. *Mentoring* usually involves an informal relationship in which an executive coaches, advises, and encourages a more junior employee. Some organizations have formal mentorship programs in which someone being considered for upward movement is assigned to another employee in the organization. A good mentor will focus on goals, opportunities, expectations, and standards and assist people in fulfilling their potential.[21]

Training Media Review
www.tmreview.com

Mentors—Peer Resources
www.mentors.ca

Canadian businesses are increasing their training budgets in efforts to increase employee effectiveness. Computers and Web-based training are exploding.

c. *Understudy assignments* groom an individual to take over a manager's job by helping the individual gain experience in handling important functions of the job.

d. *Job rotation* provides, through a variety of work experiences, the broadened knowledge and understanding required to manage more effectively.

e. *Lateral transfer* involves horizontal movement through different departments, along with upward movement in the organization.

f. *Special projects* and *junior boards* provide an opportunity for individuals to become involved in the study of current organizational problems and in planning and decision-making activities.

g. *Action learning* gives managers release time to work full-time on projects with others in the organization. In some cases, action learning is combined with classroom instruction, discussions, and conferences.

h. *Staff meetings* enable participants to become more familiar with problems and events occurring outside their immediate areas by exposing them to the ideas and thinking of other managers.

i. *Planned career progressions* utilize all these different methods to provide employees with the training and development necessary to progress through a series of jobs requiring higher and higher levels of knowledge and/or skills.

American Management Association

www.amanet.org

SEMINARS AND CONFERENCES   Seminars and conferences are useful for bringing groups of people together for training and development. In management development, seminars and conferences can be used to communicate ideas, policies, or procedures, but they are also good for raising points of debate or discussing issues (usually with the help of a qualified leader) that have no set answers or resolutions. In this regard, seminars and conferences are often used when attitude change is a goal. Check out **www.amanet.org** for a variety of conferences geared toward managers.

CASE STUDIES   Case studies use documented examples, which may have been developed from the actual experiences of participants in their own organizations. Cases help managers learn how to analyze (take apart) and synthesize (put together) facts, become conscious of the many variables on which management decisions are based, and, in general, improve their decision-making skills.

This textbook uses case studies as a way for students, with the help of the instructor, to better understand and integrate the information covered in each chapter.

MANAGEMENT GAMES   Management games are valuable for bringing a hypothetical situation to life and provide experiential learning. Many games have been designed for general use. For example, TD Bank uses a simulation called Desert Kings to encourage more open communication, to increase levels of team performance, and to increase commitment to both internal and external customer service.

ROLE PLAYING   Role playing consists of assuming the attitudes and behaviour—that is, playing the role—of others, often a supervisor and a subordinate who are involved in a particular problem. By acting out another's position, participants in the role playing can improve their ability to understand and cope with others. Role playing can also help participants learn how to counsel others by helping them see situations from a different point of view. Role playing is used widely in training health-care professionals to be empathetic and sensitive to the concerns of patients. It is also used widely in training managers to handle employee issues relating to absenteeism, performance appraisal, and conflict situations.

Phase 4: Evaluating the Training Program

Training, like any other HRM process, should be evaluated to determine its effectiveness. A variety of methods are available to assess the extent to which training and development programs improve learning, affect behaviour on the job, and have an impact on the bottom-line performance of an organization (e.g., business results and cost–benefit analysis). Unfortunately, few organizations adequately evaluate their training programs. In many ways, this lack of evaluation goes beyond poor management; it is poor business practice. Given the substantial monetary stake that organizations have in training, it would seem prudent that managers would want to maximize the return on that investment.

There are four basic methods to evaluate training: (1) reactions, (2) learning, (3) behaviour, and (4) results. Some of these are easier to measure than others, but each is important in that it provides different information about the success of the programs. The combination of these can give a total picture of the training program in order to help the organization determine if business results are improving, and for managers to decide where problem areas lie, what to change about the program, and whether to continue with a program.[22] Organizations' learning evaluation efforts are becoming more challenging with the growth in more fluid, informal, and social learning.[23] At Work with HRM 5.2 provides an example of how a Saskatchewan company uses all four ways to evaluate its training.

Method 1: Reactions

One of the simplest and most common approaches to training evaluation is assessing participant reactions. Happy trainees are more likely to focus on training principles and to utilize the information on the job. However, participants can do more than say whether they liked a program or not. They can give insights into the content and techniques they found most useful. They can also critique the instructors or make suggestions about participant interactions, feedback, and the like.

While evaluation methods based on reactions are improving, too many conclusions about training effectiveness are based on broad satisfaction measures that lack specific feedback. Furthermore, it should be noted that positive reactions are no guarantee that the training has been successful. Collecting glowing comments from trainees may be easy, but as gratifying as this information is to management, it may not be useful to the organization unless it somehow translates into improved behaviour and job performance.

Method 2: Learning

Beyond what participants *think* about the training, it might be a good idea to see whether they actually learned anything. Testing knowledge and skills before a training program provides a baseline standard on trainees that can be measured again after training to determine improvement. This approach also means that whatever the person is learning must be used at work. For example, if an employee was learning new software and the employee's computer did not have the software, the employee's inability to perform is a result of resources, not of an absence of learning.

AT WORK **with HRM 5.2**

A CLASSIC FOUR-LEVEL EVALUATION

CONEXUS is the largest credit union in Saskatchewan, with assets of $1.1 billion. According to Gayle Johnson, CHRP, VP Human Resources and Corporate Secretary, the credit union's training and development budget for its 465 employees is 6% of payroll. Three percent is spent on university education, and the other 3% is spent on training. Its largest training program develops financial service representatives (their title is to be changed to "relationship managers"). The training consists of several steps and each is measured.

In-house and classroom-based modules teach content such as computer literacy, cash duties, and introduction to CONEXUS's products and services; then employees progress through to more advanced training, such as consumer lending practices, estates, and minimal mortgage lending. Each three- to five-day module is followed by a work period of 3 to 12 months, so that employees can apply their knowledge. The four levels of measurement of the effectiveness of training are as follows:

1. *Reaction*. "Smile sheets" are completed by each participant at the end of the classroom training, asking questions such as "What did you get from this session?"

2. *Comprehensive Review.* Exams are given after each module, and the results are fed back to the employees and managers.

3. *Employee Performance Competencies.* Every job family has a number of job-specific competencies, and managers are asked to rate the participants on these performance competencies. The changes in ratings are tracked.

4. *Results*. These vary by module. For example, after the cash-lending module, the performance tracked would be the number of call-outs to customers and the number of sales.

CRITICAL THINKING QUESTIONS:

1. If the annual payroll for CONEXUS is $18,750,000, what is the annual dollar amount budgeted for training and development?

2. Are there other ways that CONEXUS could use to ensure that the training and development expenditures are worthwhile?

Method 3: Behaviour

Much of what is learned in a training program never gets used back on the job. It's not that the training was necessarily ineffective. In fact, on measures of employee reactions and learning, the program might score quite high. But for several reasons, trainees may not demonstrate behaviour change back on the job. **Transfer of training** (also called "transfer of learning") refers to the effective application of principles learned to what is required on the job. While measuring the extent of the behaviour change may not be necessary, it is important for the supervisor to expect the behaviour change and to reinforce the changes.

Transfer of training
Effective application of principles learned to what is required on the job

Ultimately, the success or failure of any training is whether or not there has been a transfer of that training. To maximize the transfer, managers can take several approaches:

1. Feature identical elements of the job in the actual training.
2. Focus on general principles that can be adapted to fit situations in the work environment.
3. Establish a climate for transfer with the manager being supportive and ensuring that the employee uses the new skills.[24]

Method 4: Results

Both the people responsible for training and the managers are under continual pressure to show that their programs produce "bottom-line" results. Most organizations measure their training in terms of its return on investment (ROI). This measure of investment is even more so during economic downturns. Organizations want to know that the training has increased

FIGURE 5.4 Measuring the Costs/Benefits of Training

In assessing the value of training (or learning), organizations will look at the costs and benefits of training and assign a dollar value. These are the typical costs included:

- trainer's salary/cost
- trainees' salary/wages
- materials for training
- expenses for trainers/trainees (e.g., travel)
- cost of facilities and equipment
- lost productivity (opportunity cost)

The benefits include the following:

- increase in productivity
- decrease in errors
- decrease in turnover
- behaviour changes
- improved safety record

For example, a revised safety training program may have the following costs: trainer time ($10,000); trainees' time ($20,000); materials ($5,000), and facilities ($1,000) for a total of $36,000. It was estimated that the training would cover two years and during that time, the company would save $50,000 in Workers' Compensation insurance and other related safety infractions. Therefore, the benefits outweigh the costs of revising the program.

business results, whether it is profit, customer satisfaction, or decreased costs.[25] Figure 5.4 provides an example of the costs and benefits of a training program and how to calculate the ROI. The Business Development Bank of Canada takes ROI very seriously, spending 5% of its payroll on training with the goal to improve business outcomes. A meta study conducted by Investing in People found that the Business Development Bank of Canada achieved a 74% ROI on training efforts to improve branch managers' coaching skills.[26]

Manager's Toolkit 5.3 provides an update on a special project in Canada to better measure training results as well as some resources to determine the ROI.

Increasingly, organizations with sophisticated training systems look to training to support long-term strategy and change more than they look for short-term financial returns from their investments. For example, WestJet sees that its investment in training will support its strategic direction to become one of the top five airlines in the world by 2016.[27]

As training and development are viewed more and more from a strategic standpoint, there is heightened interest in benchmarking developmental services and practices against those of recognized leaders in industry. While no single model for exact benchmarking exists, the simplest models are based on the late W. Edwards Deming's classic four-step process. The four-step process advocates that managers do the following:

Benchmarking
Process of measuring one's own services and practices against the recognized leaders in order to identify areas for improvement

1. *Plan.* Conduct a self-audit to define internal processes and measurements; decide on areas to be benchmarked; and choose the comparison organization.
2. *Do.* Collect data through surveys, interviews, site visits, and/or historical records.
3. *Check.* Analyze data to discover performance gaps and communicate findings and suggested improvements to management.
4. *Act.* Establish goals, implement specific changes, monitor progress, and redefine benchmarks as a continuous-improvement process.

To use **benchmarking** successfully, managers must clearly define the measures of competency and performance and must objectively assess the current situation and identify areas for improvement.

The American Society for Training and Development (ASTD) and its Institute for Workplace Learning, as well as associations such as B.C. Human Resources Management

**American Society for
Training and Development**
www.astd.org

MANAGER'S TOOLKIT 5.3

INVESTING IN PEOPLE

Organizations spend a considerable amount of money and hours on training each year. However, with the economic challenges, organizations want to be sure that value is received from the training. This desire led to an innovative project sponsored by Human Resources and Skills Development Canada (HRSDC) and undertaken by the Canadian Society of Training and Development. The purpose of the project was to have organizations determine the business impact of the training as the training was being developed, not after the training had been done. The project, called "Investing in People," designed tools and methods for monitoring and assessing the effectiveness of the training as it was implemented. The focus of the monitoring was to determine the change in business results.

Twelve Canadian organizations participated in the training ROI case studies.

Five programs determined that there was a positive relationship between formal training expenditures and performance indicators, such as employee productivity and company productivity. Additional ways to evaluate training and best training practices that organizations can use to measure ROI were found.

In seven case studies where a positive return on training investments did not occur, it was found that training was not aligned to the business strategies, initial program design was ineffective, and participants were unable to apply their new skills to their workplace. The studies also found that many training programs and practices were ineffective and that conducting ROI evaluations was challenging due to limited house resources and expertise.

Several recently researched tools and resources to measure training are available at the Web site "Investing in People" (www.cstd.ca/?IIP_Tools). Another useful tool for developing Return on Training Investment (ROTI) can be found at the Web site of FutureEd Inc. (www.futured.com/audited/returned.htm).

Sources: Adapted from "Investing in People," Canadian Society for Training and Development, www.cstd.ca/?page=IIP (accessed May 1, 2012); and Lynette Gillis and Allan Bailey "Investing in People—Meta Study of Evaluation Findings," Centre for Learning Impact, CSTD, March 2010, www.cstd.ca/resource/resmgr/iip/metastudy.pdf (accessed May 1, 2012).

Canadian Society for Training and Development
www.cstd.ca

Outcome 5

What are some characteristics of an effective orientation process?

Association (BC HRMA), have established projects that allow organizations to measure and benchmark training and development activities against each other.[28] These benchmarking forums compare data such as costs, staffing, administration, design, development, and delivery of training programs.[29]

Other helpful articles and publications on training and development can be found through the Canadian Society for Training and Development at **www.cstd.ca**.

Orientation

Orientation is a very particular type of training. The first objective in the orientation process is to get new employees off to a good start. This goal is generally achieved through a formal orientation program. Orientation is the formal process of familiarizing new employees with the organization, their job, and their work unit and embedding organizational values, beliefs, and accepted behaviours. The benefit for new employees is that it allows them to get "in sync" so that they become productive members of the organization. Orientation is a process—not a one-day event. Further, it is important to remember that orientation is a socialization process and that how employees are treated when they first join the organization makes a huge impact on their views of supervisors, managers, and the organization.

Benefits of Orientation

In some organizations a formal new-hire orientation process is almost nonexistent or, when it does exist, is performed in a casual manner. Some readers may remember showing

Video streams and video conferencing are frequently used in remote locations to orient new employees.

Thomas Northcut/Riser/Getty Images

up the first day on a new job, being told to work, and receiving no instructions, introductions, or support. This situation is unfortunate since a number of practical and cost-effective benefits can be derived from conducting a well-run orientation. Benefits frequently reported by employers include the following:

1. Lower turnover
2. Increased productivity
3. Improved employee morale
4. Lower recruiting and training costs
5. Facilitation of learning
6. Reduction of anxiety

The more time and effort an organization devotes to make new employees feel welcome, the more likely they are to identify with the organization and the more quickly to become productive. Unlike training, which emphasizes the "what" and "how," orientation stresses the "why." It is designed to develop in employees a particular attitude about the work they will be doing and their role in the organization. It defines the philosophy behind the rules and provides a framework for their work in that organization.

Continuous Process

www.okanagan.bc.ca/
administration/
human-resources/Joining_
Okanagan_College.html.

Since an organization is faced with ever-changing conditions, its plans, policies, and procedures must change with these conditions. Unless current employees are kept up-to-date with these changes, they may find themselves embarrassingly unaware of activities to which new employees are being oriented. While the discussion that follows focuses primarily on the needs of new employees, it is important that all employees be continually reoriented to changing conditions. Many companies are using intranets (internal Web sites) and online orientation modules to keep new and current employees up-to-date. For an example of online orientation, check out **www.okanagan.bc.ca/administration/human-resources/Joining_Okanagan_College.html**.

Co-operative Endeavour

For a well-integrated orientation process, co-operation between line and staff is essential. The HR department is ordinarily responsible for coordinating orientation activities and for providing new employees with information about conditions of employment, pay, benefits, and other areas not directly under a supervisor's direction. However, the supervisor has the most important role in the orientation process. New employees are interested primarily in what their supervisor says and does and what their new co-workers are like. Before the arrival of a new employee, the supervisor should inform the work group that a new worker is joining the unit. It is also common practice for supervisors or other managerial personnel to recruit co-workers to serve as volunteer "sponsors" or "buddies" for incoming employees. In addition to providing practical help to newcomers, this approach conveys an emphasis on teamwork.

Careful Planning

An orientation process can make an immediate and lasting impression on an employee that can mean the difference between the employee's success and failure at work. Thus, careful planning—with emphasis on goals, topics to be covered, and methods of organizing and presenting them—is essential. Successful orientation processes emphasize the individual's needs for information, understanding, and a feeling of belonging.

To avoid overlooking items that are important to employees, many organizations devise checklists for use by those responsible for conducting the orientation. Orientation information can also be printed and given to the new employee. Companies are also beginning to use their intranets to make the information more readily available to their employees. Manager's Toolkit 5.4 suggests items to include in an orientation checklist for supervisors. Orientation should focus on matters of immediate concern, such as important aspects of the job and organizational behaviour expectations (e.g., attendance and safety). Since orientation focuses on helping the new employee become familiar, comfortable, and productive, it is important not to overwhelm or provide too much information at one time. HRM and the Law 5.1 describes the steps employers must take to provide health and safety orientations to new and young workers.

Those planning an orientation process should take into account the anxiety employees feel during their first few days on the job. It is natural to experience some anxiety, but if employees are too anxious, training costs, turnover, absenteeism, and even production costs may increase. Early in the orientation, steps should be taken to reduce the anxiety level of new employees. This anxiety reduction can be accomplished by establishing

---

MANAGER'S TOOLKIT **5.4**

SUPERVISORY ORIENTATION CHECKLIST

1. A formal greeting, including introduction to colleagues

2. Explanation of job procedures, duties, and responsibilities

3. Training to be received (when and why)

4. Supervisor and organization expectations regarding attendance and behaviour norms

5. Job standards and production and service levels

6. Performance appraisal criteria, including estimated time frame to achieve peak performance

7. Conditions of employment, including hours of work, pay periods, and overtime requirements

8. Organization and work unit rules, regulations, and policies

9. Overview of health and safety expectations, as well as when specific training will occur

10. Those to notify or turn to if problems or questions arise

11. Chain of command for reporting purposes

12. An overall explanation of the organization's operation and purpose

13. A review of the organizational chart or structure indicating departments and work flow

14. Offers of help and encouragement, including a specific time each week (in the early stages of employment) for questions or coaching

HRM and the Law 5.1

"NEWNESS" AND WORKPLACE INJURY

A recent study, "'Newness' and the Risk of Occupational Injury," states that being new to a job or unfamiliar with the work or its hazards is a contributing factor to increased risk of occupational injury. "New to the job" can refer to young workers, short-term workers, recent immigrants, and new companies.

These finding are not surprising considering the death of the 24-year-old gas-bar attendant in Maple Ridge, B.C., who was killed when dragged under a vehicle driven by two men who had not paid for the gas. As a result of this fatality, amendments were made to the occupational health and safety legislation in the province. Organizations are now required to provide workers with health and safety orientation and training according to the systems approach to training, described in this chapter. Other provinces have also expanded their legislation because youth and new workers are more likely to be injured on the job.

Employers have had these training responsibilities for some time, but for the first time, it is stated clearly that they must do a needs assessment to evaluate the workplace situation, provide orientation and training in these specific areas, and evaluate the workers after the training to ensure that the knowledge and skills are transferred to the workplace. The general legislation states that health and safety orientation and training must occur before they begin working and that the supervisor must continue to coach and train the new workers after the initial orientation and training.

CRITICAL THINKING QUESTION:

How would you apply the systems approach to occupational health and safety orientations and training in your workplace?

Sources: Adapted from: "'Newness' and the Risk of Occupational Injury," *Institute for Work & Health*, May 2009, www.iwh.on.ca/briefings/newness (accessed May 1, 2012); and "Training and Orientations for New Workers," WorkSafeBC, www2.worksafebc.com/PDFs/YoungWorker/employer_training_backgrounder_OHSReg_part3.pdf (accessed May 1, 2012)

---

specific times in which the supervisor will be available for questions or coaching. Furthermore, reassuring newcomers that the performance levels they are observing among their co-workers will be attained within a predetermined time frame, based on experiences with other newcomers, can decrease anxiety. This reassurance is particularly important for employees with limited work experience who are learning new skills.

In addition, if the organization has a number of new immigrants, the time period for such employees to feel comfortable and part of the organization can take years. Immigrants face many barriers to integrating into the workplace. These range from lack of recognition of foreign credentials and work experience to language and culture issues.[30] A recent study found that immigrant workers are more likely to be injured on the job, a finding that reinforces the importance of orientation and training in health and safety.[31]

And, of course, like other training initiatives, the orientation process would need to be evaluated to ensure it is meeting organizational outcomes. For additional information and tips about planning an orientation, read the article "A Quick Guide to Employee Orientation" at **www.work911.com/articles/orient.htm**.

Work 911

www.work911.com/articles/
orient.htm

SPECIAL TOPICS IN TRAINING AND DEVELOPMENT

Outcome 6

What are some current popular special training programs?

Although this chapter has focused almost exclusively on the processes underlying a systems model of training (needs assessment, principles of learning, implementation methods, and evaluation), it may be useful to discuss some of the more popular topics that are covered in these training programs. As noted in Figure 5.2, there is a wide variety of skills and capabilities required in today's workplace. In addition to the training that addresses the competencies associated with a particular job, many employers develop training programs to meet the needs of a broader base of employees. This section summarizes some of these programs, including orientation, basic skills training, team training, and diversity training.

Basic Skills Training

The Canadian Council on Learning finds that almost one-half of Canadian adults and 40% of working-age Canadians are below the internationally accepted literacy standard for functioning in today's world.[32] Experts define an illiterate individual as one having a sixth-grade education or less. Working adults who improve their literacy skills gain better pay and more promotions and are employed for longer periods of time. Employers launch literacy training in order to improve productivity. Dofasco Steel in Ontario provides not only training in basic English and computer-related skills, but also advanced computer courses and business writing.[33]

These figures on literacy have important implications for society at large and for organizations that must work around these skill deficiencies. Never has this been truer, given tight labour markets on the one hand, and increasing skill requirements (related to advances in technology) on the other. Basic skills have become essential occupational qualifications, having profound implications for product quality, customer service, internal efficiency, and workplace and environmental safety. In the last several years, the number of businesses that require a high-level of knowledge has grown due to globalization and a knowledge-based economy.[34] A recent study by the Canadian Chamber of Commerce found that Canada's slipping global competitiveness is due to the shortage of skilled and educated workers. At Work with HRM 5.3 describes how Canada's labour-force participation can be increased by tapping into under-represented workers.[35] Canadian employers report that the top five skills they need in employees today are the ability to

- read and understand information
- listen, ask questions, and understand
- work in teams
- assess situations and identify problems
- share information orally and work with others

But adults don't learn the way children do, so many of the traditional basic skills training techniques are not successful with adults. To implement a successful program in basic and remedial skills, managers should do the following:

1. Explain to employees why and how the training will help them in their jobs.
2. Relate the training to the employees' goals.
3. Respect and consider participant experiences, and use these as a resource.
4. Use a task-centred or problem-centred approach so that participants "learn by doing."
5. Give feedback on progress toward meeting learning objectives.

Team Training

As discussed in Chapter 3, organizations rely on teams to attain strategic and operational goals. Whether the team is an air crew, a research team, or a manufacturing or service unit, the contributions of the individual members of the team are not only a function of the skills and capabilities (competencies) of each individual but also of the interaction of the team members. To give an example of how important this can be to an organization, Dofasco had 6,700 employees participate in four-day workshops on interpersonal and group skills over a three-year period. The company wanted all its employees to learn to work with one another in new and different ways.

Teamwork skills fall under two broad categories: task related and team related. Teamwork skills that characterize effective teams include a balance between the use of technical skills, such as time management and problem solving, and interpersonal skills, such as conflict resolution and collaboration. As noted earlier, Figure 5.2 highlights the

AT WORK **with HRM 5.3**

BRIDGING THE EDUCATION GAP

In March 2012, the Canadian Chamber of Commerce released a report, "Top 10 Barriers to Competiveness: Skills Development Discussion Paper." The report outlined several labour-force challenges faced by Canadian businesses and posed the following questions to stimulate discussion and gain new insights into potential solutions to the challenges.

1. How can businesses attract and retain older workers?

2. How can businesses leverage the Aboriginal populations in their regions more effectively to meet their business needs? What are the obstacles?

3. How can businesses encourage their employees to upgrade their skills?

4. How can businesses, high schools, and postsecondary institutions work together to prepare students for the workforce?

5. What initiatives would encourage young people to pursue post-secondary studies alongside work?

6. How can the business community help promote skilled trade occupations?

7. What steps can the business community take to integrate people with disabilities into the workplace?

8. What are the interprovincial/territorial barriers affecting businesses?

9. What changes should be implemented in order to improve the efficiency of the Federal Skilled Workers Program and the Temporary Foreign Worker Program?

10. What measures would help businesses recruit and retain foreign students as future employees?

11. How can businesses, education institutions, and government work together to improve the evaluation of foreign credentials, qualifications, and certification?

CRITICAL THINKING QUESTION:

Discuss the questions and consider possible solutions to Canada's labour force challenges.

Source: "Top 10 Barriers to Competitiveness—Skills Development Discussion Paper," The Canadian Chamber of Commerce, March 2012.

importance of teamwork skills in today's workplace. Teams need to evaluate themselves periodically to ensure that the goal(s) is being achieved and that there are no concerns about interpersonal relationships.

Managers who want to design team training for their organization should keep the following points in mind:

1. Team building is a difficult and comprehensive process. Since many new teams are under pressure to produce, there is little time for training. Everything cannot be covered in a 24-hour blitz. Team training works best when it is provided over time and parallels team development.

2. Team development is not always a linear sequence of "forming, storming, norming, and performing." Training initiatives can help a team work through each of these stages, but managers must be aware that lapses can occur.

3. Additional training is required to assimilate new members. Large membership changes may result in teams reverting to a previous developmental stage.

4. Skills need to be acquired through practice and reviewing the performance of the teams.[36]

Diversity Training

Many large organizations sponsor some sort of diversity training. This emphasis is sparked by an awareness of the varied demographics of the workforce, the challenges of employment

Employees are more diverse and expect to be involved in decision making.

Patrick Ryan/Lifesize/Getty Images

equity, the dynamics of stereotyping, the changing values of the workforce, and the potential competitive payoffs from bringing different people together for a common purpose.

There are basically two types of diversity training: (1) awareness building, which helps employees appreciate the benefits of diversity, and (2) skill building, which provides the capabilities necessary for working with people who are different. For example, a skill-building diversity program might teach managers how to conduct performance reviews with people from different cultures or teach male supervisors how to coach female employees toward better career opportunities. When designing a diversity-training program, it is important to take a systems approach (similar to that mentioned at the beginning of this chapter) and ensure that the existing policies, practices, and procedures are examined for anything that might be hampering diversity.

CAREER DEVELOPMENT—INDIVIDUAL AND ORGANIZATIONAL NEEDS

Outcome 7

How does a career development program integrate individual and organizational needs?

Career development programs, with their greater emphasis on the individual, introduce a personalized aspect to the term "development." Most training and development programs have a career development component. Most career development programs should be viewed as a dynamic process that attempts to meet the needs of managers, their employees, and the organization.

Career planning, on the other hand, is a systematic approach where you would assess your values, interests, abilities, and goals, and identify the path(s) you would need to take to realize your career goals. Through career development programs you would then journey along the career path.

Ultimately, in today's organizations, individuals are responsible for initiating their own career planning. It is up to individuals to identify their knowledge, skills, abilities, interests, and values, and seek out information about career options in order to set goals and develop career plans. Managers should encourage employees to take responsibility for their own careers, by offering continuing assistance in the form of feedback on individual performance, and making available information about the organization, the job, and career opportunities that might be of interest.

The organization should be responsible for supplying information about its mission, policies, and plans, and for providing support for employee self-assessment, training, and development. Significant career growth can occur when individual initiative combines with organizational opportunity. Career development programs benefit managers by giving them increased skill in managing their own careers, greater retention of valued employees, increased understanding of the organization, and enhanced reputations as people developers.

Some organizations make use of leadership career development programs. Enbridge, an Alberta-based company in the energy transportation and distribution business, changed the way in which it provided leadership development. For several years it sent a few executives each year to Queen's University for a three-week residential program. However, in assessing ways to maximize the training budget, the organization decided it could provide leadership training to a larger number of employees by custom-developing a program that could be delivered in-house. By changing the approach to delivery, Enbridge is now able to offer a leadership development program to 130 employees each year instead of five.[37] For more information about the types of programs available for leadership development, visit the Web site of The Banff Centre at **www.banffcentre.ca** and the Center for Creative Leadership at **www.ccl.org**.

As shown in Figure 5.5, organizational needs should be linked with individual career needs in a way that joins personal effectiveness and satisfaction of employees with the achievement of the organization's strategic objectives.

The Banff Centre
www.banffcentre.ca

Center for Creative Leadership
www.ccl.org

Creating Favourable Conditions

While a career development program requires many special processes and techniques, some basic conditions must be present if it is to be successful. These conditions create favourable conditions for the program.

Management Support

If career development is to succeed, it must receive the complete support of top management. The system should reflect the goals and culture of the organization, and the people philosophy should be woven throughout. A people philosophy can provide employees with a clear set of expectations and directions for their own career development. For a

FIGURE 5.5   Balancing Individual and Organizational Needs

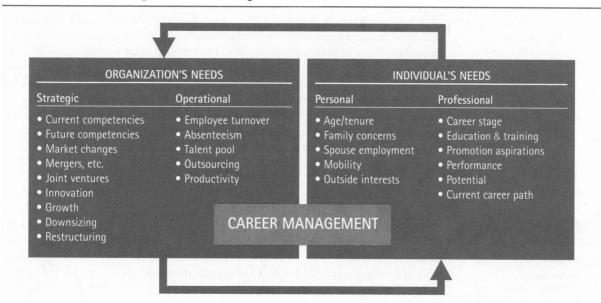

program to be effective, managerial staff at all levels must be trained in the fundamentals of job design, performance appraisal, career planning, and coaching.

Goal Setting

Before individuals can engage in meaningful career planning, they must not only have an awareness of the organization's philosophy but also a clear understanding of the organization's more immediate goals. Otherwise, they may plan for personal change and growth without knowing if or how their own goals match those of the organization. For example, if the technology of a business is changing and new skills are needed, will the organization retrain to meet this need or hire new talent? Is there growth, stability, or decline in the number of employees needed? How will turnover affect this need? Answers to these kinds of questions are essential to the support of individual career planning.

Changes in HRM Practices

To ensure that its career development program will be effective, an organization may need to alter its current HRM practices. For example, a practice of job rotation can counteract obsolescence and maintain employee flexibility. Another practice that can aid development involves job transfers and promotions. A **transfer** is the placement of an employee in another job for which the duties, responsibilities, status, and remuneration are approximately equal to those of the previous job (or work requirements). A transfer may require the employee to change work group, workplace, work shift, or organizational unit; it may even necessitate moving to another geographic area. Transfers make it possible for an organization to place its employees in jobs where there is a greater need for their services and where they can acquire new knowledge and skills. A downward transfer, or demotion, moves an individual into a lower-level job that can provide developmental opportunities, but such a move is usually considered unfavourably by the individual who is demoted.

A **promotion** is a change of assignment to a job at a higher level in the organization. The new job (or work) normally provides an increase in pay and status and demands more skill or carries more responsibility. Promotions enable an organization to utilize the skills and abilities of its staff more effectively, and the opportunity to gain a promotion serves as an incentive for good performance. The two principal criteria for determining promotions are merit and seniority. Often, the problem is to determine how much consideration to give to each factor.

As organizations continue to change, including their structure and number of employees, the ability to promote people as part of career development is becoming more difficult. The issues of balancing work and family, mentioned in Chapter 1, can become paramount when considering a promotion. Even though there has been growth in the number of women working, the proportion of women in senior management positions has not changed over the past two decades. A 2011 report by the Conference Board of Canada outlined practices that organizations are using to encourage the advancement of women: succession planning, mentoring, coaching, job rotation, and training.[38] Canadian Pacific Railway, Manitoba Lotteries Corporation, and TD Financial Group use a range of these practices to recruit and retain diverse talent, supporting their organizational goals of equity and performance.[39]

Specialized Development Needs

As mentioned earlier in this chapter, "development" is a long-term approach for acquiring and utilizing new skills. Since the purpose of a development program is to give employees enhanced capabilities, there are a number of ways in which this can occur. The responsibility to develop the talent lies with all managers in the organization—not just the person's immediate supervisor or team leader.

Transfer
Placement of an individual in another job for which the duties, responsibilities, status, and remuneration are approximately equal to those of the previous job

Promotion
Change of assignment to a job at a higher level in the organization

Outcome 8

What are some specialized career development needs?

Mentoring

When one talks with men and women about their employment experiences, it is common to hear them mention individuals at work who influenced them. They frequently refer to immediate managers who were especially helpful as career developers. But they also mention others at higher levels in the organization that provided guidance and support to them in the development of their careers. These managers (and executives) who coach, advise, and encourage less experienced employees are called **mentors**.

Generally, the mentor initiates the relationship, but sometimes an employee will approach a potential mentor for advice. Most mentoring relationships develop over time on an informal basis. However, many organizations emphasize formal mentoring plans that assign a mentor to those employees considered for upward movement in the organization. A good mentorship is a reciprocal relationship—with both the mentee and the mentor learning from each other. In recent years there has been a growth in the different types of mentoring relationships that range from reverse mentoring to peer and team mentoring. It is important to remember that a mentor relationship is very personal.

Manager's Toolkit 5.5 provides guidelines for establishing and maintaining successful mentor and mentee relationships.

Organizations with formal mentoring programs include Shell International, Sun Microsystems, Johnson & Johnson, and the Bank of Montreal. Alternatively, given the importance of the issue, a number of mentoring organizations have begun to spring up. When done well, the mentoring process is beneficial for both the mentee and the mentor. A new form of mentoring, sponsored by the Ms. Foundation for Women, provides an opportunity for both girls and boys, 8 to 18 years old, to spend a day with parents or friends on the job. The program is designed to give young people more attention and to provide them with career role models. American Express, Chevron, and Estée Lauder Companies participate in this program.

Not surprisingly, mentoring is also being done electronically. E-mentoring brings experienced business professionals together with individuals needing advice and guidance. Even though participants in e-mentoring typically never meet in person, many form long-lasting e-mail connections that tend to be very beneficial. Still, most participants see these connections as supplements to—rather than substitutes for—in-person mentors.

There are a number of resources for mentoring. A few examples include the following:

Society for Canadian Women in Science and Technology (SCWIST) is an association that has assembled thousands of women in technology fields who act as online mentors to visitors to its Web site.

National Mentoring Partnership is an online site for a variety of different resources for mentors and mentees, including information about how to find a mentor.

Women's Enterprise Centre is an organization that encourages, helps, and supports women in British Columbia who want to own, operate, and grow their own business.

Mentors
Managers who coach, advise, and encourage less experienced employees

Society for Canadian Women in Science and Technology
www.scwist.ca

National Mentoring Partnership
www.mentoring.org

Women's Enterprise Centre
www.womensenterprise.ca

Mentoring helps people at all levels in the organization develop their special skills and talents.

Huntstock/The Agency Collection/Getty Images

MENTORING GUIDELINES

Successful mentoring is built on a common understanding of interests and "ground rules." Here are some to consider before establishing a mentor–mentee relationship:

1. Formalize the expectations with a written agreement that outlines the behaviours of each person.

2. Monitor progress. Understand that either party can withdraw from the relationship at any time, and it is not necessary to provide an explanation.

3. All documents exchanged, such as company plans or résumés, will be treated as confidential.

4. The mentor cannot be solicited for a job. Doing so is grounds for breaking the relationship. There must be dedication to the process.

5. Respect each other's time. Arrive on time and prepare with a list of questions or topics to be discussed.

6. Provide feedback honestly. For example, the mentee could state, "This is not the kind of information I need at this stage," or the mentor might advise, "You should not skip meetings just because they are tedious; it is an important part of this company's culture to be visible at these meetings."

Specialized Career Development for a Diverse Workforce

Today, some organizations offer extensive career development programs geared to special groups, such as women, minorities, youth, and dual-career couples. For example, male managers have traditionally had an informal network of interpersonal relationships that has provided a means for senior (male) members of the organization to pass along news of advancement opportunities and other career tips to junior (male) members. Women have typically been left outside this network, lacking role models to serve as mentors. To combat their difficulty in advancing to management positions, women in several organizations have developed their own women's networks. At the Bank of Montreal, a women's network serves as a system for encouraging and fostering women's career development and for sharing information, experiences, and insights.

Another example is an organization actively creating conditions that recognize and reward performance on the basis of objective, non-discriminatory criteria. Many organizations are taking the position that their employees should reflect the communities in which they function. At the Bank of Montreal, each manager is required to set diversity targets.

Keeping a Career in Perspective

It is important in any training and development program to keep everything in perspective. While work is a very important part of someone's life, it is only a part. Organizations want people who maintain an appropriate balance between their work life and their personal life, and therefore can continue to grow and develop for personal satisfaction and success for the organization.

Some of the other areas of life that must be considered are the following:

1. Off-the-job interests can provide a break from the demands of a career while allowing employees to gain satisfaction from non-work-related activities.
2. Family life can be negatively affected if the organization does not provide recognition of a person's life outside of work. Conflict between work and family may arise over such issues as number of hours worked per week, the need to relocate for career advancement, and the amount of overtime that may be required.

3. Planning for retirement is an important consideration given the aging workforce. Many companies are now providing pre-retirement programs to allow an employee to be productive in the organization while minimizing problems that can arise in the retirement years.
4. Dual-career families are a factor in the contemporary business world. Therefore, career development and progress may need to take the goals of the partner into consideration.

As mentioned in Chapter 1, the workforce of today is very different than the workforce of yesterday. The organization may have as many as four generational cohorts—each with its own view and expectations about career development. Therefore, it will be important to maintain a balanced perspective on career development and to structure opportunities to fit the needs of both the diverse employee base and the organization. HRM and SME 5.1 discusses mentoring Gen Ys.

Emerging Trends 5.1 provides some additional information about what is on the horizon in relation to orientation, training, and development.

HRM and SME 5.1

THE NEXT GREAT ONES

Much has been written, discussed, and debated about the succession crisis facing financial advisors over the next 10 years. The problem is perceived as being twofold: many advisors edging toward retirement age do not have a proper succession plan in place; and there will not be enough new advisors to take over from the retiring advisors.

This dilemma does not just apply to financial advisors; succession is a challenge facing many industries, most notably oil, construction, and technology. In a nutshell, as the Baby Boom generation prepares to leave the workforce en masse, there will be a large job void to fill—a "labour crunch," as it is often called. This situation presents a huge opportunity for the youngest generation in today's workforce, the Gen Ys, as the demand for employees continues to rise.

This generation is known for caring less about the pay cheque and more about workplace flexibility. Work–life balance is more important to than it was to previous generations; they work hard, but they like to play harder. They are confident, ambitious, and achievement oriented and team players.

GenYs have high expectations of their employers and continuously seek new challenges. They're extremely tech savvy and rely on technology to do their jobs better. Because they crave constant feedback, Gen Y employees are ideal candidates for a mentoring relationship.

Today's Gen Ys are tomorrow's leaders. It behooves any financial advisor looking for a successor to reach out to them and get to know them, to understand their values, what's important to them, and how they work. Offering to mentor would be a good idea. The learning will go both ways.

CRITICAL THINKING QUESTION:

Mentoring relationships are dynamic and complex, requiring particular care to ensure compatibility between the mentor and the novice mentee. How might understanding generational differences help the personal relationship and communication between older Baby Boom workers and younger Gen Y workers? What are some knowledge retention methods SMEs can use? Refer to Emerging Trends 5.1, below.

Source: "The Next Great Ones," Editor's Note, Kristin Doucet, *Forum: The Magazine for Financial Advisors*. May 2011, 4. Reprinted with permission.

EMERGING TRENDS **5.1**

1. **Leadership development and succession planning.** The unexpected retirements of several high-profile CEOs continues to raise concern about the loss of organizational leadership experience and knowledge as the Baby Boom generation prepares to withdraw from the workplace. According to a Korn/Ferry Global Executive Survey, 98% of survey respondents regarded CEO succession planning as important yet only 35% of respondents were prepared for the departure of their CEO. Building leadership competencies is becoming a top priority for many organizations.

2. **Bridging the gap.** The transfer of knowledge in today's multi-generational workplace requires understanding, adapting to, and choosing best knowledge transfer practices and methods that accommodate the different generations working together. Organizations are facing knowledge retention challenges due to shifting demographics from older to younger workers and future labour shortages. Some knowledge retention methods include leadership transition workshops, mentoring, books, Web sites, electronic documents, interviews, and events.

3. **Learning 2.0.** Learning 2.0 is a term used to describe the reinvention of learning and development in the 21st century. It represents the paradigm shift from face-to-face and/or online instructor–controlled, structured one-way adaptive training to the learner-driven, collaborative, and problem-focused learning made possible by Web 2.0 technologies that provide a massive forum for sharing information and working collaboratively.

4. **Diversity in delivery.** Social, mobile, and cloud-computing technological advances, convergence, and the increase in collaborative work have led to changes in how organizations approach learning. They have also expanded the breadth and diversity of delivery methods: blogs, communities of practice, podcasts, instant messaging, wikis, and team learning. Tablets and emerging mobile technology tools will allow employees to manage their professional development digitally.

5. **Talent management.** The concept of training and development has evolved into the concept of "talent management." It means looking at the people in the organization as "talent" and then creating a plan to have the people at the appropriate skill level when needed. At the same time, it recognizes that a culture of lifetime employment no longer exists. Leadership development and succession planning are two of the most critical challenges that Canadian CEOs expect to face in the future.

Sources: Adapted from "Korn/Ferry Survey Reveals More Interest Than Action in CEO Succession Planning among Top Companies," press release, Korn/Ferry International, accessed May 1, 2012, www.kornferry.com/PressRelease/11916; "Bridging the Gaps: How to Transfer Knowledge in Today's Multigenerational Workplace," The Conference Board of Canada, 2008; "Learning and Development Outlook 2011: Are Organizations Ready for Learning 2.0?" The Conference Board of Canada, October 2011; Manual London and M.J. Hall, "Unlocking the Value of Web2.0 Technologies for Training and Development: The Shift from Instructor-Controlled, Adaptive Learning to Learner-Driven, Generative Learning," *Human Resource Management* 50, no. 6 (2011): 757–75; John Markoff, "Online Education Venture Lures Cash Infusion and Deals with 5 Top Universities, *The New York Times*, April 18, 2012, www.nytimes.com/2012/04/18/technology/coursera-plans-to-announce-university-partners-for-online-classes.html?_r=2&scp=1&sq=online%20education%20venture&st=Search; and The Conference Board, CEO Challenge 2011: *Fueling Business Growth with Innovation and Talent Management*, Ottawa: The Conference Board of Canada, April 2011.

SUMMARY

1. Discuss the systems approach to training and development.
   - Training and development need to be linked to the organization's goals and objectives.
   - A systems approach to training and development creates this link.
   - A systems approach consists of five phases: needs analysis, training program design, implementation, evaluation, and transfer to work environment.

2. Describe the components of a training-needs assessment.
   - Contributes to the organization's overall goals.
   - Involves four phases: needs assessment, program design, implementation, and evaluation.

3. Identify the principles of learning and how they facilitate training.
   - Goal setting.
   - Meaningfulness of presentation.
   - Modelling.
   - Individual differences.
   - Active practice and repetition.
   - Feedback.
   - Rewards and reinforcement.

4. Identify the types of training and development methods used for all levels of employees.
   - On-the-job.
   - Apprenticeship.
   - Co-operative and internship programs.
   - Computer and Web based.
   - Seminars and conferences.
   - Role playing and management games.

5. List some characteristics of an effective orientation process.
   - Familiarizing new employees with the organization, their job, and their work unit.
   - Embedding organizational values, beliefs, and accepted behaviours.
   - Active involvement and participation from the supervisor.

6. Describe the special training programs that are currently popular.
   - Basic skills training (such as literacy), where people learn the basics of reading and math.
   - Teamwork, where people learn new behaviours and skills to work in teams.
   - Diversity, where people develop an appreciation of the benefits of diversity.

7. Explain how a career development program integrates individual and organizational needs.
   - It blends employee effectiveness and satisfaction with the achievement of the organization's strategic objectives.
   - HRM practices must fit so that both individual and organizational needs can be achieved.

8. Discuss specialized career development needs.
   - Mentoring programs where more senior individuals coach and encourage more junior staff.
   - Specialized career programs for a diverse workforce, the organization gears the development to special groups, such as women, youth, etc.

NEED TO KNOW

- Definition of orientation, training, development, and learning
- Definition of employee involvement and empowerment
- Variety of training methods
- Ways to reinforce training in the work environment
- Basic approaches to development

NEED TO UNDERSTAND

- Importance of the line manager in identifying training needs
- Relationship of orientation to organizational performance
- Importance of ensuring appropriate method is used to enhance learning
- Role supervisor or line manager plays in helping the trainee use the new skills and behaviours
- Organizational and individual responsibility in a person's development

KEY TERMS

apprenticeship training 163

behaviour modification 161

benchmarking 169

co-operative training 163

development 154

e-learning 164

instructional objectives 160

internship programs 163

mentors 179

on-the-job training (OJT) 162

orientation 154

promotion 178

trainee readiness 160

training 154

transfer 178

transfer of training 168

REVIEW QUESTIONS

1. What are the steps in developing a training and development program?
2. What are the principles of learning?
3. What are the various methods for training and development?
4. What is mentoring?
5. What are the four issues in evaluating training programs? Describe why each is important.
6. What are the benefits of a well-designed orientation process?
7. Why is there an increased emphasis on career development programs?

CRITICAL THINKING QUESTIONS

1. Access the Cisco news release, "The New Workplace Currency—It's Not Just Salary Anymore: Cisco Study Highlights New Rules for Attracting Young Talent into the Workplace and the Implications for Organizations Serious about Attracting, Retaining, Engaging and Training Generation Y." Discuss the impact career choice, social media, and mobile device policies, mobile devices, and flexible work. Have on attracting and retaining young professionals. You can gain access to the news release, issued November 2, 2011, at **http://newsroom.cisco.com/press-release-content?type=webcontent&articleId=532138**.
2. Your employer has approached you to assume a supervisory role. While you feel flattered, you are also concerned about your ability to carry out the role successfully. What type of training or development might you want to help you succeed? What would be the "hard skills" and "soft skills"?
3. Discuss what it means for businesses and leaders to act ethically. How might you promote learning initiatives designed to help leaders strengthen their ethical decision-making competencies? Access the Web site of Canadian Business Ethics Research Network for examples on how this not-for-profit organization is including technology and social media initiatives to engage Canadians to participate in dialogues and activities related to business ethics in Canada: **http://www.cbern.ca**.
4. Discuss this statement: Effective 21st century organizational learning is a blend of formal, informal, and social learning strategies.
5. You have recently joined an organization as an administrative assistant. The company places a high value on the use of Web 2.0 technology. Specifically, describe the type of training you ought to have and the development that could be provided in order to meet the company's expectations on its use of communication technologies.
6. You have been asked to assist in developing an e-learning orientation program. Debate the advantages and limitations of using e-learning for "on boarding" new employees. How would you ensure the effective design, implementation, and transfer of learning?
7. What are MOOCs (Massive Open Online Courses)? Two Stanford computer scientists have developed an interactive online learning system, secured $16 million in venture capital, and partnered with four major universities to provide

free Web-based courses in the humanities, social sciences, physical sciences, and engineering that can reach hundreds of thousands of students. Access the Web site and read the article "Online Education Venture Lures Cash Infusion and Deals with 5 Top Universities," *The New York Times,* April 18, 2012. Debate whether traditional classroom training will be replaced by MOOCs and whether technology will support more partnerships between organizations and educational institutions to provide training. See **www.nytimes.com/2012/04/18/technology/coursera-plans-to-announce-university-partners-for-online-classes.html?_r=2&scp=1&sq=online%20education%20venture&st=Searchl**.

8. You work in an organization that focuses on wine sales and marketing. Recently, there have been a number of complaints about a particular customer service representative in terms of accuracy of wine knowledge shared with customers and timeliness of work orders. Complete the four steps in the systems approach to training and development. Specifically, consider these questions: (1) How will you determine whether training is the answer? (2) What is a possible learning or training objective you could identify? (3) What methods would you use to implement training? (4) How would you evaluate if the training was effective?

DEVELOPING YOUR SKILLS

1. In groups of three or four, develop a list of behaviours or skills that would improve your performance as a team member. For each behaviour or skill, identify one or two training methods that would be appropriate for learning that behaviour or skill.
2. Providing training to employees is a significant retention tool in a tight labour market. In groups of four to five, discuss the benefits of training for individuals and organizations. Prepare a response to the following statement: "Employees should be required to repay the cost of any training if they leave the organization before one year."
3. In groups of three or four, access two Web sites for major corporations that use a number of different approaches for learning and development. Write a one- to two-page paper describing the similarities and the differences.
4. Technology, demographics, and culture change combine to create new career roles all the time. Access the Kiplinger.com Web site and watch the slideshow or read the Liz Ryan article "Ten Jobs That Did Not Exist 10 Years Ago" (**www.kiplinger.com/columns/onthejob/archive/10-jobs-that-didnt-exist-10-years-ago.html**). Discuss how these job titles are illustrative of the increased complexity of job roles and the introduction of Web 2.0 into workplace learning and development.
5. YouTube videos have been created as teaching resources. Find a YouTube video and critique its effectiveness in assisting learning. Discuss whether it utilized the four components of the systems approach to the training and development model. Choose one aspect of the model you observed on the video and be prepared to present it to the larger class.

Case Study  1

Learning 2.0 at East Coast Tech Inc.?

After 10 years of managing one of the leading sales departments, Jan O'Brien was excited about her promotion to the position of learning and development manager for East Coast Tech Inc. (ECT). She had always been able to deploy new sales practices to keep the company ahead of their competitors and felt that her knowledge and experience would be valuable to her new position as the company restructured its workforce. This shift toward a more flattened organizational structure and distribution of leadership to the lower levels of the organization had created her new position.

ECT, a global telecommunications provider with more than 8,000 employees, was experiencing increased competition, requiring the company and employees to "work smarter" and "produce results." The recessionary impacts on their business resulted in a decline in finances to all departments, one of which was budget cuts to the learning and development department. In strategic planning meetings with the leadership team, it was clear to Jan that ECT was not decreasing its commitment to learning, but needed a new more cost-effective learning strategy able to meet the "on-demand" learning needs of all employees and managers at distant locations. The employee roles were increasingly complex, requiring collaboration and teamwork to effectively meet client needs. The president of ECT clearly stated that that one of her first tasks was to conduct a thorough review of the learning and development function within the organization. The president wanted hard evidence, a "return on investment," to back up learning and development initiatives.

Being in the telecommunications industry, Jan was aware of how social media were catching on among public, and, in particular, ECT employees. ECT had adopted policies that banned the use of social media in the workplace and had installed blocking software so that employees could not gain access to Facebook, MySpace, and LinkedIn at work. Most of the managers had expressed concerns that employees were spending countless hours on social media. Issues ranged from inappropriate use of social media in meetings to worries about confidential organizational information being divulged.

Through her reading, Jan knew that a few competitors had introduced a new learning approach and philosophy called Learning 2.0. This approach represented a shift from face-to-face or online instructor–controlled, structured, one-way adaptive training to the learner-driven, collaborative, and problem-focused learning made possible by Web 2.0 technologies—these provide a massive forum for sharing information and working collaboratively. Jan felt that this approach was radical but could realize the president's productivity goals. She thought the introduction of social media capabilities would encourage employee innovation and engagement. Jan did not want to miss the opportunity but did not have the confidence and support within her department. Most employees expressed resistance.

Questions

1. How would you approach the development of Learning 2.0 at ECT to ensure its success?
2. What key factors would enable ECT to implement its new learning approach?
3. Does ECT have the culture, leadership, and resources necessary to support this change?
4. How would you make a case for this direction to the leadership team?

Case Study 2

Interaction between RCMP and People with Mental Illness

Over the past decade there has been a shift towards integrating individuals with mental illness into the community with the downsizing of psychiatric hospitals. Our communities have also seen an increase use of drugs such as cocaine. The shortage of mental health facilities and social support services has resulted in RCMP officers being the first responders to individuals experiencing irrational and violent behaviour. Some of the factors of such behaviour are psychosis, suicidal intentions, substance abuse, depression or emotional anxiety.

A recent study found that in 25% of fatal RCMP shootings, the individual had a history of mental illness. The study identified that crisis intervention training and less lethal compliance tools may have facilitated a more successful intervention. Another recent study found that in more than one-third of calls received by the RCMP in some Canadian jurisdictions involved people with mental illness and that the number and frequency of interactions between the RCMP and individuals with mental illness have increased significantly. These findings suggest that responding to situations involving individuals experiencing mental illness has grown to become an integral part of the job of an RCMP officer. These situations are complex as officers are trained to protect themselves and the public and deal with the immediate threat in which they are confronted. RCMP officers are increasingly challenged in differentiating between a situation that requires force and one that can be de-escalated verbally.

RCMP training in crisis intervention and de-escalation varies considerably across Canada. Some police agencies provide little or no learning and others providing more comprehensive education that ranges from 10–40 hours. However, there is little evidence on the effectiveness of these training programs. Some jurisdictions use first responder teams of mental health professionals and RCMP officers.

As a member of the RCMP steering committee responsible for RCMP education and training your team has been asked to make recommendations and outline action steps that will address the growing challenges the RCMP face in their interactions with individuals who are vulnerable as a result of their mental or emotional state. You take the systems approach to training as outline in this chapter to answer the following questions.

Questions

1. Identify the problem and causes of the problem.
2. What are the organization-wide, job-wide, and individual training needs?
3. What are the learning objectives for the training, and what training methods would be most appropriate?
4. How would you evaluate and ensure the transfer of the training?

Sources: Dorothy Cotton. "The Attitudes of Canadian Police Officers Toward the Mentally Ill," *International Journal of Law and Mental Health*, 27(2004):135–146; Fiona Wilson-Bates, "Lost in Transition: How a Lack of Capacity in the Mental Health System Is Failing Vancouver's Mentally Ill and Draining Policing Resources," Vancouver, British Columbia: Vancouver Police Department (2008); Dorothy Cotton and Terry Coleman, "Understanding Mental Illness: A Review and Recommendations for Police Education & Training in Canada," Canadian Alliance on Mental Illness and Mental Health (2010); Dorothy Cotton and Terry Coleman, "A Study of Police Academy Training and Education for New Police Officers Related to Working with People with Mental Illness," The Police/Mental Health Subcommittee of the Canadian Association of Chiefs of Police and The Mental Health and the Law Advisory Committee of the Mental Health Commission of Canada, November 2008; and Rick Parent, "The Police Use of Deadly Force in British Columbia: Mental Illness and Crisis Intervention," *Journal of Police Crisis Negotiations* 11 (2012): 57–71.

NOTES AND REFERENCES

1. Faryal Siddiqui, "Human Capital Management: An Emerging Human Resource Management Practice," *International Journal of Learning & Development* 2, no. 1 (2012): 353–67.
2. Ibid.
3. "The Conference Board CEO Challenge: 2011: Fueling Business Growth with Innovation and Talent Management," The Conference Board of Canada, April, 2011.
4. "Learning and Development Outlook 2011: Are Organizations Ready for Learning 2.0?" The Conference Board of Canada, October 2011.
5. Ibid.
6. "Cisco Canada, from the Winners," Aon Hewitt, accessed May 1, 2012, http://was2.hewitt.com/bestemployers/canada/pages/winners.htm.
7. Douglas Watt, "Treading Water: Canada Is Gradually Losing Its Competitive Edge," The Conference Board of Canada, September 2011.
8. "Learning and Development Outlook 2011: Are Organizations Ready for Learning 2.0?"
9. Ibid.
10. *Claudine Kapel,* "Declining Investments in Training Raise Concerns," *Canadian HR Reporter*, November 28, 2011, www.hrreporter.com/blog/compensation-rewards/archive/2011/11/28/declining-investments-in-training-raise-concerns.
11. Susan M. Heathfield, "Performance Development Planning," About.com, accessed May 1, 2012, http://humanresources.about.com/cs/perfmeasurement/a/pdp.htm.
12. "Learning and Development Outlook 2011: Are Organizations Ready for Learning 2.0?"
13. Ibid.
14. Ibid.
15. Tony Bates, "Strategic Directions for E-learning in Canada," Contact North, February 2010, accessed May 1, 2012, www.contactnorth.ca/sites/default/files/pdf/trends-and-directions/strategic_directions_for_e-learning_in_canada.pdf.
16. "Global Writers Apprentice Program," Banff World Media Festival, accessed May 1, 2012, www.banffmediafestival.com/global-writers-apprentice-program.php.
17. "Saint Elizabeth First Nations, Inuit and Métis Program," accessed May 1, 2012, http://fnim.atyourside.ca/home.
18. "Embracing Opportunities for Better Patient Care," *News Canada's Healthcare Newspaper*, April 3, 2012, www.hospitalnews.com/embracing-opportunities-for-better-patient-care.
19. "Learning and Development Outlook 2011: Are Organizations Ready for Learning 2.0?"
20. Industry Canada, "Does E-learning Help Companies Save Money and Improve Productivity?" Canadian Training Solutions, accessed May 1, 2012, www.ic.gc.ca/eic/site/cts-scf.nsf/eng/sl00044.html.
21. Peer Resources—The Mentors Corporation, accessed May 1, 2012, www.mentors.ca.
22. Jim Kirkpatrick and Wendy Kirkpatrick, "The Kirkpatrick Philosophy," Kirkpatrick Partners, accessed May 21, 2012, www.kirkpatrickpartners.com.
23. Reuben Tozman, "New Learning Analytics for a New Workplace," *T+D Magazine*, February 2012, www.astd.org/Publications/Magazines/TD/TD-Archive/2012/02/New-Learning-Analytics-for-a-New-Workplace.
24. Monica Belcourt, George Bohlander, and Scott Snell, *Managing Human Resources*, 6th Canadian ed. (Toronto: Nelson Thomson, 2011), 298.
25. Lynette Gillis and Allan Bailey, "Investing in People—Meta Study of Evaluation Findings," Canadian Society for Training and Development, March 2010, accessed May 1, 2012, www.cstd.ca/?page=IIP.
26. Lynette Gillis and Allan Bailey, "Business Development Bank of Canada: Measuring The ROI of a Coaching Program for Banking Branch Managers," Canadian Society for Training and Development, accessed May 1, 2012, www.cstd.ca/resource/resmgr/iip/bdc_report_final_english.pdf.
27. Lynette Gillis and Allan Bailey, "WestJet: Measuring the ROI of Meeting Management Training," Canadian Society for Training and Development, accessed May 1, 2012, www.cstd.ca/resource/resmgr/iip/westjet_report_final_english.pdf.
28. ASTD Forum, accessed May 1, 2012, www.astd.org/Enterprise-Solutions/ASTD-Forum.aspx.
29. BC HRMA Metrics Service, accessed May 1, 2012, www.bchrma.org/researchvoice/overview.htm.
30. "'Newness' and the Risk of Occupational Injury," Institute for Work & Health, May 2009, accessed May 1, 2012, www.iwh.on.ca/briefings/newness.
31. Ibid.
32. "Workplace Literacy Facts," ABC Life Literacy Canada, accessed May 1, 2012. http://abclifeliteracy.ca/workplace-literacy-facts.
33. "In for the Long Run," ABC Life Literacy Canada, accessed May 1, 2012, http://abclifeliteracy.ca/long-run-0.
34. Watt, "Treading Water."
35. "Canada's Demographic Crunch: Can Underrepresented Workers Save Us?" The Canadian Chamber of Commerce, October 2010.
36. Lisa Gueldenzoph Snyder, "Teaching Teams about Teamwork: Preparation, Practice and Performance Review," *Business Communications Quarterly* 72 (March 2009): 74–79.
37. Shannon Klie, "Training Important during Recession," *Canadian HR Reporter*, June 1, 2009, 1.
38. "Women in Senior Management: Where Are They?" The Conference Board of Canada, August 2011.
39. Ibid.

CHAPTER 6

MANAGING PERFORMANCE

OUTCOMES

After studying this chapter, you should be able to

1. Define a performance management system.

2. Explain the purpose of a performance management system.

3. Describe the management practices necessary for a good performance management system.

4. Identify the steps in an effective performance management system.

5. Describe the different sources of performance review information.

6. Explain the various methods used for performance reviews.

7. Outline the characteristics of an effective performance review interview.

OUTLINE

HRM CLOSE-UP

"To see someone reach a goal or receive a promotion is the biggest compliment to a manager."

Tyler Gorrell.

In his role as manager at the GoodLife Fitness Club in Saskatoon, Saskatchewan, Tyler Gorrell leads a team of personal trainers, membership development staff, and customer service representatives as well as team leaders who have direct responsibility for the front-line staff. It's a large group to oversee, but he's dedicated to ensuring a quality performance management process and sees it as integral to his staff's success. "Their success reflects on my success," he says. "To see someone reach a goal or receive a promotion is the biggest compliment to a manager."

Corporately, GoodLife Fitness supplies guidelines and templates to use in personal development plans and performance management discussions. These are all found on the company's intranet site. "I also rely on the People Department at GoodLife who are available to help with any specific circumstances I have. Other club managers and colleagues are also there to support me," explains Gorrell.

GoodLife's performance management process begins with a goal-setting exercise where employees articulate personal, professional, development, and financial goals. "All of these goals tie together," says Gorrell. "An employee might be motivated by saving money for a personal trip, and they might want to know what they can do to improve performance and earn more money."

To gather information on how employees are doing, Gorrell uses a combination of tools and techniques. Managers, in particular, receive "360-degree feedback," whereby direct reports and peers provide input on their performance. Customer feedback is an important source of information as is systems data, such as numbers of new memberships, numbers of personal training sessions, revenue generated, and product sales. "I also look for a self-evaluation from staff. I like to understand the strengths and successes that the employee perceives and compare that to my own observations," says Gorrell.

Gorrell practises "Ten Minute Meetings" with his team leaders, and the team leaders do the same for their employees. These short coaching sessions are used to ask how a shift went yesterday, what risks or opportunities were presented, and what support staff need to reach specific goals. Even when the club is busy and there's lots to do, Gorrell makes sure he takes time to do this. "It's a matter of priority," he says. "It only takes an hour to go through this process with all of your employees and it's worth it."

Managers at GoodLife submit performance reviews electronically. Scores are captured in the system, giving the corporate office a way to ensure that reviews are being conducted. "But they also do 'Caring Audits' where the actual file is inspected," explains Gorrell. "Quality and integrity is important, and the company wants to ensure the employee is being cared for in terms of goal-setting and performance management. It ties in with staff retention and the employee's ability to grow with the company. This matters to GoodLife," he adds.

Finding the time to coach staff and follow through on performance management commitments can be challenging, but Gorrell knows this has to be done regularly and consistently. "Once a year is never enough," he says. "As a manager, you have to be prepared. Know the metrics. Know what the employee needs to do to improve. Look at 'skill versus will' in order to understand reasons for poor performance. Ask if they are willing to try, and find out if they might be hindered by a lack of skill in a certain area."

Meeting outside the work environment to discuss performance can also be beneficial for both manager and employee. "How you meet is important," stresses Gorrell. "Ensuring there are no distractions helps the employee know that the meeting is important and that they are special." Gorrell feels that connecting with the employee this way should take precedence over everything else a people manager does.

Personally, Gorrell enjoys working through the performance management process with his staff. He even enjoys being on the receiving end. "I like feedback," he says. "For me, performance reviews are the best opportunity to hear how I'm doing and to discover what I can improve."

INTRODUCTION

In the preceding chapters, we discussed how an organization hires and develops a productive workforce. In this chapter, we turn to performance management, which is one of the most critical processes that managers use to maintain and enhance productivity and facilitate progress toward strategic goals. While we will focus mainly on a formal system, the processes of managing and reviewing performance can be informal as well. All managers monitor the way employees work and assess how this matches organizational needs. Supervisors and managers form impressions about the relative value of employees to the organization and seek to maximize the contribution of every individual. Yet while these ongoing informal processes are vitally important, most organizations also have a system that includes a formal review of the person's performance once or twice a year, or on an ongoing basis. In the HRM Close-up, Tyler Gorrell explains the successes of regular and continuous feedback, and coaching.

The success or failure of a performance management system depends on the philosophy underlying it, its connection with business goals, the attitudes and skills of those responsible for using it, and the individual components of the system. A performance management system is more than the actual review—it is an overall approach to getting the maximum contribution from each individual.

A PERFORMANCE MANAGEMENT SYSTEM

Outcome 1

What is a performance management system?

Performance management system
A set of integrated management practices

Outcome 2

What is the purpose of a performance management system?

A **performance management system** is a set of integrated management practices. While the formal review of employees' performance is a key component, a good performance review program does not make a good performance management system. A systems approach to performance management (1) allows the organization to integrate the management functions in order to maximize employee potential and (2) helps increase employees' satisfaction with their work and with the organization.

Formal programs for reviewing performance are by no means new to organizations. Performance review programs are used in large and small organizations in both the public and private sectors. Advocates see these programs as among the most logical means to review, develop, and thus effectively utilize the knowledge and abilities of employees. A recent survey by Ceridian Canada determined that employees feel more valued by their companies when performance reviews occur.[1] Robert Bacal, a long-time observer of performance management systems, reminds us that the primary purpose for performance reviews is to improve future performance.[2]

It is important that the organization is clear about the purpose, but this is not always the case. Sometimes, companies want systems to communicate what work is valued; at other times, performance management systems are used to base pay decisions. For example, an organization that employs a team-based structure might have a performance management system that focuses on reviewing individual performance. This focus gives mixed messages about who owns the responsibility for the results and what is being valued in the performance review. Performance management needs to be leading toward improved organizational performance; if it doesn't, then it isn't worth doing.[3]

There is no doubt that managing performance is not always easy. Managers and supervisors frequently avoid discussing employee performance—whether it is good or poor. Yet, when reviews are done well, an opportunity is created to support good performance and to help poor performers improve.[4]

Managing performance is not an added activity in the busy supervisor's life—it is central to the everyday work of managers. For years managers have struggled with the performance process, as have employees. However, as companies look for better ways of keeping and motivating employees, more managers are finding that the process is evolving.[5] Even for small businesses, taking the time to provide feedback to employees is key to success. Read HRM and SME 6.1 to learn more about the experiences of small businesses.

HRM and SME 6.1

BUT THERE IS NO TIME!

Small organizations frequently do not have any formalized HR processes, especially when it comes to assessing employee performance. One reason often cited is that the company is so busy just making the business grow that there is no time for such things as reviewing performance.

Noseworthy Chapman is an accounting firm in St. John's, Newfoundland. With a workforce of only 50 people, it felt that it didn't need much in the way of any formal systems. However, in late 2008, it decided that it was important to take time for more formal reviews of employee performance. The company is now fully supportive of ensuring that the firm's partners take the time to provide employees with a frank assessment of their performance.

Likewise, Kitchen Stuff Plus Inc., a housewares company in Toronto, resisted as the owners felt that doing performance reviews was too complicated. However, as one HR manager indicated, a company does not need anything fancy to provide basic feedback to employees. As Kitchen Stuff Plus found, there are many Web sites, which can be accessed for guidance and templates.

Right Management, a consulting business that provides help to small businesses, informs its clients that they can lose good talent when feedback isn't provided. Also, with specific and explicit about goals, a small business can increase accountability, drive firm performance, and allow employees to feel part of the growing business.

QUESTION:

What are some of the reasons a small business may take the time to do performance reviews?

Sources: Mario Johne, "Performance reviews are more than worth it," *The Globe and Mail*, October 25, 2011, http://www.theglobeandmail.com/report-on-business/small-business/sb-managing/human-resources/performance-reviews-are-more-than-worth-it/article2211780/ (accessed November 17, 2011).

A number of different research studies in a variety of industries, including engineering, health care, and education, demonstrate the strong link between performance management systems and organizational success. These studies consistently demonstrate, however, that the employee's performance needs to be connected to achieving the larger goals of the organization and that it is critical to determine what will be measured.[6] Further, there is evidence that an effective system contributes to a constructive work environment by providing coaching, feedback, recognition, and open dialogue.[7] With such clear evidence of the value of performance management systems, it will be useful for managers and HR practitioners to use these research findings when building a business case for the implementation of such a system.

MANAGEMENT PRACTICES

Outcome 3

What are the management practices for a good performance system?

The following management practices are essential for an effective performance management system:

1. Setting and communicating clear performance expectations for all work and all jobs.
2. Ensuring clear and specific performance objectives (or standards of performance) for all work.
3. Providing supportive and helpful coaching by the supervisor to enable staff to reach their objectives.
4. Focusing on the accomplishment of objectives during performance reviews.
5. Recognizing and celebrating good performance.
6. Creating action plans to improve performance, if necessary.

As shown, the actual review step (item 4) is only one component of the system. However, the vast majority of performance management systems focus primarily on the review and typically use that step for making compensation decisions or making decisions about the continued employment of people. For example, as Groupon, a Web-based company that provides discount coupons for local businesses, started selling shares in the company, it aggressively increased sales targets, reviewed the performance of all employees, and terminated those employees who did not meet targets.[8]

Purposes of Managing Performance

There are several purposes for performance reviews, all intended to benefit both the organization and the employee, and to ensure that any decisions are based on objective information.

Compensation Purposes

The most frequent use of performance management systems is to make compensation decisions. It is also important that employees believe that any compensation decisions have been made fairly.[9] And the form of compensation can be everything from an increase in base salary to some other type of incentive—all with the intended outcome of motivating employees to meet business goals.[10]

Administrative Purposes

A performance management system also integrates a number of other major HR processes, such as promotion, transfer, and layoff decisions. Further, it can be used as part of HR planning—particularly when the organization has a succession plan. As well, the system provides a "paper trail" for documenting HRM processes that may result in legal action. For example, if a person were being disciplined regarding very poor customer service, the system would be able to identify what the goals were, how well the person met the goals, and the discussions and coaching sessions to improve performance in relation to customer service.

Measurement of Performance

In order to assess the overall success of the organization, it is important to be able to measure the employees' accomplishments. Thus, you want to know how the employees performed compared to the established goals. A well-designed performance management system will be able to measure the performance of the organization and the employees. Studies have also shown that an effective performance management system can positively influence the behaviours within the organization, thereby leading to business success.[11]

It is also important that the measures are reliable and valid. You were introduced to these concepts in Chapter 4 in relation to assessing skills in potential employees. These same concepts apply to measuring accomplishments. Performance measures must be consistent (reliable) and able to measure the performance (valid).[12] This issue will be explored further in the section "Complying with the Law" on page 201.

Developmental Purposes

From the standpoint of individual development, a performance system provides the feedback essential for discussing strengths and areas where performance needs improving— at both the individual and organizational levels. In this way, training and development needs can be highlighted. For example, if, through setting objectives, many supervisors identify that people have to improve their computer literacy skills, then the organization can provide a solution that meets those needs. From this information, the organization may set up a formal training program for all employees. This approach can be better than having each supervisor deal with each person on an individual basis. Without such a step in the system, the manner in which developmental needs are identified can be hit-and-miss.

Regardless of the employee's level of performance, the system provides an opportunity to identify issues for discussion, eliminate any potential problems, and work on ways of achieving high performance. Newer approaches to performance management emphasize training as well as development and growth plans for employees. A developmental approach recognizes that the purpose of a manager is to support and help the person (or team) achieve results for good organizational performance. Having a sound basis for identifying performance goals, coaching, reviewing, and recognizing performance leads to successful organizations.

Figure 6.1 provides a summary of the purposes of managing performance.

Why Performance Management Systems Sometimes Fail

In actual practice, formal performance management systems sometimes yield disappointing results. Figure 6.2 shows that some of the reasons include the manager believing that it is only for the HR department, or that it is used to punish employees, or it isn't clear what is expected. Further, if a review is used to provide a written assessment for salary action and at the same time to motivate employees to improve their work, the administrative and developmental purposes may be in conflict. As a result, the actual review interview may become a discussion about salary in which the manager seeks to justify the action taken. In such cases, the discussion might have little influence on the employee's future job performance.

As with all HR processes and systems, if the support of top management is lacking, the system will not be successful. Even the best-conceived process will not work in an environment where managers are not encouraged and expected by their superiors to take their responsibilities seriously in managing performance. To underscore the importance of this responsibility, top management should ensure that managers and supervisors are also part of the overall performance management system and that their performance will be reviewed for how well they are managing their employees' performance.

Other reasons performance management systems can fail include the following:

1. Managers feel that little or no benefit will be derived from the time and energy spent on the process.
2. Managers dislike the face-to-face discussion and performance feedback.
3. Managers are not sufficiently adept in setting goals and performance measures, in coaching and supporting, or providing performance feedback.
4. The judgmental role of a review can conflict with the helping role of developing employees.

FIGURE 6.1 Purposes for Managing Performance

Compensation

- Salary increases
- Bonuses and pay-for-performance awards

Administrative

- Promotion decisions
- Transfer decisions
- Layoff decisions
- Succession planning
- Paper trail for documenting HRM actions

Measurement of Performance

- Determine accomplishment of goals
- Influence employee behaviour
- Improve organizational performance

Developmental

- Feedback for discussing strengths and areas for improvement
- Elimination of potential problems
- Identify training needs

FIGURE 6.2   Reasons Performance Management Systems Can Fail

1. Performance management is seen as a punishment tool.
2. The performance management system is perceived to belong to the HR department.
3. Performance management is a separate system and not linked to other processes such as rewards and succession planning.
4. The performance review interview is seen as unpleasant.
5. Employees are not clear on how they will be assessed.
6. Continuous coaching and frequent feedback are not done.
7. Constantly forcing out poor performers without attempting to help those employees improve.
8. There is little or no training for managers on how to use the performance management process.
9. Employees don't know what is expected of them.
10. There is no process for involving employees in setting goals.

Sources: Adapted from Susan M. Heathfield, "When Management Systems Fail," http://humanresources.about.com/od/motivationsuccess/a/manage_systems. htm (accessed November 18, 2011); and "Performance Management Process: Avoiding the Traps," Mercer Consulting, July 15, 2011, www.mercer.com/ articles/performance-management-process-avoiding-traps (accessed November 18, 2011).

In many organizations performance management is a once-a-year activity in which the review interview becomes a source of friction for both managers and employees. An important principle of performance management is that continual feedback and employee coaching must be a positive regular activity—be it daily or hourly. The annual or semiannual performance review should be a logical extension of the day-to-day supervision process. For example, Mead Johnson Canada, a subsidiary of Bristol-Myers Squibb, a large pharmaceutical firm, changed its performance management system so that employees receive ongoing reviews. This system now has a future growth and expectations focus with immediate and specific feedback. Furthermore, other companies are encouraging frequent feedback sessions instead of only annually. At Work with HRM 6.1 describes how some companies are making use of more frequent reviews.

One of the main concerns of employees is the fairness of the performance management system, since the process is central to so many HRM decisions. Employees who believe the system is unfair may consider the review interview a waste of time and leave the interview feeling anxious and frustrated. They may also view compliance with the system as mechanical and thus play only a passive role during the interview process. By addressing these employee concerns during the planning stage of the system, the organization will help the performance management system succeed in reaching its goals. Employees can help ensure that the review is fair by being well prepared. This can include keeping track of positive (and negative) feedback from the supervisor and keeping records of courses, workshops, and any other training activities.

Finally, managers can have biases even in a well-run system.[13] For example, managers may inflate reviews because they desire higher salaries for their employees or because higher subordinate ratings make them look good as managers. Alternatively, managers may want to get rid of troublesome employees, passing them off to another department by inflating their ratings. Supervisors and managers have to be watchful for the same types of errors in performance reviews as in selection interviews. The supervisor may make decisions about a person's performance based on recent events (recency error) or judging performance favourably or unfavourably overall by putting emphasis on only one area that is important in the supervisor's mind (halo error). Likewise, the supervisor may be unwilling to give either extremely low or extremely high assessments and decide to rate everyone as "above average" (central tendency). A supervisor can also be biased by comparing one employee's performance to another's (contrast error) instead of assessing the employee against a set of standards.

It is not just biases that can create problems with performance management. Organizational politics and how the manager wants to be perceived can also creep into performance reviews. For example, the manager may base the assessment on how the manager feels about the employee—not on factual observations.[14] Or the manager may

AT WORK **with HRM 6.1**

WHAT'S WRONG WITH ONCE A YEAR?

Many managers and employees dread the annual performance review meeting. But it doesn't need to be that way. Many younger employees want more feedback—good or bad. However, with "bad" feedback, what the employee is looking for is something constructive—how can they improve.

The annual performance review started about 60 years ago and hasn't changed much since then. However, with both younger people and new technology, some organizations have turned to social media to create a much more dynamic approach to performance review.

Rypple, a Toronto-based software company that develops workplace applications for real-time feedback, was approached by Facebook to design an interactive performance review process. Rypple was a natural choice as it uses a Facebook-type approach. Managers, for example, have the ability to "like" tasks, ask for input from others, and monitor goal accomplishment set by employees. Such an approach is particularly appropriate for the Gen Ys—the very users of instant communication through computers and smartphones.

Other companies have moved to more frequent feedback sessions as the once-per-year session was completely overloaded with information: reviewing past performance, setting new goals, and discussing pay. With so much information to absorb, employees tended to focus on anything not positive and didn't "hear" any of the constructive suggestions for improvement.

Some of these changes are also appealing to older employees. If people believe that the performance review process is meaningless, then using tools that provide more frequent ways to both praise and correct allows people to make better use of the information.

Even with these new tools, there is still the issue of ensuring that managers find the time to provide the feedback. If managers don't use the tools, then such capability soon becomes irrelevant. But this type of software isn't for all workplaces—it is not a magical solution. The type of workplace that can benefit most from social media applications for performance reviews are those that are tech savvy and have younger workers. The company also needs engaged managers who want to support and encourage their employees in real time. The tools will not work for those organizations where managers like to be aloof from their staff or where the work environment is hierarchical and top-down driven. These are tools for engaging employees and supporting them in achieving their goals—through frequent real-time feedback.

CRITICAL THINKING QUESTIONS:

1. Would you like to work at an organization that uses the tools described above? Why or why not?
2. What are the advantages of a real-time, online performance management system? Can you think of some potential problems with this approach?

Sources: Adapted from Iain Marlow, "Fixing the dreaded performance review," *The Globe and Mail*, July 15, 2011, B13; and Rachel Emma Silverman, "Every year not enough, try weekly performance reviews," *The Globe and Mail*, September 12, 2011, B8.

---

want to maintain as much discretion as possible and therefore may not use the performance management system as intended. Likewise, the manager may want to avoid any conflict and therefore inflate the performance review.[15]

STEPS IN AN EFFECTIVE PERFORMANCE MANAGEMENT SYSTEM

Outcome 4

What are the steps in a performance management system?

The HR department ordinarily has the primary responsibility for overseeing and coordinating the performance management system. HR may also design or select a performance management system to use. Managers from the operating departments must also be actively involved, particularly in helping to establish the objectives for the system. Furthermore, employees are more likely to accept and be satisfied with the performance management system when they have the chance to participate in its development. Their concerns about fairness and accuracy in determining raises, promotions, and the like tend to be alleviated

About.com
humanresources.about.com

Free Management Library
http://managementhelp.org

Development Dimensions International
www.ddiworld.com

somewhat when they have been involved at the planning stage and have helped develop the performance standards. This section describes the steps that are key to an effective performance management system. In addition, other useful information on performance management can be found at About.com (**humanresources.about.com**), Free Management Library (**http://managementhelp.org**), and Development Dimensions International (**www. ddiworld.com**).

Clarifying the Work to Be Done

Before any goals can be established or any performance standards identified, it is important to clarify the work to be accomplished. And this is done by identifying the expected outcomes or results and determining how those results will be measured. For example, an expected result for a cook at a fast-food restaurant may be "no food wastage." The supervisor and cook would then decide how this would be measured. It could be measured by determining the number of kilograms of food in the garbage pail or the number of voided customer orders. Note that the clarification step is done jointly with the supervisor and the employee. The key to a good performance management system is the involvement of the employee in the entire process.

Setting Goals and Establishing a Performance Plan

Once the supervisor and employee (or team) are clear on expected results and how those results will be measured, goals must be set. And for the system to really work, these goals must be linked to overall business objectives. For example, an overall business objective for the fast-food restaurant is to reduce costs. Since food costs are a large proportion of overall costs, the restaurant may decide to focus on reducing food costs. Therefore, for the individual employee, the ability to cut down on wasted food will reduce the overall food costs and the goal may be "to reduce food waste by 10% within the next three months." You will note that this is a very specific goal that includes a time frame.

To ensure that there is a strong link to business goals, the supervisor may also need to establish performance measures that are not quantitative (e.g., revenue), but qualitative such as customer satisfaction or customer loyalty.[16] With the use of both financial results (e.g., cost of food) and soft measures (e.g., customer satisfaction), the results are more strongly linked to the overall restaurant outcomes. This step also involves discussion between both the supervisor and the employee, which leads to greater involvement and commitment to the specific goals.

Setting specific, measurable performance goals is a key step in a performance management system.

Ryouchin/The Image Bank/Getty Images

With the ongoing concern about business ethics, more and more organizations are including standards of performance related to ethics and reviewing ethical behaviour as part of the performance management system. Ethics in HRM 6.1 discusses some of the issues regarding assessing unethical behaviour.

There are other types of methods, such as trait and behavioural, in addition to goals, which can be used in establishing the performance plan. These will be discussed later in the chapter.

Regular and Frequent Coaching

Coaching sessions are designed to help employees achieve their results. Coaching should not involve fault-finding or blaming. Most people want to do a good job, and, therefore, it is important that a supervisor approach coaching in a helpful and supportive way. If the

---

ETHICS in HRM 6.1

WERE THESE ETHICAL DECISIONS?

How do you distinguish between ethical and unethical behaviour and performance at work? The answer frequently is "Not easily." As there continue to be business scandals even in recessionary times, boards of directors and senior managers are looking at ways to review and assess ethical behaviour.

But what are some actions by employees that create ethical dilemmas on which performance might be measured? A recent incident at Safeway highlights what can happen. A young couple with their toddler was accused of stealing $5 worth of sandwiches after they had spent $50 on groceries. When approached, the couple indicated that they were going to pay for the sandwiches and had gotten them while shopping. Even with asking them to pay, Safeway officials called the police; the couple was arrested and their toddler taken from them. This procedure took 18 hours before Safeway finally dropped the matter. The store manager indicated that the store was just following company policy, and Safeway apologized for the error. However, during this incident, Safeway's name was splashed across many media outlets talking about Safeway's actions.

There is no doubt that the action of the manager spoke volumes to the other employees. The action basically said, "Follow store policy no matter what and do not use common sense." On the other hand, the behaviour of managers sets the tone for how others are to behave in similar situations. In organizations that value employee empowerment and expect ethical decision-making, employees can feel more engaged. So, if the intention is for managers to behave ethically and provide a role model for others, does that mean that those same managers can use their own judgment when making certain decisions?

Many of the companies that take this view have also developed codes of ethics—a set of statements that indicate correct behaviour and actions in the organization. It is from this code that specific and measurable behaviours of performance can be established. For example, frequently in a code of ethics, there is a statement about "being respectful to each other." Therefore, the performance measure might be "Demonstrates respect for all staff and customers" or "Demonstrates respect for customers in unusual circumstances." This particular measure would also need to have clear definitions for "respect," as this word can mean different things to different people.

Organizations are driven to be fair minded and to be as transparent as possible in all their dealings. And this will work when organizations link performance to more than short-term goals. People pay attention to what they are measured on.

QUESTION:

Do you think the manager at Safeway did the right thing? Explain your reasons.

Sources: Adapted from "Wayward at Safeway," *Workforce*, November 8, 2011, www.workforce.com/article/20111108/BLOGS05/111109969; Amanda Silliker, "Management behaviours closely linked to engagement," *Canadian HR Reporter*, April 25, 2011, www.hrreporter.com/articleview? &articleid=10086&headline=management-behaviours-closely-linked-to-engagement-study (accessed November 23, 2011); and Sam H. DeKay, "Doing What's Right: Communicating Business Ethics," *Business Communications Quarterly*, September 2011, Vol. 74 Issue 3, 287–288.

employee is having difficulty reaching a goal, the supervisor and employee can explore together the reasons why and what can be done to fix the difficulty.

Coaching is also a good way to avoid costs of firing employees and hiring new employees. It is difficult for employees to improve on mistakes if the supervisor does not take the time to help them understand what they need to do. For coaching to be effective, the supervisor needs to describe what the specific behaviours that need to be reinforced or redirected, along with the specific situations where the behaviour was observed.[17] Providing feedback on behaviours is not just describing what the supervisor might want to see differently but also describing the positive behaviours. Read Manager's Toolkit 6.1 for some coaching tips.

Conducting a Formal Review of Performance

Most performance management systems include an annual formal review of the employee's overall performance. This occasion allows both the supervisor and employee to consider the employee's accomplishments and to discuss development areas for the next year. It is also usually at this point that the organization uses the results of the annual performance review for salary adjustments.

Since the employee was involved in the original goal setting, and since there has been regular and frequent feedback and coaching, this step is more of a review—there shouldn't be any surprises.

Recognizing and Rewarding Performance

No system will be effective without recognition of accomplishments. Although we usually think of recognition in monetary terms, some nonfinancial rewards for the employee include the following:

1. Being considered for a promotion.
2. Being given the opportunity to work on a special project.

MANAGER'S TOOLKIT **6.1**

"HOW-TO" TIPS ON COACHING

1. Coaching is between two people.

2. Coaching is based on a relationship of trust and respect between the two, not on control.

3. Coaching is about personal development for the person being coached.

4. Both people must want to be involved in the coaching relationship.

5. The coach asks questions and asks person to expand on comments.

6. Coaching draws out the person's potential.

7. Coaching is sharing one's own experiences and knowledge.—particularly those of the coach.

8. Coaching is about helping the person come to their own conclusions: the coach does not impose a solution.

9. Coaching requires active listening and full participation for both people.

10. Coaching is helping the other person learn and become self-sufficient.

11. Coaching is enabling,—not training.

12. Coaching is about reflection and conversation.

13. Coaching provides support and discovery.

14. Coaching focuses on real-world situations so that the person can learn and act or behave differently.

Sources: Adapted from Susan M. Heathfield "Tips for Effective Coaching," *About.com*, accessed February 28, 2012, http://humanresources. about.com/od/coachingmentoring/a/coaching.htm; "Life Coaching and Personal Coaching," businessballs.com, accessed February 29, 2012, www.businessballs.com/lifecoaching.htm; Eileen Chadnick, "Giving Feedback That Fuels Success," *Canadian HR Reporter*, September 6, 2010, www.hrreporter.com/articleview/8192-giving-feedback-that-fuels-success; Robert Hicks and John McCracken, "A Coaching Blueprint," *Physician Executive*, January/February 2012: 62–64; and Garry Kranz, "Organizations Need Coaching on How to Coach," *Workforce Management*, February 24, 2012, www.workforce.com/article/20111212/NEWS01/111219998/organizations-need-coaching-on-how-to-coach-report.

3. Being praised by the supervisor.
4. Being profiled in a business journal about a particular achievement or receiving an award of excellence.

These types of rewards cost little or no money. People like to know that their good work and achievements are noticed. Appropriate rewards can be a great tool in helping the organization be successful.[18] During the recent economic recession, managers were reminded that their praise is a valuable corporate resource and can be used to improve employee performance. By careful use of praise and positive feedback, the manager can energize the individual, and the person's work will improve in related areas.[19]

Complying with the Law

Since performance assessments are used as a basis for HRM actions, they must meet certain legal requirements. The legality of any performance management system is measured against criteria of reliability, fairness, and validity. *Reliability* refers to whether performance is measured consistently among the employee participants. *Fairness* refers to the extent to which the system avoids bias caused by any factors unrelated to performance. *Validity* refers to the extent to which the system is job related and accurate. Under the *Charter of Rights and Freedoms*, and other federal and provincial human rights requirements, performance management systems must be, above all, valid. Worker performance must be assessed on the basis of job requirements to ensure legal compliance.

Although currently there are few lawsuits pertaining to performance management systems in Canada, the spillover effect of lawsuits in the United States has prompted organizations to try to eliminate vagueness in descriptions of traits, such as attitude, co-operation, dependability, initiative, and leadership. For example, the trait "dependability" can be made much less vague if it is spelled out as employee tardiness and/or unexcused absences. In general, reducing room for subjective judgments will improve the entire performance review process.

Employers might face legal challenges to their performance management systems when reviews indicate acceptable or above-average performance but employees are later passed over for promotion, disciplined for poor performance, discharged, or laid off from the organization. In these cases, the performance reviews can undermine the legitimacy of the subsequent decision. And legal challenges can be very costly. For example, if an organization terminated someone due to a downsizing, but then subsequently said it was for poor performance, the company would not be successful in defending its action if the personnel file did not contain a poor performance review. More information regarding performance reviews and discipline is discussed in Chapter 9.

Performance reviews should therefore meet the following guidelines:

- Performance ratings must be job related, with performance standards related to the work as identified through job analysis.
- Employees must be given a written copy of their performance standards in advance of any formal performance review.
- Managers who conduct the review must be able to observe the behaviour they are assessing. This implies having a measurable standard with which to compare employee behaviour.
- Managers and supervisors should be trained to understand their role in managing performance, specifically on (1) how to set goals and performance standards, (2) how to coach and conduct a formal review session, and (3) how to write a review report or use any other written materials associated with the performance system.
- Reviews should be discussed openly with employees and coaching or corrective guidance offered to help poor performers improve their performance.
- An appeals procedure should be established to enable employees to express disagreement with the formal evaluation.

Employers must ensure that managers and supervisors document reviews and reasons for subsequent HRM actions. This information may prove decisive should an employee take legal action. An employer's credibility is strengthened when it can support performance results by documenting instances of poor performance. Read HRM and the Law 6.1 to gain an understanding of the importance of documenting poor performance and expectations for improvement.

Deciding Who Should Provide Performance Information

Outcome 5

Who should provide performance review information?

For many years, the traditional approach to reviewing an employee's performance was based solely on information the supervisor gathered through first-hand knowledge of the person. However, given the complexity of today's jobs, it is often unrealistic to presume that one person can fully observe and assess an employee's performance. There may also be a desire to gather information directly from those who are best acquainted with the person's performance, such as a customer. Consequently, information about a person's performance may come from supervisors, the employee being reviewed, peers, team members, subordinates, and customers.

The Canadian Institute of Chartered Accountants and the Ontario Ministry of Northern Development and Mines have begun using information gathered from a number of sources. Since supervisors spend much of their time on gathering data for and conducting the performance review, the remainder of this section will focus on that portion of the performance management system.

HRM and the Law 6.1

BUT HE ISN'T PERFORMING!

If someone is being disciplined for poor performance serious enough to warrant termination, then good documentation is critical. A recent court case in Saskatchewan reinforces this point.

A radio station in a small town in Saskatchewan hired a person to function as program director, music director, and morning show host as the station transitioned to an "oldies" station from a country-western station. In addition to this new person, a consulting firm was retained to manage the transition. During the consulting firm's work, a number of areas for performance improvement for the program director were put forward to the station's management. The company worked with the program director, communicated in writing the required improvement, and frequently met with the program director to work toward improved performance. Eventually, the radio station did not see the required improvements and terminated the program director. The director subsequently sued the radio station for wrongful dismissal.

Initially, the court determined that the radio station had not given the program director sufficient opportunity to improve and therefore the program director had been wrongfully dismissed. The radio station appealed that decision, and the case went to the Saskatchewan Court of Appeal. At the appeals hearing, the court ruled in favour of the radio station and said it had a legitimate right to terminate the program director for poor performance. The court also identified four factors that need to be present to terminate for poor performance: (1) the employer must have provided reasonable performance standards; (2) the employee must fail to meet the standards; (3) the employer must give clear warning as to consequences of not meeting standards; and (4) the warning must clearly state termination if performance is not met.

QUESTION:

What could the radio station have been done differently?

Source: Adapted from Andrew Treash, "Terminating underperforming employees a delicate act," *Canadian HR Reporter*, September 26, 2011, www.hrreporter.com/articleview?&articleid=11295&headline=terminating-underperforming-employees-a-delicate-act-(toughest-hr-questions). Reprinted by permission of Canadian HR Reporter. © Copyright Thomson Reuters Canada Ltd., Toronto, Ontario, 1-800-387-5164. Web: www. hrreporter.com.

Manager and/or Supervisor Review

Manager and/or supervisor review
Performance review done by the employee's supervisor

Manager and/or supervisor review has been the traditional approach to assessing an employee's performance. In most instances, supervisors are in the best position to perform this function, although it may not always be possible for them to do so. Managers often complain that they do not have the time to fully observe the performance of employees. These managers must then rely on performance records to review an employee's performance. For example, American Express Canada uses telephone monitors to assess the quality of the communication between a service centre representative and a customer. Employees are aware that they are being monitored for developmental purposes. If such reliable and valid measures are not available, the review may be less than accurate.

Where a supervisor reviews employees independently, the supervisor's superior often makes provision for an analysis of the reviews. Having reviews examined by a supervisor's superior reduces the chance of superficial or biased reviews. Reviews by superiors generally are more objective and provide a broader perspective of employee performance than do reviews by immediate supervisors.

Self-Review

Self-review
Performance review done by the employee being assessed, generally on a form completed by the employee prior to the performance interview

Sometimes employees are asked to assess themselves on some or all aspects of their performance. **Self-review** is beneficial when managers seek to increase an employee's involvement in the review process. Such an approach may require an employee to complete a review form prior to the performance interview. At a minimum, this gets the employee thinking about strengths and areas for improvement and may lead to discussions about barriers to effective performance. During the performance interview, the manager and the employee discuss job performance and agree on a final assessment. This approach also works well when the manager and the employee jointly establish future performance goals or employee development plans.

Critics of self-review argue that employees are more lenient than managers in their assessments and tend to present themselves in a highly favourable light. However, one of the authors has found through personal experience that people tend to underrate their overall performance. Research also suggests that people may also understate their performance as they may feel that they are boasting.[20] Therefore, managers are able to build on employees' views of themselves and make employees feel better about their performance. When used as part of a review process, self-reviews can be a valuable source of information.[21]

Subordinate Review

Subordinate review
Performance review of a superior by an employee, which is more appropriate for developmental than for administrative purposes

Some organizations use **subordinate review** to give managers feedback on how their subordinates view them. Subordinates are in a good position to provide feedback on their managers since they are in frequent contact with their superiors and occupy a unique position from which to observe many performance-related behaviours. Those performance dimensions judged most appropriate for subordinate input include leadership, oral communication, delegation of authority, coordination of team efforts, and interest in subordinates. However, dimensions related to managers' specific job tasks, such as planning and organizing, budgeting, creativity, and analytical ability, are not usually appropriate for subordinate feedback.

Since subordinate feedback gives employees power over their bosses, the managers themselves may be hesitant to endorse such an approach, particularly when it might be used as a basis for compensation decisions. However, when the information is used for developmental purposes, managers tend to be more open to the idea. Available evidence suggests that when managers heed the advice of their subordinates, their own performance can improve substantially. To ensure that subordinate feedback is as objective as possible, it is important that everyone receives training on how to do this.[22]

Peer Review

Individuals of equal rank who work together are increasingly asked to assess each other. A **peer review** provides information that differs to some degree from information by a superior since peers often see different dimensions of performance. Peers can readily identify leadership and interpersonal skills along with other strengths and weaknesses of their co-workers. A superior asked to provide input about a server in a restaurant on a dimension such as "dealing with the public" may not have had much opportunity to observe it. Fellow servers, on the other hand, have the opportunity to observe this behaviour regularly.

One advantage of peer input is the belief that these assessments furnish more accurate and valid information than assessments by superiors. The supervisor often sees employees putting their best foot forward, while those who work with their fellow employees on a regular basis may see a more realistic picture. With peer input, co-workers are asked to provide input on specific areas, usually in a structured, written format. The information is then compiled into a single report for use in the final review.[23]

Despite evidence that peer reviews are possibly the most accurate method of judging employee behaviour, there are reasons why they are not used.[24] Some of the reasons commonly cited are:

1. Peer reviews are simply a popularity contest.
2. Managers are reluctant to give up control over the assessment process.
3. Those receiving low ratings might retaliate against their peers.
4. Peers rely on stereotypes in ratings.
5. Peers, through discussion, can have more extreme views of the person's performance.

When peers are in competition with one another (e.g., sales associates), peer reviews may not be advisable for administrative decisions, such as those relating to salary or bonuses. Also, employers who use peer reviews must make sure to safeguard confidentiality in handling the review forms. A breach of confidentiality can create interpersonal rivalries or hurt feelings and foster hostility among fellow employees.

Team Review

An extension of the peer assessment is the **team review**. While peers are on equal standing with one another, they may not work closely together. In a team setting, it may be nearly impossible to separate out an individual's contribution. Advocates of team review argue that, in such cases, individual reviews can be dysfunctional since they detract from the critical issues of the team. To address this issue, organizations will occasionally use team reviews to assess the performance of a team as a whole.

A company's interest in team reviews is frequently motivated by its commitment to TQM principles and practices. At its root, TQM is a control system that involves setting standards (based on customer requirements), measuring performance against those standards, and identifying opportunities for continuous improvement. In this regard, TQM and performance reviews are perfectly complementary. However, a basic tenet of TQM is that performance is best understood at the level of the system as a whole, whereas performance reviews traditionally have focused on individual performance. Team input can be a helpful source of information on team members.[25]

Customer Input

Also driven by quality and customer satisfaction concerns, an increasing number of organizations use internal and external **customer input** as a source of performance review information. While external customers' information has been used for some time to review restaurant, hotel, and car rental company personnel, companies such as FedEx, UPS, and Sears have begun utilizing external customers as well. For example, Sears's customers receive a coupon asking them to call a 1–800 number within the next week. In exchange for answering prerecorded questions on a touch-tone phone, they receive $5 off their next purchase. Each call can be linked to a particular transaction (and sales associate) based on the receipt number. With 468 million transactions a year, enough survey data are generated for each sales associate to provide meaningful feedback on such performance measures as service and product knowledge. Customer information can also tell an organization if employees are following procedures. Secret shoppers at the Radisson Hotel Saskatoon provided feedback to hotel management that employees were failing to provide accurate accounting on some customers' bills.

Managers establish customer service measures (CSMs) and set goals for employees that are linked to company goals. Often, the CSM goals are linked to employee pay through incentive programs. Customer survey data are then incorporated into the performance evaluation. By including CSMs in their performance reviews, managers hope to have more effective employees, more satisfied customers, and improved business results.[26]

In contrast to external customers, internal customers include anyone inside the organization who depends on an employee's work output. For example, managers who rely on the HR department for recruitment and training services would be candidates for seeking internal customer feedback of that department. For both developmental and administrative purposes, internal customers can provide extremely useful feedback about the value added by an employee or team of employees.

Putting It All Together: 360-Degree Review

As mentioned previously, many companies are combining various sources of performance appraisal information to create multi-person—or 360-degree—appraisal and feedback systems. Jobs are multi-faceted, and different people see different things. As the name implies, 360-degree feedback is intended to provide employees with as accurate a view of their performance as possible by getting input from all angles: supervisors, peers, subordinates, customers, and the like. Although in the beginning, 360-degree systems were purely developmental and were restricted mainly to management and career development, they have migrated to performance appraisal and other HR purposes. Over 90% of Fortune 1000 companies have implemented some form of 360-degree feedback for career development, performance review, or both.

Because the system combines more information than a typical performance appraisal, it can become administratively complex. For that reason, organizations are using Web-based technology, including cloud computing, for managing performance information.[27] For example, PerformancePlus and Competency Plus, developed by Exxceed, allow managers and employees to develop performance plans, goals, and objectives, and then track their progress over time. Managers can see all of an employee's goals and action steps on a single screen, and self-appraisals and multiple-rater reviews can be combined into a 360-degree format. After rating an employee's performance on each goal, raters can provide summary comments in three categories: victories and accomplishments, setbacks and frustrations, and general comments. To ensure security, a user ID and password are required, and all the data are captured and saved in the employee's history file. Other types of performance management software can support an online recognition and rewards program.[28]

Figure 6.3 is a graphical depiction of 360-degree input sources.

Software used to help prepare 360-degree feedback systems is available from a number of companies. Among these are Halogen Software (**www.halogensoftware.com**) and SurveyConnect (**www.surveyconnect.com**) that not only give a list of resources for anyone interested in using 360-degree systems but also provide information about "best practices."

Figure 6.4 lists the pros and cons of 360-degree feedback.

Although 360-degree feedback can be useful for both developmental and administrative purposes, most companies start with an exclusive focus on development. Employees may be understandably nervous about the possibility of everyone "ganging up"

Halogen Software
www.halogensoftware.com

SurveyConnect
www.surveyconnect.com

FIGURE 6.3 360-Degree Review Information

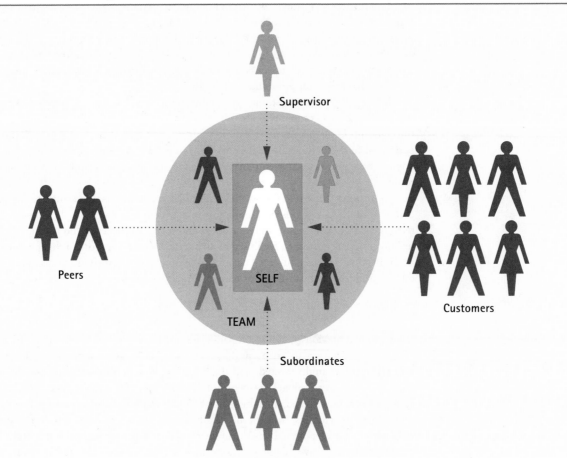

on them in their evaluations. If an organization starts with only developmental feedback—not tied to compensation, promotions, and the like—employees will become accustomed to the process and will likely value the input they get from various parties.

When Erik Djukastein of Contech Electronics, a Victoria, B.C.-based company introduced a 360-degree system, he made sure that, as CEO, he was included in the process. He knew that he could sometimes do things impulsively but was surprised when staff said he didn't always follow through on commitments.

While it is unusual to have the CEO involved in a 360-degree process, Djukastein found that even though the feedback was scary, he appreciated the honesty of his staff. And he wasn't about to ignore the feedback. In order to make it real, he hired a coach as well as inviting his staff to "call him" on any commitments he didn't deliver on.

In order to make the system effective and easy to use, Djukastein recommends the following:

- *Use expertise.* Retain a consultant or a firm that has expertise in implementing and administering 360 reviews.
- *Customize the system to your organization.* It is important that the input documents are customized to fit the organization's competencies.
- *Include many sources of input.* The input should include all direct reports and others who work closely with the person—the more the better.
- *Make use of feedback.* It doesn't help the person or the organization, if the feedback is not acted on.[29]

Source: Susan Bowness, "Full-Circle Feedback: 360-Degree Performance Reviews," *Canadian Business-Profit,* April 2006, www.canadian-business.com/entrepreneur/managing/article.jsp?content=20060406_150353_1772

FIGURE 6.4 Pros and Cons of 360-Degree Feedback

Pros

- The feedback provides a broader perspective on employee performance.
- Employees can become more aware of areas for improvement.
- Having input from customers and direct reports is helpful.
- Strong performance from one area can help offset poor performance in another area.
- Feedback is good for identifying developmental areas.
- Provides more qualitative information.
- Employee can determine who provides input.
- Approach is more consistent with new types of organizational structures (e.g., "flat").
- Encourages more accountability and employee empowerment.

Cons

- Organizational culture isn't ready.
- Managers can focus too much on specific feedback instead of looking at overall performance.
- Manager doesn't take time to review report with employee.
- People say what they want to say and aren't objective.
- System requires training to work well.
- Employees may see as a way to get back at boss.
- People can feel "ganged up on."
- System provides only a snapshot in time.
- Can damage morale.
- Confidentiality needs to be protected.

Sources: Adapted from George Vukotich, "The 360° Process," *OD Practitioner* 42, no. 3 (2010): 24–29; Steve Taylor, "Assess Pros and Cons of Performance Appraisal," Society for Human Resource Management, July 12, 2011, http://www.shrm.org/hrdisciplines/employeerelations/articles/Pages/360DegreePerformance.aspx; "How Do We Answer Questions of Unfairness in 360 Reviews?" May 17, 2011, *Workforce Management*, www.workforce.com/article/20110517/DEAR_WORKFORCE/305179988#crit=.

At Work with HRM 6.2 provides information about the success Canadian Tire has had with a 360-degree approach.

Based on the experiences of companies such as Celestica, Allstate Insurance, and Canadian Tire, it appears that 360-degree feedback can provide a valuable approach to performance review. Its success, as with any performance review method, depends on how managers use the information and how fairly employees are treated. Further, it is important to remember that there may be inconsistencies in the feedback depending on the rater. For example, the rater may not have worked with the employee long and as such may rate differently than raters who have known the person longer. Research has also indicated that if the rating isn't kept confidential from the employee, then the rating might be inflated. In addition, raters may have more or less confidence in the accuracy of their rating if the rating is lower. Finally, research has indicated that the most "accurate" of raters is the boss whereas any direct reports tend to not see much difference between high and low performers.[30]

Manager's Toolkit 6.2 provides sample competency descriptors and how they might be assessed on a 360-degree performance review.

Training Reviewers

A weakness of many performance management systems is that managers and supervisors are not adequately trained for setting performance goals or assessing performance and therefore provide little meaningful feedback to subordinates. Because they lack precise standards for reviewing subordinates' performance and have not developed the necessary observational and feedback skills, their reviews often become general, unspecific, and meaningless. Therefore, training people who will conduct performance reviews can

CANADIAN TIRE 360-DEGREE MATRIX

"Accentuate the positive; build on leadership strengths" is the principal theme of leadership performance evaluation and development conducted by the Canadian Tire Corporation as described by Janice Wismer, vice–president, Human Resources. Canadian Tire is a network of interrelated businesses with retail, financial, and petroleum interests. About 45,000 employees work in 1,000 retail stores across Canada.

The customized 360-degree feedback process used at Canadian Tire is research based and designed to build a cadre of great leaders. The first step in the design of the 360-degree feedback instrument was to benchmark other organizations that had effective 360-degree feedback processes. Twenty-seven key employees at Canadian Tire were interviewed to identify the attributes of their great leaders as measured by the standards of the organization. These key leadership attributes were then discussed and evaluated in workshops with important stakeholders. A total of 16 competencies were identified: seven related to "who one is"—characteristics, such as trustworthy, passionate, and curious. Nine others focused on "what one can do for the team, business, and enterprise," such as make strategic choices, motivate and celebrate, communicate authentically.

To date, about 170 managers have been assessed by an average of nine colleagues, including peers, subordinates, and bosses. Colleagues complete a self-survey, and all feedback assessment is analyzed relative to their own organization and to industry standards, which are maintained in a database. A confidential feedback report is given to each individual.

According to Ed Haltrecht, PhD, CHRP, who specializes in measurement and organizational leadership development, in most organizations when performance feedback is presented, both the employee and the manager focus on the reds—the weaknesses—and try to work out methods of development to improve this area. What is unique about Canadian Tire is that the focus is on the positive. It has found that improvements in weak areas (provided it is not a fundamental flaw) do not affect overall performance, while improvements in areas of strength bring managers from good to extraordinary. The goal is to identify and strengthen attributes so employees will distinguish and present themselves as extraordinary. Individuals first address any "fundamental flaws"—either a very weak attribute of the individual or, more importantly, elements regarded as critical to the organization.

Canadian Tire's leadership development system also recognizes two other significant research findings: first, extraordinary leaders have about three competencies that they excel at, and developing a few strengths to very high performance levels has a greater impact than improving several competencies from poor to average. Second, competencies travel together and improvement in one leads to significant progress in others. Identifying these companion competencies has proven to be extremely worthwhile. In a nutshell, these are the findings: start with the right set of competencies or attributes; focus on strengths; eliminate any fundamental flaws; and pay attention to companion attributes.

The assessment feedback process at Canadian Tire is seen as a tool for dialogue and for focusing on what makes a great company and what matters in leadership. Those employees who try to improve are given a developmental opportunities guidebook. Canadian Tire has discovered that the best development methods are stretch challenging assignments, coaching and mentoring, personal feedback, talks with consultants, and training programs.

CRITICAL THINKING QUESTION:

What would be your reaction to this approach if you were working for Canadian Tire? Explain your answer.

vastly improve the overall performance management system. Thus it is important that supervisors and managers be trained in how to conduct performance reviews. The training needs to help remove the barriers of time constraints, lack of knowledge, and interpersonal conflicts. By overcoming these barriers, the performance review process will be more effective.

MANAGER'S TOOLKIT 6.2

SAMPLE 360-DEGREE STATEMENTS WITH DESCRIPTORS

Based on interaction that you have had with the individual, select the level that best describes the individual's performance in each competency area.

Level 4: Consistently demonstrates the behaviour.

Level 3: Usually demonstrates the behaviour.

Level 2: Sometimes demonstrates the behaviour.

Level 1: Rarely demonstrates the behaviour.

Competency 1: Teamwork—Works effectively with others within own department and across departments for benefit of company. Specifically, displays an openness to ideas, works collaboratively with team members, participates in development of the team, celebrates team successes, and treats team members with respect.

Competency 2: Customer service—Shows a commitment to understanding customer needs and strives to exceed their expectations. Specifically, displays knowledge of customer needs, provides exceptional service to customers, exhibits knowledge of products, shows steady gains in response time without sacrificing positive interaction.

As mentioned earlier (see "Why Performance Management Systems Sometimes Fail"), people may not be made aware of some of the rater errors that can occur. Part of the training needs to include such information as well as the ability to practise giving feedback.

PERFORMANCE REVIEW METHODS

Outcome 6

What are the various performance review methods?

Since the early years of their use by the federal government, methods of reviewing staff have evolved considerably. Old systems have been replaced by new methods that reflect technical improvements and legal requirements and are more consistent with the purposes of a performance management system. In the discussion that follows, you will be introduced to those methods that have found widespread use; methods that are used less frequently will be touched on briefly. Performance review methods can be broadly classified as measuring traits, behaviours, or results; many organizations may incorporate all three into their system.

Trait Methods

Trait approaches to performance reviews are designed to measure the extent to which an employee possesses certain characteristics—such as dependability, creativity, initiative, and leadership—that are viewed as important for the job and the organization in general. Trait methods are popular as they are easy to develop but can be notoriously biased.

Frequently in the trait method, the supervisor is asked to numerically rate the person on the specific characteristics. For example, on the characteristic of "dependable," the supervisor might be asked to rate the person on a scale of 1 to 5, with 1 being unsatisfactory and 5 being exceptional. This is called a **graphic rating scale**, a sample of which is shown in Manager's Toolkit 6.3. The supervisor may also be asked to provide a short paragraph commentary on the person's dependability.

Graphic rating scales
A trait approach to performance review whereby each employee is rated according to a scale of characteristics

Behavioural Methods

As mentioned above, one potential drawback of a trait-oriented performance review is that traits tend to be vague and subjective. Behavioural methods have been developed to

When using the trait method of performance review, a customer service representative may be reviewed on being friendly and helpful.

© Jennifer Steck/iStockphoto.com

specifically describe which actions should (or should not) be exhibited on the job. Since behavioural methods are becoming more common, this section describes three approaches that use them: the behavioural checklist method, the behaviourally anchored rating scale (BARS), and the behaviour observation scales (BOS).

Behavioural Checklist Method

This method consists of having the supervisor check those statements on a list that are believed to be the characteristics of the employee's performance or behaviour. A checklist developed for computer salespeople might include a number of statements like these:

_____   Is able to explain equipment clearly
_____   Keeps abreast of new developments in technology
_____   Tends to be a steady worker
_____   Reacts quickly to customer needs
_____   Processes orders correctly

Behaviourally Anchored Rating Scale (BARS)

Behaviourally anchored rating scale (BARS)
A behavioural approach to performance review that consists of a series of vertical scales, one for each important dimension of job performance

The **behaviourally anchored rating scale (BARS)** approach consists of a series of 5 to 10 vertical scales—one for each important dimension or component of performance. These components are then given a numerical scale based on critical incidents of on-the-job performance. Manager's Toolkit 6.4 displays an example of this for an employee in a service-based industry such as hospitality.

MANAGER'S TOOLKIT **6.3**

GRAPHIC RATING SCALE WITH PROVISION FOR COMMENTS

Appraise employee's performance in PRESENT ASSIGNMENT. Check (✔) most appropriate square. Appraisers are *urged to freely use* the "Remarks" sections for significant comments descriptive of the individual.

1. KNOWLEDGE OF WORK: Understanding of all phases of his/her work and related matters	Needs instruction or guidance ☐	Has required knowledge of own and related work ☐	☐	Has exceptional knowledge of own and related work ☑	☐

Remarks: *Is particularly good on gas engines.*

2. INITIATIVE: Ability to originate or develop ideas and to get things started	Lacks imagination ☐	☑	Meets necessary requirements ☐	☐	Unusually resourceful ☐

Remarks: *Has good ideas when asked for an opinion, but otherwise will not offer them. Somewhat lacking in self-confidence.*

3. APPLICATION: Attention and application to his/her work	Wastes time Needs close supervision ☐	☐	Steady and willing worker ☑	☐	Exceptionally industrious ☐

Remarks: *Accepts new jobs when assigned.*

4. QUALITY OF WORK: Thoroughness, neatness, and accuracy of work	Needs improvement ☐	☐	Regularly meets recognized standards ☐	☐	Consistently maintains highest quality ☑

Remarks: *The work he turns out is always of the highest possible quality.*

5. VOLUME OF WORK: Quantity of acceptable work	Should be increased ☐	☐	Regularly meets recognized standards ☑	☐	Unusually high output ☐

Remarks: *Would be higher if he did not spend so much time checking and rechecking his work.*

Behaviour Observation Scales (BOS)

A behaviour observation scale (BOS) is similar to a BARS in that both are based on critical incidents. The value of BOS is that it enables the reviewer to play the role of observer rather than judge. In this way, he or she can more easily provide constructive feedback to the employee.

Results Methods

Rather than look at the traits of employees or the behaviours they exhibit on the job, many organizations review employee accomplishments—the results they achieve through their work. Advocates of results methods argue that they are more objective and empowering for employees. Looking at results, such as sales figures, production output, and the like, involves less subjectivity and therefore this method may be less open to bias.

MANAGER'S TOOLKIT **6.4**

EXAMPLE OF BARS FOR SERVICE-BASED INDUSTRY

High	7 / 6	Consistently demonstrates exceptional verbal and written communication skills. Demonstrates exceptional sensitivity and empathy. Improves lines of communication throughout hotel.
	5	Frequently demonstrates exceptional verbal and written communication skills. Correctly assesses and responds to sensitive situations.
Average	4	Facilitates the clear, concise communication of information in appropriate forms in a timely fashion. Adapts communication style to meet the needs of others.
	3	Inconsistent ability to communicate effectively or in a timely manner. Does not always adapt communication style to meet the needs of others.
Low	2 / 1	Receives and imparts information inaccurately.

Furthermore, this approach often gives employees responsibility for their outcomes, while giving them discretion (within limits) over the methods they use to accomplish them. This is empowerment in action. And with ongoing concerns about business ethics, more and more organizations are including standards of performance related to ethics and reviewing ethical behaviour as part of the performance management system. Ethics in HRM 6.1 (see page 199) discusses how this might be done.

Productivity Measures

A number of results measures are available to use in reviewing performance. Salespeople are reviewed on the basis of their sales volume (both the number of units sold and the dollar amount in revenues). Production workers are reviewed on the basis of the number of units they produce and perhaps the scrap rate or number of defects that are detected. Customer service people are reviewed on the number of customers handled. Executives are frequently reviewed on the basis of company profits or growth rate. Each of these measures directly links what employees accomplish with results that benefit the organization. In this way, results reviews can directly align employee and organizational goals.

Results methods may inadvertently encourage employees to "look good" on a short-term basis, while ignoring the long-term ramifications. Line supervisors, for example, may let their equipment suffer to reduce maintenance costs. Further, in any job involving interaction with others, it is not enough to simply look at production or sales figures. Factors such as co-operation, adaptability, initiative, and concern for human relations may be important to job success. If these factors are important job standards, they should be added to the review. For productivity measures to be successful, what is being measured must relate to business outcomes.[31]

Management by Objectives

A method that was very popular for a number of years attempted to overcome some of the limitations of results-oriented reviews. Management by objectives (MBO), pioneered by management guru Peter Drucker, focused on employees establishing objectives (e.g., production costs, sales per product, quality standards, profits), through consultation with their superiors and then using these objectives as a basis for review.[32]

MANAGER'S TOOLKIT 6.5

SAMPLE GOAL-SETTING WORKSHEET

PERFORMANCE MANAGEMENT SYSTEM

Name		Performance Period	
Key Results	Measure	Goal	By When

Over time as organizations became more mature and management styles actively involved employees in making decisions, the concept of MBO evolved into the Balance Scorecard. However, depending on the maturity and management style of the organization, the principles of MBO can be helpful in involving employees in setting objectives.

Even without an MBO approach, an organization can create a simple goal-setting system. Manager's Toolkit 6.5 presents a sample goal-setting worksheet used in organizations. You will note the column titled "Key Results." This is a description of what the goal will look like once it has been achieved. For example, a key result might be "Increased customer satisfaction." It would be measured by the percentage of satisfied customers, and the goal might be "To increase the customer satisfaction level from 75 to 80%."

The Balanced Scorecard

One of the most enthusiastically adopted performance management innovations over the past decade has been the **Balanced Scorecard** (BSC). Developed by Harvard professors Robert Kaplan and David Norton, the BSC is a measurement framework that helps managers translate strategic goals into operational objectives. The generic model, shown in Manager's Toolkit 6.6, has four related categories: (1) financial, (2) customer, (3) processes, and (4) learning. The logic of the BSC is that learning and people management help organizations improve their internal processes. These internal processes—product development, service, and the like—are critical for creating customer satisfaction and loyalty. Customer value creation, in turn, is what drives financial performance and profitability.

Evolving from the MBO, the BSC enables managers to translate broad corporate goals into divisional, departmental, and team goals in a cascading fashion. The value of this is that each individual can see more clearly how his or her performance ties into the overall performance of the firm.

The effectiveness of a BSC framework is also highly dependent on the culture of the organization. A recent study concluded that organizations that support and encourage learning, are clear on their mission, have core values, and create an atmosphere of employee involvement have a higher success rate of BSC effectiveness.[33]

Which Performance Review Method to Use?

The approach used should be based largely on the purpose of the system. Figure 6.5 provides a helpful summary of the advantages and disadvantages of the specific performance review methods discussed in this section. Note that the simplest and least expensive techniques often yield the least accurate information and focus only on the

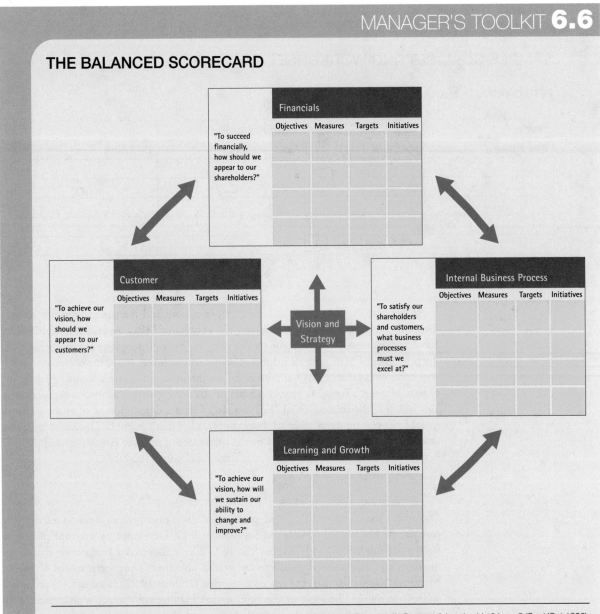

THE BALANCED SCORECARD

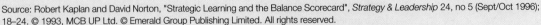

Source: Robert Kaplan and David Norton, "Strategic Learning and the Balance Scorecard", *Strategy & Leadership* 24, no 5 (Sept/Oct 1996); 18–24. © 1993, MCB UP Ltd. © Emerald Group Publishing Limited. All rights reserved.

actual review. While there has been a lot of discussion about which approach to use, whatever method is chosen needs to fit the organization's culture and strategy.[34] For example, designing and producing a form for supervisors to use in reviewing an employee's performance is relatively simple and inexpensive. On the other hand, implementing a 360-degree performance management system may require a change in management thinking and philosophy. This could take a long time with many meetings and the involvement of expensive consultants.

The bigger picture here focuses on how the performance management system is used. Having a first-rate approach does no good if the manager simply "shoves it in a drawer." Alternatively, even a rudimentary system, when used properly, can initiate a discussion between managers and employees that genuinely gives rise to superior performance. These issues are discussed next under the topic of performance review interviews.

For additional information on performance reviews, look at Emerging Trends 6.1.

FIGURE 6.5 Summary of Various Review Methods

	Advantages	Disadvantages
Trait Methods	1. Are inexpensive to develop 2. Use meaningful dimensions 3. Are easy to use	1. Have high potential for rating errors 2. Are not useful for employee counselling 3. Are not useful for allocating rewards 4. Are not useful for promotion decisions
Behavioural Methods	1. Use specific performance dimensions 2. Are acceptable to employees 3. Are useful for providing feedback 4. Are fair for reward and promotion decisions	1. Can be time-consuming to develop/use 2. Can be costly to develop 3. Have some potential for rating error
Results Method	1. Have less subjectivity bias 2. Are acceptable to employees and superiors 3. Link individual performance to organizational performance 4. Encourage mutual goal setting 5. Are good for reward and promotion decisions	1. Are time-consuming to develop/use 2. May encourage short-term perspective 3. May use contaminated criteria 4. May use deficient criteria

EMERGING TRENDS 6.1

1. ***Just-in-time feedback.*** With Gen X and Gen Y having grown up with interactive technology, there is an expectation of ongoing feedback in a work environment, not something most supervisors are comfortable with. However, with a focus on coaching and supporting managers, and the use of social media, more organizations are providing more frequent feedback.

2. ***Alignment with business strategy.*** More and more organizations are ensuring that whatever performance management system they use is aligned with and supports their business strategies and goals. By doing so, employees can see how their performance affects the overall success of the company.

3. ***Improving managers' skills to give feedback.*** Organizations are providing more training, coaching, and support to managers so that they, in turn, can provide helpful and constructive feedback to

employees. For example, L'Oréal Canada was selected as one of Canada's Top 100 Employers for 2012 because of the training provided managers in effective performance feedback.

4. ***Web-based technology.*** As organizations become more complex and the need to evaluate performance at all levels increases, online technology will become more prevalent. Such technology, including social media and cloud computing, will not only make it easier for managers to provide ongoing feedback and review previous information but will also allow the information to be kept more secure.

5. ***More emphasis on performance management as a process and not just an event.*** As managers become better equipped to coach and mentor, the focus of the review will be on continual feedback to the employee.

Sources: Adapted from Michael Benyamin, Sarah Clark, and Tom Keebler, "Turning the Tables on Talent Management," *Workforce Solutions Review*, December 2010-January 2011, 5–8; "Software-Aided Performance Management," The Business Forum, accessed November 24, 2011, http://www.bizforum.org/knowledgepoint-sf.htm; Amanda Silliker "Leaders Ineffective at Driving Success: Survey," *Canadian HR Reporter*, November 7, 2011, 10; and Ian Marlow, "Fixing the Dreaded Performance Review," *The Globe and Mail*, July 15, 2011, B13.

PERFORMANCE REVIEW INTERVIEWS

The coaching and review discussions are perhaps the most important parts of the entire performance management process. These discussions give a manager the opportunity to discuss a subordinate's performance record and to explore areas of possible improvement and growth. They also provide an opportunity to identify the subordinate's attitudes and feelings more thoroughly and thus to improve communication.

The format for the coaching sessions and the formal performance review interview will be determined in large part by the purpose of the interview, the type of system used, and the organization of any interview form. Most performance interviews attempt to give feedback to employees on how well they are performing their jobs and on planning for their future development. Interviews should be scheduled far enough in advance to allow the interviewee, as well as the interviewer, to prepare for the discussion. Usually 10 days to two weeks is a sufficient amount of lead-time.

Conducting the Formal Performance Interview

Outcome 7

What are the characteristics of an effective performance interview?

While there are no hard-and-fast rules for how to conduct a formal review, there are some guidelines that may increase the employee's acceptance of the feedback, satisfaction with the interview, and intention to improve in the future. Many of the principles of effective interviewing, discussed in Chapter 4, apply to performance review interviews as well. Here are some other guidelines that should also be considered.

1. *Ask for a self-assessment.* As noted earlier in the chapter, it is useful to have employees review their own performance prior to the interview. Recent research evidence suggests that employees are more satisfied and view the performance management system as providing more procedural justice when they have input into the process. The interview can then be used to discuss those areas where the manager and the employee have reached different conclusions—not so much to resolve the "truth," but to work toward a resolution of problems.

2. *Invite participation.* The basic purpose of a performance interview is to initiate a dialogue that will help employees improve their performance. Research evidence suggests that participation is strongly related to an employee's satisfaction with the review feedback as well as that person's intention to improve performance. It is also important to link performance to organizational goals.[35] During the conversation, it is important that the supervisor actively listens to the employee's comments and responses to questions.

3. *Express appreciation.* Praise is a powerful motivator, and in a performance interview, particularly, employees are seeking positive feedback. Start the interview by expressing appreciation for what the employee has done well. In this way, the employee may be less defensive and more likely to talk about aspects of the job that are not going so well.

4. *Minimize criticism.* If an employee has many areas in need of improvement, managers should focus on those few objective issues that are most problematic or most important to the job.

5. *Change the behaviour, not the person.* Avoid suggestions about personal traits to change; instead, suggest more acceptable ways of performing. For example, instead of focusing on a person's "unreliability," a manager might focus on the fact that the employee "has been late to work seven times this month."

6. *Focus on solving problems.* In addressing performance issues, it is frequently tempting to get into the "blame game" in which both manager and employee enter into a potentially endless discussion of why a situation has arisen. The interview should be directed at devising a solution to the problem.

7. *Be supportive.* One of the better techniques for engaging an employee in the problem-solving process is to ask: "What can I do to help?" By being open and supportive, the manager conveys to the employee that the manager will try to eliminate external roadblocks and work with the employee to achieve higher standards.

8. *Establish goals.* Since a major purpose of the performance review is to make plans for further growth and development, it is important to focus the interviewee's attention on the future rather than the past.
9. *Follow up day to day.* Ideally, coaching and ongoing feedback should be a regular part of a manager's job. Feedback is most useful when it is immediate and specific to a particular situation.
10. *Meeting set-up.* Providing feedback is better when done in private and scheduled when both people can take the time to focus on the review.

There may be times that the performance interview is very difficult—either because the manager is uncomfortable or the employee is not willing to take responsibility. Therefore, it is, very important that the supervisor remain calm and is very clear on what the problem is and what specifically needs to be done differently. You may enjoy seeing the YouTube video "Do's and Don'ts of an Appraisal," which provides some tips in a humorous way (http://www.youtube.com/watch?v=WVPpNoRdoEk&feature=related). For further resources on handling this type of interview, check out the various video clips produced by TrainingABC at **www.trainingabc.com**.

TrainingABC
www.trainingabc.com

Improving Performance

In many instances, the performance interview will provide the basis for noting deficiencies in employee performance and for making plans for improvement. Unless these deficiencies are brought to the employee's attention, they are likely to continue until they become quite serious. Sometimes, underperformers do not understand exactly what is expected of them. However, once their responsibilities are clarified, they are in a position to take the corrective action needed to improve their performance.

People in retail are frequently assessed on their customer service interactions.

Iconica/Getty Images

Identifying Sources of Ineffective Performance

There are many reasons why an employee's performance might not meet the standards. First, each individual has a unique pattern of strengths and weaknesses that play a part. In addition, other factors—such as the work environment, the external environment (including home and community), and personal problems—have an impact on job performance. To provide a better understanding of possible sources of ineffective performance related to these environments, the comprehensive list shown in Figure 6.6 has been devised.

It is recommended that a diagnosis of poor employee performance focus on three interactive elements: skill, effort, and external conditions. For example, if an employee's performance is not up to standard, the cause could be a skill problem (knowledge, abilities, technical competencies), an effort problem (motivation to get the job done), some problem in the external conditions of work (poor economy), or a combination of these problems. Any one of these problem areas could cause performance to suffer.

Managing Ineffective Performance

Once the sources of performance problems are known, a course of action can be planned. This action may lie in providing training in areas that would increase the knowledge and/ or skills needed for effective performance. A transfer to another job or department might give an employee a chance to become a more effective member of the organization. In other instances, greater attention may have to be focused on ways to motivate the individual.

If ineffective performance persists, it may be necessary to transfer the employee, take disciplinary action, or discharge the person from the organization. Whatever action is taken to cope with ineffective performance, it should be done with objectivity, fairness, and a recognition of the feelings of the individual involved. More information on dealing with ineffective performance is covered in Chapter 9.

FIGURE 6.6   Sources of Ineffective Performance

Organizational Policies and Practices

- Ineffective placement
- Insufficient job training
- Ineffectual employment practices
- Permissiveness with enforcing policies or job standards
- Heavy-handed management
- Lack of attention to employee needs or concerns
- Inadequate communication within organization
- Unclear reporting relationships

Job Concerns

- Unclear or constantly changing work requirements
- Boredom with job
- Lack of job growth or advancement opportunities
- Management–employee conflict
- Problems with fellow employees
- Unsafe working conditions
- Unavailable or inadequate equipment or materials
- Inability to perform the job
- Excessive workload
- Lack of job skills

Personal Problems

- Marital problems
- Financial worries
- Emotional disorders (including depression, guilt, anxiety, fear)
- Conflict between work demands and family demands
- Physical limitations, including disabilities
- Low work ethic
- Other family problems
- Lack of effort
- Immaturity

External Factors

- Industry decline or extreme competition
- Legal constraints
- Conflict between ethical standards and job demands
- Union–management conflict

SUMMARY

1. Define a performance management system.
   - Set of integrated management practices.

2. Explain the purpose of a performance management system.
   - Allows the organization to get the right things done.
   - Helps increase employees' satisfaction with their work and the organization.

3. Describe the management practices necessary for a good performance management system.
   - Setting and communicating clear performance expectations.
   - Clear and specific performance objectives.
   - Supportive and helpful coaching by the supervisor.
   - Focusing on accomplishment of objectives during performance appraisals.
   - Recognizing and celebrating good performance.

4. Identify the steps in an effective performance management system.
   - Clarifying the work (job) to be done.
   - Setting goals and establishing a performance plan.
   - Regular and frequent coaching.
   - Conducting formal review of performance.
   - Recognizing and rewarding performance.

5. Describe the different sources of performance review information.
   - Manager or supervisor who is able to provide feedback on contribution.
   - Self—provides a personal review of accomplishments.
   - Subordinate—provides a perspective on certain behaviours such as leadership.
   - Peers and team members—who are able to describe how the person works with others.
   - Customers—provide input about the quality of service.

6. Explain the various methods used for performance reviews.
   - Trait approaches are designed to measure the extent to which an employee possesses certain characteristics.
   - Behavioural methods specifically describe which actions should (or should not) be exhibited on the job.
   - Productivity measures look at results or outputs.
   - Balanced Scorecard (BSC) is a measurement framework that helps managers and employees translate strategic goals into operational objectives.

7. Outline the characteristics of an effective performance review interview.
   - Ask the employee to review and assess own performance prior to the interview.
   - Invite and encourage active participation by employee in the discussion of performance.
   - Express appreciation for what the employee has done well.
   - Minimize criticism.
   - Change the behaviour, not the person.

NEED TO KNOW

- Definition of performance management system
- Purpose and reasons for introducing a performance management system
- The characteristics of an effective performance management system
- Various methods used to gather performance information
- Advantages and disadvantages of various performance review methods
- Guidelines for conducting a performance appraisal interview

NEED TO UNDERSTAND

- Link of management practices with performance management systems
- Relationship of organizational performance with performance management systems
- Role the supervisor or line manager plays in the effectiveness of any system
- Relationship of methods to the overall system and the style of management
- Importance of good coaching and interviewing skills for appraising overall performance

KEY TERMS

balanced scorecard 213

behaviourally anchored rating scale (BARS) 210

customer input 204

graphic rating scale 209

manager and/or supervisor review 203

peer review 204

performance management system 192

self-review 203

subordinate review 203

team review 204

REVIEW QUESTIONS

1. What are the major purposes of a performance management system?
2. Describe the relationships among performance management systems and selection, training, and development.
3. Describe the steps of an effective performance management system.
4. Discuss the guidelines that performance reviews should meet in order to be legally defensible.
5. Who could provide input on the performance of people working in the following jobs?
   a. Sales representative
   b. Flight attendant
   c. Concierge in a hotel
   d. Activity coordinator in an eldercare centre
   e. Customer service representative in a financial institution
6. In many organizations, evaluators submit the reviews of their subordinates to their immediate superiors for review before discussing them with the individual employees they have evaluated. What advantages are there to this procedure?
7. What are the pros and cons of trait, behaviour, and results performance review methods?
8. What are the suggested guidelines for conducting an effective performance review?

CRITICAL THINKING QUESTIONS

1. Your study group at school has been asked to develop a set of performance standards by which you could measure your performance. What would you include and why?
2. Assume you have just been hired as a customer service representative at a financial services company. The branch manager has asked that you work with a small task force to develop an appropriate set of performance standards and an appropriate review method. What would you recommend and why?

3. An auto part's purchasing department is responsible for ordering and receiving all deliveries, including rush deliveries. Recently the person who checked the received orders failed to identify that an urgent part had been received for a key client. When discovered by the supervisor after the client complained, the person confirmed that this arrival was not noted. This was not the first time that a shipment had not been properly checked. The supervisor was also aware that during the employee's vacation, the replacement worker had been able to perform all the duties without any difficulty. Explain how a performance management system might have prevented such a situation.

4. You've just started working at a high-end retail store in a large city. The store manager wishes to develop a BARS rating scale for front-line staff. Identify three critical areas of the job (e.g., "interactions with customers") and develop the appropriate 7-point descriptive scale for each area.

5. Do you think students ought to be able to provide input into their instructor's performance? Why or why not? Explain your reasoning.

6. Your friend works as a supervisor in a large call centre and has asked your advice on how to give feedback to a staff member who did not handle a call particularly well. What suggestions would you give?

DEVELOPING YOUR SKILLS

1. Working in groups of two or three, prepare a list of pros and cons for each of the performance review methods (trait, behaviour, results). When completed, review your list with another group. What was similar? What was different?

2. On an individual basis, use the worksheet shown in Manager's Toolkit 6.4 to establish goals in relation to either this course or a job you are currently doing. After completing the worksheet, pair up with another student. Review and critique each other's work. In particular, look for realistic measurements and dates of completion.

3. Working in pairs, identify three to four performance characteristics on which your instructor ought to be reviewed. Share your responses with the entire class. Develop a single list of three to four performance characteristics. Discuss as an entire class. Determine whether the instructor agrees with your list; if not, enquire as to what ought to be on the list.

4. Working in groups of four, review the following descriptions of three different employees. Describe the potential causes of poor performance in each case. Once the possible reasons for poor performance are identified, pair off and create a role-playing scenario to practise giving performance feedback. (For assistance, review the role-playing information in Chapter 5.) While one pair conducts the performance feedback session, the other pair is asked to observe and then provide feedback to the role-playing pair.

    a. *Carl Spackler* is the assistant greens keeper at Bushwood Country Club. Over the past few months, members have been complaining that gophers are destroying the course and digging holes in the greens. Although Carl has been working evenings and weekends to address the situation, the problem persists. Unfortunately, his boss is interested only in results. Because the gophers are still there, he contends that Carl is not doing his job. He has accused Carl of "slacking off" and threatened his job.

    b. *Sandeep Dhillon* works in research and development for a chemical company that makes non-nutritive food additives. His most recent assignment has been the development of a nonstick aerosol cooking spray, but the project is way behind schedule and seems to be going nowhere. CEO Frank Shirley is decidedly upset and has threatened that if things don't improve, he will suspend bonuses this year just like he did last year. Sandeep feels dejected because without the bonus, he won't be able to take his family on vacation.

SurveyConnect
surveyconnect.com

Performance Appraisal
www.businessballs.com/
performanceappraisals.htm

**What Makes a Good
Leader?**
www.whatmakesagoodleader.
com/Performance-Appraisal-
Download.html

Government of Canada
www.jobsetc.gc.ca/eng/
home-accueil.jsp

c. *Soon Tan* is the host of a local television talk show called *Morning Winnipeg.* Although she is a talented performer and comedian, Soon has an unacceptable record of tardiness. The show's producer, David Bellows, is frustrated, because the problem has affected the quality of the show. On several occasions, Soon was unprepared when the show went on the air. Bellows has concluded that Soon is not a morning person and has thought about replacing her with a different host.

5. Access **www.survey connect.com**. Click the link "Demo" and review the information about the process to create a 360–degree feedback system. Would such a system be easy or difficult to implement in an organization? Why?

6. Access the following two Web sites:
   • **www.businessballs.com/performanceappraisals.htm**
   • **www.whatmakesagoodleader.com/Performance-Appraisal-Download.html**
   Each of these sites has a sample performance assessment tool. The "What Makes a Good Leader" site has both a Graphics Rating and MBO samples. Try each tool, using information about you. As you go through the samples, identify features that are useful for the supervisor and ones that might not be as useful. Write a one-page summary of the tools, explaining which you would use and why.

7. Access the Government of Canada's Web site for small business (**www.jobsetc.gc.ca/eng/home-accueil.jsp**) and click the link titled "Managing Employees" and then "Performance Appraisals." Review the information and prepare a one-page summary explaining how the information would help a small business owner deal with performance management.

Case Study ❶

Smelly Fish

A grocery chain has a central warehouse that is responsible for checking deliveries of all frozen food that is then delivered to each separate store in Halifax. In handling the frozen food, the warehouse is responsible for checking what has been received against what has been ordered, verifying the quality of the merchandise received, and ensuring that any special orders are immediately dispatched. In April 2012 an employee failed to check a case of flash-frozen fish for a restaurant. The fish was delivered to the restaurant without the receiver looking at the condition of the box. The fish had thawed on its way to the warehouse and was not able to be used once it got to the restaurant. The receiver, who had been with the company for 15 years, admitted that he had not checked the box's condition. As a result, his supervisor gave him a written warning. The employee grieved, stating that he was too busy because the workload was excessive and there was a deadline that had to be met.

There was an investigation, which indicated that the griever had not worked any overtime, nor had he requested permission to work any overtime. It was also noted that during the receiver's vacation period, the replacement worker had been able to perform the job without any difficulty. There was also evidence that the receiver was taking excessive breaks.

As a result of this investigation, the grievance was denied. In addition, the employee was sent a letter reminding him of his job responsibilities and of the need to restrict himself to the scheduled breaks. As a last step, he was given a procedure to follow if he believed that the work was becoming excessive.

Questions

1. Discuss how a performance management system might have prevented this situation.
2. Which performance appraisal method would you recommend for this type of job?

Case Study  2

A New Performance System—Will It Work?

At the beginning of 2011, a large graphics and printing company in Toronto decided that its current performance management system was not meeting its expectations. The company had 10 sites throughout Metro Toronto with approximately 250 people providing services to individuals, and small- and medium-sized companies.

The existing system had the following components:

1. The review was done once per year.
2. The employee had to develop a written document outlining accomplishments.
3. The manager reviewed the employee's accomplishments, made an assessment, and assigned a rating from 1 to 5, with 5 being "superior" and 1 being "unsatisfactory."
4. Pay adjustments were tied to the rating.
5. Feedback to the employee about performance was done at the same time as pay adjustment.

While this approach had worked well for a number of years, the company began to experience complaints from both managers and employees. Managers were restricted in what they could reward for superior performance, and as a result, everyone got the same pay adjustment. In fact, in a recent employee engagement survey, the issue of the company's approach to performance management was severely criticized.

The company decided it needed a new system and put together a task force representing managers and employees from several different sites. Everyone wanted a system that would provide ongoing feedback as well as one that included goals and developmental plans.

With members of the task force communicating with all the employees regularly, the new performance management system became a reality and was ready for implementation in early 2012. The components of the new system included:

- a meeting between the manager and employee to develop and agree to performance goals and development plans at the beginning of each calendar year
- reviews of performance goals on a quarterly basis with feedback from the manager on accomplishments as well as discussions on the progress of development plans
- a formal review of the goals, accomplishments, and development plan at the end of the year, also the completion of the performance cycle

The formal review also includes the preparation of a written assessment by both the manager and the employee that is discussed at the review meeting. If the differences regarding the manager's and employee's perceptions of accomplishments, the meeting is also used to develop a common understanding. Development plans are reviewed with a preliminary discussion about development plans for the next performance year.

Discussions regarding pay adjustments occur in a separate meeting about a month later, where the manager can better explain the reasons behind the pay adjustment.

Is the new system working? The answer seems to be yes. According to the most recent employee engagement survey, 85% of employees thought the new system was fair; 80% felt that they better understood on what basis pay adjustments were made; and 82% believed that their career development was effectively handled.

Questions

1. How do you think managers have responded to the new system and why?
2. What is key to the effectiveness of this new system?
3. What might be some potential negative aspects of this new system?
4. What might the emphasis on development plans mean for promotions?

NOTES AND REFERENCES

1. "Performance Reviews, Training Helping Workers Feel Valued: Survey," *Canadian HR Reporter*, October 24, 2011. http://www.hrreporter.com/articleview/11517-performance-reviews-training-helping-workers-feel-valued-survey.
2. Robert Bacal, "What Is the Point of Performance Appraisal," accessed November 17, 2011, http://work911.com/articles/pointperformance.htm.
3. Sarah Dobson, "Performance Reviews Valued by Employees: Poll," *Canadian HR Reporter*, December 19, 2011, 1.
4. Rebecca Knight, "Delivering an Effective Performance Review," *Harvard Business Review*, November 3, 2011, http://blogs.hbr.org/hmu/2011/11/delivering-an-effective-perfor.html.
5. Rita Pyrillis "Is Your Performance Review Underperforming?" *Workforce*, May 5, 2011, www.workforce.com/article/20110505/NEWS02/305059995.
6. Jack N. Kondrasuk, "The Ideal Performance Appraisal Is a Format, Not a Form," *Academy of Strategic Management Journal* 11, no. 1 (January 2012): 115–130.
7. Claudine Kapel, "In Praise of Performance Management," *Canadian HR Reporter*, April 18, 2011, www.hrreporter.com/blog/Compensation-Rewards/archive/2011/04/18/in-praise-of-performance-management.
8. John Pletz, "Groupon Puts Employees—and Investors—on Notice as IPO Nears," *Workforce*, October 28, 2011, www.workforce.com/article/20111028/NEWS02/111029969.
9. Ethan Rouen, "Thinking beyond Pay to Keep Your Star Employees," *Fortune*, August 10, 2011, http://management.fortune.cnn.com/2011/08/10/thinking-beyond-pay-to-keep-your-star-employees/.
10. "Firms Looking to Increase Employee Motivation through Incentive Programs: Survey," *Canadian HR Reporter*, June 8, 2011, www.hrreporter.com/articleview?&articleid=10494&headline=firms-looking-to-increase-employee-motivation-through-incentive-programs-survey.
11. Mike Schraeder and Mark Jordan, "Managing Performance: A Practical Perspective on Managing Employee Performance," *Journal for Quality & Participation* 34, no. 2 (July 2011): 4–10.
12. "Performance Appraisal," accessed November 19, 2011, www.enotes.com/performance-appraisal-reference/performance-appraisal.
13. "Performance Appraisal Biases," *Management Study Guide*, accessed November 19, 2011, www.managementstudyguide.com/performance-appraisal-bias.htm.
14. "The Politics of Performance Appraisal," *Thinking Leaders*, April 4, 2011, www.thinkingleaders.com/archives/1119.
15. Dennis Gioia, "Confronting the 'Politics' in Performance Appraisal," accessed November 19, 2011, www.allbusiness.com/human-resources/workforce-management/722568-1.html.
16. Roger Martin, "The Secret to Meaningful Customer Relations," *Harvard Business Review*, March 24, 2010, accessed November 19, 2011, http://blogs.hbr.org/martin/2010/03/the-secret-to-meaningful-custo.html.
17. Jay Forte, "Give Feedback, Get Performance," *Supervision* 70, no. 3 (March 2009): 3–4.
18. "Firms Looking to Increase Employee Motivation through Incentive Programs," *Canadian HR Reporter*, June 8, 2011, www.hrreporter.com/articleview?&articleid=10494&headline=firms-looking-to-increase-employee-motivation-through-incentive-programs-survey.
19. Diana Arbutina, "Saying 'Thank You' Doesn't Hurt Budget," *Canadian HR Reporter*, May 9, 2011, www.hrreporter.com/articleview?articleid=10207&headline=saying-thank-you-doesnt-hurt-budget.
20. Adrienne Fox, "Curing What Ails Performance Reviews," *HR Magazine*, January 2009, 52–56.
21. Ibid.
22. Susan M. Heathfield, "360 Degree Feedback: The Good, the Bad, and the Ugly," accessed November 21, 2011, http://humanresources.about.com/od/360feedback/a/360feedback_3.htm.
23. Marcie Levine, "A Litmus Test for Leaders," *Canadian HR Reporter*, August 9, 2010, accessed November 21, 2011, www.hrreporter.com/articleview?&articleid=8102&headline=a-litmus-test-for-leaders.

24. Jerry K. Palmer and James M. Loveland, "The Influence of Group Discussion on Performance Judgments: Rating Accuracy, Contrast Effects, and Halo," *The Journal of Psychology* 142, no. 2 (2008): 117–30.

25. George Vukotich, "The 360° Process," *OD Practitioner* 42, no. 3 (2010): 24–29.

26. Brooke Bates, "Fresh Take," *Smart Business Cleveland*, July 1, 2010, 66–74.

27. David Vanheukelom, "HR Tech's Future (and Present) in the Cloud," *Canadian HR Reporter*, October 10, 2011, www.hrreporter.com/articleview?articleid=11414& headline=hr-techs-future-%28and-present%29-in-the-cloud.

28. Sandra Reder, "Making Performance Reviews Work for Younger Employees," *Canadian HR Reporter*, November 15, 2010, accessed November 21, 2011, www.hrreporter.com/ articleview?&articleid=8455&headline=making-performance-reviews-work-for-younger-employees.

29. Jack N. Kondrasuk, "The Ideal Performance Appraisal Is a Format, Not a Form."

30. Robert W. Eichinger and Michael M. Lombardo, "Patterns of Rater Accuracy in 360-Degree Feedback," Star, www.star 360feedback.com/patterns-of-rater-accuracy-in-360-degree-feedback.

31. John Haggerty, "Be Careful What You Ask For or Measure!" *Workforce*, May 29, 2011, www.workforce.com/article/ 20110529/NEWS02/305299997#crit.

32. Stephen Bungay, "How to Make the Most of Your Company's Strategy," *Harvard Business Review*, January/ February 2011, 132–40.

33. Jackie W. Deem et al., "The Relationship of Organizational Culture to Balance Scorecard Effectiveness," *SAM Advanced Management Journal* (Autumn 2010): 31–39.

34. "Raising the Bar on Performance Management Best Practices to Optimize Performance Reviews and Goal Management," *Success Factors*, accessed November 23, 201, www.successfactors. com/articles/optimize-performance-management.

35. Cori Maedel, Putting Performance Programs to the Test," *HRVoice.org*, January 19, 2011, www.hrvoice.org/putting-performance-programs-to-the-test.

7

REWARDING AND RECOGNIZING EMPLOYEES

OUTCOMES

After studying this chapter, you should be able to

1 Explain an organization's concerns in developing a strategic rewards program.

2 Identify the various factors that influence the setting of pay levels.

3 Describe the major job evaluation systems.

4 Illustrate the compensation structure.

5 List the types of incentive plans.

6 Explain the employee benefits that are required by law.

7 Describe voluntary benefits.

OUTLINE

HRM CLOSE-UP

"There's nothing more rewarding to any leader than managing to build a winning team."

Rajwinder Nijjer.

At her Walmart store in New Westminster, B.C., manager Rajwinder Nijjer has a knack for recognizing and rewarding talent. On occasion, she even comes into the store at 4:00 a.m. to make personal contact with employees on the night shift so that she can get to know them and how they contribute to the store's success. Even with seven assistant managers who have direct responsibility for staff, Nijjer still feels strongly about making personal contact. "I didn't realize, until I was a store manager, how much I impact people directly and indirectly," says "RJ," as she's known by staff.

In a retail environment, where many employees are making minimum wage, reward and recognition programs play a key role in retaining a good workforce. With recognition programs, Nijjer says, "You can feel and sense your team's excitement. People will care and show more interest in profitability of the business. Rewards and recognition offer a solid foundation for building a winning team."

"People like to be recognized for a good job," Nijjer continues. "And I strongly believe that the quicker performance is recognized, the more impact it will have on your business and on the associate's personal development." To do this, Nijjer makes a point of spending at least 10 to 15 minutes per day with five different employees every day. She will work alongside them and get to know them as they get to know her. Then, a couple of days later, she will approach each of them and offer words of encouragement that recognize their effort and contribution on the job.

Walmart has corporately sponsored recognition programs such as "Shining Star," where staff can nominate fellow staff members via e-mail. Submissions are read aloud at meetings held three times daily to accommodate all work shifts. Once monthly, a star is recognized with a $75 gift card. Nijjer says this is a simple way to recognize staff and share success stories. It's especially effective for staff who work hard but may not yet be interested in

making a career in retail business. It helps to motivate staff and increase the ownership they take in the store's success. It may even influence their interest in a future at the company.

Nijjer also implements her own programs at the store, such as "Coffee with the Coach," where she dedicates time one-on-one to further recognize and reward staff. "Reward people who show initiative, who experiment, and who pursue innovation," she advises. "And be very specific when appreciating someone."

Several years ago, Nijjer hired a man for the part-time job of unloader. At his 90-day evaluation, she let him know how confident she was in his work ethic and his potential for a future with the company. He went on to master four key positions and is now her administrative manager. When Nijjer sent a congratulatory note to her management team after a store-wide initiative, the employee approached Nijjer and said "RJ, I am going to frame this e-mail of yours. I cannot believe that I am a part of management today only because you recognized my ability and helped me develop my skills. Now I'm in a position to afford a car and better living standards."

Recognizing team effort is also important to Nijjer. "You need to keep the team together," she says, recalling the store's recent expansion and reopening. "In a project like that, we had two teams of 15 people overseeing the expansion and it was really important to recognize everyone together." She adds, "There's nothing more rewarding to any leader than managing to build a winning team."

INTRODUCTION

You will note from the HRM Close-up that rewards and recognition are big issues not just for employees but also for the managers of those employees. Although companies may set guidelines about how much each position or job is worth, it is the manager who has to implement those guidelines. It is the manager who will make decisions about who gets paid what. And it is the manager's everyday interactions with the employees that influence how the employees feel about the organization. Therefore, it is important for the manager and supervisor to have an understanding of rewards and recognition, and its link to the success of the organization. It is also important for the manager to understand how compensation is derived and what factors influence the setting of the wage and benefits structure.

Literature and research indicates that important work-related variables leading to job satisfaction include challenging work, flexibility in work practices, appropriate rewards and recognition, supportive work environment, amount and type of supervision, and the ability to enhance skills and capabilities.[1] It is doubtful, however, that many employees would continue working were it not for the money they earn. Employees want reward and recognition systems that are fair and commensurate with their skills and expectations. Compensation, therefore, is a major consideration in HRM because it provides employees with a tangible reward for their services, as well as a source of recognition and livelihood. As mentioned earlier, the effectiveness of the manager has a large impact on the employee's job satisfaction, and it is usually the manager who is the first one to deal with any concerns or issues regarding compensation. While an HR professional in the organization may be responsible for gathering compensation information and developing approaches to how compensation is managed, the manager typically makes decisions on how much a person is compensated. Further, with the continuing sluggish economy, a 2011 study conducted by Towers Watson, a global management consulting firm, reinforces that organizations are reducing the overall budget pool for compensation changes, but adjustments are being made to recognize and reward staff with critical skills.[2]

It is important to know that employee recognition and rewards include all forms of pay and rewards received by employees for the performance of their jobs. **Direct compensation** encompasses employee wages and salaries, incentives, bonuses, and commissions. **Indirect compensation** comprises the many benefits supplied by employers, such as extended health and dental plans, life insurance coverage, and *nonfinancial compensation* includes employee recognition programs, rewarding jobs, and flexible work hours to accommodate personal needs. Direct and indirect compensation are referred to as "total compensation" or "total rewards approach." This latter phrase helps communicate to employees that their compensation doesn't have just a monetary value, but that it includes other forms of recognition and reward.

Both managers and scholars agree that the way rewards are allocated among employees sends a message about what management believes is important and the types of activities it encourages. Furthermore, for an employer, total rewards (direct and indirect) constitute a sizable operating cost. In manufacturing firms, compensation is seldom as low as 20% of total expenditures, and in service enterprises it often exceeds 80%. A strategic rewards program, therefore, is essential so that compensation can serve to motivate employee production sufficiently to keep labour costs at an acceptable level.

While the focus of this chapter is on pay and benefits, it is important to state that more organizations are beginning to think about and create "reward strategies." The thrust of this approach is to develop an organizational mindset to recognize and reward people with links to organizational success.[3] Further, it is important to ensure that the recognition and rewards are seen as valuable to the employees and help in the retention of employees.[4] In doing so, organizations will tend to have components of the rewards program, particularly direct compensation, that are tied to the success of the organization and to the contributions of that success through individual (or team) performance.

Towers Watson
www.towerswatson.com

Direct compensation
Employee wages and salaries, incentives, bonuses, and commissions

Indirect compensation
Benefits, such as extended health and dental plans, supplied by employers

REWARDS AS PART OF COMPANY STRATEGY

Outcome 1

What are the strategic organizational concerns when developing a rewards program?

Companies structure their rewards in ways that enhance employee motivation and growth while aligning the employees' efforts with the objectives, philosophies, and culture of the organization. Designing the rewards system goes beyond determining what market rates to pay employees—although market rates are one element of compensation planning. Research has shown that companies that make the rewards strategy a part of the overall organizational framework have better performance than those companies that don't.[5] This finding prompts a compelling argument to ensure that the organization takes into consideration what employees see as important in the reward equation.

Looking at the reward system in a strategic fashion serves to mesh the overall rewards for employees with specific business objectives. Such a strategic approach can provide a competitive advantage for the company.[6] For example, in the recruitment of new employees, the overall rewards for jobs can increase or limit the supply of applicants. Employers have adopted special reward strategies to attract job applicants with highly marketable skills, such as high-tech workers, and engineers and scientists with financial knowledge and good people skills. Organizations also use rewards to retain people with scarce skills. According to the 2012 Conference Board of Canada survey of 381 Canadian companies, there was still concern about retaining people with critical skills despite the continuing poor economic climate.[7] This problem was further reinforced by a study conducted by Deloitte: it identified a sluggish economy which potentially keeps reward levels low with the need of employers to attract and retain people with critical skills in a shrinking labour market.[8]

If rewards are high, creating a large applicant pool, then organizations may choose to raise their selection standards and hire better-qualified employees. This, in turn, can reduce training costs for the employer. When employees perform at exceptional levels, their performance assessments may justify an increased pay rate. For these reasons and others, an organization should ensure that it has a systematic way to manage employee rewards and that it is linked to business performance. Recent research has demonstrated that there is a strong link between appropriate reward systems (for that particular organization) and achieving strong business results.[9]

It is important to remember that the concept of "total rewards" is a broader set of elements and includes the tangible rewards of pay, benefits, etc., but also factors such as career development, work climate/culture, and work–life balance.[10] Other items in total rewards include peer-to-peer recognition programs, an extra day off to spend time with family, or organization of some type of fun event. For example, Dimension Data Canada Inc., a specialty IT firm, has created a "chief fun officer" role that promotes excitement, energy, and team building at work.[11] At Work with HRM 7.1 discusses the importance of communicating the total rewards program and its various components.

Linking Rewards to Organizational Objectives

Rewards have been revolutionized by heightened domestic competition, globalization, increased employee skill requirements, and new technology. Therefore, an outcome of today's dynamic business environment is that managers are needed to change their reward philosophies from paying for a specific position or job title to rewarding employees on the basis of their individual competencies or group contributions to organizational success. A recent study showed that 81% of responding organizations listed *improving employee's focus on achieving business goals* as a significant objective influencing reward changes (see Figure 7.1). A total rewards program, therefore, must be tailored to the needs of the organization and its employees. And in doing so, it is important to ensure that employees feel they are being rewarded.

Looking at total rewards is particularly helpful for small businesses. Read HRM and SME 7.1 to better understand the variety of components that are used to attract and retain talent.

AT WORK with HRM 7.1

MAKING SURE EMPLOYEES KNOW THE WHOLE STORY ON REWARDS

"The biggest problem we ran into a few years ago was that nobody understood what we had," says Tara Deegan, Director of Total Rewards and HR Services at Holt Renfrew, one of Canada's premier clothing stores. The company, with more than 2,000 employees, primarily in shift work, had a great rewards program, but the program hadn't been marketed to its staff. So, a decision was taken to consider branding its rewards program using the same principles that would be used when looking at branding from a customer perspective.

Deegan goes on to say, "The challenge was to design a marketing tool that highlighted the value of what we offer employees. We wanted to create the same feelings internally as we do for customers: luxury, special, ownership."

The objective of taking a marketing approach was not just to communicate what the total rewards program was all about but to ensure that the employees could "feel" what Holt Renfrew wanted them to feel—the outcome needed to have an emotional connection. Since this goal also involved educating the employees, a collaborative approach was developed between Deegan and Kelly Hadden, Director of Learning and Development.

One consideration was to look at how to reach all the employees. This was not easy as most of the employees work part time and in shifts, and do not have access to computer technology in the same way that someone in an office would have. Even with the limitations of computer technology, the solution was to develop a highly interactive e-magazine, including embedded videos of employee interviews. This tool provided a way for employees to speak to their peers about what was in the total rewards program and how they felt about the overall program and the individual parts.

Hadden describes the most effective part of the e-magazine as a calculator that allowed people to compute the value of their rewards. For example, a sales associate who might be earning $11 per hour could start with that as the base wage and then include the various benefits provided. By doing this, the employee could then see the true value of the overall rewards program provided by Holt Renfrew. As Hadden concludes, "We need to attract and retain the talent we have, and this allows us to do both."

CRITICAL THINKING QUESTIONS:

1. If you are working, do you know the value of your total rewards? Would you think differently about the organization if you did?
2. Do you think that being provided with information about your total rewards would encourage you to remain with an employer? Why or why not?

Source: Adapted from Melissa Mancini, "Total Rewards at Holt Renfrew," *Canadian HR Reporter TV*, June 21, 2011, www.hrreporter.com/videodisplay/161-total-rewards-at-holt-renfrew (accessed January 21, 2012).

FIGURE 7.1   Significant Goals Driving Pay and Reward Changes

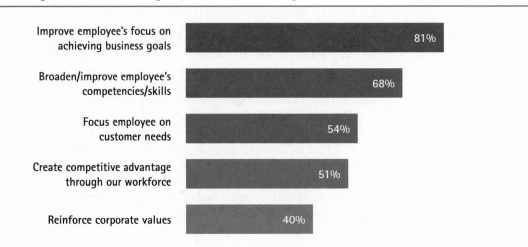

HRM and SME 7.1

HOW CAN WE COMPETE?

Attracting and retaining talent for small businesses that are involved in the online world is not easy. That's where the concept of "total rewards" can be extremely useful.

Take the case of Myplanet Digital, a Toronto start-up focusing on user experiences for the Web and mobile devices. Currently, it employs about 40 people—graphic designers, developers, and salespeople—with expectations that it will grow to over 100 employees by the beginning of 2013. As co-founder Dustin Walper states, "In our business revenues are really closely tied to how many people we have able to deliver services."

Competition for employees comes from such huge and well-known organizations such as Google and Microsoft. Since Myplanet is small, it needed a different approach than other similar companies had for rewards to encourage people to join the firm and to make it stand out from its competition. Being a start-up makes it particularly difficult to attract the talent—it is accessing a labour pool where there is more demand than talent available.

So, Walper got creative.

What Myplanet decided to do was create a fellowship program for students about to graduate. Since ongoing education for employees forms part of the total rewards philosophy, a fellowship program seemed a natural fit. The program provides students with an opportunity to work (with pay) for 10 hours a week throughout their final year, self-directed learning and hands-on experience. Based upon students' experiences, both in terms of the work and the pay, the graduates are in a much better place to assess whether this is where they wanted to work. The ultimate reward for them is to have a job opportunity waiting when they graduate.

QUESTION:

What are other ways that Myplanet Digital might have attracted talent?

Source: Adapted from Christine Dobby, "Shooting for stars," *Financial Post*, January 24, 2012, C4.

Recent research suggests that there are five components of a total rewards program: compensation, benefits, work–life balance, recognition of performance, and development and career opportunities.[12]

Fundamental to the framework of total rewards is the compensation component. It is not uncommon for organizations to establish specific goals for aligning their objectives with their compensation program.[13] Formalized compensation goals serve as guidelines for managers to ensure that wage and benefit policies achieve their intended purpose. Some of the more common goals are the following:

1. To reward employees' past performance.
2. To remain competitive in the labour market.
3. To maintain salary equity among employees.
4. To mesh employees' performance with organizational goals.
5. To control the compensation budget.
6. To attract, motivate, and retain staff.[14]
7. To influence employee work behaviours and job attitudes.[15]

To achieve these goals, specific actions or steps must be taken. Three areas of action are discussed below.

The Motivating Value of Compensation

Pay is a quantitative measure of an employee's relative worth. For most employees, pay has a direct bearing not only on their standard of living, but also on the status and recognition they may be able to achieve both on and off the job. Since pay represents a reward received in exchange for an employee's contributions, it is essential that the pay be equitable in relation to those contributions. It is also important that an employee's pay be equitable in relation to what other employees are receiving for their contributions.

Equity can be defined as anything of value earned through the investment of something of value. Equity theory is a motivation theory that explains how employees respond to situations in which they feel they have received less (or more) than they deserve.[16] Central to the theory is the role of perception in motivation and the fact that individuals make comparisons. The theory states that individuals form a ratio of their inputs (abilities, skills, experiences) in a situation to their outcomes (salary, benefits) in that situation. They then compare the value of that ratio with the value of the input/output ratio for other individuals in a similar class of jobs either internal or external to the organization. If the value of their ratio equals the value of another's, they perceive the situation as equitable and no tension exists. However, if they perceive their input/output ratio as inequitable relative to others', tension is created and they are motivated to eliminate or reduce the inequity. The strength of their motivation is proportional to the magnitude of the perceived inequity. If a person feels that someone is getting more compensation for similar work, this perception can negatively affect that employee's view of the value of the employee's own work. HR practitioners who specialize in compensation systems are particularly concerned not only that employees are paid fairly for the work they do, but also that they are paid equitably relative to other people in the organization.

Equitable pay
Compensation received is perceived to be equal to the value of the work performed

For employees, pay is **equitable** when the compensation given is perceived to be equal to the value of the work performed. Research clearly demonstrates that employees' perceptions of equity, or inequity, can have dramatic effects on their work behaviour and productivity, and therefore the employees' perception of the overall rewards system.[17] Although line managers do not design compensation systems, they do have to respond to employee concerns about being paid equitably. Compensation policies are internally equitable when employees believe that the wage rates for their jobs approximate the worth of the jobs to the organization. Perceptions of external equity exist when the organization is paying wages and benefits that are relatively equal to what other employers are paying for similar types of work. At Work with HRM 7.2 provides an interesting perspective on pay-for-performance and equity in today's volatile economic climate.

Variable Pay and Incentives

Pay-for-performance standard
Standard by which managers tie direct compensation to employee or organizational effort and performance

Aon
www.aon.com

A **pay-for-performance standard** serves to raise productivity and lower labour costs in today's economic environment. It is agreed that managers must tie at least some reward to employee effort and performance. Employees need to see and understand the link between their performance and the business performance.[18]

The term "pay for performance" or "variable pay," as described by Aon (**www.aon.com**), a world leader in management consulting, refers to a wide range of direct compensation options, including merit-based pay, bonuses, salary commissions, and team or group incentive programs.[19] Each of these compensation systems seeks to differentiate between the pay of average performers and that of outstanding performers. For example, Electronic Arts, a world gaming giant, announced that it was tying compensation to its overall company performance. It decided to do this to achieve a closer alignment between employee incentives and the overall company's performance, and minimizing the focus on an individual employee's performance record.[20] Interestingly, productivity studies show that employees will increase their output by 15 to 35% when an organization institutes a pay-for-performance program.

Unfortunately, designing a sound pay-for-performance system is not easy. Considerations must be given to how employee performance will be measured, what monies will be allocated for compensation increases, which employees will be covered, what payout method will be used, and when payments will be made. A critical issue concerns the size of the monetary increase and its perceived value to employees, as a pay-for-performance program will lack its full potential when pay increases only approximate the rises in the cost of living.

A recent study has suggested that such linkages may focus people only on the short term, and therefore, the meaningfulness of the work—not the pay—may be more important.[21] Further, since the 2008 economic turmoil, some academics and practitioners have been advocating that the link between pay and performance be stopped. The basis for this criticism lies in the number of employees—particularly at senior management levels—who undertake business risk-taking actions that may actually harm the company. In addition,

AT WORK **with HRM 7.2**

WILL THIS MOTIVATE ME?

Much has been written over the last several years about the use of incentives—particularly as a way to link employee performance to the overall success of the organization. Do incentives work and will they motivate people?

The answer in recent studies suggests "yes" and "no," or "it all depends." Whether it is as a result of the economic turmoil over the last few years or the changing expectations of the workforce, there is no simple solution, and one size does not fit all. The real issue is whether or not people are satisfied with their compensation and whether it motivates them to perform well.

According to Mercer, a global human resources consulting firm based in Canada, the majority of employees surveyed indicated that pay was the most important component of the employment relationship and yet only about one half felt satisfied with the base pay and that they were paid fairly. Further, those with bonus plans felt motivated to perform.

What was perhaps more interesting in the survey is the link between satisfaction and performance feedback. Employees that received regular feedback felt more positive about the organization and their contribution.

However, there is also contrary evidence that suggests while pay is important, recognizing achievement is more memorable and creates a more engaged employee. Recognition has been shown to motivate employees to work harder.

What appears to be equally important when designing a pay-for-performance component is the company's culture. Specifically, here are some questions that need answering: Is the organization prepared to share business and financial results with its employees? What does the organization want to pay for—results? behaviours? Is the organization prepared to identify differences in performance and pay accordingly? Is management supportive of this, and will there be a mutual discussion between employee and manager on goals and what will be rewarded?

CRITICAL THINKING QUESTIONS:

1. Would you like to have your pay tied directly to your performance? Why or why not?
2. Would pay-for-performance motivate you? Why or why not?

Sources: Adapted from Annette Cyr, "Is Your Firm Ready for Pay for Performance?" *Canadian HR Reporter*, January 25, 2010, www.hrreporter.com/articleview/7492-is-your-firm-ready-for-pay-for-performance; Mercer, *Inside Employees' Minds*, June 2011; Chris Vyse, "If You Build It, Will They Come?" *Canadian HR Reporter*, October 10, 2011, 29; Derek Irvine, "Debunking 10 Recognition and Rewards Myths," *Canadian HR Reporter*, December 5, 2011, 16.

these individuals make reference to the incredibly high CEO compensation packages; that business challenges emerge daily and therefore tying pay to performance isn't realistic; and that people will manipulate the criteria to achieve better results.[22] Figure 7.2 provides a summary of the advantages and disadvantages of different pay-for-performance systems.

The Bases for Compensation

Hourly work
Work paid on an hourly basis

Piecework
Work paid according to the number of units produced

Work performed in most private, public, and not-for-profit organizations has traditionally been compensated on an hourly basis. This is referred to as **hourly work**, in contrast to **piecework**, in which employees are paid according to the number of units they produce. Hourly work, however, is far more prevalent than piecework as a basis for compensating employees.

Employees compensated on an hourly basis are classified as *hourly employees*, or wage earners. Those whose compensation is computed on the basis of weekly, biweekly, or monthly pay periods are classified as *salaried employees*. Hourly employees are normally paid only for the time they work. Salaried employees, by contrast, are generally paid the same for each pay period, even though they occasionally may work more hours or fewer than the regular number of hours in a period. They also usually receive certain benefits not provided to hourly employees.

FIGURE 7.2   Advantages and Disadvantages of Pay-for-Performance Systems

Type of System	Advantages	Disadvantages
Individual	• Simple to compute • Clearly links pay to organizational outcomes • Motivates employees • Employees focus on clear performance targets • Distributes success among those responsible for producing success	• Standards of performance may be difficult to establish • May not be an effective motivator • Difficult to deal with missed performance targets • Available money may be inadequate • Employees may be unable to distinguish merit pay from other types of pay increases
Team	• Supports group planning • Builds team culture • Can broaden scope of contribution that employees are motivated to make • Tends to reduce jealousies and complaints • Encourages cross-training	• Individuals may perceive efforts contribute little to group success • Intergroup social problems can limit performance • Can be difficult to compute and therefore difficult to understand
Organization	• Creates effective employee participation • Can increase pride in organization • Can be structured to provide tax advantages • Has variable costs	• Difficult to handle if organization's performance is low • Can be difficult to compute and therefore difficult to understand • More difficult for individual effort to be linked to organizational success

DETERMINING COMPENSATION

Outcome 2

What are the factors when determining pay levels?

A combination of *internal* and *external* factors can influence, directly or indirectly, the rates at which employees are paid, as shown in Figure 7.3.

Internal Factors

The internal factors that influence wage rates are the employer's compensation policy, the worth of a job, an employee's relative worth in meeting job requirements, and an employer's ability and willingness to pay.

FIGURE 7.3   Factors Affecting the Wage Mix

INTERNAL FACTORS

Compensation strategy of organization

Worth of job

Employee's relative worth

Employer's ability to pay

WAGE MIX

EXTERNAL FACTORS

General economy

Conditions of the labour market

Area wage rates

Cost of living

Collective bargaining

Legal requirements

Employer's Compensation Strategy

Organizations will usually state objectives regarding compensation for their employees. For example, a public-sector employer may wish to pay fairly and at the market average. (Remember: "Market" means the geographical area in which the organization typically finds qualified candidates for work.) On the other hand, a software development company may wish to pay fairly but be the industry leader to attract and retain high-calibre staff.

Usually, both large and small employers set pay policies reflecting (1) the internal wage relationship among jobs and skill levels, (2) the external competition or an employer's pay position relative to what competitors are paying, (3) a policy of rewarding employee performance, and (4) administrative decisions concerning elements of the pay system, such as overtime premiums, payment periods, and short- or long-term incentives.

Worth of a Job

As discussed in Chapter 3, the design of work or of a job leads to the organization being able to achieve its objectives. Organizations without a formal compensation program generally base the worth of jobs on the subjective opinions of people familiar with the jobs. In such instances, pay rates may be influenced heavily by the labour market or, in the case of unionized employees, by collective bargaining. Organizations with formal compensation programs, however, are more likely to rely on a system of job evaluation to aid in rate determination. Even when rates are subject to collective bargaining, job evaluation can assist the organization in maintaining some degree of control over its wage structure.

Job evaluation
Systematic process of determining the relative worth of jobs in order to establish which jobs should be paid more than others within an organization

Job evaluation is the systematic process of determining the *relative* worth of jobs in order to establish which jobs should be paid more than others within the organization. Job evaluation helps to establish internal equity between various jobs. Job worth is usually measured by the following criteria: level of skill, effort, responsibility, and working conditions of the job, no matter which particular formal system is used. The relative worth of a job is then determined by comparing it with others within the organization using these criteria. Furthermore, each method of comparison may be made on the basis of the jobs as a whole or on the basis of the parts that constitute the jobs. Refer to the four methods of comparison explored at "Job Evaluation Systems," which starts on page 239.

Employee's Relative Worth

In both hourly and salaried jobs, employee performance can be recognized and rewarded through promotion and with various incentive systems. Superior performance can also be rewarded by granting merit raises on the basis of steps within a rate range established for a job class. If merit raises are to have their intended value, however, they must be determined by an effective performance appraisal system that differentiates between those employees who deserve the raises and those who do not. This system, moreover, must provide a visible and credible relationship between performance and any raises received. Unfortunately, too many so-called merit systems provide for raises to be granted automatically. As a result, employees tend to be rewarded more for just being present than for being productive on the job.

In some situations, supervisors will also compare the performance of one employee to another. While proponents of performance stress that a person is to be assessed against standards of performance, there is a tendency to compare employees against each other. This is particularly true in the absence of any performance management system.

Employer's Ability and Willingness to Pay

In the public sector, the amount of compensation (pay and benefits) employees can receive is limited by the funds budgeted for this purpose and by the willingness of taxpayers to provide them. Federal government employees had their pay frozen for six years, in response to the drive to balance the budget and because of the public's perception of highly paid government workers. In the private sector, profits and other financial resources available to employers often limit pay levels. Economic conditions and competition faced by employers can also significantly affect the rates they are willing to pay. Competition and recessions can force prices down and reduce the income from which compensation payments are derived. In such situations, employers may have little choice but to reduce wages and/or lay off employees, or, even worse, go out of business.

External Factors

The major external factors that influence wage rates include overall economy, labour-market conditions, area wage rates, cost of living, collective bargaining if the employer is unionized, and legal requirements.

Economy

Although Canada's economic woes are not as bad as elsewhere, given that it is an export-driven economy, businesses have to be sensitive to business projections. This situation is a backdrop to a potential labour shortage, particularly in key skill areas. To deal with this situation, companies are adopting a number of approaches. The study by Towers Watson, mentioned at the beginning of this chapter, identified the following actions:

- making a better link between rewards and business outcomes
- paying attention to job security as part of retention
- creating short-term incentive plans
- ensuring internal pay equity when new hires occur[23]

Labour-Market Conditions

The labour market reflects the forces of supply and demand for qualified labour within an area. These forces help to influence the wage rates required to recruit or retain competent employees. It must be recognized, however, that counterforces can reduce the full impact of supply and demand on the labour market. The economic power of unions, for example, may prevent employers from lowering wage rates even when unemployment is high among union members. Employment laws also may prevent an employer from paying at a market rate less than an established minimum.

Area Wage Rates

A formal wage structure should provide rates that are in line with those being paid by other employers for comparable jobs within the area. Data pertaining to area wage rates may be obtained at minimal cost from local area wage surveys. Wage-survey data also may be obtained from consulting firms, such as Towers Watson and the Hay Group. Smaller employers use government or local board of trade surveys to establish rates of pay. Many organizations conduct their own surveys. Others engage in a co-operative exchange of wage information or rely on various professional associations, such as the Professional Engineering Association of Ontario or British Columbia, for these data.

Statistics Canada
www.statcan.gc.ca

Consumer price index (CPI)
Measure of the average change in prices over time in a fixed "market basket" of goods and services

Cost of Living

Because of inflation, compensation rates tend to be adjusted upward periodically to help employees maintain their purchasing power. To do this, organizations frequently use the **consumer price index (CPI)**. The CPI is a broad measure of the cost of living in Canada and it measures the change in prices over time.[24] The index is based on prices in a "shopping basket" and the contents of this basket can change over time depending on people's spending choices. Among the close to 600 items typically measured are food, clothing, shelter, and fuels; transportation fares; charges for medical services; and prices of other goods and services that people buy for day-to-day living. Statistics Canada collects price information monthly and calculates the CPI for Canada as a whole and for various Canadian city averages. Figure 7.4 illustrates wage increases for unionized and non-unionized employees, compared with the inflation rate.

FIGURE 7.4 Inflation and Wage Increases (1993–2012)

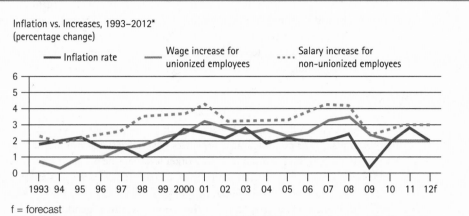

Inflation vs. Increases, 1993–2012*
(percentage change)

— Inflation rate   Wage increase for unionized employees   ···· Salary increase for non-unionized employees

f = forecast
*Wage increases for unionized employees from 1993 to 2010 are actuals as reported by Human Resources and Skills Development Canada, Workplace Information Directorate. Wage increases for unionized employees for 2011 (actual) and 2012 (projected) are from the Compensation Outlook 2012 survey.
Sources: The Conference Board of Canada; Human Resources and Skills Development Canada, Workplace Information Directorate.

Using the CPI to determine changes in pay rates can also compress pay rates within a pay structure, thereby creating inequities among those who receive the wage increase. For example, an increase of 50 cents an hour represents a 10% increase for an employee earning $5 an hour, but only a 5% increase for someone earning $10 per hour.

Collective Bargaining

As you will see in Chapter 10, one of the primary functions of a labour union is to bargain collectively over conditions of employment, the most important of which is compensation. The union's goal in each new agreement is to achieve increases in **real wages**—wage increases larger than the increase in the CPI—thereby improving the purchasing power and standard of living of its members. This goal includes gaining wage settlements that equal if not exceed the pattern established by other unions within the area.

Real wages
Wage increases larger than rises in the consumer price index; that is, the real earning power of wages

An employee's contribution to the organization (relative worth) is often considered when making salary decisions.

The agreements negotiated by unions tend to establish rate patterns within the labour market. As a result, wages are generally higher in areas where organized labour is strong. To recruit and retain competent personnel and avoid unionization, non-union employers must either meet or exceed these rates. The "union scale" also becomes the prevailing rate that all employers must pay for work performed under government contract. The impact of collective bargaining therefore extends beyond that segment of the labour force that is unionized.

Legal Requirements

As discussed in Chapter 2, legislation that either influences or requires certain pay rates is in place. For example, most provinces have a legislated minimum hourly wage, meaning that an employer cannot pay any worker less than the per-hour rate. In addition, pay equity legislation obliges certain companies to pay the same wage rate for jobs of a dissimilar nature and is based on comparing jobs performed mostly by men to jobs performed mostly by women. Under pay equity, a company must use a "gender-neutral" system, comparing jobs based on the amount and type of skill, effort, and responsibility needed to perform the job and on the working conditions in which the job is performed. Some provinces also consider male–female pay rates under human rights legislation. Read HRM and the Law 7.1 for a recent human rights decision that has taken almost 30 years to resolve.

HRM and the Law 7.1

WHY DID IT TAKE SO LONG?

The Supreme Court of Canada has upheld a decision by the Canadian Human Rights Tribunal regarding pay equity at Canada Post. This case started in 1983 and was finally resolved in late 2011!

The initial complaint was launched by the Public Service Alliance, the union representing about 2,300 employees who were mostly women. The complaint was in relation to pay equity—a claim that the clerical workers (primarily women) were paid less than comparable workers such as operations staff or letter carriers (primarily men). The claim was for $300 million.

While the case was not decided at the Canadian Human Rights Tribunal until 2005, that tribunal ruled in favour of the employees. Canada Post, however, appealed the decision, and the Federal Court heard the case in 2008, overturning the tribunal decision. This decision was then appealed by the Public Service Alliance, and the case went to the Federal Court of Appeal, which also upheld the lower court's decision and ruled in favour of Canada Post. All parties eventually applied to have the case heard at the Supreme Court of Canada.

The initial complaint indicated that there was a 50% wage gap and this is what the union is seeking. During the intervening 28 years, Canada Post modified its wage structure so that, in 2002, the basis of the complaint was eliminated. The Supreme Court noted this, so it awarded $150 million instead of the $300 million sought. The decision does mean, however, that anyone working in clerical roles at Canada Post between 1982 and 2002 is eligible to receive pay equity adjustments. There are no further appeals available, and Canada Post must distribute the amount awarded.

The laws governing pay equity for federal employees were changed in 2009 so that public employees can no longer use the court system to obtain settlements in pay equity cases. The law now requires that any challenges regarding wages be handled through collective bargaining.

QUESTION:
What do you think?

Sources: Adapted from Kathryn May, "After 28-Year Pay-Equity Fight, Female Clerical Workers Awarded $150-Million," *National Post*, November 17, 2011, news.nationalpost.com/2011/11/17/after-28-year-pay-equity-fight-female-postal-workers-awarded-150-million/; and "PSAC Wins Canada Post Pay Equity Case at the Supreme Court of Canada," Public Service Alliance of Canada, November 17, 2011, www.psac-afpc.com/news/2011/issues/20111117-e.shtml; and Public Service Alliance of Canada and Canada Post Corporation and Canadian Human Rights Commission, Nos. 33668, 33669, 33670, November 17, 2011.

Job Evaluation Systems

As mentioned earlier in this chapter, job evaluation is a way to determine the relative worth of jobs in an organization. The most typical job evaluation systems are described below.

Job Ranking System

The simplest and oldest system of job evaluation is the job ranking system, which arrays jobs on the basis of their relative worth. Job ranking can be done by a single individual knowledgeable about all jobs or by a committee composed of management and employee representatives. The basic weakness of the job ranking system is that it does not provide a very refined measure of each job's worth and therefore is not used frequently except in smaller organizations.

Job Classification System

In the job classification system, jobs that are sufficiently alike with respect to duties and responsibilities are grouped and will have a common name and common pay. Jobs that require increasing amounts of job responsibility, skill, knowledge, ability, or other factors selected to compare jobs would then be grouped together, with a different common name and a different common pay. For example, the "General Labour and Trade" classification of the federal government's Public Service Commission uses nine different factors, including "hazards," such as working under conditions that result in unavoidable exposure to illness or injury, to group positions together.[25]

The descriptions of each of the job classes constitute the scale against which the specifications for the various jobs are compared. Managers then evaluate jobs by comparing job descriptions with the different wage grades in order to "slot" the job into the appropriate grade. While this system has the advantage of simplicity, it is less precise than the point and factor comparison systems (discussed in the next sections) because the job is evaluated as a whole.

Point System

The point system is a quantitative job evaluation procedure that determines a job's relative value by calculating the total points assigned to it. It has been successfully used by high-visibility organizations, such as Boeing and Honeywell, and by many other public and private organizations, both large and small. Although point systems are rather complicated to establish, once in place they are relatively simple to understand and use. The principal advantage of the point system is that it provides a more refined basis for making judgments than either the ranking or classification systems. It thereby can produce results that are more valid and less easy to manipulate.

The point system permits jobs to be evaluated quantitatively on the basis of factors or elements—commonly called *compensable factors*—that constitute the job. The skills, efforts, responsibilities, and working conditions that a job usually entails are the more common major compensable factors that serve to evaluate the worth of a job as more or less important than another.

Factor Comparison System

The factor comparison system, like the point system, permits the job evaluation process to be accomplished on a factor-by-factor basis. A factor comparison system is typically used for legislated pay equity purposes. It differs from the point system, however, in that the compensable factors of the jobs to be evaluated are compared against the compensable factors of key jobs within the organization that serve as the job evaluation scale.

Key jobs are evaluated against five compensable factors—skill, mental effort, physical effort, responsibility, and working conditions—resulting in a ranking of the different factors for each key job. An example of a factor comparison system can be found on the University of British Columbia Web site (**www.hr.ubc.ca**), where the HR unit has posted

University of British Columbia

www.hr.ubc.ca

What system would you use to determine the worth of a rescue worker's job?

Donovan Reese/Photodisc Green/Getty Images

its job evaluation program. You will note that things such as the type and amount of independent decision-making are sub-factors of responsibility.

Regardless of the methodology used, be sure to remember that all job evaluation methods require varying amounts of judgment made by individuals. Supervisors or managers make decisions on the components of any job. Supervisors will also make decisions on how much responsibility and authority any particular job may have. Therefore, as careful an organization is in having objective ways of measuring the value of a job, subjective decisions are made regarding the content of the job. As mentioned previously, organizations frequently use a committee or panel for job evaluation assessments to help ensure objectivity in the process.

Whatever system a company uses, employees and managers will ask why the system is used. To better understand the reasons behind having some type of job evaluation system, look at the considerations in Manager's Toolkit 7.1.

MANAGER'S TOOLKIT **7.1**

WHY USE A JOB EVALUATION SYSTEM?

Organizations that have formal job evaluation systems are often questioned as to the reasons behind a particular system. It is helpful for managers to review the considerations companies give when making such a decision.

- Wages form a large portion of a company's operating cost, and job evaluation helps ensure that appropriate pay for the work is occurring.

- A job evaluation system helps establish a fair and equitable pay system.

- The system can highlight organizational design by creating appropriate job hierarchies.

- It ensures careful thinking and consistency in the making of pay allocation decisions.

- The system can help in dealing with any real or perceived pay equity issues.

Sources: Adapted from Muhammad Ali EL-Jajji, "An Analytical Approach to the Unequivocal Need of Organizations for Job Evaluation," *International Journal of Business and Social Science*, Vol. 2, No. 18, October 2011: 8–13; and Claudine Kapel, "The joy of job evaluation," *Canadian HR Reporter*, May 16, 2011, www.hrreporter.com/blog/Compensation-Rewards/archive/2011/05/16/the-joy-of-job-evaluation (accessed January 24, 2012).

THE COMPENSATION STRUCTURE

Outcome 4

What does a compensation structure look like?

Job evaluation systems provide for internal equity and serve as the basis for wage-rate determination. *They do not in themselves determine the wage rate.* The evaluated worth of each job based on its rank, class, points, or monetary worth must be converted into an hourly, daily, weekly, or monthly wage rate. The compensation tool used to help set wages is the wage and salary survey.

Wage and Salary Surveys

Wage and salary survey
Survey of the wages paid to employees of other employers in the surveying organization's relevant labour market

The **wage and salary survey** is a survey of the wages paid by employers in an organization's relevant labour market—local, regional, or national, depending on the job. The labour market is frequently defined as that area from which employers obtain certain types of workers. The labour market for office personnel would be local, whereas the labour market for engineers would be national. It is the wage and salary survey that permits an organization to maintain external equity—that is, to pay its employees wages equivalent to the wages similar employees earn in other establishments.

Collecting Survey Data

Although many organizations conduct their own wage and salary surveys, a variety of "preconducted" wage and salary surveys are available to satisfy the requirements of most public, not-for-profit, or private organizations. For example, you might want to see what the average hourly rate is for an accounting clerk in the Toronto area. Or you might want to know the average hourly rate for a Web designer anywhere in Canada. Companies such as Towers Watson (**www.towerswatson.com**), Aon (**www.aon.com**), Mercer (**www.mercer.ca**), and Hay Group (**www.haygroup.com**) conduct annual surveys.

Towers Watson
www.towerswatson.com

Aon
www.aon.com

Mercer
www.mercer.ca

Hay Group
www.haygroup.com

The Wage Curve

The relationship between the relative worth of jobs and their wage rates can be represented by means of a wage curve. This curve may indicate the rates currently paid for jobs within an organization, the new rates resulting from job evaluation, or the rates for similar jobs currently being paid by other organizations within the labour market. Figure 7.5 provides an example of a wage curve for a data conversion clerk working with the federal government in 2013. What does the slope of the wage curve suggest?

FIGURE 7.5   Wage Curve: Data Conversion Clerk, Federal Government, 2013

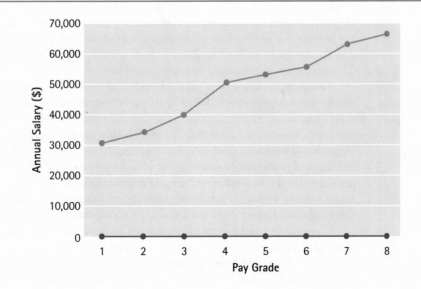

Source: Treasury Board of Canada, http://www.tbs-sct.gc.ca/pubs_pol/hrpubs/coll_agre/pa/pa08-eng.asp

FIGURE 7.6   Salary Structure with Increasing Pay Ranges: Data Conversion Clerk, Federal Government, 2013

Pay Grade	Step 1	Step 2	Step 3	Step 4
1	30,990	31,857	32,731	33,608
2	34,038	35,001	35,967	36,993
3	39,998	41,119	42,240	43,363
4	50,322	51,554	52,801	54,040
5	53,382	54,746	56,115	57,479
6	55,692	57,197	58,693	60,192
7	63,168	64,826	66,479	68,140
8	66,405	68,234	70,056	71,897

Source: Treasury Board of Canada, http://www.tbs-sct.gc.ca/pubs_pol/
hrpubs/coll_agre/pa/pa08-eng.asp

Pay Grades

Pay grades
Groups of jobs within a particular class that are paid the same rate or rate range

From an administrative standpoint, it is generally preferable to group jobs into **pay grades** and to pay all jobs within a particular grade the same rate or rate range. When the classification system of job evaluation is used, jobs are grouped into grades as part of the evaluation process. When the point and factor comparison systems are used, however, pay grades must be established at selected intervals that represent either the point or the evaluated monetary value of these jobs.

Rate Ranges

Although a single rate may be created for each pay grade, it is more common to provide a range of rates for each pay grade. The rate ranges may be the same for each grade or proportionately greater for each successive grade, as shown in Figure 7.6 using the same information for all the pay grades associated with the data conversion clerk. Rate ranges constructed on the latter basis provide a greater incentive for employees to accept a promotion to a job in a higher grade.

Other Ways to Determine Wages

The predominant approach to employee compensation is still the job-based system. Unfortunately, such a system often fails to reward employees for their skills or the knowledge they possess or to encourage them to learn a new job-related skill. Additionally, job-based pay systems may not reinforce an organizational culture stressing employee involvement or provide increased employee flexibility to meet overall production or service requirements. Therefore, many organizations have introduced competency-based or skill-based pay plans.

Competency-based pay
Pay based on how many capabilities employees have or how many jobs they can perform

Competency-based pay—also referred to as knowledge-based pay, skill-based pay, pay-for-knowledge, or multiskilled-based pay—compensates employees for the different skills or increased knowledge they possess or the collective behaviours or characteristics that they demonstrate rather than for the job they hold in a designated job category.[26] Regardless of the name, these pay plans encourage employees to earn higher base wages by learning and performing a wider variety of skills (or jobs) or displaying an array of competencies that can be applied to a range of organizational requirements. For example, in a manufacturing setting, new tasks might include various assembly activities carried out in a particular production system or a variety of maintenance functions.

Competency-based pay systems represent a fundamental change in the attitude of management regarding how work should be organized and how employees should be paid for their work efforts. The most frequently cited benefits of competency-based pay include attraction and retention of people with key skills, greater productivity, increased employee learning and commitment to work, improved staffing flexibility to meet production or service demands, and the reduced effects of absenteeism and turnover, since managers can assign employees where and when needed.[27] Competency-based pay also encourages employees to acquire training when new or updated skills are needed by an organization. Therefore, when considering the introduction of competency-based pay, it is important to:

- Clarify objectives of such an approach.
- Identify which jobs or types of work could benefit from broader and/or deeper development that is both possible and desirable.
- Identify competencies that demonstrably affect performance.
- Devise methods to measure achievement of each competency.
- Determine appropriate amount of pay for acquired skill.
- Provide mechanisms to review overall effectiveness.[28]

For example, the Government of Canada has developed a competency framework for all employees hired into public service. Competency is defined as "the knowledge, skills, abilities and behaviours that are used in performing their work."[29] The framework further indicates that the competencies used are both observable, measurable, and relevant to the work. For example, the complete competency profile for administrative services staff can be accessed through the Treasury Board of Canada Secretariat at **www.tbs-sct.gc.ca/gui/ cmas2-eng.asp**.

Treasury Board of Canada Secretariat

www.tbs-sct.gc.ca/gui/ cmas2-eng.asp

BROADBANDING   Organizations that adopt a skill-based pay system frequently use broadbanding to structure their compensation payments to employees. Broadbanding simply collapses many traditional salary grades into a few wide salary bands. Broadbands may have midpoints and quartiles, or they may have extremely wide salary ranges or no ranges at all. Broadbanding encourages lateral skill building while addressing the need to pay employees performing several jobs with different skill-level requirements. Additionally, broadbands help eliminate the obsession with grades and, instead, encourage employees to move to jobs where they can develop in their careers and add value to the organization. Paying employees through broadbands enables organizations to consider job responsibilities, individual skills and competencies, and career mobility patterns in assigning employees to bands.

INCENTIVE PLANS

Outcome 5

What are the various types of incentive plans?

For several years, a continuing trend in rewards has been the use of incentive plans, also called variable pay programs, for employees throughout the organization. However, with the economic downturn, many companies are reexamining whether or not these are appropriate in the current circumstances. A study by Deloitte Consulting found that 53% of employees indicated that promotion or job advancement retained them in their organization. However, this same study also indicated that 34% of employees wanted bonuses and other types of financial incentives as well as base salary.[30]

A recent study indicated that while the economic climate increased the need to contain reward costs, organizations were using incentive plans across many different job categories to encourage attainment of both individual and company-wide goals.[31] Incentive plans create an operating environment that champions a philosophy of shared commitment through the belief that every individual contributes to organizational performance and success.

By linking rewards with organizational objectives, managers believe that employees will assume "ownership" of their jobs, thereby improving their effort and overall job performance. Incentives are designed to encourage employees to put out more effort to complete their job tasks—effort they might not be motivated to expend under hourly and/or seniority-based compensation systems. Financial incentives are therefore offered to improve or maintain high levels of productivity and quality which, in turn, improve the market for Canadian goods and services in a global economy.

Do incentive plans work? Various studies have demonstrated a measurable relationship between incentive plans and improved organizational performance. It is important to remember that a one-size incentive plan does not fit all organizations. For such plans to work, there must be a "clear line of sight" from employee performance to organizational performance.[32]

FIGURE 7.7   The Pros and Cons of Team Incentive Plans

Pros	Cons
Team incentives support group planning and problem solving, thereby building a team culture.	Individual team members may perceive that "their" efforts contribute little to team success or to the attainment of the incentive bonus.
The contributions of individual employees depend on group co-operation.	Intergroup social problems/pressure to limit performance (e.g., team members are afraid one individual may make the others look bad) and the "free-ride" effect (one individual puts in less effort than others but shares equally in team rewards) may arise.
Unlike incentive plans based solely on output, team incentives can broaden the scope of the contribution that employees are motivated to make.	Complex payout formulas can be difficult for team members to understand.
Team bonuses tend to reduce employee jealousies and complaints over "tight" or "loose" individual standards.	
Team incentives encourage cross-training and the acquiring of new interpersonal competencies.	

A variety of individual and group incentive plans exists for both hourly and salaried employees. These include the following:

1. *Individual bonus*—an incentive payment that supplements the basic pay. It has the advantage of providing employees with more pay for exerting greater effort, while at the same time giving employees the security of a basic wage. Bonuses are common among managerial employees but as indicated earlier, organizations are increasingly providing bonuses to front-line staff.

2. *Team- or group-based incentive*—a plan that rewards team members with an incentive bonus when agreed-upon performance standards are exceeded. Figure 7.7 provides the pros and cons of team incentive plans.

3. *Merit raises*—an incentive, used most commonly for salaried employees, based on achievement of performance standards. One problem with merit raises is that they may be perpetuated year after year even when performance declines.

4. *Profit-sharing*—any plan by which an employer pays special sums based on the profits of the organization.

5. *Employee stock ownership plans (ESOPs)*—stock plans in which an organization contributes shares of its stock to an established trust for the purpose of stock purchases by its employees. With the recent economic turmoil, stock and stock options have not been as popular. And there is also always the issue of what happens to stock ownership when there is a change in ownership. For example, when Aon recently purchased Hewitt Consulting, Aon agreed to let employees have Aon stock, but it was valued differently.[33]

But do incentive plans work? Read At Work with HRM 7.3, which provides some insights.

EMPLOYEE BENEFITS

Outcome 6

Which benefits does the law require?

Employee benefits constitute an indirect form of compensation intended to improve the quality of the work and personal lives of employees. The cost of benefits can be as high as 40% when you include premiums for health and welfare, government-mandated coverage such as workers' compensation, vacation, and paid sick leave. In return, employers generally expect employees to be supportive of the organization and to be productive.

AT WORK with HRM 7.3

DO INCENTIVE PLANS REALLY WORK?

Companies will use incentive pay as a strategic tool to attract, motivate, and retain employees, and to improve organizational performance. And with the ongoing economic issues, organizations want to keep key talent while keeping costs down. Is this goal achievable with incentive plans?

Yes, but careful attention has to be paid in the objectives, design, and implementation.

1. Companies will need to reward the most valued employees, which means that the organizations need to know who matters to business performance.

2. Consider how the incentive plan is to be paid out—salary or a larger lump sum?

3. Effective programs usually pay more to those who demonstrate better results.

4. Components need to be examined periodically to ensure that outcomes are being achieved.

5. To be effective, incentives must be linked to corporate goals, such as increased customer satisfaction.

6. Plan design needs to address both short-term and long-term business performance.

For example, WestJet is proud to provide a profit-sharing program for its employees. It feels that this type of recognition and reward has enabled it to be the most profitable North American airline.

QUESTION:

Would you like to have an incentive plan? Why or why not? Explain your reasons.

Sources: Adapted from "Vision and Values Help WestJet Soar," *National Post*, January 21, 2009, FP11; Joanne Dahm and Pete Sanborn, "Addressing Talent & Rewards in 'The New Normal,'" Aon Hewitt, 2010; Brian Townley, "Motivate Employees with Incentives," *ABA Bank Marketing* 43, no. 8 (2011): 28–31; and Raphaela Finkenauer O'Day, "Effective Incentive Design," *Benefits Magazine*, February 2012, 36–40.

Since employees have come to expect an increasing number of benefits, the motivational value of these benefits depends on how the benefits program is designed and communicated. Once viewed as a gift from the employer, benefits are now considered rights to which all employees are entitled.

Too often, a particular benefit is provided because other employers are doing it, because someone in authority believes it is a good idea, or because there is union pressure. However, the contributions that benefits will make to the compensation package (and therefore, to organizational performance) depend on how much attention is paid to certain basic considerations.

Linking Benefits to the Overall Rewards Program

Like any other component of the compensation plan, an employee benefits program should be based on specific objectives. The objectives an organization establishes will depend on many factors, including the size of the firm, its profitability, its location, the degree of unionization, and industry patterns. Most important, these objectives must be compatible with the organization's strategic rewards and recognition plan, including its philosophy and policies.

The chief objectives of most benefits programs are to:

- improve employee work satisfaction
- meet employee health, security, and environment concerns and requirements
- attract and motivate employees
- retain top performing employees
- maintain a favourable competitive position

For example, Johnson, an insurance company in St. John's, Newfoundland, recognizes that there are many components in a benefits program. Its inclusion of a $500 annual payment to its 1,500 employees for use in a wellness activity has resulted in the company being listed in Canada's Top 100 Employers for 2012.[34]

But it is important to remember that not all benefits work for everyone. As a result, it is important that organizations design their benefits program to fit the employees in the organizations.[35] As with other good HR practices, it is a good idea to consult with employees when a new benefit is being considered. Many organizations establish committees composed of managers and employees to administer, interpret, and oversee their benefits policies. Opinion surveys are also used to obtain employee input. Having employees participate in designing benefits programs helps to ensure that management is satisfying employee wants.

Cost Concerns

Organizations can typically spend about 35% to 45% of their annual payroll costs on benefits such as group health plans, pension contributions, EI premiums, CPP premiums, and workers' compensation premiums. The increasing costs, particularly of health-care provisions, have made more and more organizations strive to manage those costs.

Since many benefits represent a fixed rather than a variable cost, management must decide whether it can afford this cost under less favourable economic conditions. As managers can readily attest, if an organization is forced to discontinue a benefit, the negative effects of cutting it may outweigh any positive effects that accrued from providing it.

To minimize negative effects and avoid unnecessary expense, many employers enlist the co-operation of employees in evaluating the importance of particular benefits. For example, Staples provides an opportunity every year for its 15,000 employees to review their benefits and make adjustments as necessary. To make this work, and to help manage its costs, Staples has worked with its internal communications group to get out information that would be useful and informative to the employees. Staples credits this with helping the employees be "better shoppers" when using their benefits plans, such as getting preventive dental cleanings and generic drugs.[36]

The escalating cost of health-care benefits is a major concern to employers, who must strike an appropriate balance between offering quality benefits and keeping costs under control. Some recent evidence suggests a strong relationship between effective health programs and productivity, thereby lowering the health-care costs.[37] At Work with HRM 7.4 describes what Shoppers Drug Mart has done in using its business model to improve the benefits program for its employees while reducing costs.

Providing medical benefits will be a growing burden on employers in years to come.

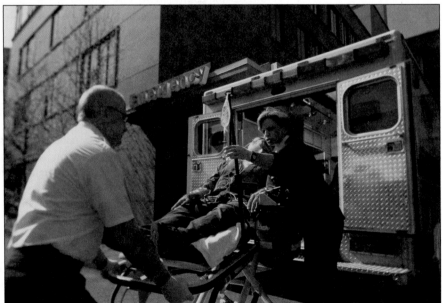

Keith Brofsky/Photodisc Green/Getty Images

AT WORK **with HRM 7.4**

LEVERAGING THE BUSINESS TO MANAGE THE COSTS OF BENEFITS

Shoppers Drug Mart, a Canada-wide retail drugstore chain with headquarters in Toronto, has taken an innovative approach with its employee benefits program. Specifically, in 2009, it began a review of its program and soon discovered that it had a unique opportunity to use its existing pharmacy expertise and business model to improve the health and wellness of its employees.

It undertook the review by creating a cross-functional team with input from pharmacy, procurement, operations, marketing, and HR with the objective of designing a leading-edge benefits plan. The result, which was launched in 2011, has three parts: chronic care management, generic drugs, and wellness—the foundation of its business model as a pharmacy.

With about one year of results, the outcomes are impressive. Expenditures for drugs have fallen by more than 10% with the Ontario claims showing a 15% reduction. The wellness portion has people enrolled in a diabetes management program as well as 80% of its employees taking part in a health-risk assessment.

Basil Rowe, Vice President Total Rewards and Shared Services, stated that the reinvesting of the drug savings into the health and wellness parts was the cornerstone of the new plan. "Our high participation rates with the health-risk assessments and the self-help programs show that our employees understand and they are committed," reports Rowe. He further noted that Shoppers Drug Mart wants its employees to have a positive experience with the new benefits plan—by being partners in improving and maintaining their health and wellness.

CRITICAL THINKING QUESTIONS:

1. Do you think it is important for an employer to focus on the health of its employees? Why or why not?
2. Isn't managing employee health care and wellness just another way to reduce costs? Why or why not?

Source: Adapted from Sonya Felix, "Shoppers Drug Mart capitalizes on company strengths," *Benefits Canada*, January 4, 2012, http://www.benefitscanada.com/benefits/health-benefits/shoppers-drug-mart-capitalizes-on-company-strengths-24129. Used with permission from Benefits Canada and Shoppers Drug Mart.

Benefits Canada

www.benefitscanada.com

While organizations still have ongoing concerns for the costs of benefits, particularly in the pension area, there is some suggestion that the increases are slowing down.[38] Part of the reason for this is the use of generic drugs and the results of wellness programs initiated a number of years ago. In addition, some organizations are approaching their costs of health-care benefits from a value-based perspective. Specifically, "value-based health care" is a systematic and holistic approach to creating a culture of health for employees. It does this by better aligning financial and nonfinancial incentives for a healthier lifestyle.[39] For additional articles on managing the cost of health care, check out the Web site of Benefits Canada (**www.benefitscanada.com**).

BENEFITS REQUIRED BY LAW

Legally required employee benefits can cost over 15% of an organization's annual payroll. These benefits include employer contributions to the Canada or Quebec pension plan, unemployment insurance, workers' compensation insurance (covered in Chapter 8), and, in some provinces, provincial medicare.

Canada and Quebec Pension Plans (CPP/QPP)

The Canada and Quebec pension plans cover almost all Canadian employees between the ages of 18 and 70. Both plans require employers to match the contributions made by employees. The revenues generated by these contributions are used to pay three main types of benefits: retirement pensions, disability benefits, and survivors' benefits. With Canada's population aging, funds from the CPP will not be able to meet the needs of retirees unless those currently working, and their employers, significantly increase their contributions.

Employment Insurance (EI)

Employment insurance (EI) benefits have been available for more than 50 years and were provided as income protection to employees who were between jobs. Employees and employers both contribute to the Employment Insurance fund. The amount of benefit paid is a formula (which can change) based on the number of hours of employment in the past year and the regional unemployment rate.

Provincial Hospital and Medical Services

Most provinces fund health-care costs from general tax revenue and federal cost sharing. Ontario, Quebec, and Newfoundland also levy a payroll tax, while other provinces, such as Alberta and British Columbia, charge premiums that are payable by the resident or an agent, usually the employer (subsidies for low-income residents are provided).

The cost of the government providing health care has escalated to the point where major reform in Canada's health-care system is occurring. As of 2011, 27% of the Canadian population was over 55 with those over 80 comprising 4%.[40] As has been discussed by policy makers, politicians, and journalists, the increasing longevity of people and the major health problems that do occur mean that our health-care system will need significant redesign to be sustainable in the future.[41]

Leaves without Pay

Most employers grant leaves of absence to employees who request them for personal reasons. In some provinces, legislation mandates that these types of leaves must be granted. These leaves are usually taken without pay, but also without loss of seniority or benefits.

Other Required Benefits

In addition to the benefits described, through provisions in employment standards legislation, provinces do require employers to pay for statutory holidays, minimum vacation pay, premiums when people work overtime, and in some provinces, a severance payment when employees are terminated.

VOLUNTARY EMPLOYEE BENEFITS

Outcome 7

Describe voluntary benefits.

**International Foundation
of Employee Benefit Plans**
www.ifebp.org

In addition to the benefits that are required by legislation, employers can choose to provide more benefits as part of the overall compensation package. Organizations do this to ensure that they are able to attract and retain the kinds of employees they want. These benefits are called "voluntary benefits." While there can be many types of these benefits, we will look at the more typical ones. You can review some of the other voluntary benefits at the International Foundation of Employee Benefit Plans Web site (**www.ifebp.org**).

Health and Welfare Benefits

Due to sharply rising costs and employee concern, the benefits that receive the most attention from employers today are health-care benefits. In the past, health insurance plans covered only medical, surgical, and hospital expenses. Today, employers include prescription drugs as well as dental, optical, and mental health–care benefits in the package they offer their workers. As mentioned earlier in this chapter, employers are attempting to ensure that the benefit provided will be of value to the person. Listed below is a brief description of typical health and welfare benefits.

Dental Coverage

Dental plans are designed to help pay for dental-care costs and to encourage employees to receive regular dental attention. Typically, the insurance pays a portion of the charges and the employee pays the remainder.

Extended Health Coverage

This benefit provides for additional payments beyond the basic provincial medical coverage. It typically provides such things as semi-private or private hospital rooms, prescription drugs, private nursing, ambulance services, out-of-country medical expenses that exceed provincial limits, and vision care.

It should be noted that there could be duplication of coverage if both partners in a relationship have access to health coverage. In some cases, if there is better coverage in one plan than in another, the partner with the better coverage will enroll and include the partner.

One aspect of extended health coverage that is increasing greatly is the cost of prescription drugs. This situation becomes worse when provincial health plans reduce coverage or make use of generic drugs—private plans typically will pick up thereby increasing costs.[42] To counter this increase, many plans make use of generic drugs as well, but this only goes so far. Other ways to reduce the costs are to encourage employees to have a healthy lifestyle that eliminates the need for increased health-care coverage.[43] Employers and benefits' carriers are also watching the increased use of genetic testing and its impact on extended health coverage. The concern is that as it becomes more widely available, it won't be covered by public plans, and hence, employees will want the testing covered under private plans.[44]

Life Insurance

One of the oldest and most popular employee benefits is group term life insurance, which provides death benefits to beneficiaries and may also provide accidental death and dismemberment benefits.

Retirement and Pension Plans

Retirement is an important part of life and requires sufficient and careful preparation. In convincing job applicants that theirs is a good organization to work for, employers usually emphasize the retirement benefits that can be expected after a certain number of years of employment.

Many employers offer additional health benefits, such as dental coverage.

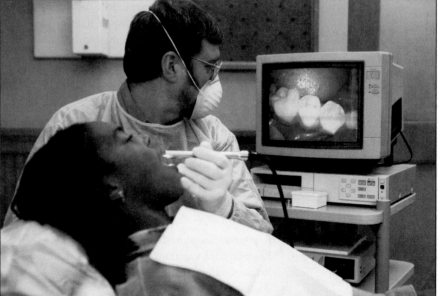

Keith Brofsky/Photodisc Green/Getty Images

Pension plans are classified into two primary categories: (1) defined benefit, and (2) defined contribution. In a *defined benefit plan (DBP)*, a person receiving benefits receives a specific amount (usually based on years of service and average earnings), regardless of the amount of contributions. On the other hand, a *defined contribution plan (DCP)* provides to the recipient an amount that is based on the amount of accumulated funds and how much those funds can purchase (at the time of retirement) for retirement benefits.

Since defined benefit plans have to provide the specific payment whether or not the employee has made sufficient contributions, the organization becomes liable for the difference. With the aging workforce, more and more organizations and employees are expressing concern about whether their plan will be able to fund what has been promised. The ongoing economic turmoil has continued and increased the concern about the viability of companies having a defined benefit plan. For example, RBC, Canada's biggest bank, decided that all new hires as of January 1, 2012, would no longer be enrolled or eligible for its defined benefit pension plan.[45] In doing so, the bank indicated that the changes were a responsible way to ensure retirement plans in the future and manage the costs prudently. To ensure that RBC remained competitive, it also enhanced its defined contribution plan for those new employees by increasing its contribution on behalf of employees.

Unfortunately, the concerns about the value of pension plans are not new. For some time, Canadian organizations have been faced with the dilemma of potentially having insufficient resources in the future to pay pensions to the people who will be retiring in the future. These concerns have led some employers to consider changing pension plan design from defined benefit to defined contribution. Within the private sector, the defined benefit plans have seen a reduction from 90 to 56% in the proportion of pension plan members who were in one.[46] While labour unions will be discussed more fully in Chapter 11, it is worthwhile to note that the primary issue between Air Canada's sales and service agents, represented by CAW, in their labour negotiations is the issue of pensions. According to Air Canada, it has a $2.1 billion shortfall in its pension liabilities. It is proposing to fix this by reducing its contributions as well as changing the provisions for new employees.[47] Other suggestions to keep defined benefit plans viable are to have multi-employer pension plans, such as the Ontario Municipal Employees Retirement System, or ensuring that the pension plan is professionally invested.[48]

There is also concern from various levels of government that the overall pension system needs to improve, and hence, a number of reports have called for new models that are more flexible and appealing to employers and employees. One suggestion is for a super CPP.[49] In late 2011, the federal government introduced the *Pooled Registered Pension Plans Act*, a framework for businesses—particularly small businesses—to allow people to save for retirement through payroll deductions.[50]

Given the current volatility of the stock market and the concern about future payments from pension plans, it is no wonder that there is a push to improve the performance of all pension plans, including government-funded ones. Ethics in HRM 7.1 discusses the dilemma of investments of pension plans.

Pay for Time Not Worked

The "pay for time not worked" category of benefits includes statutory holiday pay, vacation pay (above any legislated minimum), bereavement leave, rest periods, coffee breaks, sick leave, and parenting benefits (salary continuance). These benefits typically account for a large portion of overall benefit costs.

Vacations with Pay

It is generally agreed that vacations are essential to the well-being of an employee. Eligibility for vacations varies by industry, locale, and organization size. To qualify for longer vacations of three, four, or five weeks, one may expect to work for 7, 15, and 20 years, respectively.

ETHICS in HRM 7.1

IS THIS A WISE INVESTMENT?

The Canada Pension Plan is the federal government's provision for employees to have retirement income based on their years of work. Overseen by Service Canada, it states that it is there to "provide you with a stable and dependable pension you can build on for retirement." When created in 1966, the CPP was not intended to be the sole component of a person's retirement income but only a portion.

To ensure that the CPP would be healthy and well funded in the future, the federal government and all the provinces reached agreement to create an arms-length agency (an agency free from political interference) to professionally manage the investments for the benefit of future generations. Hence the CPP Investment Board (CPPIB) was launched in 1996 when it was determined that the government was paying out $6 billion more than it was receiving in contributions and that the investment returns needed to improve.

The CPPIB does this by taking a long-term view of its investments. In its 2010 Responsible Investment Policy, it stresses that the overriding duty of the Board is to "maximize return without undue risk of loss." It currently manages about $150 billion.

The CPPIB made financial headlines in late 2011 when it joined with Microsoft Corp. to purchase Skype and offered to purchase a significant portion of Yahoo. Over the last several years, Yahoo's performance has declined as a search engine, as it is being eclipsed by Google, and Facebook is becoming an alternative for online advertisers. Concerns about the future of Yahoo resulted in its founder (Jerry Yang) resigning in the fall of 2011; the new CEO is faced with many challenges. The joint proposal would cost about $3 billion.

Yet, many Canadians do not have much confidence in the health of their pension plans. They are concerned that the financial underpinnings are not sound and that the payments will be reduced. This perception increased when the federal government announced in early 2012 that it would need to do something in the future to contain the costs of providing income to an increasing retirement population.

CRITICAL THINKING QUESTIONS:

1. Is it ethical for the CPPIB to invest in the stock market? Why or why not?
2. Given the CPPIB's policy about investing without "undue risk of loss," is it ethical for CPPIB to make an offer to purchase an interest in Yahoo? Why or why not?

Sources: Adapted from Service Canada, "Canada Pension Plan (CPP), accessed January 30, 2012, www.servicecanada.gc.ca/eng/isp/cpp/cpptoc.shtml; "Summary Facts and Figures," CPP Investment Board, November 2011; "Policy on Responsible Investing, CPP Investment Board, August 10, 2010; Laurie Segall, "Yahoo: New CEO, Same Results," CNNMoney Tech, January 24, 2012, money.cnn.com/2012/01/24/technology/yahoo_earnings/index.htm; Anupreeta Das and Gina Chon, The Globe and Mail, October 20, 2011, A7; Brian Womack, Jeffrey McCracken, and Serena Saitto, "CPPIB in Group Bidding for Stake in Yahoo," The Globe and Mail, December 1, 2011, B7; Tammy Burns, "Pension Plans Shaking Canadians' Confidence," Benefits Canada, January 12, 2012, www.benefitscanada.com/pensions/other-pensions/pension-plans-shaking-canadians-confidence-24442; and "Harper Tells Davos That Hard Choices Needed Now," CBC News, January 26, 2012, www.cbc.ca/news/world/story/2012/01/26/davos-harper-thurs.html.

Paid Holidays

Both hourly and salaried workers can expect to be paid for statutory holidays as designated in each province. The standard statutory holidays in Canada are New Year's Day, Good Friday, Canada Day (Memorial Day in Newfoundland and Labrador), Labour Day, and Christmas Day. Other holidays that are recognized by various provinces are Victoria Day, Thanksgiving Day, Remembrance Day, and Family Day. Additionally, each province may designate special holidays important to that province only. Many employers give workers an additional one to three personal days off. With the increasing diversity in culture and religions in the workforce, situations may arise where governments feel a need to change the number and type of statutory holidays so that there are more general kinds of observations rather than holidays tied to any one faith. For example, Broadcast Services International, a technical production and engineering services company for radio and television broadcasts, provides an opportunity for employees to take days off to celebrate their cultures or attend religious conferences.[51]

Sick Leave

Employees may be compensated in several ways during periods when they are unable to work because of illness or injury. Most public employees, as well as many in private firms (particularly in white-collar jobs), receive a set number of sick-leave days each year to cover such absences. Where permitted, sick leave that employees do not use can be accumulated to cover prolonged absences. Accumulated vacation leave may sometimes be used as a source of income when sick-leave benefits have been exhausted. Group insurance that provides income protection during a long-term disability is also becoming more common. As discussed earlier in the chapter, income lost during absences resulting from job-related injuries may be reimbursed, at least partially, through workers' compensation insurance.

According to a Statistics Canada report, workplace absences have risen over the last several years. In 2010, an average of nine work days (approximately 3%) were lost due to illness or family responsibilities.[52] Much of this amount is due to the aging workforce. Workers aged 55 and over missed 11 days of work on average each year, while workers aged 35 to 44 missed only 8 days.[53] It is also interesting to note that absence due to family responsibilities accounts for about 20% of the overall days absent.

Wellness Programs

In recent years, new types of services have been offered to make life at work more rewarding and to enhance employee well-being. Excellence Canada (formerly the National Quality Institute) provides annual awards for organizations that have outstanding wellness programs. Ceridian Canada, a full-service company specializing in payroll support, has won the award three years in a row.[54] Recent research suggests that for every $1 spent on wellness programs, the return in terms of lower health-care costs, increased production, and higher employee morale is close to $6.[55] For a creative approach to encouraging wellness, read At Work with HRM 7.5.

Employee Assistance Programs

To help workers cope with a wide variety of problems that interfere with the way they perform their jobs, organizations have developed employee assistance programs (EAPs). An employee assistance program typically provides diagnosis, limited counselling, and referral for advice or treatment when necessary for problems related to substance abuse (alcohol, drug), emotional difficulties, and financial or family difficulties. (EAPs will be discussed in detail in Chapter 8.) Approximately 75% of employers have an EAP for their employees and families.[56] The main intent of these programs is to help employees solve their personal problems or at least to prevent problems from turning into crises that affect their ability to work productively. With the economic difficulties over the last several years, however, employees are also using the EAP to help them with credit and debt issues; when people have financial issues, they become stressed and are less able to handle work issues.[57]

Educational Assistance Plans

One of the benefits most frequently mentioned in literature for employees is the educational assistance plan. The primary purpose of this plan is to help employees keep up-to-date with advances in their fields and to help them get ahead in the organization. Usually, the employer covers—in part or totally—costs of tuition, books, and related fees, while the employee is required to pay for meals, transportation, and other expenses. Depending on the organization, some companies are willing to pay for courses not directly related to a specific job. Employees who have had access to such programs and, therefore, advanced their education believe that they are more efficient, produce higher quality, are more satisfied, and that their increased knowledge was helpful on the job.[58]

AT WORK **with HRM 7.5**

10,000 STEPS A DAY!

Early in 2011, Standard Life, one of Canada's largest insurance companies, wanted to improve its wellness program in such a way that everyone could participate without concern about where they lived or how physically fit they were. Eric Pfeiffer, a senior consultant at the company, indicated that simplicity was also important. To meet these expectations, Standard Life got involved with the Global Corporate Challenge (GCC). This program challenges people to take 10,000 steps each day. As Pfeiffer states, "It's just walking, so it's inclusive for everyone … it is something that can bring all the offices together."

To get the program started, employees walked together at lunch and went out dancing. Pfeiffer commented that he had never seen so many people using the stairs in the company's Toronto office. Standard Life has had great success with employees averaging 13,000 steps per day.

The Global Corporate Challenge, now more than 10 years old, is the largest corporate health initiative in the world, with participants in 83 countries. It has sponsored research to better understand the health risks associated with the contemporary sedentary life.

The results from the research have demonstrated that something as simple as walking can improve mental health, sleep patterns, and energy levels, and help reduce weight. Specifically, 71% of the GCC participants reported an increase in energy levels, 54% had reduced blood pressure, and 90% reported an improvement in their overall health.

Other research has demonstrated that people who are sedentary for more than 30 hours per week are at a greater risk of obesity. The more active people are, the better. The Global Corporate Challenge focuses on the word "active" and doesn't call it "exercise" because vigorous activity is not the only way to become and stay fit.

Being involved in the Global Corporate Challenge is also cost effective. Currently, employers can participate at $99 per person with lower costs for more participants. A small price to pay for 10,000 steps each day for 16 weeks!

QUESTION:

What are some of the reasons why an organization may not want to invest in a wellness program? Explain your reasons.

Sources: Adapted from Amanda Silliker, "Global Corporate Challenge combats obesity," *Canadian HR Reporter*, December 19, 2011, www.hrreporter.com/articleview/12004-global-corporate-challenge-combats-obesity (accessed January 30, 2012); and The Global Corporate Challenge, www.gettheworldmoving.com (accessed January 30, 2012).

Childcare and Eldercare

Consider these statistics:

- Over 14% of the Canadian population is 65 or older.[59]
- 2.3 million employees aged 45 and over combine work and caregiving.[60]
- Caregivers miss 1.5 million work days per month because of care duties.[61]
- Lost productivity due to caregiving is the equivalent of 157,000 full-time employees.[62]

In the past, working parents had to make their own arrangements with sitters or with nursery schools for preschool children. Today, benefits may include financial assistance, alternative work schedules, and family leave. For many employees, on-site or near-site childcare centres are the most visible, prestigious, and desired solutions.

A growing benefit offered employees with children experiencing a short illness is called "mildly ill childcare." Medical supervision is the primary difference between these facilities and traditional daycare arrangements.

Responsibility for the care of aging parents and other relatives is another fact of life for more and more employees. The term **eldercare**, as used in the context of employment, refers to situations where an employee provides care to an elderly relative while remaining actively at work. Most caregivers are women. According to Statistics Canada, at the end of 2011 close to 5 million Canadians were 65 or older, of which close to 30% were over 80.[63] By 2036, it is estimated that approximately 9.9 million Canadians, or about 25%, will be 65 and older.[64] As a consequence

Eldercare
Care provided to an elderly relative by an employee who remains actively at work

of the expected shortfall in eldercare facilities, the responsibility for the care of these seniors will be borne by their children and other relatives. The majority of caregivers are women.

To reduce the negative effects of caregiving on productivity, organizations may offer eldercare counselling, educational fairs and seminars, printed resource material, support groups, and special flexible schedules and leaves of absence.

Interest in and demand for eldercare programs is increasing dramatically as the Canadian population ages and lives longer. One author of this text (Stewart) found herself in just this situation: raising a young child and having to care for aging parents at a distance.

It is important to consider the impact of childcare on the Canadian workplace, as well. Most people who are responsible for childcare are female. Given that the labour force is approximately 55% female,[65] significant issues can occur in the workplace when childcare duties need attention. Of the women working, 65% had infants and toddlers.[66] As mentioned earlier in this section, 20% of the absences in the Canadian workplace are due to family responsibilities—a huge loss to the Canadian economy.

And it isn't just the impact that absences have on the performance of the organization, but the challenge of women to obtain appropriate childcare and return to work partially explains the wage gap between men and women.[67]

Organizations have been involved in a number of initiatives to improve this situation. For example, Central 1 Credit Union, with offices in Ontario and British Columbia, has a daycare benefit that is available throughout Canada.[68] The specific plan is a corporate membership with a daycare company. Since the plan is nationwide in scope, employees can access guaranteed childcare whenever needed.

Other Services

The variety of benefits and services that employers offer today could not have been imagined a few years ago. Some are fairly standard, and we will cover them briefly. Some are unique and obviously grew out of specific concerns, needs, and interests. Some of the more creative and unusual benefits are group insurance for employee pets, free baseball tickets for families and friends, and summer boat cruises. At Work with HRM 7.6 describes the special benefits at Bayer Canada.

There are many emerging trends in relation to rewards and recognition. See Emerging Trends 7.1 for some of the more prominent ones.

Many organizations recognize the needs of working parents and ensure that appropriate childcare is available.

Nelson Education

AT WORK **with HRM 7.6**

GREAT BENEFITS!

Bayer Canada, which develops a number of health-care solutions, has about 800 employees across Canada and is rated one of Canada's top employers. The benefits it offers employees is one of the reason for its success. In addition to the usual health coverage, Bayer Canada offers flexible benefit options such as savings, pension, and stock purchase plans.

However, as stated by Gord Johnston, vice-president of HR, Bayer wanted to add more value to its benefits. It decided to offer a program of employee discounts. But this wasn't just any employee discount program. What Bayer did was become involved in a national organization called WorkPerks. As Johnston put it, "Field employees sometimes feel like they miss out on all this stuff so, yeah, we have a gym on-site, but where is their gym?"

Belonging to WorkPerks provides employees with access to discounts on a variety of items, from restaurants to travel to clothing. Many brand names such as Apple and Empire Theatres are included in the offerings. These discounts can also be shared with families.

For Bayer, the program is also very cost effective—it costs about $15 annually per employee. For larger organizations, such as one with 5,000 employees, the cost is only about $3 per year per employee. Employees in the program create an account through the WorkPerks Web site, which allows people to browse through the various discounts. The employees then either print the coupon or get the access code for the discount. For some organizations involved, access to WorkPerks can also be done through the organization's Web site.

Johnston believes that these types of programs enhance the total rewards program and as such, are able to attract and retain key talent.

CRITICAL THINKING QUESTIONS:

1. Do you think these special benefits are attractive? Why or why not?
2. Would the inclusion of an employee-discount program draw you to work for Bayer? Why or why not?

Sources: Amanda Silliker, "Employee discount programs appeal to all levels of employees," *Canadian HR Reporter*, September 12, 2011, 26; "Bayer: Science for a Better Life," www.bayer.ca/?q=en/node/46 (accessed January 31, 2012); and WorkPerks, www.bayer.ca/?q=en/node/46

EMERGING TRENDS **7.1**

1. ***Incentives and innovative programs for adopting a healthier lifestyle.*** As costs of health care—both publicly funded and through work benefits—continue to rise, employers are encouraging and supporting employees to be healthier. This includes providing health-risk assessments and specialized interventions such as smoking-cessation aids. Employers are concerned not just about the rising costs to health plans, but also about a less productive workforce.

2. ***Increased use of nonfinancial rewards.*** Organizations are looking at new ways to reward and recognize employees in order to encourage

creativity and innovation. Some of the ways will be giving employees challenging work, career development, training, and the opportunity for older employees to mentor younger employees.

3. ***Creating different approaches to compensation.*** Organizations are being unorthodox as they look at the value of rewards and their overall purpose: to attract and retain employees. Fusion Home in Ontario, for example, pays for the gasoline costs of employees who have to travel farther than other employees. Likewise, Walmart has decided to adjust pay based on the person's length of time as an employee.

continued

4. ***Phased retirement.*** Despite economic problems, organizations remain concerned about losing the knowledge base from the retirement of workers. Therefore, some organizations are looking at ways and means to allow their employees to retire partially. Employees would receive a combination of pay for work plus some portion of their company pension. Walmart Canada, for example, won an award for its Progressive Retirement Services program, which provides flexible work options.

5. ***Range of voluntary options.*** Primarily to deal with the changing demographics, employers will be looking at ways to provide a range of options from which employees can select. These include employee discount vendors, health spending accounts, and transit passes.

6. ***More emphasis on pensions.*** With the heightened awareness of the sluggish economy as more people move into retirement, employers are looking at better ways to fund pensions as well as ensuring that employees understand what pension benefits they have.

7. ***Rise of self-insured benefit plans.*** With self-insured plans, employers may pay less in overall benefit costs but take on an additional risk of paying for the actual benefit not just the premium costs.

8. ***Executive compensation.*** While the depths of the recession have passed, there is still a concern among the general public and an organization's employees in regard to executive and CEO pay. Not long ago we witnessed the Occupy Wall Street movement in a few major cities across Canada. CEOs in North America have been enjoying annual compensation increases of 23 to 27% while the average employee's comparable increase has been less than 1%. Further, the top CEOs in Canada are paid almost 190 times more than the average wages of an employee.

Sources: Sarah Dobson, "Health Incentives More Popular: Survey," *Canadian HR Reporter*, December 19, 2011, 3; "One-Quarter of Firms Planning to Offer Incentive Pay for Health Programs: Towers Watson," *Canadian HR Reporter*, November 22, 2011, www.hrreporter.com/articleview/11781-one-quarter-of-firms-planning-to-offer-incentive-pay-for-health-programs-towers-watson; "3 Organizations Earn Best Employers Award for 50-Plus Canadians," *Canadian HR Reporter*, February 25, 2011, www.hrreporter.com/articleview/9602-3-organizationsearn-best-employers-award-for-50-plus-canadians; Wallace Immen, "Employers Seek New Ways to Foster Growth, Creativity," *The Globe and Mail*, January 27, 2012, B13; Sarah Dobson, "Health Incentives More Popular: Survey," *Canadian HR Reporter*, December 19, 2011, www.hrreporter.com/articleview/12006-health-incentives-more-popular-survey; Rachel Von Sturner, "Self-Funded Benefits Appealing Approach," *Canadian HR Reporter*, December 19, 2011, 16; Todd Henneman, "Workers Pick Their Perfect Perquisite," *Workforce Management*, January 2012, 4; Daniel Dumas, "Giving the Straight Goods on Pensions," *Canadian HR Reporter*, September 26, 2011, 18; Susan Adams, "Compensation Is Going Up—But Only at the Top," *Forbes*, July 6, 2011, www.forbes.com/sites/susanadams/2011/07/06/salaries-are-going-up-but-mainly-at-the-top/; "Top CEOs See Pay Gain of 27 Per Cent in 2010," *Canadian HR Reporter*, January 3, 2012, www.hrreporter.com/articleview/12029-top-ceos-see-pay-gain-of-27-per-cent-in-2010; David Creelman, "Embracing the Unorthodox: Welcome to the High Commitment Workplace," *HR Voice.org*, January 26, 2012, www.hrvoice.org/embracing-the-unorthodox-welcome-to-the-high-commitment-workplace/; and Lisa Beyer, "Transit Perks: A Driving Force for Workers and Employers," *Workforce Management*, January 2012, 3.

SUMMARY

1. Explain an organization's concerns in developing a strategic rewards program.
   - Companies structure compensation in ways that enhance employee motivation and growth.
   - Compensation must be tailored to fit the needs of the company and its employees.
   - Companies are concerned that employees believe the compensation to be equitable.
2. Identify the various factors that influence the setting of pay levels.
   - There are internal and external factors.
   - Internal factors include the organization's compensation policy, the perceived worth of the job, the performance of the employee, and the employer's willingness to pay.
   - The external factors include labour-market conditions, cost of living, collective bargaining, and legal considerations.

3. Describe the major job evaluation systems.
   - Job ranking system, which groups jobs on the basis of their relative worth.
   - Job classification system, where jobs are grouped according to a series of predetermined grades based on a number of factors.
   - Point system, which determines a job's relative worth by using a quantitative system of points.
   - Factor comparison system, where a job is evaluated on a factor-by-factor basis; this type of system is typically used for legislated pay equity purposes.
4. Illustrate the compensation structure.
   - Wage and salary survey, which provides information about average wage rates external to the organization.
   - Development of a wage curve, which indicates the rates currently paid for jobs within the organization.
   - Development of pay rates for paying individuals based on the job.
5. List the types of incentive plans.
   - Individual bonus.
   - Team- or group-based.
   - Merit raises.
   - Profit-sharing.
   - Employee stock ownership plan.
6. Explain the employee benefits that are required by law.
   - Canada and Quebec pension plans, which provide for a pension for all employees working in Canada.
   - Employment Insurance, which provides income protection to employees who are between jobs.
   - Workers' compensation insurance, which pays people for work-related accidents or illnesses.
7. Describe voluntary benefits.
   - Benefits that are considered indirect compensation.
   - Benefits that an organization chooses to provide.
   - Can include health and welfare coverage, pay for time not worked (vacation, sick leave), wellness programs, and childcare assistance.

NEED TO KNOW

- Definition of rewards, compensation, and compensation management
- Internal and external factors that affect compensation
- Types of incentive plans
- Types of voluntary and mandatory benefits

NEED TO UNDERSTAND

- Relationship of rewards and organizational objectives
- Complexity of factors in relation to compensation decisions
- Role of line manager in making individual employee reward decisions
- Impact of benefits costs on costs of running business

KEY TERMS

competency-based pay 242

consumer price index (CPI) 236

direct compensation 228

eldercare 253

equitable pay 232

hourly work 233

indirect compensation 228

job evaluation 235

pay grades 242

pay-for-performance standard 232

piecework 233

real wages 237

wage and salary survey 241

REVIEW QUESTIONS

1. What are the goals of a reward strategy?
2. Explain why rewards are considered motivational.
3. Describe the internal and external factors used in determining compensation levels.
4. Describe the various methods of job evaluation and explain what job evaluation is.
5. What are incentive plans?
6. What are the components of a compensation structure?
7. Which benefits are required by law?
8. What are some of the voluntary benefits offered by employers?

CRITICAL THINKING QUESTIONS

1. A large-chain grocery store in your community has many part-time employees, primarily in the 18 to 25 year age range. Each store in the chain has some flexibility on how it designs part of the rewards program. The local manager knows that you are taking an introductory course in human resources management and has approached you to give some ideas about additional rewards and recognition. What items would you suggest and why?
2. You have recently been promoted to a supervisor. Your company is in the fast-food business and has a policy that supervisors are paid a salary instead of on an hourly wage basis. Why would the company do this? What are the advantages and disadvantages to you and your company?
3. You work for a small fitness centre in your community as a fitness coach. The manager has approached you about your thoughts on introducing a bonus based on the number of clients each person works with. How would you respond and why?
4. Would it be better to grant pay increases on a percentage basis or by a fixed amount? Why? Explain your reasoning.
5. What benefits would be the greatest value to you? Why?
6. What other rewards and/or recognition could employers offer to motivate and retain employees?
7. Many younger people are attracted to companies that promote themselves as "green" or environmentally friendly. What kinds of incentives could a "green" company offer its employees?
8. You are the owner-operator of a small graphics company in a medium-size city. You have decided that you need to hire someone who can assist you, particularly in taking orders and working with customers. You're not sure how much you might have to pay someone for this work, though. Where would you get the information and what other factors might you need to consider?

DEVELOPING YOUR SKILLS

Monster
www.monster.ca

1. Do you know how much you are worth? What about your dream job? How much does it pay? Working in pairs, go to Monster.ca and use its Salary Wizard to find out how much you could earn in that dream job. Is information about the methodology used provided? What would you need to do to determine whether the information was good data? Share your results with your classmates.
2. Since pay-for-performance is an important factor governing compensation increases, managers must be able to defend the compensation recommendations they make for their employees. Merit raises granted under a pay-for-performance policy must be based on objective performance ratings if they are to achieve their intended purposes of rewarding outstanding employee performance. As managers

know, however, they must deal with other factors that can affect compensation recommendations. These may include the opinions of the employee's peers or extenuating circumstances, such as illness or family responsibilities. The purpose of the following exercise is to provide you with the experience of granting salary increases to employees based on their work performance and other information.

3. Assume you have just been hired as the store manager for a high-volume discount store in Regina. Other stores in Ontario are owned by the same person. The previous manager has recently hired 10 part-time employees. The store has more than 50 full-time employees. While the part-time employees in Ontario have a benefits program, the employees in Regina do not. The store owner wants to know whether there should be consistency on benefits across the country. What would you need to consider in your response? Prepare a one-page summary of your thoughts for the store owner.

4. Working in groups of three or four, access the Competency Profile for Supervisors in the federal government at **www.tbs-sct.gc.ca/gui/cmgs-eng.asp**. Read the descriptions and the detail for each of the nine competencies listed. Once you have reviewed them, discuss whether pay ought to be based on these competencies, and if pay is to be based on each competency, how would you weight each and why?

5. Working in groups of four or five, develop a rewards objective to match the following organization and its business goals. Luxor Corporation has 400 employees and a dynamic business strategy. It wishes to employ a high-quality workforce capable of responding to a competitive business environment. Share your results with the class, including an explanation of your results.

Treasury Board of Canada Secretariat

www.tbs-sct.gc.ca/gui/
cmgs-eng.asp

EXERCISE

Following are the work records of five employees. As their supervisor, you have just completed their annual performance reviews, and it is now time to make recommendations for their future salaries. Your department budget has $8,000 allocated for salary increases. Distribute the $8,000 among your employees based on the descriptions for each person.

1. Siri Sandhu currently earns $40,000. Her performance review rating was very high. She is respected by her peers and is felt to be an asset to the work group. She is single with three young children to support.

2. John Smith earns a salary of $35,000. His annual performance review was average. Several members of the work group have spoken to you about the difficulty involved in John's job. They feel that it is a tough and demanding job and that he is doing his best.

3. Jennie Lee earns $36,000. Her performance review rating was below average, and she seems to have difficulty with other members of her team. Jennie has had a difficult time this past year. Both her parents, with whom she lived, have died recently.

4. Ricardo Martinez earns $33,000. His performance review rating was above average. He is respected by his co-workers and is generally considered to be helpful and outgoing.

5. Sheila Reed earns $34,000. Her performance review rating was very high. Her peers resent her because she comes from a very wealthy family and they feel that she is trying to impress everyone.

Share your results with other class members. Be prepared to explain your allocation of money.

Case Study 1

This Isn't Fair!

Some time ago Mike received a phone call from his friend Pardeep, and he could feel the emotion in her voice when they began their conversation. A few minutes later Pardeep said that she had just learned that one of her colleagues, who started one year after she had started at the organization was being paid 20% more than she was. Pardeep said, "I really want to know why. And what should I do?"

Mike began asking several standard questions, such as:

1. Is there a difference in the pay grade?
2. How about the tasks performed?
3. Can you tell me about the performance review?

Pardeep responded that the pay grade as well as the tasks were the same. In relation to the performance review, Pardeep indicated that her rating was "exceed the expectations and perform above the peer group." Mike suggested she speak with her manager.

Mike didn't forget this story and became more curious as he began to reflect. So, he did two things. First, he did some research on labour-market conditions and then, he conducted a focus group of 30 people, some students and some working professionals.

The research showed a trend the year Pardeep was hired: the demand and supply for talent were balanced whereas the following year, when the other person was hired, the economy was getting stronger and the demand for talent was higher. Mike spoke to several HR professionals and was informed that this was standard practice: it is fine to pay more to new recruits when the demand is high and make no adjustments for existing employees.

The results got Mike thinking. How can you keep your top talent in the dark for a long time? And what will happen when they do find out? He decided to investigate further and put this simple question to his focus group: What would you do in Pardeep's situation? And what did the 30 people say? Ninety-five percent of them responded that they would leave the organization.

Yes, there are times that the economy or the industry is booming, and we need to recruit new talent at the current market rate, but in relation to existing employees, there can be consequences for the organization.

Questions

1. Should the organization inform current employees? If so, what should be communicated and how?
2. How can the organization make sure that experienced employees feel that they are being rewarded fairly?
3. What would you do if you were Pardeep?

Source: Case study based on research done by Mory Mosadegh, Research Assistant, February 2012.

Case Study 2

Do Legislated Wage Rates Work?

All provinces in Canada have legislated minimum wage rates. Nova Scotia raised its rate to $10.15 in April 2012 and British Columbia raised its rate to $9 in May 2012. The other provinces range from a low of $9.40 in Alberta to $11 in Nunavut.

Governments do this they want to provide workers with a guaranteed minimum that will enable them to support themselves and their families. Setting rates is also intended to help the general economy—the more people are able to support themselves with increased incomes, the more tax revenues as well as an improved standard of living for the family there will be. In some places, such as with Nova Scotia, the government is making the adjustments to align with an increased CPI.

Unfortunately, some sectors of the economy do not always see the benefit of raising minimum wage rates. For example, the Canadian Federation of Independent Business is concerned that such increases create challenges for many businesses. The Canadian economy relies heavily on small businesses, and increased costs in a poor economic climate puts additional strain on those businesses.

Of particular concern with the new rate in British Columbia is the impact on the hospitality sector. This sector has faced the introduction of a new statutory holiday and added taxes, too, all of which have reduced revenues and created some situations of reduced staffing levels.

On the other hand, many small employers pay more than the minimum wage to retain key staff. Those employers are concerned that increases in minimum wage will force them to raise rates for all existing staff. A survey done by the Business Council of British Columbia noted that only 2.3% of B.C. employees were paid the minimum wage in 2011.

Questions

1. Should governments legislate minimum wage rates? Why or why not?
2. Why would employers want to pay more than the minimum wage? Explain your reasons.
3. Do you feel that small businesses are at risk of laying staff off when the minimum wage increases? Explain your reasons.

Sources: Adapted from Darah Hansen, "Hospitality sector bemoans latest hike to minimum wage," *The Vancouver Sun*, November 1, 2011, C1; "Nova Scotia minimum wage increasing to $10.15 on April 1," *Canadian HR Reporter*, January 25, 2012, www.hrreporter.com/articleview/12191-nova-scotia-minimum-wage-increasing-to-1015-on-april-1 (accessed February 4, 2012).

NOTES AND REFERENCES

1. John Annakis, Antonio Lobo, and Soma Pilla, "Exploring Monitoring, Work Environment and Flexibility as Predictors of Job Satisfaction within Australian Call Centres," *International Journal of Business and Management* 6, no. 8 (August 2011): 75–93; Asta Savanevicience and Zivile Stankeviciute, "Human Resource Management Practices Linkage with Organizational Commitment and Job Satisfaction," *Economics and Management* 16 (2011): 921–27; Tamela D. Ferguson and Ron Cheek, "How Important Are Situational Constraints in Understanding Job Satisfaction?" *International Journal of Business and Social Science* 2, no.22 (December 2011): 221–27; and Ghulam Mustafa Kazi and Zainab F. Zadeh, "The Contribution of Individual Variables: Job Satisfaction and Job Turnover," *Interdisciplinary Journal of Contemporary Research in Business* 3, no 5 (September 2011): 985–92.

2. Towers Watson, *Leading through Uncertain Times: The 2011–2012 Talent Management and Rewards Study, North America*, 2011.

3. Gail Evans and Arden Dalik, "Vanilla Compensation Strategies Fall Flat," *Canadian HR Reporter*, June 20, 2011, www.hrreporter.com/articleview/10578-vanilla-compensation-strategies-fall-flat.

4. Claudio Fernandez-Araoz, Boris Groysberg, and Nitin Nohria, "How to Hang On to Your High Potentials," *Harvard Business Review*, October 2011, 76–83.

5. Teresa M. Amabile and Steven J. Kramer, "The Power of Small Wins," *Harvard Business Review* 89, no. 5, (May 2011): 70–80; and Gretchen Spreitzer and Christine Porath, "Creating Sustainable Performance," *Harvard Business Review* 90, no. 1 (January/February 2012): 92–99.

6. Claudine Kapel and Alina Mitchell, "5 Questions for Maximizing Total Rewards," *Canadian HR Reporter*, August 9, 2010, www.hrreporter.com/articleview/8099-5-questions-for-maximizing-total-rewards.

7. Nicole Stewart, *Compensation Planning Outlook 2012—Winter Update,* Conference Board of Canada, October 2011.

8. Deloitte, "Human Capital Trends, 2011—Revolution and Evolution," 2011.

9. Hafiz Abdur Rashid, Ammar Asad, and Mian Muhammad Ashraf, "Factors Persuading Employee Engagement and Linkages to Personal & Organizational Performance," *Interdisciplinary Journal of Contemporary Research in Business* 3, no. 5 (September 2011): 98–108; and Yi Hua Hsieh and Hai Ming Chen, "Strategic Fit among Business Competitive Strategy, Human Resource Strategy, and Reward System," *Academy of Strategic Management Journal* 10, no. 2 (2011): 11–32.

10. "Success Uncovered: *Fortune* World's Most Admired Companies," sponsored by Hay Group, 2011.

11. Tavia Grant, "Thanking Staff without a Fistful of Dollars," *The Globe and Mail*, March 21, 2009, B15.

12. Stephanie C. Payne et al., *The Relative Influence of Total Rewards Elements on Attraction, Motivation and Retention*, SR-02-10, Washington, DC: WorldAtWork, March 2010.

13. "Firms Looking to Increase Employee Motivation through Incentive Programs: Survey," *Canadian HR Reporter*, June 8, 2011, www.hrreporter.com/articleview/10494-firms-looking-to-increase-employee-motivation-through-incentive-programs-survey.

14. Demetrice Branch, "Employee Motivation, Recognition, Rewards, and Retention: Kicking It Up a Notch," *CPA Practice Management Forum* 7, no. 11 (2011): 5–7; and "Human Capital Trends," Deloitte Consulting.

15. Richard E. Kopelman, Naomi A. Gardberg, and Ann Cohen Brandwein, "Using a Recognition and Reward Initiative to Improve Service Quality," *Public Personnel Management* 40, no. 2 (Summer 2011): 133–49.

16. Michaeline Skiba and Stuart Rosenberg, "The Disutility of Equity Theory in Contemporary Management Practices," *Journal of Business & Economic Studies* 17, no. 2 (Fall 2011): 1–19.

17. Ibid.

18. Claudine Kapel, "Achieving High Performance in 2012," *Canadian HR Reporter*, January 4, 2012, www.hrreporter.com/blog/Compensation-Rewards/archive/2012/01/04/achieving-high-performance-in-2012.

19. Brian Kreissl "Does HR Differ in Theory and in Practice?" *Canadian HR Reporter*, December 6, 2011, www.hrreporter.com/blog/HR-Policies-Practices/archive/2011/12/06/does-hr-differ-in-theory-and-in-practice; and Ken Abosch, "Aftermath of the Recession on 2009–2010 Compensation Spending," Aon Consulting, accessed January 24, 2011, www.aon.com/human-capital-consulting/thought-leadership/compensation/article_compensation_spending.jsp.

20. "Gaming Giant Electronic Arts Ties Compensation to Company Performance," *Financial Post*, June 7, 2011, FP 9.

21. Claudine Kapel, "The Great Motivation Debate," *Canadian HR Reporter*, August 1, 2011, www.hrreporter.com/blog/Compensation-Rewards/archive/2011/08/01/the-great-motivation-debate.

22. Bruno S. Frey and Margit Osterloh, "Stop Tying Pay to Performance," *Harvard Business Review*, January/February 2012, 51.

23. Towers Watson, "Leading through Uncertain Times"; and Rachel Finan, "2012 Looking a Lot Like 2011 on Wage Front," *Canadian HR Reporter*, December 5, 2011, www.hrreporter.com/articleview/11873-2012-looking-a-lot-like-2011-on-wage-front.

24. Bank of Canada/Banque du Canada, *The Consumer Price Index,* October 2011.

25. "Classification Standard, General Labour and Trade Operational Category," Treasury Board of Canada Secretariat, accessed January 24, 2012, www.tbs-sct.gc.ca.

26. Gerald E. Ledford Jr. and Herbert G. Heneman III, "Skill-Based Pay," Society for Industrial & Organizational Psychology and Society for Human Resource Management, June 2011.

27. Abul Mitra, Nina Gupta, and Jason D. Shaw, "A Comparative Examination of Traditional and Skill-Based Pay Plans," *Journal of Managerial Psychology* 26, no. 4 (2011): 278–96.

28. Ledford and Heneman, "Skill-Based Pay"; and Criyan de Silva, "An Introduction to Performance and Skill-Based Pay Systems," International Labour Office, 2011.

29. "Competencies," Treasury Board of Canada, Secretariat, December 2, 2011, www.tbs-sct.gc.ca/tal/comp-eng.asp.

30. Deloitte, "Human Capital Trends, 2011."

31. Allison A. Gordon and Jennifer L. Kaswin, "Effective Employee Incentive Plans: Features and Implementation Processes," *Corner HR Review*, May 2010, 1–6.

32. Claudine Kapel, "Who Is Eligible for a Bonus?" *Canadian HR Reporter*, July 25, 2011, www.hrreporter.com/blog/Compensation-Rewards/archive/2011/07/25/who-is-eligible-for-a-bonus.

33. Steve Daniels, "Aon Employees Face Tax Hit in HQ Move to London," *Workforce Management*, January 24, 2012, www.workforce.com/article/20120124/NEWS01/120129979/aon-employees-face-tax-hit-in-hq-move-to-london.

34. Amanda Silliker "Top Employers Focus on Safety, Engagement," *Canadian HR Reporter*, November 7, 2011, www.hrreporter.com/articleview/11660-top-employers-focus-on-safety-engagement.

35. Susan Ladika, "No Perfect Fit," *Workforce Management*, September 23, 2011, 1–3.

36. Sonya Felix, "Staples Gets the Message Out," *Benefits Canada*, January 11, 2012.

37. "2011/2012 Staying@Work Report," Towers Watson, 2011.

38. "Increases to Health Benefit Plan Costs Slowing Down," *Canadian HR Reporter*, October 27, 2011, www.hrreporter.com/articleprint.aspx?articleid=11554.

39. "Value-Based Health Care," *International Foundation*, accessed January 29, 2012, www.ifebp.org/News/FeaturedTopics/ValueBasedHealthCare/default.htm.

40. Statistics Canada, "Population by Sex and Age Group," accessed January 29, 2012, www40.statcan.gc.ca/l01/cst01/demo10a-eng.htm.

41. Information gathered by the current author from a presentation by Vancouver Coastal Health Authority, November 29, 2011.

42. Marilee Mark, "Beyond Drugs," *Benefits Canada*, August 16, 2010, www.benefitscanada.com/benefits/health-benefits/beyond-drugs-8255.

43. "Employers Keen to Evolve Health Programs: Survey," *Canadian HR Reporter*, January 13, 2012, www.hrreporter.com/articleview/12118-employers-keen-to-evolve-health-programs-survey.

44. John Halls, "Genetic Testing Will Only Continue to Grow," *Canadian HR Reporter*, November 7, 2011, 22.

45. Barbara Shecter, "New Hires at RBC Won't Get Fixed Pension," *Financial Post*, September 24, 2011, FP5.

46. Bill Gooden, "DB Plans Struggle to Survive," *Canadian HR Reporter*, November 7, 2011, 20.

47. Scott Deveau, "Companies Draw Line with New Pensions," *Financial Post*, June 14, 2011, FP1.

48. Tony Keller, "All for One," *Report on Business*, July/August 2011, 10; and John Crocker, "DB Pension Plans Still Viable: HOOPP," *Canadian HR Reporter*, November 7, 2011, 29.

49. Jonathan Chevreau, " 'Big CPP' Gets New Wind," *Financial Post*, July 6, 2011, FP6.

50. Bill Curry, "New Pooled Pension Plan's Success Will Depend on Business Owners," *The Globe and Mail*, November 17, 2011, www.theglobeandmail.com/news/politics/new-pooled-pension-plans-success-will-depend-on-business-owners/article2240522.

51. Amanda Silliker, "Holiday Parties Should Be More Inclusive: Survey," *Canadian HR Reporter*, November 7, 2011, www.hrreporter.com/articleview/11630-holiday-parties-should-be-more-inclusive-survey.

52. Statistics Canada, *Work Absence Rates 2010*, Catalogue no. 71-211-X (Ottawa: Statistics Canada, Labour Statistics Division, 2011), 21.

53. Ibid.

54. "All Canada Awards for Excellence," Excellence Canada, accessed January 30, 2011, www.excellence.ca/en/awards/All_CAE_Recipients_Alpha.

55. Leonard L. Berry, Ann M. Mirabito, and William B. Baun, "What's the Hard Return on Employee Wellness Programs?" *Harvard Business Review*, December 2010, 104–12.

56. Morneau Shepell, "EAP Improves Health Status and Productivity, and Demonstrates a Positive ROI," June 20, 2011.

57. Amanda Silliker, "More Staff Turning to EAPs for Credit, Debt Help," *Canadian HR Reporter*, October 10, 2011, www.hrreporter.com/articleview/11426-more-staff-turning-to-eaps-for-credit-debt-help-report.

58. "Tuition Assistance Programs Increase Job Satisfaction, Productivity: Survey," *Canadian HR Reporter*, November 3, 2011, www.hrreporter.com/articleview/11606-tuition-assistance-programs-increase-job-satisfaction-productivity-survey.

59. Statistics Canada, "Population by Sex and Age Group."

60. Nora Spinks and Donna Lero, "Caregiving and Work: HR's Next Big Challenge," *Canadian HR Reporter*, December 19, 2011, www.hrreporter.com/articleview/11996-caregiving-and-work-hrs-next-big-challenge-guest-commentary.

61. Ibid.

62. Statistics Canada, "Population Projections: Canada, the Provinces and Territories," *The Daily*, May 26, 2010, accessed January 30, 2012, www.statcan.gc.ca/daily-quotidien/100526/dq100526b-eng.htm.

63. Ibid.

64. Statistics Canada, "Employment by Age, Sex, Type of Work, Class of Worker and Province," December 2011, www40.statcan.ca/l01/cst01/LABR66A-eng.htm.

65. Laurie Monsebraaten, "Lack of Child Care Costing Canada: Report," *Toronto Star*, March 6, 2011, www.thestar.com/news/article/949585—lack-of-child-care-costing-canada-report.

66. Sarah Dobson, "'Motherhood Gap' Partly Explains Wage Loss for Female Workers," *Canadian HR Reporter*, November 15, 2010, accessed January 31, 2012, www.hrreporter.com/articleview/8468-motherhood-gap-partly-explains-wage-loss-for-female-workers.

67. Amanda Silliker, "A Solution for Child-Care Nightmare?" *Canadian HR Reporter*, September 12, 2011, 20.

68. "Top Employers 2012," *Financial Post*, February 1, 2012.

Employee Relations

CHAPTER 8

CREATING A SAFE AND HEALTHY WORK ENVIRONMENT

OUTCOMES

After studying this chapter, you should be able to

1 Describe the legal responsibilities of supervisors and managers to create a safe and healthy work environment.

2 Cite the measures that should be taken to create a safe work environment.

3 Describe current workplace health and safety hazards and controls.

4 Explain a proactive strategic approach to improving employee health and well-being.

5 Describe the organizational services and programs for building better health.

OUTLINE

HRM CLOSE-UP

"It's like wearing a seatbelt. There can be long-term effects if you work too fast and don't take safety seriously."

Ilda Palermo.

Any traveller who has had the pleasure of sleeping on a Fairmont Hotel bed will know the comfort and good night's sleep that come from the chain's promise of "bigger, softer mattresses."

"The bed is the major part of the room," says Ilda Palermo, a senior manager at the Queen Elizabeth Hotel in downtown Montreal, "but for our cleaning staff, old habits are hard to change. Dealing with bigger, softer mattresses, huge duvets, three sheets, and six pillows is double the work it used to be."

It's therefore a health and safety concern for workers.

Palermo supervises the implementation of the company's health and safety policy, ensuring the health and well-being of staff. The largest employee group she is responsible for is the cleaning staff, comprised of 180 room attendants. Each attendant has 14 rooms to clean daily and that can mean dealing with up to 28 of those big, comfortable beds. The part of the job that involves lifting mattresses is where employees are most likely to get hurt. "We hired an ergo-therapist to evaluate the movements, and we then provided training to staff to ensure they use the right movements when making a bed," explained Palermo. "Staff are trained to slide sheets under mattresses without lifting them."

The Queen Elizabeth Hotel and its parent company, Fairmont Hotels, are recognized as an environmentally friendly company. Although some operational practices cross over into health and safety, the company maintains separate policies in this regard. One example is the use of toxic-free cleaning products, now for many years. Not only have they benefited the environment, but there are no longer any staff health issues related to the use of cleaning chemicals. Palermo points out that employees have more knowledge today and are more aware of issues affecting health. "They ask more questions, and they are health conscious and concerned about their working environment," she says. "So, whenever there is an issue, the health and safety committee will invite staff to give suggestions. Management tends to take their advice because they are the ones who do the job."

Years ago, the hotel had an incident of a mini-bar attendant who injured his shoulder and neck with the constant bending required. After treatment, the employee had a progressive return to work. "With his input, we worked with our engineering department to adapt a cart with wider, larger wheels which was much easier to push. We also rearranged the placement of items on the cart," said Palermo. "Other staff have benefited as well because we reorganized the stocking area to make items more accessible, requiring less bending and lifting, especially with heavier items."

Taking a proactive approach is key. The hotel pays into Workers' Compensation and is inspected whenever there is a staff complaint. "We do internal inspections ourselves via our health and safety committee," said Palermo. "And our internal leaders have the responsibility to make sure employees are following the safety procedures we have in place."

Management also holds general assemblies with all staff to discuss workplace health and safety. Palermo feels it's important for employees to share responsibility for safety. "It's like wearing a seatbelt. There can be long-term effects if you work too fast and don't take safety seriously," she commented.

To Palermo, the key measures taken to ensure health and safety are communication and training. Staff are made aware of the hazards of different tasks or products they utilize, and how to use proper safety equipment. "Every position has a safety shoe to wear," says Palermo. "The work is very physical throughout the hotel, and shoes are an important part of the process."

In terms of wellness, the company has an employee assistance program and 17% of employees have used the program at some point. "The program is well received by staff," explained Palermo, "and it enables us to provide specific assistance to our employees which we are not able to directly provide ourselves."

You might say that a good night's sleep is not only paramount for guests, but integral for the well-being of Queen Elizabeth Hotel employees as well.

INTRODUCTION

You will note from the HRM Close-up that Fairmont Hotels is proactive in assessing and managing workplace health and safety risks. It is also an example of the many health and safety concerns faced by managers. Occupational health and safety (OHS) accidents are numerous and costly to employers; they can even result in criminal charges. For example, in 2012, a B.C. demolition and drywall contractor was sentenced to 60 days in jail for contempt of court for ignoring orders from both WorkSafeBC and the Supreme Court of British Columbia to stop exposing youth and vulnerable workers to asbestos.[1]

Employers must be aware that neglect of OHS duties can lead to unlimited fines for the corporation and possible fines and jail time for individuals. HRM and the Law 8.1 describes three organizations and individuals that have recently been charged with criminal negligence causing death under Bill C-45, resulting in fines and jail terms. To prevent workplace accidents and fatalities such as these, employers are required by law to provide working conditions that do not impair the safety or health of their employees.

Although the laws safeguarding employees' physical and emotional well-being are an incentive to provide desirable working conditions, many employers are motivated to comply by virtue of their sensitivity to human needs and rights. The more cost-oriented employer recognizes the importance of avoiding accidents and illnesses wherever possible. Costs associated with sick leave, disability payments, replacement of employees who are injured or killed, and workers' compensation far exceed the costs of maintaining a safe and healthy workplace. Accidents and illnesses attributable to the workplace may also have pronounced effects on employee morale and on the goodwill that the organization enjoys in the community and in the business world.

Although managers at all levels are expected to know and enforce health and safety standards throughout the organization, in reality the supervisor has the biggest role. The supervisor must ensure a work environment that protects employees from physical hazards, unhealthy conditions, and unsafe acts of other personnel. Through effective safety and health practices, the physical and emotional well-being of employees may be preserved and even enhanced. This chapter will discuss health and safety in the workplace, including the legal responsibilities of employers, supervisors, and workers to recognize, assess, and control workplace hazards. You will also be presented with information about how to create a safe and healthy work environment and culture.

HEALTH AND SAFETY: THE LAW

Consider these facts about Canadian workers (most recent statistics available):

- In 2010, more than one million workplace incidents occurred.
- In 2010, 1,014 employees died in work-related accidents.
- Workers' compensation boards throughout Canada pay out over $12 billion to injured workers and their families each year.
- In 2010, over 335,000 work-related injuries were reported.
- In 2010, 10,479 young adults between the ages of 15 and 24 were injured.[2]

The burden on the country's commerce as a result of lost productivity and wages, medical expenses, and disability compensation is staggering. And there is no way to calculate the human suffering involved.

The federal, provincial, and territorial governments regulate occupational health and safety. While statutes and standards differ slightly from jurisdiction to jurisdiction, attempts have been made to harmonize the various acts and regulations. Health and safety legislation has had an impact on workplace injuries and illnesses. The number of workplace accidents in Canada has declined even though there has been an increase in the number of workers.

Occupational injury
Any cut, fracture, sprain, or amputation resulting from a workplace accident

Occupational illness
Abnormal condition or disorder resulting from exposure to environmental factors in the workplace

An **occupational injury** is any cut, fracture, sprain, or amputation resulting from a workplace accident or from an exposure involving an accident in the work environment. An **occupational illness** is any abnormal condition or disorder, other than one resulting from an occupational injury, caused by exposure to environmental factors associated with employment. It includes acute and chronic illnesses or diseases that may be caused by inhalation, absorption, ingestion, or direct contact. With regard to parts of the body affected by accidents, injuries to the back occur most frequently, followed by leg, arm, and finger injuries.

Acts and Regulations

All supervisors, managers, and HR professionals should become familiar with the occupational health and safety legislation governing the jurisdiction under which their organization operates. The applicable legislation for each jurisdiction, the Web addresses, and the agency that administers the legislation are shown in Manager's Toolkit 8.1.

Duties and Responsibilities

The fundamental duty of every employer is to take every reasonable precaution to ensure employee safety. The motivating forces behind workplace legislation were effectively articulated in the landmark case *Regina v. Wholesale Travel Group*, which dealt with the legal liability and obligation of employers to behave in accordance with legislation:

> Regulatory legislation is essential to the operation of our complex industrial society; it plays a legitimate and vital role in protecting those who are most vulnerable and least able to protect themselves. The extent and importance of that role have increased continuously since the onset of the Industrial Revolution. Before effective workplace legislation was enacted, labourers—including children—worked unconscionably long hours in dangerous and unhealthy surroundings that evoke visions of Dante's inferno. It was regulatory legislation with its enforcement provisions that brought to an end the shameful situations that existed in mines, factories and workshops in the nineteenth century.

Duties of Employers

Outcome 1

What legal responsibilities guide supervisors and managers in creating a safe and healthy work environment?

In addition to providing a hazard-free workplace and complying with the applicable statutes and regulations, employers must inform their employees about health and safety requirements. Employers are also required to keep certain records, to compile an annual summary of work-related injuries and illnesses, and to ensure that supervisors are familiar with the work and its associated hazards (the supervisor, in turn, must ensure that workers are aware of those hazards). In most jurisdictions, employers are required to ensure that the employees are knowledgeable about workplace health and safety. At Work with HRM 8.1 describes how UPS focuses on employee involvement, ownership, and responsibility as the foundation of its health and safety program.

In all jurisdictions, employers are required to report any accidents that cause injuries and diseases to the Workers' Compensation Board. An accident resulting in death or critical injury must be reported immediately; the accident must then be investigated and a written report submitted. Finally, employers must provide safety training and be prepared to discipline employees for failing to comply with safety rules.

The high incidence of youth injuries is attributable to lack of work experience and insufficient training. To help build the awareness of safety at work in young people, the Ontario agency has created a separate Web site as a resource for young people (**www. ywap.ca**). Its objective is to help younger workers protect themselves and others in the workplace. The poster in Manager's Toolkit 8.2 is targeted toward young people—making them aware of workplace risks.

WSIB-Young Worker Awareness Program
www.ywap.ca

WORKERS' COMPENSATION REFERENCE CHART

Jurisdiction	Body of Legislation	Administration Agency	Web Site
Canada			www.canoshweb.org
Alberta	Occupational Health and Safety Act	Workers' Compensation Board of Alberta	www.wcb.ab.ca
British Columbia	Workers' Compensation Act	WorkSafeBC	www.worksafebc.ca
Manitoba	The Workers' Compensation Act	Workers Compensation Board of Manitoba	www.wcb.mb.ca
New Brunswick	Occupational Health and Safety Act	WorkSafeNB	www.worksafenb.ca
Newfoundland and Labrador	Occupational Health and Safety Act	Workplace Health, Safety and Compensation Commission (Newfoundland)	www.whscc.nf.ca
Northwest Territories	Workers' Compensation Act	Workers' Safety and Compensation Commission	www.wcb.nt.ca
Nova Scotia	Occupational Health and Safety Act	Workers' Compensation Board of Nova Scotia	www.wcb.ns.ca
Nunavut	Workers' Compensation Act	Workers' Safety and Compensation Commission	www.wcb.nt.ca
Ontario	Occupational Health and Safety Act/Workplace Safety and Insurance Act	Workplace Safety and Insurance Board (Ontario)	www.wsib.on.ca
Prince Edward Island	Occupational Health and Safety Act/Workers' Compensation Act	Workers' Compensation Board of Prince Edward Island	www.wcb.pe.ca
Quebec	Act Respecting Occupational Health and Safety	Commission de la santé et de la sécurité du travail of Quebec	www.csst.qc.ca
Saskatchewan	The Workers' Compensation Act	Saskatchewan Workers' Compensation Board	www.wcbsask.com
Yukon	Workers' Compensation Act/Occupation Health and Safety Act	Yukon Workers' Compensation Health and Safety Board	www.wcb.yk.ca

Duties of Workers

Employees are required to comply with all applicable acts and regulations, to report hazardous conditions or defective equipment, and to follow all employer safety and health rules and regulations, including those prescribing the use of protective equipment, such as wearing hard hats or steel-toed boots at a construction site or protective eyewear in a laboratory.

Workers have many rights that pertain to requesting and receiving information about safety and health conditions. They also have the right to refuse unsafe work without fear of reprisal. (Some professionals, such as police, firefighters, teachers, and health-care workers have only a limited right of refusal in the sense that their work is inherently dangerous.) For example, in Ontario, an employee who suspects hazardous work conditions may refuse to do the work but must immediately report this concern to the supervisor, triggering an investigation by the supervisor and a worker representative.

AT WORK **with HRM 8.1**

UPS: EMPLOYEE-POWERED SAFETY

UPS is the largest express carrier and package delivery company in the world. UPS Canada has more than 850 stores, 9,887 employees, and 3,049 vehicles. The company was confronted with high injury rates, particularly sprains and strains from loading and unloading packages, and getting into and out of trucks. How did they reduce their injury rates?

UPS implemented the Comprehensive Health and Safety Process (CHSP), starting with committees of non-management employees supported by management representing 10% of the workforce. The goal was to improve health and safety by involving employees first. The employees were able to address the sources of workplace risks such as lifting and lowering, slips and falls, pushing and pulling, and powered equipment that led to musculoskeletal injuries, or MSI (injuries to the muscles, tendons, ligaments, nerves, blood vessels, and joints of the neck, shoulders, arms, wrists, legs, and back). In their safety committees, they began to help develop health and safety processes, conduct regular inspections, investigate accidents, conduct facility and equipment audits, coach employees on how to perform their jobs more safely, and report and keep records on all incidents and accidents.

Employee empowerment is the foundation of the health and safety process established by UPS. The company's approach can be illustrated as a pyramid in which the base of the pyramid consists of employees' personal values toward safety practices. The next level is built on management commitment and employee involvement. The remaining three tiers are worksite analysis, hazard prevention and control, and education and training. Worksite analysis is based on past data, prevention reports, audits, employee concerns, observation, and feedback. Hazard assessment and control utilizes an employee concern logbook as well as observation and feedback processes. Train-the-Trainer is the approach used to provide a range of comprehensive and ongoing training from mentoring to certification workshops.

Wellness is emphasized through educational programs and other benefits and services. Employee recognition and performance feedback are linked to healthy and safe employee workplace behaviours. The senior leadership teams meet twice a year to focus solely on safety.

CRITICAL THINKING QUESTION:
UPS's CHSP approach relies on individual employee commitment and responsibility in the development and maintenance of its comprehensive health and safety program. Consider a past or current workplace with which you are familiar. Would this approach work?

Sources: "Fact Sheet," UPS Canada, http://pressroom.ups.com/Fact+Sheets/UPS+Canada+Fact+Sheet (accessed March 15, 2012); "Safety Training Fact Sheet," UPS Canada, www.ups.com/content/ca/en/about/facts/canada.html (accessed March 15, 2012); and Jayanth Jayaram, Jeff Smith, Sunny Park, and Dan McMackin, "A Framework for Safety Excellence: Lessons from UPS," *Supply Chain Management Review*, January/February 2012, www.scmr.com/article/A_Framework_for_Safety_Excellence_Lessons_from_UPS (accessed March 15, 2012).

Workplace Safety and Insurance Board

www.wsib.on.ca

A work-refusal investigation can result in either the employee's return to work in a safer environment or the employee's continued refusal. In the latter case, the appropriate ministry is notified, and an investigator is dispatched to the job site to provide a written decision. If a replacement worker is used, that individual must be notified of the previous employee's refusal to work. Employees cannot be suspended, fired, or docked pay for refusing unsafe work, and they can continue to refuse the work until the situation is corrected.[3] For more information on the standards in Ontario, check out the province's agency responsible for workplace safety (**www.wsib.on.ca**).

Duties of Supervisors

A *supervisor* is generally defined as a person (with or without a title) who has charge of a workplace and authority over a worker. Occupational health and safety laws require supervisors to advise employees of potential workplace hazards; ensure that workers use or wear safety equipment, devices, or clothing; provide written instructions where applicable; and take every reasonable precaution to guarantee the safety of workers. As you will read later in this chapter, the supervisor is key in creating a healthy and safe work environment. The supervisor is the point-of-contact for almost every question regarding health and safety. Further, the supervisor will reinforce safety and health training, and the supervisor will be

Source: © WorkSafeBC. Used with permission. The image "Young worker, be on guard" on page 240 is © WorkSafeBC, from Student WorkSafe Planning 10, and is available free of charge at WorkSafeBC.com.

The more complex and diverse your workplace, the more difficult managing safety can be.

Comstock Images

the person held accountable for the employees' understanding and behaviour regarding health and safety in the workplace.

Duties of Joint Health and Safety Committees

Most jurisdictions require the formation of health and safety committees operated jointly by employee and management representatives. This arrangement is intended to create a nonadversarial climate in which labour and management work together to create a safe and healthy workplace. In Ontario, at least one management committee member and one worker representative must be certified. The certification program provides training in such subjects as safety laws, sanitation, general safety, rights and duties, and indoor air quality.

In addition, the legislation in British Columbia requires that a joint worker–employer committee must be formed in a company with 20 or more employees. Further, the employer is obligated to provide at least eight hours of annual educational leave for training and upgrading on health and safety issues.[4]

Figure 8.1 summarizes the legally required duties and responsibilities of those directly involved in health and safety issues.

Penalties for Employer Noncompliance

Penalties for violations of occupational health and safety regulations vary across provinces and territories. The Ontario *Health and Safety Act* provides for fines of up to $500,000, and offenders can be sent to jail. Saskatchewan and Manitoba continue to have the two highest workplace injury rates in the country. Both provinces have proposed increased penalties to reflect the serious nature of violating laws that protect worker health and safety. The current maximum fines under Manitoba's *Workplace Safety and Health Amendment Act* are $150,000 for the first offence and $300,000 for a second or subsequent offence. These fines are proposed to increase to $250,000 for a first offence and $500,000 for a second or subsequent offence.[5] The maximum penalty under Saskatchewan's *Occupational Health and Safety Act* is proposed to increase from $300,000 to $1.5 million. All other fines would double, except the maximum fine, from current penalties that range from $2,000 to $300,000.[6] Financial penalties for federally regulated companies range from $100,000 to $1 million.[7]

FIGURE 8.1 Health and Safety Duties and Responsibilities

Employers

- Provide a hazard-free workplace.
- Comply with laws and regulations.
- Inform employees about safety and health requirements.
- Keep records.
- Compile annual summary of work-related injuries and illnesses.
- Ensure supervisors are familiar with work and associated hazards.
- Report accidents to WCB.
- Provide safety training.

Workers

- Comply with all laws and regulations.
- Report hazardous conditions or defective equipment.
- Follow employer safety and health rules.
- Refuse unsafe work.

Supervisors

- Advise employees of potential workplace hazards.
- Ensure workers use or wear safety equipment.
- Provide written instructions.
- Take every reasonable precaution to guarantee safety of workers.

Joint Health and Safety Committees

- Advise employer on health and safety matters.
- Create nonadversarial climate to foster a safe and healthy work environment.
- Investigate accidents.
- Train others in safety obligations.

The federal government was so concerned about employers' responsibilities for workplace health and safety that the *Criminal Code* was changed to make it easier to bring criminal charges against co-workers, supervisors, executives, and employers when a worker is killed or injured on the job. The legislation was a direct result of a public inquiry into the Westray Mine disaster in 1992 that killed 26 workers. Numerous safety infractions occurred at Westray, and it was determined that senior managers and executives knew of the infractions but did nothing to fix them. There is no doubt that violations of health and safety laws can have significant consequences. HRM and the Law 8.1 describes the recent implementation of Bill C-45.

Workers' Compensation

Under workers' compensation, injured workers or workers who become ill as a result of their work environment can receive benefits in the form of a cash payout (if the disability is permanent) or wage-loss payments (if the worker can no longer earn the same amount of money). Unlimited medical aid is also provided, along with vocational rehabilitation, which includes physical, social, and psychological services. The goal is to return the employee to the original job (or some modification thereof) as soon as possible. Sun Life Assurance Company of Canada has a return-to-work awards program, which will give premium credits to employers that allow injured workers to change jobs or duties to enable these employees to return to work. A person who has been off work for six months has a 50% chance of returning; after 12 months, a 20% chance; and after two years, a 10% chance. A carefully designed return-to-work program can shorten work absences by providing early assessment and graduated transitional programs.[8]

HRM and the Law 8.1

BILL C-45: ARE CANADIAN WORKPLACE DEATHS CLIMBING?

Bill C-45 has been enforced since its 2004 introduction into the *Criminal Code*, creating criminal liability for health and safety violations. The amendment to the *Criminal Code* emerged in response to the Westray coal mine disaster yet new health and safety criminal negligence charges have been laid against only three Canadian businesses in the construction industry since that time.

In 2008, a small Quebec paving-stone manufacturer was the first organization to be charged with criminal negligence causing death under Bill C-45, resulting in a fine of $100,000. A 23-year-old worker was fatally crushed when he tried to clear a jam in a machine with its motion detector safety mechanism deactivated.

A Quebec landscape contractor in 2011 was the second employer convicted of criminal negligence in the workplace resulting in a conditional sentence of two years of imprisonment, which he served in the community. An employee died after being pinned against a wall when an unmaintained backhoe failed to brake.

In 2011, the owner, director, and supervisor of an Ontario construction company and a scaffold platform supplier were charged with criminal negligence causing bodily harm and four counts of criminal negligence causing death, in addition to 61 provincial health and safety legislation charges. Five migrant workers fell 13 stories from a high-rise building when the faulty scaffolding broke, and they were not attached to harnesses.

CRITICAL THINKING QUESTION:

Canadian workplace fatalities increased from 939 in 2009 to 1,014 in 2010. Do you think Bill C-45 has made workplaces safer?

Sources: *Workers Compensation Board of British Columbia v. Moore*, Court of Appeal for British Columbia, 2011 BCSC 459, accessed February 27, 2012, www.worksafebc.com/news_room/resources/2011/ArrestWarrantBCEmployer.asp; "Quebec Employer Going to Jail," *Canadian Employment Law*, February 25, 2011, www.employmentlawtoday.com/ArticleView.aspx?l=1&articleid=2427; "Danger Pay," *Canada's Occupational Health & Safety Magazine*, March 4, 2011, www.ohscanada.com/news/danger-pay/1000403671/; "Number of Fatalities by Jurisdiction 1993–2010," Association of Workers' Compensation Boards of Canada, accessed February 27, 2012, http://awcbc.org/en/nationalworkinjuriesstatisticsprogramnwisp.asp.

Industrial disease

A disease resulting from exposure relating to a particular process, trade, or occupation in industry

Equally problematic is compensation for stress, which is discussed in more detail later in the chapter. Stress-related disabilities are usually divided into three groups: physical injuries leading to mental disabilities (e.g., clinical depression after a serious accident); mental stress resulting in a physical disability (ulcers or migraines); and mental stress resulting in a mental condition (anxiety over workload or downsizing leading to depression). Most claims, it should be pointed out, result from accidents or injuries.

In some industrial sectors, employers are working together to establish rules and training programs to further the cause of accident prevention. For further information on the specific objectives of each provincial and territorial workers' compensation agency, visit the Web sites listed in Manager's Toolkit 8.1.

Compensation has become a complex issue. Workers are now able to receive payment if they have contracted an **industrial disease**. An industrial disease is a disease resulting from exposure to a substance relating to a particular process, trade, or occupation in industry. Cause and effect can be difficult to determine. Consider, for example, the case of a mine worker who has contracted a lung disease, but who also smokes heavily.

While the number of Canadians injured at work every year is decreasing, there are still close to one million people injured and the cost of these injuries is over $12 billion in compensation claims.[9] This has left workers' compensation boards with a huge deficit to pay existing claims. To encourage employers to introduce better prevention and claims management practices, the emphasis of workers' compensation has been shifting from assessments and payments to the creation of a safety-conscious environment intended to reduce the number of work-related accidents, disabilities, and diseases. Figure 8.2 lists some ways in which employers can reduce their workers' compensation costs.

FIGURE 8.2   Ways to Reduce Workers' Compensation Costs

1. Perform an audit to assess high-risk areas within a workplace.
2. Prevent injuries by proper ergonomic design of the job (such as position of keyboard) and effective assessment of job candidates.
3. Provide quality medical care to injured employees by physicians with experience and preferably with training in occupational health.
4. Reduce litigation by effective communication between the employer and the injured worker.
5. Manage the care of an injured worker from the injury until return to work. Keep a partially recovered employee at the worksite.
6. Provide extensive worker training in all related health and safety areas.

CREATING A SAFE WORK ENVIRONMENT

Outcome 2

What measures can be taken to create a safe work environment?

Canada Safety Council
www.safety-council.org

We have seen that employers are required by law to provide healthy and safe working conditions for their employees. To achieve this objective, most employers have a formal safety program. The success of a safety program depends largely on managers and supervisors of operating departments, even though an HR department may have responsibility for coordinating the safety communication and training programs, and maintaining safety records required by occupational health and safety regulations. Above all else, the CEOs and other senior leaders in unique positions of influence set the tone for safe and healthy work practices. Mike Moore and Sons, the winner of the 2011 Ontario General Contractors Association Award for safety, works with owners, subtrades, and partners to ensure that everyone, including management, labourers, and suppliers, is included in safety training, meetings, worksite and equipment inspections, and audits. The owner views safety as a culture to be promoted, not just a job task, adopting an inclusive safety leadership approach. He encourages all the workers to participate in activities that create a healthy and safe worker environment; as a result, no time has been lost to injuries in 13 years.[10]

Organizations with formal safety programs generally have an employee–management safety committee that includes members from management, each department or manufacturing or service unit, and the pool of employees. Committees are typically involved in investigating accidents and helping to publicize the importance of safety rules and their enforcement.

The Canada Safety Council Web site (**www.safety-council.org**) provides resources to assist in the development of a safe work environment.

Promoting Safety Awareness

Probably the most important role of a safety program is motivating managers, supervisors, and subordinates to be aware of safety considerations. While there is a requirement by law to do this, success comes when a manager or supervisor willingly promotes a safe work environment. If managers and supervisors fail to demonstrate awareness, their subordinates can hardly be expected to do so. Unfortunately, most managers and supervisors wear their "safety hats" far less often than their "production, quality control, and methods improvement hats."

While discipline may force employees to work safely, the most effective enforcement of safety expectations occurs when employees willingly obey and champion safety rules and procedures. This goal can be achieved when management actively encourages employees to participate in all aspects of the organization's safety program, and the organization provides incentives to do so.

As an example, Hydro One in Ontario determined that it needed to not only have management encourage employees but that it also needed to recognize that there were four generational cohorts, each thinking about the workplace differently. With the expected retirements and the hiring of younger people, Hydro One determined that through the orientation process, it needed to instill the importance of having a safe and

In certain workplaces, safety standards require the use of protective clothing.

Jimmy Lee/Shutterstock.com

healthy work environment. This was then reinforced through mentoring, where different generations used different approaches to meet the needs of the mentees in relation to health and safety. And, of course, there was the ongoing leadership from the senior team in demonstrating its commitment to health and safety. It was important that they modelled the type of behaviour that they were expecting from the rest of the employees. Hydro One also extends its safety practices beyond employee safety awareness to educating the public about possible electrical hazards to partnering with four colleges to educate and attract future workers, creating a more inclusive community culture of safety awareness.[11]

Ontario Power Generation, the other electrical company in Ontario, uses an incentive program as a way to continuously improve its safety performance, health and safety management systems, and safety culture. Performance is regularly measured and evaluated; good health and safety behaviour and performance are recognized and rewarded, and poor behaviour and performance are identified and corrected. One limitation of an incentive program is that employees may feel pressure not to report incidents.[12]

Manager's Toolkit 8.3 provides some steps in setting up a safety incentive program.

Safety Awareness Programs

Most organizations have a safety awareness program that entails the use of several different media. Safety lectures, commercially produced films, specially developed videocassettes, and other media, such as pamphlets, are useful for teaching and motivating employees to follow safe work procedures. Posters have been found to be very effective because they can be displayed in strategic locations where workers will be sure to see them. For example, a shipyard found that placing posters at the worksite helped reduce accidents by making employees more conscious of the hazards of using scaffolds.

The Key Role of the Supervisor

One of a supervisor's major responsibilities is to communicate to an employee the need to work safely. Beginning with new employee orientation, safety should be emphasized continually. Proper work procedures, the use of protective clothing and

MANAGER'S TOOLKIT **8.3**

STEPS TO A SUCCESSFUL SAFETY INCENTIVE PROGRAM

- Obtain the full support and involvement of management by providing cost benefits.

- Review current injury and health statistics to determine where change is needed.

- Decide on a program of action and set an appropriate budget.

- Select a realistic safety goal, such as reducing accidents by a set percentage, improving safety suggestions, or achieving a period of time without a lost-time injury. Communicate your objectives to everyone involved.

- Select incentive rewards on the basis of their attractiveness to employees and their fit with your budget.

- Develop a program that is both interesting and fun. Use kickoff meetings, posters, banners, quizzes, and/or games to spark employee interest. Give all employees a chance to win.

- Communicate continually the success of your program. Provide specific examples of positive changes in behaviour.

- Reward safety gains immediately. Providing rewards shortly after improvements reinforces changed behaviour and encourages additional support for the safety program.

devices, and potential hazards should be explained thoroughly. Furthermore, employees' understanding of all these considerations needs to be verified during training sessions, and employees encouraged to take some initiative in maintaining a concern for safety. Since training by itself does not ensure continual adherence to safe work practices, supervisors must observe employees at work and reinforce safe practices. Where unsafe acts are detected, supervisors should take immediate action to find the cause. Supervisors need to foster a team spirit of safety among the work group. Again, it is important to identify that while this is a legal requirement, the success of any safety awareness depends on the willingness of the supervisor to actively support the employees in creating a safe work environment.

Proactive Safety Training Program

What are the most popular subjects in safety training programs? Frequent topics are (1) first aid, (2) accident investigation, (3) accident prevention techniques, (4) hazardous materials, and (5) emergency procedures.

Most programs emphasize the use of emergency first-aid equipment and personal safety equipment. Furthermore, many organizations provide training in off-the-job safety—at home, on the highway, and so on—as well as in first aid. Injuries and fatalities away from the job occur much more frequently than do those on the job and are reflected in employer costs for insurance premiums, wage continuation, and interrupted production. The Industrial Accident Prevention Association (IAPA) offers six diploma programs for workers, supervisors, managers, and health and safety representatives. Course topics include health and safety legislation, hazard identification, and workplace inspection. Visit the Web site of the IAPA (**www.iapa.ca**).

HR professionals and safety directors, in particular, advocate employee involvement when designing and implementing safety programs.[13] Employees can offer valuable ideas regarding specific safety and health topics to cover, instructional methods, and proper teaching techniques. Furthermore, acceptance for safety training is heightened when employees feel a sense of ownership in the instructional program.

At Work with HRM 8.2 describes how CN encourages employee involvement in safety.

Industrial Accident Prevention Association (IAPA)

www.iapa.ca

AT WORK with HRM 8.2

CN RAIL: SaFE OBSERVERS

Canadian National Railway (CN) is a transportation company that offers integrated transportation services: rail, intermodal, trucking, freight forwarding, warehousing, and distribution. CN is committed to the safety of its employees, customers, and the public. Its safety management system includes elements such as safety goals and performance targets, risk assessments, responsibilities and authorities, policies and procedures, and monitoring and evaluation processes.

CN's focus on two-way health and safety communication fosters a culture of safety. The organization invests in safety training, coaching, awareness, motivation, and employee involvement initiatives. Its performance management process provides for employee recognition. Drug and alcohol policies stress prevention as well as assistance for employees confronting substance abuse problems.

Daily job safety briefings and risk assessments enable work teams to discuss possible safety hazards and emergency procedures.

The **S**afety **F**or **E**veryone (**SaFE**) program encourages peer-on-peer safety. "SaFE observers" provide positive and constructive feedback to peers during a shift. At-risk behaviours are discussed in confidence and corrected on the spot. General observations are noted by the SaFE observer and shared with supervisors for future analysis. Communication training is provided to employees on how to give and receive feedback.

CRITICAL THINKING QUESTION:

In relation to CN's approach, what do you think is meant by "It's not about enforcing rules, but encouraging safe behaviours."?

Source: Safety Management System," Safety, CN http://www.cn.ca/en/corporate-citizenship-safety.htm (accessed March 15, 2012).

Information Technology and Safety Awareness and Training

Health and safety professionals, educators, workers, students, and employers can instantly access health and safety regulations, guidelines, videos, publications, articles, posters, and safety-meeting guides through communication technology. The expanded broadband access and the availability of tablets and smartphones have allowed individuals and groups access to information and learning materials from anywhere and anytime. E-learning modules are being converted to play on mobile devices. Even YouTube and various safety videos can be accessed on personal hand-held devices, providing current updated information 24/7. Expanded use of e-books and online instructional materials are becoming the main learning resources for education institutions.

Whether connecting through telephone networks or across the Internet, workers and students have instant connectivity to learning materials and information systems. For example, WorkSafeBC has a new leading-edge Web-based apprenticeship portal (http://www2.worksafebc.com/Topics/Apprenticeships/Home.asp) that provides health and safety resources for apprentices and other trade workers: carpenters, electricians, plumbers, cooks, and automotive service technicians. The training is aligned to the Industry Training Authority (ITA) curriculum for B.C. apprenticeship programs. This new site emphasizes the importance of learning about workplace safety at an early stage and accommodating learners who use their own mobile technology.[14]

The increased use of safety management information systems that address the multiple facets of a health and safety program ranging from risk assessments and control measures to training, certification, and promotion is improving organizations' safety practices through the integration and sharing of critical safety information. For example, BC Ferries Inc. has replaced its fleet manuals with a new user-friendly eFleet Electronic Documentation System, which has significantly improved employee access to accurate and up-to-date safety information through intranet or local computers on board vessels.

In recognizing the importance of managing risk, BC Ferries Inc. has integrated a formal fleet-wide risk identification and assessment process into its safety management system. Training for this new system includes basic risk awareness, risk management, and risk facilitation training.[15]

Enforcement of Safety Rules

Specific expectations and standards concerning safety are communicated through supervisors, bulletin-board notices, employee handbooks, and signs attached to equipment. Safety rules are also emphasized in regular safety meetings, at new employee orientations, and in paper and online manuals of standard operating procedures. Such rules typically refer to the following types of employee behaviours:

- using proper safety devices
- using proper work procedures
- following good housekeeping practices
- complying with accident and injury reporting procedures
- wearing required safety clothing and equipment
- avoiding carelessness or horseplay

Penalties for violation of safety rules are usually stated in the employee handbook. In a large percentage of organizations, the penalties imposed on violators are the same as those imposed for violations of other standards and expectations. They include an oral or written warning for the first violation, suspension or disciplinary layoff for repeated violations, and, as a last resort, dismissal. However, for serious violations—such as smoking around volatile substances—even the first offence may be cause for termination.

Sometimes, the consequences of poor safety behaviours result in serious injuries. For example, an employee was seriously injured after being run over by a BobCat loader while working on the construction site; the employee had not been alerted to the site being dangerous. The company was fined $100,000 in Alberta.[16]

Accident Investigations and Records

The supervisor and a member of the safety committee should investigate every accident, even those considered minor. Such an investigation may determine the factors contributing to the accident and may reveal what corrections are needed to prevent a similar accident from happening again. Correction may require rearranging workstations, installing safety guards or controls, or, more often, giving employees additional safety training and ensuring that they understand the importance of safe work practices.

Employers are also required to keep certain records and to compile and post an annual summary of work-related injuries and illnesses. From these records, organizations can compute their *incidence rate*, the number of injuries and illnesses per 100 full-time employees during a given year. The standard formula for computing the incidence rate is shown by the following equation, where 200,000 equals the base for 100 full-time workers who work 40 hours a week, 50 weeks a year:

$$\text{Incidence rate} = \frac{\text{Number of injuries and illnesses} \times 200,000}{\text{Total hours worked by all employees during period covered}}$$

It should be noted that the same formula can be used to compute incidence rates for (1) the number of workdays lost because of injuries and illnesses, (2) the number of nonfatal injuries and illnesses without lost workdays, and (3) cases involving only injuries or only illnesses.

Incidence rates are useful for making comparisons between work groups, between departments, and between similar units within an organization. They also provide a basis for making comparisons with other organizations doing similar work. Occupational health and safety departments in each province and Human Resources and Skills

Safety begins with preparedness, as these employees demonstrate in a practice situation.

Photodisc Collection/Getty Images

Development Canada compile data that an organization can use as a basis for comparing its safety record with those of other organizations. Progressive organizations can also use this information to benchmark "best practices." As Ethics in HRM 8.1 indicates, reporting and investigating accidents can make an organization subject to more inspections, higher insurance premiums, and possible lawsuits.

ETHICS in HRM 8.1

SUPERVISOR AND EMPLOYEES BURY THE RECORD

A supervisor was instructing a group of new recruits in the cleaning of metal parts in an assembly plant. She was attempting to demonstrate the cleaning technique to two employees at one workstation, while at another workstation, a third new employee was trying to clean the parts himself. The cleaning liquid was highly toxic. The employee felt restricted by his safety gloves and so removed them. His eyes started to water, and instinctively he rubbed them with his solution-soaked hands. The pain was overwhelming, and no water for rinsing his eyes was immediately available. The employee suffered some temporary vision loss.

Who is to blame? The worker who started to clean without receiving full instructions and without using the issued gloves? The supervisor who could have forbidden the worker to start work until she explained the safety aspects? Or the company that failed to post warning signs about the hazardous nature of the cleaning solvent and to have an eye-washing facility available?

Because workplace accidents increase workers' compensation premiums and the number of inspections, the company had an interest in not reporting the accident. Furthermore, because the company had instituted a rewards program that provided incentives to employees for accident-free days, even the employees did not want to report the accident. Thus, the supervisor and the employees agreed to "bury the record."

CRITICAL THINKING QUESTION:

What are the consequences of this decision?

CREATING A HEALTHY WORK ENVIRONMENT

Occupational health and safety legislation was clearly designed to protect the health, as well as the safety, of employees. Because of the dramatic impact of workplace accidents, however, managers and employees alike may pay more attention to these kinds of immediate safety concerns than to job conditions or work environments that may be dangerous to their health. It is essential, therefore, that health hazards be identified and controlled. Attention should also be given to nonwork-related illnesses and injuries and their impact on the organization and its members. Special health programs may also be developed to provide assistance to employees with health problems.

Largely because of the growing public awareness of the efforts of environmentalists, factors in the work environment that affect health are receiving greater attention. Unprecedented air and water pollution throughout the world has made everyone more conscious of the immediate environment in which they live and work. Articles about workers who have been exposed to potential dangers at work can frequently be found in the newspapers. Pressure from the federal government and unions, as well as increased public concern, has given employers a definite incentive to provide the safest and healthiest work environment possible. Small organizations have particular challenges regarding the creation of a healthy work environment. Read HRM and SME 8.1 to gain a better understanding.

As part of "Developing Your Skills" at the end of this chapter, you will be asked to explore the Web site for the Canadian Centre for Occupational Health and Safety (**www.ccohs.ca**).

Canadian Centre for Occupational Health and Safety

www.ccohs.ca

Outcome 3

What are some current workplace health and safety hazards and controls?

Health Hazards and Controls

At one time health hazards were associated primarily with jobs found in industrial processing operations, such as coal mining. In recent years, however, hazards in jobs outside the plant, such as in offices, health-care facilities, and airports, have been recognized and preventive methods adopted. Substituting materials, altering processes, enclosing or isolating a process, issuing protective equipment, and improving ventilation are some common methods to prevent problems. General conditions of health with respect to sanitation, housekeeping, cleanliness, ventilation, water supply, pest control, and food handling are also important to monitor.

Workplace Hazardous Materials Information Systems

Believing that workers have the right to know about potential workplace hazards, industry, labour, and government joined forces several years ago to develop a common information system for labelling hazardous substances. The Workplace Hazardous Materials Information System (WHMIS) is based on three elements:

Material Safety Data Sheet (MSDS)
Documents that contain vital information about hazardous substances

1. *Labels.* Labels are designed to alert the worker that the container holds a potentially hazardous substance. The two types of labels (supplier labels and workplace labels) must contain specified and regulated information, including product identifiers and data on safe handling and material safety. WHMIS class symbols and subclass designations are shown in Figure 8.3.
2. *Material Safety Data Sheet (MSDS).* The **MSDS** identifies the product and its potentially hazardous ingredients, and suggests procedures for the safe handling of the product. The MSDS information must be comprehensive, current, and available in English and French.
3. *Training.* Workers must be trained to check for labels and to follow specific procedures for handling spills. Training workers is part of the due diligence required of employers; it also becomes an important factor in the event of a lawsuit. The Peel Board of Education in Ontario has developed a computer-based program to train workers in WHMIS, allowing illiterate workers to respond to audio commands by touching the screen, thus giving the right response.

HRM and SME 8.1

HEALTH AND SAFETY VALUES AND ATTITUDES

SMEs have a much higher injury rate than larger companies, requiring them to pay even more attention to workplace health and safety. Five million Canadians work for SMEs which account for more than two-thirds of employment in moderately to highly dangerous industries: non-institutional health care, forestry, other services, construction, accommodation, and food. SMEs created over 15,000 jobs in 2010, expanding the number of entry-level positions for new young workers. Workers who have been on the job for less than a month have much higher injury rates than more experienced workers. Young workers are at a higher risk for injury in the workplace than any other demographic. Smaller firms may have limited resources for safety equipment and limited occupational health and safety knowledge. SMEs that utilize part-time and temporary employees may experience a weak safety culture and poorer safety education and training. A single workplace injury can have a devastating effect on a small business and the small, family-like group of employees. An extreme sense of tragedy is associated with the serious injury or death of a young person.

Research suggests that there are a variety of young worker and workplace characteristics that can lead to an elevated risk of youth injuries in the workplace: lack of confidence, lack of information about their rights as workers, lack of preparation for the workplace, amount of physical work, sense of invincibility, intimidation and shyness about voicing concerns, focus on performance, fear of losing a good position, a perception that minor injuries are part of the job, mentally or emotionally assessing hazards differently, and feeling distracted. Recent research suggests that newness to the job, insufficient training, perceived work pressure, or inexperience (relative to their peers) can lead to youth workplace injuries.

CRITICAL THINKING QUESTIONS:

Determining why youth workplace injuries occur can be difficult because there are many complex factors. At the root of our behaviours are our attitudes and values. Individuals and organizations often state certain convictions and values, but act on other more deeply rooted values that they feel are more important.

1. Discuss the competing health and safety values and attitudes you have experienced in your workplace.
2. What are the non-transparent values and attitudes that youth who are new to a SME job may act upon?

Sources: Adapted from Infrastructure Health and Safety Association, "Small Business Owners, Improve Your Bottom Line by Investing in Health and Safety," accessed March 1, 2012, www.ihsa.ca/small_business/smallbusiness_owners_improve_hs.cfm; Small Business and Tourism Branch Industry Canada, "Key Small Business Statistics," July 2011; Institute for Work & Health, " 'Newness' and the Risk of Occupational Injury," issue briefing, May 2009; "Young Workers Focus Report," Workers' Compensation Board of British Columbia, 2010; and Curtis F. Breslin, Peter Smith, and James R. Dunn, "An Ecological Study of Regional Variation in Work Injuries among Young Workers," *BMC Public Health* 7 (2007): 91.

Canada has been working with other countries to develop a standardized global system. This new system, Globally Harmonized System of Classification and Labelling of Chemicals (GHS), is intended to ensure that the symbols used by many countries, such as Japan, the United States, and some countries in the EU, are more universal. Through this joint effort workers throughout the world will have common education and training in the handling of hazardous materials.[17]

Indoor Air Quality

As a consequence of energy concerns, commercial and residential construction techniques have been changed to increase the energy efficiency of heating, ventilating, and air-conditioning systems. This effort has included sealing windows, reducing outside air intake, and, in general, "buttoning up" buildings—thus resulting in the "sick building syndrome" (SBS) and "building related illnesses" (BRI) that give rise to such employee complaints as

FIGURE 8.3   WHMIS Class Symbols and Subclass Designations

Source: Do You Know These Vital Signs: The Hazard Symbols of WHMIS, http://www.hc-sc.gc.ca/ewh-semt/alt_formats/hecs-sesc/pdf/occup-travail/whmis-simdut/poster_symbols-eng.pdf. Health Canada. Reproduced with the permission of the Minister of Public Works and Government Services, 2012.

headaches and nausea, etc. Popular office equipment, including photocopying machines, computer terminals, fax machines, and laser printers, contributes to these health complaints.

Four basic ways to overcome polluted buildings are to (1) eliminate tobacco smoke, (2) provide adequate ventilation, (3) maintain the ventilating system, and (4) remove sources of pollution. It is now common practice in office and industrial settings, as well as public facilities (airports, hotels, schools, and so on), to monitor and manage the quality of indoor air.

TOBACCO SMOKE   Probably the most talked-about workplace health issue in recent years is smoking. Nonsmokers, fuelled by studies linking "passive smoking" (inhaling other people's smoke) with disease and death and irritated by smoke getting in their eyes, noses, throats, and clothes, have been extremely vocal in demanding a smoke-free environment. The number of organizations restricting smoking in the workplace has risen dramatically, motivated by legislation in most provinces. Banning smoking releases employers from concerns about future lawsuits or being forced into installing ventilating systems for smokers.

Because of health research over the last several years, smokers have been banned from lighting up on airplanes, at work, and in restaurants and hotels. Furthermore, nonsmokers have demanded a smoke-free environment that will also benefit employers. Smokers cost employers an additional $3,396 each due to increased absenteeism, decreased productivity, and costs of smoking facilities.[18] For this reason, some employers are charging smokers more for health insurance or are reducing their benefits. However, many employers prefer positive reinforcement through wellness programs to encourage employees to stop smoking.

FRAGRANCES   More attention is now placed on keeping fragrances such as perfumes, colognes, oils, and other personal care products with scents, clear of the workplace. Many people can suffer painful reactions even if the scent is a very low concentration. If an employee expresses concern about fragrances, it is important for the organization to treat the concern seriously, openly, and honestly. Depending on the number of employees that may be negatively impacted, the organization may need to educate the employees and develop a scent-free policy.

Technology

As discussed in Chapter 3, the rapid advances in communication technology has changed how, when, where, and why work is done, and how we interact with other workers. The increasing use of technology has been associated with increased health risks ranging from musculoskeletal injuries caused by repetitive movements involved in computer and technical device use to reduced psychological well-being caused by isolation, reduced privacy, and increased surveillance, increased job demands, increased expectations for continuous learning, and frustration due to technical malfunctions.[19]

The constant use of e-mail can be another psychological strain on workers. A growing number of Canadians have a difficult time resisting the use of a smartphone, and 68% of employed Canadians check work e-mails or voicemails while on vacation.[20] Employers are beginning to reduce after-work use of company-issued smartphones, expressing concerns ranging from unpaid overtime to encroachment on family time. Citizenship and Immigration Canada and Volkswagen either block or ban e-mail use from company-issued smartphones after work hours.[21]

Research examining the impact of cell-phone radiation states that there is not clear evidence of any negative side effects of cell-phone use, although Health Canada suggests that users can take the following, practical measures to reduce their radio frequency exposure by limiting the length of cell-phone calls, using hands-free devices, and replacing cell-phone calls with text messages.[22]

Texting on your iPhone and listening to music on your iPad can be distracting, which may result in accidents or hearing loss. Can you resist the buzz-buzz-buzzing of your smartphone? Have you turned the volume down?

Cumulative Trauma Disorders

Cumulative trauma disorders
Injuries involving tendons of the fingers, hands, and arms that become inflamed from repeated stresses and strains

Meat cutters, cooks, dental hygienists, textile workers, violinists, flight attendants, office workers at computer terminals, and others whose jobs require repetitive motion of the fingers, hands, or arms are reporting injuries in growing percentages. Known as **cumulative trauma disorders** or repetitive motion injuries, these musculoskeletal disorders (MSDs) are injuries of the muscles, nerves, tendons, ligaments, joints, and spinal discs caused by repeated stresses and strains. One of the more common conditions is *carpal tunnel syndrome*, which is characterized by tingling or numbness in the fingers occurring when a tunnel of bones and ligaments in the wrist narrows and pinches nerves that reach the fingers and base of the thumb.

Ergonomics attempts to design equipment and systems that can be easily and efficiently used by people. As a result, ergonomics techniques are also successfully used to improve or correct workplace conditions that cause or aggravate cumulative trauma disorders.[23]

Continuous developments in office furniture, video display terminals, tool design, computer keyboards, and adjustable workstations are all attempts to make the work setting more comfortable—and, hopefully, more productive—but also to lessen musculoskeletal disorders. Mini-breaks involving exercise and the changing of work positions have been found helpful. Importantly, these kinds of injuries often go away if they are caught early. If they are not, they may require months or years of treatment or even surgical correction. Also, when cumulative trauma disorders result from work activities, they can be as high as 40% of the workers' compensation claims.[24]

Communicable Diseases

Communicable diseases, such as herpes simplex (cold sores), influenza, and athlete's foot, and AIDS (acquired immune deficiency syndrome), are covered in public health legislation, not occupational health and safety legislation. In recent years, no issue has received as much attention as SARS (severe acute respiratory syndrome). SARS is a pneumonia-like and potentially fatal illness that infected areas such as Hong Kong, Taiwan, Singapore, and Toronto earlier this decade. The U.S.-based Centers for Disease Control and Prevention advised business travellers to avoid these areas. Employers in Canada had to make decisions about travel bans, quarantines, the right to refuse work, and what constituted a safe work environment.

Since the SARS issue, public health officials and, therefore, employers have become concerned about pandemics, particularly those caused by the avian flu virus. As a result, provinces and organizations have prepared emergency health plans to both take care of their employees and the public.[25]

Workplace Violence and Security

Perhaps the most significant event that has affected workplace security has been the events that occurred on September 11, 2001. From that day forward, organizations throughout Canada have placed renewed emphasis on personal safety and security at work. On a recent study tour, one author of this book was acutely aware of the heightened security

Many employers were unprepared to deal with SARS issues, such as employee quarantines.

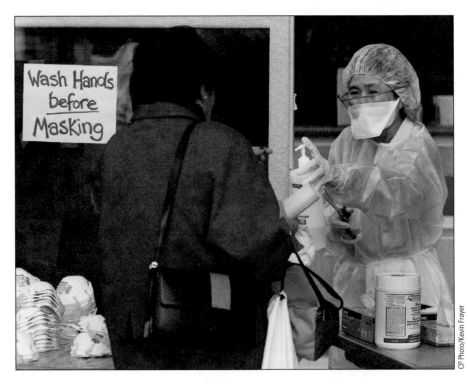

CP Photo/Kevin Frayer

measures to get into certain government buildings. In some cases, unless you were employed there, you could not enter. Further, if you were an employee, you had to go through substantive security checks, including metal detectors, prior to being authorized to enter.

Once largely confined to foreign countries, terrorism is now a major concern to many Canadian employers, such as airlines, sporting facilities, energy plants, high-tech companies, and financial institutions. The heightened security procedures at these facilities show the importance employers place on the prevention of terrorist attacks. Some of the steps taken to have more secure facilities are increased video surveillance, blast-resistant glass, tightened garage security, and off-site emergency offices.

And the concerns of employees are not restricted to those from terrorism or bomb threats. In fact, changes to the *Canada Labour Code* have provided an expanded definition of the reasons that employees can refuse work that they perceive as dangerous. Employees can now refuse on the basis of any "potential" condition that could reasonably be expected to cause injury or illness.[26]

In Canada tragic incidents such as that at L'École Polytechnique, in which 14 women were shot and killed, and the death of Grant De Patie, who was killed after chasing a car that drove away from the gas station without paying, have brought our attention to workplace violence. Unfortunately the incidents and costs of Canadian workplace violence are increasing.[27] The challenge of understanding workplace violence is that it has so many forms of which not all are legislated against, bullying, aggression, intimidation, ganging, and emotional abuse among them.

Many people think of workplace violence as a physical assault, but there are many forms, including these:

- threatening behaviour, such as shaking fists or throwing objects
- verbal or written threats
- harassment—any behaviour that demeans, embarrasses, or humiliates
- verbal abuse, including swearing, insults, or condescending language
- physical attacks, including hitting, shoving, pushing, or kicking[28]

Recent legislative changes have broadened the responsibility of employers to ensure their work environment is free of violence. Several provinces, including Alberta, British Columbia, Saskatchewan, Manitoba, Nova Scotia, Prince Edward Island, Quebec, Newfoundland, and Labrador, as well as Canadian federally regulated workplaces, have implemented regulations dealing with workplace violence as part of their Occupational Health and Safety regulations. Among the requirements of these regulations are a risk assessment, development of policies and procedures to handle the risks identified, instruction and training of workers in handling violence, emergency response plan, and a requirement that incidents be reported.[29] A recent case in Alberta where an employee at Garda Canada Security Corp. was sexually assaulted resulted in the government charging the company with failing to ensure the health and safety of workers. While the legislation requires employers to conduct a hazard assessment, implement safety measures to reduce risks, and ensure that workers have an effective way of communicating with other employees, the government feels that given the nature of the business, there was a failure on the part of the employer to do what was expected. The company was fined $92,750 in 2011 for failing to protect a female worker who was attacked while working alone at an isolated worksite.[30] Most provinces have begun to expand legislation requiring employers to have procedures in place to eliminate or reduce the risks associated with working alone and at night.

So, what are the risk factors in industries such as hospitality, health care, and retail? An informal and effective way to answer this question is to conduct a risk assessment by involving your employees in a discussion around the following three questions:

1. What violence have you been exposed to on this job?
2. Do you know of any violence that has happened to others in similar jobs?
3. What violence-related concerns do you have on this job?[31]

Exposure to workplace violence results in employees fearing more incidents of violence, leading to personal strains (such as stress) and organizational strains (such as reduced commitment). To implement some preventive measures, the Canadian Centre for Occupational Health and Safety suggests the following:

- workplace designs, such as locks or physical barriers, lighting, and electronic surveillance
- administrative practices, such as keeping cash register funds to a minimum, varying the time of day that cash is emptied, and using a security firm to deliver cash
- work practices (particularly for those working alone or away from an office) that include having a designated contact, checking the credentials of a client, and having an emergency telephone source[32]

Kevin Kelloway, director of the CN Centre for Occupational Health and Safety at Saint Mary's University, has identified specific risk factors that can be subsumed under the acronym SAV-T; Scheduling, Authority, Valuables, and Taking care of others.[33] For example, a home care nurse who works alone with ill patients has an increased risk of violence. Workers who work around money and other valuables have an increased risk of violence. Employers must make an effort to prevent workplace violence, for example, by developing policies and providing employees with violence prevention training. In 2012, the Vancouver Island Health Authority was fined in $97,500 because of three incidents of violence by psychiatric patients against the staff.[34]

Keloway's SAV-T acronym can also be used as a way to recognize the signs of escalating violence: Swearing, Agitation, Volume, and Threat.[35] For example, if a worker is agitated and swearing, workers can respond by defusing the situation, establishing clear boundaries around appropriate behaviour, and accessing supervisory help. If the worker is shouting and swearing, workers should remove themselves from the situation and alert security. Awareness of such threatening behaviours can provide an opportunity to intervene and prevent disruptive, abusive, or violent acts.

Finally, organizations can establish formalized workplace violence prevention policies, informing employees that aggressive employee behaviour will not be tolerated. Manager's Toolkit 8.4 lists violence prevention measures that organizations can take.

Organizations are also using a number of different ways to inform employees about security issues. For example, Seneca College in Ontario uses its intranet as a communication tool to inform employees of internal security as well as external security issues in the surrounding geographic area of the college. Another innovative approach to learning more about preventing workplace violence is the Canadian Initiative on Workplace Violence (**www.workplaceviolence.ca**). The Canadian Initiative is a research firm with partners from universities, unions, and employers. It researches the impact of workplace violence and provides educational resources to help organizations eliminate such violence.

Some organizations have formal crisis management teams. These teams conduct initial risk assessment surveys, develop action plans to respond to violent situations, and perform crisis intervention during violent, or potentially violent, encounters. For example, a crisis management team would investigate a threat reported by an employee. The team's mandate would be to gather facts about the threat, decide if the organization should intervene, and, if so, to determine the most appropriate method of doing so. Organizations, as part of their corporate social responsibility, have created emergency telephone lines for their employees and families in the event of a crisis, such as a blackout or severe weather conditions.

When violent incidents, such as the death of a co-worker, happen at work, employees can experience anxiety, shock, guilt, grief, apathy, resentment, cynicism, isolation, and a host of other emotions. Such incidents may require the violence response team to perform crisis intervention through positive counselling techniques.

Canadian Initiative on Workplace Violence

www.workplaceviolence.ca

Stressors in the Workplace

According to a 2011 Statistics Canada report on the main sources of workplace stress, one in four Canadian workers described their daily lives as highly stressed.[36] But what is

MANAGER'S TOOLKIT 8.4

VIOLENCE STOPS HERE!

Everyone in the workplace must be committed to, and involved in creating, a workplace violence prevention program: employers, workers, the joint health and safety committee, and unions.

Follow these steps to prevent workplace violence:

1. Establish violence prevention policy and standards.

2. Conduct a risk assessment.

3. Control violence hazards through workplace design and work practices.

4. Regularly inspect your workplace, and review your program to ensure that standards are maintained.

5. Include domestic violence issues in workplace violence prevention policies and programs.

6. Educate employees on these policies and programs, appropriate actions to take, signs of domestic violence, how to prevent violence, and resources for victims of domestic violence.

7. Develop a safety plan, if an employee reports domestic violence, to ensure that the victim is protected while at the workplace.

8. Ensure that all employees are aware the employee assistance provider is available.

9. Encourage the victim to contact a professional.

10. Screen for the abuser (with the victim's permission) by providing a photo or description to reception and security.

11. Inform all workplace parties that they must report any abuse or violent behaviour.

12. Act upon any reports immediately.

Source: "Addressing Domestic Violence in the Workplace: A Workbook," Public Services Health and Safety Association, 2010, www.healthandsafetyontario.ca/HSO/media/PSHSA/pdfS/DomVioWkplace.pdf?ext=.pdf (accessed March 15, 2012).

Stress
Any adaptive demand caused by physical, mental, or emotional factors that requires coping behaviour

stress? People frequently talk about being stressed at work, yet they are often unable to explain what they mean. **Stress** is simply any demand on the physical or emotional self that requires a person to cope with that demand. For example, while running 5 km an individual may become short-winded after 3 km. Thus, the body is "stressed" as the individual deals with being short of breath. Likewise, a student may have just received a special award at school and be excited about the recognition. Again, the student has to cope with this. Stress can be either positive or negative, and each person handles stress differently.

Six in 10 of highly stressed Canadian workers identified work as their main source of stress.[37] So, then, what work processes (the way work is designed and performed) and organizational practices are stressing the stressed at work? The 2012 survey report by Towers Watson found that excessive workload or long hours, lack of work–life balance, inadequate staffing, technologies that expand availability during nonwork hours, and unclear or conflicting job expectations are the top sources of workplace stress.[38] A 2011 Conference Board of Canada survey report that looked at mentally healthy workplaces from the perspectives of Canadian workers and front-line managers found that most leaders think that their work environment supports mental health, but most employees do not share the same view.[39] These employees share what they feel represents a mentally healthy workplace in Manager's Toolkit 8.5. Recognizing and dealing with the **workplace stressors** is the first step toward managing workplace stress. A corporate culture and work environment that promote a healthy, safe, and environmentally protected work environment can have a positive impact on worker stress.

Workplace stressor
A workplace event, process, or practice that has the potential to cause worker stress

Court decisions across Canada have created an increasing legal obligation for employers to provide psychologically safe workplaces, which generally means being aware of worker mental health and establishing plans to manage it.[40] One 2012 example is British Columbia's Bill 14, now passed as the *Workers' Compensation Amendment Act*, 2011, which expands the compensation for mental stress beyond post-traumatic stress to include a reaction to a significant work-related stressor.[41] Other jurisdictions now recognize exposure to workplace violence, bullying, and ongoing sexual harassment as

WHAT IS A MENTALLY HEALTHY WORKPLACE?

Workplace Strategies for Mental Health outlines factors in building a psychologically healthy workplace. Many of the same characteristics noted by employees and managers during the course of the research are included on this list. Other characteristics include role clarity, job security, removal of class distinctions, and the physical environment.

WORKLOAD

- Workloads are monitored to ensure they are not excessive.
- "Face time" at the office does not equate to better job performance.
- There is sufficient staff to do the work required.
- Overtime is compensated.

WORK SCHEDULING

- Flexible work arrangements—including flexible schedules, compressed workweeks, and telework—exist.

WORK–LIFE BALANCE

- Work–life balance is promoted.
- Employees are encouraged to take their allotted vacation time.
- Employees are not expected to respond to e-mail 24/7.

WORK ENVIRONMENT

- People are friendly, empathetic, understanding, and supportive in the workplace.
- Employee morale is high.

- The organization holds social activities for staff.
- Employees are respected.
- Bullying, harassment, and discrimination are not tolerated.
- People are not manipulated.
- Policies and procedures are in place and enforced (e.g., overtime practices, anti-discrimination policies).
- It is not a high-stress environment.
- There is an absence of hostility and conflict.
- Employees are acknowledged, rewarded, and recognized for a job well done.
- There is not widespread negativity.

MANAGEMENT STYLE

- Managers are well trained and good people managers.
- Managers are not autocratic, authoritarian, controlling, and aggressive.
- Managers do not bully employees.
- Employees have autonomy over their work.
- Employees are not blamed or punished for mistakes.
- Employees are appreciated.

COMMUNICATION

- There is open communication between management and employees.
- Human resource professionals and managers are approachable.
- Discussions are kept confidential.

Source: "Building Mentally Healthy Workplaces, Perspectives of Canadian Workers and Front-Line Managers," June 2011, The Conference Board of Canada. Reproduced with permission from the Conference Board of Canada.

workplace stressors.[42] Such legislation as well as the new federal standards, will encourage employers to actively promote mental health in the workplace. The new 2012 National Standard on Psychological Health and Safety in the Workplace will provide organizations with the tools to achieve measurable improvement in psychological health and safety of Canadian employees. It will help employers prevent the loss and liability associated with mental injuries—estimated to cost $20 billion a year in workplace losses alone—by nurturing psychologically safe working environments.[43]

Stress management programs involve both employees and employers working together to take initiatives to reduce aspects of their work environments that result in negative impacts on employee health.

Many employers have developed stress management programs to teach employees how to minimize the negative effects of job-related stress. A typical program might include instruction in relaxation techniques, coping skills, listening skills, methods of dealing with difficult people, time management, and assertiveness. Organizational techniques, such as flexible work hours, learning opportunities, and regular feedback on job performance, should not be overlooked in the process of teaching employees how to handle stress.[44]

Even though the number and severity of organizational stressors can be reduced, everyone encounters situations that may be described as distressful. Those in good physical health are generally better able to cope with the stressors they encounter.

Before concluding this discussion, we should observe that stress that is harmful to some employees might be healthy for others. Most managers learn to handle distress effectively and find that it can stimulate better performance. However, there will always be those who are unable to handle stress and need assistance in learning to cope with it. The increased interest of young and old alike in developing habits that will enable them to lead happier and more productive lives will undoubtedly be beneficial to them as individuals, to the organizations where they work, and to a society where people are becoming more and more interdependent. Progressive companies are also discovering that other interventions, such as rewarding employees for exhibiting appropriate behaviours, encouraging employees to be innovative, and taking a holistic approach to wellness, are also reducing stressors for employees.[45] Further, organizations that focus on having an engaged workforce (as discussed in Chapter 3) have shown an association between engagement and reduced stress.[46] Overall employee well-being and health are more likely in organizations with highly engaged staff. Therefore, there is additional rationale to ensure that work stressors are kept to a minimum. Figure 8.4 provides some suggestions on how individuals can reduce stress.

Building Better Health

Outcome 4

How can a comprehensive strategic approach to health and safety improve employee well-being?

Along with improving working conditions that are hazardous to employee health, many employers provide health services and have programs that encourage employees to improve their health habits. It is recognized that better health benefits not only the individual but also the organization in reduced absenteeism, increased efficiency, and better morale. An understanding of the close relationship between physical and emotional health and job performance has made broad health-building programs attractive to employers as well as to employees. Further, recent surveys suggest that 39% of employers have adequate budgets and value statements indicating their commitment to building and maintaining a culture of heath for employees.[47] These programs, it has been found, could be more

FIGURE 8.4 Tips for Reducing Job-Related Stress

- Build rewarding relationships with co-workers.
- Talk openly with managers or employees about job or personal concerns.
- Prepare for the future by keeping abreast of likely changes in job demands.
- Don't greatly exceed your skills and abilities.
- Set realistic deadlines; negotiate reasonable deadlines with managers.
- Act now on problems or concerns of importance.
- Designate dedicated work periods during which time interruptions are avoided.
- When feeling stressed, find time for detachment or relaxation.
- Don't let trivial items take on importance: handle them quickly or assign them to others.
- Take short breaks from your work area as a change of pace.

effective with more leadership involvement.[48] As public expectations for ethical business practices are increasing, organizations are beginning to follow through on their social and environmental commitment responsibilities, creating new opportunities to improve the quality of work life and organizational performance. These organizations are using individual health promotion programs as the first step toward a more comprehensive approach to employee wellness. Health services, alternative health care, wellness, disability management, and employee assistance programs can begin to address the underlying causes of presenteeism, absenteeism, stress, and work–life imbalance. Also critical is the understanding of the work environment and how work processes and practices can be improved to enhance employee health and organizational performance. Graham Lowe, a leading researcher on healthy organizations, states that a positive culture, inclusive leadership, engaged employees, and a vibrant workplace are the building blocks of a healthy organization.[49] Yet, it was found that only 26% of Canadian organizations are taking a strategic approach to improving employee wellness.[50] Seventy-two percent of Canadian organizations indicated that they offer specific initiatives targeted at specific health risks such as smoking and high blood pressure.[51]

Studies have demonstrated a strong link between high-performance work systems and healthy organizations.[52] In such a system, employees are the primary source of the company's competitive advantage, are treated accordingly, and therefore are motivated to perform at high levels. Employees who are treated respectfully and experience quality interpersonal relationships tend to be more committed and to participate more fully in workplace safety.[53]

As described in At Work with HRM 8.3, Hamilton Utilities Corporation is an example of a healthy workplace initiative that is comprehensive in scope, integrated with other human resource initiatives, and has an implementation strategy based on effective communication, inclusive leadership, employee participation, and wellness teams.

Health Services

Outcome 5

What are the services and programs an organization can provide to build better health?

The type of health services that an employer provides is primarily related to the size of the organization and the importance of such services. Small organizations have only limited facilities, such as those needed to handle first-aid cases, while many larger firms offer complete diagnostic, treatment, and emergency medical services. Since employers are required to provide medical services after an injury, the larger firms may have nurses and physicians on full-time duty or certainly have arrangements with local physicians for preferred attention. Medium-size and smaller organizations have one or more physicians on call.

Effective handling of workplace violence involves intervention from specialists trained in handling workplace traumas.

Bruce Ayres/Stone/Getty Images

Alternative Approaches

In a discussion of health services as well as health benefits, it should be emphasized that there are many non-traditional approaches to better health. These are typically referred to as alternative approaches. Many of the approaches differ from traditional medicine in that they are less invasive, and they empower the patient by enlisting patient participation in health-care decisions.

Relaxation techniques, chiropractic, therapeutic massage, acupuncture, homeopathy, megavitamin and herbal therapy, special diets, and many other alternative approaches are used to treat a wide variety of health problems.

Wellness Programs

The 2011 Sun Life Canadian Health Index found that Canadian employees and employers are failing to take the preventive measures to ensure a healthy lifestyle. The study found that money and time, second to motivation, were the primary barriers to healthy living, and suggested that employee-sponsored wellness programs could address these barriers.[54] Since Canadians spend half of their working hours at work, the worksite is an ideal setting to address health and well-being. While the trends toward wellness programs is growing, only 28% of Canadians have access to these healthy lifestyle programs.[55]

The elements that employees are looking for in a wellness program include access to flexible work hours, healthy food, fitness facilities, health professionals, health groups, activities, mentoring, and education.[56] For example, the employee health management program at Xerox includes cardiovascular fitness through aerobic exercises, such as jogging, skipping rope, and racquet sports. These types of programs support The Public Health Agency of Canada's findings that physical activity can prevent serious illnesses such as heart disease, obesity, diabetes, and stress.[57] Companies such as BC Hydro and Toronto Life Insurance found that workplace fitness programs reduced employee turnover.[58] Other Canadian companies with wellness programs have been able to reduce absenteeism.[59] Even in difficult economic situations, a modest approach to wellness in the workplace can occur with things such as encouraging employees to get some exercise or take stretch breaks each day. BC Hydro's wellness program is also described in At Work with HRM 8.3.

In a *Health Affairs* article published in 2011, Harvard University researchers reported on a meta-analysis of the literature on costs and saving associated with such wellness programs. The researchers found that medical costs fall by about $3.27 for every dollar spent on wellness programs and that absenteeism costs fall by about $2.73 for every dollar spent on wellness programs. They contended that wellness programs can generate savings that outweigh costs in addition to improving health outcomes and employee productivity.[60]

Disability Management

Disability management
Integrated approach to managing disability-related benefits

More and more organizations are taking an integrated approach to dealing with short- and long-term absences. Initially, **disability management** programs were linked to workplace injuries as a way to get employees back to work as soon as possible. These programs have now evolved to an approach that combines a strong organizational commitment centred on line supervisors, overseen by expert internal resources, and supported by clinical case management.[61] This means that the focus is also on creating a work environment where employees want to return to work as soon as they are medically able. Part of an effective disability management program includes a graduated return-to-work where the employee works fewer hours and, in some situations, is accommodated by having a different shift.[62] Even in difficult economic times, a carefully designed and well-managed program can be effective in getting capable staff back to work while understanding that the employer is interested in their well-being.[63]

Facilitating a return-to-work plan would include maintaining contact with the employee while he or she is on leave, providing organizational support to the supervisor and team by discussing implementation and anticipated challenges and solutions,

WHY WORK FOR AN ENERGY COMPANY?

Two Canadian energy companies have recognized the connection between employee health, productivity, and health insurance costs. They highlight their wellness initiatives in their recruitment publications as a human resources plan to deal with growing shortages of workers.

BC Hydro has a comprehensive employee wellness program that supports employee physical and mental health through health promotion, employee and family assistance, a respectful workplace, subsidized healthy meals, and return-to-work programs. Its fitness facility offers a range of services: yoga, massage therapy, physiotherapy, and meditation.

The workplace wellness initiatives of Ontario's Hamilton Utilities Corporation are comprehensive in scope and integrated with the corporation's business strategy, human resources processes and practices, health, safety, environmental protection, and social responsibility initiatives and programs. The leadership in the company is committed to and convinced of the value of wellness programs, as stated in their workplace wellness value and policy statements. The focus of the program is to improve understanding of workplace issues that have an impact on health and to provide an environment that addresses these workplace stressors. Through a shared employer and employee responsibility approach, employees are assisted in achieving ownership of their physical, mental, and emotional health. Hamilton Utilities believes that the key elements of a healthy workplace include the physical environment, health practices, the social environment, and personal resources, and that these independent, broad-based factors must be considered as part of a holistic approach to a healthy workplace and employee well-being. The corporation has well-designed implementation and evaluation strategies that include the active involvement of managers, employees, and the workplace wellness team.

CRITICAL THINKING QUESTION:

If wellness programs can save a company money, why don't more organizations have them? Explain your answer.

Sources: "Why Work for BC Hydro," BC Hydro Media Release, www.bchydro.com/careers/why_work_for_bc_hydro.html (accessed March 15, 2012); "British Columbia Top Employers 2012," *The Vancouver Sun* and MediCorp Canada, March 3, 2012; and "Hamilton Utilities Corporation's Workplace Wellness Policy," Hamilton Utilities Corporation, www.hamiltonucorp.com/html/social/social_workplace.shtml (accessed March 15, 2012).

understanding the tasks and responsibilities that need to be modified, and having a clear diagnosis and plan. This approach would reduce any anxiety, alienation, fears of reinjury and job loss, and stigma that the employee involved might feel.

Employee Assistance Programs

Employee assistance program (EAP)
Program to provide short-term counselling and referrals to appropriate professionals

A broad view of health includes the emotional as well as the physical aspects of one's life. While emotional problems, personal crises, alcoholism, and drug abuse are considered to be personal matters, they become organizational problems when they affect behaviour at work and interfere with job performance. It is estimated that psychological problems, including depression, anxiety, and stress in the workplace, cost the Canadian economy about $51 billion each year with a third of that attributed to productivity losses.[64]

Employee assistance programs (EAPs) can provide a useful way to deal with problems, such as stress and depression, which could lead to more serious mental health problems. Supervisors are often given training and policy guidance in the type of help they can offer their subordinates. Figure 8.5 outlines the types of EAP services offered to employees in Canada. While many companies do not offer programs due to concerns over the cost/benefits of such initiatives, research has shown that 80% of mental health problems can be successfully treated with early detection and treatment.

For additional information on EAP service providers, access **www.easna.org**.

**Employee Assistance
Society of North America**
www.easna.org

FIGURE 8.5 Employee Assistance Programs

Listed below are some of the usual services in EAPs:

- personal issues
- job stress
- relationship issues
- eldercare, childcare, and parenting issues
- harassment
- substance abuse
- separation and loss
- balancing work and family
- financial or legal
- family violence

In addition, and depending on the wishes of the company, there may be services for retirement and layoff assistance, wellness and health promotion, fitness, and disability issues.

Source: Employee Assistance Programs, Canadian Centre for Occupational Health and Safety, www.ccohs.ca/oshanswers/hsprograms/eap.html (accessed March 12, 2012).

PERSONAL CRISES   The most prevalent problems among employees are personal crises involving marital, family, financial, or legal matters. Such problems often come to a supervisor's attention. In most instances, the supervisor can usually provide the best help simply by being understanding and supportive and by helping the individual find the type of assistance needed. In many cases, the person is referred to the EAP program. Many organizations that have an EAP also have operations and offices that are in many different locations yet want to use the same EAP provider. Therefore, in recent years, many EAP providers have begun to offer 24/7 telephone access to bilingual expert counsellors, telephonic counselling sessions, and online assistance to support managers.[65] Managers would want to ensure that they leverage the online support services offered by EAP providers: these include training, guides, checklists, videos, assessment tools, and articles.

EMOTIONAL PROBLEMS   In 2011, the Conference Board of Canada reported that 44% of employees surveyed had said they experienced a mental health issue.[66] Mental health claims are the fastest-growing reason for days lost to disability. In 2012, 78% of short-term disability claims and 67% of long-term disability claims were related to mental health issues.[67] Only 50% of employees feel comfortable using an organization's EAP or speaking to their manager or colleague about mental health issues for fear of hurting potential career advances.[68] A persistent focus on awareness, communication, and education would begin to reduce the fear, stigma, and discrimination around mental illness. Whether such individuals will be able to perform their jobs must be determined on an individual basis. In reviewing such cases, the organization should pay particular attention to workplace safety factors, since there is general agreement that emotional disturbances are primary or secondary factors in a large proportion of industrial accidents and violence.

SUBSTANCE ABUSE   Business and industry lose billions of dollars each year because of substance abuse. According to the most recent study by the Canadian Centre on Substance Abuse, the total cost is close to $40 billion yearly, or $1,267 for every Canadian. In addition, legal substances such as tobacco and alcohol account for 80% of the abuse. Specifically, the following losses occur:

- $14.6 billion from alcohol abuse
- $8.2 billion from illicit drugs
- $17 billion from tobacco[69]

In confronting the problem, employers must recognize that substance addiction is considered a disease that follows a rather predictable course. Thus, they can take specific actions to deal with employees showing symptoms of the disease at particular stages of its progression. Substance abuse typically begins with social drinking or drug taking that gets out of control. As the disease progresses, the person loses control over how much to use and when to use. The person uses denial to avoid facing the problems created by the substance abuse and often blames others for these problems. The first step in helping the substance abuser is to awaken the person to the reality of the situation.

To identify substance abuse as early as possible, it is essential that supervisors monitor the performance, attendance, and behaviour of all employees regularly and systematically. A supervisor should carefully document evidence of declining performance, behaviour, and/or attendance, and then bring the matter to the attention of the employee with evidence that the individual's work is suffering. The employee should be assured that help will be made available without penalty. In fact, through court decisions concerning substance addiction, the courts have confirmed that substance addiction is a disability, and employers are legally obliged to deal with the problem. This decision means that the employer can no longer terminate a person's employment because of an abuse problem. Specifically, a supervisor needs to set clear expectations, be consistent, act, and follow any other health and safety regulations. Since the assessments are made solely with regard to poor job performance, attendance, or behaviour, a supervisor can avoid any mention of the abuse and allow such employees to seek aid as they would for any other problem. A supervisor cannot discipline an employee because a person is suspected of abusing a substance: discipline is dependent on the degree of problem with job performance, attendance, or behaviour. Between 70 and 80% of employees accept the offer to get help and resolve their problems. Therefore, it is important for supervisors and managers to recognize that any discipline, whether it is a verbal warning or a termination, has to be related to the job. Further, as mentioned in previous chapters, there are many constraints on employers to legally ensure that the workplace is safe, secure, and free of discrimination.

Consider Emerging Trends 8.1 for information about what is on the horizon for workplace health and safety.

EMERGING TRENDS **8.1**

1. ***Enhanced EAP services.*** With the economic upheaval, more employees have had higher levels of anxiety. To help employees through these difficult times, EAP services have expanded to include financial counselling, retirement planning, and career transition support as well as services dealing with bankruptcy and divorce. Online services and resources are expanding.

2. ***Increased fines for workplace health/safety infractions.*** With the increase in fatalities in the workplace, the various workers' compensation boards across Canada are increasing penalties. For example, in Alberta, the occupational health and safety fines and penalties doubled in 2011 to $3.4 million, and Syncrude Canada received a fine of $376,000.

3. ***Dealing with "presenteeism."*** In many situations, employees who are ill still come to work, creating a situation where the person is present but not productive or engaged. Sometimes, employees do this because they have irrational expectations of themselves or in some workplaces, such as education and health care, there are not enough people to do the work. However, employers are now realizing that an unwell employee is not only unproductive but could possibly spread the illness to healthy workers. As a result, employers are supporting employees to stay home and take care of themselves.

4. ***Increasing workplace mental health standards***. Quebec's Groupe de promotion pour la prévention en santé (GP2S) is an

continued

organization that has established an ISO standard for workplace wellness. The factors include leadership commitment, integration of wellness into the business strategy and management systems, a communication strategy, and diagnostic health evaluation.

5. ***Ensuring harassment and bullying are not present in the work environment.*** Although harassment and bullying were discussed in Chapter 2 in relation to human rights legislation, many organizations consider these elements as a form of workplace violence and are taking more proactive steps to eliminate them from the work environment. Health and safety legislation is targeting the reduction and elimination of workplace violence, harassment, and bullying by modifying the laws requiring the investigation and compensation of workplace harassment and bullying incidents. Examples include Ontario's Bill 168 and B.C.'s Bill 14.

Sources: Karla Thorpe and Louise Chénier, "Building Mentally Healthy Workplaces: Perspectives of Canadian Workers and Front-Line Managers," Ottawa: The Conference Board of Canada, June 2011; "Alberta Government Reports Workplace Safety Fines Increase," *Daily Commercial News and Construction Record*, January 10, 2012, http://dcnonl.com/article/id48248/ohs; Towers Watson, *Pathway to Health and Productivity, 2011/2012 Staying@Work Survey Report*, December 2012, www.towerswatson.com/united-states/research/6031; "Boost Health and Productivity with a Wellness Program," *Benefits Canada*, August 25, 2011, www.benefitscanada.com/benefits/health-wellness/boost-employee-health-and-productivity-with-a-wellness-program-19628; and Bill M 212—2012: *Workplace Bullying Prevention Act, 2012*, Legislative Assembly British Columbia, accessed March 15, 2012, www.leg.bc.ca/index.htm.

SUMMARY

1. Describe the legal responsibilities supervisors and managers have to create a safe and healthy work environment.
   - Become familiar with the occupational health and safety legislation governing their operation.
   - Enforce health and safety standards throughout the organization.
   - Protect employees from physical hazards, unhealthy conditions, and unsafe acts of other employees.

2. Cite the measures that should be taken to create a safe work environment.
   - Take every reasonable precaution to ensure employee safety.
   - Inform and train employees about safety and health requirements in the organization.
   - Keep records and investigate any accidents.
   - Involve employees in identifying and eliminating health and safety problems.
   - Provide safety training programs and emphasize the importance of health and safety in the workplace.
   - Enforce safety procedures.

3. Describe the current workplace health and safety hazards as well as the related control measures.
   - WHMIS.
   - Indoor air quality, including second-hand smoke.
   - Technology.
   - Cumulative trauma disorders.
   - Communicable diseases.
   - Workplace violence and security.
   - Workplace stressors.

4. Explain a proactive strategic approach to improving employee health and well-being.
   - Leadership and management commitment.
   - Culture conducive to health and safety.
   - Communication and integrated strategies.

5. Describe the organizational services and programs for building better health.
   • Health services.
   • Alternative approaches.
   • Wellness programs.
   • Disability management.
   • Employee assistance programs.

NEED TO KNOW	NEED TO UNDERSTAND
• Elements of a workplace health and safety program • Definition of WHMIS • Types of health and safety hazards and controls in the workplace	• Role of legislation in occupational health and safety • Responsibilities of employer, supervisor, and employee regarding health and safety • A proactive strategic approach to employee well-being • Prevention and control of workplace violence • Role managers can play in preventing workplace stress

KEY TERMS

cumulative trauma disorders 285

disability management 293

employee assistance
  program (EAP) 294

industrial disease 275

Material Safety Data
  Sheet (MSDS) 282

occupational illness 269

occupational injury 269

stress 289

workplace stressors 289

REVIEW QUESTIONS

1. What are the primary duties and responsibilities in relation to health and safety for each of the following?
   • employers
   • workers
   • supervisors
2. What is the purpose of workers' compensation legislation?
3. What can employers do to reduce the cost of workers' compensation?
4. What are two ways an employer can create a safe work environment?
5. What questions would you ask to assess the risk of violence in the workplace?
6. What are two services an organization can provide to build better workplace health?
7. What is stress, and what are the specific causes of workplace stress?

CRITICAL THINKING QUESTIONS

1. You've just been hired by Rim Auto Parts as a management trainee. Part of your responsibilities includes introducing a "Safety First" mindset. How would you approach this task, and what elements would you want in the mindset?
2. Refer to HRM and the Law 8.1. The vulnerability of youth and migrant workers was noted in the investigation reports. What are the reasons for this vulnerability? How would you tackle this health and safety issue?

3. Refer to the HRM Close-up on the Queen Elizabeth Hotel. Recently the hotel manager has noticed an increase in the number of back injuries and wrist strains. The hotel also received notification from the provincial agency that its Workers' Compensation premiums would be increased in the following calendar year as a result of the increased claims. What else can the hotel do to ensure employee safety and health, and reduce their injury claims and premiums?

4. Refer to Emerging Trends 8.1. Comment on the slogan "Wellness is not just a mission—it's a message. How you deliver it makes a difference."

5. Refer to At Work with HRM 8.3 and Emerging Trends 8.1. Describe how you would build a comprehensive corporate wellness program. What factors would affect the success of your wellness program?

6. Refer to At Work with HRM 8.1. Describe the essential elements of a health and safety program.

DEVELOPING YOUR SKILLS

Canada Safety Council
www.safety-council.org

Canadian Centre for Occupational Health and Safety
www.ccohs.ca

Association of Workers' Compensation Boards of Canada
www.awcbc.org

1. Working in pairs, identify health and safety concerns at your school or workplace. Suggest ways in which these concerns could be addressed and outline how you would go about solving them. Share your responses with the rest of the class.

2. Working in small groups, address this scenario. One of your group members has recently joined the staff of a retail clothing store or a restaurant. On the person's first full shift your group member noticed a number of safety and health violations. Discuss the hazards, risks, and controls at the workplace. What advice would you give your classmate to deal with these violations and why?

3. Access the following Web sites or your provincial workers' compensation Web site.

   - **www.safety-council.org** (Canada Safety Council)
   - **www.ccohs.ca** (Canadian Centre for Occupational Health and Safety)
   - **www.awcbc.org** (Association of Workers' Compensation Boards of Canada)

   Identify three companies that have violated health and safety regulations in your province. Prepare a one-page summary describing the losses to the organizations in work (hours), the dollar penalties, and any other considerations such as family impact.

4. On your own, think about a situation where employees follow the safety rules when the supervisor is watching yet violate the rules when the supervisor is not watching. How would you motivate these employees to follow the rules when the supervisor isn't there? Now, in groups of four or five, develop a plan to improve safety under these conditions. Share your information with the rest of the class, and identify any common approaches.

5. You have been appointed to a task group to undertake a workplace violence audit and then develop appropriate procedures. Working in groups of four, consider what steps you could take to do the audit and what procedures you could adopt to minimize the possibility of workplace violence.

Case Study

Emergency Room Shutdown

On Saturday, February 30, 2012, Ciara Michaluk, the human resource manager at Stathcona Hospital, made a decision to shut down the hospital's emergency room. A second registered nurse had refused to work a 12-hour shift due to fears concerning the spread and infection of several communicable diseases. Patients had to be directed to another hospital, 260 km away. Michaluk had spent the last several hours fielding questions and concerns from hospital staff, the public, and government representatives about the hospital emergency room closure. Several additional health and safety concerns were brought to her attention, pointing to a larger problem.

Doctors and nurses were particularly concerned about the risk of patients contracting C. difficile virus as the incidents of infection had increased 300% in two years. There had been two recent needle-stick injuries: one involving a rushed emergency room cleaning staff person and the other, a practicum nursing student. These incidents posed both physical and emotional threats related to the hepatitis B virus, the hepatitis C virus, and HIV.

All emergency room staff, as well as paramedics and emergency social services staff, are concerned about the shortage of hospital beds and the makeshift system of creating an overflow ward in the hallways and cafeteria. Hallway beds don't have the safety equipment available, leading to mistakes and poor care. Extension cords run across the floors in order to reach an electrical outlet. Patients with acute problems are seen in chairs, and some are tucked way into corners where they cannot be observed. These stressful working conditions are having an adverse impact on emergency room health-care workers. It was felt that a serious employee or patient accident was bound to happen.

Source: Catherine Fitzgerald, Okanagan College, 2012.

Question

Michaluk has asked you, the health and safety advisor, to investigate and assess the root causes of these problems. You are also to outline the action steps that need to be taken to ensure a healthy and safe work environment.

Case Study

Patient Shot Staff with Pellet Gun

Kyle Jon was a Health and Safety advisor for East Coast Regional Health Services (ECRHS), which has more than 50 community care facilities. In addition to being responsible for the health, safety, and well-being of the health-care workers, he was a member of the violence prevention steering committee responsible for the 2013 online "Violence in Health Care" survey. A total of 11,791 health-care workers responded, representing more than two-thirds of the ECRHS workers and all the health-care facilities.

Survey results indicated that violence remains extremely prevalent in health care. Participants responded as outlined below:

- Seventy-four percent had experienced some kind of violence in their workplace.
- Types of violence experienced included swearing/verbal abuse (64%), threats of assault (32%), throwing/striking objects (70%), intimidating gestures (40%), spitting (27%), physical assault (18%), and use of weapon (11%).

- Sixty-two percent reported violence verbally; 38% reported violence in writing.
- Twenty-four percent accepted violence as part of the job.
- Eighty-one percent felt patient illness or delays in attending to patient needs contributed to violence.
- Fifty-three percent felt insufficient staffing contributed to violence.

What Jon found most troublesome was that the nurses, licensed practical nurses, and care aides in the community care facilities reported experiencing more violence than their colleagues at the hospitals and other health-care facilities. More than 70% of home care providers felt unsafe in their workplaces and did not perceive their workplace control measures as effective in protecting them against violence.

Last year, violence was the leading cause of injury to ECRHS home care workers, resulting in over 1,000 injuries. Investigations into these violent incidents frequently revealed that the patient who exhibited violent behaviour had a history, or a known risk, of violent behaviour that had not been communicated to workers by way of assessments, charts, and care plans.

Over the past two years there had been two incidents of violence by patients against staff at the Northern Rim residential care facility. One psychiatric patient was involved in firing a pellet gun that hit several employees, and another irritable and agitated patient had thrown a worker into a wall and then punched him repeatedly after being asked to return to his room.

Source: Catherine Fitzgerald, Okanagan College, 2012.

Question

What violence prevention efforts should be targeted to eliminate, reduce, and/or control violence at ECRHS community care facilities?

NOTES AND REFERENCES

1. *Workers' Compensation Board of British Columbia v. Moore*, Court of Appeal for British Columbia, 2011 BCSC 459, accessed March 15, 2012, www.worksafebc.com/news_room/resources/2011/ArrestWarrantBCEmployer.asp.
2. "Key Statistical Measures for 2010," Association of Workers' Compensation Boards of Canada; "Number of Fatalities, by Age and Jurisdiction, 2008–2010," Association of Workers' Compensation Boards of Canada; and "Number of Accepted Time-Loss Injuries, by Age and Jurisdiction, 2008–2010," Association of Workers' Compensation Boards of Canada, http://awcbc.org/en/nationalworkinjuriesstatisticsprogramnwisp.asp (all accessed March 15, 2012).
3. "Your Health and Safety Rights and Responsibilities," Workplace Safety and Insurance Board, accessed March 15, 2012, www.wsib.on.ca/en/community/WSIB/230/ArticleDetail/24338?vgnextoid=6c44e35c819d7210VgnVCM100000449c710aRCRD.
4. "Workers Compensation Act (British Columbia)," accessed March 25, 2012, www2.worksafebc.com/Publications/OHSRegulation/WorkersCompensationAct.asp#SectionNumber:Part3Division4.
5. "Increased Fines under Workplace Safety and Health Act," Workers Compensation Board of Manitoba, accessed March 15, 2012, http://safemanitoba.com/increased_fines_under_workplace_safety_and_health_act.aspx.
6. "The Province of Saskatchewan Proposes Increasing Penalty Amounts to $1.5M," *Canadian OH&S News*, January 10, 2012, http://www.ohscanada.com/news/sask-proposes-increasing-penalty-amounts-to-1-5m/1000812373.
7. Canada Labour Code Part II-Overview, *Canada Labour Code*, accessed March 15, 2012, www.hrsdc.gc.ca/eng/labour/health_safety/overview.shtml.
8. Karla Thorpe and Louise Chénier, *Building Mentally Healthy Workplaces: Perspectives of Canadian Workers and Front-Line Managers*, Ottawa: The Conference Board of Canada, June 2011.
9. "Key Statistical Measures for 2010," Association of Workers' Compensation Boards of Canada.
10. "Moore Wins 2011 OGCA Doug Chalmers Award," *Daily Commercial News*, September 26, 2011.
11. "Educating Future Energy Professionals," Hydro One, accessed March 15, 2012, www.hydroone.com/Our Commitment/Safety/Pages/Default.aspx.

12. "2012 Health & Safety Policy," Ontario Power Generation, accessed March 15, 2012, www.opg.com/safety/nsafe/.

13. "Basic OH & S Program Elements," Canadian Centre for Occupational Health and Safety, accessed March 15, 2012, www.ccohs.ca/oshanswers/hsprograms/basic.html.

14. "Apprenticeship Programs," WorkSafeBC, accessed March 15, 2012, www2.worksafebc.com/Topics/Apprenticeships/Home.asp.

15. George L. Morfitt, *Safety and BC Ferries: A Follow-up Review of the 2007 Report on Operational Safety at British Columbia Ferry Services Inc.*, January 2012, www.bcferries.com/about/More_Information.html.

16. "The Last Resort: Reporting on Recent Convictions under the Occupational Health and Safety Act," *Occupational Health and Safety*, WorkSafe Alberta, January 2012.

17. "Boost Health and Productivity with a Wellness Program," *Benefits Canada*, August 25, 2011, www.benefitscanada.com/benefits/health-wellness/boost-employee-health-and-productivity-with-a-wellness-program-19628.

18. Towers Watson, *Pathway to Health and Productivity, 2011/2012 Staying@Work Survey Report*, December 2011, www.towerswatson.com/united-states/research/6031.

19. Kevin Kelloway and Lori Francis, *Management of Health and Safety*, 5th ed. (Toronto: Nelson Education, 2011).

20. "Canadians Not Letting Go of Work on Holiday," *The Canadian HR Reporter*, November 30, 2011, www.hrreporter.com/articleview/11825-canadians-not-letting-go-of-work-on-holiday.

21. "Step Away from That BlackBerry," *Canadian HR Reporter*, accessed March 15, 2012, www.hrreporter.com/blog/editor/archive/2012/01/17/step-away-from-that-blackberry.

22. Health Canada, "Safety of Cell Phones and Cell Phone Towers," *It's Your Health*, October 2011, www.hc-sc.gc.ca/hl-vs/iyh-vsv/prod/cell-eng.php.

23. "NIOSH Releases Fact Sheet on Preventing Musculoskeletal Disorders," *Occupational Health and Safety*, February 15, 2012, http://ohsonline.com/articles/2012/02/15/niosh-releases-fact-sheet-on-preventing-musculoskeletal-disorders.aspx.

24. "Prevent Musculoskeletal Disorders (MSD)," WSIB Ontario, accessed March 15, 2012, www.wsib.on.ca/wsib/wsibsite.nsf/Public/PreventMSD.

25. "What You Should Know about a Flu Pandemic," Ministry Programs, Ontario Ministry of Health and Long Term Care, accessed March 15, 2012, www.health.gov.on.ca/en/public/programs/emu/pan_flu.

26. "The Right to Refuse Dangerous Work," *Canada Labour Code*, accessed March 15, 2012, www.hrsdc.gc.ca/eng/labour/publications/health_safety/refuse/page00.shtml.

27. Lisa Hughes and Bjorn Rutten, "Managing the Risks of Workplace Violence and Harassment," Ottawa: The Conference Board of Canada, October 2010.

28. Canadian Centre for Occupational Health and Safety, accessed March 15, 2012, www.ccohs.ca.

29. Ontario, Ministry of Labour, Occupational Health and Safety Branch, "Introduction to *Safe at Work Ontario* Sector Plans, 2011–2012," *Safe at Work Ontario*, June 2011, accessed March 15, 2012, www.labour.gov.on.ca/english/hs/pdf/sp_11intro.pdf.

30. "The Last Resort: Reporting on Recent Convictions under the Occupational Health and Safety Act," *Occupational Health and Safety*, WorkSafe Alberta, January 2012.

31. "Take Care: How to Implement and Develop a Violence Prevention Program," *WorkSafe BC, Violence Prevention*, accessed March 15, 2012, www2.worksafebc.com/Topics/Violence/Home.asp.

32. Canadian Centre for Occupational Health and Safety, accessed March 15, 2012, www.ccohs.ca.

33. Kelloway and Francis, Management of Health and Safety.

34. Carla Wilson, "Vancouver Island Health Authority Fined $97,500 over Violent Attacks on Staff," *Post Media News*, February 29, 2012, www.canada.com/Vancouver+Island+Health+Authority+fined+over+violent+attacks+staff/6230105/story.html.

35. Kelloway and Francis, *Management of Health and Safety*.

36. Susan Crompton, "What's Stressing the Stressed? Main Sources of Stress among Workers," *Canadian Social Trends* (Statistics Canada Catalogue no. 11-008-X), October 13, 2011.

37. Crompton, "What's Stressing the Stressed?"

38. Towers Watson, *Pathway to Health and Productivity*.

39. Thorpe and Chénier, *Building Mentally Healthy Workplaces*.

40. Martin Shain and Mary Ann Baynton, *Preventing Workplace Meltdown: An Employer's Guide to Maintaining a Psychologically Safe Workplace,* Toronto: Carswell, 2011.

41. Bill 14—2011: *Workers Compensation Amendment Act, 2011, Legislative Assembly British Columbia*, accessed March 15, 2012, www.leg.bc.ca/39th4th/1st_read/gov14-1.htm.

42. B.C. Ministry of Labour, Citizens' Services, and Open Government, "Workers Compensation Act Expands Mental Stress Coverage," news release, November 3, 2011, www.bcpffa.org/docs/BC%20Govt%20Media%20Release_Backgrounders%20for%20WC%20Act%20to%20recognize%20Mental%20Stress.pdf.

43. Mental Health Commission of Canada, "Psychological Health and Safety Standard for Canadian Workplaces," news release, June 16, 2011.

44. World Health Organization, "Mental Health: Strengthening Our Response," Fact Sheet no. 220, September 2010, accessed March 15, 2012, www.who.int/mediacentre/factsheets/fs220/en/index.html.

45. Towers Watson, *Pathway to Health and Productivity*.

46. Ibid.

47. Ibid.

48. Ibid.

49. Graham Lowe, *Creating Healthy Organizations*, Rotman/UTP Publishing, 2010.

50. Sun Life Assurance Company of Canada, *2011 Buffett National Wellness Survey*, 2011, accessed March 15, 2012, www.sunlife.ca/canada/v/index.jsp?vgnextoid=e1a651efcefdf210VgnVCM10000047d2d09fRCRD&appInstanceName=default.

51. Ibid.

52. Towers Watson, *Pathway to Health and Productivity*.

53. Lowe, *Creating Healthy Organizations*.

54. "Sun Life Canadian Health Index: 2011 Canadian Health Index Report."

55. Ibid.

56. Ibid.

57. "Business Case for Active Living at Work," Public Health Agency of Canada, accessed March 15, 2012, www.phac-aspc.gc.ca/alw-vat/execsum-resumexec-eng.php#a6.

58. Ibid.

59. Ibid.

60. Katherine Baicker, David Cutler, and Zirui Song, "Workplace Wellness Programs Can Generate Savings," [Harvard University] *Health Affairs*, February 2010, accessed March 15, 2012, http://content.healthaffairs.org/content/29/2/304.abstract.

61. "Disability Case Management," BC Public Service, accessed March 15, 2012, www.bcpublicservice.ca/dismgmt.

62. Thorpe and Chénier, *Building Mentally Healthy Workplaces*.

63. Ibid.

64. "Treat Depression to Boost Productivity," *Benefits Canada*, January 11, 2012, www.benefitscanada.com/benefits/health-wellness/treat-depression-to-boost-productivity-24333.

65. Thorpe and Chénier, *Building Mentally Healthy Workplaces*.

66. Ibid.

67. Towers Watson, *Pathway to Health and Productivity*.

68. Ibid.

69. Canadian Centre on Substance Abuse, *The Costs of Substance Abuse in Canada,* Ottawa: Canadian Centre on Substance Abuse, accessed March 12, 2012, www.ccsa.ca/Eng/Priorities/Research/CostStudy/Pages/default.asx.

9

MANAGEMENT RIGHTS, EMPLOYEE RIGHTS, AND DISCIPLINE

OUTCOMES

After studying this chapter, you should be able to

1 Describe statutory rights, contractual rights, due process, and legal implications of those rights.

2 Identify the job expectancy rights of employees.

3 Explain the process of establishing disciplinary practices, including the proper implementation of organizational rules.

4 Discuss the meaning of discipline and how to investigate a disciplinary problem.

5 Outline the differences between progressive and positive discipline.

6 Identify the different types of alternative dispute-resolution procedures.

7 Discuss the role of ethics in the management of human resources.

OUTLINE

HRM CLOSE-UP

"I'm fair to a point of not asking my staff to do anything I wouldn't do myself."

Emily Donahue, owner, Pure Esthetics.

As the owner of an aesthetics salon in the small town of Saint Andrews, New Brunswick, Emily Donahue's staff perform a full range of aesthetics such as manicures, pedicures, facials, and massage therapy. In this type of business, cleanliness and sanitation standards are of utmost importance. For a small business owner, this means that employees not only have their manager's rules to follow, but also the rules of the governing body: the Cosmetology Association.

"The Association inspects salons regularly and could send in a secret shopper at any time," said Donahue, owner of Pure Esthetics, "so it's key that I make sure procedures are followed." Staff, once certified, must register and renew with the Association annually, which helps them stay focused and attentive to industry practices and procedures.

Donahue refers to her management style as "firm but fair as well. I'm fair to a point of not asking my staff to do anything I wouldn't do myself." That includes rules such as hours of work, where Donahue and her team of professionals cater to the needs of the client as much as possible. "If someone wants an appointment at seven and our hours are posted till five, we will stay open for them," said Donahue. Offering this kind of flexibility certainly requires specific understanding between manager and employee, and is covered in the contracts she has with each of her staff.

In terms of employee discipline, Donahue feels lucky that she doesn't have to discipline staff very often. When she does, she typically asks them what they would do in the situation. "I ask them if they were in my shoes, what would they do?" She feels this approach helps staff to think through issues and gives them the power to help solve a problem. "I also get them to tell their side of the story," explained Donahue, "and then afterwards, I always finish with the good work they have done and how very glad I am that they work for me."

"I think if you are honest with them and you are a good manager, the situation won't turn into a finger-pointing one," commented Donahue. "But if you are dealing with someone who always needs to be talked to, they can poison the work environment for the other staff members." Getting a handle on issues quickly is paramount, and Donahue ensures she

steps up, has a discussion, gives a warning, and communicates the consequences clearly. Then if the problem persists, "you need to follow through with what you said would happen," explained Donahue.

Donahue once had an issue with an employee who came to work smelling of liquor. The employee would try to do her job but couldn't, and Donahue would send her home. A pattern developed, where the employee would come to work "dressed and ready to work but not mentally alert enough to do her job properly, and fully expecting to be sent home." Donahue spoke to the employee a number of times, each time the employee promising that she would not let the problem happen again. Recognizing her own actions as part of the problem, Donahue decided **not** to send the employee home when the pattern repeated next. By the end of the workday, the employee apologized for the times she had come in with a hangover, "and she never came to work like that again!"

Even though staff can be very good at their jobs and a manager may be hesitant to address a problem, Donahue is sensitive to the message it sends to other employees if she does not address an issue. "I try not to be too lenient and always want to be fair," she said. "At the same time, I'm aware of what other employees are seeing."

Asked what she enjoys most about being a people manager, even when she has to deal with the occasional downside, Donahue responded, "I know my staff left other more stable positions to come and work for me. They tell me that they couldn't imagine working for anyone else."

And for a manager in the business of wellness, that's a pretty good feeling to have.

Courtesy of Emily Donahue

INTRODUCTION

In this chapter, employee rights, management rights, workplace privacy, and employee discipline are discussed. Managers note that these topics have a major influence on the activities of both employees and supervisors. Managers are discovering that the right to discipline and discharge employees—a traditional responsibility of management—is more difficult to exercise in light of the growing attention to employee rights. In addition, disciplining employees is a difficult and unpleasant task for most managers and supervisors; many of them report that taking disciplinary action against an employee is the most stressful duty they perform. Balancing employee rights and employee discipline may not be easy, but it is a universal requirement and a critical aspect of good management. As Emily Donahue expressed in the HRM Close-up, the role of the supervisor is to help employees understand their rights as well as the company's expectations.

Because the growth of employee rights issues may lead to an increase in the number of lawsuits filed by employees, this chapter includes a discussion of alternative dispute resolution as a way to foster a less legalistic approach to solving disagreements. As managers are the people who take disciplinary actions that are subject to challenge and possible reversal through governmental agencies or the courts, managers should make a positive effort to prevent the need for such action. Further, managers often avoid difficult performance reviews and thus may create a situation where disciplinary action is considered. When disciplinary action becomes impossible to avoid, however, that action should be taken in accordance with carefully developed HR policies and practices. Since ethics is an important element of good managerial practice, this chapter concludes with a discussion of organizational ethics in employee relations. Most of this chapter applies to both non-unionized and unionized workplaces. Where a concept applies only to a non-union workplace, this will be identified.

MANAGEMENT RIGHTS AND RESPONSIBILITIES

All companies have people, usually called "managers," who make fundamental decisions such as how the business is run or how much the company should charge for its products or services. In making these decisions, they have both rights and responsibilities. One of the more basic rights is that the company can hire or terminate whomever it wants.

However, as discussed in both this chapter and in Chapter 10, those rights now have to be exercised in certain ways, and managers have increased responsibilities in how those rights are exercised. Managers function as the representative of the organization and therefore have the legal responsibilities and liabilities that go with the managerial role.

One illustration of this is "negligent hiring." Negligent hiring refers to a situation where a person is hired and then involved in job-related misconduct that could have been determined if the person's previous work background and behaviours were referenced.[1] While any claim would be against the employer, the action (or lack of action) of the manager creates the situation. Think about a situation in a long-term residential care facility where a resident is physically assaulted by an employee who has a long (and verifiable) history of physical violence. Negligent hiring would occur if the manager did not do a thorough enough background check to identify the history or did and still hired the person.

In addition, supervisors and managers are expected to behave and act in ways that acknowledge that employees also have certain rights. Managers are no longer able to make decisions or take actions without being aware of their obligations as to how an employee must be treated in today's workplace.

EMPLOYEE RIGHTS

Various human rights laws, wage and hour regulations, and safety and health legislation have secured basic employee rights and brought numerous job improvements to the workplace. Now employee rights litigation has shifted to such workplace issues as employees' rights to protest unfair disciplinary action, to refuse to take drug tests, to have access to their personnel files, to challenge employer searches and surveillance, and to whether employers use social media activity to gather information about potential employees.[2] All these things make it very important that managers act and behave in fair and objective ways.

The current emphasis on employee rights is a natural result of the evolution of societal, business, and employee interests. The term **employee rights** refers to the expectation of fair treatment from employers in the employment relationship. These expectations become rights when they are granted to employees by the courts, legislatures, or employers. Employee rights frequently involve an employer's alleged invasion of an employee's right to privacy. Unfortunately, the difference between an employee's legal right to privacy and the moral or personal right to privacy is not always clear. The confusion is due to the lack of a comprehensive and consistent body of privacy protection, whether from laws or from court decisions.

There can be a perceived invasion of privacy when the employer uses electronic monitoring or surveillance to observe or monitor employees while they are doing their work. Although such action is not illegal, employers are well advised to let employees know when and why they are doing it. For example, companies that have a call-centre operation frequently will use electronic means to monitor customer calls. However, employees are provided full information about the purpose and, in some situations, given guarantees that the data will be used only to help the employees learn and improve their customer-service skills.

Balanced against employee rights is the employer's responsibility to provide a safe workplace for employees while guaranteeing safe, high-quality goods and services to consumers. An employee who uses drugs may exercise a privacy right and refuse to submit to a drug test. But should that employee produce a faulty product as a result of drug impairment, the employer can be held liable for any harm caused by that product. Employers must therefore exercise *reasonable care* in the hiring, training, and assignment of employees to jobs. As mentioned earlier, without the exercise of reasonable care, employers can be held negligent by outside parties or other employees injured by a dishonest, unfit, or violent employee.[3] In law, **negligence** is the failure to use a reasonable amount of care where such failure results in injury to another person. Several years ago, the federal government established occupational health and safety negligence as a criminal offence. In late 2011, an employer in Quebec was found guilty of criminal negligence causing death in a workplace accident.[4]

It is here that employee rights and employer responsibilities can come most pointedly into conflict. The failure of an employer to honour employee rights can result in costly lawsuits, damage the organization's reputation, and hurt employee morale. But failure to protect the safety and welfare of employees or consumer interests can invite litigation from both groups. At Work with HRM 9.1 discusses the practical implications for managers of the balance between employee rights and employer responsibilities. The remainder of this section will discuss various rights that employees have come to expect from their employers.

Employment Protection Rights

It is not surprising that employees should regard their jobs as an established right—a right that should not be taken away lightly. Without the opportunity to hold a job, personal well-being would be greatly curtailed. This line of reasoning has led to the emergence of three legal considerations regarding the security of one's job: statutory rights, contractual rights, and due process.

Statutory Rights

Statutory rights are rights that derive from legislation. As we saw in Chapter 2, human rights legislation protects employees from discrimination on the basis of such grounds as age, sex, and race.

For example, a case involving two airline pilots with Air Canada was heard by the Canadian Human Rights Tribunal. The complaint revolved around the mandatory retirement at age 60 provision. The two pilots stated that this was age discrimination and, therefore, they ought to be allowed to not retire. Air Canada had maintained age 60 for

---

Employee rights
Expectations of fair treatment from employers

Negligence
Failure to provide reasonable care where such failure results in injury to consumers or other employees

Statutory rights
Rights that derive from legislation

Outcome 1

What are the various rights and legal implications?

AT WORK **with HRM 9.1**

EMPLOYEE RIGHTS LITIGATION

For a number of years, two court cases[5] demonstrated the special recognition to the employer–employee relationship given through decisions of the Supreme Court of Canada. These decisions focused on the fair and individual treatment of each person. This meant that managers should pay greater attention to individual employees before, during, and at the end of employment.

One of the cases, *Wallace v. United Grain Growers*, pointed to the need for employers to pay more attention to the way in which people are terminated. Besides compensation for lack of notice, employees were seeking damages if they felt they were poorly treated during the actual termination. This perspective meant that the manager's behaviour during the process could have a bearing on how much the termination would cost the employer.

However, a significant case decided by the Supreme Court in mid-2008 changed this approach. In *Honda Canada Inc. v. Keays*, the Court determined that earlier decisions had been inappropriate. In lower court decisions, the employee had been awarded $100,000 in punitive damages for the manner in which Honda conducted itself in the termination. The employee had been diagnosed with chronic fatigue syndrome, resulting in his eventually being placed in Honda's disability program. That program required employees to provide Honda with medical information from a physician that absences were due to the medical condition. What the employee's physician provided was insufficient, so Honda requested that the employee meet with an occupational medical specialist. The employee refused.

Honda then terminated the employee. The employee sued for wrongful dismissal, stating that Honda had demonstrated bad faith. The Court disagreed, saying that the employee had not been treated poorly— either in terms of compensation or behaviour.

This case eliminated a number of principles established through the *Wallace* case. The most significant was that employees were not entitled to additional severance or punitive damages, only to receive compensation for "actual" damages—i.e., loss of wages. But the case maintained that employers must act in good faith when dismissing employees, and the employees must be treated respectfully.

In a recent Saskatchewan court decision, the judge concluded that Capital Pontiac Buick Cadillac GMC Ltd. failed to meet its obligations when it terminated an employee. Specifically, Capital Pontiac acted harshly and vindictively when it wrongly dismissed the person. The damage suffered by the employee was as a result of false accusations of fraudulent conduct. The judge went on to say, "I am of the view that Mr. Coppola is entitled to a substantial award for aggravated damages for mental distress caused by the false allegation…. I have decided that a reasonable award for aggravated damages in this case is $20,000."

CRITICAL THINKING QUESTIONS:

1. Do you believe that employees have too many rights? Why or why not?
2. What would you have decided in these cases and why?

Sources: Adapted from Stuart Rudner, "The latest word on the 'damages formerly known as Wallace,'" *Canadian HR Reporter*, September 26, 2011, www.hrreporter.com/blog/Canadian-HR-Law/archive/2011/09/26/the-latest-word-on-the-damages-formerly-known-as-iwallacei (accessed February 5, 2012); *Coppola v Capital Pontiac Buick Cadillac GMC Ltd.*, August 31, 2011, 2011 SKQB 318.

many years as a bona fide occupational requirement. Earlier age discrimination cases had resulted in Air Canada being allowed to continue with its practice. This case was no different: the complaint was dismissed, and Air Canada did retire the pilots.[6] Nonetheless, in early 2012, Air Canada announced that it was abandoning this requirement. Air Canada said it was doing this as part of the requirement for federally regulated companies to eliminate mandatory retirement.[7] Such a change means that age discrimination is no longer a valid complaint for Air Canada pilots.

Provincial employment standards acts establish basic rights for such things as overtime pay and minimum vacation pay. However, these laws were developed at a time when use of technology, such as e-mail and smartphones, was not blurring work and personal life. Not being aware of the requirements for overtime pay has created issues for large organizations such as CIBC and Bank of Montreal.[8] Specifically, one of the more interesting cases dealing with statutory rights are the various class-action suits against CIBC and Scotiabank in relation to unpaid overtime. Employees at retail branches who thought they were eligible for overtime pay initiated these lawsuits. The focus of the lawsuits revolves around whether any of the employees were considered exempt from overtime provisions. Specifically, "overtime" refers to employees. People in certain occupations, such as accountants and engineers, are exempt. Likewise, positions such as manager are exempt. So, if a person isn't a manager or in a profession, then the person is entitled to overtime. For many years, though, organizations have considered employees who are paid a salary exempt from overtime; however, according to the law, this thinking is not correct. While the CIBC class action suit was dismissed, the Scotiabank case was "certified." In other words, that case can proceed to trial with a claim that seeks $250 million in damages.[9]

The problem is not just with overtime pay. A common complaint is in relation to employees not receiving vacation pay on incentive compensation.[10] Think about the materials in Chapter 7 on incentive plans and the number of organizations that have or are thinking of implementing such plans to motivate and reward key staff. Not knowing the impact of such plans on the provincial employment standards can result in liabilities for the employers.

Occupational health and safety legislation aims to ensure safe and healthy working conditions while labour relations laws (discussed in Chapter 10) give employees the right to form and belong to unions, and to bargain for better working conditions. All these laws are statutory and grant certain rights to people.

Contractual Rights

Contractual rights
Rights that derive from contracts

While law establishes statutory rights, **contractual rights** are derived from contracts. A *contract* is a legally binding agreement; if one party breaches the contract, a remedy can be sought through an appeal to the courts. Although formal contracts between employers and full-time employees are rare, they are standard practice when it comes to contingent workers, a growing segment of the Canadian labour force. Such a contract, referred to as the "employment contract," will contain such items as the type of work, length of work, the amount of pay for the work, including any benefits, and whether or not there is any obligation on the employer if the employee is terminated.

Not all contracts are written. An implied contract can occur when an employer extends to an employee a promise of some form of job security. Implied contractual rights can be based on either oral or written statements made during the pre-employment process or subsequent to hiring. Promises of job security are sometimes contained in employee handbooks, HR manuals, or employment applications. Whether explicit or implicit, promises of job security are generally ruled by the courts to be binding. A recent case of an employee's contractual rights revolved around an employer's attempt to order an employee to hide a tattoo on the employee's shoulders. The case involved a daycare worker in Quebec who had a dragon tattoo on the shoulder. The employer had not allowed the employee to show the tattoo while at work. This issue went on for five years until a judge in the Quebec Superior Court ruled that forcing the cover-up violated the employee's rights.[11]

The following are circumstances in which an implied contract may become binding:

- telling employees their jobs are secure as long as they perform satisfactorily and are loyal to the organization
- stating in the employee handbook that employees will not be terminated without the right of defence or access to an appeal procedure (i.e., due process)
- urging an employee to leave another organization by promising higher wages and benefits, and then reneging after the person has been hired

To lessen their vulnerability to implied-contract lawsuits, employers can do the following:

1. Train supervisors and managers not to imply contract benefits in conversations with new or current employees.
2. Include in employment offers a statement that an employee may voluntarily terminate employment with proper notice, and the employee may be dismissed by the employer at any time and for a justified reason (just cause). The language in this statement must be appropriate, clear, and easily understood while conveying a tone of welcome to the company.
3. Explain the nature of the employment relationship in documents—for example, employee handbooks, employment applications, and letters of employment.
4. Have written proof that employees have read all documents pertaining to the employment relationship. This proof can be in the form of an offer-of-employment letter that the person signs or another type of sign-off document.

It is important that in a contractual situation, employees also have obligations and responsibilities. For example, the federal Department of Citizenship and Immigration terminated an employee with 27 years of service for spending more than half of his working day trolling the Internet, including news and sports Web sites, and downloading more than 300 pornographic photos. The employee was charged with "time theft," and the federal government hoped that the termination would set an example for other employees who wasted time online. However, it didn't quite work out the way the government wanted. The employee claimed that he was bored, didn't have enough work to do, and had repeatedly informed his supervisor. The adjudicator ruled that while the employee had violated federal employment policies by downloading porn, the employee had not committed "time theft." The employee was given back his job.[12]

Due Process

Due process
Employee's right to a fair process in making a decision related to employment relationship

Management has traditionally had the right to direct employees and to take corrective action when needed. Nevertheless, many individuals also believe that a job is the property right of an employee and that the loss of employment has such serious consequences that an employee should not lose employment without the protection of due process. Managers normally define **due process** as the employee's right to a fair treatment in the handling of an employment matter.[13] However, proactive employers will additionally incorporate the following principles—or rights—in their interpretation of due process:

1. The right to know job expectations and the consequences of not fulfilling those expectations.
2. The right to consistent and predictable management action for the violation of rules.
3. The right to fair discipline based on facts, the right to question those facts, and the right to present a defence.
4. The right to appeal disciplinary action.
5. The right to progressive discipline—to be informed about an incident and be given a chance to improve.

Employment Rights Not a Guarantee

It should be understood that although employees might have cause to regard their jobs as an established right, there is no legal protection affording employees a permanent or continuous job. Furthermore, in general, the concept of due process does not guarantee employees any assurance of employment. However, the concepts of due process and of job as a right do obligate management to act in a consistent and fair manner.

Employees *do* have the right to expect sound employment practices and to be treated respectfully as individuals. In Canada, in absence of a formal contract specifying the duration of employment, the employment relationship can be construed as ongoing. While employment is not considered necessarily to be permanent, the employer must provide reasonable notice and grounds for termination. Thus, Canada functions under statutory and common (contract) law.[14]

Job Expectancy Rights

Outcome 2

What are the job expectancy rights of employees?

Canadian Centre on Substance Abuse

www.ccsa.ca

Once hired, employees expect certain rights associated with fair and equitable employment. Employee rights on the job include those regarding substance abuse and drug testing, privacy, plant closing notification, and just-cause disciplinary and discharge procedures.

Substance Abuse and Drug Testing

In Canada, the social costs of substance abuse, including lost productivity, as well as the health-care costs, have been estimated at more than $39 billion.[15] Most human rights legislation considers substance abuse as a disability and therefore needs to be accommodated.[16]

According to a recent survey by Statistics Canada, 25% of men and 10% of women aged 19 to 70 reported consuming more than five alcoholic drinks per occasion at least 12 times a year.[17] The trend in the general population continues to find daily and heavy drinking significantly higher for males than for females, highest marijuana use levels in the 18 to 39 age group, and approximately twice as many males as marijuana users as females. Since illicit drugs are available and increasingly available in high quality throughout Canada, studies are finding cannabis use is up among Canadian adults. Recent student surveys in Ontario find use patterns increasing for most drug categories. Various studies have indicated that alcohol and other drug use (both prescription and non-prescription) contribute to issues of job performance, work productivity, absenteeism, increased workplace accidents, and problems with interpersonal relationships.[18]

As mentioned earlier in this chapter, the failure of an employer to ensure a safe and drug-free workplace can result in astronomical liability claims when consumers are injured because of a negligent employee or faulty product. Because of this, Canadian companies are ensuring that they have policies and programs on alcohol and other drugs.[19] Although the Canadian government has not introduced legislation on drug testing, such legislation exists south of the border. Companies with drug-testing policies report reductions in absenteeism, sick days, and accidents. Some of the issues surrounding drug testing are discussed in At Work with HRM 9.2.

Employee Searches and Electronic Monitoring

Consider these practices:

- General Electric employs tiny fish-eye lenses installed behind pinholes in walls and ceilings to observe employees suspected of crimes.
- DuPont uses long-distance cameras to monitor its loading docks.
- An Alberta IDA drugstore requires cashiers to place their fingers on a pad that scans their fingerprints and allows them access to the cashiering system.

While these examples may seem a violation of privacy rights, it is not uncommon for employers to monitor employee conduct through surveillance techniques. Most retailers use some form of monitoring, and almost all of us have made a phone call where we are informed that our call might be monitored.

Employees have no reasonable expectation of privacy in places where work rules that provide for inspections have been put into effect. They must comply with probable-cause searches by employers. And they can be appropriately disciplined, normally for insubordination, for refusing to comply with search requests. It is advisable that employers inform new employees through either the final employment interview or an orientation session that mandatory or random searches are done. See Figure 9.1 for the tools and techniques for monitoring employees.

WHEN ARE THERE PROBLEMS WITH DRUG AND ALCOHOL POLICIES?

Many employers express concern about the impact of an employee being impaired at work. The concerns range from loss of productivity to safety for customers and employees. While legislation exists in the United States to allow random and regular drug testing, no legislation in Canada allows this. Further, since most human rights tribunals see drug or alcohol abuse as a disability, any testing for these substances can be a form of discrimination or a challenge on the rights to privacy.

So, what can employers do? Some recent cases across Canada will help shed some light.

Irving Pulp & Paper implemented a random drug and alcohol testing policy for safety-sensitive positions. In the application of the policy, a millwright, claiming that his religion forbade him from drinking, felt that such a test was unreasonable. The union grieved the policy, and the arbitration panel determined that the policy was unreasonable. Irving appealed the decision, and the New Brunswick Court of Queen's Bench agreed with the employer and overturned the arbitration decision. The court found that it was reasonable to do random testing on safety-sensitive positions.

In another case, Rio Tinto, at its aluminum smelter in B.C., had a substance abuse policy that required employees to have a medical exam if a supervisor removed the employee from the worksite due to suspected impairment. The union grieved the policy, stating that the medical exam was done without the employee's consent and that if the employee refused, the person was subject to discipline. The arbitrator determined that while the overall policy was appropriate, requiring a medical examination was not.

More recently, the Toronto Transit Commission (TTC) instituted a random drug and alcohol testing policy after a fatal bus accident. The accident investigation concluded that the driver had drugs in his possession at the time. The union representing the driver is challenging the policy saying that the TTC has no legal right to intrude in a person's life outside of work and that such random testing could identify a substance used outside of work.

CRITICAL THINKING QUESTIONS:

1. Do you think employers ought to have the right to test for drug or alcohol use? Why or why not?
2. How would you feel if your employer did random drug and alcohol tests? Explain your answer.

Sources: Irving Pulp & Paper Limited and Communications, Energy and Paperworkers Union of Canada, Local 30, and Queen's Court, New Brunswick, September 17, 2010, NBQB 294 (CanLII); Jeffrey R. Smith, "No Need for History of Workplace Accidents for Random Drug and Alcohol Testing: Court," *Canadian HR Reporter*, December 13, 2010, accessed February 2, 2012, www.hrreporter.com/articleview/8666-no-need-for-history-of-workplace-accidents-for-random-drug-and-alcohol-testing-court-legal-view; Jeffrey R. Smith, "Right Idea, Wrong Application for Drug, Alcohol Policy," *Canadian HR Reporter*, August 15, 2011, www.hrreporter.com/articleview/11001-right-idea-wrong-application-for-drug-alcohol-policy-legal-view; and David Whitten, "Deconstructing Random Drug, Alcohol Testing," *Canadian HR Reporter*, November 21, 2011, www.hrreporter.com/articleprint.aspx?articleid=11775.

Managers must be diligent when conducting employee searches. Improper searches can lead to employee complaints under various privacy legislation (see Chapter 2) and possible lawsuits claiming defamation of character and negligent infliction of emotional distress.

It is not uncommon for employers to monitor the conduct of employees through surveillance techniques. One of the most common means of electronic surveillance by employers is telephone surveillance to ensure that customer requests are handled properly or to prevent theft.

With the *Personal Information Protection and Electronic Documents Act* (PIPEDA), there is an expectation that employers are reasonable in their use of any type of surveillance technique. For example, a recent arbitration case in Quebec determined that while the employer, a public transit authority, had the to install video cameras around its workplace, it also determined that some cameras were an invasion. Specifically, the cameras outside its premises were used to monitor trespassing and tracking the bus fleet. However, the panel determined that the indoor cameras had no purpose as the employer did not have any concern about employee theft. The use of these cameras was an invasion, and the

FIGURE 9.1 Tools and Techniques for Monitoring Employees

Performance	Output, keystrokes, telephone call content
	Use of resources
	Communications content: e-mail and Web
	Location: cards, pages CCTV, GPS, RFID
	Covert: mystery shoppers, counter employee theft
Behaviours	Communications content: e-mail and Web
	Location: cards, pages CCTV, GPS, RFID
	Covert: mystery shoppers, counter employee theft
	Psychometric, testing, drug testing, biometrics
	Lie detector tests
Personal characteristics	Covert: mystery shoppers, counter employee theft
	Psychometric, testing, drug testing, biometrics
	Lie detector tests
	Predisposition to health risk, genetic testing
	Data mining; headhunting; e-recruitment

Source: Adapted from Kirstie Ball, "Workplace surveillance: an overview," *Labor History*, Vol. 51, No. 1, February 2010: 87–106. Copyright © 2010 Routledge.

panel ordered that they be removed.[20] When an employer is considering using surveillance, it is suggested that the following "best practices" be used.[21]

1. Establish, communicate, and enforce written policies.
2. Have policies that clearly identify what types of uses are either permitted or prohibited.
3. Communicate the consequences for failing to abide by the policy.
4. If an employee is suspected of misconduct, confront the employee before undertaking an extensive investigation; the employee may be deterred from future misconduct.

Video monitoring is frequently used in retail operations.

UpperCut Images/Getty Images

Employers have the right to monitor employees and to disclose certain information to another agency. Specifically, the Alberta Information and Privacy Commissioner determined that an employer was able to provide information to the RCMP to minimize danger to the health or safety of a person.[22] As technology continues to change, privacy commissioners are requested to examine the appropriateness of the technology. Recently, the Canadian Privacy Commissioner was asked to consider whether cloud computing could be a breach of an employee's privacy. The commissioner noted that as technology changed, there needed to be a balance between business needs and privacy rights.[23] Ethics in HRM 9.1 highlights some of these issues.

ETHICS in HRM 9.1

CAN MONITORING AN EMPLOYEE BECOME AN INVASION OF PRIVACY?

Many employers use a variety of electronic surveillance techniques to monitor employee activities in the workplace—everything from attendance reporting to controlling employee access to certain areas of work. Organizations with off-site assets use GPS (global positioning systems) to monitor the use of company vehicles or use video cameras to monitor employees on extended sick leave. There is the monitoring of a person's profile on any of the social networking Web sites such as Facebook or LinkedIn, too. But when does this become an invasion of one's privacy? The answer is usually "it all depends."

The Greater Toronto Transit Authority (GTAA) fired a long-service employee for sick-leave fraud. In making the decision, the GTAA relied upon video surveillance that was used in observing another employee. The long-service employee had been off work due to knee surgery and was seen driving to the physio, reaching high, and standing on tiptoes. When the GTAA asked for further medical information, the employee's doctor said with certain limitations, work could be resumed. However, after the first day, the employee was seen limping. The GTAA confronted the employee and disclosed the videotape. The employee maintained that there had been no wrongdoing and was terminated by the GTAA. The employee who had been with the GTAA for 23 years had an exemplary record. At arbitration, not only did the arbitrator rule against the GTAA, but it ruled that the GTAA had acted in bad faith in treating the employee the way it did. The result: The GTAA was ordered to pay $50,000 for mental distress and another $50,000 in damages.

In another arbitration, the ruling was different. A packaging operator at a food manufacturer in Ontario produced a doctor's certificate stating that the employee was unable to perform repetitive shoulder activities. The employer tried to accommodate the disability, but the nature of the work didn't allow modification and the company couldn't find any other work. The company ceased to find other work when the employee did not supply additional medical information, and the employee continued on paid sick leave. The company was suspicious, however, and began video surveillance. The videotaping showed the employee doing activities that didn't appear to have any physical restrictions. These included carrying groceries, picking up and carrying a child, and carrying a child's car seat. With these inconsistencies and the three discipline actions the employee had received in the last year, the company terminated the employee for serious misconduct. The arbitrator ruled not only that the video surveillance was acceptable but that the employee showed little understanding of the seriousness of the misconduct. The firing was upheld.

QUESTIONS:

1. Would you work differently if you knew that your performance was continually monitored?

2. Is it ethical for employers to monitor employees in this way? Why do you think that?

Sources: Adapted from Jeffrey R. Smith, "Airport Worker Receives Big Payout after Suffering False Accusation, Firing," *Canadian HR Reporter*, May 31, 2010, accessed February 8, 2012, www.hrreporter.com/articleview/7904-airport-worker-receives-big-payout-after-suffering-falseaccusation-firing-legal-view; Sheena Harrison, "Court Rules Video Can Be Used as Evidence to Discontinue Disability Benefits," *Workforce Management*, November 9, 2011, www.workforce.com/article/20111109/NEWS01/111109964/court-rules-video-can-be-used-as-evidenceto-discontinue-disability; and Jeffrey R. Smith, "Video of Injured Worker Shows Injury Not So Bad," *Canadian HR Reporter*, January 18, 2010, accessed February 8, 2012, www.hrreporter.com/articleview/7481-video-of-injured-worker-shows-injury-not-so-bad.

Access to Employee Files

The information kept in an employee's official employment record or employee file can have a significant impact—positive or negative—on career development. The personnel file, typically kept by the HR department, can contain performance reviews, salary information, investigatory reports, credit checks, criminal records, test scores, and family data.

In compliance with legislation, most employers give their employees access to their employment files. There is virtually no organization that is exempt from privacy legislation. PIPEDA also entitles employees to examine their own personnel file—including any information that is stored in an electronic format.

In addition, any personal information cannot be used or disclosed without the prior knowledge and consent of the employee. For example, if you are seeking a car loan and the company wants confirmation of your employment, only you can authorize release of that information from your employer. The most important legal principle with regard to data privacy is the concept of consent—ahead of time from the employee. Under PIPEDA, the person must be notified of the following before any information can be provided:

• that he or she is about to provide personal data
• the purposes for which the information is to be processed
• the people or bodies to whom the information might be disclosed
• the proposed transfer of information to other countries
• the security measures protecting the information

It is also important to remember that any medical information is not only personal but confidential. It is to be accessed only by authorized people on a need-to-know basis.[24]

It is also important to ensure that appropriate items reside in the employee file. For example, in its revised Employment Standards Code, Manitoba is allowing individual flextime agreements.

Employers and employees will be able to adjust daily hours to meet the needs of the employees and create a better work–life balance.[25] The employer will need to have the employee sign the agreement, and it will need to remain in the employee file until any changes occur. Employment professionals recommend that organizations develop a policy on employee files that includes, as a minimum, the points noted in Manager's Toolkit 9.1.

MANAGER'S TOOLKIT 9.1

POLICY GUIDELINES ON HANDLING PERSONNEL FILES

• Ensure compliance with legislation.
• Define exactly what information is to be kept in employee files.
• Ensure informed consent has been received from employees regarding types of information that will be collected and stored.
• Develop different categories of personnel information, depending on legal requirements and organizational needs.
• Specify where, when, how, and under what circumstances employees may review or copy their files.

• Ensure appropriate security measures are in place to safeguard information.
• Identify company individuals allowed to view personnel files.
• Prohibit the collection of information that could be viewed as discriminatory or could form the basis for an invasion-of-privacy suit.
• Audit employment records regularly to remove irrelevant, outdated, or inaccurate information.

Electronic Privacy

The benefits of electronic communication, including e-mail, voice mail, and use of social media, are many: they encourage openness and sharing of information; they diffuse power throughout the organization; and they provide a means to create more transparency in the running of the business.[26]

Unfortunately, the growth of management and financial information systems can create privacy problems by making personnel information more accessible to those with prying eyes, or "hackers," who might use the information inappropriately. Messages can be read or heard, and deleted messages can be accessed.

Further, there is the issue of an employee bad-mouthing co-workers in more public forms, such as blogs or tweets. In a somewhat similar situation, a sportscaster was terminated for making certain comments on his Twitter account. Specifically, his tweeted comments were in relation to an NHL player's decision to participate in a commercial supporting gay marriages. Fortunately for the employer, the cellphone belonged to the employee so the employer could not be sued by listeners or the NHL player for defamation.[27] Moreover, messages can be forwarded, replicated, and printed with ease. In addition, social media networks, such as Facebook, can expose both employers and employees to inappropriate comments by co-workers, thereby creating a hostile work environment. For example, two employees at a car dealership in B.C. were terminated for using their Facebook accounts to make threatening and vitriolic comments about management.[28]

Technology creates the need for a critical balance between employee privacy and the employer's need to know. Although employees may assume that their right to privacy extends to e-mail and voice-mail messages, it does not. The *Freedom of Information and Protection of Privacy Act* (federal legislation) applies only to records in the custody or control of public bodies, such as a Crown corporation, a school board, or a government ministry. This act does not apply to the employment relationship in many organizations.

Employees often assume that they have a right to privacy on the company's telephone.

© ThinkStock/SuperStock

That means employers have the right to monitor materials created, received, or sent for business-related reasons.[29] Employers are strongly encouraged to develop clear policies and guidelines that explain to employees how any form of electronic communication is to be used, including when and under what conditions employees can be monitored (see Manager's Toolkit 9.2). In addition, employees should be reminded of their responsibilities under the company's policy every time they log on to the company's computer system. More and more decisions by courts and arbitrators are reaffirming the organization's right to monitor e-mail or any other electronic transmission on the company-owned computers. This trend holds true for companies that monitor employee use of the Internet.

Therefore, it is important for managers and supervisors, as well as employees, to understand that employers have the right to monitor any and all electronic transmissions at work. Where e-mail and voice-mail policies do exist, employees should be required to sign a form indicating that they have read and understand the policy. In most cases, courts will find disciplining an employee for Internet abuse to be a reasonable action. For example, a construction worker in Ontario was terminated for posting a YouTube video of him nailing his "private parts" to a board. Even though the union grieved the termination, the arbitration panel said the termination was appropriate for the "patently unacceptable in any workplace" behaviour.[30] In another case, a manager at a credit union was terminated for sending inappropriate and degrading jokes to office colleagues.[31]

Employee Conduct Outside the Workplace

Consider the following case. On Monday morning the owner of ABC Corporation reads in the newspaper that a company employee has been charged with robbery and assault on a local convenience store owner. The employee has been released pending trial. A phone call to the employee's supervisor reveals that the employee has reported to work. What should the owner do?

New technologies enable employers to monitor staff very closely, even on their personal time. As well, with the widespread use of smartphones, pictures and videos can be taken, posted in blogs and on Facebook, and become public. While most courts uphold

---

MANAGER'S TOOLKIT 9.2

E-MAIL, INTERNET, SOCIAL MEDIA, AND VOICE-MAIL POLICY GUIDELINES

- Decide on whether policy will promote use or prohibit misuse.
- Ensure other relevant policies, such as computer use, privacy, confidentiality, and harassment/discrimination are aligned.
- Consistently apply policy.
- Clearly specify anything that is prohibited, such as certain Internet sites or file sharing.
- Clearly specify use or no use of social media sites and whether usage on company equipment will be monitored.

- Communicate consequences of breaches of policy.
- Through the organization's systems, block any sites the organization does not want employees to access.
- Inform employees that any confidential information is not to be shared or sent electronically.
- Advise employees that e-mail and computer use, including any personal information stored on computer, is not private and therefore may be reviewed by others.

Sources: Adapted from materials presented at a seminar presented by Roper Greyell, March 31, 2010; Madeleine Loewenberg, "Balancing Risks, Benefits of Social Media," *Canadian HR Reporter*, January 31, 2011, www.hrreporter.com/articleview/8936-balancing-risks-benefitsof-social-media; Charles Dervarics, "Establishing an Employee Internet Policy," *Business.com*, accessed February 10, 2012, www.business.com/human-resources/internet-and-employee-policy; Bettina Burgess, "Debunking Common Misconceptions around Employee Privacy," *Canadian HR Reporter*, August 15, 2011, www.hrreporter.com/articleview/10993-debunking-common-misconceptions-around-employeeprivacy; and "Intel Social Media Guidelines," accessed February 10, 2012, www.intel.com/content/www/us/en/legal/intel-social-mediaguidelines.htm.

the right of the employer to monitor employees at the workplace, particularly if there is a justifiable reason to collect evidence, the monitoring of employees outside the workplace is more complex. For example, during the Stanley Cup riots in Vancouver in the June 2011, many videos were taken of participants and widely publicized. As a result, some individuals who were observed were subsequently terminated from their employment.[32] In some cases, people have not been hired because of information on Facebook or LinkedIn.[33] Organizations that want to discipline employees for off-duty misconduct must establish a clear relationship between the misconduct and its negative effect on other employees or the organization. This link might be established, for example, in cases where off-duty criminal misconduct (e.g., child molestation) creates a disruptive impact on the workplace. Another example might be where the public nature of the employee's job (e.g., police or fire department personnel) creates an image problem for the organization. Ultimately, whether an employer can terminate someone for activities outside the work will depend on the profession, the profession's code of conduct, and the role the profession plays in our general society.[34] Read At Work with HRM 9.3 to read about the behaviour of two senior managers at Research in Motion (RIM) and their termination.

Further legal resources on the topics discussed in this chapter can be found at Canadian Legal Information Online (**canadaonline.about.com/cs/law/a/legalinfo.htm**) or Law Central Canada (**www.lawcentralcanada.ca/CanadianLaw/default.aspx**).

**Canadian Legal
Information Online**

canadaonline.about.com/cs/
law/a/legalinfo.htm

Law Central Canada

www.lawcentralcanada.ca/
CanadianLaw/default.aspx

AT WORK **with HRM 9.3**

BAD BEHAVIOUR RESULTS IN TERMINATION

Perhaps the most written-about termination in Canada in late 2011 was about two senior managers at Research in Motion (RIM). Further, the incident that led to the termination was when the company was experiencing significant challenges in the business.

So, what happened?

Between Beijing and Toronto, Air Canada had to divert a flight and make an unscheduled landing at Vancouver to remove the two individuals due to alcohol-fuelled behaviour. Specifically, the pair were disorderly and belligerent, and had to be subdued by flight attendants and passengers and then restrained by the crew. When the plane landed, RCMP officers boarded the plane and removed the two people. When appearing at court, both employees pleaded guilty and received a court-ordered payment of $71,757 to Air Canada. The payment, with each paying half, represented the amount for fuel, landing, and other related costs to the incident.

Besides the heavy financial penalty, the two employees were immediately suspended and then subsequently terminated. As stated by RIM, "RIM expects that its employees conduct themselves in a manner reflective of our strong principles and standards of business behaviour. RIM does not condone behaviour that conflicts with applicable laws and employees are expected to act, at all times, with integrity and respect."

Most legal specialists commenting on this case indicated that executives are typically held to a higher standard. Thus, having two vice-presidents behave in the manner that they did put RIM in a very bad light and created much negative publicity for a company that was struggling with its products. While other employees might have to be reminded of expectations of behaviour, senior managers getting drunk and creating problems do not need a policy to cover their behaviour.

CRITICAL THINKING QUESTION:

Do you think the employees ought to have been terminated? Why or why not?

Sources: Adapted from "Drunks on a plane fired by RIM," *The Vancouver Sun*, December 7, 2011, A11; Ian Bailey, "Rowdy RIM pair plead guilty after Beijing flight disrupted," *The Globe and Mail*, December 2, 2011, A10; and Sarah Dobson, "Employees behaving badly," *Canadian HR Reporter*, January 16, 2012, 1.

With the Internet increasingly becoming a place where people's movements are tracked, logged, bought, and sold, it is important for users to understand how to protect and secure their information.

Adam Berry/Getty Images

DISCIPLINARY POLICIES AND PROCEDURES

Outcome 3

What is the process of establishing disciplinary practices?

The rights of managers to discipline and discharge employees are increasingly limited. There is thus a great need for managers at all levels to understand discipline procedures. Disciplinary action taken against an employee must be for justifiable reasons, and there must be effective policies and procedures to govern its use. Such policies and procedures serve to assist those responsible for taking disciplinary action and help to ensure that employees receive fair and constructive treatment. Equally important, these guidelines help to prevent disciplinary action from being voided or from being reversed through the appeal system.

If an organization has an HR department, it will have a major responsibility in developing the disciplinary policies and procedures. While the HR department will get top-management approval, it is also critical that supervisors and managers be involved in the development of the policies and procedures. It will be the supervisors and managers who carry out the policies, any of their experiences can contribute to more effective coordination and consistency in the use of disciplinary action throughout the organization. As part of the manager–HR partnership, the HR department will work with the manager to ensure that any actions taken against employees are consistent with any collective agreements and conform to current law.

The primary responsibility for preventing or correcting disciplinary problems rests with an employee's immediate supervisor. This person is best able to observe evidence of unsatisfactory behaviour or performance and to discuss the matter with the employee. Discussion is frequently all that is needed to correct the problem, and disciplinary action becomes unnecessary. However, when disciplinary action is needed, the supervisor should strive to use a problem-solving attitude. Causes underlying the problem are as important as the problem itself, and any attempt to prevent recurrence will require an understanding of them.

Admittedly, it is often difficult for supervisors to maintain an objective attitude toward employee infractions. But if supervisors can maintain a problem-solving stance, they are likely to come up with a diagnosis that is nearer the truth than would be possible were they to use the approach of a trial lawyer. For example, if an employee is late for work several days in a row, the supervisor needs to discuss the situation with the employee and try to determine the reasons for the lateness. The supervisor needs to remember that the objective is to get the employee to work on time—not to discipline the individual for being late. Therefore, by attempting to find out the reasons for the lateness, the supervisor is in a better position to work with the employee to find an acceptable solution.

Office Depot Business Tools
www.officedepot.com

Business Owner's Toolkit
www.toolkit.com

For additional resources in disciplining employees, see Office Depot (**www.officedepot.com**; access the link Business Resource Centre and then link to Small Business Tools) and Business Owner's Toolkit (**www.toolkit.com**; access the Business Tools link).

Setting Organizational Rules

Clearly stating expectations of performance and behaviour is the foundation for an effective disciplinary system. These expectations govern the type of behaviour expected of employees. Since employee behaviour standards are established through the setting and communicating of organizational procedures and rules, the following suggestions may help reduce problems in this area:

1. Information about rules should be widely distributed and known to all employees. It should not be assumed that employees know what is expected of them.
2. Rules, especially those critical to work success, should be reviewed periodically, perhaps annually.
3. The reasons for rules concerning performance and behaviour should always be explained. Acceptance is greater when employees understand the reasons behind rules.
4. Organization policies and rules should always be written. Ambiguity should be avoided, since this can result in different interpretations by different supervisors.
5. Rules must be reasonable and relate to the safe and efficient operation of the organization. They should not be made simply because of personal likes or dislikes.
6. If management has been lax in the enforcement of a policy or rule, it must be restated, along with the consequences for its violation, before disciplinary action can begin.
7. Have employees sign that they have read and understand the organizational rules regarding their behaviour and performance in the organization.

When seeking reasons for unsatisfactory performance, supervisors must keep in mind that employees may not be aware of certain expectations. Before initiating any disciplinary action, therefore, it is essential that supervisors determine whether they have given their employees careful and thorough orientation in what is expected of them in relation to their jobs.

Defining Discipline

Outcome 4

What is discipline and how do you investigate?

Discipline
(1) Treatment that punishes;
(2) Orderly behaviour in an organizational setting; or (3) Training that moulds and strengthens desirable conduct—or corrects undesirable conduct—and develops self-control

In dictionaries, **discipline** normally has three meanings:

1. Treatment that punishes;
2. Orderly behaviour in an organizational setting; or
3. Training that moulds and strengthens desirable conduct—or corrects undesirable conduct—and develops self-control.

To some managers, discipline is synonymous with force. They equate the term with the punishment of employees who violate rules or regulations. Other managers think of discipline as a general state of affairs—a condition of orderliness where employees conduct themselves according to standards of acceptable behaviour. Discipline, viewed in this manner, can be considered positive when employees willingly practise self-control and respect organizational values and expectations.

The third definition considers discipline a management tool used to correct undesirable employee performance or behaviour. Discipline is applied as a constructive means of getting employees to conform to acceptable standards of behaviour and performance. Figure 9.2 provides examples of common disciplinary problems.

Many organizations, such as Goodyear Aerospace, define the term "discipline" in their policy manuals as training that "corrects, moulds, or perfects knowledge, attitudes, behaviour, or conduct." Discipline is thus viewed as a way to correct poor employee performance rather than simply to punish for an offence. As these organizations emphasize, discipline should be seen as a method of training employees to perform better or to

FIGURE 9.2 Common Disciplinary Problems

Attendance Problems
- Unexcused absence
- Chronic absenteeism
- Unexcused or excessive tardiness
- Leaving without permission

Dishonesty and Related Problems
- Theft
- Falsifying employment application
- Willfully damaging organizational property
- Punching another employee's time card
- Falsifying work records

Work Performance Problems
- Failure to complete work assignments
- Producing substandard products or services
- Failure to meet established production requirements

On-the-Job Behaviour Problems
- Intoxication at work
- Insubordination
- Horseplay
- Smoking in unauthorized places
- Fighting
- Gambling
- Failure to use safety devices
- Failure to report injuries
- Carelessness
- Sleeping on the job
- Using abusive or threatening language with supervisors
- Possession of narcotics or alcohol
- Possession of firearms or other weapons
- All forms of harassment, such as sexual innuendo or actions, teasing, racial slurs, inappropriate jokes, and bullying

improve their job attitudes or work behaviour. It is also interesting to note that the word "discipline" is derived from the word "disciple," which means follower or pupil. Figure 9.3 shows one disciplinary model, which consists of several steps that must be carried out to ensure that the termination is justifiable.

Investigating the Disciplinary Problem

It's a rare manager who has a good, intuitive sense of how to investigate employee misconduct. Too frequently, investigations are conducted in a haphazard manner; worse, they overlook one or more investigative concerns. In conducting an employee investigation, it is important to be objective and to avoid the assumptions, suppositions, and biases that often surround discipline cases. Manager's Toolkit 9.3 lists things that need to be considered when doing workplace investigations. Paying attention to each item will help ensure a full and fair investigation while providing reliable information free from personal prejudice. And as mentioned in Chapter 2, many actions an organization would take in relation to an employment issue require a careful and full investigation. Further, some employment concerns, such as absences, may need "reasonable accommodation" (see Chapter 2), and therefore discipline would be an inappropriate action.[35]

When preparing documentation, it is important that the manager records the incident immediately after the infraction takes place. Then, the memory of the incident is still fresh, and the manager can ensure that the record is complete and accurate. It is critical

FIGURE 9.3 A Disciplinary Model

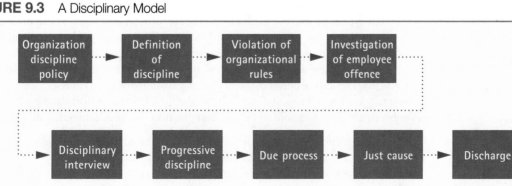

that the documentation be complete. This information will include whether there had been any previous warnings with an opportunity to improve. These documents are necessary to prove that the employer had the right to discipline.[36]

The Investigative Interview

Before any disciplinary action is initiated, an investigative interview should be conducted to make sure employees are fully aware of the offence. This interview is necessary because the supervisor's perceptions of the employee's behaviour may not be entirely accurate. The interview should concentrate on how the offence violated the performance standards of the job. It should avoid getting into personalities or areas unrelated to job performance. Most important, the employee must be given a full opportunity to explain so that any deficiencies for which the organization may be responsible are revealed. In fact, it is critical to the outcome of any discipline to conduct a careful investigation as quickly as possible and to ensure that the investigation is approached quickly, respectfully, and independently.[37]

Approaches to Disciplinary Action

Outcome 5

What are the differences between progressive and positive discipline?

When taken against employees, disciplinary action should never be thought of as punishment. Discipline can embody a penalty as a means of obtaining a desired result; however, punishment should not be the intent of disciplinary action. Rather, discipline must have as its goal the improvement of the employee's future behaviour. To apply discipline in any other way—as punishment or as a way of getting even with employees—can invite only problems for management, including possible wrongful-dismissal suits. If a thorough investigation shows that an employee has violated some organization rule, disciplinary action must be imposed. Two approaches to disciplinary action are progressive discipline and positive discipline.

Progressive Discipline

Progressive discipline
Application of corrective measures by increasing degrees

Generally, discipline is imposed in a progressive manner. By definition, **progressive discipline** is the application of corrective measures by increasing degrees. Progressive discipline is designed to motivate employees to correct their misconduct voluntarily. The technique is aimed at correcting unacceptable behaviour as soon as it starts, using only enough corrective action to remedy the shortcoming. However, the sequence and severity of the disciplinary action vary with the type of offence and the circumstances surrounding it. Since each situation is unique, a number of factors must be considered in determining how severe a disciplinary action should be.

To highlight the uniqueness of situations, a recent case involved an employee who was disciplined for talking about her deceased daughter all the time at work. After co-workers complained, the supervisor told her that the pictures of her dead daughter must come down and that she could no longer speak about her daughter at work.[38] Given that people react differently to loss, perhaps a more appropriate response for the supervisor was to refer the employee to the company's EAP program. Some of the factors to consider are listed in Manager's Toolkit 9.3.

The typical progressive discipline procedure includes four steps: (1) an oral warning (or counselling) that subsequent unsatisfactory behaviour or performance will not be tolerated, (2) a written warning, (3) a suspension without pay, and (4) termination.

The progressive discipline used by several organizations is described in At Work with HRM 9.4. The "capital punishment" of discharge is utilized only as a last resort. Organizations normally use lower forms of disciplinary action for less severe performance problems. It is important for organizations to follow "best practices" when documenting discipline:

1. Use an employee discipline form—this helps in ensuring that there is a uniform process and all the important information is gathered.
2. Conduct a fair and full investigation.
3. Get the facts.

MANAGER'S TOOLKIT **9.3**

WHAT MAKES AN EFFECTIVE INVESTIGATION?

1. Decide as soon as possible if an investigation is necessary.
2. Arrange for the investigation to be conducted by an individual who is trained and experienced.
3. Ensure that the investigator is as independent as possible.
4. Identify all relevant issues and explore them as appropriate.
5. Plan the investigation—create a road map for the conduct of the investigation.
6. Ensure that the investigation has sufficient resources to be completed.
7. Control the investigation—don't lose sight of purpose.
8. Be aware that the speed of investigation is critical to minimize workplace disruptions.
9. Ensure that all evidence (both physical and digital) is collected, examined, and preserved.
10. Review and secure all relevant documents.
11. Identify and interview any witnesses.
12. Analyze information based on facts.

Sources: Adapted from Gareth Jones, "Workplace investigations: Getting beyond 'he said, she said,'" *Canadian HR Reporter*, January 30, 2012, 22. Reprinted by permission of Canadian HR Reporter. © Copyright Thomson Reuters Canada Ltd., Toronto, Ontario, 1-800-387-5164. Web: www.hrreporter.com.

4. Be objective.
5. Be clear and specific.
6. Complete the form while the information is fresh.
7. Get the employee's acknowledgment.
8. Allow the employee to explain the actions.
9. Be fair.
10. To the degree possible, use the discipline process as a positive experience.[39]

Positive Discipline

Although progressive discipline is the most popular approach to correcting employee misconduct, some managers have questioned its logic. They have noted that it has certain flaws, including its intimidating and adversarial nature, which prevent it from achieving the intended purpose. For these reasons, some organizations are using an approach called **positive**, or **nonpunitive, discipline**. Positive discipline is based on the concept that employees must assume responsibility for their personal conduct and job performance.[40]

Positive discipline requires a co-operative environment in which the employee and supervisor engage in joint discussion and problem solving to resolve incidents of employee irresponsibility. It also requires that the supervisor takes a coaching and supportive role.[41] The approach focuses on the early correction of misconduct, with the employee taking total responsibility for resolving the problem. Management imposes nothing; all solutions and affirmations are jointly reached. While positive discipline appears similar to progressive discipline, its emphasis is on giving employees reminders rather than reprimands as a way to improve performance. Figure 9.4 illustrates the procedure for implementing the three-step positive discipline procedure.

Compiling a Disciplinary Record

In applying either progressive or positive discipline, it is important for managers to maintain complete records of each step of the procedure. When employees fail to meet the obligation of a disciplinary step, they should be given a warning, and their manager should document

Positive, or nonpunitive, discipline
System of discipline that focuses on the early correction of employee misconduct, with the employee taking total responsibility for correcting the problem

PROGRESSIVE DISCIPLINE APPROACHES

A number of organizations have readily available guidelines aimed at changing unwanted employee behaviour. Before discipline begins, it is expected that the supervisor can show that the employee is aware of desired behaviour and that he or she is choosing to act otherwise. Frequently, all that is needed is to let employees know that a particular behaviour inappropriate. Employees usually react positively to this. Progressive discipline definitely is not used as a way of punishing an employee. Typical steps in a discipline process are the following:

Step 1: Establish cause for action. Employer needs to determine that an incident which warrants discipline has occurred. If for performance, the employer must be able to prove to an arbitrator or judge that the employee knew of expectations and that supervision occurred to ensure the standard.

Step 2: Coaching. This is a supportive discussion in which the supervisor reinforces expectations of either performance or behaviour. It is important that this conversation is noted in the supervisor's calendar.

Step 3: Verbal warning. This is a private discussion between the employee and the supervisor that takes place if there has been a repeat after the coaching session. The supervisor describes the incident and ensures that all sides of the story are heard. Human Resources and Skills Development Canada's verbal warning step also states that the supervisor needs to be very clear on outlining the consequences if expectations are not met.

Step 4: Written warning. If the employee's behaviour continues, a meeting is held with the supervisor and the employee. At the meeting the supervisor describes the events, reviews expectations as discussed in step 1, seeks solutions from the employee, and indicates what will happen if unacceptable behaviour continues. The meeting is summarized in writing and placed in the employee's personnel file. It is also helpful if the written warning includes a plan to ensure that the employee has sufficient time to improve.

Step 5: Suspension. If the inappropriate behaviour continues, the supervisor will next consider suspension. A meeting is held, similar to the meeting in step 2. At the conclusion of the meeting, a suspension may be imposed with a length that is linked to the nature of the problem. The suspension can be for one day or for several days. A letter of suspension is written and placed in the employee's file.

Step 6: Dismissal. This is a very serious step and is taken only when all other options have been exhausted. Again, a meeting is held to review facts and expectations and to summarize previous meetings and actions. Even at this meeting, it is important to provide an opportunity for the employee to explain. At the end of the meeting, a letter of dismissal is presented. One copy is given to the employee, and one copy is placed in the employee's file.

CRITICAL THINKING QUESTION:

Are there any other steps that ought to be taken in corrective discipline? Describe and explain.

Sources: Adapted from Sabine Bell, "Motivation a goal of progressive discipline," *Canadian HR Reporter*, May 31, 2010, http://www.hrreporter.com/articleprint.aspx?articleid=7895 (accessed February 8, 2012); "Progressive Discipline," Human Resources and Skills Development Canada, 2011; and Robert Olson, "Terminating a worker for poor performance," *Canadian HR Reporter*, November 21, 2011, 19.

the warning. A copy of this warning is usually placed in the employee's personnel file. After an established period—frequently six months—the warning is usually removed, provided that it has served its purpose. Otherwise, it remains in the file to serve as evidence should a more severe penalty become necessary later.

An employee's personnel file contains the employee's complete work history. It serves as a basis for determining and supporting disciplinary action and for evaluating the organization's disciplinary policies and procedures. Maintenance of proper records also

FIGURE 9.4   Positive Discipline Procedures

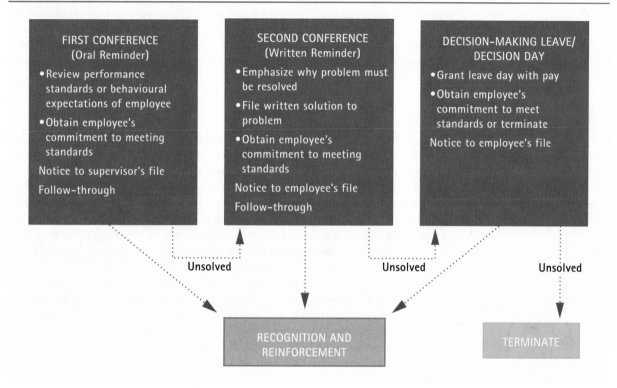

provides management with valuable information about the soundness of its rules and regulations. Those rules that are violated most frequently should receive particular attention, because the need for them may no longer exist, or some change might be required to facilitate their enforcement. If the rule is shown to have little or no value, it should be revised or rescinded. Otherwise, employees are likely to feel they are being restricted unnecessarily.

Documentation of Employee Misconduct

"It's too complicated." "I just didn't take time to do it." "I have more important things to do." These are some of the frequent excuses used by managers who have failed to document cases of employee misconduct. The most significant cause of inadequate documentation, however, is that managers have no idea what constitutes good documentation. Unfortunately, the failure of managers to record employee misconduct accurately can result in the reversal of any subsequent disciplinary action. Written records are key in discipline.[42] For documentation to be complete, the following nine items should be included:

1. Employee's name and job title.
2. Names of others involved or who witnessed the incident.
3. Date, time, and location of the incident(s).
4. Creation of a factual account of what happened and why it is a problem.
5. Identification of which policies were broken.
6. Noting of the impact of the behaviour on other employees.
7. Identification of changes that are required to correct problem and by what date.
8. Prior discussion(s) with the employee about the problem.
9. Consequences if improvement is not made, and a follow-up date.[43]

It is critical that managers at all levels understand the guidelines for appropriate discipline. For additional resources on discipline, do a search on "discipline" at **humanresources. about.com.**

About Human Resources

humanresources.about.com

Grounds for Dismissal

No matter how helpful and positive a supervisor is with an employee who is not abiding by the organization's policies and rules, there may come a time when the employee must be dismissed. Since dismissal has such serious consequences for the employee—and possibly for the organization—it should be undertaken only after a deliberate and thoughtful review of the case.

Wrongful Dismissal

When an employer dismisses or terminates an employee for not performing as expected or not following the company's rules, this is called dismissal for "just cause." To do this, the employer must document and prove serious misconduct or incompetence on the part of the employee. In recent years, a growing number of employees have sued their former employers for "**wrongful dismissal**," claiming the termination was "without just or sufficient cause," implying a lack of fair treatment by management or insufficient reasons for the termination. Termination for cause also expects that the employee could do something different and had been informed of this prior to termination. This means that a termination resulting from a job redefinition/redesign, downsizing, restructuring, or lack of organizational fit is not just cause. However, poor performance, poor interpersonal relationships, and technical incompetence might be just cause if the employee had been informed of expectations and had been given a chance to improve but failed to conform. Figure 9.5 lists some "just-cause" reasons.

Many managers are faced with having to terminate someone when there are sufficient and legitimate grounds for doing so. Some companies may suggest that just cause includes the organization's financial difficulties. It is important for managers and supervisors to know that the economic hardship of the company is not a justifiable reason to terminate someone's employment. HRM and the Law 9.1 gives two examples of wrongful dismissal cases. For additional information on wrongful dismissals, see **www.duhaime.org**.

Managers must be able to document that any performance problems have been brought to the attention of the employee and that sufficient time, training, and assistance

Wrongful dismissal
Terminating an employee's employment without just cause

Duhaime Law
www.duhaime.org

The final stage of discipline is termination.

Ariel Skelley/Photographer's Choice/Getty Images

FIGURE 9.5 Sample "Just-Cause" Reasons

- Excessive lateness or absenteeism
- Theft from the company
- Improper or wrong conduct, such as fighting with a co-worker

Depending on the seriousness of the wrongdoing, the individual may be terminated immediately, bypassing the steps of progressive discipline. For example, a hotel concierge who makes threatening statements to a guest could be terminated right away.

have been given to improve the weak performance. If the organization has an HR professional, the line manager needs to work closely with the HR person to ensure that the appropriate type of documentation occurs. Other tips to prevent a challenge by a terminated employee are discussed later in the chapter.

If an employee termination is to be upheld for just cause, what constitutes fair employee treatment and valid reasons? This question is not easily answered, but standards governing just-cause dismissal have evolved from the field of labour arbitration. These standards are

HRM and the Law 9.1

WRONGFUL DISMISSALS: TWO CASES AND TWO DIFFERENT OUTCOMES

An Ontario arbitration board found that the firing of two employees involved in a sit-in at their workplace was appropriate. Specifically, the employer (a credit union) had been on strike for some time and even though the labour dispute wasn't settled, the parties reached an agreement about the behaviour of picketers. The agreement stated that while the premises could be picketed, the picketers were expected to be peaceful and respectful to people entering the employer's premises. Shortly after the agreement came into force, several employees decided to stage a sit-in at one of the branches and refused to leave when the branch closed and chained the doors shut, forcing non-union employees to remain. The employees were subsequently fired, and the union at the arbitration stated that the misconduct was during a legal strike and therefore "just cause" did not apply. The arbitration panel did not agree, saying that the misconduct was serious as it removed the freedom of people to leave when they wanted to.

In another case, an employee was terminated when the employee did not return to work after a significant personal situation. Early in the new year, the employee's house burned down, and the employee informed the employer that work would be missed and the employee wasn't sure about the return date. While the employer tried to contact the employee during the month that followed, the phone had been disconnected. Eventually, the employer sent a Record of Employment, indicating the employee had quit. Shortly after this, the employee was diagnosed with severe depression and contacted the employer regarding medical leave. The employer did indicate that the person could come back to work when well. The employee did not return but commenced a wrongful dismissal lawsuit. The court determined that it was unclear that the employee had resigned and concluded also that the employer had terminated unjustly. The court awarded $20,000 in damages to the former employee because it concluded that the employer did not make the kinds of efforts it thought the employer ought to have made in determining the status of the employee after the tragedy.

QUESTION:

How would you have ruled in these two cases?

Sources: Adapted from Jeffrey R. Smith, "Dismissal for some, suspension for others after sit-in during strike," *Canadian HR Reporter*, April 6, 2010, www.hrreporter.com/articleview/7706-dismissal-for-some-suspension-for-others-after-sit-in-during-strike (accessed February 13, 2012); and Steve Winder, "Avoiding Wrongful Termination Claims," *BC Business*, March 18, 2011, www.bcbusinessonline.ca/bcb/bc-blogs/conference/2011/03/17/avoiding-wrongful-termination-claims (accessed February 12, 2012).

"JUST-CAUSE" DISMISSAL GUIDELINES

1. Did the organization forewarn the employee of the possible disciplinary consequences of his or her action?

2. Were management's requirements of the employee reasonable in relation to the orderly, efficient, and safe operation of the organization's business?

3. Did management, before changing the working conditions or discharging the employee, make a reasonable effort to establish that the employee's performance was unsatisfactory?

4. Was the organization's investigation conducted in a fair and objective manner?

5. Did the investigation produce sufficient evidence or proof of guilt as charged?

6. Has management treated this employee under its rules, orders, and penalties as it has other employees in similar circumstances?

7. Did the discharge fit the misconduct, considering the seriousness of the proven offence, the employee's service record, and any mitigating circumstances?

applied by arbitrators in dismissal cases to determine whether management had just cause for the termination. These guidelines are normally set forth in the form of questions, as provided in Manager's Toolkit 9.4. For example, before dismissing an employee, did the manager warn the person of possible disciplinary action in the past? A "no" answer to any of the seven questions generally means that just cause was not established and that management's decision to terminate was arbitrary, capricious, or discriminatory. These guidelines are being applied not only by arbitrators in dismissal cases but also by judges in wrongful-dismissal suits.

It is also important for small business to be aware of the consequences of wrongful dismissals. Read HRM and SME 9.1 for the costs of terminating an employee who was fired for cancer medical treatment. Therefore, it is important for an employer to represent itself respectfully when terminating someone.[44]

Constructive Dismissal

Constructive dismissal

Changing an employee's working conditions such that compensation, status, or prestige is reduced

Another type of dismissal is constructive. **Constructive dismissal** occurs when an employer changes an employee's working conditions such that compensation, status, or prestige is reduced. Even if the employee agrees to the changed conditions (the only other option might be unemployment) or resigns, the court may consider the employee to have been dismissed.[45]

Two cases illustrate the concept.

One involved Sobeys, a grocery chain throughout Canada, and an employee who had worked with the company for 28 years. The company eliminated the food experience manager's role, which was part of the marketing department, at its head office in Nova Scotia. The head of marketing wanted to make the operation more efficient while not having any negative impact on existing employees. To that end, the management team made a proposal that included the employee. A month later, however, the employee was informed that while the position was eliminated, the company wanted to maintain the employment relationship; the employee was offered a choice of two positions: assistant store manager in another town or demo coordinator at head office. Both positions had lower salaries, but the company offered a lump sum payment (one-time only) that represented the difference in the first year. All other aspects of the compensation would remain the same. The employee was devastated and shocked, and after taking a week to review options, decided both would be "humiliating and embarrassing." The employee commenced constructive dismissal litigation. At trial, the court concluded that if the employee had been able to get past the emotional response that one of the positions would not be a demotion and she therefore could not refuse to take the position. The court confirmed

HRM and SME 9.1

EMPLOYER ACTED BADLY!

Not long ago, a small employer in Ontario was ordered to pay $55,000 to a former employee for breaching a duty and for punitive damages because of the way the employer handled the termination. This amount is quite sizable for a small company.

The employer, a musical instrument company, fired an employee who had worked for the company 30 years for failing to work the minimum number of hours required. It all started when the employee was diagnosed with lung cancer in December. Early the next year, the employee had part of the lung removed and took a month off work. After that, chemo- and radiotherapy occurred for several months, during which time the employee worked reduced hours. During this time, the company kept the employee on full salary. In the fall of that year, the company sent a letter to the employee, indicating that the employee frequently came in late, left early, and did not always provide prior notice when absent. Because of the long service with the family-run business, the employee was shocked but went to work the next day, being fearful for the job. Unfortunately, the employee had to take another medical leave right after returning; the employee informed the employer a return-to-work would be in three months. Shortly thereafter, the employer wrote another letter indicating that the employee's position had been abolished and that the company had no obligation to find other work when the employee was able to return to work.

The court determined that not only was the termination inappropriate but the manner in which it was handled was "callous and insensitive."

QUESTION:

What do you think? Why?

Source: Adapted from Jeffrey R. Smith, "30-year employee fired after getting cancer," *Canadian HR Reporter*, April 25, 2011, www.hrreporter.com/articleview/10084-30-year-employee-fired-after-getting-cancer-legal-view (accessed February 13, 2012). Reprinted by permission of Canadian HR Reporter. © Copyright Thomson Reuters Canada Ltd., Toronto, Ontario, 1-800-387-5164. Web: www.hrreporter.com.

that Sobeys had provided a reasonable solution. It determined that the employee had quit and no constructive dismissal had occurred.[46]

In another case, involving Thrifty Foods, a subsidiary of Sobeys, the employee was demoted due to performance and work attendance issues. Specifically, the employee of 16 years had married a relative of the president, couldn't get along with the spouse's daughters, became depressed, and eventually left the spouse. The employee said that the guilt and embarrassment over the situation led to poor performance and attendance. A new manager laid out very specific expectations of attendance and performance, had the employee sign the document, and then put the employee on three months' short-term medical leave to seek treatment. The performance and attendance problems continued after the employee returned, and the employee was demoted to a clerical position. The employee agreed to this, indicating that a demotion might reduce the pressure. Before starting the new role, the employee again went on short-term medical leave for one month. However, at the end of the month the employee did not contact the store and was therefore terminated. During the court hearing, the court found that the employee had been constructively dismissed due to the size of the salary cut (16%). However, the court did find that Thrifty's had not given sufficient warning of the performance issues—and therefore had failed to establish a "just-cause" termination.[47]

These two different cases both deal with performance improvement plans yet have different outcomes. To access the latest information on constructive dismissals, Carswell's *The Wrongful Dismissal Handbook* is a helpful resource.

In a non-union setting, employers can give notice of future changes in compensation (wages and benefits), working hours, location, and other similar items so long as they provide notice equivalent to that given for dismissal. For example, if the company wished to reduce the amount of paid sick leave, it could do so with sufficient notice.

Dismissing Employees

Regardless of the reasons for a dismissal, it should be done with personal consideration for the employee affected. Every effort should be made to ease the trauma a dismissal creates. The employee must be informed honestly, yet tactfully, of the exact reasons for the action. Such candour can help the employee face the problem and adjust to it in a constructive manner.

Managers need to discuss, and even rehearse, with their peers the upcoming termination meeting. This practice can ensure that all important points are covered while giving confidence to the manager. Although managers agree that there is no single right way to conduct the dismissal meeting, the following guidelines will help to make the discussion more effective:

1. Hold the meeting as early in the week as possible and in a neutral meeting place.
2. Come to the point within the first two or three minutes, and list in a logical order all reasons for the termination.
3. Be straightforward and firm, yet tactful, and remain resolute in the decision; avoid debating reasons and decisions.
4. Make the discussion private, businesslike, and fairly brief; make notes of the meeting.
5. Avoid making accusations against the employee and injecting personal feelings into the discussion; be courteous and respectful at all times.
6. Avoid bringing up any personality differences.
7. Provide any information concerning severance pay and the status of benefits and coverage.
8. Explain how employment inquiries from future employers will be handled.
9. Arrange a mutually agreed upon time for the employee to clear out personal belongings and for the return of any company property.
10. Have another manager present as a witness.

Termination meetings should be held in a neutral location, such as a conference room, so that the manager can leave if the meeting gets out of control. The prudent manager will also have determined, prior to the termination decision, that the dismissal does not violate any legal rights the employee may have.

Finally, when terminated employees are escorted off the premises, the removal must not serve to defame the employee. Managers should not give peers the impression that the terminated employee was dishonest or untrustworthy. Furthermore, managers are advised never to discuss the discharge with other employees, customers, or any other individual.

Providing Career Transition Assistance

Employers often use career transition or outplacement services to assist employees who are being dismissed. Assistance is especially likely to be provided for employees of long tenure.

And not just the usual organizations we think of provide help. For example, with the return of soldiers from fighting in the Middle East, career transition services are being offered to veterans to help them secure work in a challenging economy.[48] These services are especially helpful for people who have spent much time in the military and may not know how to translate their military work experience into the "civilian world."[49] They provide both job search technique help and emotional support. While terminations do not have the negative stigma they once did, they are still traumatic for the employee.

Managers cite the following reasons for providing outplacement services: concern for the well-being of the employees, protection against potential lawsuits, and the psychological effect on remaining employees. Outplacement consultants assist employees being terminated by reducing their anger and grief, and helping them regain self-confidence as they begin searching in earnest for a new job. Since many terminated workers have been out of the job market for some time, they may lack the knowledge and skills needed to look for a new job. Outplacement specialists can coach them in how to develop contacts, probe for job openings through systematic letter and telephone campaigns, and handle employment interviews and salary negotiations.

Job-site learning joins the electronic age, where those wanting to learn certain trades can get some of their training online through Web-based learning.

Sean Gallup/Getty Images

The Results of Inaction

Failure to act implies that the performance or behaviour of the employee concerned is acceptable. If disciplinary action is eventually taken, the delay will make it more difficult to justify the action, if appealed. In defending against such an appeal, the employer is likely to be asked why an employee who had not been performing or behaving satisfactorily was kept on the payroll. An even more probing question might be "Why did that employee continue to receive pay adjustments if there was a question about the performance?"

Such contradictions in practice can only aid employees in successfully challenging management's corrective actions. Unfortunately, some supervisors try to build a case to justify their corrective actions only after they have decided that a particular employee should be dismissed. The following are common reasons given by supervisors for their failure to impose a disciplinary penalty:

1. The supervisor had failed to document earlier actions, so no record existed on which to base subsequent disciplinary action.
2. Supervisors believed they would receive little or no support from higher management for the disciplinary action.
3. The supervisor was uncertain of the facts underlying the situation requiring disciplinary action.
4. Failure by the supervisor to discipline employees in the past for a certain infraction caused the supervisor to forgo current disciplinary action in order to appear consistent.
5. The supervisor wanted to be seen as a likable person.

It is critical to remember that any grounds for discipline must be well documented. Failure to do so can result in the disciplinary action being invalid.

APPEALING DISCIPLINARY ACTIONS

With growing frequency, organizations are taking steps to protect employees from arbitrary and inequitable treatment by their supervisors. A particular emphasis is placed on creating a climate in which employees are assured that they can voice their dissatisfaction with their superiors without fear of reprisal. This safeguard can be provided through the implementation of a formal procedure for appealing disciplinary actions.

Alternative Dispute-Resolution Procedures

Outcome 6

What are the different types of alternative dispute-resolution procedures?

Alternative dispute resolution (ADR)
Term applied to different types of employee complaint or dispute-resolution procedures

ADR Institute of Canada

www.amic.org

Conflict Resolution Network

www.crnhq.org

Mediation
The use of an impartial third party to help facilitate a resolution to employment disputes

In unionized workplaces, grievance procedures are stated in virtually all collective agreements. In non-union organizations, however, **alternative dispute resolution (ADR)** processes are increasingly being used to keep employers out of court. The employer's interest stems from the desire to meet employees' expectations for fair treatment in the workplace while guaranteeing them due process—in the hope of minimizing discrimination claims or wrongful-dismissal suits.

Some organizations prefer these procedures as an avenue for upward communication for employees and as a way to gauge the mood of the workforce. Others view these systems as a way to resolve minor problems before they mushroom into major issues, thus leading to improved employee morale and productivity.

The appeal procedures described in this chapter are mediation, the step-review system, the use of a hearing officer, the open-door policy, the use of an ombudsperson, and arbitration. A helpful resource for additional information on ADR can be found at **www.amic.org** and **www.crnhq.org**.

Mediation

Mediation is fast becoming a popular way to resolve employee complaints and labour disputes involving unions. The essence of mediation is facilitating face-to-face meetings so that the employee and manager can reach an agreement. Mediation is a flexible process that is shaped to deal with the particular conflict between the parties.[50] It can also be used to resolve a wide range of employee complaints, and is particularly helpful when an organization has a very diverse workforce.[51] Employees like the process because of its informality. Settlements fashioned through mediation are readily accepted by the parties, thus promoting a favourable working relationship.

Conciliation is another form of mediation. It is used in labour relations, primarily in disputes involving governments as the employer. For example, in 2012 there were two significant labour disputes in Nova Scotia (transit workers in Halifax and professors at Dalhousie University) that were settled with the assistance of a conciliator.[52]

Step-Review Systems

Step-review system
System for reviewing employee complaints and disputes by successively higher levels of management

As Figure 9.6 illustrates, a **step-review system** is based on a pre-established set of steps—normally four—for the review of an employee complaint by successively higher levels of management. These procedures are patterned after the union grievance systems, which will be discussed in Chapter 10. For example, they normally require that the employee's complaint be formalized as a written statement. Managers at each step are required to provide a full response to the complaint within a specified time period, perhaps three to five working days.

Use of a Hearing Officer

Hearing officer
Person who holds a full-time position with an organization but assumes a neutral role when deciding cases between management and aggrieved employees

This procedure is ordinarily confined to large organizations, where unions may represent employees. The **hearing officer** holds a full-time position with the organization but assumes a neutral role when deciding cases between an aggrieved employee and management. Hearing officers are employed by the organization; however, they function independently

FIGURE 9.6 Step-Review Appeal Procedure

from other managers and occupy a special place in the organizational hierarchy. Their success rests on being perceived as neutral, highly competent, and completely unbiased in handling employee complaints. They hear cases upon request, almost always made by the employee. After considering the evidence and facts presented, they render decisions or awards that are normally final and binding on both sides.

Open-Door Policy

Open-door policy
Policy of settling grievances that identifies various levels of management above the immediate supervisor for employee contact

The open-door policy is an old standby for settling employee complaints. In fact, most managers, regardless of whether their organization has adopted a formal open-door policy, profess to maintain one for their employees. The traditional **open-door policy** identifies various levels of management above the immediate supervisor that an aggrieved employee may contact; the levels may extend as high as a vice-president, president, or chief executive officer. Typically, the person who acts as "the court of last resort" is the HR director or a senior staff official.

Ombudsperson System

Ombudsperson
Designated individual from whom employees may seek counsel for the resolution of their complaints

An **ombudsperson** is a designated individual from whom employees may seek counsel for the resolution of their complaints. The ombudsperson listens to an employee's complaint and attempts to resolve it by mediating a solution between the employee and the supervisor. This individual works co-operatively with both sides to reach a settlement, often employing a clinical approach to problem solving. Since the ombudsperson has no authority to finalize a solution to the problem, compromises are highly possible, and all concerned tend to feel satisfied with the outcome. To function successfully, an ombudsperson must be able to operate in an atmosphere of confidentiality that does not threaten the security of the managers or subordinates who are involved in a complaint. Such a system also allows the ombudsperson to make recommendations to improve workplace practices.[53]

Arbitration

Private employers may require that employees submit their employment disputes for a binding resolution through arbitration. (Arbitration is fully explained in Chapter 10.) Arbitration can save court costs and avoid time delays and unfavourable publicity.

ORGANIZATIONAL ETHICS IN EMPLOYEE RELATIONS

Outcome 7

What is the role of ethics in the management of human resources?

Ethics
Set of standards of conduct and moral judgments that help to determine right and wrong behaviour

Throughout this textbook the legal requirements of HRM are emphasized. Laws and court decisions affect all aspects of the employment process—recruitment, selection, performance appraisal, safety and health, labour relations, and testing. Managers must comply with governmental regulations to promote an environment free from litigation.

However, beyond what is required by the law is the question of organizational ethics and the ethical—or unethical—behaviour engaged in by managers. **Ethics** can be defined as a set of standards of acceptable conduct and moral judgment. Ethics provides cultural guidelines—organizational or societal—that help decide between proper and improper conduct. Therefore, ethics, like the legal aspects of HR, permeates all aspects of the employment relationship. For example, managers may adhere to the organization's objective of hiring more members of designated groups, but how those employees are supervised and treated once employed gets to the issue of managerial ethics. Compliance with laws and the behavioural treatment of employees are two completely different aspects of the manager's job.

While ethical dilemmas will always occur in the supervision of employees, how employees are treated is what largely distinguishes the ethical organization from the unethical one. An ethical organization recognizes and values the contributions of

**Canadian Centre
for Ethics and
Corporate Policy**

www.ethicscentre.ca

employees and respects their personal rights. And certainly the court cases mentioned earlier in this chapter are reinforcing this belief.

Many organizations have their own codes of ethics that govern relations with employees and the public at large. These codes are formal written statements of the organization's primary values and provides a basis for the organization, and individual managers, for behaviours and actions. For example, the Canadian Centre for Ethics and Corporate Policy (**www.ethicscentre.ca**) is an organization designed to promote and practise ethical decision-making, and in doing so ensures that its members have codes that are widely publicized. Among its members are Books for Business, BMO Financial Group, Four Seasons Hotels, Starbucks, and Walmart Canada.[54] Organizations now have ethics committees and ethics ombudspersons to provide training in ethics to employees.

In addition, the Government of Canada has an ethics commissioner, reporting directly to the prime minister. The role of the commissioner is to help appointed and elected officials prevent and avoid conflicts between their public and private interests.[55] Provincial governments such as Alberta and New Brunswick also have ethics commissioners. The ultimate goal of ethics training and ethics commissioners is to avoid unethical behaviour and adverse publicity; to gain a strategic advantage; but most of all, to treat employees in a fair and equitable manner, recognizing them as productive members of the organization.

Yet even with codes of ethics and ethics committees, people do not always behave ethically. When this happens, employees will sometimes report an organization's unethical practices outside the organization. This is referred to as "whistle-blowing." Organizations, such as Canada Post, encourage high standards of business conduct by encouraging employees to report any improper activities through an independent company that can handle reports 24/7.[56] However, not all whistle-blowers are applauded for their reporting of unethical practices. One high-profile case was the situation at ORNGE, the provincial air ambulance service in Ontario. In late 2011 a number of staff had alerted the public to problems in the organization. Some of the more notable problems were poor equipment and inexperienced staff, creating patient safety issues while large sums of money were being paid to senior managers by helicopter vendors once their helicopters were selected for purchase. When new management came into the organization in early 2012, employees were told not to speak with the media but to use the internal whistle-blowing policy. Employees responded by saying they had done that, but it didn't work.[57]

As demonstrated above, organizations have frequently attempted to discipline or punish an employee for whistle-blowing. But with the renewed interest in business ethics, more and more companies are taking steps to ensure that any unethical behaviour or action by an employee is punished and that people are encouraged to report unethical actions. In order to ensure that employees understand the importance of dealing with unethical behaviour, top management needs to visibly support ethical actions by behaving ethically themselves, encouraging a culture of ethical practices, have a whistle-blower policy, have ethics training, and that ensuring whistle-blowing issues are handled quickly and that employees can see that the issue has been handled.[58]

There are things each of us can do. when faced with an ethical dilemma. Some suggestions by a leading ethics author are: (1) Have a personal commitment to preventing harm—such as not coming to work when you are very sick; (2) Always try to make a positive difference, such as providing exceptional customer service; (3) Always be respectful of others, which includes not talking in a public place about a co-worker; (4) Always be fair, for example, informing your employer if you know that your friend is stealing; and (5) Be loving toward others.[59]

For trends in the areas covered in this chapter, see Emerging Trends 9.1.

EMERGING TRENDS 9.1

1. **Encouraging employees to become more involved in charities—even on company time.** As a way to encourage better ethical practices and be good corporate citizens, organizations are providing opportunities for employees to take work time to do charitable work. For example, Starbucks has provided employees with an opportunity to help clean up cities, repaint schools, etc. when natural disasters have occurred. Also, Cisco's professional development program for top leaders allows them to spend time working in nonprofit organizations.

2. **Improving systems for "due process."** Many organizations have faced court challenges for not providing good internal processes for investigating incidents of misconduct, particularly when dealing with long-service employees.

3. **Increased attention to privacy issues.** Companies have legitimate rights to protect their products and their employees through monitoring. However, recent court decisions have also held companies liable, and therefore open to lawsuits by employees, for not ensuring that the employees' information is protected from other employees.

4. **Making better use of social media.** Not too many years ago organizations were creating very restrictive practices for use of Internet access on work time. Now as many organizations use the Internet as part of business information retrieval, companies have decided that social media sites might provide helpful contacts and that the benefits can outweigh the risks of people wasting time.

Sources: Howard Schultz, "How Starbucks Fought for Its Life without Losing Its Soul," *Onboard*, March 2011, accessed February 21, 2012, news.starbucks.com/article_display.cfm?article_id=514; Stuart Rudner, "Invasion of Privacy," *Canadian HR Reporter*, January 24, 2012, www.hrreporter.com/blog/Canadian-HR-Law/archive/2012/01/24/invasion-of-privacy; Stuart Rudner, "Another Botched Investigation and Dismissal," *Canadian HR Reporter*, February 21, 2012, www.hrreporter.com/blog/Canadian-HR-Law/archive/2012/02/21/another-botched-investigation-and-dismissal; and Brian Kreissl, "Employers Should 'Friend' Social Media in the Workplace," *Canadian HR Reporter*, February 15, 2012, www.hrreporter.com/blog/HR-Policies-Practices/archive/2012/02/15/employers-should-friend-social-media-in-the-workplace.

SUMMARY

1. Describe statutory rights, contractual rights, due process, and legal implications of those rights.
   - Statutory rights derive from legislation, such as human rights legislation.
   - Contractual rights are derived from contracts, such as an employment contract.
   - Due process is the employee's right to be heard through a complaint process.
   - Legal implications flow from how the employee is treated.
2. Identify the job expectancy rights of employees.
   - Fair and equitable treatment.
   - A workplace that is safe and drug-free.
   - Reasonable treatment regarding privacy.
   - Access to one's own personnel files.
   - Not being subject to discipline for off-duty behaviour.
   - Being notified of any plant closings.
3. Explain the process of establishing disciplinary practices, including the proper implementation of organizational rules.
   - The primary purpose of having disciplinary procedures is to prevent or correct discipline problems.
   - Failure to take disciplinary action serves only to aggravate a problem that eventually must be resolved.
   - Organizations need to clearly outline rules and expectations regarding performance and behaviour.

4. Discuss the meaning of discipline and how to investigate a disciplinary problem.
   - Discipline is action that results in desirable conduct or performance.
   - If a problem occurs, the supervisor needs to determine when the situation occurred and to have a full discussion with the employee to get the employee's view of the situation.
5. Outline the differences between progressive and positive discipline.
   - Progressive discipline is the application of corrective measures by increasing degrees.
   - Progressive discipline is designed to motivate an employee to correct misconduct.
   - Positive discipline is based on the concept that the employee must assume responsibility for personal conduct and job performance.
   - Positive discipline requires a co-operative environment for joint discussion and problem solving between the supervisor and the employee.
6. Identify the different types of alternative dispute-resolution procedures.
   - Step-review systems.
   - Peer-review systems.
   - Use of hearing officers.
   - Open-door system.
   - Ombudsperson system.
   - Arbitration.
7. Discuss the role of ethics in the management of human resources.
   - Ethics in HRM extends beyond the legal requirements of managing employees.
   - Managers engage in ethical behaviour when employees are treated in a fair and objective way and when an employee's personal and work-related rights are respected and valued.

NEED TO KNOW

- Definition of termination with cause, and wrongful dismissal
- Types of disciplinary approaches
- Types of discipline appeal mechanisms for non-union staff
- Definition of ethics

NEED TO UNDERSTAND

- How employee rights are protected
- How to conduct a discipline investigation
- How to dismiss an employee
- Factors used to determine if termination was for cause
- Relationship of organizational ethics to employee rights and expectations

KEY TERMS

alternative dispute resolution (ADR) 332

constructive dismissal 328

contractual rights 309

discipline 320

due process 310

employee rights 307

ethics 333

hearing officer 332

mediation 332

negligence 307

ombudsperson 333

open-door policy 333

positive, or nonpunitive, discipline 323

progressive discipline 322

statutory rights 307

step-review system 332

wrongful dismissal 326

REVIEW QUESTIONS

1. Define management rights and employee rights.
2. What are statutory rights and contractual rights?
3. List some of the guidelines for developing a policy on employee searches.
4. What are some of the guidelines employers ought to use when developing policies for e-mail, Internet, voice-mail, and social media usage?
5. Explain why documentation is so important in the disciplinary process.
6. What are the differences and similarities between progressive and positive discipline?
7. What is "just-cause" dismissal and "wrongful" dismissal?
8. How would you define mediation?
9. Explain a code of ethics.

CRITICAL THINKING QUESTIONS

1. Anjana has recently created a blog where she describes her working conditions, colleagues, and boss. Does her employer have the right to control what she posts? Why?
2. Janet works as a machine operator in a highly automated manufacturing company. The company is considering redesigning its discipline procedures to be oriented toward positive discipline. Janet has been asked to provide some input from the shop floor regarding the advantages and disadvantages of this change. What might she say?
3. You have recently been promoted to a supervisory position. In your new role, you've just discovered that one of your staff has not been updating client files as is required. Outline the steps that you would use to deal with this issue.
4. You have taken a student job monitoring students while they are writing exams. While on duty, you notice that one student is behaving oddly—looking at a smartphone all the time, and looking at the palm of the hand. What would you do?
5. You are a new manager in a large financial institution. You are aware that there is a code of ethics that applies to dealing with client information. You observe that several staff are behaving badly toward some clients. What would you do and why?

DEVELOPING YOUR SKILLS

Privacy Commissioner of Canada

www.priv.gc.ca

Privacy Rights Clearinghouse

www.privacyrights.org

Electronic Frontier Foundation

www.eff.org/issues/privacy

Canadian Internet Policy and Public Interest Clinic

www.cippic.ca/ workplace-privacy

1. Working in groups of three or four, discuss the following questions:
   a. If you are working, do you know whether you are monitored at work?
   b. If you don't know whether you are monitored or not, how could you determine this?
   c. Do you object to monitoring? Why or why not?
2. On an individual basis, access the Web site of the Office of the Privacy Commissioner of Canada (**www.priv.gc.ca**). Click the "Privacy Quiz" and take the "My Privacy Quiz." You may take the quiz as often as you like as the questions change. Were there any surprises for you? Share any surprises with your classmates.
3. Working in a group of four or five, identify an ethical dilemma you had at work or school. What did you do and why? Review your response in relation to the five guidelines listed at the end of the chapter.
4. Access the following Web sites, which discuss employee privacy rights in the workplace. Prepare a one- to two-page report summarizing what each site has to offer. Indicate if there are any areas of the site that might be more helpful to an employee rather than an employer.

   - **www.privacyrights.org**
   - **www.eff.org/issues/privacy**
   - **www.cippic.ca/workplace-privacy**

Fair Measures Inc.
www.fairmeasures.com

5. Access the Fairmeasures Inc. Web site at **www.fairmeasures.com** and go to the "Workplace Issues" drop-down menu, and click on "Business Ethics." Read the various FAQs and pick one to explore further. Access each specific example and read the explanation. Prepare a one-page analysis about why you picked the question and what you learned.

6. Conduct your own Internet search, using any search engine, under the heading of "alternative dispute resolution." Share with your classmates what you learned about alternative dispute resolution, and provide at least two URLs you found helpful.

Case Study 1

When Is Discipline Discriminatory?

Many organizations have policies and programs that deal with employees who are absent from work regularly. Coast Mountain Bus, the public transportation company in Metro Vancouver, implemented an Attendance Management Program (AMP) to deal with chronic absenteeism. The company had an average absence rate of 35 days (seven weeks) and it deemed that 20 to 25% of its operators were "chronic," which means that they were above the 35 days on a regular and consistent basis. The chronic absences were costing the company over $8 million annually. It decided something had to be done.

The AMP has five steps: (1) an informal discussion with the person, in which the employer could explain and advise the employee to minimize absences; (2) a formal interview where the employee is informed of the employer's concerns and asked to provide medical information; (3) a request from the employer that the employee obtain a medical assessment with the outcome of any necessary accommodation if a chronic illness is identified; (4) a request for a further medical assessment and a warning that continued absences could result in termination; and (5) a meeting to inform the employee that attendance has not improved and the employee is being terminated.

Coast Mountain had great results: a reduction in the overall rate of absenteeism and significant cost savings. However, the union representing the operators challenged the program, and the B.C. Human Rights Tribunal decided that the program was discriminatory. The tribunal based its decision because of Step 3: it felt that dealing with an accommodation need at that stage was too late. Coast Mountain appealed the decision, and at the level of the B.C. Supreme Court, the tribunal decision was overturned. The court did say that while steps 1 and 2 were not discriminatory, steps 3 and 4 could be. These "could be" discriminatory if the employee had a chronic illness and attendance expectations were out of line with the need to accommodate. In other words, if a person had a chronic illness that meant missing a fair bit of work, the court indicated that the person ought not to be disciplined. The court concluded that each employee with a disability had to be treated as an individual case and could not have attendance measured in the same way as the other employees.

Source: Case written from information provided at a workshop sponsored by Fasken Martineau, Vancouver, February 22, 2012.

Questions

1. Do you think it was necessary for Coast Mountain Bus to implement such an attendance program? Why or why not?
2. Do you think any kind of discipline is appropriate when people miss work frequently? Why or why not?
3. Do you think that this program will continue to achieve the results being sought? Why or why not?

Case Study 2

The Polluter's Dilemma

Jonica Gunson is the environmental compliance manager for a small plastics manufacturing company. She is currently faced with the decision whether or not to spend money on new technology that will reduce the level of a particular toxin in the wastewater that flows out the back of the factory and into a lake.

The factory's emission levels are already within legal limits. However, Jonica knows that environmental regulations for this particular toxin are lagging behind scientific evidence. In fact, a scientist from the university has been quoted in the newspaper recently, saying that, if emission levels stay at this level, the fish in the lakes and rivers in the area might soon have to be declared unsafe for human consumption.

Further, if companies in the region don't engage in some self-regulation on this issue, there is reason to fear that the government—backed by public opinion—may force companies to begin using the new technology, and may also begin requiring monthly emission level reports (which would be both expensive and time consuming).

The company's environmental compliance budget is tight, however. Asking for this new technology to be installed would put Jonica's department over budget, and could jeopardize the company's ability to show a profit this year.

Source: Chris MacDonald, Businessethics.ca. Reprinted with permission through www.businessethics.ca. (http://www.businessethics.ca/cases/pollutersdilemma1.html).

Questions

1. What motives would the company have to install the new technology?
2. What motives would the company have to *delay* installing the new technology?
3. Why might the companies in this region *prefer* for the government to impose new regulations?

NOTES AND REFERENCES

1. "Pre-employment Screening Services," accessed February 5, 2012, www.dataresearch.com/frame.htm.

2. "Social Media Activity Rarely a Factor in Hiring Decisions: SHRM," *Canadian HR Reporter*, August 26, 2011, www.hrreporter.com/articleview/11069-social-media-activity-rarely-a-factor-in-hiring-decisions-shrm.

3. Sarah Dobson, "Manitoba Gets Tougher on Risk of Violence at Work," *Canadian HR Reporter*, September 12, 2011, www.hrreporter.com/articleview/11207-manitoba-gets-tougher-on-risk-of-violence-at-work.

4. Norm Keith and Anna Abbott, "Criminal Conviction in Death of Worker," *Canadian HR Reporter*, October 10, 2011, www.hrreporter.com/articleview/11412-criminal-conviction-in-death-of-worker.

5. *Wallace v. United Grain Growers* (1997), 152 DLR (4th) 1 (SCC); *BC(PSERC) v. BCGEU* (1999), SCJ No. 46 (SCC).

6. Canadian Human Rights Tribunal, George Vilven and Canadian Human Rights Commission and Air Canada and Air Canada Pilots Association, July 8, 2011, 2011 CHRT 10.

7. Brent Jang, "Air Canada Plans to End Forced Retirement at Age 60," *The Globe and Mail*, January 28, 2012, B8.

8. Peter Eastwood, "Employment Standards Mistakes Can Be Costly for Employers," *Canadian HR Reporter*, June 14, 2010, accessed February 6, 2012, www.hrreporter.com/articleview/7958-employment-standards-mistakes-can-be-costly-for-employers.

9. Lisa Stam, "Certification of Overtime Class Action," February 22, 2010, accessed February 6, 2012, www.canadaemploymenthumanrightslaw.com/articles/overtime-1; and George Waggott, "Overtime and the Salaried Employee in Ontario: A Disaster Waiting to Happen," April 2010, accessed February 6, 2012, www.mcmillan.ca/Overtime-and-the-Salaried-Employee-in-Ontario-A-Disaster-Waiting-to-Happen.

10. Eastwood, "Employment Standards Mistakes Can Be Costly for Employers."

11. Ingrid Peritz, "Visible Tattoos Okay on the Job, Quebec Judge Rules," *The Globe and Mail*, June 11, 2009, A10.

12. Paul Waldie, "But Was It Time Theft?" *The Globe and Mail*, September 9, 2011, A3.

13. *Canadian Online Legal Dictionary*, accessed February 6, 2012, www.irwinlaw.com/cold/term/134.

14. Canada, Department of Justice, "The Canadian Legal Framework," accessed February 6, 2012, http://www.justice.gc.ca/eng/pi/franc/dual/index.html.

15. Canadian Centre for Occupational Health and Safety, "Substance Abuse in the Workplace," accessed February 6, 2012, www.ccohs.ca/oshanswers/psychosocial/substance.html.

16. "Canadian Human Rights Commission's Policy on Alcohol and Drug Testing," accessed February 6, 2012, www.chrc-ccdp.ca/legislation_policies/padt_pdda/toc_tdm-eng.aspx.

17. Statistics Canada, "Heavy Drinking 2009," April 29, 2011, www.statcan.gc.ca/pub/82-625-x/2010002/article/11261-eng.htm.

18. Dr. Joti Samra, "Substance Use in the Workplace," *Benefits Canada*, August 5, 2011, www.benefitscanada.com/benefits/health-wellness/substance-use-and-the-workplace-19182.

19. Ibid.

20. Lukasz Granosik, "Video Surveillance in Workplace: Limits on Employer Rights," *Canadian Employment Law Today*, February 3, 2012, www.employmentlawtoday.com/ArticleView.aspx?l=1&articleid=2645.

21. Bettina Burgess, "Debunking Common Misconceptions around Employee Privacy," *Canadian HR Reporter*, August 15, 2011, 21.

22. Alberta Office of the Information and Privacy Commissioner, Order F2012-01, January 12, 2012.

23. Office of the Privacy Commissioner of Canada, *Consultations on Online Tracking, Profiling and Targeting, and Cloud Computing*, May 2011.

24. Alexander Hamilton, "Organizing Personnel Files: Record Retention," *Business Management*, January 26, 2012, www.businessmanagementdaily.com/19717/organizing-personnel-files-record-retention-faqs.

25. "Individual Flex-Time Agreements Coming to Manitoba," *Canadian HR Reporter*, December 19, 2011, www.hrreporter.com/articleview/11984-individual-flex-time-agreements-coming-to-manitoba.

26. Jocelyn Brodie, "Leave Workers in the Dark at Your Peril," *Canadian HR Reporter*, January 17, 2011, www.hrreporter.com/articleview/8780-leave-workers-in-the-dark-at-your-peril.

27. Amanda Silliker, "Workers' Tweets Could Spell Trouble for Employer," *Canadian HR Reporter*, June 6, 2011, 1.

28. Jeffery R. Smith, "Status Update: You're Fired," *Canadian HR Reporter*, November 8, 2010, accessed February 9, 2012, www.hrreporter.com/blog/Employment-Law/archive/2010/11/08/status-update-youre-fired.

29. Marino J. Sveinson (Roper Greyell LLP, presentation, March 30, 2010).

30. Jeffrey R. Smith, "Construction Worker Sacked for YouTube Stunt," *Canadian HR Reporter*, October 24, 2011, 5.

31. Darah Hansen, "Court Awards Ex-manager More Than $220,000 for Wrongful Dismissal," *The Vancouver Sun*, October 20, 2011, D3.

32. Graeme McFarlane, "Reacting to Riots: Firing from the Hip," *PeopleTalk*, Fall 2011, 30.

33. Andrea Siedsma, "Are Background Checks on Web Posts Too Much Information?" *Workforce Management*, January 2012, 11.

34. Jeffrey R. Smith, "B.C. Worker Fired after Encounter with Prostitute during Shift," *Canadian HR Reporter*, January 16, 2012, www.hrreporter.com/articleview/12092-bc-worker-fired-after-encounter-with-prostitute-during-shift-legal-view.

35. "Labour, Employment, and Human Rights National Update" (Fasken Martineau workshop, February 22, 2012).

36. HR Council for the Nonprofit Sector, "Keeping the Right People: Discipline," accessed February 11, 2012, http://hrcouncil.ca/hr-toolkit/keeping-people-discipline.cfm#top.

37. Gareth Jones, "Workplace Investigations: Getting beyond 'He Said, She Said,'" *Canadian HR Reporter*, January 30, 2012, 22.

38. Matthew Heller, "Court Ruling Puts Workplace Grief on Trial," *Workforce Management*, January 2012, 10.

39. Thadford A. Felton, "Best Practices in Documenting Employee Discipline," *Workforce Management*, January 15, 2009, accessed February 11, 2012, www.workforce.com/article/20090115/NEWS02/301159997.

40. Readers interested in the pioneering work on positive discipline should see James R. Redeker, "Discipline, Part 1: Progressive Systems Work Only by Accident," *Personnel* 62, no. 10 (October 1985): 8–12; James R. Redeker, "Discipline, Part 2: The Nonpunitive Approach Works by Design," *Personnel* 62, no. 11 (November 1985): 7–14. See also Alan W. Bryant, "Replacing Punitive Discipline with a Positive Approach," *Personnel Administrator* 29, no. 2 (February 1984): 79–87; and Chimezie A. B. Osigweh Yg and William R. Hutchison, "Positive Discipline," *Human Resource Management* 28, no. 3 (Fall 1989): 367–83.

41. Shannon Klie, "Moving from Managing to Coaching," *Canadian HR Reporter*, January 25, 2010, accessed February 11, 2012, www.hrreporter.com/articleview/7497-moving-from-managing-to-coaching.

42. HR Council for the Nonprofit Sector, "Keeping the Right People: Discipline."

43. Ibid.

44. Dan Gleadle, "So What Exactly Constitutes Just Cause?" *Canadian HR Reporter*, January 16, 2012, 13.

45. "Constructive Dismissal," accessed February 13, 2012, www.duhaime.org/LegalDictionary/C/Constructive Dismissal.aspx.

46. Jeffrey R. Smith, "Opportunity Knocks But Worker Doesn't Answer," *Canadian HR Reporter*, January 30, 2012, www.hrreporter.com/articleview/12206-opportunity-knocks-but-worker-doesnt-answer-legal-view.

47. Howard Levitt, "Constructive Tips on Demotions," *The National Post*, January 4, 2012, www.nationalpost.com/related/topics/Constructive+tips+demotions/5943184/story.html.

48. Rebecca Olles, "Returning Veterans Unarmed for Job Searches," *Workforce Management*, November 9, 2011, www.workforce.com/article/20111109/NEWS02/111109966/returning-veterans-unarmed-for-job-searches.

49. Sarah Dobson, "Bringing the Troops Home," *Canadian HR Reporter*, January 30, 2012, www.hrreporter.com/articleview/12210-bringing-the-troops-home.

50. Jennifer Myers, "When Employee Conflict Gets in the Way of Doing Business," *The Globe and Mail*, April 28, 2011, www.theglobeandmail.com/report-on-business/careers/career-advice/on-the-job/article2002782.ece.

51. Ray Friesen, "Turning Differences into Creativity," *Canadian HR Reporter*, March 8, 2010, accessed February 13, 2012, www.hrreporter.com/articleview/7616-turning-differences-into-creativity.

52. Jane Taber, "A Hidden Elevator and Two Labour Disputes Unlocked at One Go," *The Globe and Mail*, March 13, 2012, A1.

53. Ian Darling and Suzanne Belson, "Ombuds a Valuable Alternative for Dispute Resolution," *Canadian HR Reporter*, July 12, 2010, accessed February 13, 2012, www.hrreporter.com/articleview/8032-ombuds-a-valuable-alternative-for-dispute-resolution.

54. "Current Membership," Canadian Centre for Ethics and Corporate Policy, accessed February 20, 2012, www.ethicscentre.ca/EN.

55. "Welcome to the Office," Office of the Conflict of Interest and Ethics Commissioner, accessed February 20, 2012, http://ciec-ccie.gc.ca/Default.aspx?pid=1&lang=en.

56. Canada Post Corporation, "Whistleblowing," accessed February 20, 2012, www.canadapost.ca/cpo/mc/aboutus/corporate/whistleblowing.jsf.

57. Kevin Donovan and Tanya Talaga, "ORNGE Scandal: Tougher Legislation, But Whistleblowers Muzzled," *The Star*, February 18, 2012, www.thestar.com/news/canada/politics/article/1133433—ornge-scandal-tougher-legislation-but-whistleblowers-muzzled.

58. Muel Kaptein, "From Inaction to External Whistleblowing: The Influence of the Ethical Culture of Organizations on Employee Responses to Observed Wrongdoing," *Journal of Business Ethics* 98, no. 3 (2011): 519–30; Tara J. Shawver, "Can Ethics Education Impact Whistleblowing?" *Management Accounting Quarterly* 12, no. 4, (Summer 2011): 29–37.

59. Harvey Schachter, "The Business of Acting Ethically," *The Globe and Mail*, February 22, 2012, B19.

10

LABOUR RELATIONS AND COLLECTIVE BARGAINING

OUTCOMES

After studying this chapter, you should be able to

1 Explain the federal and provincial legislation that provides the framework for labour relations.

2 Cite the reasons employees join unions.

3 Outline the process by which unions organizes employees and gains recognition as their bargaining agent.

4 Illustrate the functions labour unions perform at the national and local levels.

5 Describe the bargaining process and the bargaining goals and strategies of a union and an employer.

6 List the forms of bargaining power that a union and an employer may utilize to enforce their bargaining demands.

7 Identify the major provisions of a collective agreement, including the issue of management rights.

8 Describe a typical grievance procedure, and explain the basis for arbitration awards.

OUTLINE

HRM CLOSE-UP

"We share a common goal and that is to serve our customers. If the company is successful, the unions will also be successful."

Eric Poirier.

Eric Poirier remembers his first union meeting in the mid-1990s. He was a university student studying electrical engineering and felt fortunate to have a great job as a technician with a telephone company in New Brunswick. He recalls his union membership as being an important part of his work. But he didn't really appreciate the importance of good management–labour relations until he began to manage his own team years later.

In his first role as a manager for Bell Aliant, a telecommunications company with customers throughout Atlantic Canada and rural areas in Ontario and Quebec, Poirier spent time getting to know what each employee did. He also wanted to show his support for staff by being available when they needed him. "When the phone rang, I answered it. If I received a voice mail, I responded as soon as I could," he said. "It was an effort to build relationships and develop trust and respect."

In a subsequent position, Poirier managed people who did maintenance and provisioning of more advanced inter-networking technology. "Those jobs were new to me, and it was important for me to understand more about the employees' work," he recalls. "When I learned that some maintenance activities had to be done between the hours of 2:00 a.m. and 6:00 a.m., I came in at that time to learn first-hand from them." According to Poirier, working on strengthening the manager-employee relationship helps the manager when there's a business issue that needs attention.

Managing a unionized group has its benefits, says Poirier. "There are rules of engagement, and when it comes to making decisions about things like vacation and sick time, being able to refer to the collective agreement makes it easier." He feels that some managers may be nervous the first time they have to deal with a grievance, for example. "But really, the grievance process just gives us a way to have a discussion. It's a process that's laid out for us and enables us to talk through an issue and find a resolution."

Recently, Bell Aliant began monthly meetings between senior executive leaders from both the union and the company. The goal of this "Common Interest Forum" is to bring both parties together to discuss business strategy. "We share a common goal, and that is to serve our customers. If the company is successful, the unions will also be successful," Poirier explains.

Perhaps the greatest challenge for Poirier is how to recognize and reward employees who do outstanding work. In an environment where all employees must be treated fairly and equally, and everyone is compensated in the same way, he must find creative ways to recognize performance excellence. Sometimes, assigning a special project allows Poirier to provide additional job satisfaction to top performers. "I've had staff getting involved in test installations when we do a trial for a new service offering. This kind of thing becomes a source of pride for staff and lets them become role models for others who are developing their skills."

Building great relationships with staff is Poirier's secret. "If you've built a solid foundation, you can drive improvements and introduce change that will strengthen the business. It's a win-win."

INTRODUCTION

Mention the word "union" and most people will have some opinion, positive or negative. To some, the word evokes images of labour–management unrest—grievances, strikes, picketing, and boycotts. To others, the word represents fairness, opportunity, equal representation, and someone who will look after them. Many think of unions as simply creating an adversarial relationship between employees and managers, while others feel that unions are necessary to counterbalance the power employers have.

Regardless of how people feel about them, unions have been an important force shaping organizational practices, legislation, and political thought in Canada since the mid-1800s. Consider Eric Poirier's statements in the HRM Close-up. Some people might say that fears about unionization have helped employers become better at managing people. Today, unions remain of interest because of their influence on organizational productivity and competitiveness, the development of labour law, and HR policies and practices. Like business organizations themselves, unions are undergoing changes in both operation and philosophy. Labour–management co-operative programs, company buyouts by unions, and labour's increased interest in global trade are examples of labour's new role in society. Currently, of the 17.3 million people employed, approximately 4.3 million are unionized, of which the vast majority (71%) are in the public sector.[1]

In spite of the long history of unions, the intricacies of labour relations are unfamiliar to many individuals. Therefore, this chapter describes government regulation of labour relations, the labour relations process, the reasons workers join labour organizations, the structure and leadership of labour unions, contemporary challenges to labour organizations, and the role a supervisor or manager plays in labour relations.

Unions and other labour organizations can significantly affect the ability of managers to direct and control the various HR processes. For example, union seniority provisions in the labour contract may influence who is selected for job promotions or training programs. Pay rates may be determined through union negotiations, or unions may impose restrictions on management's employee evaluation methods. Therefore, it is essential that managers understand how unions operate and familiarize themselves with the growing body of laws governing labour relations. It is also important for the supervisor to understand how unionization affects the actions of the union and those of the HR professional.

THE LAWS GOVERNING LABOUR RELATIONS

Unions have a long history in North America, and the regulations governing labour relations have evolved over time. Initially, employers strongly opposed union growth, using court injunctions (e.g., court orders forbidding various union activities, such as picketing and strikes) and devices, such as the "yellow-dog contract." A yellow-dog contract was an employer's anti-union tactic by which employees had to agree not to join a union while working for the employer's organization. Using strikebreakers, blacklisting employees (e.g., circulating the names of union supporters to other employers), and discriminating against those who favoured unionization were other anti-union tactics.

Today, the laws governing labour relations seek to create an environment in which both unions and employers can exercise their respective rights and responsibilities. Chapter 2 provided an overview of the various employment laws, including those governing labour relations. This chapter now looks at the laws in more detail.

Labour Relations Legislation

Outcome 1

Which laws govern federal and provincial labour relations?

The first labour relations legislation, the *Trades Unions Act*, was passed by the federal Parliament in 1872. This act exempted unions from charges of criminal conspiracy, allowed them to pursue goals of collective bargaining without persecution, and gave them the ability to strike. Between 1872 and 1900, legislation to settle industrial disputes was enacted in a number of provinces, including Quebec, Ontario, British Columbia, and

Nova Scotia. Although these acts are no longer in effect, they did mark Canada's early recognition of the rights of unions.

Several different laws at the federal and provincial levels currently regulate labour relations. These laws make up a labour relations "system" consisting of government, unions, and employers. The government makes the laws that regulate how unions and employers behave with each other.[2] In making laws, the government will determine who can unionize and where they can unionize. There are specific laws, or acts, for different sectors, industries, and workers.

Canada's labour relations system is highly decentralized, whereas the U.S. system is highly centralized. For example, in Canada, the federal law governs interprovincial transportation and communications, while provincial legislation governs manufacturing and mining. However, 90% of the workforce is governed by provincial legislation. As mentioned earlier in this book, the *Canada Labour Code* governs federally regulated companies such as Bell, Rogers, Canadian National Railway, and Telus, whereas the province in which they operate governs companies such as Molson Breweries. Labour legislation, whether federal or provincial, has certain features in common:

- the right of people to join unions
- the requirement that employers recognize a certified union as the rightful and exclusive bargaining agent for that group of employees
- the identification of unfair labour practices
- the right of unions to strike and right of employers to lock out workers[3]

The Canada Industrial Relations Board (CIRB) was established to administer and enforce the *Canada Labour Code*. Similarly, each province has a labour relations board (LRB) whose members are appointed by the provincial government and who administer the labour law. (The exception is Quebec, which has a labour court and commissioners.) The LRB is generally separate from the government and is composed of representatives from labour and management. The duties of the LRB include, but are not limited to:

- processing union applications to represent employees;
- processing applications to terminate union bargaining rights;
- hearing unfair labour practice complaints; and
- hearing complaints and issuing decisions regarding strikes, lockouts and picketing.[4]

It is important to remember that the administrative regulations are greatly influenced by the politics of any provincial government. Therefore, the legislation can be relatively similar, but the interpretation of the law can vary greatly from one province to another. The law typically gets interpreted by the decisions made by the respective labour boards that then influence the actions a union or company can take in the future. To learn more about the administration of labour relations, Manager's Toolkit 10.1 lists the Web sites of the labour relations boards.

WHY EMPLOYEES UNIONIZE

Outcome 2

What are some of the reasons employees give for unionizing?

Labour relations process
Logical sequence of four events: (1) Workers desire collective representation, (2) union begins its organizing campaign, (3) collective negotiations lead to a contract, and (4) the contract is administered

Employees frequently feel that individually, they will be unable to exercise power regarding their employment conditions at any particular employer. The treatment and benefits they receive depend in large part on how their employers view their worth to the organization. Of course, if they believe they are not being treated fairly, they have the choice of quitting. However, another way to correct the situation is to organize and bargain with the employer collectively. When employees pursue this direction, the labour relations process begins. As Figure 10.1 illustrates, the **labour relations process** consists of a logical sequence of four events: (1) employees desire collective representation, (2) union organizers or employees begin the organizing campaign, (3) collective negotiations lead to a collective agreement, and (4) the collective agreement is administered. Laws and administrative rulings influence each of the separate events by granting special privileges to, or imposing defined constraints on, employees, employers, and union officials.[5]

MANAGER'S TOOLKIT **10.1**

LABOUR RELATIONS BOARDS

Labour relations boards are making it easier for employers and employees to access information. The following Web sites are a valuable resource for the supervisor and HR professional.

Jurisdiction	Name	Web site
Federal government	Canada Industrial Relations Board	www.cirb-ccri.gc.ca
Alberta	Alberta Labour Relations Board	www.alrb.gov.ab.ca
British Columbia	Labour Relations Board	www.lrb.bc.ca
Manitoba	Manitoba Labour Board	www.gov.mb.ca/labour/labbrd
New Brunswick	Labour and Employment Board	www.gnb.ca/leb-cte
Newfoundland	Labour Relations Board and Labrador	www.hrle.gov.nl.ca/lrb
Nova Scotia	Labour Relations Board	www.gov.ns.ca/lae/labourboard
Ontario	Ontario Labour Relations Board	www.olrb.gov.on.ca
Prince Edward Island	Labour Relations Board	www.gov.pe.ca/labour/index.php3?number=1006679&lang=E
Quebec	The Labour Code is administered through investigations and commissions created at the time of a complaint.	
Saskatchewan	Labour Relations Board	www.sasklabourrelationsboard.com

FIGURE 10.1   Labour Relations Process

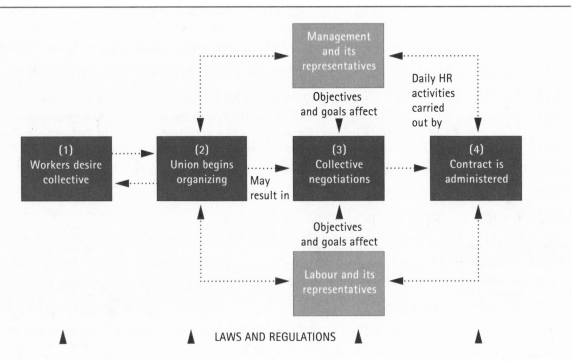

The majority of research on why employees unionize comes from the study of blue-collar employees in the private sector. These studies generally conclude that employees unionize as a result of:

1. Economic need
2. General dissatisfaction with managerial practices
3. A desire to fulfill social and status needs

Union shop

Provision of the collective agreement that requires employees to join the union as a condition of their employment

It should be pointed out that some employees join unions because of the **union shop** provisions of the collective agreement that require employees to join as a condition of their employment. Others join because the employer is a **closed shop**—only members of a union will be hired—or because they choose to under an **open shop** provision. Even when forced to join, many employees eventually accept the concept of unionism. The sections that follow look at some of the more specific reasons people unionize and what role the supervisor and/or organization plays in the unionization process.

Closed shop

Provision of the collective agreement that requires employers to hire only union members

Pay, Benefits, and Working Conditions

Open shop

Provision of the collective agreement that allows employees to join or not join the union

Whether or not a union can become the bargaining agent for a group of employees will be influenced by the employees' degree of dissatisfaction, if any, with their overall employment conditions. For example, employees may feel their concerns about health and safety are ignored or they may be required to wear uniforms without being reimbursed for the cost. It will also depend on whether the employees perceive the union as likely to be effective in improving these conditions. However, unhappiness with wages, benefits, and working conditions appear to be the strongest reasons to join a union. Unions will generally try to convince potential members that they can deliver pay increases and benefits. Other issues that have concerned unions include changes in business practices such as using contract workers, outsourcing, and providing a way for employees to have more voice in their work environment.[6]

At Work with HRM 10.1 explains why workers may wish to improve their conditions by joining a union.

Dissatisfaction with Supervisors and Managers

Employees may seek unionization when they perceive that managerial practices regarding promotion, transfer, shift assignment, or other job-related policies are decidedly unfair.

AT WORK **with HRM 10.1**

HOMEWORKERS: CANADA'S INVISIBLE LABOUR FORCE

Rosanna Gonzalez (not her real name) works in the basement of her home in a small room crowded with industrial sewing machines. Rosanna is in the process of making 410 sweatshirts. To meet her deadline she will have to put in 40 hours of work in two days. There is no natural light in the airless basement room and no way to escape the flying dust and thread particles. Last week the assignment was T-shirts. Rosanna received 38 cents per shirt. She can churn one out in five minutes, but even at that speed, she still earns only about $4.50 per hour—not even minimum wage.

In most provinces the law requires that homeworkers be paid at least one dollar above minimum wage to compensate them for the use of space and equipment in their homes. But enforcement of the law is rare. Canadians are quick to condemn working conditions in developing countries, yet they are noticeably silent about abuses in their own country.

Joining a union is a traditional response to abysmal working conditions.

For homeworkers, unionization is a remote possibility at best. These individuals (most of whom speak little English) work in scattered and unlicensed locations and are usually unaware of their rights. Those who are aware are afraid that if they complain, they will suffer retribution at the hands of the retailers, contractors, and subcontractors with whom they do business. These women have few employment options and are often the sole providers for their children. For them, the choice is clear: put up with the exploitation or don't work at all.

QUESTION:

Do you think that employees working in their own home ought to be able to unionize? Explain your reasons.

Winnipeg Strike of 1919, showing a group of strikers lining a downtown street in Winnipeg. In the centre of the photo is a burning streetcar. Metal workers started the strike to force their employers to improve their working conditions.

Employees cite favouritism shown by managers as a major reason for joining unions. This is particularly true when the favouritism concerns discipline, promotion, and wage increases. Unions will describe the structured complaint process in the collective agreement (the grievance or arbitration process) as a formal way in which employees can have their complaints heard and acted on.

This book has noted that today's employees are better educated than those of the past and often express a desire to be more involved in decisions affecting their jobs. Chapter 3 discussed the concepts of employee engagement and employee empowerment, and highlighted various ways for managers to behave. The failure of employers to give employees an opportunity to participate in decisions affecting their welfare may encourage union membership. It is widely believed that one reason managers begin employee involvement programs and seek to empower their employees is to avoid collective action by employees.

Social and Status Concerns

Employees whose needs for status and recognition are being frustrated may join unions as a means of satisfying these needs. Through their union, they have an opportunity to fraternize with other employees who have similar desires, interests, and problems. Joining the union also enables them to put to use any leadership talents they may have. In the final analysis, the deciding factor is likely to be whether employees perceive that the benefits of joining a union outweigh the costs associated with membership.

Sometimes, employees in similar industries may feel that they can improve their pay and working conditions only by joining a union. For example, the pilots at Porter Airlines have started a drive to unionize. Porter is a relatively new airline that competes directly with Air Canada, whose pilots are unionized.[7]

HOW EMPLOYEES ORGANIZE

Once employees desire to unionize, a formal organizing campaign may be started either by a union organizer or by employees acting on their own behalf. Contrary to popular belief, most organizing campaigns are begun by employees rather than by union organizers. Large national unions such as the Canadian Auto Workers, the United Brotherhood of Carpenters, the United Steelworkers, and the Teamsters, however, have formal organizing departments whose purpose is to identify organizing opportunities and launch organizing campaigns. It has been no secret that the labour movement has targeted certain types of employers. Larger unions have moved out of their traditional industries into other areas. This has been due to changes from a goods-producing society to a service-based society as well as a decline in union membership in resource-based industries such as mining and forestry.[8]

One of the more interesting unionization cases in 2012 relates to the entry of Target retail stores to Canada. Specifically, Target has for a number of years resisted attempts by employees to unionize. Target's business model operates on flexibility in assigning shifts and tasks as well as competitive pay.[9] Similar to Walmart, Target has successfully remained non-union in North America. While Target continues to resist, this status could change given that Target is taking over some of the Zellers stores in Canada—and these are unionized. Most of the labour laws in Canada have had a principle that when a company takes over a similar company in the same area, the employees remain unionized.[10] To test this principle, the United Food and Commercial Workers' union (UFCW), Local 1518, that represents the 120 employees in a Zellers store in Burnaby, B.C., had filed an application with the B.C. labour board to have Target declared the "successor employer" for Zellers. As yet, no decision has been made.[11]

Since organizing campaigns can be expensive, union leaders carefully evaluate their chances of success and the possible benefits to be gained from their efforts. Important in this evaluation is the employer's vulnerability to unionization. Union leaders also consider the effect that allowing an employer to remain non-union may have on the strength of their union within the area. A non-union employer can impair a union's efforts to standardize employment conditions within an industry or geographic area, as well as weaken the union's bargaining power with employers it has unionized. Unions will also assess whether there is a possibility that future employees may wish to decertify. Just as the costs of unionizing can be high, so can the challenges coming from employees wanting to cease having the union represent them.

Organizing Steps

Outcome 3

What is the process to unionize?

The typical organizing campaign follows a series of progressive steps that can lead to employee representation. The organizing process normally includes the following steps:

1. Employee–union contact
2. Initial organizational meeting
3. Formation of in-house organizing committee

Employees will frequently consider a union if there is dissatisfaction with how they are treated.

4. Application to labour relations board
5. Issuance of certificate by labour relations board
6. Election of bargaining committee and contract negotiations

STEP 1   The first step begins when employees and union officials make contact to explore the possibility of unionization. During these discussions, employees will investigate the advantages of representation, and union officials will begin to gather information on employee needs, problems, and complaints as well as information on the employer's financial health and supervisory styles. To win employee support, union organizers must build a case against the employer and for the union.

Supervisors and managers can become familiar with the questions unions ask employees during organizing drives and therefore better assess the effectiveness of their management practices. Manager's Toolkit 10.2 presents these questions.

STEP 2   As an organizing campaign gathers momentum, the organizer will schedule an initial union meeting to attract more supporters. The organizer will use the information gathered in Step 1 to address employee needs and explain how the union can secure these goals.

STEP 3   The third important step in the organizing drive is to form an in-house organizing committee composed of employees willing to provide leadership to the campaign. The committee's role is to interest other employees in joining the union and in supporting its campaign. An important task of the committee is to have employees sign a **membership card** (or authorization card), indicating their willingness to be represented by a labour union in collective bargaining with their employer. The number of signed membership cards demonstrates the potential strength of the labour union. Legislation across Canada states that unions must have a majority of employees as members in a bargaining unit before they can apply for certification election. However, most jurisdictions now interpret

Membership card
A statement signed by an employee authorizing a union to act as a representative of the employee for purposes of collective bargaining

MANAGER'S TOOLKIT **10.2**

FREQUENTLY ASKED QUESTIONS

Many organizations find themselves unionized and are surprised that it has happened. There is also a mistaken belief that unions do not actively recruit new members. The following are the questions union organizers usually ask employees:

1. Do you think people get paid more in other organizations? (Unions will know how much people are paid in the industry and geographic area.)

2. Are decisions about how much employees are paid based on logic or favouritism? (Usually, unions will have received information that supervisors make decisions in an arbitrary fashion.)

3. Are decisions about promotions based on merit or favouritism? (Unions usually have information about a particular individual who was promoted for reasons other than merit.)

4. If something happens that you feel is unfair, do you have recourse? Can you get your complaint heard? Who will hear it? Can they fix it? (Many small companies do not have a way to handle employee complaints. Unions will talk about the formal grievance procedure and the protections that can be provided to employees who feel helpless in dealing with a problem.)

5. How are shift schedules determined? (Unions will say that shifts ought to be determined by seniority.)

6. How are performance problems handled? (Unions will convince potential members that a union can ensure that people are treated fairly if there are performance issues.)

7. Do you feel that your manager criticizes you unfairly? (Unions will describe the processes that can be used if employees feel that they have not been treated fairly.)

8. Does your boss treat you with respect? (Unions will indicate that the power of a collective group of people will make the employer treat everyone respectfully.)

this to mean that at least 50% of those voting constitute a majority. In other words, those who do not cast ballots are not assumed to be voting against the certification of the union. The union membership card, once signed, is confidential, and only the labour relations board has access to the cards.

STEP 4   Application is made to the appropriate labour relations board. In Canada, a majority of unions are certified without a vote if the labour relations board finds that the union has the support of the majority of the employees, based on the number of signed cards. However, in Ontario, if 40% or more of the employees sign membership cards, then a vote can be requested.

STEP 5   The labour relations board reviews the application and initially informs both the employer and the employees about the application. This application is posted so that either employees or the employer have an opportunity to challenge.

STEP 6   Once the labour relations board determines that the union is certified, a bargaining committee is put in place to start negotiating a collective agreement. If the union is a national union, such as the Canadian Auto Workers, usually a national representative works with the bargaining committee to negotiate the collective agreement with the company.

Canadian Auto Workers
www.caw.ca

Employer Tactics

Employers must not interfere with the certification process. They are prohibited by law from dismissing, disciplining, or threatening employees for exercising their rights to form a union. Employers cannot promise better conditions, such as increased vacation days, if the employees vote for no union or choose one union over another. Employers cannot unilaterally change wages and working conditions during certification proceedings or during collective bargaining. Like unions, they must bargain in good faith, meaning that they must demonstrate a commitment to bargain seriously and fairly. In addition, they cannot participate in the formation, selection, or support of unions representing employees.

None of these prohibitions prevents an employer from making the case that the employees have a right not to join a union or that they can deal directly with the employer on any issue. Employer resistance to unionization is the norm in Canada; however, employers need to recognize that employees must be free from threats, intimidation, pressure, or coercion, such as threatening job loss if employees unionize.[12]

Attempts by employers to influence employees are scrutinized closely by officials of the organizing unions and the labour relations board. In one recent case, the Communications, Energy and Paperworkers Union of Canada (CEP) accused Bell Mobility of unfair labour practices in relation to a unionization drive for all of its workers. Specifically, Bell Mobility was charged with pressuring its employees into signing forms against the union by telling the employees they would lose their jobs if the union comes in.[13] The Canada Industrial Relations Board ruled against the company in a unanimous decision. A certification vote was held in July 2011, and the employees voted not to have a union.[14]

Union Tactics

Bargaining unit
Group of two or more employees who share common employment interests and conditions and may reasonably be grouped together for purposes of collective bargaining

Unions also have a duty to act in accordance with labour legislation. Unions are prohibited from interfering with the operation of an employer's organization. They cannot intimidate or coerce employees to become or remain members of a union. Nor can they force employers to dismiss, discipline, or discriminate against non-union employees. They must provide fair representation for all employees in the **bargaining unit**, whether in collective bargaining or in grievance procedure cases. Unions cannot engage in activities such as strikes before the expiration of the union contract.

Unfair labour practices
Specific employer and union illegal practices that operate to deny employees their rights and benefits under labour law

Any of the prohibited activities discussed above for both employers and unions are considered **unfair labour practices**. Charges of unfair labour practices are made to the labour relations board, whose duty is to enforce the applicable labour laws and decide if

FIGURE 10.2 Unfair Labour Practices

Unfair labour practices by employers include the following:

- helping to establish or administer a union
- altering the working conditions of the employees while a union is applying for certification without the union's consent
- using intimidation, coercion, threats, promises, or exercising undue influence while a union is being organized
- failing to recognize or bargain with the certified union
- hiring professional strike breakers

Unfair labour practices by unions include the following:

- contributing financial or other support to an employees' organization
- not representing fairly the employees in the bargaining unit
- bargaining or negotiating a collective agreement with an employer while another union represents the employees in the bargaining unit
- calling or authorizing an unlawful strike, or threatening to do so

---

an unfair labour practice occurred. An example of an unfair labour practice by an employer would be to threaten to fire people who wanted to join a union. Similarly, a union cannot threaten harm to employees if they don't join the union. Figure 10.2 provides a list of unfair labour practices on both the union and the management sides.

An unusual union tactic for organizing employees was attempted in Quebec. Specifically, the Confédération des syndicats nationaux (CSN) made proposals to the shareholders of Couche-Tard convenience stores at its annual shareholders meeting. The union has been trying to organize the Couche-Tard outlets in the greater Montreal area for some time. The proposals included one to "promote respect of freedom of association and collective bargaining."[15] While the proposals did not succeed, the union might have influenced the senior management to comment on the company's successful performance as a result of the employees.[16]

CERTIFICATION PROCEDURES

Certification
Acquisition of exclusive rights by union to represent the employees

The procedures for union **certification** vary across Canadian jurisdictions. As mentioned earlier, if an applicant union can present documentation that it has sufficient support in the proposed bargaining unit, labour boards will grant certification to the union or grant a vote. The labour relations board must certify a union before it can act as a bargaining unit for a group of employees. The union normally provides evidence by submitting signed authorization cards and proof that initiation dues or fees have been paid.[17] Recognition of a union may be obtained through voluntary recognition, regular certification, or a prehearing vote.

However, there can be a situation whereby the legal framework of labour relations forces a person to join a particular union if the person wants to work. For example, the government of Quebec has legislation that requires all construction workers to belong to one of five unions. This also means that any construction company must hire only unionized workers.

Voluntary Recognition

All employers, except those in the province of Quebec, may voluntarily recognize and accept a union. This has not happened often, except in the construction industry where there is a great reliance on union hiring halls. Recently, however, many of the craftspeople associated with the film industry in British Columbia achieved voluntary recognition.

This resulted in an application to the Labour Relations Board by CEP and the board acknowledged that the production-by-production basis of the labour supply in the industry was done on a production-by-production basis that occurred when the producers "voluntarily recognized" each of the individual craft unions. The LRB decision puts all the craftspeople in one union for collective bargaining purposes.[18]

Regular Certification

The regular certification process begins with the union submitting the required minimum membership evidence to the labour relations board. Generally, if an applicant union can demonstrate that it has sufficient support in the proposed bargaining unit, labour boards may grant certification on that basis. (However, with changes in government, labour relations legislation is often reformed. Therefore, requirements for granting certification may change.) The labour relations board may order a representative vote if a sizable minority of workers have indicated either support for or opposition to the unionization.

Prehearing Votes

If there is evidence of irregularities, such as unfair labour practices taking place during the organizing drive, a prehearing vote may be taken. The purpose of this vote is to establish the level of support among the workers. Depending on the particular labour relations legislation, votes can be called if less than 50% of the employees indicate support for a union.

Once a union has been certified, employees are part of a collective and can no longer individually make special arrangements on pay, hours of work, and so on. Likewise, this means that the manager and supervisor can no longer treat individuals differently—that is, they can't make individual deals.

Contract Negotiations

Once a bargaining unit has been certified by the labour relations board, the employer and the union are legally obliged to bargain in good faith over the terms and conditions of a collective agreement. The collective agreement is for at least one year. As the contract expiry date approaches, either party must notify the other of its intention to bargain for a renewal collective agreement or contract negotiation.

The CAW is Canada's largest private-sector union.

Courtesy of CAW Local 195

Decertification

All legislation allows for decertification of unions under certain conditions. If the majority of employees indicate that they do not want to be represented by the union or that they want to be represented by another union, or if the union has failed to bargain, an application for decertification can be made to the labour relations board. If a collective agreement has been reached with the employer, this application can be made only at specified times, such as a few months before the agreement expires. The application for decertification can be initiated by either employees or the employer if the union fails to bargain.

Impact of Unionization on Managers

The unionization of employees can affect managers in many ways. Perhaps most significant is the effect it can have on the ability of managers to make decisions about employees. A union can assist employees if they believe they haven't been treated in accordance with the agreed-to employment conditions. As an example, if a company doesn't have a formal complaint mechanism, there is now a structured grievance procedure. And the decisions of a structured grievance procedure can be enforced through the courts (as will be discussed later in this chapter). Unionization also restricts the freedom of management to formulate HR policy and practices unilaterally.

Challenges to Management Decisions

Management rights
Decisions regarding organizational operations over which management claims exclusive rights

Unions typically attempt to achieve greater participation in management decisions that affect their members. Specifically, these decisions may often involve such issues as the subcontracting of work, productivity standards, and job content. Employers quite naturally seek to claim many of these decisions as their exclusive **management rights** (discussed more fully later in this chapter). However, these rights are subject to challenge and erosion by the union. They may be challenged at the bargaining table, through the grievance procedure, and through strikes. In changing business environments, challenges can include rotating work stoppages to protest the impacts on workers when the company has to make difficult decisions regarding staffing levels. That occurred in mid-2011 when Canada Post workers began job action in protest. Read At Work with HRM 10.2 to gain a fuller understanding of this action.

Loss of Supervisory Flexibility

At a labour–management conference, a union official commented, "Contract terms covering wages, benefits, job security, and working hours are of major importance to our membership." However, for managers and supervisors, the focal point of the union's impact is at the operating level (the shop floor or office facility), where the terms of the collective agreement are implemented on a daily basis. For example, these terms can determine what corrective action is to be taken in directing and disciplining employees. When disciplining employees, supervisors must be certain that they can demonstrate just cause (see Chapter 9) for their actions because these actions can be challenged by the union, and a supervisor can be called as defendant during a grievance hearing. If the challenge is upheld, the supervisor's effectiveness in coping with subsequent disciplinary problems may be impaired. Specific contract language can also reduce the supervisor's flexibility to manage in such areas as scheduling, training, performance evaluation, and promotions, to name a few.

The list provided in Manager's Toolkit 10.3 offers guidelines to help managers and supervisors understand what they can do to create a work environment where employees will see no need to unionize.

The impact of unionization on small businesses can have some, special issues. Read HRM and SME 10.1 to learn more.

CANADA POST NO LONGER HAS A MONOPOLY

It wasn't that many years ago, when the majority of written communications (letters, bills, announcements, etc.) were sent through Canada Post. That is no longer the case. Canada impacted by the changing business of communications and must continue to find ways to make its services relevant.

The post office is no longer the sole supplier of ways and means to transfer documents. As a result, the consumer is not as dependent on its services as it was in the past. Much of what is sent through Canada Post now are wedding invitations, greeting cards, and magazines. Businesses, both large and small, also have more choices in how to move goods and documents.

With the changing nature of the postal business, Canada Post has sought ways and means to trim costs and provide good service. The impact of this has been fewer staff, including on delivery routes. In many new community developments, people have to pick up their mail at a central location of mailboxes.

In spring 2011, the postal workers, represented by the Canadian Union of Postal Workers (CUPW), began rotating work stoppages to protest these decisions. The union said that by having a disruption in different cities, people would be minimally impacted.

Canada Post reacted by shutting down its operations, putting almost 50,000 employees out of work. As a Crown corporation, it felt it had to take such drastic action as the rotating work stoppages had caused almost $100 million in losses.

The federal government eventually passed a law ordering the employees back to work.

CRITICAL THINKING QUESTIONS:

1. What do you or your family use Canada Post for? Has this changed over the last five years?
2. What could both the union and Canada Post have done differently?
3. What do you see as the future for Canada Post?

Sources: Adapted from Richard Blackwell and Brent Jang, "Post workers engineer Strike 2.0," *The Globe and Mail*, June 7, 2011, B11; "Canada Post shuts down operations nationwide," *The Vancouver Sun*, June 15, 2011, B1; and "Angry postal workers rally before returning to work," *CTV News*, www.ctv.ca/CTVNews/TopStories/20110627/strike-canada-post-mail-delivery-resuming-tuesday-110627 (accessed March 7, 2012).

CREATING A POSITIVE WORK ENVIRONMENT

1. If you have something to say to one of your employees, say it directly—and soon.

2. Praise employees publicly; criticize in private.

3. Remember that actions speak louder than words. Be sure your actions "say" what you want them to.

4. Be respectful of all your employees—even the poor performers.

5. Set up a file system for employee information, where you can keep documentation on pay raises, performance reviews, and the like.

Allow employees access to their files, and encourage them to review their files.

6. Create performance goals with each employee—goals that are challenging but attainable; monitor performance and provide feedback.

7. Share business information.

8. Seek input from employees when making changes that will affect them.

9. Ask employees for suggestions on how to improve business operations.

HRM and SME 10.1

UNIONS IN SMALL BUSINESSES

With the majority of unionization occurring in medium to large organizations, what happens when a small business is unionized?

A recent case of attempts to organize workers in a small, family-run and -operated construction company highlights some of the issues. Most labour relations boards will make decisions in the construction industry based on the number of workers on a certain day. For this small company, the day that the union applied for certification, there were five workers at the job site, and most of those were already union members at another construction company. On top of this, the employees were engaging in misuse of company property and obvious insubordination toward the owner/manager. The employer was concerned about saying or doing anything about the

inappropriate behaviour of the workers for fear of the union filing an unfair labour practice complaint.

The owner eventually decided not to be coerced and initiated progressive discipline procedures against the employees who were being insubordinate. The owner wanted to be clear that just because the employees wished to be represented by a union at the company, this was not a rationale to do what they wanted. The owner decided to run the company as it always had been run and not permit the behaviour the owner wouldn't tolerate in any other circumstances.

QUESTIONS:

1. What actions do you think the union took?

2. If you were the owner, what would you have done?

Source: Adapted from "Employers should stand their ground," *The Financial Post*, January 25, 2012, http://business.financialpost.com/2012/01/25/employers-should-stand-their-ground/ (accessed March 11, 2012).

HOW UNIONS OPERATE

International Brotherhood of Electrical Workers

www.ibew.org

International Brotherhood of Boilermakers

www.boilermakers.org

Canadian Union of Postal Workers

www.cupw.ca

Ontario Secondary School Teachers' Federation

www.osstf.on.ca

Canadian Labour Congress

canadianlabour.ca

Unions that represent skilled craft workers, such as carpenters or masons, are called craft unions, such as the International Brotherhood of Electrical Workers (IBEW) and the Brotherhood of Boilermakers. Unions that represent unskilled and semiskilled workers employed along industry lines are known as industrial unions, for example, the Canadian Union of Postal Workers and the Ontario Secondary School Teachers' Federation. While the distinction between craft and industrial unions still exists, technological changes and competition among unions for members have helped to reduce it. Today, skilled and unskilled workers, white-collar and blue-collar workers, and professional groups are being represented by both types of union.

Besides unions, there are also employee associations representing various groups of professional and white-collar employees. Examples of employee associations include the Federation of Quebec Nurses and the Alberta Teachers' Association. In competing with unions, these associations may function as unions and become just as aggressive as unions in representing members. These associations are non-union; however, if the employee association met the necessary criteria under labour legislation, the association could become certified as a union.

Regardless of their type, labour organizations are diverse, each with its own method of governance and objectives. And it is important to remember that unions are primarily political organizations. That is, they have elected leaders who can be voted out of office if the wishes of the members are not met.

Because of the political nature of unions, many unions have come together under an umbrella organization, called the Canadian Labour Congress (CLC). Through this organization, the CLC attempts to influence government policy by commenting on economic conditions, such as the unemployment rate. Also, since most of the major unions in Canada are members of the CLC, the CLC also helps to referee between unions if they are seeking to organize the same group of workers. Because of its size and resources, the

CLC is a very influential organization in Canada, and globally. For example, the head of the CLC, Ken Georgetti, spoke to the House of Commons Committee on Foreign Affairs and International Development in late February 2012. The CLC was challenging the federal government's desire to partner more with the private sector to fund foreign aid to improve the lives of the world's poor. The CLC believes strongly that this work should continue to be done through non profit organizations and not through organizations that are profit-taking.[19] For further information on the CLC, go to its website at **canadianlabour.ca**.

History of Unions in Canada

Trade unions began in Canada during the War of 1812. However, it wasn't until the 1860s that unionism really took root and became more prevalent. Some of the influence to unionize came from British and U.S. immigrants who were involved with unions in their home countries. Laws that protected union members from employer actions such as firing or not hiring union members were enacted much later.

It was not until 1944 that laws were passed that allowed employees to join unions, to be able to bargain collectively and to be protected from unfair labour practices by employers.

Membership in trade unions continued to grow so that by the 1950s, one-third of the Canadian workforce was unionized. And their impact on businesses was being felt: non-union employers had to pay competitive wages in order to keep workers.

In 1956, the Canadian Labour Congress was created with a mission to "explore and develop coordination of action in the legislative and political fields." As mentioned in the previous section, the CLC remains very influential in Canada. The CLC is frequently credited for encouraging the expansion of Canada's social network, such as the universal health-care system and Canada Pension Plan.[20]

Over the years unions have been instrumental in highlighting bad management and helping employees achieve improvements in their work lives.

Structure, Functions, and Leadership of International and National Unions

International unions tend to be affiliates of American unions, with headquarters in the United States. In Canada, there are 39 international unions (with membership of about 1.3 million workers) and 179 national unions (with membership of more than 3 million).[21] There are about the same number of international and national unions as there has been for many years, although the size and composition have changed.

Both international and national unions are made up of local unions. The objectives of these unions are to help organize local unions, to provide strike support, and to assist local unions with negotiations, grievance procedures, and the like. These unions also represent membership interest with internal and external constituents. By ensuring that all employers pay similar wages to their unionized workers, they fulfill the additional role of removing higher wages as a competitive disadvantage.

Outcome 4

What are the functions of unions at both national and international levels?

Structure and Functions of Local Unions

Employees of any organization can form their own union, with no affiliation to a national or international union. In this case, the local is the union. However, most local unions are members of national or international unions or the Canadian Labour Congress, which make available to them financial resources and advice. There are approximately 14,700 locals in Canada—less than in previous years.[22] Some of the reduction is due to mergers of smaller locals into larger entities. For example, two United Food and Commercial Workers (UFCW) locals merged in late 2011 to create one local that will represent 60,000 workers.[23] The UFCW indicated that by doing so, it created better benefits such as a more powerful negotiating position and reduced chance of friction between locals.

Canadian Auto Workers
www.caw.ca

Union (shop) steward
Employee who, as a nonpaid union official, represents the interests of members in their relations with management

Business agent
Normally a paid labour official responsible for negotiating and administering the collective agreement and working to resolve union members' problems

Canadian Union of Public Employees
cupe.ca

National Union of Public and General Employees
www.nupge.ca

Public Service Alliance of Canada
www.psac-afpc.com

Unionized employees pay union dues that finance the operation of the local union. The officers of a local union are usually responsible for negotiating the local collective agreement, for ensuring that the agreement is adhered to, and for investigating and processing member grievances. At Work with HRM 10.3 describes how the Canadian Auto Workers union operates (see also **www.caw.ca**).

Role of the Union (Shop) Steward

The **union (shop) steward** represents the interests of union members in their relations with their immediate supervisors and other members of management. Union stewards are employees of the company and are normally selected by union members within their department. They serve without union pay.

A union steward can be viewed as a "person in the middle," caught between conflicting interests and groups. It cannot be assumed that stewards will always champion union members and routinely oppose managerial objectives. Union stewards are often insightful individuals working for the betterment of employees and the organization. Therefore, supervisors and managers at all levels are encouraged to develop a positive working relationship with stewards and all union officials. This relationship can have an important bearing on union–management co-operation and on the efficiency and morale of the workers.

Role of the Business Agent

Negotiating and administering the collective agreement and working to resolve problems arising in connection with it are major responsibilities of the **business agent**. In performing these duties, business agents must be all things to all people within their unions. They frequently are required to assume the role of counsellor in helping union members with both personal and job-related problems. They are also expected to satisfactorily resolve grievances that cannot be settled by the union stewards. Administering the daily affairs of the local union is another significant part of the business agent's job.

Union Leadership Approaches and Philosophies

To evaluate the role of union leaders accurately, one must understand the nature of their backgrounds and ambitions, and recognize the political nature of the offices they occupy. The leaders of many national unions have been able to develop political machines that enable them to defeat opposition and to perpetuate themselves in office. Tenure for the leaders of a local union, however, is less secure. If they are to remain in office, they must be able to convince a majority of the members that they are serving them effectively.

Although true that union leaders occupy positions of power within their organizations, rank-and-file members can and often do exercise a strong influence over these leaders, particularly with respect to the negotiation and administration of the collective agreement. It is important for managers to understand that union officials are elected to office and, like any political officials, must be responsive to the views of their constituency. The union leader who ignores the demands of union members may risk (1) being voted out of office, (2) having members vote the union out as their bargaining agent, (3) having members refuse to ratify the union agreement, or (4) having members engage in wildcat strikes or work stoppages.

To be effective leaders, union officials must also pay constant attention to the general goals and philosophies of the labour movement. Unions also have historically been politically active, backing such parties as the NDP. However, at times a union will comment on government policy. For example, the Canadian Auto Workers and United Steelworkers jointly criticized the federal government at the beginning of the Great Recession for not making a "buy Canadian" policy a part of the economic stimulus package.[24]

As mentioned earlier, unions are expanding their memberships by organizing employees in a number of different sectors in the economy. To get a fuller appreciation of the range of different unions in different industries, review At Work with HRM 10.4.

A DAY IN THE LIFE OF THE CANADIAN AUTO WORKERS

Ken Lewenza, president of the Canadian Auto Workers (CAW), oversees the operations of Canada's largest private-sector union. The CAW was established in 1985 after breaking away from its American affiliate, the United Auto Workers. Membership had increased from 118,000 to 255,000 through mergers with other unions, until recently when membership dropped to 195,000 as a result of losses in its traditional base of the auto industry. It does, however, represent employees in all major sectors of the Canadian economy, including aerospace, health care, and hospitality, in addition to the auto industry.

The CAW has also amalgamated smaller locals into larger ones. For example, one local in Brantford, Ontario, was very powerful while it represented the employees at the Massey Ferguson manufacturing plant. When the plant closed, that local was merged with another one. Doing so created better support from the CAW as well as provided an ongoing identity for the terminated workers. Even though the original local was very powerful, neither it nor the CAW could stop the closing of the plant.

While the CAW is noted for its negotiations in the auto industry, its most high-profile negotiations were with Caterpillar Inc., with plants in Ontario. Specifically, Caterpillar acquired 425 production workers when it acquired Electro-Motive Diesel Inc. in 2010. The CAW was suspicious of Caterpillar's intentions regarding its investment in Canada when it invested in other locomotive plants in the U.S. The suspicions grew when negotiations for a new collective agreement for the plant started in late 2011, and Caterpillar wanted to reduce pay by 50% and eliminate the pension plan.

The CAW resisted the proposals and sought a strike-mandate from the workers. Caterpillar pre-empted any strike by locking out the workers on January 1, 2012, to pressure the union into agreeing to the wage cuts.

Observers of negotiations and international trade were surprised by Caterpillar's actions. Normally, companies will seek large wage cuts when the business is in trouble. That was not the case for Caterpillar. It is the world's largest heavy machinery maker with sales increasing 35% in one year (2011). These same observers shared some of the CAW's earlier suspicions about whether Caterpillar had intentions of keeping the work in Canada or moving it to the U.S.A., where unions are weaker and labour is cheaper. The observers and the CAW were correct in their suspicions: on February 3, 2012, Caterpillar closed the plant and now appears to be shifting the work to the U.S.A.

On top of dealing with the plant closure, the CAW has been in discussions with another union, the Communications, Energy and Paperworkers, about a possible merger. As noted at the beginning of this story, the CAW's membership has declined, and it feels that by merging with another large union, it can prevent declining union membership. Perhaps a larger union entity could have had a different outcome for the Caterpillar plant.

CRITICAL THINKING QUESTIONS:

1. What are the advantages and disadvantages of creating large unions such as a merger between the CEP (129,000 members) and the CAW (195,000 members)?

2. What would have happened in the Caterpillar plant closing if the CAW had merged with the CEP? Why?

3. Do you think unions ought to be able to organize workers in any industry, such as retail or fast food? Why?

Sources: Adapted from "About the CAW," accessed March 7, 2012, www.caw.ca/en/about-the-caw.htm; Danielle Harder, "UFCW Creates 'Super Local' of 60,000," *Canadian HR Reporter*, August 15, 2011, 8; Lynn Adler, "CAW Seeks Strike Mandate at Cat Plant," *Financial Post*, December 30, 2011, FP3; James R. Hagerty and Caroline Van Hasselt, "Caterpillar Lockout a High-Profile Test of Union Clout," *The Globe and Mail*, January 30, 2012, B5; Strategic Policy, Analysis, and Workplace Information Directorate, Labour Program, Human Resources and Skills Development Canada, *Union Membership in Canada—2010*, 3; Linda Nguyen, "Union Standoff at Caterpillar a Threat to Labour Relations," *The Financial Post*, January 27, 2012, FP2; and Tavia Grant and Greg Keenan, "Severance Packages Bring an End to Acrimonious Chapter in Closing of Caterpillar Factory," *The Globe and Mail*, February 24, 2012, B11.

AT WORK **with HRM 10.4**

DIFFERENT UNIONS IN DIFFERENT INDUSTRIES

SERVICE EMPLOYEES INTERNATIONAL UNION (SEIU)

- Buro Design
- Canadian Linen and Uniform Supply
- Moose Jaw and District EMS
- Saskatchewan Association of Health Organizations
- Queen's Park Racetrack

CANADIAN AUTO WORKERS (CAW)

- Brinks
- Windsor Casino
- Canadian Salt Company
- Xstrata Mining
- No Frills Grocery Stores
- St. Martha's Regional Hospital

COMMUNICATION, ENERGY, AND PAPERWORKERS UNION OF CANADA (CEP)

- SaskEnergy
- Terra Nova Mining
- Mosaic Mine Construction
- CTV
- Bell Aliant

CRITICAL THINKING QUESTION:

Do you think unions can effectively represent the interests of their members in such diverse industries? Why or why not?

Sources: Information accessed on union Web sites: www.seiu.ca; www.caw.ca; www.cep.ca (accessed March 7, 2012).

One success story of union philosophy is a worker-owned pulp mill in British Columbia. The Harmac mill, located in Nanaimo, had been one of the assets of Pope & Talbot, which was declared insolvent in 2008 and then placed into receivership. A group of employees, including members of the Pulp, Paper and Woodworkers of Canada, with the help of investors, put together an offer to take over the operation. The employees also agreed to buy into the mill at $25,000 per person. The mill not only survived, but it has been upgraded so that it is now producing 365,000 tonnes of pulp per year. Furthermore, success seems to breed success. In early 2012, Harmac announced that it had reached a 15-year deal with B.C. Hydro to build an electrical generation plant and produce 25 megawatts of power per year. Wood by-products from the mill will be used to generate the steam to run the power plant.[25]

Labour Relations in the Public Sector

Collective bargaining among federal, provincial, and municipal government employees, and among employees in parapublic agencies (private agencies or branches of the government acting as extensions of government programs) has increased dramatically since the 1960s. Over 71% of all public employees are now unionized compared to 16% for the private sector.[26] The three largest unions in Canada represent public-sector employees. The Canadian Union of Public Employees (CUPE) is the largest union in Canada, representing more than 600,000 members. The second-largest union, with 340,000 members, is the National Union of Provincial Government Employees (NUPGE), which represents employees at the provincial level. The largest union representing employees at the federal level is the Public Service Alliance of Canada (PSAC), with more than 188,000 members.[27] Growth in these unions is threatened by increased cost-cutting efforts of governments at all levels, resulting in employee reductions.

While public- and private-sector collective bargaining have many features in common, a number of factors differentiate the two sectors. However, two key distinctions are the political nature of the labour–management relationship and public-sector strikes.

Political Nature of the Labour–Management Relationship

Government employees are not able to negotiate with their employers on the same basis as their counterparts in private organizations. It is doubtful that they will ever be able to do so because of inherent differences between the public and private sectors.

One significant difference is that labour relations in the private sector have an economic foundation, whereas in government their foundation tends to be political. Since private employers must stay in business in order to sell their goods or services, their employees are not likely to make demands that could bankrupt them. Governments, on the other hand, must stay in business because alternative services are usually not available. For example, the transit strike in Halifax in early 2012 was a way for the union to force the city to agree to its bargaining proposals. The strike created transportation difficulties for students and commuters but did not force the municipal government to agree to union demands.[28] Workers, after being on strike for over a month, escalated job action by blocking snowplows. The union stated again that it was doing this not to upset the public but to force the municipal government to meet its demands.[29] Through the use of a conciliator (discussed in Chapter 9), a settlement was eventually reached in mid-March 2012.[30]

Strikes in the Public Sector

Strikes by government employees create a problem for lawmakers and for the general public. Because the services that government employees provide, such as police work and firefighting, are often considered essential to the well-being of the public, public policy is opposed to such strikes. However, various provincial legislatures have granted public employees the right to strike. Where striking is permitted, the right is limited to specific groups of employees—those performing nonessential services—and the strike cannot endanger the public's health, safety, or welfare. Public-sector unions contend, however, that denying them the same right to strike as employees in the private sector greatly reduces their power during collective bargaining.

Public employees who perform essential services do, in fact, strike. Teachers, sanitation employees, police, transit employees, firefighters, and postal employees have all engaged

Public-sector workers picket to publicize their disputes and discourage people from entering the premises.

Dick Hemingway Editorial Photographs

in strike action. To avoid a potentially critical situation, various arbitration methods are used for resolving collective-bargaining deadlocks in the public sector. One is compulsory binding arbitration for employees such as police officers, firefighters, and others in jobs where strikes cannot be tolerated. Another method is final-offer arbitration, under which the arbitrator must select one or the other of the final offers submitted by the disputing parties. With this method, the arbitrator's award is more likely to go to the party whose final bargaining offer has moved the closest to a reasonable settlement. The government can also enact back-to-work legislation, an option being used with increasing frequency when concerns about public health or safety arise.

THE COLLECTIVE BARGAINING PROCESS

Outcome 5

What are the key activities in the bargaining process?

Once a union wins bargaining rights for employees, its two primary functions are to negotiate the collective agreement and resolve member complaints, usually through the grievance-arbitration process. Interestingly, according to labour law, once the union is certified to negotiate for bargaining-unit members, it must represent everyone in the unit equally, regardless of whether employees subsequently join the union or elect to remain nonmembers. The collective agreement that is ultimately negotiated establishes the wages, hours, employee benefits, job security, and other conditions under which represented employees agree to work.

Those unfamiliar with contract negotiations often view the collective bargaining process as an emotional conflict between labour and management, complete with marathon sessions and fist pounding. In reality, negotiating a collective agreement entails long hours of extensive preparation combined with diplomatic manoeuvring and the development of bargaining strategies. Furthermore, negotiation is only one part of the collective bargaining process. Collective bargaining may also include the use of economic pressures in the form of strikes and boycotts by a union. Lockouts, plant closures, and the replacement of strikers are similar pressures used by an employer. In addition, either or both parties may seek support from the general public or from the courts as a means of pressuring the opposing side. To help you understand the collective bargaining process, review Figure 10.3.

FIGURE 10.3   The Collective Bargaining Process

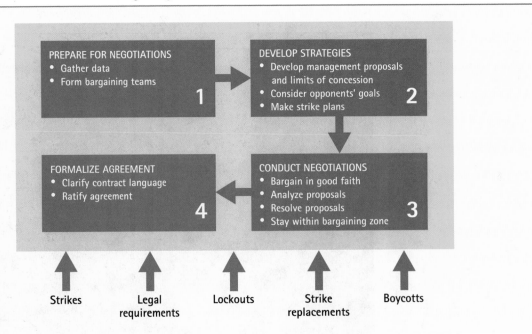

Good-Faith Bargaining

Once a union has been recognized as the representative for employees, an employer is obligated to negotiate in good faith with the union's representatives over conditions of employment. Good faith requires the employer's negotiators to meet with their union counterparts at a reasonable time and place to discuss these conditions. In discussing the other party's proposals, each side will put forward their demands and attempt to justify their position.[31] Finally, at the conclusion of negotiations, a written document—the collective agreement—is produced, which governs the day-to-day employment relationship.[32] Furthermore, an employer cannot override the bargaining process by making an offer directly to the employees. Figure 10.4 illustrates several common examples of bad-faith employer bargaining.

Preparing for Negotiations

Preparing for negotiations includes planning the strategy and assembling data to support bargaining proposals. It will permit collective bargaining to be conducted in an orderly fashion and on a factual and positive basis with a greater likelihood of achieving desired goals. Negotiators often develop a bargaining book that serves as a cross-reference file to determine which contract clauses would be affected by a demand. Assuming that the collective agreement is not the first to be negotiated by the parties, preparation for negotiations ideally should start soon after the current agreement has been signed. This practice will allow negotiators to review and diagnose weaknesses and mistakes made during the previous negotiations while the experience is still current in their minds.

Gathering Bargaining Data

Internal data relating to grievances, disciplinary actions, transfers and promotions, layoffs, overtime, former arbitration awards, and wage payments are useful in formulating and supporting the employer's bargaining position. In addition, information can be obtained from other collective agreements negotiated in the company's industry. These agreements are usually available through the labour relations boards.

The supervisors and managers who must live with and administer the collective agreement are the key sources of ideas and suggestions concerning changes that are needed in the next agreement. Their contact with union members and representatives provides them with a firsthand knowledge of the changes that union negotiators are likely to propose. Any concerns that supervisors and managers might have with the collective

FIGURE 10.4 Examples of Bad-Faith Bargaining

Employer

- Using delaying tactics, such as frequent postponements of bargaining sessions
- Insisting that the union stop striking before resuming negotiations
- Unilaterally changing bargaining topics
- Negotiating with individual employees other than authorized union representatives
- Going through the motions of bargaining rather than conducting honest negotiations
- Refusing to meet with authorized union representatives

Union

- Using delaying tactics, such as frequent postponements of bargaining sessions
- Withdrawing concessions previously granted
- Unilaterally changing bargaining topics
- Going through the motions of bargaining rather than conducting honest negotiations
- Refusing to meet with authorized employer representatives

agreement should be thoroughly understood, considered, and incorporated as appropriate into the overall bargaining approach. And since supervisors work with the collective agreement on a daily basis, it is important that the supervisors and managers be involved in the data-collection process so that they understand and feel part of the bargaining process.

Developing Bargaining Strategies

It is critical that the organization develop a strategy for negotiations. Without adequately planning what it wants to achieve, a company could end up with an unwanted outcome. Negotiators for an employer should develop a written plan covering their bargaining strategy. The plan should consider the proposals that the union is likely to submit, based on the most recent agreements with other employers and the demands that remain unsatisfied from previous negotiations. The plan should also consider the goals the union is striving to achieve and the extent to which it may be willing to make concessions or to resort to strike action in order to achieve these goals. Likewise, it is essential that the company identify the point at which it is willing to let the employees strike or to lock out the employees. Not knowing the organization's limits can create difficulties at negotiations and perhaps incur job action that could have been avoided.

At a minimum, the employer's bargaining strategy must address these points:

- Identify the likely union objectives, including specific proposals and management responses to them.
- Develop a list of organizational objectives, including management demands, limits of concessions, and anticipated union responses.
- Identify the nature of the union–management relationship and the relationship the union has with its members.
- Determine whether the company is prepared to lock out or take a strike.
- Develop a database to support management bargaining proposals and to counteract union demands.
- Determine whether the company will operate if employees strike and prepare a contingency operating plan.

Certain elements of strategy are common to both the employer and the union. Generally, the initial demands presented by each side are greater than those it may hope to achieve. This approach is taken in order to provide room for compromise. Moreover, each party will usually avoid giving up the maximum it is capable of conceding in order to allow for further compromise that may be needed to break a bargaining deadlock.

Forms of Collective Bargaining

Traditionally, the collective bargaining relationship between an employer and a union has been adversarial. The union has held the position that, while the employer has the responsibility for managing the organization, the union has the right to challenge certain actions of management. Unions also have taken the position that the employer has an obligation to operate the organization in a manner that will provide adequate compensation to employees. Moreover, unions maintain that their members should not be expected to subsidize poor management by accepting less than their full entitlement.

With adversarial bargaining, negotiators start with defined positions and through deferral, persuasion, trade, or power, the parties work toward resolving individual bargaining demands. In traditional bargaining, with its give-and-take philosophy, the results may or may not be to the complete satisfaction of one or both parties. In fact, when one side feels it has received "the short end of the stick," bitter feelings may persist for the life of the agreement.

To overcome these negative feelings, labour and management practitioners may follow a nonadversarial approach. **Interest-based bargaining** (IBB), or interest-based negotiations, is based on the identification and resolution of mutual interests rather than the resolution of specific bargaining demands. IBB is "based on relationships of mutual

Interest-based bargaining
Problem-solving bargaining based on a win-win philosophy and the development of a positive long-term relationship

respect and trust among the parties, in lieu of the adversarial nature of traditional collective bargaining."[33] The focus of bargaining strategy is to discover mutual bargaining interests with the intent of formulating options and solutions for mutual gain.

Interest-based bargaining is novel in both its philosophy and process. Also distinct are the bargaining tools used to expedite a successful nonadversarial negotiating experience. Rather than using proposals and counterproposals to reach agreement (as with adversarial negotiations), participants use brainstorming, consensus decision making, active listening, process checking, and matrix building to settle issues. This style of negotiations was pioneered by Roger Fisher and William Ury, two professors at the Harvard Business School, and published in their highly successful book, *Getting to Yes*. Fry and Ury stressed the need to focus on the problem (not the positions of the parties); to separate the people from the problem; and to create options for mutual benefit. In this fashion, the parties strive to find solutions to problems and thus improve their overall relationship.[34]

Conducting the Negotiations

Among the factors that tend to make each bargaining situation unique are the economic conditions under which negotiations take place, the experience and personalities of the negotiators on each side, the goals they are seeking to achieve, and the strength of the relative positions. Some collective agreements can be negotiated informally in a few hours, particularly if the contract is short and the terms are not overly complex. Other agreements, such as those negotiated with large organizations, such as Air Canada and CP Rail, require months before settlements are reached. The economic problems in the last several years have resulted in fewer work stoppages.[35]

Bargaining Teams

The composition and size of bargaining teams are often a reflection of the desires and practices of the parties. Normally, each side will have four to six representatives at the negotiating table. The chief negotiator for management is usually the senior HR person; the chief negotiator for the union is usually the local union president or union business agent. Others making up management's team may include representatives from accounting or finance, operations, and other HR staff. The local union president is likely to be supported by the chief steward, various local union vice-presidents, and a representative from the national union. In some cases, the representative from the national union will be the chief negotiator for the local union.

Labour negotiations have become increasingly complex and legalistic. Therefore, it is advisable that the parties have an experienced negotiator.

The initial meeting of the bargaining teams is particularly important because it establishes the climate that will prevail during the negotiations that follow. A cordial attitude, with perhaps the injection of a little humour, can contribute much to a relaxation of tensions and help the negotiations to begin smoothly.

Analyzing the Proposals

The negotiation of a collective agreement can have some of the characteristics of a poker game, with each side attempting to determine its opponent's position while not revealing its own. Each party will normally try to avoid disclosing the relative importance that it attaches to a proposal so that it will not be forced to pay a higher price than is necessary to have the proposal accepted. As with sellers who will try to get a higher price for their products if they think the prospective buyer strongly desires them, negotiators will try to get greater concessions in return for granting those their opponents want most.

As they develop their collective bargaining proposals, astute negotiators know that some demands are more important to their side than others—either for economic or for political reasons. Therefore, the proposals that each side submits generally may be divided into those it feels it must achieve, those it would like to achieve, and those it is submitting primarily for trading purposes. As bargainers discuss the proposals from each side, they are constantly trying to determine the intensity with which each side is committed to its demands. The ability to accurately gauge "commitment" to various proposals can spell the difference between an agreement and a bargaining impasse.

Resolving the Proposals

For each bargaining issue to be resolved satisfactorily, the point at which agreement is reached must be within limits that the union and the employer are willing to accept. The area within these two limits is called the "bargaining zone." In some bargaining situations, the solution desired by one party may exceed the limits of the other party. Thus, that solution is outside the bargaining zone. If that party refuses to modify its demands sufficiently to bring them within the bargaining zone, or if the opposing party refuses to extend its limit to accommodate the demands of the other party, a bargaining deadlock will result.[36] For example, when bargaining a wage increase for employees, if the union's lowest limit is a 2% increase and management's top limit is 3%, an acceptable range—the bargaining zone—is available to both parties. If management's top limit is only 1%, however, a bargaining zone is not available to either side and a deadlock is likely to occur.

The Union's Power in Collective Bargaining

Outcome 6

What forms of bargaining power do unions and employers have?

During negotiations, it is necessary for each party to retreat sufficiently from its original position to permit an agreement to be achieved. If this does not occur, the negotiations will become deadlocked, and the union may resort to the use of economic power to achieve its demands. Otherwise, its only alternative will be to have members continue working without a collective agreement once the old one has expired. The economic power of the union may be exercised by striking, picketing, or boycotting the employer's products and encouraging others to do likewise. As managers know well, the ability to engage in or even threaten to engage in such activities also can serve as a form of pressure. And in some cases, employees do not actually strike, but slow down their work and create pressure on the company. Or the employees will "work to rule"—strictly following the terms of the collective agreement. This means that if the collective agreement specifies that employees will have a 45-minute lunch break, yet most employees take only 30 and work the other 15 minutes, in a work-to-rule, the employees would take the full 45 minutes.

Striking

Strike
A situation in which unionized workers refuse to perform their work during labour negotiations

A **strike** is the refusal of a group of employees to perform their jobs. It is legal only during negotiations after the collective agreement has expired. Employees cannot strike during the collective agreement as proscribed by labour legislation. Although strikes account for only a small portion of total workdays lost in industry each year, they are a costly and emotional event for all concerned. For example, in 2010, when a Hertz outlet went on strike, there were reports of harassment by picketers of both management staff and customers. Hertz, in seeking a court injunction to stop the harassing behaviour, discovered that some of the picketers were not employees but individuals who had been hired by the union to picket.[37] Unions usually will seek strike authorization from their members to use as a bargaining ploy to gain concessions, making a strike unnecessary. A strike vote by the members does not mean they want or expect to go out on strike. Rather, it is intended as a vote of confidence to strengthen the position of their leaders at the bargaining table. The threat of a strike creates as much of a problem as an actual strike.

Since a strike can have serious effects on the union and its members, the prospects for its success must be analyzed carefully by the union. For example, the elementary/secondary school teachers' strike in British Columbia in 2012 created issues for parents and students. Parents were concerned about how to have their children both educated and cared for during the strike while students, particularly those graduating, were concerned about getting marks for entrance into postsecondary schools. Because of these concerns, the British Columbia government introduced legislation to end the strike.[38]

**International Association
of Machinists and
Aerospace Workers**

www.iamaw.ca

**Canadian Union of Public
Employees**

cupe.ca

**International Brotherhood
of Electrical Workers**

www.ibew.org

Work stoppages continue to create issues for the Canadian economy. In a recent study, it was determined that during the 2000s, most of the stoppages were in the telecommunications, broadcast, or transportation sectors, and that most of the days lost came from only two or three work stoppages a year.[39] Strikes can be disruptive and challenging to the organizations struck. Of critical importance is whether the employer will be able to continue operating using supervisory and nonstriking personnel and replacement workers. In organizations with high levels of technology and automation, and consequently fewer employees, continuing service with supervisors and managers is more likely. For example, among the highly automated telephone companies, supervisors can maintain most services during a strike. The greater the ability of the employer to continue operating the company's services, the smaller the union's chances of achieving its demands through a strike.

To understand more about the issues over which unions will strike, check out the Web sites of the International Association of Machinists and Aerospace Workers (**www.iamaw.ca**), Canadian Union of Public Employees (**cupe.ca**), and the International Brotherhood of Electrical Workers (IBEW) (**www.ibew.org**).

Picketing

When a union goes on strike, it will picket the employer by placing persons at business entrances to advertise the dispute and to discourage people from entering the premises. Even when the strikers represent only a small proportion of the employees within the organization, they can cause the shutdown of an entire organization if a sufficient number of the organization's remaining employees (i.e., sympathy strikers) refuse to cross their picket line. Furthermore, because unions often refuse to cross another union's picket line, the pickets may serve to prevent trucks and railcars from entering the business to deliver and pick up goods.

Pickets are used during a strike to make customers and the general public aware of the dispute.

If a strike fails to stop an employer's operations, the picket line may serve as more than a passive weapon. Employees who attempt to cross the line may be subjected to verbal insults and even physical violence. Mass picketing, in which large groups of pickets try to block the path of people trying to enter an organization, may also be used. However, the use of picket lines to exert physical pressure and incite violence is illegal and may harm more than help the union cause.

Boycotting

Another economic weapon of unions is the boycott, which is a refusal to patronize the employer. For, example, production employees on strike against a hand-tool manufacturer might picket a retail store that sells the tools made by the struck employer. Unions will also use handbills, radio announcements, and notices in newspapers to discourage purchase of the employer's product or service.

The Employer's Power in Collective Bargaining

The employer's power in collective bargaining largely rests in being able to shut down the organization or certain operations within it. The employer can transfer these operations to other locations or can subcontract them to other employers through outsourcing. General Motors outsources to foreign manufacturers many parts used in the assembly of North American cars. In exercising their economic freedom, however, employers must be careful that their actions are not interpreted by the provincial labour relations board to be an attempt to avoid bargaining with the union.

Operating During Strikes

When negotiations become deadlocked, typically it is the union that initiates action and the employer that reacts. In reacting, employers must balance the cost of taking a strike against the long- and short-term costs of agreeing to union demands. They must also consider how long operations might be suspended and the length of time that they and the unions will be able to endure a strike. An employer who chooses to accept a strike must then decide whether to continue operating if it is possible to do so. Air Canada, in preparation for a possible strike by its sales and service agents, began training non-union staff on those duties.[40]

Should employees strike the organization, employers in certain jurisdictions are limited in their ability to hire replacement workers. Quebec and British Columbia have passed "anti-scab" laws, forbidding the use of replacement workers during a strike. Employers have the right to dismiss workers who engage in sabotage or violence during a strike.

Workers are entitled to return to their jobs, but not necessarily their previous position, once a strike is settled. The right to return to work is often an issue to be negotiated. Although laws vary, in many cases employees must submit, in writing, their intention to return to their job once a strike is finalized.

Using the Lockout

Lockout
Strategy by which the employer denies employees the opportunity to work by closing its operations

Although not often used, a **lockout** occurs when an employer takes the initiative to close its operations. Besides being used in bargaining impasses, lockouts may be used by employers to combat union slowdowns, damage to their property, or violence within the organization that may occur in connection with a labour dispute.

While this approach hasn't been used often, more incidences of lockouts began to occur as of 2010. For example, U.S. Steel locked out its employees at its Hamilton, Ontario, plant in late 2010. By Fall 2011, the company was warning that the plant had lost money and that it wouldn't be subsidized by any profits made at other plants. The company was demanding that the union (United Steelworkers) agree to end the indexing of retiree pension payments and to create a defined contribution pension plan (as discussed in Chapter 7) for new employees.[41] Another major lockout, previously discussed, was Canada Post in 2010.

Under Labour Relations Board provisions, an employer cannot enforce a lockout within a prescribed number of hours (48 to 72) of a strike vote. Lockouts affect nonstriking workers. For example, when miners at Inco are locked out, administrative work ceases, and office staff are also locked out or laid off. Employers may be reluctant to resort to a lockout because of their concern that denying work to regular employees might hurt the organization's image.

Resolving Bargaining Deadlocks

When a strike or a lockout occurs, both parties are soon affected by it. The employer will suffer a loss of profits and customers, and possibly of public goodwill. The union members suffer a loss of income that is likely to be only partially offset by strike benefits or outside income. The union's leaders risk the possibility of losing members, of being voted out of office, of losing public support, or of having the members vote to decertify the union as their bargaining agent. As the losses to each side mount, the disputing parties usually feel more pressure to achieve a settlement.

Mediation and Arbitration

When the disputing parties are unable to resolve a deadlock, a third party serving in the capacity of a conciliator, a mediator, or an arbitrator may be called on to provide assistance. In many jurisdictions, conciliation is compulsory before a legal strike or lockout. The conciliator, appointed by the provincial ministry of labour, helps the parties reconcile their differences in an attempt to reach a workable agreement. If the conciliation effort is unsuccessful, a report is filed with the ministry of labour, which, in rare instances, may appoint a conciliation board that accepts presentations from both parties and makes nonbinding formal recommendations. If a settlement cannot be reached at this stage, a strike is permitted, except in Manitoba, Alberta, Saskatchewan, and Quebec, where strikes are permissible during conciliation. This two-stage conciliation process is normally reserved for high-profile cases in which significant social and economic consequences would result from a strike.

Mediation is similar to conciliation except that it is voluntary (the two parties contract a neutral third party to help them), and the mediator assumes a more active role as a negotiator. A **mediator** serves primarily as a fact finder and someone to open up a channel

Mediator
Third party in a labour dispute who meets with one party and then the other in order to suggest compromise solutions or to recommend concessions from each side that will lead to an agreement.

Target is challenging whether some of its stores will remain unionized when it opens outlets in former Zellers operations.

The Canadian Press/Stephen C. Host

Arbitrator
Third-party neutral who resolves a labour dispute by issuing a final and binding decision in an agreement

Interest arbitration
A mechanism to renew or establish a new collective agreement for parties

Rights arbitration
A mechanism to resolve disputes about the interpretation and application of a collective agreement during the term of that collective agreement

of communication between the parties. Recent research has demonstrated that mediation can produce higher satisfaction with outcomes and that the relationship between the parties remains good after the conflict has been resolved.[42] Typically, the mediator meets with one party and then the other in order to suggest compromise solutions or to recommend concessions from each side that will lead to an agreement without causing either to lose face. Mediators have no power or authority to force either side toward an agreement. They must have exceptional communication skills (listening and handling strong emotions), a variety of assessment skills to identify causes of conflict, and the ability to respond to cultural and power issues.[43]

One of the newer forms of mediation is online mediation. Through using Internet-based help, ways can be found to use experts in helping solve the dispute without having the expert present. Check out some of these resources by visiting the following Web sites: Mediate.com (**www.mediate.com/odr**), ADR Resources (**www.adrr.com**), and ADR Institute of Canada (**www.adrcanada.ca**).

Arbitration is the only third-party resolution form that results in binding decisions. An **arbitrator** assumes the role of a decision maker and determines what the settlement between the two parties will be. In other words, arbitrators write a final contract that the parties must accept. Compared with mediation, arbitration is not often used to settle private-sector bargaining disputes. In those essential-service areas within the public sector where strikes are prohibited, the use of **interest arbitration** is a common method to resolve bargaining deadlocks. Because one or both parties are generally reluctant to give a third party the power to make the settlement for them, a mediator typically is used to break a deadlock and assist the parties in reaching an agreement. Once an agreement is concluded, an arbitrator may be called on to resolve disputes arising in connection with the administration of the agreement. This type of arbitration is called grievance arbitration, or **rights arbitration**.

THE COLLECTIVE AGREEMENT

Outcome 7

What are the major provisions of a collective agreement?

At the conclusion of negotiations, a collective agreement is put in writing and ratified by the union membership. The union typically does this by asking that the members vote on the new terms. The representatives of both parties then sign the agreement—a legal, binding contract. The scope of the agreement (and the length of the written document) will vary with the size of the employer and the length of the bargaining relationship. Manager's Toolkit 10.4 shows some of the major articles in a collective agreement and also provides examples of some new and progressive contract clauses.

Two important items in any collective agreement pertain to the issue of management rights and the forms of security afforded the union.

The Issue of Management Rights

Management rights have to do with conditions of employment over which management is able to exercise exclusive jurisdiction. Since virtually every management right can and has been challenged successfully by unions, the ultimate determination of these rights will depend on the relative bargaining power of the two parties. Furthermore, to achieve union co-operation or concessions, employers have had to relinquish some of these time-honoured rights.

Residual Rights

Residual rights
Concept that management's authority is supreme in all matters except those it has expressly conceded to the union in the collective agreement

In the collective agreement, management rights may be treated as **residual rights** or as defined rights. The residual rights concept holds that

management's authority is supreme in all matters except those it has expressly conceded in the collective agreement, or in those areas where its authority is restricted by law. Put another way, management does not look to the collective

MANAGER'S TOOLKIT **10.4**

TYPICAL ITEMS IN A COLLECTIVE AGREEMENT

TYPICAL CLAUSES WILL COVER

- wages
- vacations
- holidays
- work schedules
- management rights
- union security
- transfers
- discipline
- grievance procedures
- no strike/no lockout clause
- overtime
- safety procedures
- severance pay
- seniority
- pensions and benefits

PROGRESSIVE CLAUSES WILL COVER

- employee access to records
- limitations on use of performance evaluation
- eldercare leave
- flexible medical spending accounts
- protection against hazards of technology (repetitive strain injuries or chemicals, such as PCBs)
- limitations against electronic monitoring
- procedures governing drug testing (or other substances)
- bilingual stipends
- domestic partnership benefits (same-sex benefits)

agreement to ascertain its rights; it looks to the agreement to find out which and how much of its rights and powers it has conceded outright or agreed to share with the union.[44]

Residual rights might include the right of management to determine the product to produce or to select production equipment and procedures. Employers who subscribe to the residual rights concept prefer not to mention management rights in the collective agreement on the grounds that they possess such rights already. To mention them might create an issue with the union.

Defined Rights

Defined rights

Concept that management's authority should be expressly defined and clarified in the collective agreement

The **defined rights** concept, on the other hand, is intended to reinforce and clarify which rights are exclusively those of management. This concept means that the employer has only those rights that are written into the collective agreement. It serves to reduce confusion and misunderstanding and to remind union officers, union stewards, and employees that management never relinquishes its right to operate the organization. For example, a defined right would include the right of management to take disciplinary action against problem employees. The great majority of collective agreements contain provisions covering management rights. The following is an example of a general statement defining management rights in one collective agreement:

It is the exclusive right of the Company to manage the enterprise and direct the workforce and exercise all of its functions except to the extent that these functions are expressly limited by this Collective Agreement and provided however that this Article will not be used in a discriminatory manner against any employee or group of employees. Without restricting the generality of the foregoing it is the exclusive function of the employer to:

a) maintain order, discipline, and efficiency

b) hire, promote, assign, demote, classify, transfer, layoff and to discipline and discharge any employee for just cause subject to any part of this agreement which is relevant thereto and which may be cause for a grievance to be filed.

c) determine the nature and kind of business, the kinds of equipment and materials to be used, the methods and techniques of work, the content of jobs, the schedules of production, the schedule of shifts, the number of employees to be employed, and the cessation of operations or any part thereof.

d) transfer, shift or divert employees from one work area or department to another from time to time, subject to any part of the agreement which is relevant, thereto.[45]

Forms of Union Security

When a labour organization is certified by a labour relations board as the exclusive bargaining representative of all employees in a bargaining unit, it must, by law, represent all employees in the unit, non-union and union members alike. In exchange for its obligation to represent all employees equally, union officials will seek to negotiate some form of compulsory membership as a condition of employment. Union officials argue that compulsory membership prevents the possibility that some employees will receive the benefits of unionization without paying their share of the costs. A standard union security provision is dues checkoff, which gives the employer the responsibility of withholding union dues from the paycheques of union members who agree to such a deduction.

The more common forms of union security found in collective agreements are the following:

1. The *closed shop* states that employers will hire only union members.
2. The *union shop* provides that any employee not a union member upon employment must join the union within 30 days or be terminated.
3. The *agency shop* states that union membership is voluntary yet all bargaining unit members must pay union dues and fees.
4. The *open shop* allows employees to join the union or not. Nonmembers do not pay union dues. This is the rarest form of union security.

Few issues in collective bargaining are more controversial than the negotiation of these agreements. Though rare, closed-shop clauses are perhaps the most adversarial because they require employers to recruit employees from a union hiring hall.

Working in conjunction with the union-shop clause are the various seniority provisions of the collective agreement. Unions prefer that many personnel decisions (e.g., promotions, job transfers, shift assignments, vacations) be based on seniority, a criterion that limits the discretion of managers to make such decisions on the basis of merit.

Administration of the Collective Agreement

Negotiation of the collective agreement, as mentioned earlier, is usually the most publicized and critical aspect of labour relations. Strike deadlines, press conferences, and employee picketing help create this image. Nevertheless, as managers in unionized organizations know, the bulk of labour relations activity comes from the day-to-day administration of the agreement. Once the collective agreement is signed, each party frequently will interpret clauses differently. These differences are traditionally resolved through the grievance procedure.

Manager's Toolkit 10.5 provides some examples of clauses from collective agreements.

GRIEVANCE PROCEDURES

Grievance procedure
Formal procedure that provides for the union to represent members and nonmembers in processing a grievance

The **grievance procedure** typically provides for the union to represent the interests of its members (and nonmembers as well) in processing a complaint that something in the collective agreement has been violated. It is considered by some authorities to be the heart of the bargaining agreement—the safety valve that gives flexibility to the whole system of collective bargaining.[46] When negotiating a grievance procedure, one important concern

MANAGER'S TOOLKIT **10.5**

CLAUSES FROM COLLECTIVE AGREEMENTS

1. Leave with or without Pay for Other Reasons

At its discretion, the Employer may grant:

(a) leave with pay when circumstances not directly attributable to the employee prevent his or her reporting for duty; such leave shall not be unreasonably withheld;

(b) leave with or without pay for purposes other than those specified in this Agreement. (Between Canada Revenue Agency and the Public Service Alliance of Canada)

2. Layoffs

The Employer shall give all permanent Employees with one (1) or more years of service, two (2) consecutive working days notice of lay off or two (2) days pay.

[Between Communications, Energy, and Paperworkers Union and A.B.C. Press (1979) Limited]

3. Seniority

SENIORITY LIST The Company shall at least once every six (6) months, post in a conspicuous place on its premises an up-to-date list of all employees covered by this Agreement showing the date when each commenced his employment with the Company. The Company shall forward to the Union a copy of each list on the date of its posting.

LAYOFFS In the event of layoffs, seniority shall be recognized. The principle of last man on, first man off, shall prevail, subject to job classification. The Company shall give at least forty-eight (48) hours' notice on layoffs, exclusive of Saturdays, Sundays, and General Holidays.

(Between Robinson Rentals and Sales and International Union of Operating Engineers)

for both sides is how effectively the system will serve the needs of employees and management. A well-written grievance procedure will allow grievances to be processed quickly and with as little red tape as possible. Furthermore, it should serve to foster co-operation, not conflict, between the employer and the union.

Outcome 8

How does a grievance procedure work?

The operation of a grievance procedure is unique to each individual collective bargaining relationship but is required under Canadian labour relations codes. Grievance procedures are negotiated to address the organization's structure and labour–management philosophy and the specific desires of the parties. Although each procedure is unique, there are common elements among systems. For example, grievance procedures normally specify how the grievance procedure is to be initiated, the number and timing of steps that are to compose the procedure, and the identity of representatives from each side who are to be involved in the hearings at each step (see Figure 10.5). The purpose of this multi-step process is to allow higher levels of union and management representatives to look at the issue from different perspectives. When a grievance cannot be resolved at one of the specified steps, most agreements provide for the grievance to be submitted to a third party—usually an arbitrator—whose decision is final and binding. It is not the function of an arbitrator to help the two parties reach a compromise solution. Rather, it is the arbitrator's job to mandate how the grievance is to be resolved.

Initiating the Formal Grievance

In order for an employee's grievance to be considered formally, it must be expressed orally and/or in writing—ideally to the employee's immediate supervisor. If the employee feels unable to communicate effectively with the supervisor, the grievance may be taken to the union steward, who will discuss it with the supervisor. Since grievances are often the result of an oversight or a misunderstanding, many of them can be resolved at this point. Whether or not it is possible to resolve a grievance at the initial step will depend on the

FIGURE 10.5   Grievance Procedure

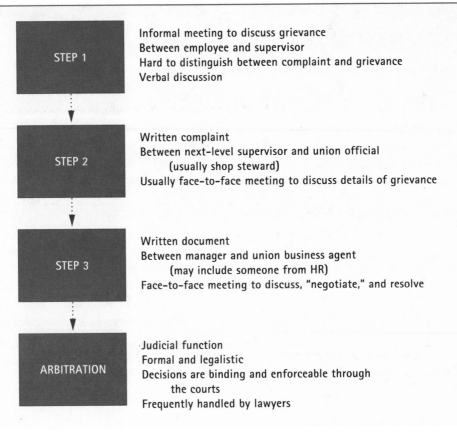

STEP 1 — Informal meeting to discuss grievance
Between employee and supervisor
Hard to distinguish between complaint and grievance
Verbal discussion

STEP 2 — Written complaint
Between next-level supervisor and union official
      (usually shop steward)
Usually face-to-face meeting to discuss details of grievance

STEP 3 — Written document
Between manager and union business agent
      (may include someone from HR)
Face-to-face meeting to discuss, "negotiate," and resolve

ARBITRATION — Judicial function
Formal and legalistic
Decisions are binding and enforceable through
      the courts
Frequently handled by lawyers

supervisor's ability and willingness to discuss the problem with the employee and the steward. Supervisors should be trained formally in resolving grievances. This training should include familiarization with the terms of the collective agreement and the development of counselling skills to facilitate a problem-solving approach.

In some instances, a satisfactory solution may not be possible at the first step because there are legitimate differences of opinion between the employee and the supervisor, or because the supervisor does not have the authority to take the action required to satisfy the griever. Personality conflicts, prejudices, emotionalism, stubbornness, or other factors may also be barriers to a satisfactory solution at this step.

One of the more entertaining grievances occurred when Molson Canada decided to eliminate the supply of free beer to its 2,400 retirees. Molson determined that it could save about $1 million per year and that by doing this, it would not have to cut employees or reduce pensions. The union representing the retirees launched the grievance.[47]

Grievance Resolution

If a grievance is to be resolved successfully, representatives of both management and the union must be able to discuss the problem in a rational and objective manner. A grievance should not be viewed as something to be won or lost. Rather, both sides must view the situation as an attempt to solve a problem. Throughout the process, both parties will try to resolve the issue. However, if the conflict cannot be resolved through discussion and compromise, all collective agreements in Canadian jurisdictions contain a provision for arbitration, or **grievance resolution**. An arbitrator (usually a lawyer or professional skilled in the arbitration process) or a board or panel (consisting of a union nominee, a management nominee, and a neutral chair) hears the case and submits a decision, including the rationale. The decision is final, and the parties are legally bound

Grievance resolution
Process in which a neutral third party assists in the resolution of an employee grievance

to accept the decision unless there is a serious concern over the arbitrator's competence or integrity.

One criticism of the arbitration process is that it is slow (up to two years) and costly. One solution is expedited arbitration, which is an agreement to bypass some steps in the grievance process when the issue is particularly important or urgent, as in the case of employee dismissals or layoffs of employees. For example, the Regina (Saskatchewan) Health Region and CUPE went to an expedited arbitration hearing when the Region contracted out certain services to a third party.[48]

Rights Arbitration

The function of rights (or grievance) arbitration is to provide the solution to a grievance that a union and an employer have been unable to resolve by themselves. As mentioned earlier, arbitration is performed by a neutral third party (an arbitrator or impartial umpire). This third party's decision dictates how the grievance is to be settled. Both parties are obligated to comply with the decision. Even if one of the parties believes the arbitrator's award is unfair, unwise, or inconsistent with the collective agreement, that party may have no alternative but to comply with the decision. Read HRM and the Law 10.1 for what might be considered an unusual decision.

HRM and the Law 10.1

ISN'T IT OK TO DRINK AT WORK?

You might think that drinking on the job and then wrecking a company vehicle would be grounds to terminate someone. But that isn't always the case. SaskTel attempted to fire two employees who had been drinking, as well as having open beer cans in the truck, before crashing the truck. However, when the union pushed the grievance to arbitration, the arbitrator determined that while the behaviour/action was serious and warranted discipline, termination was too severe.

The individuals were field technicians responsible for installing and maintaining telephone lines in the southeastern part of the province. What was key in the mind of the arbitrator was that they had been long-service employees (one with 12 years and the other with 11 years) with no discipline record and very good performance reviews.

Details of the employees' activities leading up to the accident were reported during the arbitration. Specifically, as per standard operation, the two had surveyed a site prior to commencing work the following day. At the completion of the survey, they decided to visit the parents of a co-worker who had recently died. During the visit, the two individuals joined the parents in a small glass of rum mixed with pop. After the visit, they left and the father gave them a beer. They opened the beer on the way to the truck. Both indicated that they felt fine and felt that they could drive. On their way home, they ran into a patch of black ice and the driver lost control, ran into a ditch, and rolled. Fortunately, neither employee was injured, but the truck was written off.

The police arrived on the scene, administered an alcohol road test, which the driver failed. However, when re-tested at the police station, the driver did not fail but did receive a 24-hour suspension. When the two field technicians reported the accident to their manager, they admitted to the drinking and open beer can. After SaskTel investigated, a decision was made to terminate them for violating the company's code of conduct. The arbitrator, in reversing the termination, did institute a four-month suspension without pay.

QUESTIONS:

1. If you had been the arbitrator, what would have been your decision?

2. Would you have made the suspension longer or shorter? Why?

Source: Adapted from Jeffrey R. Smith, "SaskTel workers brew up trouble with truck," *Canadian HR Reporter*, December 5, 2011, 5. Reprinted by permission of Canadian HR Reporter. © Copyright Thomson Reuters Canada Ltd., Toronto, Ontario, 1-800-387-5164. Web: www.hrreporter.com.

The Decision to Arbitrate

If a grievance cannot be resolved through the grievance procedure, each disputing party must decide whether to use arbitration to resolve the case. The alternatives would be for the union to withdraw the grievance or for the employer to agree to union demands.

In deciding whether to use arbitration, each party must weigh the costs involved against the importance of the case and the prospects of gaining a favourable award. It would seem logical that neither party would allow a weak case to go to arbitration if there were little possibility of gaining a favourable award. But there may be other reasons for advancing a grievance. For example, it is not unusual for a union to take a weak case to arbitration in order to demonstrate to the members that the union is willing to exhaust every remedy in looking out for their interests. Union officers also are not likely to refuse to take to arbitration the grievances of members who are popular or politically powerful in the union, even though their cases are weak. Moreover, unions have a legal obligation to provide assistance to members who are pursuing grievances. Because members can bring suit against their unions for failing to process their grievances adequately, many union officers are reluctant to refuse taking even weak grievances to arbitration.

Management, on the other hand, may allow a weak case to go to arbitration to demonstrate to the union officers that management "cannot be pushed around." Managers at lower levels may also be reluctant to risk the displeasure of top management by stating that a certain HR policy is unworkable or unsound. Stubbornness and mutual antagonism may force many grievances into arbitration because neither party is willing to make concessions to reach an agreement, even when it may recognize that it is in the wrong.

The Arbitration Process

The issues to be resolved through arbitration may be described formally in a statement. Each party makes a joint submission to the arbitrator, indicating the rationale for the grievance. The submission to arbitrate must state the nature of the dispute with reference to the section of the collective agreement that has allegedly been breached. Such a statement might read: "Was the three-day suspension of Alex Hayden for just cause? If not, what is the appropriate remedy?" However, the two parties at the beginning of the hearing also present grievable issues orally to the arbitrator. The purpose of an arbitration hearing is to provide a full and fair hearing of the matter in dispute. If minutes and memoranda covering the meetings held at earlier stages of the grievance procedure have been prepared, these are sometimes submitted prior to the formal hearing to acquaint the arbitrator with the issues.

In arbitrating a dispute, the arbitrator is responsible for ensuring that each side receives a fair hearing, during which it may present all the facts it considers pertinent to the case. The procedures for conducting arbitration hearings and the restrictions governing the evidence that may be introduced during these hearings are more flexible than those permitted in a court of law. Hearsay evidence, for example, may be introduced, provided it is considered as such when evaluated with the other evidence presented. The primary purpose of the hearing is to assist the arbitrator in obtaining the facts necessary to resolve a human resources problem rather than a legal one. The arbitrator, therefore, has a right to question witnesses or to request additional facts from either party.

Depending on the importance of the case, the hearings may be conducted in an informal way or in a very formal manner not unlike that of a court trial. If the proceedings have witnesses who will testify, the witnesses are sworn in. After conducting the hearing and receiving all written evidence, or any other submissions allowed, the arbitrator customarily has 30 days in which to consider the evidence and to prepare a decision. In the majority of labour contracts, the parties share the costs of arbitration equally. In all grievance arbitrations except those involving any form of discipline, the "burden of proof" rests with the union. This means that the union must prove that the employer violated the written collective agreement.

The Arbitration Award

Arbitration award
Final and binding award
issued by an arbitrator in
a labour–management dispute

The **arbitration award** should include not only the arbitrator's decision but also the rationale for it. The reasoning behind the decision can help provide guidance concerning the interpretation of the collective agreement and the resolution of future disputes arising from its administration. In pointing out the merits of each party's position, the reasoning that underlies the award can help lessen the disappointment and protect the self-esteem of those representing the unsuccessful party. In short, tact and objective reasoning can help to reduce disappointment and hard feelings.

The foundation for an arbitrator's decision is the collective agreement and the rights it establishes for each party. In many instances, the decision may hinge on whether management's actions were justified under the terms of this agreement. Sometimes, it may depend on the arbitrator's interpretation of the wording of a particular provision. Established HR policies and past practices can also provide the basis for determining the award. And it must be remembered that an arbitration decision, if need be, is enforceable through the courts.

In many grievances, such as those involving employee performance or behaviour on the job, the arbitrator must determine whether the evidence supports the employer's action against the griever. The evidence must also indicate whether the employee was accorded the right of due process, which is the employee's right to be informed of unsatisfactory performance and to have an opportunity to respond to these charges. Under most collective agreements, an employer is required to have just cause (i.e., a good reason) for the action it has taken, and such action should be confirmed by the evidence presented.

If the arbitration hearing indicates that an employee was accorded due process and the disciplinary action was for just cause, the severity of the penalty must then be assessed. Where the evidence supports the discipline imposed by the employer, the arbitrator will probably let the discipline stand intact. However, it is within the arbitrator's power, unless denied by the submission agreement, to reduce the penalty. It is not uncommon, for example, for an arbitrator to reduce a discharge to a suspension without pay for the period the griever has been off the payroll.

Because of the importance and magnitude of arbitration in grievance resolution, the process by which arbitrators make decisions and the factors that influence those decisions are of continuing interest to managers. Typically, arbitrators use four factors when deciding cases:

1. The wording of the collective agreement.
2. The submission agreement as presented to the arbitrator.
3. Testimony and evidence offered during the hearing about how the collective agreement provisions have been interpreted.
4. Arbitration criteria or standards (i.e., similar to standards of common law) against which cases are judged.

When deciding the case of an employee discharged for absenteeism, for example, the arbitrator would consider these factors separately and/or jointly. Arbitrators are essentially constrained to decide cases on the basis of the wording of the collective agreement and the facts, testimony, and evidence presented at the hearing. For example, in a recent termination case, the employee (a field gas worker) was lying about having a prostitute in the company car while on shift. The arbitration panel determined through the facts, testimony, and evidence presented that the person had been terminated with cause. The cause in this case was not for having the person in the car, but for lying about it; being truthful, no matter what the circumstances, was key to an employment relationship.[49]

Given the ongoing economic climate, labour relations and collective bargaining continue to undergo many changes. See Emerging Trends 10.1 for some of the more important ones.

Arbitration is a formal process to solve a grievance.

PhotoLink/Getty Images

NEL

EMERGING TRENDS **10.1**

1. ***Tougher negotiations.*** With the continuing issues in the Canadian economy, more organizations are taking a firmer approach and stand at bargaining. Examples of lockouts were discussed earlier, and there is also the lockout at an Alcan smelter in Quebec. In another example, GM Canada wanted to reduce the amount of money it contributes to the health-care costs of its retirees. Governments are also considering legislation to take away union power such as in Quebec, where the construction industry, long considered corrupt, no longer wants unions to determine who works at job sites.

2. ***Labour unrest.*** Coupled with tougher negotiations, there is considerable turmoil among unionized employees. Many unions believe that the unrest is being fuelled by employers. Unions believe that their members are frustrated because the economy hasn't recovered as much as it was expected to. This problem is on top of

any concessions that were made when the economy first went into recession in 2008. Also, federal and provincial governments have been more vocal about getting their debts under control, which typically means fewer employees or less for wage adjustments.

3. ***Change in labour–management relations.*** Even though there is unrest and tougher negotiations, organizations are developing new relationships with their unions. As organizations continue to change and evolve, unions can be helpful in providing the employer with insights into how the employees are feeling. For example, when a care centre in Ontario had to lay off workers due to the economy, the employer worked closely with the union to ease the situation for the employees. For these positive relations to occur, however, it is important for the company to treat the union as a partner in the overall enterprise and to develop a true collaboration.

4. ***Different bargaining demands.*** Perhaps as a result of the economy and the low rate of return on investments, pensions for workers are again becoming prominent. For example, a three-day strike by customer service agents at Air Canada was over the airline's demand to change their pension plan. Unions are also demanding that employers work harder to create healthier work environments by dealing more visibly with bullying and harassment. Another area on the union bargaining agenda concerns challenging what an employer can do to employees regarding off-work conduct. This issue was highlighted during the Stanley Cup riots in Vancouver in 2011 when a number of employees, mostly younger workers, were terminated because newscasts showed them participating in the riots.

5. ***Unionization.*** Union density in Canada continues to decline—currently about 29%. Much of the decline is due to the shift from an industrial economy to one of service and knowledge. People in these sectors are usually more educated and therefore tend to resist collective action. Further, some provinces have enacted labour legislation that restricts the union certification process. Beyond that, Gen X and Y, as well as Millennials, have different expectations and views of their role in the workplace. These younger workers see themselves as more independent, able to make their own way, and they expect to be encouraged to contribute. They also see the unionized workplace as adversarial and thus do not want to be associated with that type of environment.

6. ***Changes in employer communications.*** Since the time unions came into existence, unions and employees have wanted better communications from their employers. With the deluge of social media in the workplace, employers are finding new ways of communicating. Employers have always been particularly eager to inform their employees about what is occurring in negotiations. With the use of social media, employees can now instantaneously know what is being discussed—far quicker than unions have traditionally been able to inform their members.

Sources: Greg Keenan, "GM Canada Eliminates Key Legacy Cost with Deal on Health-Care Trust Fund," *The Globe and Mail*, August 15, 2011, B3; Rheal Segin, "Construction Union Conflict Turns Nasty," *The Globe and Mail*, October 25, 2011, A1; Karla Thorpe, "Are Unions Relevant in Canada Today?" November 9, 2011, The Conference Board of Canada, www.conferenceboard.ca/topics/humanresource/commentaries/11-11-09/Are_Unions_Relevant_in_Canada_Today.aspx; Michelle Miner, "Striking Right Balance in Labour Relations," *Canadian HR Reporter*, December 5, 2011, 8; Amanda Silliker, "Canada's Labour Relations at Crossroads: Survey," *Canadian HR Reporter,* December 5, 2011, 1; Darah Hansen, "Pensions Challenge Labour in 2012," *The Vancouver Sun*, January 3, 2012, D3; Craig Wong, "Tough Year of Labour Negotiations Ahead, Warns Union," *The Globe and Mail*, January 4, 2012, B5; Derek Sankey, "Social Media Carries Benefits and Risks," *The Vancouver Sun*, February 4, 2012, D5; and Jane Taber, "Halifax Labour Wars about to Get Bloody," *The Globe and Mail*, March 7, 2012, A4.

SUMMARY

1. Explain the federal and provincial legislation that provides the framework for labour relations.
   - Laws determine who can unionize.
   - Laws require that unions and employers bargain in good faith.
   - Laws provide for unions to strike and for employers to lock out.

2. Cite the reasons employees join unions.
   - Dissatisfaction with pay and benefits.
   - Dissatisfaction with managerial practices.
   - Desire for recognition and status.

3. Outline the process by which unions organize employees and gain recognition as their bargaining agent.
   - Employees make contact with a union representative.
   - Union schedules meeting with other employees.
   - Application is made to labour relations board.
   - Labour relations board grants bargaining rights.

4. Illustrate the functions labour unions perform at the national and local levels.
   - National unions help organize local unions.
   - National unions help train and educate local unions.
   - Local unions negotiate collective agreements and process member grievances.

5. Describe the bargaining process and the bargaining goals and strategies of a union and an employer.
   - Each side will prepare a list of goals it wishes to achieve while additionally trying to anticipate the goals desired by the other side.
   - Both employer and union negotiators will be sensitive to current bargaining patterns within the industry, general cost-of-living trends, and geographical wage differentials.
   - The collective bargaining process includes not only the actual negotiations but also the power tactics used to support negotiating demands.

6. List the forms of bargaining power that a union and an employer may utilize to enforce their bargaining demands.
   - The union's power in collective bargaining comes from its ability to picket, strike, or boycott the employer.
   - The employer's power during negotiations comes from its ability to lock out employees or to operate during a strike by using managerial or replacement employees.

7. Identify the major provisions of a collective agreement, including the issue of management rights.
   - Typical collective agreements will contain numerous provisions governing the labour–management employment relationship.
   - Major areas of interest concern wages (rates of pay, overtime differentials, holiday pay), hours (shift times, days of work), and working conditions (safety issues, performance standards, retraining).
   - Management rights refers to the supremacy of management's authority in all issues except those shared with the union through the collective agreement.

8. Describe a typical grievance procedure and explain the basis for arbitration awards.
   - The procedure will consist of three to five steps—each step having specific filing and reply times.
   - Higher-level managers and union officials will become involved in disputes at the higher steps of the grievance procedure.
   - The final step of the grievance procedure may be arbitration.
   - Arbitrators render a final decision for problems not resolved at lower grievance steps.
   - Arbitrators consider the wording of the collective agreement, testimony, and evidence offered during the hearing, including how the parties have interpreted the collective agreement.

NEED TO KNOW

- Legislation in your province governing labour relations
- Steps employees go through to unionize
- Definition of collective bargaining
- Definition of grievance
- Difference between mediation and arbitration
- Definition of defined rights and residual rights

NEED TO UNDERSTAND

- Relationship of supervisory actions and behaviours in employees unionizing
- Expected behaviours from employers and unions during organizing drive
- Impact of unionization on supervisory actions
- Steps and importance of preparation for negotiations
- Steps in grievance process

KEY TERMS

arbitration award 377

arbitrator 370

bargaining unit 351

business agent 358

certification 352

closed shop 347

defined rights 371

grievance procedure 372

grievance resolution 374

interest arbitration 370

interest-based bargaining 364

labour relations process 345

lockout 368

management rights 354

mediator 369

membership card 350

open shop 347

residual rights 370

rights arbitration 370

strike 366

unfair labour practices 351

union shop 347

union (shop) steward 358

REVIEW QUESTIONS

1. How are labour relations regulated at both the federal and provincial levels?
2. Describe the unfair labour practices that apply to employers. Are they the same for unions? If not, what are the differences?
3. What is the impact on supervisors of employees becoming unionized?
4. Describe the role of a union business agent and a union shop steward.
5. What are the components of the bargaining process?
6. Describe both a strike and a lockout. What is the difference?
7. Describe mediation and arbitration. What is the difference?
8. Describe some of the employment conditions covered in a collective agreement.
9. Describe a rights (or grievance) arbitration.

CRITICAL THINKING QUESTIONS

1. The Service Employees International Union (SEIU) uses business-savvy techniques to organize workers. One example is when the SEIU had difficulty in organizing office cleaners who were primarily women and immigrants. When the union organizer learned that many office buildings were financed by large pension funds, he persuaded one pension fund to insert a "responsible contractor" clause into each financing policy, and then in one fast way, organized all the office cleaners. Is this a "fair labour practice"? Why or why not?
2. Using the same example above, what other non-traditional organizing tactics might unions use to increase union membership?
3. What arguments might a union present to encourage someone to join a union? What might an employer present?
4. Provincial labour laws typically do not cover individuals who are self employed. Should labour laws be changed to allow self-employed individuals to become union members? If so, what could the benefits be and why?
5. You have recently been appointed as a shop steward for your work unit. The supervisor of the unit tends to be fairly controlling and direct in the approach to staff; however, you feel that the supervisor has always been fair in dealing with members of the bargaining unit. What type of relationship would you want to develop with the supervisor? Why?
6. You are part of the negotiating team representing all the workers in a medium-size, high-end clothing manufacturer. Some of your fellow workers are in the 18 to 27 age bracket, and another large number are in the 45 to 50 age bracket. What are some items these workers might want in relation to hours of work and benefits?
7. Indira Singh has decided to file a grievance with her union steward, alleging that she was not promoted and a more junior (in seniority) employee was. Describe the steps in her grievance and whether you think her grievance ought to go to arbitration.

DEVELOPING YOUR SKILLS

Fast Food High

www.youtube.com/
watch?v=0XR84-v1Fqk

UNI Global Union

www.uniglobalunion.org

Canadian Union of Public Employees

www.cupe.ca

Canadian Auto Workers

www.caw.ca

Ontario Teachers' Federation

www.otffeo.on.ca

The Manitoba Teachers' Society

www.mbteach.org

Canadian Industrial Relations Board

www.cirb-ccri.gc.ca/
decisions/index_eng.asp

1. *Fast Food High* is a film produced by CTV and inspired by the real story about how a group of teenage workers tried to organize a union at McDonald's in Orangeville, Ontario. Watch the YouTube clip of the opening scene at **www.youtube.com/ watch?v=0XR84-v1Fqk**, and then in groups of three or four, identify the reasons that these young people may want to form a union.

2. Access to technology has and is changing the dynamics in bargaining. Go to UNI Global Union at **www.uniglobalunion.org** and explore the various items in a global union that represents 900 unions and 20 million workers worldwide. Prepare a two- or three-page summary explaining how the use of Web technology, including Facebook and Twitter, can affect labour relations.

3. About 16% of working Canadians are self employed. Some see this as a positive sign (i.e., evidence of an increase in entrepreneurial activity); others see it as a response to the lack of ongoing employment opportunities. The labour laws in each province do not have any provisions for independent workers. These workers may have low contract rates (wages) and no income security. Divide the class into two groups, and assign each group to prepare to debate solutions to this issue, taking one of two sides: "Governments should change labour laws to recognize and protect self-employed workers," or, "Unions should organize self-employed workers and fight for better treatment by the organizations that use them."

4. During a union organizing drive, labour and management will develop a plan to present their positions to employees. A goal of each side will be to collect information on the other that can be used to build a case for or against the union. In addition, each side will seek to avoid committing unfair labour practices. Working in teams of union and management representatives, answer the following questions, and be prepared to present your findings during a discussion period.

   a. What methods might the union use to contact employees?

   b. What information might the union collect on management in order to obtain employee support?

   c. What information might management want to collect on the union?

   d. What methods might unions and management use to tell their story to employees? What illegal actions will the union and management want to guard against?

5. Access the following union Web sites:

   - **www.cupe.ca**
   - **www.caw.ca**
   - **www.otffeo.on.ca**
   - **www.mbteach.org**

   Review the profile of the union and the current issues it supports. Compare each union with regard to membership and issues. Bring your information to class and share it in groups of four or five. Identify at least one aspect of the Web site that surprised you and one thing that impressed you.

6. Access the Canadian Industrial Relations Board Web site (**www.cirb-ccri.gc.ca/ decisions/index_eng.asp**), where summaries of cases can be found. Access, too, the Web site of your provincial labour relations board (see Manager's Toolkit 10.1 on page 346) and access the link to decisions. Retrieve two or three decisions from each site. Prepare a two- to three-page report comparing the decisions.

Case Study 1

Will This Be a Strike or a Lockout?

With the election of Rob Ford as mayor of Toronto, new challenges faced the city's unions. Ford, a champion of reducing spending, felt that the city was being coerced by some of the unions. As a result, he planned to be a different mayor.

In March 2012, the City of Toronto declared that it was at an impasse in bargaining with its 23,000 "inside" workers (planners, daycare workers, ambulance dispatchers, etc.) represented by the Canadian Union of Public Employees (CUPE), Local 79. The City also requested that no recommendation for conciliation be brought in. It is up to the Ontario Ministry of Labour to determine whether conciliation does or does not occur. However, if the ministry decided not to assign a conciliation board, then the City would be in a legal position to lock out employees and the union would be in a legal position to strike. The City indicated that it did not want conciliation as it wanted to have new collective agreements bargained.

However, the union maintained that the city hadn't changed any of its demands in the three months since negotiations commenced. While the union and the City couldn't confirm, it was generally agreed that the major issues were job security and pay.

As part of its desire to cut the costs of running the city and provide better value to the taxpayer, the City had negotiated some major concessions with its outside workers (labourers, truck drivers, sanitation workers, etc.) in early 2012. The most significant change was that the union agreed to a new layoff policy whereby employees had to have 15 years of seniority before there was any layoff protection. During these negotiations, the mayor was accused of "attempting to gut the collective agreement" by demanding that the "jobs-for-life" clause be removed.

The general suspicion regarding the City's motivation had fuelled union concerns regarding the City's request for noconciliation efforts.

In mid-March, CUPE Local 79 filed an unfair labour practice complaint with the Ontario Labour Relations Board, charging that the City was not bargaining in good faith and was not engaging in meaningful discussion. The City responded by saying that the union had begun to escalate its demands when the City requested no conciliation.

The ministry accepted the City's request for no conciliation, which meant that at the end of March, the City and the union would both be in the power positions of either locking out or striking.

Sources: Adapted from: Sue-Ann Levy, "Union Bullies Yield to City," *The Toronto Sun*, February 5, 2012, www.torontosun.com/2012/02/05/levy-union-bullies-yield-to-city; "Toronto Outside Workers Ratify New Contract," *Canadian Labour Reporter*, February 14, 2012, www.labourreporter.com/articleview/12353; "Toronto Inside Workers Can Strike or Be Locked Out March 25," *Canadian Labour Reporter*, March 8, 2012, www.labour-reporter.com/articleview/12500-toronto-inside-workers-can-strike-or-be-locked-out-march-25; and "Union Accuses Toronto of Bad-Faith Bargaining," *Canadian Labour Reporter*, March 13, 2012, www.labour-reporter.com/articleview/12553-union-accuses-toronto-of-bad-faith-bargaining.

Questions

1. Striking or locking out has very serious consequences for both parties. Decide which of the above (City or union) has more power and why.
2. Should public-sector unions, such as those representing the employees at the City of Toronto, be able to strike? Should the City be able to lock out? Why or why not?
3. As a class exercise, determine the outcome of the dispute outlined above and identify when it occurred.

Case Study

The Union Vice-President Is Barred from Entering Company Property

Beginning in the summer of 2011, a long and bitter strike took place at a mining company in northern Canada. Sometime in early 2012, several employees decided to cross the picket line and go to work. Tempers flared and an employee (Jones) with a good work record was involved in an incident where one employee who crossed the picket line was assaulted. The company investigated the incident, but Jones refused to co-operate, and the company concluded that Jones had physically assaulted the employee crossing the picket line. Besides Jones, two other striking employees were charged with assault and criminal harassment, respectively.

The company decided to fire all the striking workers involved in the picket line incident, including Jones. In addition to being fired, all were banned from the mining company's property. The strike eventually ended in the summer of 2012.

At the conclusion of the strike, Jones, although terminated from the company, became a vice-president of the union. Jones needed access to the mining company property to represent the union members, and the company refused to recognize Jones in his union role, saying that Jones must be an employee per terms of the collective agreement to be on the union executive. However, in the handling of several grievances, the company did deal with Jones in his vice-president role by telephone.

Through separate court action, Jones was found not guilty of criminal harassment, but the company still refused access to its property, saying that Jones would pose a risk to those other employees who had crossed the picket line. Further, the company noted that Jones was not on the union executive at the time of the termination and was not a member of the union when Jones was appointed vice-president.

The union filed a grievance, stating that the company was interfering with the union doing its rightful job and that since Jones was acquitted on all charges, the company had no right to treat Jones differently than other union members. At arbitration, the panel determined that there was no specific language in the collective agreement that required the vice-president of the union to be an employee. The arbitration panel also determined that since the company had handled grievances with Jones on the phone, it meant that the company was prepared to deal with Jones. The panel went on to state that not allowing Jones on the property denied union members access to their vice-president and that it could find no proof of Jones being a risk to others. The panel did find that the company had interfered with union activities and ordered that Jones be allowed on the property.

Source: Adapted from Jeffrey R. Smith, "Value must open its gates to fired worker," *The Canadian HR Reporter*, February 13, 2012, 5; names are fictitious. Reprinted by permission of Canadian HR Reporter. © Copyright Thomson Reuters Canada Ltd., Toronto, Ontario, 1-800-387-5164. Web: www.hrreporter.com.

Questions

1. In your opinion, should the company have refused the union vice-president access to the mining property? Why or why not?
2. What else could the company have done initially when it fired Jones and learned that Jones had become the union vice-president?

NOTES AND REFERENCES

1. Statistics Canada, "Table 1, Labour Force Characteristics by Age and Sex, Canada, Seasonally Adjusted," *Labour Force Information*, March 9, 2012, www.statcan.gc.ca/pub/71-001-x/2012002/t001-eng.htm; Sharanjit Uppal, "Unionization 2011," *Perspectives on Labour and Income*, Statistics Canada Catalogue no. 75-001-X (October 26, 2011), 8; Strategic Policy, Analysis, and Workplace Information Directorate, Labour Program, Human Resources and Skills Development Canada, *Union Membership in Canada—2010*, 1.

2. For a more complete understanding of the labour relations system in Canada, refer to Morley Gunderson and Daphne G. Taras, *Canadian Labour and Employment Relations*, 6th ed. (Toronto: Pearson, 2009); Larry Suffield, *Labour Relations*, 3rd ed. (Toronto: Pearson, 2012); and William H. Holley, Kenneth M. Jennings, and Roger S. Wolters, *The Labor Relations Process* (Toronto: Nelson Education, 2012).

3. Labour Canada, "Labour Law," accessed March 4, 2012, www.hrsdc.gc.ca/eng/labour/labour_law/index.shtml.

4. Suffield, *Labour Relations*, 3rd ed., 82.

5. To read more about the labour relations process, consult Gunderson and Taras, *Canadian Labour and Employment Relations*; Suffield, *Labour Relations*, 3rd ed.; Bruce Kaufman, "The Theoretical Foundation of Industrial Relations and Its Implications for Labor Economics and Human Resource Management," *Industrial and Labor Relations Review* 64, no. 1 (October 2010): 74–108.

6. Elisabetta Magnani and David Prentice, "Outsourcing and Unionization: A Tale of Misallocated (Resistance) Resources," *Economics Inquiry* 48, no. 2 (April 2010) 460–82; Yuval Feldman, Amir Falk, and Miri Katz, "What Workers Really Want: Voice, Unions, and Personal Contracts," *Employee Rights and Employment Policy Journal* 15, 237–78; Noah Zatz, "Beyond Misclassification: Tackling the Independent Contractor Problem without Redefining Employment," *Journal of Labor and Employment Law* 26, no. 2 (Winter 2011): 279–94.

7. Claire Sibonney, "Porter Airlines Pilots Attempt to Unionize," *Canadian Labour Reporter*, February 23, 2012, http://www.labour-reporter.com/articleview/12399-porter-airlines-pilots-attempt-to-unionize.

8. Uppal, "Unionization 2011," *Perspectives on Labour and Income*.

9. Marina Strauss, "Target Takes on Union as Retailer Readies Launch in Canada," *The Globe and Mail*, November 29, 2011, B1.

10. Ibid.

11. Darah Hansen, "Zellers Staff Want Union Agreement Honoured," *The Vancouver Sun,* December 2, 2011, C4.

12. Danielle Harder, "Labour Board Orders Certification at Boehmer Box," *Canadian HR Reporter*, March 19, 2010, accessed March 5, 2012, http://www.hrreporter.com/articleview/7646-labour-board-orders-certification-at-boehmer-box.

13. Bell Mobility Inc., and Communications, Energy and Paperworkers Union of Canada, Canada Industrial Relations Board, 28361-C, April 18, 2011.

14. Mobility Union Update, Issue 6, July 21, 2011.

15. Nicolas Van Praet, "Quebec Labour Targets Couche," *The Financial Post*, July 19, 2011, FP1.

16. Alimentation Couche-Tard Inc., Annual General Meeting, English, September 6, 2011,

17. Canada Industrial Relations Board Regulations and *Ontario Labour Relations Act.*

18. The Association of Canadian Film Craftspeople, Local 2020, "About Us," accessed March 6, 2012, http://www.acfcwest.com/about.html; and British Columbia Labour Relations Board, BCLRB No. B176/2010.

19. Ken Georgetti, "CLC President Speaks to the House of Commons Standing Committee on Foreign Affairs and International Development," February 27, 2012, www.canadianlabour.ca/news-room/speeches/clc-president-ken-georgetti-speaks-house-commons-standing-committee-foreign-affai.

20. Armand Roy, "Canadian Labour History," Canadian Labour Congress; and "History and Development of Unions in Canada—General," Canadian Legal FAQs, January 15, 2010, accessed March 7, 2012, www.law-faqs.org/wiki/index.php/History_and_Development_of_Unions_in_Canada/General.

21. *Union Membership in Canada—2010*, 6.

22. *Union Membership in Canada—2010*, 7.

23. Danielle Harder, "UFCW Creates 'Super Local' of 60,000," *Canadian HR Reporter,* August 15, 2011, 8.

24. "CAW and USW Leaders Make Joint Call for Buy Canadian Policy," February 10, 2009, www.caw.ca.

25. Harmac Pacific, "Employees," accessed March 7, 2012, http://harmacpacific.com/employees.php; and "Harmac Pulp Mill to Build Electrical Generation Plant," ForestTalk.com, January 5, 2012, http://foresttalk.com/index.php/2012/01/05/harmac-pulp-mill-to-build-electrical-generation-plant/.

26. Uppal, "Unionization 2011," 8.

27. *Union Membership in Canada—2010*, 3.

28. "Transit Strike Sends Haligonians Scrambling," *The Globe and Mail*, February 3, 2012, A5.

29. "Striking Transit Workers Block Halifax Snowplows," *CBC News Nova Scotia*, March 5, 2012, www.cbc.ca/news/canada/nova-scotia/story/2012/03/05/ns-transit-strike-snowplow.html?cmp=rss.

30. "Buses, Ferries Free as Halifax Strike Ends," *The Globe and Mail*, March 14, 2012, A5.

31. Suffield, *Labour Relations*, 3rd ed., 201–18.

32. Gunderson and Taras, *Canadian Labour and Employment Relations*, 6th ed., 294–300.

33. Margie Wheeler, Issam A. Ghazzawi, and Marie Palladini, "The Los Angeles County Metropolitan Transportation Authority: Interest Based Bargaining as an Alternative Approach to Collective Bargaining," special issue, *Journal of the International Academy for Case Studies* 17, no. 1 (2011): 90–116.

34. Roger Fisher and William Ury, *Getting to Yes* (Toronto: Penguin Books, 1991).

35. "Collective Bargaining Highlights, 2011," Ministry of Labour, Dispute Resolution Services.

36. Ross Stagner and Hjalmar Rosen, *Psychology of Union–Management Relations* (Belmont, CA: Wadsworth, 1965), 95–97. This is another classic in the field of labour–management relations.

37. Jeffrey R. Smith, "Flare-ups on the Picket Lines: Who's Responsible?" *Canadian HR Reporter*, June 7, 2010, accessed March 8, 2012, www.hrreporter.com/blog/Employment-Law/archive/2010/06/07/flare-ups-on-the-picket-lines-whos-responsible.

38. Wendy Stueck, "Returning B.C. Teachers Stay Defiant," *The Globe and Mail*, March 8, 2012, S1.

39. Human Resources and Skills Development Canada, "Work Stoppages in the Federal Private Sector: Innovative Solutions," January 13, 2012, www.hrsdc.gc.ca/eng/labour/labour_relations/wsfps/page00_sum.shtml.

40. Brent Jang, "Air Canada Union Protests Replacement Worker Training," *The Globe and Mail*, September 12, 2011, B4.

41. Greg Keenan, "U.S. Steel Warns Employees at Embattled Hamilton Mill," *The Globe and Mail*, September 29, 2011, B4.

42. Rory Ridley-Duff and Anthony Bennett, "Towards Mediation: Developing a Theoretical Framework to Understand Alternative Dispute Resolution," *Industrial Relations Journal* 42, no. 2 (2011): 106–23

43. Queen's University, Industrial Relations Centre, "Dispute Resolution Skills," May 4, 2012.

44. For an expanded discussion of management's residual rights, termed "reserved rights" in the United States, see Paul Prasow and Edward Peters, *Arbitration and Collective Bargaining*, 2nd ed. (New York: McGraw-Hill, 1983): 33–34. This book is considered an authority on management rights issues.

45. Collective Agreement, Stork Craft Manufacturing Inc. and United Steelworkers, November 1, 2009–October 31, 2012.

46. B.C. Labour Relations Board, "The Steward and Grievance Procedure," CEP, accessed March 8, 2012, www.cep1133.com/grievance.html.

47. "Union Grieves the Demise of Free Beer for Old Guys," *The Vancouver Sun*, June 10, 2009, D5.

48. "In the Matter of an Expedited Arbitration between Regina Qu'Appelle Health Region and Canadian Union of Public Employees, Local 3967," September 28, 2010.

49. Jeffrey R. Smith, "Worker Fired after Encounter with Prostitute during Shift," *Canadian HR Reporter*, January 16, 2012, www.hrreporter.com/articleview/12092-bc-worker-fired-after-encounter-with-prostitute-during-shift-legal-view.

INTERNATIONAL HUMAN RESOURCES MANAGEMENT

OUTCOMES

After studying this chapter, you should be able to

1 Identify the types of organizational forms used for competing internationally.

2 Explain the economic, political-legal, and cultural factors in different countries that need to be considered from an HR perspective.

3 Illustrate how Canadian and international HRM differ.

4 Describe the staffing process for individuals working internationally.

5 Discuss the unique training needs of employees that work internationally.

6 Outline the characteristics of a good international recognition and rewards program.

7 Reconcile the difficulties of home- and host-country performance management systems.

8 Explain how labour relations differ around the world.

OUTLINE

HRM CLOSE-UP

Xiomara Carrillo, Sandra Grant.

Canadian company StarTech.com's tagline is "Hard-to-find made easy®." As the name implies, the company specializes in providing hard-to-find parts and making it easier for customers to obtain the parts they need. With more than 2,000 products in its inventory, from cables and adapters to switches and extenders, StarTech.com supports business connectivity needs from legacy systems to the latest technology used in business today. Currently, approximately 70% of StarTech.com's sales come from the United States, but the market is growing rapidly internationally. To facilitate sales and service outside of Canada, the company has staff in distribution centres in the United States and in the United Kingdom. The company has also hired business development managers in France, Spain, and Belgium, and is currently hiring in Italy, Mexico, and Germany. One such manager is Xiomara Carrillo. As a managing director, she has responsibility for eight team members in Europe.

"Speaking four languages has been an asset in developing the European business, but most importantly, in building a cohesive European team," she says. Carrillo explains that she works hard with head office in Canada to ensure that local differences in each country are understood and considered when developing plans, strategies, and procedures. In terms of human resources practices, Carrillo says, "It's vital that specific cultural differences and nuances always be observed in and during the process."

In Europe, Sandra Grant, a senior manager, explains, most countries where StarTech.com has initiated business to date have the entire workforce regulated by a government-mandated collective agreement. This is not the kind of collective agreement found in unionized environments in North America but rather a set of stipulations outlining all aspects of labour for all types of employees hired. To navigate these varying agreements, StarTech.com relies on a European payroll provider that assists in creating employment contracts and is also responsible for tax remittances, compliance with legislation, anything applicable to her overseas employees. After a hire in Belgium in late 2011, Grant was surprised to immediately receive notice of a 3% payroll increase mandated by the government. "Expect the unexpected," she advises. "There are unique nuances in every country, and they can be vastly different."

In terms of managing employees who work outside Canada, both Grant and Carrillo agree that communication and employee engagement is key. "Most of our international staff work on their own, from their homes, and this can create a feeling of being in a silo," commented Grant. "My challenge is to keep them feeling connected and engaged in our company."

"Working remotely makes the dynamics of personal interaction very challenging," adds Carrillo. "We use as much technology as is available to us. Skype, for example, helps to create a virtual office environment. For interaction with several individuals at the same time, we use conference software called WebEx to share documents while we are video conferencing."

As well as Skype, the company uses other common applications such as MSN, e-mail, and smartphones to stay connected. A company people directory, with names, photos, and optional short profiles, also helps employees put faces to names.

Once yearly, StarTech holds an annual conference called "One Team Conference," where the entire team is brought to the London, Ontario, head office. "We fly everyone here regardless of position or country," explains Grant. "It's an opportunity for the executive and leadership team to share our corporate strategy for the next 12 to 18 months, for our staff to exchange different perspectives, and for us to obtain feedback from employees."

"These regular face-to-face meetings are fundamental in building a cohesive group," adds Carrillo. "This contributes to the employees' sense of belonging to a great company and a great global team."

INTRODUCTION

Even with the continuing recession, there are many examples of companies competing in a global environment. These examples might include acquisitions of international companies, such as Glencore in 2012 acquiring Canada's largest grain handler, Viterra. Or they might highlight companies expanding into other markets, such as Hitachi into Canada, Bombardier in Asia, or BMO in the United States or StarTech as described in the HRM Close-up. Or, examples might focus on international companies gaining dominance here in Canada, such as Starbucks, Walmart, and Lowes. Lastly, the examples might include companies acquiring a Canadian company and shutting it down, such as the acquisition of Electro-Motive in Ontario by Caterpillar.

Whatever the angle, we see clearly that globalization is a chief factor driving Canadian business. Nearly all organizations today are influenced by international competition. Some handle the challenge well, while others fail miserably when they try to manage across borders. More often than not, the difference boils down to how people are managed, the adaptability of cultures, and the flexibility of organizations. Because of this, many organizations are focusing on their human resources management practices.[1]

The importance of globalization notwithstanding, we have—for the most part—emphasized HRM practices and systems, as they exist in Canada. This is not so much an oversight on our part as it is a deliberate decision to explain the HR practices in the most fundamental way. However, the topic of international HRM is so important that we wanted to dedicate an entire chapter to its discussion. Our thinking is that now after you have read (and, we hope, discussed) some of the best practices for managing people at work, it may be appropriate to see how some of these HRM practices may change as we begin to manage people in an international arena.

MANAGING ACROSS BORDERS

Outcome 1

What types of organizational forms are used internationally?

International corporation
Domestic firm that uses its existing capabilities to move into overseas markets

Multinational corporation (MNC)
Firm with independent business units operating in several countries

Global corporation
Firm that has integrated worldwide operations through a centralized home office

International business operations can take several different forms. A large percentage of them carry on their international business with only limited facilities and minimal representation in foreign countries. Others, particularly Fortune 500 corporations, have extensive facilities and personnel in various countries of the world. For example, Dell employs more people outside the United States than within it. Managing these resources effectively, and integrating their activities to achieve global advantage, is a challenge to the leadership of these companies.

Figure 11.1 shows four basic types of organizations and how they differ in the degree to which international activities are separated to respond to the local regions and integrated to achieve global efficiencies. The **international corporation** is essentially a domestic firm that builds on its existing capabilities to penetrate overseas markets. Companies such as Honda, General Electric, and Procter & Gamble used this approach to gain access to Europe—they essentially adapted existing products for overseas markets without changing much else about their normal operations. One such adaptation, for example, was P&G's extremely successful introduction of a detergent brick used on washboards in India.

A **multinational corporation (MNC)** is a more complex form that usually has fully autonomous units operating in several countries. Shell, Philips, and ITT are three typical MNCs. These companies have traditionally given their foreign subsidiaries a great deal of latitude to address local issues such as consumer preferences, political pressures, and economic trends in different regions of the world. Tata Communications, a part of the Mumbai-based Tata Group, purchased the Canadian Crown corporation, Teleglobe Inc., and then entered into an agreement with the British Telecom Group to be the primary supplier of international direct dial outside the United Kingdom and other European countries served by British Telecom.[2] Another company within the Tata Group, Tata Motors, produced a very cheap car which has not made the inroads in global sales as expected even though people in India like it.[3] Frequently, these subsidiaries are run as independent companies, without much integration. The **global corporation**, on the

FIGURE 11.1   Types of Organizations

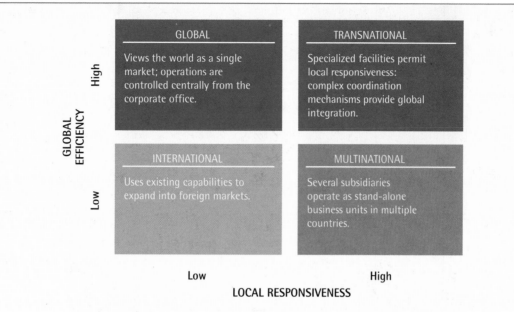

other hand, can be viewed as a multinational firm that maintains control of operations back in the home office. Japanese companies such as Matsushita and NEC, for example, tend to treat the world market as a unified whole and try to combine activities in each country to maximize efficiency on a global scale. These companies operate much like a domestic firm, except that they view the whole world as their marketplace.

Finally, a **transnational corporation** attempts to achieve the local responsiveness of an MNC while achieving the efficiencies of a global firm. To balance this "global/local" dilemma, a transnational uses a network structure that coordinates specialized facilities positioned around the world. By using this flexible structure, a transnational provides autonomy to independent country operations but brings these separate activities together into an integrated whole. For most companies, the transnational form represents an ideal, rather than a reality. Barrick Gold Corporation, one of the largest gold producers in the world, is headquartered in Canada and is considered a transnational company.[4]

Although various forms of organization exist, in this chapter we will generally refer to any company that conducts business outside its home country as an international business. Canada, of course, has no monopoly on international business. International enterprises are found throughout the world. In fact, some European and Pacific Rim companies have been conducting business on an international basis much longer than their Canadian counterparts. The close proximity of European countries, for example, makes them likely candidates for international trade. Figure 11.2 shows a list of the top global companies, measured by sales, profits, assets, and market value.[5] You will note significant changes in the composition of the lists between 2008 and 2009 as a result of the worldwide market crisis.

These companies are in a strong position to affect the world economy in the following ways:

1. Production and distribution extend beyond national boundaries, making it easier to transfer technology.
2. They have direct investments in many countries, affecting the balance of payments.
3. They have a political impact that leads to co-operation among countries and to the breaking down of barriers of nationalism.

Although Figure 11.2 is showing financial measures to demonstrate "top" or "best," Figure 11.3 lists the world's "Most Admired Companies." This list was determined by surveying executives, directors, and industry analysts in a methodological "peer review"

Transnational corporation
Firm that attempts to balance local responsiveness and global scale via a network of specialized operating units

FIGURE 11.2 Top International Companies—2011 and 2012

2012 Rank	2011 Rank	Company	Country	Sales 2012	Sales 2011	Profits 2012	Profits 2011	Assets 2012	Assets 2011	Market Value 2012	Market Value 2011
1	4	ExxonMobil	United States	$433.5	$341.6	$41.1	$30.5	$331.1	$302.5	$407.4	$407.2
2	1	JP Morgan Chase	United States	$220.8	$115.5	$19	$17.4	$2,265.8	$1,227.6	$170.1	$182.2
3	3	General Electric	United States	$147.3	$150.2	$14.2	$11.6	$717.2	$751.2	$213.7	$216.2
4	5	Royal Dutch Shell	Netherlands	$470.2	$329.1	$30.9	$20.1	$340.5	$317.2	$227.6	$212.9
5	7	ICBC	China	$82.6	$69.2	$25.1	$18.8	$2,039.1	$1,723.5	$237.4	$239.5
6	2	HSBC Holdings	United Kingdom	$102	$103.3	$16.2	$13.3	$2,550	$2,467.9	$164.3	$186.5
7	6	PetroChina	China	$310.1	$222.3	$20.6	$21.2	$304.7	$251.3	$294.7	$320.8
8	8	Berkshire Hathaway	United States	$143.7	$136.2	$10.3	$13	$392.6	$372.2	$202.2	$211
9	11	Wells Fargo	United States	$87.6	$93.2	$15.9	$12.4	$1,313.9	$1,258.1	$178.7	$170.6
10	8	Petrobras-Petroleo Brasil	Brazil	$145.9	$121.3	$20.1	$21.2	$319.4	$313.2	$180	$238.8
14	9	Citigroup	United States	$102.6	$111.5	$11.1	$10.6	$1,873.9	$1,913.9	$107.5	$132.8
20	10	BNP Paribas	France	$119	$130.4	$7.9	$10.5	$2,539.1	$2,680.7	$61.5	$88

FIGURE 11.3 Most Admired Companies

Company	Headquarters
1. Apple	United States
2. Google	United States
3. Amazon.com	United States
4. Coca-Cola	United States
5. IBM	United States
6. FedEx	United States
7. Berkshire Hathaway	United States
8. Starbucks	United States
9. Procter & Gamble	United States
10. Southwest Airlines	United States

Source: From *Fortune Magazine*, "The World's Most Admired Companies 2012," March 19, 2012. © 2012 Time inc. Used under license.

of reputation. Conducted jointly by *Fortune* and Hay Group, it is done in this way as there is a belief that a company's reputation is positively related to measurable outcomes, such as innovation, social responsibility, financial soundness, and global competitiveness. Interestingly enough, the top three on the Most Admired list—Apple, Google, and Amazon—had only recently started when the list was originally compiled 15 years ago.[6] *Fortune* also prepared the list "The 100 Best Companies to Work For," which identified Google as the top company to work for, primarily for its unique benefits program which includes free food and massages.[7]

Another more recent list measures the world's most sustainable organizations—those that are equipped to prosper in the long term because of their approach to relationship building with all the various stakeholders. This 2012 list included the following Canadian companies: Suncor Energy Inc., Enbridge Inc., Encana Corporation, Nexen Inc., Sun Life Financial Inc., and Royal Bank of Canada.[8] It is important to remember that Canada is an export nation, and therefore most of our major companies do business outside Canada. For example, Bombardier Inc. was awarded a $214-million contract to supply rail equipment for the Mumbai Railway in central India.[9] It is listed as one of Canada's top companies.[10]

So, how do Canadian companies compare to those on the world lists? Figure 11.4 lists the top 10 publicly traded companies for 2011.

The Society for Human Resource Management provides current news updates on issues concerning HRM from around the world. Currently, the information can be found at "Global HR" under its HR Disciplines category.

Society for Human Resource Management

www.shrm.org

How Does the Global Environment Influence Management?

In Chapter 1, we highlighted some of the challenges facing business and therefore affecting human resources management. One of the major economic issues we discussed was the creation of free trade zones within Europe, North America, and the Pacific Rim. As of March 2009, there were 27 member countries within the European Union (EU), whose goal is to have a single market for the movement of goods, services, people, and money across certain national borders.[11] A similar transition has been occurring within North America since the passage of NAFTA (discussed in Chapter 1). While there had been fears that NAFTA would lead to a loss of jobs for companies in the three countries, just the opposite has occurred. In the more than 15 years since NAFTA was created, a study

FIGURE 11.4   Top 10 Canadian Companies

Rank	Company	2011 Profits (Billions US$)	2011 Revenues (Billions US$)
1	Royal Bank of Canada	5,223	36,026
2	Toronto-Dominion Bank	4,644	25,409
3	Bank of Nova Scotia	4,239	23,775
4	Suncor Energy	3,571	36,820
5	Research in Motion	3,411	19,915
6	Barrick Gold	3,274	11,068
7	Bank of Montreal	2,810	15,453
8	CIBC	2,452	14,976
9	BCE Inc.	2,277	18,207
10	Imperial Oil	2,210	25,092

Source: "2011 Rankings of Canada's top 1000 public companies by profit," *The Globe and Mail*, September 26, 2011, www.theglobeandmail.com/report-on-business/rob-magazine/top-1000/2011-rankings-of-canadas-top-1000-public-companies-by-profit/article2071184/ (accessed March 26, 2012).

reports, trade has totalled over $1,884 trillion, and employment has risen in all three countries (although not as much in Mexico as in the United States and Canada), even with the Great Recession.[12] The United States is Canada's largest partner; the EU is Canada's second-largest economic partner; and China is now the third-largest trading partner.[13]

Similar to NAFTA, numerous trade associations, including the Association of Southeast Asian Nations (ASEAN), East Asia Economic Group, and Asia-Pacific Economic Cooperation (APEC), have significantly facilitated trade among Asian countries, making Asia the fastest-growing region in the world. China—Asia's fastest-growing country—has emerged as a dominant trade leader since instituting trade reforms in the late 1970s. In the last 15 years, China's economy has grown fourfold, drastically altering political and trading relations among nations. Some industry analysts estimate that the country now produces 50% of the world's cameras, 30% of air conditioners and televisions, 25% of washing machines, and 20% of refrigerators worldwide. In addition, China's 1.3 billion people represent a massive, largely untapped consumer market for global companies. Even with the continuing global economic instability, China's GDP still expanded by almost 9% in 2011 and is predicted to do about the same in 2012.[14] Today more cars are sold in China than in Europe. Driving this trend are multinational corporations, such as General Electric, Toyota, and Intel, which are building or expanding their manufacturing units in the country.

The automaking industry has undergone tremendous global change. Fiat, which purchased Chrysler automaker a few years ago, recently merged its management structure, moving closer to being a fully merged company. When Chrysler was first purchased, Fiat left the management structures in place, but it has since decided that costs must be reduced and Chrysler should become fully integrated. Companies moving into other countries are not about size or structure of the company.[15] The auto industry saw a Chinese firm purchase Saab, saving it from bankruptcy.[16]

In addition to China, other key countries for trade are Brazil, Russia, and India. With China, these countries are called "BRIC." and are considered to have the fast-growing economies, capturing about 18% of the world's $62-billion economy.[17] Even with growing economies in places such as India, certain types of businesses can suffer, though. For example, Kingfisher Airlines, started by the "Richard Branson of India," is on the verge of collapse. The airline is reported to owe more than $1 billion in loans to Indian banks.[18] On the other hand, Molson Coors has announced that it is expanding its operations into India—the fastest-growing beer market.[19]

Canada has launched free-trade talks with Japan in order to encourage more trade between the two countries.[20] And Fruits & Passion, a small Canadian personal care product company, have been opening stores in places such as Korea, the United Arab Emirates, and Qatar.[21] Similarly, countries such as Japan continue to expand their businesses overseas. For example, in late 2011, Bridgestone Corporation, the Japanese tire manufacturer, announced it would build a $1.1 billion plant in the United States to produce tires for heavy vehicles.[22]

The fact that international corporations can choose the countries in which they do business or relocate operations generally results in the selection of countries that have the most to offer. In addition to economic factors, political-legal factors are a huge consideration. In many countries, particularly those in Africa, governments poorly protect property rights. Whoever has the political power or authority can seize others' property with few or no consequences. Civil unrest can also lead to the poor enforcement of property rights. This situation gives companies less incentive to locate factories or invest in those countries. Another issue relates to intellectual property rights—rights related to patents, trademarks, and so forth. Despite the fact that private property rights are now generally enforced in China, intellectual property rights have seen little protection. For example, when General Motors formed a joint venture with a Chinese company to produce and sell a new automobile in the country, a knockoff version of the car could be seen on China's streets even before GM and its partner were able to manufacture their first car.

Environmental restrictions also make some countries more attractive to do business in than others. Read At Work with HRM 11.1 to learn more about a Canadian company that expanded its global presence.

Beyond the economic and political-legal issues just mentioned, a country's **cultural environment** (communications, religion, values and ideologies, education, and social structure) also has important implications when it comes to a company's decision about when and how to do business in another country. Because of language and culture similarities, many Canadian companies are finding the United States, Ireland, and the United Kingdom attractive places to locate their facilities, particularly call centres. Eastern Europe has also begun to attract interest because citizens there are well educated and, for the most part, possess English-speaking skills. Figure 11.5 summarizes the complexity of the cultural environment in which HR must be managed.

Culture is an integrated phenomenon. By recognizing and accommodating taboos, rituals, attitudes toward time, social stratification, kinship systems, and the many other components listed in Figure 11.5, managers stand a better chance of understanding the culture of a **host country**—a country in which an international business operates. Different cultural environments require different approaches to human resources management.

Strategies, structures, and management styles that are appropriate in one cultural setting may lead to failure in another. Even in countries that have close language or cultural links, HR practices can be dramatically different. In some countries night shifts are taboo. In other countries employers are expected to provide employees with meals and transportation between home and work. In India, workers generally receive cash bonuses on their wedding anniversaries with which to buy gifts for their spouses, and dating allowances are provided to unmarried employees. Also in India, promotional opportunities are more highly valued than compensation. Employees in France and Japan, while on vacation, are typically linked in to their companies through e-mail and voice mail.[23] These practices would probably never occur to Canadian managers.[24]

For more information on the various trade agreements and doing business in other countries, check out NAFTA (**www.nafta-sec-alena.org**), Europa (**europa.eu**), ASEAN (**www.aseansec.org**), and Foreign Affairs and International Trade Canada (**international.gc.ca**).

Outcome 2

What are the factors that need to be considered from an HR perspective in different countries?

Cultural environment. Communications, religion, values and ideologies, education, and social structure of a country

Host country Country in which an international corporation operates

NAFTA
www.nafta-sec-alena.org

Europa
europa.eu

ASEAN
www.aseansec.org

Foreign Affairs and International Trade Canada
international.gc.ca

AT WORK **with HRM 11.1**

MOVING OUT OF MONTREAL

Gildan Activewear Inc., a Montreal-based company, is one of the largest T-shirt manufacturers in the world. But it wasn't always that way.

Gildan started in 1984 with only a few people producing blank shirts that could then be screen-printed. It now has over 30,000 workers throughout the world and manufactures socks, fleece, and underwear with annual net sales of $1.7 billion.

Gildan was able to expand into the global market primarily because of trade legislation. The company credits the reduction of trade barriers in the early 1990s for its ability to move operations beyond Canada.

After careful consideration, Gildan decided on creating facilities in Honduras with the intention of both manufacturing and shipping from there. It determined that it would be more cost effective to ship into its largest markets (U.S., Canada, Mexico, and Europe) from facilities in Central America. Not only was it able to get quality workers and management, but it found that the work ethics and ethics of the people aligned with the company's own ethics. From Honduras, Gildan was able to ship duty free, which gave it a huge cost advantage. After success in Honduras, it also set up facilities in the Caribbean— again, to provide access to more distribution points throughout the world. It is now considering investing in a manufacturing facility in Bangladesh.

The success of the company is not just about low labour costs. The CEO credits the company's success to allowing local management to oversee its operations instead of running the operations from Canada. The company actively trains and develops local talent.

However, having a more hands-off approach is not without risk and consequences. There is always the concern about political and social instability as well as natural disasters such as hurricanes. In 2010, close to 100 of Gildan's employees were killed in the Haitian earthquake.

Even with the risks and sometimes allegations about labour practices in other countries, Gildan still considers its expansion good. It has been able to continue lowering costs, which gives it a distinct competitive advantage.

CRITICAL THINKING QUESTIONS:

1. There is much controversy about some of the labour practices in developing countries— particularly about employing younger workers. Do you think Canadian companies ought to refuse to hire younger workers in developing countries? Why or why not?

2. What are the pros and cons of training local management instead of managing the entire operation from headquarters in Montreal?

Source: Adapted from Christine Dobby, "Offshore Opportunities 'Too Good to Pass Up,'" *Financial Post*, November 25, 2011, C6; and *Part of Your Life: 2011 Annual Report*, December 9, 2011, Gildan Activewear.

Canadian vs. International HRM

Outcome 3

How do Canadian HRM and international HRM differ?

International HRM differs from domestic HRM in several ways. In the first place, it necessarily places a greater emphasis on functions and activities such as relocation, orientation, and translation services to help employees adapt to new and different environments outside their own countries and to help newly hired employees in foreign countries adapt to working for companies headquartered outside their borders. Because of the complexity of HR when doing business in other countries, larger companies will have HR professionals devoted solely to assisting with the globalization process. Further, some companies will also hire international staffing firms, such as Boston Global Consulting. These firms have expertise when it comes to relocating employees, establishing operations abroad, and helping with import/export and foreign tax issues.

HR management systems have come a long way in terms of helping firms improve their international coordination. A good HR management system can facilitate communication, record keeping, and a host of other activities worldwide. Some HRMSs are designed to track the whereabouts of employees travelling or on assignment. This can be important in the event of a transportation accident, a natural disaster such as a tsunami, a terrorist attack, or

FIGURE 11.5 The Cultural Environment of International Business

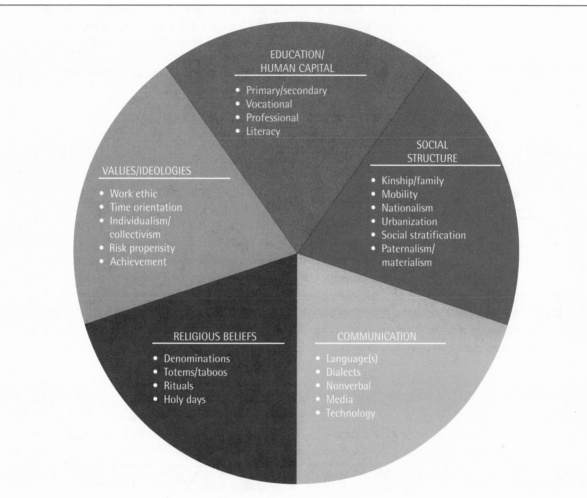

civil strife when evacuation plans may have to be implemented. Occasionally, however, even the seemingly simplest of cultural differences can be difficult to overcome when a company tries to set up a global HRIS. When Lucent Technologies rolled out a PeopleSoft system to more than 90 countries, the company's managers found that the order of employees' names was so important—and so varied—that it took two months to settle on a format allowing employee names to be entered into the system. As you can see, even small differences such as name format can create problems for international companies.

International Staffing

Outcome 4

What is the staffing process for individuals working internationally?

Expatriates, or home-country nationals
Employees from the home country who are on international assignment

Host-country nationals
Employees who are natives of the host country

Third-country nationals
Employees who are natives of a country other than the home country or the host country

International management poses many problems in addition to those faced by a domestic operation. Because of geographic distance and a lack of close, day-to-day relationships with headquarters in the home country, problems must often be resolved with little or no counsel or assistance from others. It is essential, therefore, that special attention be given to the staffing practices of overseas units. In fact, a recent study by Mercer suggests that the inability to successfully integrate cultural differences is the primary reason global mergers and acquisitions fail.[25]

There are three sources of employees with whom to staff international operations. First, the company can send people from its home country. These employees are often referred to as **expatriates**, or **home-country nationals**. Second, it can hire **host-country nationals**, natives of the host country, to do the managing. Third, it can hire **third-country nationals**, natives of a country other than the home country or the host country.

Each of these three sources of overseas workers provides certain advantages and certain disadvantages. Most corporations, such as the Four Seasons Hotels (described in At Work with HRM 11.2), use all three sources for staffing their multinational operations.

As shown in Figure 11.6, at early stages of international expansion, organizations often send home-country expatriates to establish activities (particularly in less-developed countries) and to work with local governments. Doing this is generally very costly. Expatriate assignments cost companies, on average, $1 million over a three-year period, which can be three to five times what a domestic assignment costs. As a result, many companies are taking greater pains to more clearly outline the overall goal of the foreign

AT WORK **with HRM 11.2**

SELECTING FOR SERVICE

Four Seasons Hotels, with a staff of over 25,000, manages 50 hotels and luxury resorts around the world, from Bali to Boston. The Four Seasons brand is synonymous with luxury and first-class service standards. The execution of the strategy of being the best in the world starts with leaders who are passionate about the corporation's customer service and employee relations values. These leaders can take a concept such as "We will deliver exceptional personal service" and paint a picture for employees that is clear and motivational, and that results in the delivery of that exceptional personal service.

Does the perception of service excellence depend on the country or culture in which Four Seasons operates? John Young, executive vice-president of human resources, states that the Four Seasons guest is typically a sophisticated global traveller who has acquired a sensitivity to differences in culture without negative preconceptions. Nevertheless, Four Seasons trains service staff to be sensitive to guests' needs and to minimize or avoid culture and language problems. For example, in Asia, when an English-speaking guest gives a food or beverage order, the service staff are trained to repeat the order. They do so not only to prevent a potential service error, but also to avoid loss of face for the employee. In North America, a repetition of the order would be seen as redundant.

So that employees can meet these high performance expectations, Four Seasons selects employees based on their service attitudes. Candidates for employment must undergo four behaviourally based interviews (including one with the general manager) to determine their service attitudes and current skills and knowledge. As Young says, "Customer service is the heart and soul of our business, and we need to assess if a candidate has

sensitivity to the needs and wants of others. Of course, we also look at high levels of knowledge, skill, and experience, but these can be trained. We continuously adapt our service to match guest needs. For example, many years ago, in our Seattle hotel, one of the valet parking attendants noted that on weekends our guests were disproportionately families with children. On his own initiative, he put chocolate chip cookies and milk in cars that he was returning to these departing guests. They loved it. This practice has now become one of Four Seasons' standards."

Four Seasons does not have a rigid formula for selecting home-country nationals or expatriates for any given country. The ratios depend on three factors: regulations, economics, and corporate management development needs.

Young continues, "For example, Indonesia used to have a rule that no more than three expatriates could be employed per hotel. So we set expatriate reduction targets to meet this regulation. Economically, it made sense for us, since an expatriate general manager could cost us as much as 75 or 80 local employees. And finally, we will choose candidates based on their need for global exposure and professional development, to match our targeted needs for international expansion.

"Our biggest challenge in international HR now is management development in the context of our growth plans. We need to develop culturally appropriate leadership in preparation for specific new locations on a defined timeline. If we cannot find managers who can speak the language, and understand the culture, then our ability to grow is limited. Recently we opened a hotel in Puerto Vallarta. We found a Spanish-speaking general manager from Colombia who, over time, was able to integrate the Four Seasons way of doing business with the Mexican culture. Business culture in

Mexico tends to be very rule and policy driven. Employees continuously asked, "What is the policy ..." in HR, sales, everything. Over time, the general manager learned to deal with the questions by no longer looking to home office for all the rules, but by asking himself and his team, "What should the rule be in our situation?"

"We cannot just hire the management talent we want from other sectors or hotel chains on short lead time, because of differences in operating standards and corporate culture. For example, we were opening a hotel with a general manager recruited from Hilton International. As he toured the new facility with Issy Sharp, our founder and CEO, the general manager said that the lounge facilities ought to be larger. He explained that this would make guests more comfortable while waiting for their dinner reservations. Issy replied, 'At Four Seasons our guests do not wait for their reservations.' These cultural differences, across countries, across sectors, and across competitors, underline the importance of our investing

the time and effort in developing our own management talent, which is culturally and linguistically fluent, mobile, and imbued with our service culture."

This attention to the selection and development of high-performance employees resulted in *Fortune* magazine naming Four Seasons as one of the 100 best employers in the world for at least 10 consecutive years. Consequently, Four Seasons is now able to attract more and better applicants. Four Seasons is also widely recognized as the best luxury hotel chain in the world. Furthermore, the turnover rate at Four Seasons is one of the lowest in the hospitality sector. Even those employees who have left are often recaptured as they elect to return to the kind of culture that treats them as they treat the guests.

QUESTION:

Do you think that other international hotels have the same problem with management development? Why or why not?

FIGURE 11.6 Changes in International Staffing over Time

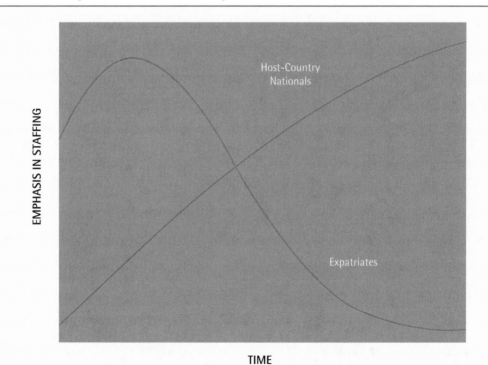

assignment and its timetable for completion. To reduce the costs some companies are considering short-term and "commuter" assignments. A short-term assignment lasts 6 to 12 months, with the employee remaining under a home-country employment contract. A "commuter" assignment lasts up to three months, and the compensation package remains with the home country. In both cases, there is either a per-day or monthly living allowance, or an expense account.[26]

Given the ever-expanding global environment, more and more people appear to be open to working in another country. A recent survey conducted by Ipsos in many countries (including Brazil, Canada, China, South Africa, and Great Britain) concluded that employees are keen to have an international assignment. Individuals felt that such work experience would be an asset to their future career opportunities.[27]

At later stages of internationalization, there is typically a steady shift toward the use of host-country nationals. This move has three main advantages:

1. Hiring local citizens is less costly than relocating expatriates.
2. Since local governments usually want good jobs for their citizens, foreign employers may be required to hire them.
3. Most customers want to do business with companies (and people) they perceive to be local versus foreign.

Because Canadian companies want to be viewed as true international citizens, there has also been a trend away from hiring expatriates to head up operations in foreign countries, particularly European countries. Bombardier and Four Seasons, which have strong regional organizations, tend to replace their expatriate managers with local managers as quickly as possible. In addition to hiring local managers to head their foreign divisions and plants, more companies are using third-country nationals. Third-country nationals are often multilingual and already acclimated to the host country's culture—perhaps because they live in a nearby region. Thus, they are also less costly to relocate and sometimes better able to cope culturally with the foreign environment. At Work with HRM 11.3 tells the story of internationalization into Canada.

AT WORK **with HRM 11.3**

EXPANDING INTO CANADA

While most Canadians think about Canadian companies expanding into other countries, we seldom think about companies expanding into Canada other than retail operations.

But that recently changed when Hitachi, for example, decided to expand an existing manufacturing plant in Ontario to build its giant mining trucks. Many manufacturing companies have moved out of Canada, usually citing high labour costs. However, Hitachi chose to expand because of the skilled workforce available as a result of the demise of some auto plants. The company's executive vice-president stated that when a welder is working on equipment as large as the 8 m–high trucks, it is an art to ensure that the weld seams are of high quality.

Hitachi's move might seem unusual, given that other international companies, such as Caterpillar and U.S. Steel, have closed down their respective manufacturing facilities, citing high wages. Hitachi, however, is so confident of its product that it is exporting these trucks to low-cost and developing markets instead of building plants in those locations. It believes that the skilled workforce it has in Canada is a significant advantage. It also believes that with the demand in growth in China and India for base metals, mining companies will be expanding, thereby increasing the demand for the 3000 horsepower trucks.

CRITICAL THINKING QUESTIONS:

1. Besides skilled labour, what other advantages might Hitachi have by producing trucks in Ontario?
2. What might be some disadvantages for Hitachi in the future with an expanded plant in Canada?

Source: Adapted from Greg Keenan, "Hitachi's Canadian Advantage," *Report on Business*, March 12, 2012, B1, http://www.theglobeandmail. com/report-on-business/economy/manufacturing/hitachi-construction-has-big-plans-for-its-big-trucks/article533781.

World Education Services
www.wes.org/ca

Companies tend to continue to use expatriates only when a specific set of skills is needed or when individuals in the host country require development. It is important to note, however, that while top managers may prefer one source of employees to another, the host country may place pressure on them that restricts their choices. Such pressure takes the form of sophisticated government persuasion through administrative or legislative decrees designed to employ host-country individuals. To encourage local hiring the host country frequently implements tax incentives, tariffs, and quotas.

Canadian employers wishing to assess thousands of academic credentials for foreign-born employees can consult the not-for-profit World Education Services at **www.wes.org/ca**.

Recruiting Internationally

Improved telecommunications and travel have made it easier to match up employers and employees of all kinds worldwide. Rolls-Royce, headquartered in the United Kingdom, hires 25% of its 25,000 employees abroad. Because its customers come from around the globe, Rolls-Royce figures its workforce should as well. Airbus, the European commercial jet maker, recruits engineers from universities and colleges all over Europe. American-based Boeing's need for engineers is so great that it also recruits internationally and has even opened a design centre in Moscow. The trend is likely to continue as the populations in developed countries age, and companies search for talent elsewhere. Even China, despite its massive population, will face labour shortages because laws there prohibit couples from having more than one child.

Companies must be particularly responsive to the cultural, political, and legal environments both domestically and abroad when recruiting internationally. For example, Starbucks and Honeywell have made a special effort to create codes of conduct for employees throughout the world to ensure that standards of ethical and legal behaviour are known and understood. PepsiCo has taken a similar approach to ensuring that company values are reinforced (even while recognizing the need for adapting to local cultures). The company has four core criteria that are viewed as essential in worldwide recruiting efforts: (1) personal integrity, (2) a drive for results, (3) respect for others, and (4) capability. However, it is important to recognize local cultures in relation to implementing ethical codes in other countries.

In general, however, employee recruitment in other countries is subject to more government regulation than it is in Canada. Regulations range from those that cover procedures for recruiting employees to those that govern the employment of foreign workers or require the employment of the physically disabled, war veterans, or displaced persons. Many Central American countries, for example, have stringent regulations about the number of foreigners that can be employed as a percentage of the total workforce. Virtually all countries have work-permit or visa restrictions that apply to foreigners. A **work permit**, or **visa**, is a document issued by a government granting authority to a foreign individual to seek employment in that government's country.

Work permit, or visa
A government document granting a foreign individual the right to seek employment

Multinational companies (MNCs) tend to use the same kinds of internal and external recruitment sources as are used in their home countries. At the executive level, companies use search firms such as Korn/Ferry in Canada or Spencer Stuart in the United Kingdom. At lower levels, more informal approaches tend to be useful. While unskilled labour may be readily available in a developing country, recruitment of skilled workers may be more difficult. Many employers have learned that the best way to find workers in these countries is through referrals and radio announcements; that's because many people lack sufficient reading or writing skills. Other firms use international recruiting firms to find skilled labour abroad. Some countries require the employment of locals if adequate numbers of skilled people are available. Specific exceptions are sometimes granted (officially or unofficially) for difficult situations such as farm workers from Mexico in Canada or for Italian, Spanish, Greek, and Turkish workers in Germany and the Benelux countries (Belgium, the Netherlands, and Luxembourg). Foreign workers invited to come to perform needed labour are usually referred to as **guest workers**. Although hiring non-nationals may result in lower direct labour costs for a company, the indirect costs—those

Guest workers
Foreign workers invited to perform needed labour

related to housing, language training, health services, recruitment, transportation, and so on—can be substantial. Some organizations, such as health authorities recruiting nursing staff, are nonetheless finding the expenditures worthwhile.[28]

With the continuing global financial issues, companies are still looking to a global workforce when recruiting. For example, in a recent survey, over one-half of respondents in Canada indicated that they recruited internationally—and more so if the companies had global operations.[29] Likewise, a report by Mercer stated that global leaders believe that human capital, the talent recruited from wherever, is the "engine of the global economy."[30] Sourcing local and skilled talent remains a problem, particularly in emerging markets, even in 2012, and thus the need to send home-country staff to foreign assignments continues.[31]

In order to ensure that global talent is attracted and retained in emerging countries, organizations need to focus on the following:

1. Brand—having a reputation for excellence, being a global leader, and having leadership that inspires others;
2. Rewards and recognition—ensuring that their rewards program is competitive and fits the local circumstances as well as what applies in the home country;
3. Opportunity—clarifying what employees will gain and what they can provide;
4. Culture—understanding the local environment and what additional supports might be necessary to attract and retain employees.[32]

Read At Work with HRM 11.4 to learn what a Canadian entrepreneur found out about recruiting in Russia.

Apprenticeships

A major source of trained labour in European nations is apprenticeship-training programs (described in Chapter 5). On the whole, apprenticeship training in Europe is superior to that in Canada. In Europe, a dual-track system of education directs a large number of youths into vocational training. The German system of apprenticeship training, one of the best in Europe, provides training for office and top jobs under a three-way responsibility contract between the apprentice, the parents, and the organization. At the conclusion of their training, apprentices can work for any employer but generally receive seniority credit

---

AT WORK **with HRM 11.4**

IT'S A WOMEN'S WORLD!

What does someone from Canada need to know about doing business in Moscow? The short answer is "lots"! However, when recruiting, there is one key cultural distinction for success.

Craig Cohon, originally from Toronto, has been doing business in Russia for over 20 years. He originally went to Russia to oversee the construction of Coca-Cola's first plant there and continued to work for Coca-Cola internationally as its brand manager. Then, in 2009, he returned to Moscow as a Russian partner for the famous Cirque du Soleil, from Quebec. Through that partnership he has really gained insight into the employment world in Moscow.

And what is the insight? As Cohon states, "This is a matriarchal society masquerading as a patriarchal society." He has learned that recruiting and hiring talented women has been the key to his incredible success in Russia. He sees these women as courageous, detail oriented, and results oriented. He reinforced the need for patience when doing business in Russia and feels that having Russian women as part of his core team helps him in forming the necessary business relationships.

CRITICAL THINKING QUESTION:
Would you like to work in Russia? Why or why not?

Source: Adapted from Matthew Fisher, "Women Run the Show," *Financial Post,* March 9, 2012, FP8.

with the training firm if they remain in it. France has been able to draw on its "Grandes Écoles" for centuries. Created during the Renaissance to fulfill a need that universities weren't meeting, the Grandes Écoles educate prospective engineers up to the equivalent level of Master of Engineering. It is said that people who have graduated from the various institutions in the Grandes Écoles run France—even the former French president.[33]

Staffing Transnational Teams

Transnational teams
Teams composed of members of multiple nationalities working on projects that span multiple countries

In addition to focusing on individuals, it is also important to note that companies are increasingly using transnational teams to conduct international business. **Transnational teams** are composed of members of multiple nationalities working on projects that span multiple countries. For example, Aon, a global insurance and human resources firm, has teams all over the world working in a number of different ways. It feels that one of the successes of transnational teams is the camaraderie that has evolved.[34]

Sometimes, companies send employees on temporary assignments abroad as part of transnational teams that last a few months. They might do so to break down cultural barriers between international divisions or disseminate new ideas and technology to other regions. Aon, for example, as part of its acquisition of the former Hewitt consulting firm, created three world teams to pass on knowledge, service, values, and client expertise to the newly merged 60,000-employee company.[35]

The fundamental task in forming a transnational team is assembling the right group of people who can work together effectively to accomplish the goals of the team. Many companies try to build variety into their teams in order to maximize responsiveness to the special needs of different countries. For example, when Heineken formed a transnational team to consolidate its production facilities, it ensured that team members were drawn from each major region within Europe. Team members tended to have specialized skills, and members were added only if they offered some unique skill that added value to the team.

Selecting Employees Internationally

As you might imagine, selection practices vary around the world. In Canada, managers tend to emphasize merit, with the best-qualified person getting the job. In other countries, however, firms tend to hire on the basis of family ties, social status, language, and common origin. The candidate who satisfies these criteria may get the job even if otherwise unqualified. Much of this is changing—there has been a growing realization among organizations in other nations that greater attention must be given to hiring those most qualified. In addition to a person's qualifications, various other hiring laws are enforced around the world. Labour union restrictions, which will be discussed later in this chapter, can also have an impact on hiring.

The Selection Process

The selection process for international assignments should emphasize different employment factors, depending on the extent of contact that one would have with the local culture and the degree to which the foreign environment differs from the home environment. For example, if the job involves extensive contacts with the community, as with a chief executive officer, this factor should be given appropriate weight. In addition, other factors that might be different in a foreign environment include the pace of business and how people interact in business.[36]

If a candidate for expatriation is willing to live and work in a foreign environment, an indication of the person's tolerance of cultural differences should be obtained. On the other hand, if local nationals have the technical competence to carry out the job successfully, they should be carefully considered for the job before the firm launches a search (at home) for a candidate to fill the job. As stated previously, most corporations realize the advantages to be gained by staffing international operations with host-country nationals wherever possible.

Selecting home-country and third-country nationals requires that more factors be considered than in selecting host-country nationals. While the latter must, of course, possess managerial abilities and the necessary technical skills, they have the advantage of familiarity with the physical and cultural environment and the language of the host country. And depending on the country, certain factors in the environment may be key as to whether or not the person is an "expat." For example, people who are managers in China need to understand that China is a collectivist society and that there is a power difference in the leadership hierarchy.[37] The discussion that follows will focus on the selection of expatriate managers from the home country.

Selecting Expatriate Managers

One of the toughest jobs facing many organizations is finding employees who can meet the demands of working in a foreign environment. There are several steps involved in selecting individuals for an international assignment. The sequencing of these activities can make a big difference.

STEP 1: BEGIN WITH SELF-SELECTION.   Employees should begin the process years in advance by thinking about their career goals and interest in international work. By beginning with self-selection, companies can more easily avoid the problems of forcing otherwise promising employees into international assignments where they would be unhappy and unsuccessful. In cases where individuals have families, the decisions about relocation are more complicated. Employees should seek out information to help them predict their chances of success in living abroad. Companies such as EDS and Deloitte & Touche give the self-selection instruments to their employees to help them think through the pros and cons of international assignments.

STEP 2: CREATE A CANDIDATE POOL.   After employees have self-selected, organizations can put together a database of candidates for international assignments. Information on the database might include availability, languages, country preferences, and skills. Fluor, a global engineering firm, has an extensive database that it uses to track all the experiences of its international managers.[38] Further, Siemens, an international company in the electronics and electrical fields, has operations in more than 190 countries with 400,000 employees. Its candidate pool consists of about 2,000 managers who work in another country three to five years.[39]

STEP 3: ASSESS CORE SKILLS.   From the shortlist of potential candidates, managers can assess each candidate on technical and managerial readiness relative to the needs of the assignment. Although many factors determine success abroad, the initial focus should be on the requirements of the job. Walmart uses shorter-term assignments to help assess international experience and the person's capabilities to move into longer-term international assignments.[40]

STEP 4: ASSESS AUGMENTED SKILLS AND ATTRIBUTES.   As shown in Figure 11.7, expatriate selection decisions are typically driven by technical competence as well as professional and international experience. In addition, however, an increasing number of organizations have also begun considering an individual's ability to adapt to different environments. Participating in a variety of different activities, such as athletic or social programs, can be very helpful in assisting the person in adapting to the host country.[41]

To be more specific, companies such as Colgate-Palmolive, Whirlpool, and Dow Chemical have identified a set of **core skills** that they view as critical for success abroad and a set of **augmented skills** that help facilitate the efforts of expatriate managers. For example, decision making, team building, and adaptability are some of the core skills; negotiation skills and change management are two of the augmented skills. It is worth noting that many of these skills are not significantly different from those required for managerial success at home.

Core skills
Skills considered critical to an employee's success abroad

Augmented skills
Skills helpful in facilitating the efforts of expatriate managers

FIGURE 11.7 Expatriate Selection Criteria

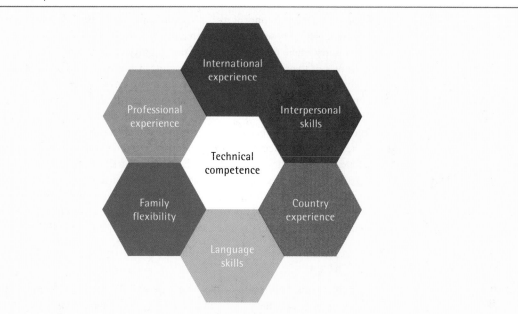

Failure rate
Percentage of expatriates who do not perform satisfactorily

Outpost Expatriate Support Network

www.outpostexpat.nl

Even companies that believe they have selected the best candidates frequently experience high expatriate **failure rates**. The primary reason for an assignment failure is the person's family—spouse and children. In studies on this topic, it was determined that inadequate attention was paid to ensuring that the family could adapt to the new conditions. Besides family issues, failures also occurred due to the person's lack of job knowledge, poor relational leadership skills, and lack of cultural openness and adaptability.[42] Samsung, another global electronics manufacturing company, has found that the most common reasons for an unsuccessful foreign assignment were inability to adapt to the different culture, lack of appropriate skills, and lack of communication skills.[43]

There are a number of ways to improve the success of expatriate assignments. One important step is to involve spouses early in the process. In addition, training and development for both expatriates and their families can have a big impact. (This matter will be discussed next.) As an example of how companies can prepare employees and their families, consider Shell, which created an online information centre called the Outpost Expatriate Support Network (**www.outpostexpat.nl**).

TRAINING AND DEVELOPMENT

Outcome 5

What are the training needs for employees working internationally?

Although companies try to recruit and select the very best people for international work, it is usually necessary to provide some type of training. Not only is this type of training important to expatriate managers; it is also important for the foreign employees they will ultimately supervise. To know and understand how the Japanese or Chinese negotiate contracts or how businesspeople from Latin America view the enforcement of meeting times, for example, can help expatriate managers and their employees deal with each other more successfully. To illustrate this latter point, Finning International, in its desire to provide global exposure to its key staff, has had to ensure that the Canadian managers understand that the concept of time is very relaxed in the operations in Chile.[44] The biggest mistake managers can make is to assume that people are the same everywhere. Corporations that seriously desire to succeed in global business are tackling these problems head-on by providing intensive training.

Content of Training Programs

Lack of training is one of the principal causes of failure among employees working internationally. Those working internationally need to know as much as possible about (1) the country where they are going, (2) that country's culture, and (3) the history, values, and dynamics of their own organizations. Figure 11.8 gives an overview of what one needs to study for an international assignment. In many cases, the employee and the family can obtain a great deal of general information about the host country, including its culture, geography, social and political history, climate, food, and so on, through the Internet, books, lectures, and DVDs. The knowledge gained will at least help the participants have a better understanding in their assignments. Sensitivity training can also help expatriates overcome ethnic prejudices they might harbour. Expatriates can simulate a field experience in sensitivity training by visiting a nearby subculture in their native countries or by visiting a foreign country before relocating there. Key elements of training and development programs that prepare employees for working internationally include cross-culture training; job-specific training; language training; and learning how business is done in the particular country.[45]

Language Training

Communication with individuals who have a different language and a different cultural orientation is extremely difficult. Most executives agree that it is among the biggest problems for the foreign business traveller. Students who plan careers in international business should start instruction in one or more foreign languages as early as possible. The top-ranked China Europe International Business School (CEIBS), jointly founded by the Chinese government and the European Union, also offers language training. Some companies do their own language training. Multinational companies, as well as businesses that outsource work abroad, stand to benefit from this type of training.

Fortunately for most Canadians, English is almost universally accepted as the primary language for international business. Particularly when many people from different countries are working together, English is usually the designated language for meetings and formal discussions. Procter & Gamble provides an opportunity for not only the manager to acquire language skills but also for children.[46] Many companies also provide instruction in English for those who are required to use English in their jobs.

Learning the language is only part of communicating in another culture, though. The following list illustrates the complexities of the communication process in international business.

1. In England, to "table" a subject means to put it on the table for current discussion. In Canada, it means to postpone discussion of a subject, perhaps indefinitely.

FIGURE 11.8   Preparing for an International Assignment

To prepare for an international assignment, one should become acquainted with the following aspects of the host country:

1. Social and business etiquette
2. History and folklore
3. Current affairs, including relations between the host country and Canada
4. Cultural values and priorities
5. Geography, especially its major cities
6. Sources of pride and great achievements of the culture
7. Religion and the role of religion in daily life
8. Political structure and current players
9. Practical matters, such as currency, transportation, time zones, and hours of business
10. The language

International assignments provide an employee with a set of experiences that are uniquely beneficial to both the individual and the firm.

Pankaj & Insy Shah/Gulfimages/Getty Images

2. In Canada, information flows to a manager. In cultures where authority is centralized (such as Europe and South America), the manager must take the initiative to seek out the information.
3. Getting straight to the point is uniquely North American. Many Europeans, Arabs, and others resent this directness in communication.
4. In Japan, there are 16 ways to avoid saying "no."
5. When something is "inconvenient" to the Chinese, it is most likely downright impossible.
6. In most foreign countries, expressions of anger are unacceptable; in some places, public display of anger is taboo.
7. The typical North American must learn to treat silences as "communication spaces" and not interrupt them.
8. In general, North Americans must learn to avoid gesturing with the hand. Nonverbal communication training can help businesspeople avoid some of these communication pitfalls.[47]

Cultural Training

Cross-cultural differences represent one of the most elusive aspects of international business. Brazilians tend to perceive North Americans as always in a hurry, serious, reserved, and methodical, whereas the Japanese view North Americans as relaxed, friendly, and impulsive. Why do these different perceptions exist, and how do they affect the way we do business across borders?

Managerial attitudes and behaviours are influenced, in large part, by the society in which managers have received their education and training. Similarly, reactions of employees are the result of cultural conditioning. Each culture has its expectations for the roles of managers and employees. On her first day on the job abroad, one expatriate manager recalls her boss ordering a bottle of wine to split between the two of them at lunch. Although this practice is common in Britain, the expatriate manager was initially taken aback. Being successful as a manager depends on one's ability to understand the way things are normally done and to recognize that changes cannot be made abruptly without considerable resistance, and possibly antagonism, on the part of local nationals. Some organizations are finding that using technology, such as online cross-cultural training, is better preparing employees and their families for international assignments.[48]

Studying cultural differences can help managers identify and understand work attitudes and motivation in other cultures. When compared with the Japanese, North Americans may feel little loyalty to their organization. In Japan, for example, employees are more likely to feel a strong loyalty to their company, although recent reports show that this may be changing. Japanese companies no longer universally guarantee an employee a job for life, and layoff decisions are increasingly being made based on merit, not seniority—a practice unthinkable in the country in the past. For example, Ricoh, the global print maker and copier headquartered in Japan, decided to cut its staff by almost 10% by 2014 through restructuring its global workforce.[49] Latin Americans tend to view themselves as working not only for a particular company but also for an individual manager. Thus, managers in Latin American countries can encourage performance only by using personal influence and working through individual members of a group.

One important dimension of leadership, whether we are talking about international or domestic situations, is the degree to which managers invite employee participation in decision making. While finding hard data on employee participation across different countries is difficult, careful observers report that Canadian managers are about in the middle on a continuum of autocratic to democratic decision-making styles. Scandinavian and Australian managers also appear to be in the middle. South American and European managers, especially those from France, Germany, and Italy, are toward the autocratic end of the continuum; Japanese managers are at the most participatory end. Additional information about living, relocating, and working globally, as well as daily news, can be found at EscapeArtist.com (**www.escapeartist.com**).

EscapeArtist.com
www.escapeartist.com

Assessing and Tracking Career Development

International assignments provide some definite developmental and career advantages. For example, working abroad tends to increase a person's responsibilities and influence within the corporation. In addition, it provides a person with a set of experiences that are uniquely beneficial to both the individual and the firm. In this way, international assignments can expand a person's career prospects.[50]

To maximize the career benefits of a global assignment, a candidate should ask two key questions before accepting an international position:

1. Do the organization's senior executives view the firm's international business as a critical part of its operation? Research shows that expatriates with clear goals that truly need to be accomplished are likely to find their assignments more rewarding. Realizing this, fewer companies are sending expatriates abroad for career development purposes only.
2. Within top management, how many executives have a foreign-service assignment in their background, and do they feel it important for one to have overseas experience? Colgate-Palmolive sees a foreign assignment as part of an extended career track rather than as a one-off assignment. A successful international assignment tends to lead to another and another. "Our top priority is to identify, develop, and retain the next two to three generations of leaders," said one Colgate-Palmolive manager. Part of that strategy includes directly using the knowledge of the company's current and former expatriates.

Managing Personal and Family Life

Culture shock
Perpetual stress experienced by people who settle overseas

As noted previously, one of the most frequent causes of an employee's failure to complete an international assignment is personal and family stress. **Culture shock**—a disorientation that causes perpetual stress—is experienced by people who settle overseas for extended periods. The stress is caused by hundreds of jarring and disorienting incidents such as being unable to communicate, having trouble getting the telephone to work, being unable to read the street signs, and a myriad of other everyday matters that are no problem at home. Soon minor frustrations become catastrophic events, and one feels helpless and drained, emotionally and physically.

In Chapter 4, it was noted that more and more employers are assisting two-career couples in finding suitable employment in the same location. To accommodate dual-career partnerships, some employers are providing informal help finding jobs for the spouses of international transferees. Many industry studies have indicated that the number-one reason people refuse international assignments or the assignment fails is due to partner/spousal issues.[51] To improve this, some companies are establishing more formal programs to assist expatriate couples. These include career- and life-planning counselling, continuing education, intercompany networks to identify job openings in other companies, and job-hunting/fact-finding trips. In some cases, a company may even create a job for the spouse, such as what Ford did when it sent two engineers married to each other to China, one as a product development manager and the other as vehicle team quality manager.[52]

Repatriation

Repatriation
Process of employee transition home from an international assignment

An increasing number of companies such as Enbridge are developing programs specifically designed to facilitate **repatriation**—that is, helping employees make the transition back home. Coming back is often difficult. An employee recently repatriated from Colombia walked outside his Edmonton office and waited for his driver, not remembering that he had driven his own car to work. Another family, repatriated from Kazakhstan, had to be restrained from purchasing all the fresh vegetables at the supermarket, because over there, if there was fresh produce, you hoarded it because it might not be there next week. Repatriation programs are designed to prepare employees for adjusting to life at home (which at times can be more difficult than adjusting to a foreign assignment). ExxonMobil employees are given a general idea of what to expect following a foreign assignment even before they leave home. Unfortunately, not all companies have career development programs designed for repatriating employees. A recent study by the Canadian Employee Relocation Council found that few organizations have a structured program to repatriate employees. It did find some insights to encourage more organizations to develop structured programs, however. These are as follows:

1. Align individual goals with organizational goals, including "personality fit" for an international assignment.
2. Provide appropriate notice of repatriation as well as clarity on what benefits will be provided such as moving costs, tax planning, home search, counselling, spousal career counselling, and settling-in services.
3. Ensure that there is appropriate employment in the home country when the international assignment is completed.
4. Have a mentoring program in place for returning employees as most expats are high performing and high potential.[53]

Employees often lament that their organizations are vague about repatriation, about their new roles within the company, and about their career progression. In many cases, employees abroad have learned how to run an entire international operation—or at least significant parts of it. When they return home, however, their responsibilities are often significantly diminished. In fact, the evidence suggests that only a fraction of them are promoted. It is also not uncommon for employees to return home after a few years to find that there is *no* position for them in the firm and that they no longer know anyone who can help them. Employees often feel that their firms disregard their difficulties in adjusting to life back in Canada.

Even where employees are successfully repatriated, their companies often do not fully utilize the knowledge, understanding, and skills developed on these global assignments. This hurts the employee, of course, but it may hurt equally the firm's chances of using that employee's expertise to gain competitive advantage. Not surprisingly, expatriates sometimes leave their company within a year or two of coming home. Since as many as 50% of returning employees leave the company soon after their return, one global expert suggests that the key to making the repatriation successful is communication—constantly so that the employees will have good information about what to expect on the return. It is also important to give the employees sufficient time to reinstall their families.[54]

At companies with good repatriation processes, employees are given guidance about how much the expatriate experience may have changed them and their families. Some firms introduce former expatriates and their spouses to other former expatriates at special social events. And more companies are making an effort to keep in touch with expatriates while they are abroad, which has been made easier by e-mail, instant messaging, and video conferencing. Colgate's division executives and other corporate staff members frequently visit international transferees. Dow appoints a high-level manager who serves as a home-country contact for information about organizational changes, job opportunities, and anything related to compensation.

As the global economy continues to be volatile, it is important that international assignments be designed to anticipate such changes. Such a program would include the following:

- Align any global assignments with the organization's overall talent management approach.
- Have different policies and processes for global assignments, such as long-term assignments, short-term assignments, and tax policy.
- Have consistent and clear information about approval process for international assignments.
- Create a written assignment letter that includes the assignment's objectives.
- Have a framework for determining who is eligible for international assignments.
- Have ongoing contact and communication with organizational leaders.
- Have ongoing communication between the organization overall and the person on international assignment.[55]

REWARDS AND RECOGNITION

Outcome 6

What are the characteristics of a good international rewards and recognition program?

One of the most complex areas of international HRM is compensation. Different countries have different norms for employee compensation. Managers should consider carefully the motivational use of incentives and rewards in foreign countries. For North Americans, while nonfinancial incentives such as prestige, independence, and influence may be motivators, money is likely to be the driving force. And the concern is not just for larger organizations. Read HRM and SME 11.1 to learn more about the concerns for access to health-care coverage.

Other cultures are more likely to emphasize respect, family, job security, a satisfying personal life, social acceptance, advancement, or power. Since there are many alternatives to money, the rule is to match the reward with the values of the culture. In individualistic cultures, such as Canada, pay plans often focus on individual performance and achievement. However, in collectivist societies such as Asian and South American societies, people may value pay less than group relationships.[56]

In general, a guiding philosophy for designing pay systems might be "think globally and act locally." That is, executives should normally try to create a pay plan that supports the overall strategic intent of the organization but provides enough flexibility to customize particular policies and programs to meet the needs of employees in specific locations. For example, in a recent study Aon concluded that companies that reduced pay adjustments during the recession increased variable pay components to higher levels.[57] Aon further noted that companies that have global operations must treat the employees comparably no matter where the home country is.[58]

After a brief discussion of compensation practices for host-country employees and managers, the focus will be on the problems of compensating expatriates.

Compensation of Host-Country Employees

As shown in Figure 11.9, hourly compensation can vary dramatically from country to country, from about $58 in Norway to $20 in New Zealand and Israel.[59] Host-country employees are generally paid on the basis of productivity, time spent on the job, or a combination of these factors. In industrialized countries, pay is generally by the hour; in

HRM and SME 11.1

MAKING IT HAPPEN!

Those of us living in Canada take for granted our basic health coverage. Even if we don't work for an organization that provides additional health insurance, such as extended health (described in Chapter 7), we at least have access to doctors and hospitals. But this isn't true of many people—particularly those who work in U.S. organizations.

A small bagel producer, Bagel Grove, with only 20 employees, has very limited coverage due to the structure of health care. The owner is keen about the new concept of "health insurance exchanges," similar to online travel sites where small businesses can access affordable health coverage.

Part of the design of the exchanges will allow small employers to offer more options to their employees while simplifying the administration of the enhanced coverage. Small businesses are looking forward to these exchanges with 60% of those who do not yet offer any health coverage planning to do so. Many feel the exchanges will enable more low-paid employees to have access to affordable health coverage.

Small businesses understand the need to attract and retain talent in a competitive environment. Having access to health coverage with options that best fit the needs of the employees will help employers keep their key employees.

QUESTIONS:

1. If you are or were working, would you want to have access to additional health coverage such as extended health? If not, would you like to have this and why?

2. In small groups and from an employer's perspective, discuss the pros and cons of not having basic health coverage provided through the provincial governments.

Source: Adapted from "Small Shops Ready to Roll Out More Variety," *Workforce Management*, March 2012, 3.

developing countries, by the day. The piece-rate method is quite common. In some countries, including Japan, seniority is an important element in determining employees' pay rates. When companies commence operations in a foreign country, they usually set their wage rates at or slightly higher than the prevailing wage for local companies. Eventually, though, they are urged to conform to local practices to avoid "upsetting" local compensation practices. And more companies are now creating targeted benefits packages for people working in global assignments so that costs can be better managed.[60]

Employee benefits can range dramatically from country to country as well. In China, for example, paid maternity leave is increasing from 90 working days to 98 working days. This compares to 273 days in the United Kingdom and 480 days in Sweden. The additional benefit in China will also provide insurance coverage for the birth.[61]

Labour costs are one of the biggest motivators for international expansion, but many managerial and administrative issues must be addressed when an organization establishes operations overseas. For example, bad press can be generated for charging hundreds of dollars for individual products while the people who make them—sometimes children in developing countries working under poor conditions—earn only a few cents. Or, the bad press can also be generated when a company is accused of violating employment laws. See Ethics in HRM 11.1 for the story of Apple in China.

Compensation of Host-Country Managers

In the past, remuneration of host-country managers has been ruled by local salary levels; however, increased competition among different companies with subsidiaries in the same country has led to a gradual upgrading of host-country managers' salaries. Overall, international firms are moving toward a narrowing of the salary gap between the host-country manager and the expatriate. For example, the expected salary for a merchandise

FIGURE 11.9   Hourly Compensation Costs in Different Countries for Production Workers in Manufacturing

Country	$/Hour (U.S. Dollars)
Norway	57.53
Switzerland	53.20
Belgium	50.70
Denmark	45.48
Sweden	43.81
Germany	43.76
Finland	42.30
Austria	41.07
Netherlands	40.92
Australia	40.60
France	40.55
Ireland	36.30
Canada	**35.67**
United States	34.74
Italy	33.41
Japan	31.99
United Kingdom	29.44
Spain	26.60
Greece	22.19
New Zealand	20.57
Israel	20.12

Source: U.S. Department of Labor, Bureau of Labor Statistics, "International Comparisons of Hourly Compensation Costs in Manufacturing, 2010," December 21, 2011.

ETHICS **in HRM 11.1**

APPLE IN CHINA

What happens when iconic Apple's reputation becomes tarnished over allegations of child labour and unsafe working conditions in its Chinese factory? The short answer: Lots and quickly.

In early 2012, Apple's ethics were questioned when a series of articles were written for the *New York Times* describing numerous labour conditions in the factories that make iPhones, iPads, and Apple computers. Very quickly, CEO Tim Cook responded that the accusations went against Apple's values and all allegations would be investigated immediately. Even though Apple monitors all its factories, it did admit that with the intense production pressure some unfortunate accidents had occurred, such as suicides, poisonings, and explosions. Unfortunately, even with increased monitoring, some of the working conditions have worsened.

Apple does not own or operate the facilities but instead contracts with Chinese factories to produce its tech gadgets. In its investigation of the contractors, Apple did find that about two-thirds of the factories (90 out of 156) had staff working more than 60 hours a week. There were also five instances of children working.

The Fair Labour Association (FLA), a worldwide organization dedicated to having its members adhere to international labour standards, conducted the investigation into the allegations. By late March 2012, the FLA found extreme violations of Chinese labour laws, including unfair pay for overtime hours and inconsistent safety standards. Apple, as a relatively new member in the association, supported the investigation and recommendations.

As a result, Apple and its principal partner in China, Foxconn, pledged to substantially improve working conditions, including increasing wages, instituting safety protocols, addressing housing, and eliminating illegal overtime. Part of the recommendations was to hire thousands of more employees to handle the excess work as a result of restricting overtime.

Since Foxconn is China's largest private-sector employer and Apple is a world giant, their partnership in improving working conditions is expected to spill over to other Chinese manufacturers. While the improvements will make the lives of Chinese workers better, they will also drive up costs for other companies, such as Dell, HP, Nokia, and Sony, to which Foxconn supplies components. The increased costs will likely be passed on to consumers.

QUESTIONS:

1. Do you think companies like Apple or Foxconn ought to be penalized for employment infractions? What types of penalties would you impose and why?

2. As a consumer, how much more are you willing to pay for electronics if you could be assured that no violations of employment laws had occurred in the Chinese manufacturers?

Sources: Adapted from Malcolm Moore, "Apple accused of having unsafe working conditions," *The Vancouver Sun*, January 28, 2012, B7; Poornima Gupta and Edwin Chan, "Apple, Foxconn vow to improve worker conditions in China," *The Globe and Mail*, March 30, 2012, B3; and Stanley James, "Foxconn violated labour code," *The Vancouver Sun*, March 30, 2012, E4.

manager in Beijing is about \$4,000 per month.[62] There is a recognition that talent is scarce and competition is intense.

The ongoing global economic challenges are putting pressures on companies to attract and retain the top talent. A number of studies have suggested that this translates into a better link between global performance expectations—both of the company and the individual—and an appropriate rewards package. Talent is mobile, and organizations are looking at different approaches to recognize and reward their top talent.[63]

Compensation of Expatriate Managers

If the assignment is going to be successful, the expatriate's compensation plan must be competitive, cost effective, motivating, fair, easy to understand, consistent with international financial management, easy to administer, and simple to communicate.

For short-term assignments, usually those that are project based, expatriates are frequently given per-diem (per day) compensation. These managers might reside in hotels and service apartments instead of leasing houses. They are also less likely to bring their family members with them. The assignment becomes more like a commuting assignment in which the expatriate spends the week in the host country and returns home on the weekend.

For longer-term assignments, there are two basic types of compensation systems. The first is home-based pay, where the pay is based on the compensation practices of the expatriate's home country. For example, an airline pilot working for KLM Dutch Airlines and living in Vancouver is paid in Euros. The second type of compensation system is host-based pay. Companies are under pressure to move expatriates to host-based pay because it is generally less costly. Host-based pay is compensation that is equivalent to that earned by employees in the country where the expatriate is on assignment. This type of pay is also done in the local currency along with the local benefits, which means that fluctuations in currency exchange can affect the expat manager.[64]

Whether a company uses home-based or host-based pay depends on whether the employee may also depend on the cost of living within a particular country. For example, Japan and Norway are very expensive countries whereas India and Paraguay are the least expensive.[65]

A serious issue related to expatriate compensation is medical care when a major event, such as the tsunami in Japan in 2011 or the political unrest in Pakistan, occurs. Employees are unlikely to consent to a global assignment if they cannot get health care comparable to what's available in their home countries, including medical evacuation if that is necessary.[66] Often, Canadian-based plans can't cover expatriate employees or efficiently deal with claims that need to be reimbursed in foreign currency. One solution is to transfer the employee to a global employment company that can provide these types of benefits.

Another issue is the need to provide expatriates and employees who travel abroad with security. If the company operates in a high-risk market, such as the Middle East, it will have particular protocols to remove expatriates when danger arises.[67]

PERFORMANCE MANAGEMENT

Outcome 7

What are the difficulties with managing performance internationally?

As we noted earlier, individuals frequently accept international assignments because they know that they can acquire skills and experiences that will make them more valuable to their companies. Frequently, however, it can be difficult for the home office to assess the performance of employees working abroad. Even the notion of performance assessment is indicative of a North American management style that focuses on the individual, something that can cause problems in Asian countries such as China, Japan, and Korea and Eastern European countries such as Hungary and the Czech Republic.

Who Should Be Involved?

In many cases, an individual working internationally has at least two allegiances: one to his or her home country (the office that made the assignment) and the other to the host country in which the employee is currently working. Superiors in each location frequently have different information about the employee's performance and may also have very different expectations about what constitutes good performance. For these reasons, the multirater (360-degree) review discussed in Chapter 6 is gaining favour among global firms.

Home- vs. Host-Country Reviews

Domestic managers are frequently unable to understand expatriate experiences, value them, or accurately measure their contribution to the organization. Geographical distances create communication problems for expatriates and home-country managers even with the use of technology such as e-mail and instant messaging. However, local managers with daily contact with expatriates are more likely to have an accurate understanding of their performance. But there can still be problems with this. First, local cultures may influence one's perception of how well an individual is performing. As noted earlier in the chapter, participative decision making may be viewed either positively or negatively, depending on the culture. Such cultural biases may not have any bearing on an individual's true level of effectiveness. In addition, local management frequently does not have enough perspective on the entire organization to know how well an individual is contributing to the firm as a whole.

Given the pros and cons of home-country and host-country reviews, most observers agree that performance reviews should try to balance the two sources of performance information. Although host-country employees are in a good position to view day-to-day activities, in many cases, the individual is still formally tied to the home office. Promotions, pay, and other administrative decisions are connected there, and as a consequence, the written evaluation is usually handled by the home-country manager. Nevertheless, the review should be completed only after vital input has been gained from the host-country manager.

Performance Criteria

Because expatriate assignments are so costly, organizations are increasingly under pressure to calculate the return on investment of these assignments. What did the firm get for the

Video conferencing is one way for remote employees to stay in close contact with their home office.

© 2009 Jupiterimages Corporation

$1 million it spent to send an expatriate abroad? Has the expatriate achieved the goals set forth in the assignment in the appropriate time frame? Obviously, the goals and responsibilities inherent in the job assignment are among the most important criteria used to assess an individual's performance, and different goals necessitate measuring different criteria. Using a return-on-investment (ROI) approach, similar to what was discussed in Chapter 5, for determining the value of training and development, can be lacking. Productivity, profits, and market share, while valid, may not capture the full range of an expatriate's responsibility. Leadership development, for example, involves a much longer-term value proposi tion. In many cases, an expatriate is an ambassador for the company, and a significant part of the job is cultivating relationships with citizens of the host country. As discussed at the beginning of this chapter, an individual's success or failure is affected by a host of technical and personal factors. For example, as one might guess, it is much easier to adjust to similar cultures than to dissimilar ones. A Canadian can usually travel to the United Kingdom or Australia and work with locals almost immediately. Send the same individual to Hungary or Malaysia, and the learning curve is steeper.

Providing Feedback

Performance feedback in an international setting is clearly a two-way street. Although the home-country and host-country superiors may tell expatriates how well they are doing, it is also important for expatriates to provide feedback regarding the support they are receiving, the obstacles they face, and the suggestions they have about the assignment. More than in almost any other job, expatriates are in the best position to evaluate their own performance.

In providing feedback to expatriates, here are some tips:

1. Prior to any performance review, ensure that there is a trusting relationship between the employee and supervisor.

2. Arrange travel schedule so that feedback can be given in person.
3. Use technology (phone calls and video conferencing) to have weekly conversations to provide informal feedback.
4. Be sensitive to cultural differences such as whether the society is individualistic or collectivist.
5. Train managers on how to give feedback to expatriates.[68]

If the performance is not successful after review and coaching, careful attention needs to be paid to the local environment before terminating an employee. In some cases, such as China, employees can be terminated only for cause (discussed in Chapter 9); in other cases, such as in France, a prescribed procedure must be followed.[69]

THE LABOUR ENVIRONMENT WORLDWIDE

Outcome 8

How do labour relations differ around the world?

Labour relations in countries outside Canada differ significantly from those in Canada. Differences exist not only in the collective bargaining process but also in the political and legal conditions. For example, the EU prohibits discrimination against workers in unions, but in many countries, labour unions are illegal. China has only one officially recognized organization of workers, the All-China Federation of Trade Unions, which has negotiated many labour contracts with foreign companies such as Walmart and KFC—which are heavily against unions in North America.[70] Even though China has enacted the *Labour Contract Law* to protect workers and clarify the rights of employers, plans are already being made to amend it to better regulate outsourcing.[71]

Other examples of the labour environment in other countries include the investigation into the death of an intern in a test-drive car at Daimler. What is unusual is that CEO Dieter Zwetsch is being investigated for potential manslaughter charges in an attempt to hold the senior manager accountable for the actions of the company.[72] To gain a basic idea about labour–management relations in an international setting, we will look at four primary areas: (1) the role of unions in different countries, (2) collective bargaining in other countries, (3) international labour organizations, and (4) the extent of labour participation in management.

The Role of Unions

The role of unions varies from country to country and depends on many factors, such as the level of employee participation, per capita labour income, mobility between management and labour, homogeneity of labour (racial, religious, social class), and unemployment levels. These and other factors determine whether the union will have the strength it needs to represent labour effectively. Nearly all of Sweden's workers are organized, giving the unions in this country considerable strength and autonomy. By contrast, in countries with relatively high unemployment, low pay levels, and no union funds with which to support social welfare systems, unions are driven into alliance with other organizations: political party, church, or government. This kind of relationship is in marked contrast to Canada, where the union selected by the majority of employees bargains only with the employer, not with other institutions. As mentioned earlier in this section, China has a central union that is more aligned with employers than the employees.

There are many examples of union unrest in the global economy. For example, throughout 2011, strikes occurred in Australian coal mines owned by BHP Billiton and Mitsubishi.[73] Unions representing gold miners in Africa were demanding wage increases of 12 to 14% while 8,000 copper and gold miners in Indonesia went on strike, wanting more than the current $1.50 per hour wage.[74] Unions in Norway expressed outrage when an insurance company installed a new surveillance system that monitors how long employee bathroom breaks are.[75] In late 2011, thousands and thousands of workers in England went on strike in protest against government-directed pension reforms as part of its plan to reduce government spending.[76] Similarly, in the spring of 2012, truck drivers in Sao Paulo, Brazil, went on strike to protest government restrictions as to where the trucks can be driven during certain hours.[77] And lastly, customs workers in Kuwait went on strike, demanding higher wages, disrupting oil shipments from its ports.[78]

Collective Bargaining in Other Countries

In Chapter 10, you studied the collective bargaining process as it is typically carried out in companies operating in Canada. When you look at other countries, you find that the whole process can vary widely, especially with regard to the role of government. In Australia and New Zealand, for most of the 20th century, labour courts had the authority to impose wages and other employment conditions on a broad range of firms. In the United Kingdom and France, the government intervenes in all aspects of collective bargaining. Government involvement is only natural where parts of industry are nationalized. Also, in countries where nationalization is heavy, government involvement is more likely to be accepted, even in the non-nationalized companies. Read HRM and the Law 11.1 to learn what an Australian tribunal did regarding Qantas Airlines and its negotiations.

International Labour Organizations

The most active of the international union organizations has been the International Confederation of Free Trade Unions (ICFTU, **www.icftu.org**), which has its headquarters in Brussels. Co-operating with the ICFTU are numerous International Trade Secretariats (ITSs), which are really international federations of national trade unions operating in the same or related industries. In addition to the ITSs, the ICFTU also co-operates with the European

International Confederation of Free Trade Unions

www.icftu.org

HRM and the Law 11.1

THEY'RE FLYING AGAIN!

In the spring of 2012, Canadians experienced the impact of the labour dispute between Air Canada and its pilots that resulted in cancelled flights for many. Australia also went through a similar situation in late 2011 regarding its flagship carrier, Qantas.

Qantas, which accounts for about 40% of the Australian domestic market and is the 10th largest airline in the world, had been experiencing labour strife for months. A variety of different unions, representing occupations from pilots to baggage handlers to engineers had been striking over Qantas's plan to established a new Asia-based airline.

As the strike escalated, Qantas's officials grounded the entire fleet, leaving about 70,000 travellers throughout the world stranded. The Australian government was concerned about the overall economic impact and referred the issue to an Australian tribunal for resolution.

The tribunal ruled that the unions are precluded from taking any more strike action to further their demands. Strike action had been blamed for steep reductions in bookings for future flights, and Qantas reported losing over $75 million. In addition, the tribunal took over authority for negotiations. It has the ability to impose binding arbitration if the unions and Qantas cannot reach a settlement. Negotiations are continuing.

QUESTIONS:

1. Do you think airline employees should have the right to strike? Why or why not?

2. When workers at airlines strike, should the unions have to compensate the passengers for the disruption? Why or why not?

Sources: Adapted from Edna Curran and Andrew Critchlow, "Australian Tribunal Ends Qantas Strike," *The Globe and Mail*, October 31, 2011, B4; "Qantas Strike 2011 Ends: Australian Court Puts Top to Grounded Fleet, Labor Dispute," *Huffington Post*, October 31, 2011, www.huffingtonpost.com/2011/10/30/qantas-strike-2011-ends_n_1066353.html; Rod McGuirk, "Aussie Court Ends Qantas Strike, Fleet Grounding," *Business Week*, October 30, 2011, www.businessweek.com/ap/financialnews/D9QMVVUO0.htm; and Adrian Schofield, "Qantas Moves Closer to Resolving Labor Dispute," December 22, 2011, www.aviationweek.com/aw/generic/story_channel.jsp?channel=mro&id=news/avd/2011/12/20/06.xml.

**European Trade Union
Confederation**

www.etuc.org

**International Labor
Organization**

www.ilo.org

Codetermination
Representation of labour on the
board of directors of a company

Trade Union Confederation (ETUC, **www.etuc.org**) that represents over 60 million trade unionists in the EU and is recognized by the EU as a social partner.[79] Another active and influential organization is the International Labor Organization (ILO, **www.ilo.org**), a specialized agency of the United Nations. The ILO perhaps has had the greatest impact on the rights of workers throughout the world. It promotes the rights of workers to organize, the eradication of forced and child labour, and the elimination of discrimination. Read At Work with HRM 11.5 to learn more about the ILO from one of Canada's representatives.

Labour Participation in Management

In many European countries, law establishes provisions for employee representation. An employer may be legally required to provide for employee representation on safety and hygiene committees, worker councils, or even on boards of directors. While their responsibilities vary from country to country, worker councils basically provide a communication channel between employers and workers. The legal codes that set forth the functions of worker councils in France are very detailed. Councils are generally concerned with grievances, problems of individual employees, internal regulations, and matters affecting employee welfare.

A higher form of worker participation in management is found in Germany, where law requires representation of labour on the board of directors of a company. This arrangement is known as **codetermination** and often by its German word, *Mitbestimmung*. While sometimes puzzling to outsiders, the system is fairly simple: Company shareholders and employees are required to be represented in equal numbers on the supervisory boards of all corporations with more than 2,000 employees.

Concluding Comments

Each of these differences makes managing human resources in an international context more challenging. But the crux of the issue in designing HRM systems is not choosing one approach that will meet all the demands of international business. Instead, organizations

---

AT WORK **with HRM 11.5**

WHAT A PRIVILEGE!

What's it like being one of Canada's representatives to the International Labour Organization (ILO)? Just ask John Beckett, Vice President, Training, Safety and Recruitment for the BC Maritime Employers Association and he will describe the privilege it is to be one of Canada's employer representatives on one of the ILO's committees.

The ILO, as an agency of the United Nations, is funded by the United Nations, which is funded by member countries. The ILO is considered to be the "house of labour," with labour, employer, and government representatives. While it started in the early 1900s, it wasn't until after World War II that it really took off. As John states, "The primary mandate is for continuous improvement on social issues throughout the world." Much of its focus has been on labour issues.

Typically, the ILO identifies 3–4 areas each year in which active work occurs by the members. John,

as a representative of Canada, sits on one of the ILO's sub-committees. This particularly committee, labour inspection protocols, has about 400 members. While it might seem that this quite a few for getting things done, in fact, things do get done and new standards, called "conventions" are agreed to. Then each member country can choose to adopt or accept the convention and develop legislation to support and action. Canada has a good track record of adopting the various conventions over the years.

What's the most interesting aspect of John's work? "It is the international reach of the ILO in social programs and reforms," says John. "And it is great being part of the changes that happen."

QUESTION:

Why else might John Beckett consider his role privilege? Explain your reasons.

facing global competition must balance several approaches and make their policies flexible enough to accommodate differences across national borders. Throughout this book we have noted that different situations call for different approaches to managing people, and nowhere is this point more clearly evident than in international HRM.

As the discussion on international HRM draws to a close, remember that whether the world is less volatile or not, today's organizations will need to be vigilant about employee engagement in a global context. There is, and will continue to be, competition for global talent, and companies will need to monitor and take actions to motivate and engage employees all over the world.[80] Furthermore, as already demonstrated, multinational companies will relocate operations that provide a competitive advantage—whether in terms of natural resources, cost of labour, or inducements by governments.

Are the factors in employee engagement different for global assignments than for domestic ones? The top factor "career opportunities" is the same whether a person is working on a global assignment or not.[81] After that, the differences depend on the country, although pay rates were low in all regions.

Moving forward with a still struggling global economy, organizations will have to continue with an emphasis on talent management in order to succeed in what is now a solid global economy. Consider the other areas to watch in Emerging Trends 11.1.

EMERGING TRENDS **11.1**

1. **Shorter international assignments.** Organizations are taking a more targeted approach to international assignments. For example, Ford sent one engineer to Mexico for 13 months to modernize a plant. By doing so, it saved significant costs on housing and education, and the employee, already a Spanish speaker, did not have to sell his house.

2. **Global talent attraction and retention.** There is a continuing expectation that the world economy will improve, which will make the workforce even more mobile. Companies will need to be watchful to ensure that they are engaging their employees and providing the career opportunities that they may be looking for.

3. **Changes to government pension plans.** More and more governments are changing the manner in which pensions for individuals are financed. Canada has recently changed the age to collect OAS from 65 to 67; Germany will levy additional taxes on individuals over the age of 25 to pay for the increasing number of elderly people and the project costs for pensions.

4. **Increasing labour unrest.** Even with an expectation of an improved global economy, unions are becoming more involved in protests. For example, a general strike occurring in Spain saw almost one million people protesting labour reforms as Spain struggles to deal with its finances.

5. **Making use of more technology in certain industry sectors.** While automakers have for a number of years used robots and other advanced technology to build cars, mining operations are looking to do the same. With increased automation, mining companies are looking to reduce maintenance costs and increase production as well as improve safety. For example, Rio Tinto will soon be the first fully automated mine, where a control centre, perhaps thousands of kilometres away, will remotely control huge hauling trucks to move ore.

6. **Improving employee health.** Whether or not there is government-provided health care, organizations throughout the world are understanding the link between productivity and worker health. Wellness programs are becoming more prevalent to deal with lifestyle risks such as stress and obesity.

Sources: Adapted from Lynette Clemetson, "Special Report on Globalization: The Globe-Trotters," *Workforce Management*, December 15, 2010, accessed April 5, 2012, www.workforce.com/article/20101215/TOOLS/312159992; "Trends in Global Employee Engagement," Aon Hewitt, 2011; Bruno Waterfield, "Germany Proposes to Tax Young to Help Old," *The Financial Post*, April 5, 2012, FP3; Daniel Silve, "Clashes Erupt in Spain during Strike," *Financial Post*, March 30, 2012, FP2; Brenda Bouw, "Miners Look to a Future of Automation," *The Globe and Mail*, February 6, 2012, B3; and "Multinational Workforce Health: Building a Sustainable Global Strategy," Towers Watson, 2011.

SUMMARY

1. Identify the types of organizational forms used for competing internationally.
   - International—domestic firm that uses existing capabilities to move into global markets.
   - Multinational—fully autonomous units operating in multiple countries.
   - Global—multinational firm that maintains control back in the home office.
   - Transnational—a firm that attempts to balance local responsiveness with efficiencies of global firm.

2. Explain the economic, political-legal, and cultural factors in different countries that need to be considered from an HR perspective.
   - Trade agreements can shift jobs from one location to another.
   - Companies will move or expand operations depending on which country provides best economic return.
   - Property rights and intellectual property rights will determine which countries companies do business in.
   - Cultural factors include language, religion, values, education, and social structure.

3. Illustrate how Canadian and international HRM differ.
   - Functions such as relocation, orientation, and translation services become more important for global assignments.
   - Decisions need to be made regarding the currency of compensation.
   - More attention is paid to the security of international staff, particularly if the geographic area is high risk.

4. Describe the staffing process for individuals working internationally.
   - Companies can send people from the home country (expatriates).
   - Firms can hire employees who are natives to the host country.
   - Employee recruitment in other countries is subject to more government regulation than in Canada.

5. Discuss the unique training needs for employees who work internationally.
   - Content needs to have information about the country and the country's culture.
   - Language training may be necessary.
   - Special attention needs to be paid to helping the employees manage personal and family life.
   - Some development programs are designed to facilitate repatriation.

6. Outline the characteristics of a good international recognition and rewards program.
   - Different cultures value recognition and rewards differently.
   - Determine whether the employee will be paid through the policies of home or host country and in what currency.

7. Reconcile the difficulties of home- and host-country performance management systems.
   - Decisions need to be made on who will be involved in performance process.
   - Domestic managers may not fully understand the expatriate experiences so it is a good idea to involve the host-country manager.
   - Performance criteria need to include more than just financial goals.
   - It is important to provide feedback regularly to the expatriate.

8. Explain how labour relations differ around the world.
   - Labour laws are different from one country to another.
   - Government may be more involved in determining wage rates even with unionized staff.
   - Some countries, such as Germany, have a high degree of worker participation.

NEED TO KNOW

- Definition of international, multinational, global, and transnational corporation
- Definition of expatriate
- Definition of culture shock

NEED TO UNDERSTAND

- Role of economic, political-legal, and cultural issues in global assignments
- Advantages of using home- or host-country nationals
- Contents of training program when someone is taking on global assignment
- Different components of recognition and rewards in an international assignment
- Role home-country manager plays in supporting expatriate
- Differences in international labour relations

KEY TERMS

augmented skills 404

codetermination 418

core skills 404

cultural environment 395

culture shock 408

expatriates, or home-country nationals 397

failure rate 405

global corporation 390

guest workers 401

host country 395

host-country nationals 397

international corporation 390

multinational corporation (MNC) 390

repatriation 409

third-country nationals 397

transnational corporation 391

transnational teams 403

work permit, or visa 401

REVIEW QUESTIONS

1. Name the types of organizational forms used for competing internationally.
2. What are the factors in different countries that need to be considered from an HR perspective?
3. How do Canadian and international HR differ?
4. What is the staffing process for individuals working abroad?
5. What are the unique training needs for an individual working internationally?
6. What are the characteristics of a good international recognition and rewards program?
7. What are the difficulties between home- and host-country performance management systems?
8. How do labour relations differ around the world?

CRITICAL THINKING QUESTIONS

1. Review Figures 11.2 and 11.3. Are there any companies that are on all the lists? If so, which ones? Is there anything in particular that you note about Figure 11.3?
2. Scotiabank operates in 50 countries and employs Canadians to staff its New Delhi office. What are the advantages of employing Canadians with roots in the host country? Would you use expatriate managers or host-country nationals to staff Scotiabank offices? Explain your thinking.
3. In what ways are Canadian managers likely to experience difficulties in their relationships with employees in foreign operations? How can these difficulties be minimized?
4. If learning about different cultures is an important outcome of an overseas assignment, how can this be worked into a performance management system? How would a manager assess the learning?

5. If the cost of living is lower in a foreign country than in Canada, should expatriates be paid less than they would be at home? Explain your answer.
6. Chrysler is planning to build a plant in St. Petersburg, Russia, to make Jeeps. Do you think it would be better to start the plant with expatriate managers or with host-country managers? Why?

DEVELOPING YOUR SKILLS

The Globe and Mail Top Publicly Traded Companies
www.theglobeandmail.com/
report-on-business/
rob-magazine/top-1000

Expatica
www.expatica.com

Wageindicator.org
www.wageindicator.org

1. Access the archives of *The Globe and Mail* rankings of the top Canadian companies at **www.theglobeandmail.com/report-on-business/rob-magazine/top-1000**. Access the 2009 list in the archives. Compare the top 10 companies there to Figure 11.4. What do you notice about any changes?
2. One of the most common reason for failure of an expatriate assignment is family issues. Go to Expatica (**www.expatica.com**) and click on a country of your choice. Read the information available on "Families and Kids." What was the most useful piece and why?
3. If you wanted to work in another country, what would be important for you to consider and why?
4. Examine Figure 11.9 in relation to manufacturing wages. Pick a country in which you might like to work; then, go to Wageindicator.org (**www.wageindicator.org/main**), find the same country and determine what wages people in other occupations are paid. How do the wages compare to those in manufacturing?

Case Study

Global Recovery and the Impact on HRM

What happens to worldwide people practices when the world begins to recover from the Great Recession? From expansions to contractions, HRM plays an important role.

For example, some Canadian businesses are relocating their call centres to Canada. The reasons for doing so include high turnover in foreign operations and rising wages in host countries. American Express Canada, BCE, and Fortis also indicated they did so to improve the customer experience. However, the rising costs in foreign call centres mean that foreign workers lose their jobs while more job opportunities are provided for Canadians.

CAE, the Montreal-based company that provides training on flight simulators, is opening its fifth centre in India. As India expands, 7,000 more pilots will be needed each year. More opportunities will be available for global staff to run the centre, including those individuals from Canada who have previously provided training. Thus, renewed emphasis on recruitment will take place in India as well as Canada.

UPS is expanding its parcel delivery service in Germany by buying Europe's TNT Express. In doing so, it will cut overlap with its existing facilities and the acquisition by job cuts. So, both German workers and some existing UPS staff will find that they will have to seek alternative employment.

More and more companies globally are enabling telecommuting as a way to attract and retain women. In India, over one half of workers telecommute; in countries such as Mexico, Indonesia, and Argentina, about one third do so. Ipsos Reid conducted a recent survey indicating that with technology and emerging markets, telecommuting was more viable than ever before. In addition, people can be working with others in different countries through their telecommuting work.

The U.S. experienced backlash from its unions when a decision was made to reject the construction of the Keystone XL pipeline from Canada to Texas. The coalition of unions representing workers involved in the construction trades were angry that so many thousands of jobs were not going to be created. This coalition was also annoyed with some other unions that opposed the construction, which is creating tension between unions. On the other hand, in its contract talks with GM, the UAW traded high wages and benefits for job security, with any pay increases being linked to the overall performance of the company.

With its expansion into the U.S., Toronto-Dominion is planning to add more than 1,600 new jobs to its operations, thereby creating a need to attract capable financial services people from both Canada and the U.S. to the South Carolina area branches. Likewise, Daimler Trucks is expanding into North Carolina and planning to recall or rehire close to 1,100 workers.

Sources: Adapted from Sean Silcoff, "Busy Signals: Why Call Centres Came Back," *The Globe and Mail*, March 14, 2012, B3; "CAE to Open Fifth Training Centre," *The Globe and Mail*, June 23, 2011, B13; "United Parcel Service Nearing Agreement to Buy Europe's TNT Express," *Financial Post*, March 9, 2012, FP5; Patricia Reaney, "One in 5 Workers Telecommute, Global Survey Suggests," *The Vancouver Sun*, March 24, 2012, E16; Sharon Terlep and Matthew Dolan, "UAW Shields Jobs, Yields on Pay," *The Wall Street Journal*, September 21, 2011, B1; Sam Hananel, "U.S. Unions at Odds over Keystone XL," *The Globe and Mail*, March 12, 2012, A11; "TD to Hire 1,600 in South Carolina," *The Globe and Mail*, November 17, 2011, B9; and "Daimler to Hire 1,100 Workers at U.S. Plant," *The Globe and Mail*, January 13, 2012, B6.

Questions

1. If you were on an international assignment and the economy began to improve, would you expect the company to change any conditions of your work assignment? If so, what and why?
2. What hardships might foreign workers have as the global economy or their home country economy improves?
3. What would be your reaction if you were on a global assignment and the company unilaterally told you that with an improving economy, you'd need to stay for another year or two?

Case Study  **2**

What a Show!

What's it like to be involved with a circus? And not just any circus! Cirque du Soleil is probably Canada's foremost and most known export. Cirque started as street performers in Montreal, where it was created by Guy Laliberté, to celebrate Quebec's 450th anniversary in 1984. With only 73 people when it started, it now has over 5,000 employees throughout the world.

Its most noted recent show is in the Kremlin—where Russian audiences have come to see a "Broadway-meets-the-Big-Top" production. It wasn't easy to move into the Russian market, but with the help of others who had been Russia for some time doing business, Cirque was able to bring clowns and jugglers to a stated-owned building.

When the company opened an office in Moscow, it decided to hire an all-Russian staff. These people knew the Russian environment, including the strong circus tradition. Also, with approximately 20% of its performers from Russia, it had the ingredients to undertake a successful enterprise. And it isn't just the Russian performers that work in Russia. A person who trained with the Moscow circus was asked to move to Canada to join the show. The acrobat, Yakimolin, had a dream of joining Cirque du Soleil and didn't hesitate to say "yes."

Of particular importance to Daniel Lamarre, the CEO, was ensuring that he and the others understood the Russian culture. "It's just as normal that we work with Russians when we're in Russia as working with Americans when in Las Vegas," he states.

Part of understanding the culture was acknowledging the respect that the Kremlin has. Even though Russian politics can be unpredictable, it was important to remember that the Kremlin is the president's theatre. It commands the same kind of respect as the White House does in the U.S. Furthermore, the show that debuted in Russia was heavily edited to reflect the political scene in early 2012—when Vladimir Putin was returned to the presidency after serving for four years as prime minister. The show, *Zarkana*, had language and scenes that dealt with revolutions. Given the unrest of the Russian people toward Putin, it was decided that the show's dialogue and scenes had to be changed to ensure they did not provoke anyone in power in Russia.

Its success is already getting the Cirque executives to look at expanding its exposure in Russia. But will it move into another country such as China? Possibly. Lamarre is doing the same thing that he did when considering a move to Russia—talking to lots of people.

Sources: Adapted from Mark MacKinnon, "Inside the Kremlin Walls, Canada's Circus Spectacular Finds a Blueprint for Growth," *The Globe and Mail*, March 24, 2012, B6; "What's New in Canada," Cirque du Soleil, accessed April 9, 2012, www.cirquedusoleil.com/en/jobs/home.aspx; and Nastassia Astrasheuskaya, "Cirque du Soleil Eclipsing Traditional Russia Circus," Reuters, January 20, 2012, www.reuters.com/article/2012/01/20/us-russia-circus-idUSTRE80J0RH20120120.

Questions

1. If Cirque du Soleil does open a show in China, what cultural factors might it need to consider?
2. What was key to Cirque moving into Russia?
3. Access the jobs site at Cirque (**www.cirquedusoleil.com/en/jobs/home.aspx**). Determine what type of work is available. Is this a company that you might enjoy working for? Why or why not?

NOTES AND REFERENCES

1. Stephan Stern, "Corporate War for Talent Is Being Waged Worldwide," *The Globe and Mail*, February 14, 2012, www.theglobeandmail.com/report-on-business/careers/management/management-advice/corporate-war-for-talent-is-being-waged-worldwide/article2337813/; and Alicia Clegg, "Managing Up Close and Personal from Far Away," *The Globe and Mail*, February 15, 2012, www.theglobeandmail.com/report-on-business/careers/management/management-advice/managing-up-close-and-personal-from-far-away/article2338569.

2. "Tata's Pact with British Telecom Could Be Worth US$1-Billion," *Financial Post*, June 26, 2009, FP 3.

3. Stephanie Nolen, "India's Nano Hits Bumps on the Road," *The Globe and Mail*, November 8, 2011, /www.theglobeandmail.com/report-on-business/international-news/asian-pacific/indias-nano-hits-bumps-on-the-road/article2229888/; and Ketan Thakkar, "Petrol Powered Entry Level Cards Like Alto, Nano and Eon Keep Pace with Diesel Cars," *The Times of India*, March 21, 2012, http://economictimes.indiatimes.com/news/news-by-industry/auto/automobiles/petrol-powered-entry-level-cards-like-alto-nano-eon-keep-pace-with-diesel-cars/articleshow/12347200.cms.

4. "Global Overview," Barrick Gold, accessed March 26, 2012, www.barrick.com/Home/default.aspx.

5. Forbes staff, "Global 2000 Methodology," *Forbes*, April 20, 2011, www.forbes.com/2011/04/20/global-2000-11-methodology.html.

6. Hay Group, "*Fortune* World's Most Admired Companies," accessed March 26, 2012, www.haygroup.com/Fortune/results/fortune-rankings.aspx; and Hay Group webinar, April 18, 2012.

7. "The 100 Best Companies to Work For," *Fortune*, February 6, 2012, 117.

8. "Six Canadian Firms on Global Top 100 List," *The Globe and Mail*, January 25, 2012, B2; and "2012 Global 100 Most Sustainable Corporations in the World," accessed March 26, 2012, www.global100.org/annual-lists/2012-global-100-list.html.

9. Ross Marowits, "Bombardier Wins $214-Million Rail Contract in India," *The Globe and Mail*, November 29, 2011, B10.

10. "2011 Rankings of Canada's Top 1000 Public Companies by Profit," *The Globe and Mail*, June 23, 2011, www.theglobeandmail.com/report-on-business/rob-magazine/top-1000/2011-rankings-of-canadas-top-1000-public-companies-by-profit/article2071184.

11. "Countries," http://europa.eu/about-eu/countries/index_en.htm; and "Basic Information on the European Union," accessed March 26, 2012, http://europa.eu/about-eu/basic-information/index_en.htm.

12. Ki Hee Kim, "NAFTA Is a Good Deal for Workers in North America: Theory and Evidence," *Proceedings of Northeast Business and Economics Association* (2010): 517–22.

13. *Canada's State of Trade: Trade and Investment Update—2011*, Foreign Affairs and International Trade Canada, March 2012.

14. "China's Gross Domestic Product (GDP) Growth," *Chinability*, November 5, 2011, www.chinability.com/GDP.htm.

15. "Marchionne Merges Fiat, Chrysler Management," *Report on Business*, July 29, 2011, B8.

16. Veronica Ek and Patrick Lannin, "Saab Escapes Bankruptcy Again as Chinese Firms Take Over," *The Globe and Mail*, October 20, 2011, B5.

17. Ray Colitt and Ben Blanchard, "BRICS Dig in Heels over World Trade Talks" *The Globe and Mail*, April 26, 2011, www.theglobeandmail.com/report-on-business/economy/trade/brics-dig-in-heels-over-world-trade-talks/article1983228.

18. Dean Nelson, "'King of Good Times' Hits Turbulence," *The Vancouver Sun*, November 15, 2011, B6.

19. "Molson Coors Enters Indian Market," *Report on Business*, June 24, 2011, B9.

20. Shawn McCarthy, "Canada, Japan Launch Free-Trade Talks," *Report on Business*, March 26, 2012, B1.

21. "What's New?" Fruits and Passion, accessed March 26, 2012, http://www.fruits-passion.ca/whats-new.

22. Jeff Bennett, "Japanese Tire Maker Sets U.S. Investment," *The Wall Street Journal*, September 22, 2011, B4.

23. "Canadians Not Letting Go of Work on Holiday," *Canadian HR Reporter*, November 30, 2011, www.hrreporter.com/articleview/11825-canadians-not-letting-go-of-work-on-holiday.

24. For more information on culture and organizations, interested readers can access the journal *Culture and Organization* published by Routledge, in affiliation with the Centre for Innovative Management at Athabasca University, Alberta.

25. "Cultural Quicksand Makes Doing Deals a Very Risky Proposition," Aon Hewitt, 2012.

26. Tim McCarney, "Relocation Policies More about Speed, Dexterity," *Canadian HR Reporter*, December 5, 2011, 20.

27. "One-Half of Employees Globally Open to Working Abroad: Survey," *Canadian HR Reporter*, February 7, 2012, www.hrreporter.com/articleview/12284-one-half-of-employees-globally-open-to-working-abroad-survey.

28. Anne Harvey, vice-president, Employee Engagement, Vancouver Coastal Health Authority, interview by author, June 2012.

29. Shannon Klie, "HR Goes Global," *Canadian HR Reporter*, February 14, 2011, www.hrreporter.com/articleview/9505-hr-goes-global.

30. *Talent Mobility Good Practice to Stimulate Economic Growth*, Mercer, 2011.

31. "Top HR Challenge in Emerging Markets Lack of Local, Skilled Talent," *Canadian HR Reporter*, February 17, 2012, www.hrreporter.com/articleview/12371-top-hr-challenge-in-emerging-markets-lack-of-local-skilled-talent.

32. Pushpendra Priyadarshi, "Employer Brand Image as Predictor of Employee Satisfaction, Affective Commitment & Turnover," *The Indian Journal of Industrial Relations* 46, no. 3 (January 2011): 510–22; Sylvia Ann Hewlett and Ripa Rashid, "The Battle for Female Talent in Emerging Markets," *Harvard Business Review*, May 2010, 101–06; Tavia Grant, "More Canadian Workers Being Transferred Abroad," *The Globe and Mail*, June 8, 2011, B21; and "Developing Your Global Know-How," *Harvard Business Review*, March 2011, 71–75.

33. "Education in France: Understanding the Grandes Écoles," accessed March 28, 2012, www.understandfrance.org/France/Education.html#ancre518687.

34. Richard Rothschild, "Aon's Premier Partnership Kicks Up Camaraderie," *Workforce Management*, November 3, 2011, www.workforce.com/article/20111103/NEWS02/111109993/aons-premier-partnership-kicks-up-camaraderie.

35. Ibid.

36. Edmond Mellina, "It's Not Easy to Work in a Global World," *Canadian HR Reporter*, November 29, 2010, accessed March 30, 2012, www.hrreporter.com/articleview/8556-its-not-easy-to-work-in-a-global-world-guest-commentary.

37. Erin Millar, "Why Chinese Workers Don't Hate the Boss," *The Globe and Mail*, November 3, 2011, www.theglobeandmail.com/report-on-business/careers/business-education/why-chinese-workers-dont-hate-the-boss/article2222620.

38. Sarah Fister Gale, "From Texas to Timbuktu—How Fluor Tracks Talent on a Global Scale," *Workforce Management*, March 7, 2012, www.workforce.com/article/20120307/NEWS02/120309967/from-texas-to-timbuktu-mdash-how-fluor-tracks-talent-on-a-global-scale.

39. Siegfried Russwurm, "On How to Embrace a Foreign Posting," *Harvard Business Review*, March 2011, 71.

40. Susan Chambers, "On the Value of Short-Term Global Assignments," *Harvard Business Review*, March 2011, 74.

41. Lynette Clemetson, "The Pepsi Challenge: Helping Expats Feel at Home," *Workforce Management*, December 15, 2010, accessed March 30, 2012, www.workforce.com/article/20101215/NEWS02/312159991.

42. Klaus J. Templer, "Personal Attributes of Expatriate Managers, Subordinate Ethnocentrism, and Expatriate Success: A Host-Country Perspective," *The International Journal of Human Resource Management* 21, no. 10 (August 2010): 1754–68.

43. Keumyong Chung, "On Training Programs for Employees Headed Abroad," *Harvard Business Review*, March 2011, 75.

44. Information supplied to current author by Doug Whitehead, chair of the board of directors, April 2012.

45. Chung, "On Training Programs for Employees Headed Abroad."

46. Marc Forgas, Human Resources Director, "Expatriates at P&G," (presentation to P & G Board of Directors, March 2010).

47. Managers who are interested in setting up a language-training program or who wish to evaluate commercially available language-training programs or finding appropriate cross-cultural training can used the following resources: Rosetta Stone, www.rosettastone.com; Berlitz, www.berlitz.com; Global Integration, www.global-integration.com; and DFA Intercultural Global Solutions, www.deanfosterassociates. com. Additional resources can be found through continuing education at many local universities or community colleges.

48. Sarah Dobson, "Technology Eases Relocation Process," *Canadian HR Reporter*, May 7, 2010, accessed March 31, 2012, www.hrreporter.com/articleview/7849-technology-eases-relocation-process.

49. Mayumi Negishi, "Ricoh to Axe 10,000 Jobs, Promises to Get Back in Shape," Reuters, May 26, 2011, http://in.reuters.com/article/2011/05/26/idINIndia-57291020110526.

50. Wallace Immen, "On the Move for Work," *The Globe and Mail*, May 14, 2010, accessed March 31, 2012, www.theglobeandmail.com/report-on-business/careers/career-advice/weekend-workout/on-the-move-for-work/article1569522.

51. Lynne Clemetson, "Special Report on Globalization: The Globe-Trotters," *Workforce Management*, December 15, 2010, accessed March 31, 2012, www.workforce.com/article/20101215/TOOLS/312159992.

52. Ibid.

53. "Survey of Corporate Repatriation Practices, 2010," Canadian Employee Relocation Council, April 12, 2010.

54. Stephen Cryne, "Homeward Bound," *Canadian HR Reporter*, March 9, 2009, accessed March 31, 2012, www.hrreporter.com/ArticleView.aspx?l=1&articleid=6721.

55. Kris Morgan and Gary Johnson, "Building and Maintaining an 'All-Weather' Global Mobility Program," *Workforce Management*, July 12, 2010, accessed March 31, 2012, www.workforce.com/article/20100712/NEWS02/307129994.

56. "Cultural Differences," Iowa State University, Center for Excellence in Learning and Teaching, October 11, 2011, www.celt.iastate.edu/international/CulturalDifferences3.html.

57. "Aftermath of the Recession on 2009–2010 Compensation Spending," Aon, 2011, accessed April 1, 2012, www.aon.com/human-capital-consulting/thought-leadership/compensation/article_compensation_spending.jsp.

58. Sandeep Chaudhary, "Globalization of Compensation," Aon, accessed April 1, 2012, www.aon.com/apac/human-resources/thought-leadership/asia-connect/2011-sep/globalization-of-compensation.jsp.

59. For those students interested in how quickly these costs have increased, look at either the 4th edition of this textbook, Figure 11.9 on page 364, or access the U.S. Department of Labor, "International Comparison" for 2008." You'll notice that most of the costs have increased substantially.

60. "Costs, Employee Demands Biggest Relocation Challenge," *Canadian HR Reporter*, January 23, 2012, www.hrreporter.com/articleprint.aspx?articleid=12176.

61. Natasha Khan, "Longer Maternity Leave Offered in China," *The Vancouver Sun*, November 26, 2011, C7.

62. "Guide to China Market Salaries 1st Quarter 2012," J. M. Gemini.

63. Annmarie Neal, "Time to Step Up: Challenges and Opportunities Facing Talent Management," The Conference Board Council of Talent Management, 2010; "People Management in the Middle East and North Africa: What Has Changed after the Crisis and the 'Arab Spring,'" Mercer, 2011.

64. "The Host-Based Salary System," ECA International, June 2010, accessed April 1, 2012, www.eca-international.com/news/articles/show_article?ArticleID=7176#.T3i-jL_IRAl.

65. Sam Barrett, "Enigmatic Variations," *Employee Benefits*, January 2010, 7–10.

66. Tynan Barton, "Care in a Crisis," *Employee Benefits*, April 2011, 36.

67. Susan Ladika, "Global Turmoil Tests Ability to Protect Workers," *Workforce Management*, April 7, 2011, www.workforce.com/article/20110407/NEWS02/304079992.

68. Steven H. Appelbaum, Michel Roy, and Terry Gilliland, "Globalization of Performance Appraisals: Theory and Applications," *Management Decisions* 49, no. 4, (2011): 570–85; and Shahzad Ghafoor et al., "Evaluation of Expatriates' Performance and Their Training on International Assignments," *The Interdisciplinary Journal of Contemporary Research in Business* 3, no. 5 (September 2011): 335–51.

69. Dan Harris, "Terminating Your Employee in China. It Ain't Easy…," *China Law Blog*, January 9, 2010, accessed April 2, 2012, www.chinalawblog.com/2010/01/terminating_your_china_employe.html; and "France Employment Law," Worldwide Consulting Group, accessed April 2, 2012, www.worldwideconsulting.com/france.htm.

70. Dierdre Griswold, "Debate over Role of Unions Opens in China," *Workers World*, July 11, 2010, accessed April 2, 2012, www.workers.org/2010/world/china_0715.

71. Chen Xin, "Labor Contract Law Needs to Be Amended," *China Daily*, March 14, 2012, www.chinadaily.com.cn/china/2012-03/14/content_14827287.htm.

72. "Daimler CEO Faces Manslaughter Investigation," *Financial Post*, September 16, 2011, http://business.financialpost.com/2011/09/16/daimler-ceo-faces-manslaughter-investigation/.

73. Brenda Bouw, "Mine Works Dig In on Labour Front," *The Globe and Mail*, July 6, 2011, B3.

74. Ibid.

75. "Norwegian Insurance Company Monitors Bathroom Breaks," *Workforce Management*, February 6, 2012, www.workforce.com/article/20120206/NEWS01/120209968/norwegian-insurance-company-monitors-workers-bathroom-breaks.

76. Stefano Ambrogi, "Union, Government Claim Strike Victory," *The Vancouver Sun*, December 1, 2011, B7.

77. "Truckers' Strike Hurts Sao Paulo," *The Globe and Mail*, March 8, 2012, B9.

78. "Kuwait Customs Workers on Strike," *The Globe and Mail*, March 14, 2012, B9.

79. The European Trade Union Confederation, accessed April 5, 2012, www.etuc.org.

80. "Trends in Global Employee Engagement," Aon Hewitt, 2011.

81. Ibid.

GLOSSARY

Achievement tests Measures of what a person knows or can do right now (page 135)

Alternative dispute resolution (ADR) Term applied to different types of employee complaint or dispute-resolution procedures (page 332)

Apprenticeship training System of training in which a worker entering the skilled trades is given thorough instruction and experience, both on and off the job, in the practical and theoretical aspects of the work (page 163)

Aptitude tests Measures of a person's capacity to learn or acquire skills (page 135)

Arbitration award Final and binding award issued by an arbitrator in a labour–management dispute (page 377)

Arbitrator Third-party neutral who resolves a labour dispute by issuing a final and binding decision in an agreement (page 370)

Augmented skills Skills helpful in facilitating the efforts of expatriate managers (page 404)

Bargaining unit Group of two or more employees who share common employment interests and conditions and may reasonably be grouped together for purposes of collective bargaining (page 351)

Behaviour modification Technique that if behaviour is rewarded it will be exhibited more frequently in the future (page 161)

Behavioural description interview (BDI) Question about what a person actually did in a given situation (page 130)

Behaviourally anchored rating scale (BARS) A behavioural approach to performance review that consists of a series of vertical scales, one for each important dimension of job performance (page 210)

Benchmarking Finding the best practices in other organizations that can be brought into a company to enhance performance (page 19)

Benchmarking Process of measuring one's own services and practices against the recognized leaders in order to identify areas for improvement (page 169)

Bona fide occupational qualification (BFOQ) A justifiable reason for discrimination based on business reasons of safety or effectiveness (page 45)

Business agent Normally a paid labour official responsible for negotiating and administering the collective agreement and working to resolve union members' problems (page 358)

Certification Acquisition of exclusive rights by union to represent the employees (page 352)

Closed shop Provision of the collective agreement that requires employers to hire only union members (page 347)

Codetermination Representation of labour on the board of directors of a company (page 418)

Competency-based pay Pay based on how many capabilities employees have or how many jobs they can perform (page 242)

Constructive dismissal Changing an employee's working conditions such that compensation, status, or prestige is reduced (page 328)

Consumer price index (CPI) Measure of the average change in prices over time in a fixed "market basket" of goods and services (page 236)

Contractual rights Rights that derive from contracts (page 309)

Co-operative training Training program that combines practical on-the-job experience with formal education (page 163)

Core competencies A combination of knowledge, skills, and characteristics needed to effectively perform a role in an organization (page 22)

Core skills Skills considered critical to an employee's success abroad (page 404)

Cultural environment Communications, religion, values and ideologies, education, and social structure of a country (page 395)

Culture shock Perpetual stress experienced by people who settle overseas (page 408)

Cumulative trauma disorders Injuries involving tendons of the fingers, hands, and arms that become inflamed from repeated stresses and strains (page 285)

Customer input Performance review that, like team review, is based on TQM concepts and seeks information from both external and internal customers (page 204)

Defined rights Concept that management's authority should be expressly defined and clarified in the collective agreement (page 371)

Designated groups Women, visible minorities, First Nations peoples, and persons with disabilities who have been disadvantaged in employment (page 57)

Development The acquisition of skills, behaviours, and abilities to perform future work or to solve an organizational problem (page 154)

Direct compensation Employee wages and salaries, incentives, bonuses, and commissions (page 228)

Disability management Integrated approach to managing disability-related benefits (page 293)

Discipline (1) Treatment that punishes; (2) Orderly behaviour in an organizational setting; or (3) Training that moulds and strengthens desirable conduct—or corrects undesirable conduct—and develops self-control (page 320)

Diversity management The optimization of an organization's multicultural workforce in order to reach business objectives (page 61)

Downsizing The planned elimination of jobs (page 13)

Due process Employee's right to a fair process in making a decision related to employment relationship (page 310)

Eldercare Care provided to an elderly relative by an employee who remains actively at work (page 253)

E-learning Learning that takes place through electronic media (page 164)

Employee assistance program (EAP) Program to provide short-term counselling and referrals to appropriate professionals (page 294)

Employee empowerment Granting employees power to initiate change, thereby encouraging them to take charge of what they do (page 92)

Employee rights Expectations of fair treatment from employers (page 307)

Employee teams An employee-contributions technique in which work functions are structured for groups rather than for individuals, and team members are given discretion in matters traditionally considered management prerogatives, such as process improvements, product or service development, and individual work assignments (page 95)

Employment equity A distinct Canadian process for achieving equality in all aspects of employment (page 56)

Equitable pay Compensation received is perceived to be equal to the value of the work performed (page 232)

Ethics Set of standards of conduct and moral judgments that help to determine right and wrong behaviour (page 333)

Expatriates, or home-country nationals Employees from the home country who are on international assignment (page 397)

Failure rate Percentage of expatriates who do not perform satisfactorily (page 405)

Global corporation Firm that has integrated worldwide operations through a centralized home office (page 390)

Globalization Moving local or regional business into global marketplace (page 10)

Graphic rating scales A trait approach to performance review whereby each employee is rated according to a scale of characteristics (page 209)

Grievance procedure Formal procedure that provides for the union to represent members and nonmembers in processing a grievance (page 372)

Grievance resolution Process in which a neutral third party assists in the resolution of an employee grievance (page 374)

Guest workers Foreign workers invited to perform needed labour (page 401)

Harassment Any unwanted physical or verbal conduct that offends or humiliates the individual (page 49)

Hearing officer Person who holds a full-time position with an organization but assumes a neutral role when deciding cases between management and the aggrieved employees (page 332)

Host country Country in which an international corporation operates (page 395)

Host-country nationals Employees who are natives of the host country (page 397)

Hourly work Work paid on an hourly basis (page 233)

Human capital The individual's knowledge, skills, and abilities that have economic value to an organization (page 21)

Human resource planning Process that the people required to run the company are being used as effectively as possible, where and when they are needed, in order to accomplish the organization's goals (page 108)

Human resources management (HRM) An integrated set of processes, programs, and systems in an organization that focuses on the effective deployment and development of its employees (page 4)

Human resources management strategy Identifying key HR processes and linking those to the overall business strategy (page 31)

Human resources management system (HRMS) Technology system that provides data and information for purposes of control and decision making (page 16)

Indirect compensation Benefits, such as dental plans and life insurance, supplied by employers (page 228)

Industrial disease A disease resulting from exposure relating to a particular process, trade, or occupation in industry (page 275)

Instructional objectives Desired outcomes of a training program (page 160)

Interest arbitration A mechanism to renew or establish a new collective agreement for parties (page 370)

Interest-based bargaining Problem-solving bargaining based on a win-win philosophy and the development of a positive long-term relationship (page 364)

Internal job posting Method of communicating information about job openings (page 115)

International corporation Domestic firm that uses its existing capabilities to move into overseas markets (page 390)

Internship programs Programs jointly sponsored by colleges, universities, and other organizations that offer students the opportunity to gain real-life experience while allowing them to find out how they will perform in work organizations (page 163)

Job A group of related activities and duties (page 78)

Job analysis Process of obtaining information about jobs by determining the duties, tasks, or activities and the skills, knowledge, and abilities associated with the jobs (page 79)

Job characteristics model An approach to job design that recognizes the link between motivational factors and components of the job to achieve improved work performance and job satisfaction (page 89)

Job description A document that lists the tasks, duties, and responsibilities of a job to be performed along with the skills, knowledge, and abilities, or competencies needed to successfully perform the work (page 81)

Job design Process of defining and organizing tasks, roles, and other processes to achieve employee goals and organizational effectiveness (page 89)

Job evaluation Systematic process of determining the relative worth of jobs in order to establish which jobs should be paid more than others within an organization (page 235)

Job specifications Statement of the needed knowledge, skills, and abilities of the person who is to perform the position. The different duties and responsibilities performed by only one employee (page 81)

Labour market Area from which applicants are recruited (page 116)

Labour relations process Logical sequence of four events: (1) workers desire collective representation, (2) union begins its organizing campaign, (3) collective negotiations lead to a contract, and (4) the contract is administered (page 345)

Lockout Strategy by which the employer denies employees the opportunity to work by closing its operations (page 368)

Management forecasts Opinions and judgments of supervisors or managers and others that are knowledge-able about the organization's future employment needs (page 110)

Management rights Decisions regarding organizational operations over which management claims exclusive rights (page 354)

Manager and/or supervisor review Performance review done by the employee's supervisor (page 203)

Markov analysis Method for tracking the pattern of employee movements through various jobs (page 111)

Material Safety Data Sheet (MSDS) Documents that contain vital information about hazardous substances (page 282)

Mediation The use of an impartial third party to help facilitate a resolution to employment disputes (page 332)

Mediator Third party in a labour dispute who meets with one party and then the other in order to suggest compromise solutions or to recommend concessions from each side that will lead to an agreement (page 369)

Membership card A statement signed by an employee authorizing a union to act as a representative of the employee for purposes of collective bargaining (page 350)

Mentors Managers who coach, advise, and encourage less experienced employees (page 179)

Multinational corporation (MNC) Firm with independent business units operating in several countries (page 390)

Negligence Failure to provide reasonable care where such failure results in injury to consumers or other employees (page 307)

Occupational illness Abnormal condition or disorder resulting from exposure to environmental factors in the workplace (page 269)

Occupational injury Any cut, fracture, sprain, or amputation resulting from a workplace accident (page 269)

Ombudsperson Designated individual from whom employees may seek counsel for the resolution of their complaints (page 333)

On-the-job training (OJT) Method by which employees are given hands-on experience with instructions from their supervisor or other trainer (page 162)

Open shop Provision of the collective agreement that allows employees to join or not join the union (page 347)

Open-door policy Policy of settling grievances that identifies various levels of management above the immediate supervisor for employee contact (page 333)

Orientation Formal process of familiarizing new employees with the organization, their jobs, and their work unit and embedding organizational values, beliefs, and accepted behaviours (page 154)

Outsourcing Contracting outside the organization for work that was formerly done by internal employees. The small-business owner saves money, time, and resources by outsourcing tasks such as accounting and payroll. (page 13)

Panel interview An interview in which a board of interviewers questions and observes a single candidate (page 129)

Pay equity The practice of equal pay for work of equal value (page 60)

Pay-for-performance standard Standard by which managers tie compensation to employee effort and performance (page 232)

Pay grades Groups of jobs within a particular class that are paid the same rate or rate range (page 242)

Peer review Performance reviews done by one's fellow employees, generally on forms that are compiled into a single profile for use in the performance interview conducted by the employee's manager (page 204)

Performance management system A set of integrated management practices (page 192)

Piecework Work paid according to the number of units produced (page 233)

Position Specific duties and responsibilities performed by only one employee (page 78)

Positive, or nonpunitive, discipline System of discipline that focuses on the early correction of employee misconduct, with the employee taking total responsibility for correcting the problem (page 323)

Progressive discipline Application of corrective measures by increasing degrees (page 322)

Promotion Change of assignment to a job at a higher level in the organization (page 178)

Real wages Wage increases larger than rises in the consumer price index; that is, the real earning power of wages (page 237)

Psychological harrassment Repeated and aggravating behaviour that affects an employee's dignity, psychological, or physical integrity that results in a harmful work environment (page 52)

Reasonable accommodation Attempt by employers to adjust the working conditions and employment practices of employees to prevent discrimination (page 47)

Recruitment The process of locating and encouraging potential applicants to apply for jobs (page 113)

Reliability The degree to which interviews, tests, and other selection procedures yield comparable data over time and alternative measures (page 126)

Repatriation Process of employee transition home from an international assignment (page 409)

Residual rights Concept that management's authority is supreme in all matters except those it has expressly conceded to the union in the collective agreement (page 370)

Reverse discrimination Giving preference to members of certain groups such that others feel they are the subjects of discrimination (page 48)

Rights arbitration A mechanism to resolve disputes about the interpretation and application of a collective agreement during the term of that collective agreement (page 370)

Selection The process of choosing individuals who have relevant qualifications and who will best perform on the job to fill existing or projected job openings (page 125)

Self-review Performance review done by the employee being assessed, generally on a form completed by the employee prior to the performance interview (page 203)

Situational question Question in which an applicant is given a hypothetical incident and asked how he or she would respond to it (page 131)

Six Sigma A process used to translate customer needs into a set of optimal tasks that are performed in concert with one another (page 18)

Skills inventory Information about the education, experiences, skills, etc. of staff (page 111)

Staffing table Graphic representations of organizational jobs along with the numbers of employees currently occupying those jobs and future employment needs (page 111)

Standards of performance Set out the expected results of the job (page 85)

Statutory rights Rights that derive from legislation (page 307)

Step-review system System for reviewing employee complaints and disputes by successively higher levels of management (page 332)

Stress Any adjustive demand caused by physical, mental, or emotional factors that requires coping behaviour (page 289)

Strike A situation in which unionized workers refuse to perform their work during labour negotiations (page 366)

Subordinate review Performance review of a superior by an employee, which is more appropriate for developmental than for administrative purposes (page 203)

Systemic discrimination The exclusion of members of certain groups through the application of employment policies or practices based on criteria that are not job-related (page 45)

Talent management Leveraging competencies to achieve high organizational performance (page 22)

Team review Performance review, based on TQM concepts, that recognizes team accomplishment rather than individual performance (page 204)

Telework Conducting work activities in different locations through the use of technology (page 15)

Third-country nationals Employees who are natives of a country other than the home country or the host country (page 397)

Trainee readiness The consideration of a trainee's maturity and experience when assessing him or her (page 160)

Training The acquisition of skills, behaviours, and abilities to perform current work (page 154)

Transfer Placement of an individual in another job for which the duties, responsibilities, status, and remuneration are approximately equal to those of the previous job (page 178)

Transfer of training Effective application of principles learned to what is required on the job (page 168)

Transnational corporation Firm that attempts to balance local responsiveness and global scale via a network of specialized operating units (page 391)

Transnational teams Teams composed of members of multiple nationalities working on projects that span multiple countries (page 403)

Trend analysis Quantitative approach to forecasting labour demand on an organizational index (page 110)

Unfair labour practices Specific employer and union illegal practices that operate to deny employees their rights and benefits under labour law (page 351)

Union shop Provision of the collective agreement that requires employees to join the union as a condition of their employment (page 347)

Union (shop) steward Employee who, as a nonpaid union official, represents the interests of members in their relations with management (page 358)

Validity How well a test or selection procedure measures a person's attributes (page 126)

Virtual team A team with widely dispersed members linked together through computer and telecommunications technology (page 96)

Wage and salary survey Survey of the wages paid to employees of other employers in the surveying organization's relevant labour market (page 241)

Work Tasks or activities that need to be completed (page 78)

Work permit, or visa A government document granting a foreign individual the right to seek employment (page 401)

Workplace stressor A workplace event, process, or practice that has the potential to cause worker stress (page 289)

Wrongful dismissal Terminating an employee's employment without just cause (page 326)

NAME AND ORGANIZATION INDEX

SUBJECT INDEX